Internet Edition

Composición práctica

Conversación y repaso

Trinidad González
Joseph Farrell

California State Polytechnic University, Pomona

JOHN WILEY & SONS
New York • Chichester • Weinheim • Brisbane • Singapore • Toronto

ACQUISITIONS EDITOR Bob Hemmer
ASSISTANT EDITOR Samantha Alducin
MARKETING MANAGER Ilse Wolf
SENIOR PRODUCTION EDITOR Kelly Tavares
COVER DESIGNER Dawn Stanley
TEXT DESIGNER Nancy Field
PHOTO EDITOR Lisa Gee
ILLUSTRATION EDITOR Anna Melhorn

This book is printed on acid-free paper.

Library of Congress Cataloging in Publication Data:
González, Trinidad.
Composición práctica / Trinidad González, Joseph Farrell. —2nd ed.
p. cm.
Spanish and English.
Includes index.
ISBN 0-471-40531-0 (pbk. : alk. paper)
1. Spanish language—Composition and exercises. 2. Spanish language—Textbooks for foreign speakers—English. I. Farrell. Joseph (Joseph R.) II. Title.
PC4420.G56 1999
808′.0461—dc21
98-39511
CIP

10 9 8 7 6

To the student

YOU CAN LEARN TO WRITE WELL IN SPANISH!

For an extremely fortunate small minority, good writing may be a natural gift, an innate endowment; unfortunately, however, the great majority of us were not born with such a talent. Nevertheless, we can all **learn** to write well—to write clearly, simply, and effectively. In order to develop good writing skills, we must practice and perfect certain important techniques. The purpose of ***Composición práctica*** is to provide the essentials you will need in learning to communicate well in written Spanish.

Our focus is on the building of **practical writing skills**, skills that will enable you to produce the kinds of writing you will very likely need in your everyday social or professional lives in our increasingly bilingual world. ***Composición práctica*** will help you to function and communicate effectively in Spanish.

Language teachers have learned that the more exposure students have to the foreign language they are studying, the better and faster they learn it. Consequently, we have written this textbook primarily in Spanish and at a level used by educated writers. For your convenience, we have included in each chapter a list of vocabulary words that you are unlikely to know. However, this list is just a point of departure, and you should expect to look up some words in the dictionary.

We include throughout the text, well-written models to demonstrate the particular writing techniques that you will integrate into your own style. Simply reading many examples of good writing—examples from a variety of styles, genres, and epochs—will not teach you how to write well; but if you read enough of such examples you will eventually acquire an appreciation of good writing. However, being able to appreciate something is not the same as being able to do it.

In order to write well you have to write! Just as in acquiring and perfecting any other skill, it is necessary to practice if you are to become proficient and successful in writing. Thomas Wolfe, for example, once confessed that he had to write a million words before he achieved his ultimate style. So, while we do encourage you to read and to recognize in the works you read all the concepts that this book presents, the emphasis in the lessons is always on practicing your writing skills actively and repeatedly.

The message, then, is clear: with a little patience, some determination, and a lot of practice, you can indeed learn to write well in Spanish.

A FINAL WORD

Most of your coursework in Spanish up to now has probably concentrated on the study of grammatical structures and oral communication. However, if you plan to continue to use Spanish either in more advanced university courses or after graduation in your personal relationships or professional life, you will need to develop your written communication skills. That is precisely our reason for writing ***Composición práctica***. We **know** that it works, and we know that you **can learn to write successfully in Spanish**!

Trinidad González
Joseph Farrell

Acknowledgements

We are grateful to Bob Hemmer, Foreign Language Acquisitions Editor at John Wiley & Sons, Samantha Alducin, Assistant Editor, and Steve Debow for their support. We also had the good fortune to have worked with an outstanding Developmental Editor, Madela Ezcurra, whose insightful observations, knowledge, and constant encouragement were instrumental in greatly improving our work. For their conscientious work on this book we are appreciative and indebted to Harriet C. Dishman, Copyeditor; Kelly Tavares, Senior Production Editor; and Lisa Gee, Associate Photo Editor, all of John Wiley & Sons. We also wish to thank our colleagues who used the first and second editions of ***Composición práctica*** for their patronage, encouragement, and suggestions—many of which have been incorporated into this 2001 Internet edition.

Trinidad González
Joseph Farrell

Preface

Write on—online that is!

Popular in both composition and conversation courses at the fourth, fifth, and sixth semester levels and offering completely integrated Internet-based discussion and writing activities, ***Composición práctica: conversación y repaso, 2001 Internet edition*** is the only text of its kind. Practical and hands-on, it is based on an error analysis of hundreds of writing assignments and conferences with undergraduate students about topics of interest to them. The authentic language models in *Composición práctica* are appropriate to each topic presented, and every chapter highlights one grammar point that is specifically related to the chapter's central task.

Composición práctica, 2001 Internet Edition offers a variety of readings, discussion topics, and writing activities—both individual and group. Together with the student-friendly format, they enhance the underlying effectiveness of the book. Most units are self-contained, making this book one of the most flexible options: instructors can easily customize ***Composición práctica*** to the particular needs of any course!

HIGHLIGHTS OF THE 2001 INTERNET EDITION

- The **Online Writing Center** (www.wiley.com/college/gonzalez) includes Internet-based discussion and writing activities and instructor's resources.

  The **On-line Writing Center** (www.wiley.com/college/gonzalez) that accompanies the 2001 Internet Edition of **Composición práctica** contains integrated Internet writing activities and exercises students can access at any time. In addition, students can link to the Wiley-Nonce Modern Language Resource Center complete with Spanish learning tools such as online dictionaries and grammars.

  Available within the Instructor's Resource section of the Online Writing Center are an electronic version of the Instructor's Manual (accessible by chapter) and sample syllabi from various users of the popular Second Edition.

- A unique *Using a Dictionary* section at the beginning of the text

  The **Lección preliminar** offers a hands-on tutorial for using the dictionary, an indispensable tool for students in developing their own vocabulary for each chapter. The chapter also includes both dictionary strategies and exercises. Students can also access various Spanish dictionary resources on the Web at the **Online Writing Center.**

- Flexible and versatile for both composition and conversation courses at the fourth, fifth, and sixth semesters

  Interesting topics and activities provide the springboard for class discussion and combine to make **Composición práctica** a versatile text suitable for conversation as well as composition.

- Practical, real world topics and assignments for non-majors as well as majors who will use Spanish in their careers

  Since many students enrolled in conversation and composition classes are non-majors, **Composición práctica** stresses the communication skills students will most likely use in their careers. Unlike other composition texts that focus almost exclusively on writing about literature, **Composición práctica** offers unique chapters on advertising, resume building, and business correspondence.

- Variety of student activities, both individual and group

  A blend of individual and group activities helps students achieve higher levels of writing proficiency. The variety of activities ensures that students experience the act of writing in different ways. Feedback from classmates and self-reflection are both useful activities for the writing process.

- Reference tools on syllabification, written accent, and documentation and bibliography

  Five appendices—Syllabification and Diphthongs, Stress and Written Accent, Capitalization, Punctuation, and Documentation and Bibliography for a Research Paper—provide easy access to important tools students will need to refer to as they complete their writing assignments. In addition, a sixth appendix contains a correction key that explains the symbols instructors may use in correcting students' work.

OVERVIEW OF THE TEXT

Composición práctica takes students from simple sentence formation to organized and complex essay and research paper writing. **Chapters 1** and **2** stress the different types of sentence structure—simple, compound, and complex—and help students avoid writing overly simple, monotonous sentences. The beginning chapters provide a solid foundation upon which to build written compositions, including the rules of punctuation.

Chapter 3 teaches students to develop a topic sentence into an effective paragraph. In **Chapter 4,** students learn techniques for revising paragraphs to make them as clear, precise, and logical as possible. In **Chapter 5,** via the topic of advertising, students learn the precise lexical selection to create an effect, motivate, or convince. In **Chapter 6** students learn how to write a summary, while **Chapter 7** teaches students to write and respond to invitations and short personal notes.

Since many students taking the course will need to apply their Spanish writing skills in business or industry, in **Chapters 8** and **9** (personal and business letters, respectively) students study the kinds of writing they would be expected to produce if they were to take a position with an organization with ties to Spanish-speaking countries, or if they simply wanted to maintain cordial social or business relations with Spanish-speaking friends or acquaintances. These are skills students will use for the rest of their lives.

Chapters 10 and **11** focus on the techniques of narrative and descriptive writing, respectively. Finally, in **Chapter 12** students combine the techniques they have learned in previous chapters to develop a thesis into an effective expository essay. Students are ultimately presented with guidelines for writing a research paper.

CHAPTER STRUCTURE

Each chapter consists of the following sections:

- *Objectives*—identify the focus and desired outcomes as well as the specific type of writing taught in the chapter.
- *Para hablar del tema* —provides a brief list of useful vocabulary related to both the chapter theme (*la familia, la rutina diaria,* and so on) and to its specific writing focus (memo, personal letter, and so on). Intended to serve as a starting point for the chapter, **Para hablar del tema** is followed by activities that encourage students to develop their own additional, personalized vocabulary
- *Análisis*—introduces and explains the chapter's specific writing topic. It analyzes writing samples and details the process involved in completing the particular writing task described.
- *Para escribir mejor*—provides an authentic writing model followed by short prewriting activities that prepare students for the chapter's writing task.
- *Estructuras en acción*—focuses on one grammar point that is **specifically related to the chapter's writing task.** For example, preterit versus imperfect appears in the chapter dealing with narration; adjective position is discussed in the chapter on description, and so on. **Composición práctica** carefully selects problematic grammar points for review; it is not a comprehensive grammar review.
- *Manos a la obra*—allows students to apply what they have learned in the previous sections to produce a finished piece of writing
- *Para los internautas*—affords students an opportunity to work with the expanding resources of the Internet through online activities and exercises.
- *Más allá*—supplements the chapter with a variety of thought-provoking topics that can serve as the basis for either conversation, additional writing activities, or both.
- *Mi diario*—encourages students to keep a record of their progress and to write about their lives.

Trinidad González
Joseph Farrell

Credits

TEXT AND REALIA CREDITS

Page 21 Pamphlet reprinted courtesy of Mission Branch, San Francisco Public Library (funded by a grant from the California State Library); **page 26** Advertisement reprinted courtesy of CETYS University, Mexicali, Mexico; **page 39** "El divorcio, transición sin pelea," (adaptation) from *Más,* May–June, 1992, courtesy of The Univision Network Limited Partnership; **page 68** "Ciclo de energía"(adaptation) from *Cosmopólitan en español,* Año 19, No. 8, reprinted with permission of Editorial América, S.A. d/b/a Editorial Televisa; **page 76** "La dieta y el supermercado" (adaptation) from *Cosmopólitan en español,* Año 20, No. 6, reprinted with permission of Editorial América, S.A. d/b/a Editorial Televisa; **page 88** "La Framboise" (adaptation) by Elly Levy. Reprinted courtesy of Miami Mensual Monthly Magazine; **page 90** Front cover, "Cosina sabrosa en pocos minutos" *Vanidades Continental,* No. 10, reprinted with permission of Editorial América, S.A. d/b/a Editorial Televisa; **page 93** Advertisement © Sunbeam Corporation, reprinted with permission. Oster® and Sunbeam® are registered trademarks of the Sunbeam Corporation; **page 95** Reprinted courtesy of Sony Electronics, Inc.; **page 104** Advertisement © The Procter & Gamble Company, reprinted with permission; **page 105** Advertisement © Goya Foods, reprinted with permission; **page 106** C/B Productions/ The Stock Market; **page 112** "Entrevista con Fernando Botero" reprinted from *Américas,* bimonthly magazine published by the Organization of American States in English and Spanish; **page 117** "Más cerca de Cristina Saralegui" (adaptation) by Diana Montané, from *Más,* July–Aug. 1991, reprinted with permission of The Univision Network Limited Partnership; **page 135** "Nuevo furor con ritmo latino" reprinted from *Américas,* bimonthly magazine published by the Organization of American States in English and Spanish; **page 142** "Las postales de felicitación," from *Vanidades Continental,* Año 32, No. 11, reprinted with permission of Editorial América, S.A. d/b/a Editorial Televisa; **page 144** "¿Qué sabes de cuidades?" from *Vanidades Continental,* Año 31, No. 13, reprinted with permission of Editorial América, S.A. d/b/a Editorial Televisa; **page 167** "Un baño en la Presa" by Magón (Manuel González Zeledón), reprinted from *Cuentos/Magón,* Editorial Costa Rica, 1980; **page 207** "El enfrentamiento," by Ann-Marie Trudeau, reprinted with permission of the author; **page 225** "El agua y la ciudad de México" (adaptation) from "El agua, cada vez más lejos de la Zona Metropolitana," by María Isabel Melchor

Sánchez, Factor Financiero, Año 1, No. 16, November 1992, reprinted courtesy of *El Financiero;* **page 229** "Calor que empobrece," by Katiana Murillo, *La Nación,* sección B, September 1992, reprinted courtesy of *La Nación* (San José, Costa Rica); **page 243** "El mundo de Frida Kahlo," reprinted from *Américas,* bimonthly magazine published by the Organization of American States in English and Spanish; **page 251** "Los hitos del modernismo," reprinted from *Américas,* bimonthly magazine published by the Organization of American States in English and Spanish.

PHOTO CREDITS

Title Page—Preliminary Page: Peter Menzel
Chapter 1—Page 9: Ulrike Welsch Photography.
Chapter 2—Page 31: Ted McCarthy/The Stock Market. **Page 39:** Michael Keller/FPG International. **Page 47:** Paul Barton/The Stock Market.
Chapter 3—Page 53: Stuart Cohen/Comstock, Inc.
Chapter 4—Page 73: Barbara Alper/Stock, Boston. **Page 88:** Peter Menzel/Stock, Boston.
Chapter 5—Page 92: Nancy D'Antonio. **Page 106:** C/B Productions/The Stock Market.
Chapter 6—Page 111: Rogers/Monkmeyer Press Photo. **Page 113:** © Fernando Botero, "Nina", 1981, courtesy Marlborough Gallery, NY. **Page 117:** Andrea Renault/Globe Photos, Inc.
Chapter 7—Page 133: Bob Daemmrich/Stock, Boston. **Page 135:** Macduff Everton/The Image Works. **Page 144** (top, left): © Stuart Cohen Photographer. **Page 144** (bottom, left): Topham/The Image Works.
Chapter 8—Page 159: Stuart Cohen/Comstock, Inc.
Chapter 9—Page 181: Paul Barton/The Stock Market.
Chapter 10—Page 205: Margaret Thompson/The Picture Cube.
Chapter 11—Page 223: Steven Rubin/The Image Works. **Page 225:** Peter Menzel. **Page 237:** A. Ramey/Stock, Boston.
Chapter 12—Page 241: Alfredo Ramos Martinez, "Casamiento Indio", circa 1930, private collection, Mexico; courtesy Louis Stern Fine Arts. **Page 243:** Frida Kahlo, "Autorretrato con el pelo suelto", courtesy Archivo Cenidiap. Reproduced with permission of Banco De Mexico. **Page 251:** Wilfredo Lam, "The Jungle," 1943, Courtesy Museum of Modern Art, New York.

Contenido

Appendices

Lección preliminar

The Dictionary

ABOUT DICTIONARIES

Dictionaries are invaluable and indispensable not only in composition classes but also in daily life. This lesson will help you to use dictionaries effectively and efficiently.

There are several types of dictionaries available in bookstores and libraries: bilingual (Spanish-English/English-Spanish), Spanish-language, etymological, of synonyms (thesaurus), etc. A Spanish thesaurus, which will help you to avoid repetition of the same word, is highly recommended. However, when writing in Spanish it is **absolutely essential** to have at least two dictionaries: one Spanish-language and one bilingual. A bilingual dictionary will help you find words that you do not know in Spanish, and a Spanish-language dictionary will help you choose the word that best represents the meaning you want to convey.

Dictionaries vary widely in quality, purpose, and price. Some are geared to commercial or technical fields (medicine, business, law, etc.); others tend to be stronger in areas such as the arts or literature, while still others are more appropriate for general use. The list of dictionaries at the end of this chapter, while not exhaustive, provides a representative sample of the variety of works currently available to writers of Spanish. Since these reference tools are so important, you should consult your professor before you purchase them in order to learn which texts are best suited for a specific class's needs.

How to use your dictionary

Even students with considerable knowledge of a foreign language often assume that the first word a dictionary gives is perfectly adequate to express the thought they have in mind. This assumption is naive, and all too often using the first word the dictionary lists results in poor word choices, which can lead to compositions that are imprecise, unclear, and sometimes difficult or even impossible to understand.

You should take the following steps to find the equivalent of an English word you don't know in Spanish. Suppose that you need to express the word **pawn**. There are several things you must consider. First, this word has several meanings in English:

1. a piece in a chess game
2. a person or entity used to further the purposes of another
3. something given in security
4. a hostage
5. the act of pawning
6. to risk
7. to give as security for payment

Which of these ideas is the closest equivalent to the thought you want to express? Suppose that the English sentence is "I pawned my watch." Look up the word **pawn** in the English-Spanish section of your bilingual dictionary. First of all, you must determine whether you are looking for a verb or a noun. In this case it's a verb; therefore, you go to the section that appears under the abbreviation *v.* (*verbo*). There you find the infinitive *empeñar* and the phrase *dejar en prenda.*

The next step is to verify whether these two translations are equivalent or not. Generally there are differences, whether slight or significant. At this point you should consult your Spanish-language dictionary. Based on the definitions of each term that you find there, you can then select the appropriate word. Some of the meanings you will find for *empeñar* are:

1. *dar o dejar una cosa en prenda*
2. *poner a uno por medianero*
3. *llenarse de deudas*
4. *insistir con fuerza*

In this case the first meaning solves the problem: both translations (*empeñar* and *dejar en prenda*) are equivalent. Therefore, the Spanish sentence can be either *Empeñé mi reloj* or *Dejé mi reloj en prenda.*

Unfortunately, the procedure is not always so simple. Sometimes the Spanish definitions are not sufficiently clear or discriminatory, or they may require you to look up other words in order to understand them. The process can become tedious and time-consuming, but it gets easier with practice, and the resultant precision and clarity of your writing are well worth the effort you invest. Consider, for example, the word **pawn** in a different context: "The pawn can move forward one square at a time." The function of the word has changed: it is now a noun associated with the game of chess. The dictionary lists several entries under the rubric *s.* (*sustantivo*):

1. *empeño*
2. *prenda*
3. *peón* (chess)

In this case the parentheses hold the key to the solution. The sentence can be expressed in Spanish as *El peón puede avanzar una casilla por jugada.*

The question of equivalency can be complicated. The remainder of this chapter looks at some of the most common problems and offers some strategies to help you resolve them.

Useful Dictionary Strategies

a) In English you can take a root word and modify its meaning by adding prepositions such as **off, back, on**, etc. Observe what happens with the English words **pay** and **pay off** (or **payoff**). As in the case of **pawn**, these two words can be used either as nouns or verbs. You cannot assume that Spanish will use a preposition to change the meaning of the root word, as is the case in English. On the contrary, the two concepts usually have two completely different forms in Spanish. Look at the following English meanings.

pay	to give money in exchange for goods or services to give an indicated amount to yield a return
payoff	to make the final of a series of payments a bribe

Now compare the words you would find in a bilingual dictionary.

pay	v. *pagar* (to remit), *costear* (to pay for), *ser provechoso* (to profit), *valer la pena* (to be worth) n. *pago* (payment), *paga* (payment), *sueldo* (salary), *recompensa* (reward)
payoff	v. *hacer el último pago* (to make the last payment), *sobornar* (to bribe) n. *arreglo* (arrangement), *pago* (payment), *soborno* (bribe), *cohecho* (bribe)

Obviously, the use of parentheses and abbreviations in dictionary definitions is extremely important. Pay close attention to them.

b) There is another way to determine if a word you find in the English-Spanish section of your bilingual dictionary is the best choice: look it up in the Spanish-English section and decide if it really has the meaning you want to convey. If you are still in doubt, then refer to your Spanish-language dictionary.

When two or more Spanish words have very similar meanings it is necessary to determine if they are truly synonyms. Perhaps one word is more appropriately used in a colloquial context while a different form has a more erudite or literary tone. Maybe the word you have found is used in Latin America but not in Spain, or vice versa. In other cases one language may have more words in a certain semantic area than the other language has, and the first language may create distinctions that cannot be translated from language to language with just one word. For example, to render the English noun **grin** into Spanish you must use a phrase such as *sonrisa burlona o maliciosa.*

c) Idiomatic expressions present yet another translation problem that can have serious implications in your writing. These are expressions whose overall meaning is not predictable from the usual, normal meaning of each of their component elements (**to kick the bucket, to hit the ceiling**, etc.). In most cases these expressions cannot be translated literally from one language into the other. For example, suppose you want to give the Spanish equivalent of the English sentence **Mark my words**! If you select one of the first options presented in the English-Spanish section of your bilingual dictionary and write *Marque mis palabras*, you have indeed translated the sentence literally into Spanish, but have not conveyed the **idea** or particular idiomatic sense of the English sentence. A small, very limited dictionary will not help you in these cases. A larger, more complete work will often prove more effective. If you explore all the possibilities you will probably find a close equivalent, such as *¡Advierte lo que te digo!* or *¡Recuerda mis palabras!* Always try to give the equivalent **sense** or **meaning** of the idiomatic expression rather than a literal translation of each individual word.

EXERCISES

A. Use your bilingual dictionary and your Spanish-language dictionary to supply information for each of the underlined words in the following sentences. Write

a. its equivalent Spanish word
b. the word's grammatical function (adjetivo, sustantivo, verbo, etc.)
c. the word's definition in Spanish

Example: They knocked the wall down.

a. derribar
b. verbo
c. echar a tierra paredes o edificios

1. He gave me an advance for my work.

a. ______________________________

b. ______________________________

c. ______________________________

2. Miguel always acts on impulse.

a. ______________________________

b. ______________________________

c. ______________________________

3. That doctor is a quack.

a. ______________________________

b. ______________________________

c. ______________________________

4. We could hear the quacking of the ducks.

a. ______________________________

b. ______________________________

c. ______________________________

5. That terrible food made me gag.

a. ____________________________

b. ____________________________

c. ____________________________

6. Those gags were not very funny.

a. ____________________________

b. ____________________________

c. ____________________________

B. The following groups of words are related and could appear together in a bilingual dictionary. Refer to your dictionaries to explain the different meaning of each Spanish word indicated.

Example: **head:** (a) *cabeza,* (b) *cabecera,* (c) *jefe*

a. *La cabeza es la parte superior de un animal.*
b. *La cabecera es la parte superior de la cama.*
c. *El jefe es el líder de un grupo.*

1. wall: (a) *pared,* (b) *muro,* (c) *muralla,* (d) *tapia,* (e) *tabique*

a. ____________________________

b. ____________________________

c. ____________________________

d. ____________________________

e. ____________________________

2. shower: (a) *regadera,* (b) *ducha,* (c) *aguacero,* (d) *chubasco,* (e) *chaparrón*

a. ____________________________

b. ____________________________

c. ____________________________

d. ____________________________

e. ____________________________

3. skin: (a) *cáscara,* (b) *piel,* (c) *cuero,* (d) *pellejo,* (e) *corteza*

a. ____________________________

b. ____________________________

c. ____________________________

d. ____________________________

e. ____________________________

4. **screen:** (a) *pantalla,* (b) *biombo,* (c) *cedazo,* (d) *mampara*

   a. ______________________________

   b. ______________________________

   c. ______________________________

   d. ______________________________

5. **chair:** (a) *silla,* (b) *taburete,* (c) *cátedra,* (d) *sillón,* (e) *presidencia*

   a. ______________________________

   b. ______________________________

   c. ______________________________

   d. ______________________________

   e. ______________________________

C. Challenge! Form groups of three or four classmates. Your professor will ask each group to find a Spanish equivalent of <u>one</u> of the following idiomatic expressions.

1. He's over the hill!

   ____

2. She hit the ceiling!

   ____

3. I freaked!

   ____

4. Don't throw in the towel!

   ____

5. That's mixing apples and oranges!

   ____

6. I lost my cool!

   ____

7. The old man finally kicked the bucket!

   ____

WWW

PARA LOS INTERNAUTAS

Vaya a **http://www.wiley.com/college/gonzalez,** busque la página que corresponde a este capítulo y haga los ejercicios indicados.

SPANISH/SPANISH DICTIONARIES

1. *Diccionario de la lengua española,* Real Academia Española.
   The official dictionary of the Royal Academy of the Spanish Language. Also available in CD-ROM.
2. *Diccionario de uso del español,* Moliner, María.
   A grammatical encyclopedia and a very complete dictionary of synonyms, in 2 volumes.
3. *Pequeño Laroussse ilustrado en color,* García-Pelayo, R.
   An up-to-date dictionary that takes into account changes in vocabulary in Latin America and Spain.
4. *Diccionario escolar de la Real Academia Española.*
   Contains 33,000 words, examples of usage, color illustrations, and a grammar section.
5. *Diccionario de dudas y dificultades de la lengua española.*
   Offers specific applications by topic, a summary of basic grammar and verb conjugation, as well as spelling and punctuation guidelines.
6. *Diccionario etimológico español e hispano,* Lapesa, Rafael.
   Provides ample information on the origins of the Spanish lexicon.
7. *Espasa diccionario de sinónimos y antónimos.*
   Offers a very comprehensive list of synonyms and antonyms, which will allow the seeker to find the precise lexical item for each idea.
8. *Larousse: sinónimos/antónimos. Práctico.*
   A concise, practical dictionary for all students.

BILINGUAL DICTIONARIES

1. *Simon and Schuster International Spanish Dictionary.*
   A very complete and up-to-date dictionary.
2. *The Oxford Spanish Dictionary: Spanish-English/English-Spanish.*
   A very comprehensive and authoritative dictionary.
3. *The American Heritage Laroussse Spanish Dictionary.*
   A good bilingual dictionary with 120,000 words and phrases.
4. *Velázquez Spanish and English Dictionary.*
   A dictionary that includes maps, phonetic and pronunciation guides.
5. *Richmond Electronic Dictionary.*
   Contains 55,000 words and entries and 160,000 translations and examples of usage. A correspondence section also included. Windows 3.1 or higher; Macintosh, System 7.0 or higher.
6. *Cassells Colloquial Spanish. Spanish-English.*
   A handbook of Spanish idioms and expressions with English equivalents. Emphasis on false cognates and levels of meaning as well as of register.

Capítulo 1

La educación superior

Estudiantes universitarios de Madrid, España, escriben una composición en grupo.

Objectives

Upon completion of this chapter you should be able to:

- identify and create simple and compound sentences
- utilize appropriate vocabulary to write about higher education
- use direct and indirect object pronouns

► Para hablar del tema

VOCABULARIO ESENCIAL

Estudie las siguientes palabras y expresiones. Le pueden resultar útiles para entender el capítulo y escribir sobre la educación superior.

Sustantivos

la actividad ex-cátedra / la actividad extracurricular	*extracurricular activity*
el alumnado	*student body*
el (la) asesor(a) / consejero(a)	*advisor*
la asignatura	*course*
el (la) aspirante	*applicant*
el auditorio	*auditorium*
el aula (f.) / la sala de clase	*classroom*
la beca	*scholarship*
la biblioteca	*library*
el campus	*campus*
la cátedra	*professorship*
el (la) catedrático(a)	*university professor*
la ciudad universitaria	*campus*
el colegio / el liceo	*secondary school*
la conferencia	*lecture*
el cuatrimestre	*quarter*
los deportes	*sports*
el diploma	*diploma*
la escuela	*school (primary, secondary); division of a university*
la facultad	*school (division of a university)*
la inscripción	*registration*
la librería	*bookstore*
el (la) licenciado(a)	*a person holding the degree similar to a Master's*
la matrícula	*registration fee*
el periódico	*newspaper*
el plan de estudios	*curriculum*
el plazo de inscripción	*registration period*
la política estudiantil	*student politics*
el profesorado	*faculty*
el recinto universitario	*university*
la residencia estudiantil	*dormitory*
el semestre	*semester*
la solicitud	*application form*
el taller	*workshop*
el título	*degree*
el torneo	*tournament*
el trimestre	*trimester*
el (la) universitario(a)	*university student*

Verbos

impartir / dar clases	*to teach classes*
solicitar	*to apply*

A. Lea la siguiente información.

Master en periodismo UAM / EL PAÍS

La Fundación Escuela de Periodismo **UAM / EL PAÍS** anuncia que el plazo de inscripción para las pruebas de acceso para el próximo curso (sexta promoción) de la Escuela de Periodismo **UAM / EL PAÍS** quedará abierto en el mes de octubre, en fechas que oportunamente se publicarán.

Los estudios seguidos en dicha Escuela permiten optar al título de 'Master en Periodismo'. Este título, de acuerdo con lo establecido en la Ley de Reforma Universitaria, tiene rango de título propio de la Universidad Autónoma de Madrid.

El número de plazas es limitado, y los aspirantes han de realizar una serie de pruebas selectivas. Se requiere ser licenciado en cualquier Facultad Universitaria, Escuela Técnica Superior o, en el caso de los extranjeros, poseer un título equivalente.

El curso, de un año de duración (de enero a diciembre), se imparte de lunes a viernes, de 10.00 a 14.30 y de 16.00 a 20.30 horas.

El Plan de Estudios comprende asignaturas teóricas y prácticas, de carácter básico o complementario, impartidas a lo largo de dos sesiones académicas cuatrimestrales. Para pasar al segundo cuatrimestre se exige un periodo de prácticas en algún medio informativo, nacional o extranjero.

A partir del 2 de septiembre, la Secretaría de la Escuela facilitará información más detallada. Los interesados deben dirigirse a la Escuela de Periodismo **UAM / EL PAÍS**, calle de Miguel Yuste, 40, 28037 Madrid. Tel. (91) 327 05 18.

rango...*equivalent (rank)*

B. Conteste las siguientes preguntas sobre la información anterior.

1. ¿Qué tipo de título ofrece la Fundación Escuela de Periodismo UAM / El País?

____

____

2. ¿Qué deben hacer los estudiantes que deseen participar en este programa?

____

____

3. ¿En qué consiste el plan de estudios?

____

____

4. ¿Cómo pueden obtener información los interesados?

____

____

5. ¿Qué ventaja ofrecen los bonos de ahorro de los EE.UU. para los padres de los futuros estudiantes universitarios?

____

____

6. ¿Cuál es el costo aproximado de una educación universitaria hoy en día? ¿Cuál será el costo en unos dieciocho años?

____

____

C. Ahora haga una lista de las palabras del Ejercicio A que usted no conocía. Añada otras expresiones que considere útiles para escribir sobre la educación superior. Si es necesario, busque su significado en el diccionario.

______________	______________	______________
______________	______________	______________
______________	______________	______________
______________	______________	______________
______________	______________	______________
______________	______________	______________
______________	______________	______________
______________	______________	______________
______________	______________	______________
______________	______________	______________

VOCABULARIO CLAVE

Las palabras de esta sección son de uso muy frecuente. Estúdielas y apréndalas. Le ayudarán en sus trabajos de redacción.

de acuerdo con *according to, in accordance with*

La petición está **de acuerdo con** lo establecido en la Ley de Reforma Universitaria.

a lo largo de *throughout*

Son asignaturas impartidas **a lo largo de** dos sesiones.

a partir de *from*

La inscripción se realizará **a partir del** 2 de septiembre.

por eso *thus, consequently*

Los bonos están exentos de impuestos; **por eso** es bueno comprarlos.

Análisis de oraciones

La manera de clasificar las oraciones en inglés y en español es similar. En esta sección podrá repasar la oración en sus variantes, familiarizarse con la nomenclatura española y aprender a usar todo tipo de oración en sus trabajos. Además, un buen conocimiento de la oración y su estructura le ayudará a entender y a usar las reglas de la puntuación.

En su forma más básica, una oración es un grupo de palabras (o una palabra) que tiene por lo menos un **verbo independiente** y su **sujeto**. Afirma o declara, pregunta, pide o manda, o exclama algo.

Ejemplos: La educación universitaria es cara. (Afirma o declara.)
¡Qué cara es la educación universitaria! (Exclama.)
¿Es la educación universitaria cara? (Pregunta.)
Piense usted más en su educación. (Manda.)

La oración es una entidad completa en sí misma; posee sentido sin necesidad de comentario adicional. Se puede clasificar en tres categorías fundamentales: **la oración simple, la compuesta y la compleja**. En este capítulo se estudian los dos primeros tipos. En el siguiente capítulo, se analizará la oración compleja.

LA ORACIÓN SIMPLE

La oración simple es una sola cláusula independiente—un grupo de palabras que tiene un sujeto y un verbo y quizás uno o más modificantes—que no depende de ninguna información externa para ser completa. En su forma más sencilla, consiste en un sujeto y un verbo.

Ejemplo: Beatriz estudia.
(sujeto) (verbo)

Algunas veces la oración simple requiere un complemento para que su sentido sea claro. Hay varios tipos de complementos. Puede ser un **complemento directo**, el cual nombra al receptor de la acción del verbo.

Ejemplo: Los señores Sáenz compraron **bonos de ahorro**.
(complemento directo)

También puede ser un **complemento indirecto**, el cual nombra el sustantivo para el que (o a quien) se hace la acción del verbo. Es el recipiente de la acción.

Ejemplo:	La Dra. Núñez	**le** da consejos *(complemento indirecto, pronombre)*	**al aspirante**. *(complemento indirecto, sustantivo)*

A. Escriba en el espacio entre paréntesis la función de las palabras subrayadas (complemento directo, complemento indirecto, sujeto, etc.).

Ejemplo: El técnico integra las estrategias de desarrollo.
(complemento directo)

1. Los estudiantes de periodismo eligieron a Pilar presidenta del consejo estudiantil.
   (______________________________)

2. Le envió la solicitud al jefe del departamento.
   (______________________________)

3. Por lo general, los universitarios no son ricos.
   (______________________________)

4. El examen estuvo muy difícil.
   (______________________________)

LOS MODIFICANTES

La oración simple puede amplificarse con el uso de **modificantes**—palabras o frases que describen un sustantivo o un pronombre, o indican cuándo, dónde o cómo se realiza la acción. En su forma más sencilla el modificante es una sola palabra: un adjetivo (palabra que califica un sustantivo) o un adverbio (palabra que califica un verbo, un adjetivo u otro adverbio).

Ejemplos: Es un curso **difícil**. (adjetivo)
Lo explicó **claramente**. (adverbio)

Modificantes de más de una palabra pueden ser frases adjetivas, adverbiales o infinitivas. Observe los diferentes tipos de modificantes en las siguientes oraciones.

Ejemplos: Esos son los libros **del curso de química**. (frase adjetiva con preposición)

Los libros están **en el escritorio**. (frase adverbial con preposición)

Pensando en sus exámenes, Ramiro no durmió en toda la noche. (frase adverbial con gerundio: **-ndo**)

Terminada la conferencia, volvimos a casa. (frase adverbial con participio pasado: **-do, -da**)

Yo puedo **comprar los textos**. (frase infinitiva)

Deseamos **obtener el máster en periodismo**. (frase infinitiva)

B. Junto con otro(a) compañero(a), complete las siguientes frases u oraciones. Sigan las indicaciones entre paréntesis. Pueden usar los siguientes modificantes o crear los suyos.

- terminada la presentación
- construir un nuevo edificio
- revisando la composición
- excelente
- declararse en huelga
- completado el ejercicio
- en agronomía
- siguiendo los consejos de su profesora
- rápidamente
- de tenis

Ejemplo: En la escuela de ingeniería se confieren títulos... (frase preposicional) *en ingeniería aeroespacial.*

1. La universidad no ofrece cursos... (frase preposicional)

   ____

2. Es un asesor... (adjetivo)

   ____

3. La escuela de odontología necesita... (frase infinitiva)

   ____

4. El cuatrimestre se pasó... (adverbio)

   ____

5. (frase de participio pasado)..., los estudiantes le hicieron preguntas al conferenciante.

   ____

6. El alumnado piensa... (frase infinitiva)

   ____

7. (frase de gerundio)..., Elisa se matriculó en el curso de informática.

   ____

8. (frase de participio pasado)..., Evangelina se lo entregó (*turned it in*) a la profesora.

   ____

9. Tendremos un torneo... (frase preposicional)

   ____

10. (frase de gerundio)..., descubrió que necesitaba más ejemplos.

    ____

LA ORACIÓN COMPUESTA

Una oración compuesta es la unión de dos oraciones simples que tienen una estructura paralela o que están íntimamente relacionadas. Ésta es su característica más importante. Si no existe una relación, las oraciones deben aparecer en su forma simple. Es necesario distinguir entre una oración compuesta y una oración simple de sujeto compuesto o verbo compuesto: la oración compuesta tiene dos pares de sujetos y verbos, ambos completos y separables.

Ejemplos: **Mercedes y Rodolfo** son universitarios. (oración simple con **sujeto compuesto**)

Mercedes estudia medicina; Rodolfo sigue cursos en derecho. (oración compuesta)

Si las oraciones simples son paralelas (íntimamente relacionadas o con ideas paralelas), se usa un punto y coma (*semicolon*) para separarlas.

Ejemplo: Luis obtuvo su título en contabilidad; Elisa se graduó en administración de empresas.

Las demás oraciones compuestas usan una conjunción coordinante (**y**[1], **mas**, **pero**, **porque**, **o**, **ni**, **sino que**, **tampoco**, **también**, **por eso**, etc.) precedida de una coma para separar las dos oraciones.

Ejemplos: Me gusta el plan de estudios, pero algunas asignaturas parecen ser muy teóricas.

No voy a matricularme este semestre, sino que voy a esperar hasta el verano.

El secretario escribió la solicitud a máquina, y Celia la envió a la escuela de periodismo.

Hice el examen, pero todavía no sé el resultado de la prueba.

Use las oraciones compuestas para crear flexibilidad y variedad en el estilo de su composición.

► Para escribir mejor

COMO IDENTIFICAR Y ESCRIBIR ORACIONES COMPUESTAS

A. Lea el siguiente trozo *(excerpt)*.

Ese Profesor Guerrero Fallas

En esta época de expertos pedagogos, de docentes con problemas y de demandas legales, encontrar un profesor como el Lic. Guerrero Fallas,

[1]Cuando las dos oraciones compuestas son muy cortas y usan la conjunción coordinante **y,** no es necesario usar la coma.

titular de la cátedra de historia, sería un escándalo digno de la radio y la televisión. Medía unos buenos dos metros, tenía voz de trueno° y vestía siempre de traje negro y corbata. Era un tirano absoluto y se enorgullecía° en serlo. Sabía que nadie escapaba a sus garras°, pero dictaba las mejores y más amenas° charlas de la facultad. Hablaba del tema que quería, y en su clase no había libros de texto ni programa de curso. Nosotros, pobres ignorantes, debíamos —según sus recomendaciones— tomar notas hasta de sus suspiros°.

Al principio de cada lección, seleccionaba una víctima a quien le correspondía resumir las ideas principales de la clase anterior. Todavía oigo sus palabras: «Señorita Quesada» o «Señor Gutiérrez, ¿de qué hablamos en la lección pasada?» Durante la exposición del pobre compañero mantenía una expresión que un jugador de póker habría envidiado°. Nadie se atrevía° a preguntar el resultado de la prueba. Al final de cada trimestre, uno a uno pasábamos por un examen oral comprensivo y la clase entera presenciaba la agonía de los condiscípulos°. En un sistema en el que las calificaciones° iban de uno como la peor nota hasta el diez como la mejor, nunca se supo de nadie que obtuviera más de un nueve.

Para sacar un diez en esta clase, decía, hay que saber más que el profesor, y eso es un imposible.

Con el transcurso de los años, se han borrado° de mi memoria los recuerdos de tantos maestros bondadosos y justos que me educaron, pero jamás podré olvidar al Lic. Guerrero Fallas.

thunder
took pride/
clutches/
pleasant
sighs
envied
dared
classmates
grades
erased

OBSERVE . . . el uso de la preposición ***de*** en la frase "*...vestía...**de** traje negro*".

B. Busque tres oraciones compuestas en el trozo del Ejercicio A. Subráyelas y cópielas.

____

____

____

____

____

C. ¿Cuáles son sus reacciones?

1. Obviamente, el profesor Guerrero Fallas era un personaje fuera de lo común. ¿Le habría gustado estar en su clase? Explique.

____

____

____

____

____

2. ¿Ha tenido usted un profesor o profesora excepcional? Escriba una descripción breve de esa persona y diga por qué la recuerda.

____

____

____

____

____

D. Forme oraciones compuestas con las siguientes oraciones simples para evitar (*to avoid*) la repetición innecesaria. No olvide el uso de la coma o el punto y coma. Siga el ejemplo.

Ejemplo: La Facultad de Economía ofrece seminarios sobre las finanzas internacionales. La Facultad de Educación tiene conferencias sobre los diferentes sistemas universitarios.

La Facultad de Economía ofrece seminarios sobre las finanzas internacionales; la de Educación tiene conferencias sobre los diferentes sistemas universitarios.

(o)

La Facultad de Economía ofrece seminarios sobre las finanzas internacionales, y la de Educación tiene conferencias sobre los diferentes sistemas universitarios.

1. No hay requisitos para inscribirse. Los aspirantes deben realizar una prueba selectiva.

____

____

____

2. Ricardo consiguió el empleo durante el verano. Ricardo no pudo pagar los derechos de matrícula este semestre.

____

____

____

3. Para inscribirse en el instituto hay que llenar una solicitud. Para inscribirse en el instituto se requiere pagar $500.

____

____

____

4. Susana obtuvo la tarjeta de la biblioteca. Susana no encontró el libro.

____

____

____

5. Olga se retiró del curso. No le devolvieron su dinero.

____

____

____

► Estructuras en acción

OBJECT PRONOUNS

In order to avoid the unnecessary repetition of direct and indirect object nouns, these words are often replaced by object pronouns.

Examples: Mariana has studied **Spanish** (direct object noun), but she doesn't speak **Spanish**. (direct object noun)
*Mariana ha estudiado **español**, pero no habla **español**.*

Mariana has studied **Spanish** (direct object noun), but she doesn't speak **it**. (direct object pronoun)
*Mariana ha estudiado **español**, pero no **lo** habla.*

Direct Object Pronouns

Direct object pronouns answer the question **Whom**? or **What**? as related to the verb. (I see **her**. He bought **it**.) Review the Spanish direct object pronouns:

Singular

me	me
te	you (familiar)
lo	him, it (masculine), you (formal, masculine)
la	her, it (feminine), you (formal, feminine)

Plural

nos	us
os	you (familiar)
los	them (masculine), you (formal, masculine)
las	them (feminine), you (formal, feminine)

Indirect Object Pronouns

Indirect object pronouns answer the questions **To whom/what?** or **For whom/what?** as related to the verb. (I'll show **her** the library. Please tell **us** where to register. Do **me** a favor.) Review the Spanish indirect object pronouns.

Singular

me	to / for me
te	to / for you (familiar)
le	to / for him, her, it, you (formal)

Plural

nos	to / for us
os	to / for you (familiar)
les	to / for them, you (formal)

NOTE: Third-person indirect object pronouns (*le, les*) usually accompany the corresponding indirect object nouns preceded by *a*. **This double usage is not considered redundant in Spanish.**

Examples: ***Le*** *solicitó ayuda a* ***la asesora.***
Les *envió la solicitud a* ***los estudiantes.***

Placement of Object Pronouns

1. Both direct and indirect object pronouns are always placed immediately in front of a conjugated verb.

   Examples: *Mariana ha estudiado español, pero no* ***lo*** *habla bien.*
   Pablo conoce al profesor y ***le*** *habla a menudo.*

2. They are always attached to an **affirmative** command,

   Examples: *Si usted quiere mejorar el español, practíque****lo.***
   *Como tú conoces al profesor, hábla****le.***

   but must precede a **negative** command.

   Example: *La profesora está ocupada; no* ***le*** *hables ahora.*

3. They **may be** attached to the end of an infinitive or a present participle (**-ndo**).

   Examples: *Yo voy a hablar****le*** (al profesor).
   (or)
   Yo ***le*** *voy a hablar.*

   *En este momento estoy hablándo****le.***
   (or)
   En este momento ***le*** *estoy hablando.*

Two Object Pronouns

1. When two object pronouns accompany the same verb, the indirect pronoun always comes before the direct. Nothing may separate them.

Examples: She told **it** (direct object) to **me** (indirect object).
*Ella **me lo** dijo.*

She's going to tell **it** to **me.**
*Ella **me lo** va a decir.*
(or)
*Ella va a decír**melo.***

2. When both object pronouns begin with the letter *l*, the first one (the indirect object) changes to *se*.

Examples: She told **it** (direct object) to **them** (indirect object).
*Ella **se*** (originally *les*) ***lo** dijo.*

She's not going to tell **it** to **them.**
*Ella no **se lo** va a decir.*
(or)
*Ella no va a decír**selo.***

EXERCISES

A. The following pamphlet exemplifies an effective use of direct and indirect object pronouns. Underline as many of these pronouns as you can, then copy each one on the lines that follow. (HINT: In this text, *se* is not an indirect object pronoun.)

BIBLIOTECA DE LA MISION

3359 de la Calle 24
SAN FRANCISCO

COMO OBTENER UNA TARJETA DE LA BIBLIOTECA

LA TARJETA DE LA BIBLIOTECA ES GRATIS

Para llevar a su casa materiales de la biblioteca usted necesita tener su propia tarjeta. Para obtenerla, los adultos necesitan llenar una solicitud y mostrar una identificación con su dirección actual. Niños menores de 14 años necesitan la firma de uno de los padres o el guardián. La información suministrada es estrictamente confidencial y es sólo para el uso de la biblioteca. En caso que se le pierda la tarjeta, se le cobrará por reemplazarla. Usted puede utilizar la tarjeta en cualquier biblioteca pública de San Francisco.

LOS LIBROS SE PRESTAN GRATIS

La mayoría de los libros se prestan por tres semanas. Cassettes, videos, revistas y algunos libros se prestan por un tiempo más limitado. Si usted regresa el material después de la fecha de vencimiento se le cobrará una multa.

PARA MAS INFORMACION LLAME AL 695-5090.

EL PERSONAL DE LA BIBLIOTECA HABLA ESPAÑOL.

Biblioteca de la Misión
3359 de la Calle 24
San Francisco, CA 94110

Teléfono: (415) 695-5090

El horario de la Biblioteca:

Lunes	10-6
Martes	10-6
Miércoles	1-9
Jueves	1-6
Viernes	1-6
Sábado	10-6

Nuestro personal habla español.

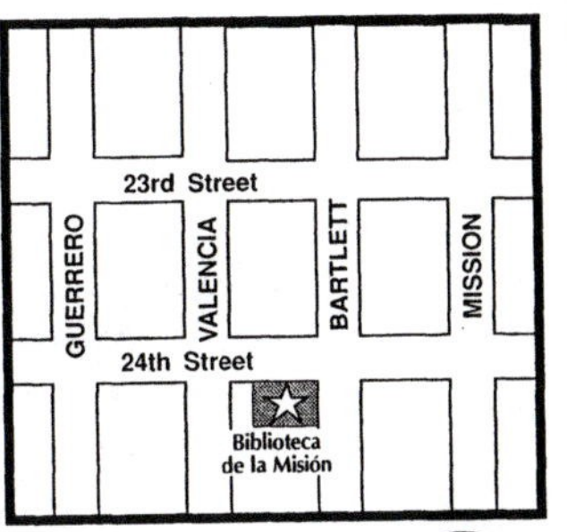

is a program of the California State Library and supported by the Library Services and Construction Act.

Tipografía, Diseño, Producción: La Raza Graphics, SF

1. ______________________ 3. ______________________

2. ______________________ 4. ______________________

5. ______________________

B. Find two direct object pronouns in the following ad.

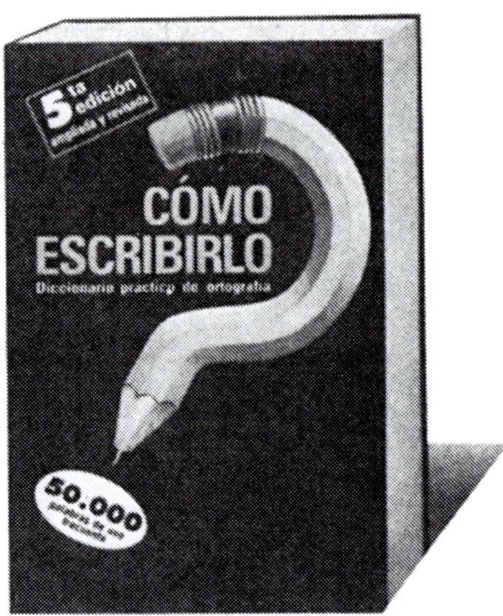

Su mejor ayudante para escribir con impecable ortografía en inglés y español.

¡Cómprelo ya en su librería o puesto de revistas favorito!

1. ______________________ 2. ______________________

Why is each pronoun attached to its verb?

1. ____

____

2. ____

____

C. Identify the direct and indirect object pronouns in the ad on page 23. (HINT: Here *lo mismo* is used to mean "the same"; *lo* is not used as a direct object.)

1. direct object pronoun: ______________________

2. indirect object pronouns:

   a. ______________________

   b. ______________________

D. Combine the following simple sentences to create a compound sentence. Use object pronouns whenever appropriate to avoid repetition. Make all necessary changes and follow the example.

Example: El asesor les explicó a los estudiantes cómo completar la solicitud. Les informó a los estudiantes que tenían que entregar la solicitud para el 2 de agosto.

El asesor les explicó a los estudiantes cómo completar la solicitud; también les informó que tenían que entregarla para el 2 de agosto.

1. Los Bonos de Ahorro de EE.UU. están exentos (*exempt*) de impuestos (*taxes*). Usar los bonos para la educación universitaria es una buena idea.

____

____

____

____

2. La Profesora Iglesias les informó a los estudiantes que habrá clase mañana. Les dijo a los estudiantes que habrá una prueba.

3. En esta clase, Omar está analizando la novela más reciente de Gabriel García Márquez. Josefina está leyendo la novela más reciente de Gabriel García Márquez para escribir un trabajo.

4. Javier compró sus libros de texto. Trajo sus libros de texto a la clase.

5. La librería universitaria no les da gratis la lista de asignaturas a los estudiantes. Les vende la lista de asignaturas a los estudiantes.

► Manos a la obra

A. He aquí (*Here is*) una lista de campos de estudio y de nombres de los profesionales que trabajan en esos campos. Familiarícese con este vocabulario.

Campo de estudio	*Profesional*
administración de empresas	administrador(a) de empresas
administración hotelera	administrador(a) de hoteles

agronomía	agrónomo(a)
antropología	antropólogo(a)
arquitectura	arquitecto(a)
astronomía	astrónomo(a)
bellas artes	pintor(a), profesor(a), etc.
biología	biólogo(a)
contabilidad	contador(a)
derecho	abogado(a)
economía	economista
educación	maestro(a), profesor(a)
filosofía	filósofo
física	físico
historia	historiador(a)
informática	técnico en informática
ingeniería	ingeniero(a)
lenguas extranjeras	profesor(a), traductor(a), intérprete
lingüística	lingüista
literatura	crítico literario, literato(a), profesor(a)
matemáticas	matemático
medicina	médico(a), doctor(a), cirujano(a)
música	músico(a), profesor(a) de música
odontología	dentista, odontólogo(a)
periodismo	periodista, reportero(a)
psicología	psicólogo(a)
química	químico
sociología	sociólogo(a)
veterinaria	veterinario(a)

B. Ahora trabaje con un(a) compañero(a) de clase. Juntos escojan dos campos profesionales. Luego digan cuál es su trabajo, de qué se ocupan y las tareas que realizan. Usen el diccionario si es necesario. Cuando sea posible, incluyan pronombres de complemento directo/indirecto.

Ejemplo: Un(a) lingüista estudia y describe la estructura de los lenguajes humanos. Puede dedicarse a enseñarla o a hacer investigación.

1. Un(a) ______________________________
____
____

2. Un(a) ______________________________
____
____

C. Con cuatro compañeros de clase, lea y estudie la siguiente descripción.

INGENIERO INDUSTRIAL EN PRODUCCION

¿QUIEN ES UN INGENIERO INDUSTRIAL EN PRODUCCION?

Es el profesionista* capacitado para el diseño, implantación y mejoramiento de sistemas integrados por personas, materiales y equipos, orientados a la producción.

AREAS DE ESPECIALIZACION

- Producción
- Métodos de Trabajo
- Sistemas de Manufactura
- Control de Calidad
- Planeación y Control de Proyectos
- Ingeniería Económica
- Simulación de Sistemas Industriales

HABILIDADES

- Elabora programas de producción.
- Diseña y mejora métodos de trabajo.
- Desarrolla modelos para pronósticos de demanda.
- Diseña e implanta sistemas de inventarios.
- Desarrolla procedimientos y políticas para el control total de calidad.
- Evalúa alternativas de inversión.
- Administra sistemas de manufactura.

¿DONDE TRABAJA?

En una empresa manufacturera en los siguientes departamentos:

- Control de Producción
- Embarques
- Ingeniería de Productos
- Superintendencia de Planta
- Mantenimiento
- Fabricación
- Aseguramiento de Calidad

En empresas comerciales, bancarias, de servicio al público y servicios en general en los siguientes departamentos:

- Ventas
- Organización y Métodos
- Ingeniería de Proyectos
- Gerencia General
- Mantenimiento
- Investigación y Desarrollo

*La palabra ***profesionista*** es un mexicanismo. En otros países se usa el término ***profesional***.

Ahora piensen ustedes en otra profesión (como contador, abogada, biólogo marino, dentista, profesora de español, etc.) y elaboren su propia descripción usando oraciones compuestas y pronombres cuando sea posible. Sigan los siguientes pasos:

1. ¿Quién es...?

___

___

___

2. ¿Cuáles son las áreas de especialización?

___

___

___

3. ¿Qué habilidades necesita?

___

___

___

4. ¿Dónde trabaja?

____

____

____

Elijan ustedes ahora a un miembro del grupo para presentar su trabajo a la clase.

D. En una hoja adicional (*an extra sheet of paper*), describa su carrera o especialización y entréguele su redacción a su profesor o profesora.

PARA LOS INTERNAUTAS

Vaya a **http://www.wiley.com/college/gonzalez,** busque la página que corresponde a este capítulo y haga los ejercicios indicados.

MÁS ALLÁ

Toda universidad tiene una serie de actividades extracurriculares. Comente los siguientes temas con sus compañeros de clase. Luego escoja uno de ellos y escriba sus opiniones al respecto. Use oraciones simples y compuestas para variar el estilo.

1. ¿Qué obras de teatro se han presentado últimamente en la universidad? ¿Han asistido a alguna? Hagan un comentario de una obra de interés del teatro universitario o de otro teatro.
2. ¿En qué deportes sobresale esta universidad? ¿Qué deportes les interesan a ustedes? Escriban un comentario sobre un partido emocionante jugado en el campus.
3. Mencionen algunas de las organizaciones estudiantiles de esta universidad. Describan una en detalle, explicando sus funciones y labores en el campus.

En esta página podrá anotar sus ideas respecto al capítulo o bien referirse a un episodio de su propia vida.

Mi diario:

Capítulo 2

La familia

Objectives

Upon completion of this chapter you should be able to:

- identify and create complex sentences
- utilize appropriate vocabulary to write about the family
- use conjunctions and relative pronouns

Integrantes de varias generaciones se encuentran en esta reunión familiar.

Para hablar del tema

VOCABULARIO ESENCIAL

Estudie las siguientes palabras y expresiones. Le pueden resultar útiles para entender el capítulo y escribir sobre la familia.

Sustantivos

el (la) abuelo(a)	*grandfather (grandmother)*
el apellido[1]	*family name, surname*
el bautizo	*baptism, christening party*
el (la) bisabuelo(a)	*great-grandfather (great-grandmother)*
el (la) bisnieto(a)	*great-grandson (great-granddaughter)*
la boda	*wedding*
la comadre	*name used reciprocally by the godmother and the parents of the child*
el compadre	*name used reciprocally by the godfather and the parents of the child*
el (la) cónyuge / esposo(a)	*spouse*
el cumpleaños	*birthday*
el (la) cuñado(a)	*brother-in-law (sister-in-law)*
la familia adoptiva	*adoptive family*
la familia extendida	*extended family*
la familia nuclear	*nuclear family*
el funeral	*funeral*
los (las) gemelos(as)	*twins*
la guardería infantil	*day-care center*
el (la) hermano(a)	*brother (sister)*
el (la) hijo(a)	*son (daughter)*
el hogar	*home, household*
el hogar de ancianos	*retirement home*
la madre	*mother*
la madrina	*godmother*
el marido / esposo	*husband*
el matrimonio	*matrimony, married couple*
la muerte	*death*
la mujer / esposa	*wife*
el nacimiento	*birth*
el (la) nieto(a)	*grandson (granddaughter)*
la niñera	*nursemaid, babysitter*
el nombre de pila	*given name*
el (la) novio(a)	*boyfriend (girlfriend) / fiancé (fiancée)*
el noviazgo	*courtship*
el padre	*father*
el padrino	*godfather*
el parentesco	*family relationship*
los parientes	*relatives*

[1]Most Hispanics use two surnames: the first is paternal, the second is maternal. Example: *Ana Rojas* (father's surname) *Loría* (mother's surname).

el parto	*act of giving birth*
la pensión alimenticia	*spouse or child support*
la primera comunión	*first communion*
el (la) primo(a)	*cousin*
la quinceañera	*girl celebrating her fifteenth birthday*
el (la) sobrino(a)	*nephew (niece)*
el (la) suegro(a)	*father-in-law (mother-in-law)*
el (la) tío(a)	*uncle (aunt)*
el (la) tío(a) político(a)	*uncle (aunt) by marriage*
la unión consensual	*common-law marriage*
la vejez	*old age*
el (la) viudo(a)	*widower, widow*

Verbos

adoptar	*to adopt*
casarse	*to get married*
comprometerse	*to get engaged*
dar a luz	*to give birth*
divorciarse	*to get divorced*
enamorarse (de)	*to fall in love (with)*
enviudar	*to become a widower or widow*
separarse	*to separate, break up*

Adjetivos

familiar	*pertaining to the family*
materno	*maternal*
paterno	*paternal*

NOTA: La forma masculina **plural** de muchos sustantivos que indican relaciones familiares puede referirse a ambos sexos.

Ejemplos:	padres	*parents*	tíos	*uncles and aunts*
	hermanos	*siblings*	nietos	*grandchildren*
	hijos	*children*	abuelos	*grandparents*

A. Lea el árbol genealógico de la familia de Arturo Soto Díaz (página 34).

B. Conteste las siguientes preguntas sobre la familia de Arturo Soto Díaz.

1. ¿Quiénes son los bisabuelos de Arturo?

____

2. ¿Cuál es el apellido materno de la abuela de Arturo?

____

3. ¿Cómo se llaman los tíos de Arturo?

____

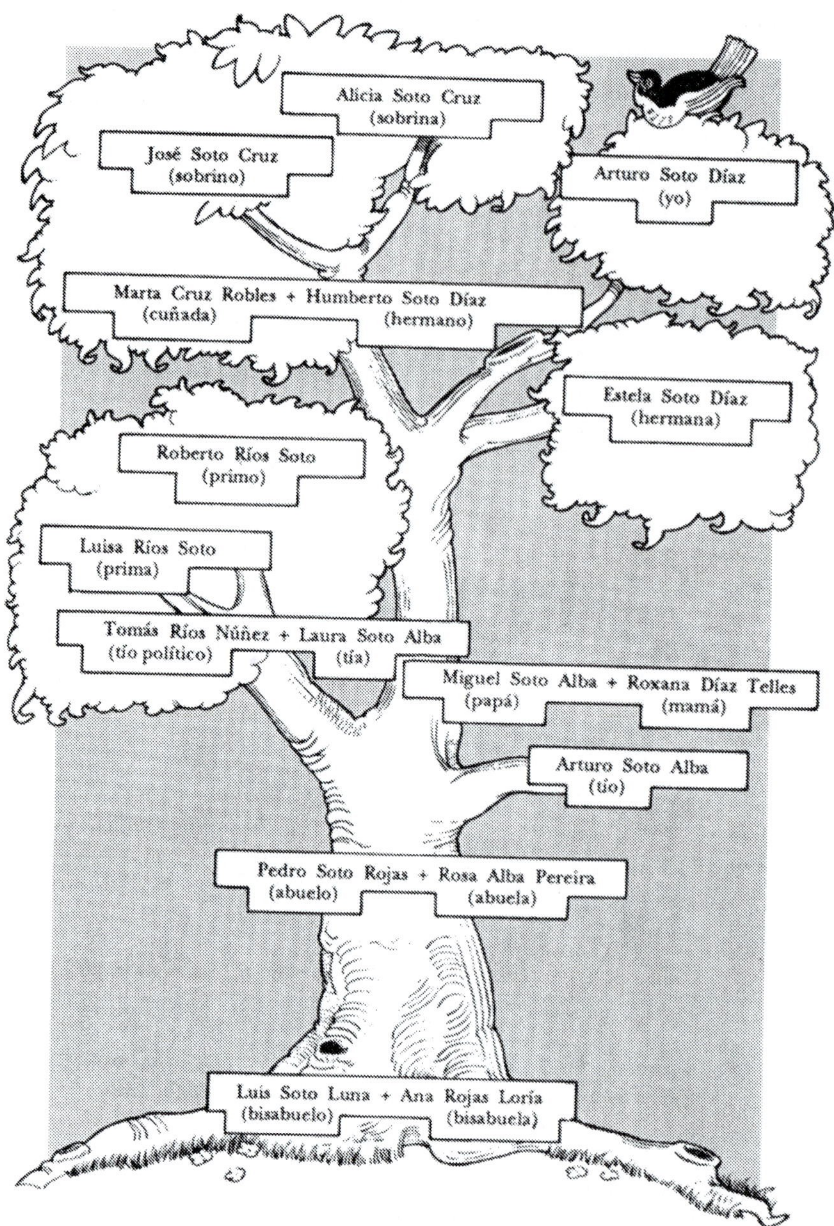

4. ¿Qué parentesco existe entre Arturo y Alicia Soto Cruz?

____

5. ¿Cuántos bisnietos tienen Pedro Soto y Rosa Alba?

____

6. ¿Qué lazos (*ties*) familiares unen a Tomás Ríos y a Laura Soto?

____

C. Haga una lista de otras palabras que le podrían ser útiles para escribir sobre la familia. Si es necesario, busque esos términos en el diccionario.

____________	____________	____________
____________	____________	____________
____________	____________	____________
____________	____________	____________
____________	____________	____________
____________	____________	____________
____________	____________	____________
____________	____________	____________
____________	____________	____________
____________	____________	____________

VOCABULARIO CLAVE

Las palabras de esta sección son de uso muy frecuente. Estúdielas y apréndalas. Le ayudarán en sus trabajos de redacción.

no obstante, sin embargo *however*

Alba y Eladio se divorciaron; **no obstante**, siguen siendo amigos.

por lo general *generally*

Por lo general nos reunimos con los parientes en el mismo restaurante.

a menudo *often*

Mis primos del Ecuador me llaman por teléfono **a menudo**.

a veces *sometimes*

A veces las responsabilidades familiares impiden dedicarse a los estudios.

► Análisis de la oración compleja

Imagine por un segundo la monotonía de la composición si sólo tuviéramos oraciones simples y compuestas. La oración **compleja** nos permite indicar en una sola oración la relación entre ideas. Contiene por lo menos **una cláusula principal** (independiente, con significado completo) y una o más **cláusulas subordinadas** (dependientes, que necesitan una cláusula principal para completar su significado). La cláusula subordinada puede aparecer al principio, intercalada (*embedded*), o al final de la oración. En los ejemplos de esta sección, las cláusulas subordinadas aparecerán entre corchetes (*brackets*).

Ejemplos: [Cuando llegan a la vejez], los ancianos continúan en sus casas.
Los ancianos continúan en sus casas [cuando llegan a la vejez].
Los ancianos, [cuando llegan a la vejez], continúan en sus casas.

Para unir la cláusula subordinada a la principal, a veces se usa un pronombre relativo (**que**, **quien**, **el que**, **la que**, **las cuales**, etc.) o el adjetivo relativo **cuyo** (whose).

Ejemplos: La tía Clara, [quien era soltera], siempre pasaba la Navidad con nosotros.
Vino la tía Esmeralda, [cuyos hijos estaban en Venezuela].

Usted encontrará más información sobre los pronombres relativos y el adjetivo **cuyo** en las páginas 41–43.

Otras veces, se emplea una conjunción subordinante para unir la cláusula subordinada a la principal. La conjunción subordinante puede expresar cualquiera de los conceptos que se indican a continuación.

Tiempo

antes (de) que	*before*
cuando	*when*
desde que	*since*
después (de) que	*after*
en cuanto	*as soon as*
hasta que	*until*
mientras que	*while*
tan pronto como	*as soon as*

Ejemplo: [**Después que** Ana se casó], se mudó a casa de sus suegros.

Sitio

donde, dondequiera	*where, wherever*

Ejemplo: La casa [**donde** vivían] estaba en el centro de la ciudad.

Causa

porque	*because*
puesto que	*since, inasmuch as*
ya que	*since, because*

Ejemplo: [**Puesto que** mi abuela enviudó], ahora vive con nosotros.

Concesión

aunque	*although*

Ejemplo: [**Aunque** el divorcio representa el final del matrimonio], no tiene que suponer el final de la familia.

Condición

a menos que	*unless*
con tal que	*provided that*
si	*if*
sin que	*without*

Ejemplo: La quinceañera tendrá la fiesta en casa de los abuelos [**si** no encuentra un salón].

Propósito

de manera que	*so that*
para que	*so that*

Ejemplo: [**Para que** la fiesta resulte más animada], invitaremos a toda la familia.

Manera

como	*as, since*

Ejemplo: [**Como** el costo de la vida es alto], a veces los recién casados viven con sus padres.

A. Subraye las cláusulas dependientes de las siguientes oraciones complejas.

1. Si la relación no mejora, Luisa piensa divorciarse.
2. La boda a la que asistí tuvo lugar en la Iglesia de la Merced.
3. La tía que más quiero vive en Cuernavaca.
4. Como te contaba, mi padrino fue un gran futbolista.
5. Para que vivieran más cómodamente, la abuela les hizo a los nietos un dormitorio en el segundo piso.

B. Relea las oraciones del Ejercicio A. Ahora, en los espacios siguientes, copie la palabra que une cada cláusula subordinada a la oración principal e indique si es un pronombre o una conjunción.

1. ______________________: ______________________
2. ______________________: ______________________
3. ______________________: ______________________
4. ______________________: ______________________
5. ______________________: ______________________

C. Forme oraciones complejas con las siguientes oraciones simples. Use las conjunciones subordinantes de las páginas 36–37.

Ejemplo:

Oraciones simples:	Los niños no pueden ir al cine. Los padres no les dieron dinero.
Oración compleja:	*Ya que los padres no les dieron dinero, los niños no pueden ir al cine.* (o) *Los niños no pueden ir al cine porque los padres no les dieron dinero.*

1. Llueve. Mi abuelo y yo jugamos a las cartas.
   Mi abuelo... porque llueve
   ____

2. El funeral terminó. Nos reunimos con los parientes y amigos de la familia.
   Nos reunimos... después del funeral.
   ____

3. Julián es pobre. Eva quiere casarse con él.
   Aunque Julian..., Eva quiere...
   ____

4. El matrimonio Rodríguez-Sánchez necesita una casa más grande. Ahora tienen cuatro hijos.
   El matrimonio... porque ahora tienen...
   ____

5. Eladio y Leticia se casaron. Los padres no lo supieron.
   Eladio y Leticia... pero los padres
   ____

► Para escribir mejor

CÓMO IDENTIFICAR Y ESCRIBIR ORACIONES COMPLEJAS

A. Subraye y copie al menos cinco cláusulas subordinadas (dependientes) de las oraciones complejas del siguiente texto.

El Divorcio, Transición Sin Pelea

Cuando uno se casa, lo hace convencido que es para toda la vida. Por eso, cuando la palabra divorcio hace su aparición, nos toma desprevenidos°. Si además se desconocen las leyes del divorcio, separarse de su esposo o esposa puede convertirse en una pesadilla° cara. Para evitar eso, es aconsejable que cada cónyuge establezca créditos a su nombre y que se paguen las deudas que tengan en común.

by surprise
nightmare

El divorcio representa el final del matrimonio, pero no tiene por qué suponer el final de la familia. La mayoría de las leyes del divorcio fueron creadas para proteger la unidad emocional y financiera entre padres e hijos. Si usted es capaz de ver el divorcio como una transición hacia otro tipo de vida familiar, le será más fácil adaptarse a su nueva situación.

1. ____

____

2. ____

____

3. ____

____

4. ____

____

5. ____

____

B. **Si usted fuera un (una) consejero(a) matrimonial, ¿qué ideas le sugeriría a un (una) cliente que está a punto de divorciarse? ¿Por qué?**

____

____

____

____

____

____

____

____

____

____

C. **Un divorciado, quien ha estado pagándoles una pensión alimenticia a su esposa y supuesto *(presumed)* hijo, acaba de enterarse (*to find out*) por medio de un examen de sangre que en realidad el hijo no es suyo. La esposa alega que ella, de buena fe, siempre pensó que él era el verdadero padre. El esposo, por su parte, ha presentado una demanda judicial para suspender el pago de la pensión. ¿Debe seguir ayudando el padre al hijo? ¿Debe ser castigada la esposa? Usted y otros cinco compañeros de clase han sido escogidos para decidir el caso. Escriban el veredicto del jurado en las líneas que siguen y prepárense para darle una explicación de sus razones al resto de la clase.**

____

____

____

____

____

____

____

____

____

____

▶ Estructuras en acción

RELATIVE PRONOUNS

As you have learned, complex sentences often contain a subordinate clause introduced by a relative pronoun. The words **who, whom, whose, what, which**, etc. are relative pronouns in English. *Que, quien, cuyo,* etc. are examples of Spanish relative pronouns. With very few exceptions, these words refer to a noun that has already been mentioned—the **antecedent**.

Examples:	*El primo*	***que** llamó...*	The cousin	***who*** called...
	(antecedent)	*(pronoun)*	*(antecedent)*	*(pronoun)*
	La niñera	*con **quien** hablé...*	The babysitter	with **whom** I spoke...
	(antecedent)	*(pronoun)*	*(antecedent)*	*(pronoun)*

It is important to note that sometimes the English relative pronoun may be omitted; however, in Spanish it is **never** omitted.

Example: *El hogar **que** visitamos es muy unido.*
The household (**that**) we visited is very close-knit.

Familiarity with the following relative pronouns and their uses is a valuable prerequisite to good writing in Spanish.

Que

This word is the most commonly used relative pronoun. Its antecedent can be a person or an object, singular or plural. *Que* functions as:

1. the subject of a **restrictive** adjective clause (a clause that provides essential, indispensable information to identify or describe the antecedent). *Que* is the **only** pronoun that can be used in this situation.

   Examples: *La tía **que** habló...* (singular subject, antecedent is a person)
   *Los hogares **que** visitamos...* (plural subject, antecedent is a thing)

2. the subject of a **nonrestrictive** adjective clause (a clause that adds some additional—but not essential—information about the antecedent). Nonrestrictive clauses are easily recognizable because they are always set off by commas.

   Example: *La abuela, **que** ya estaba cansada, decidió retirarse a dormir.*

3. the direct object.

   Example: *La casa **que** compró el abuelo está cerca de mi pueblo.*
   (direct object, antecedent is a thing)

Quien, quienes

This pronoun refers only to persons (or personified objects). *Quien* is used with a singular antecedent and *quienes* with a plural. *Quien/quienes* functions as:

1. the indirect object.

   Example: *La joven a* ***quien*** *le celebran los quince años...*

2. the object of a preposition.

   Example: *Los primos con* ***quienes*** *hablamos...*

3. the subject of a **nonrestrictive** clause. In this function, *quien/quienes* can be replaced by *que.*

   Examples: *Los hijos,* ***quienes*** *habían jugado por horas, estaban agotados.*
   (or)
   Los hijos, ***que*** *habían jugado por horas, estaban agotados.*

4. the equivalent of indefinite English expressions such as **whoever, whomever**, **the one who**, **anyone who**, etc., when the antecedent is either indefinite or not expressed.

   Examples: ***Quien*** *no trabaja, no come.*
   Tengo que buscar ***quien*** *me haga los quehaceres domésticos.*

El/La/Los/Las que or *El/La/Los/Las* cual(es)

The relative pronoun *cual(es)* is more precise than *que,* which is invariable. Both of them are preceded by the definite article (*el, la, los, las*). In **written** Spanish, *cual(es)* is usually preferred.

1. *Cual(es)* occurs in nonrestrictive clauses when the distance between the antecedent and the relative pronoun could cause confusion or when there is more than one noun that could be the antecedent.

   Examples: *Mi hermano trajo las fotos del viaje,* ***las cuales*** *me encantaron.* (*Las cuales* refers to *fotos.* The **photos** are what delighted me.)
   (but)
   Mi hermano trajo las fotos del viaje, ***el cual*** *me encantó.* (*El cual* refers to *viaje.* The **trip** is what delighted me.)

2. In written Spanish, *el cual* is used more often than *el que* after prepositions of two or more syllables (*hacia, para, contra, dentro de, desde, sobre,* etc.) and after prepositional phrases (*después de, cerca de, lejos de, junto a,* etc.). However, *el que* is grammatically correct in these instances in both written and spoken Spanish.

   Examples: *La aldea* (village) *cerca de* ***la cual*** *vivíamos está a unos veinte kilómetros de la capital.*
   (or)
   La aldea cerca de ***la que*** *vivíamos está a unos veinte kilómetros de la capital.*

3. When *el* (*la, los, las*) *que* occurs with no expressed antecedent, it is often equivalent to the English **the one(s) who**.

Example: ***El que*** *te llamó debe haber sido un pariente lejano.*

Cuyo

This word, which is really an adjective (equivalent to the English word **whose**), is used with both persons and things. It is important to remember that it must agree in number and gender with the **noun possessed**, not with the possessor. It occurs more often in written Spanish than in the spoken language.

Examples: *La familia,* ***cuyos*** *miembros asistieron a la fiesta...*
(*Cuyos* agrees with *miembros*, not with *familia.*)
The family, **whose** members attended the party...

Este es el padre ***cuya*** *hija se casó sin avisar.*
(*Cuya* agrees with *hija*, not with *padre.*)
This is the father **whose** daughter got married without letting anyone know.

Mi hermana, ***cuyo*** *auto usamos durante el viaje...*
(*Cuyo* agrees with *auto*, not with *hermana.*)
My sister, **whose** car we used during the trip...

Lo cual

This pronoun is used when the antecedent is an **entire clause**, not just a word or phrase.

Examples: *Todos los hijos de la señora Araluce son muy corteses,* ***lo cual*** *no es nada de extrañar.*
All of Mrs. Araluce's children are extremely polite, **which** is not at all surprising.

Note that the antecedent of *lo cual* is the entire clause *Todos los hijos de la señora Araluce son muy corteses,* **not** any specific noun.

Lo que

This pronoun refers to a noun or a clause **previously expressed**. It is equivalent to **what, whatever,** or **that which**.

Examples: ***Lo que*** *dijo papá nos sorprendió.*
What Dad said surprised us.

Mamá te comprará ***lo que*** *quieras si te portas bien.*
Mom will buy you **whatever** you want if you behave.

EXERCISES

A. Read the following text and underline the relative pronouns.

HOMBRES FAMOSOS QUE SE ENAMORARON DE LA HERMANA DE SU ESPOSA

1- Herodes, quien incluso ejecutó a San Juan Bautista porque cuestionó su derecho a casarse con su cuñada. 2- Enrique VIII, quien sostuvo un sonado romance con María Bolena antes de que el muy apasionado rey se enamorara de su hermana Ana, a quien terminó cortándole la cabeza. 3- Mozart, el compositor, quien se enamoró primero de Aloysia Weber y terminó casándose con su hermana Constanza, al ser rechazado por Aloysia. 4- El escritor Charles Dickens, quien se enamoró de DOS de sus cuñadas y terminó divorciándose de su esposa a los 22 años de casados y después de tener 10 hijos. 5- El famoso Sigmund Freud, quien se enamoró perdidamente de la hermana de su mujer, Minna, a quien le confió todas sus ideas sobre el sicoanálisis, y de quien se afirma fue amante por más de 40 años. Lo más curioso es que Minna vivía en la misma casa de su hermana y cuñado, y para llegar a su dormitorio tenía que atravesar el dormitorio matrimonial de los Freud. 6- Y en épocas modernas tenemos el caso del armador griego Stavros Niarchos, quien primero se casó con Eugenia Livanos (de cuya súbita muerte se le acusó, aunque fue llevado a juicio) y después se casó con su cuñada Tina Livanos, quien había sido la esposa de su archirrival en los negocios, Aristóteles Onassis.

sonado... celebrated; rechazado...*rejected*; perdidamente... *hopelessly*; súbita... sudden

OBSERVE... el uso de la preposición ***con*** unida al verbo ***casarse*** en las líneas 3, 10, 28 y 31. Note también el uso de la preposición ***de*** que sigue el verbo reflexivo ***enamorarse*** en las líneas 6, 9, 13 y 17.

B. Explain why the underlined relative pronouns are used in the following excerpt.

Example: *It is the object of a preposition* or *it introduces a nonrestrictive adjective clause whose antecedent is* ______________________________.

El famoso Sigmund Freud, quien (1) se enamoró de...Minna, a quien (2) le confió todas sus ideas sobre el sicoanálisis, y de quien (3) se afirma que fue amante por más de 40 años... . Y en épocas modernas tenemos el caso del armador griego Stavros Niarchos, quien (4) primero se casó con Eugenia Livanos (de cuya (5) súbita muerte se le acusó)... .

1. quien ____

____

____

2. a quien ______________________________

____

____

3. de quien ______________________________

____

____

4. quien ______________________________

____

____

5. cuya ______________________________

____

____

C. Using a relative pronoun, combine the following simple sentences to create a complex sentence. Eliminate unnecessary repetition where possible. Follow the example.

Example: Simple sentences: Herodes ejecutó a San Juan Bautista.
Herodes se casó con su cuñada.

Complex sentence: *Herodes, quien ejecutó a San Juan Bautista, se casó con su cuñada.*

(or)

Herodes, quien se casó con su cuñada, ejecutó a San Juan Bautista.

1. Simple sentences: Enrique VIII se casó con Ana Bolena.
Enrique VIII le cortó la cabeza a Ana Bolena finalmente.

Complex sentence: ______________________________

____

____

2. Simple sentences: Mozart se casó con Constanza Weber.
La hermana de Constanza Weber rechazó a Mozart.

Complex sentence: ______________________________

____

____

3. Simple sentences: Minna vivió en la casa de Freud.
Minna fue amante de Freud.

Complex sentence: ______________________________

____

____

4. Simple sentences: Stavros Niarchos fue un armador griego.
Stavros Niarchos se casó con Eugenia Livanos.

Complex sentence: ______________________________

____

____

D. Give Spanish equivalents of the following sentences.

1. This is the woman whose son got married last week.

____

____

____

2. The house in which the Castro family lived was destroyed by an earthquake (*un terremoto*).

____

____

____

3. My cousin invited me to her wedding, which made me very happy.

____

____

____

4. Whoever has children has responsibility.

____

____

____

5. What Aunt Marta told me is a secret.

____

____

____

► Manos a la obra

A. Lea el siguiente texto. Subraye los pronombres relativos y las conjunciones subordinantes en las oraciones complejas y observe su uso. Familiarícese con el vocabulario también.

Cambios en la familia hispanoamericana

El cuadro estereotipado de una familia hispana altamente unida, siempre numerosa y con una organización patriarcal es en mucho la imagen de tiempos pretéritos o de las zonas rurales. Para comprender mejor los cambios que han surgido, es necesario hacer cortes longitudinales de la sociedad hispanoamericana y observar el ambiente en el que se desarrolla cada familia.

La familia culta de clase media o alta en los grandes centros urbanos recuerda la europea o la norteamericana. Ambos cónyuges desempeñan actividades profesionales y el núcleo familiar es relativamente pequeño. Como el nivel de vida es superior al del resto de la población, los miembros de esta unidad disfrutan de las comodidades modernas y mantienen una actitud muy abierta hacia cambios venidos del exterior. La mujer, aunque aún juega un papel tradicional, se ha independizado bastante y ha dejado el nido hogareño° para colaborar con su marido en el plano económico. Este grupo social acepta sin muchos reparos° el aborto, la planificación familiar y el divorcio como formas legítimas de modelar la familia moderna.

home
qualms

Problemas socio-económicos han creado una emigración constante del campo hacia las ciudades. Los nuevos arribos° constituyen un cinturón de pobreza alrededor de las ciudades importantes. Estas clases

arrivals

desproveídas° en las grandes aglomeraciones metropolitanas ven un derrumbamiento° de sus valores y una desintegración de la familia. Las uniones consensuales son comunes y los hijos ilegítimos muchas veces crecen sin el padre. La madre, quien se convierte en la única responsable del bienestar del grupo familiar, es por lo general obrera o empleada doméstica. En los países donde existe la medicina social, estas mujeres tienen acceso a clínicas y hopitales donde se practica la distribución de anticonceptivos, la esterilización y, en casos especiales, el aborto. En los casos más patéticos, los hijos deambulan° por las calles solicitando limosna y muchas veces terminan con líos° judiciales.

poor
collapse
walk aimlessly
problems

Un tercer grupo está constituído por las familias de zonas rurales. Es aquí que se conservan las actitudes religiosas y tradicionales que normalmente se asocian con la familia hispanoamericana. La madre junto con las hijas mayores son típicas amas de casa, encargadas del hogar y de velar por los niños. El padre junto con los hijos mayores trabaja fuera de la casa; es el patriarca y mantiene una actitud altamente machista. El producto es una familia extendida en la cual los anticonceptivos y la planificación familiar son rechazados como pecaminosos° o dañinos. Este sector de la población sufre los altibajos° de la economía mundial y local y tiene muchos problemas para sobrevivir. No es de extrañar, pues, que gran número de estas familias emigren masivamente a las ciudades, alimentándose así el ciclo urbano descrito anteriormente.

sinful
ups and downs

Es un hecho ineludible° que las estructuras familiares son complejas en Hispanoamérica y que las diferencias que a menudo se atribuyen a la familia tradicional tienden a desaparecer. Es también verdad que los jóvenes aceptan más fácilmente los cambios, y con el advenimiento de un nivel de vida más holgado°, las nuevas estructuras adquieren vigor. Hay que apuntar, no obstante, que aunque el núcleo familiar se ha achicado°, el concepto de familia extendida donde caben los abuelos, las tías, los primos y aún parentela° distante, sigue vigente. Hasta ahora las guarderías infantiles de los centros urbanos no han logrado reemplazar totalmente a las abuelas.

unavoidable
comfortable
has become smaller
relatives

B. Con un(a) compañero(a) forme oraciones complejas de las siguientes oraciones sencillas. Usen un pronombre relativo o una conjunción subordinante para introducir la cláusula dependiente. (Consulten las páginas 36–37 si necesitan repasar las conjunciones subordinantes.)

Ejemplo: Los hijos tienen a menudo líos con la justicia. Deambulan por las calles solos.
Cuando los hijos deambulan por las calles solos, a menudo tienen líos con la justicia.

1. La familia extendida es una estructura. Aquí cabe toda la parentela.

La familia extendida es una estructura ______________________________

____

2. La madre es por lo general obrera. Es la única responsable del grupo familiar.

   La madre, ____
   ____

3. Hay que observar parámetros de clase social y de posición geográfica. Podemos caer en el esterotipo falso.

   A menos que ____
   ____

4. Vamos a explicar los cambios. Los cambios han surgido recientemente.

   Vamos a explicar los cambios ______________________________
   ____

5. Es necesario tener en cuenta el ambiente de cada familia. Cada familia vive en un ambiente específico.

   Es necesario tener en cuenta el ambiente específico______________
   ____

6. El padre aún juega el papel de proveedor. La madre también contribuye económicamente.

   ______________________________, la madre contribuye también ecómicamente.

7. Los hijos ilegítimos son comunes. Los cinturones de pobreza se hallan por todo Hispanoamérica.

   Los cinturones de pobreza, en______________________________
   ______________________________, se hallan por todo Hispanoamérica.

C. ¿Ya encontró su media naranja *(better half)* o aún la sigue buscando? En una hoja adicional, prepare una descripción de su compañero(a) ideal. Describa su personalidad, su aspecto físico y hable de sus gustos, hábitos y pasatiempos. Incluya por lo menos tres oraciones complejas en su trabajo. A continuación encontrará algunos términos que le podrían ser útiles para realizar este ejercicio.

Personalidad

inteligente, con un buen sentido del humor, de buen carácter, trabajador(a), cariñoso(a), alegre, comprensivo(a), etc.

Aspecto físico

moreno(a), rubio(a), de ojos (negros, café, azules), de pelo (rubio, castaño, negro, rizado, lacio), en forma, musculoso(a), bien vestido(a), limpio(a), etc.

Gustos, hábitos y pasatiempos

aficionado(a) al..., jugador(a) de..., etc.

D. Ahora, trabajando en grupos de cinco, lean y comenten lo que cada uno(a) ha escrito para el Ejercicio C. Escojan el mejor trabajo y léanlo al resto de la clase.

PARA LOS INTERNAUTAS

Vaya a **http://www.wiley.com/college/gonzalez,** busque la página que corresponde a este capítulo y haga los ejercicios indicados.

MÁS ALLÁ

Comente los siguientes temas con sus compañeros de clase. Luego escoja uno de ellos y escriba sus opiniones al respecto. Use oraciones simples, compuestas y complejas para variar el estilo.

1. El núcleo familiar ha cambiado mucho. En el pasado la madre se quedaba en casa y el padre salía a trabajar. Hoy, ambos (*both*) trabajan y en algunos casos es el padre quien cuida de los hijos y está encargado de las labores del hogar. ¿Qué consecuencias han tenido estos cambios? ¿Les parecen los tiempos contemporáneos más justos y beneficiosos? Den sus ideas sobre los cambios en la familia tradicional.
2. Muchos ancianos terminan sus días alejados de (*far from*) sus parientes en un asilo (*retirement, nursing home*). ¿Permitirían ustedes que sus padres murieran en una institución para ancianos? Algunos piensan que los ancianos tienen mejor cuidado médico en un asilo y que se sienten mejor con personas de su misma edad y gustos. Otros creen que los ancianos pueden vivir más y mejores años si se quedan con sus parientes y ayudan con las tareas de la casa. Además muchos afirman que los ancianos sufren muchos maltratos y abusos en esas instituciones. ¿Cuáles son sus reacciones sobre este tema?
3. Uno de los más agudos (*pressing*) problemas de nuestra sociedad es el maltrato y abuso de niños y adolescentes. ¿Cuáles creen ustedes que son las causas? ¿Qué se podría hacer para disminuir este flagelo (*calamity*)?

En esta página podrá anotar sus ideas sobre este capítulo o bien referirse o a un episodio de su propia vida.

Mi diario:

Capítulo 3

La rutina diaria

Objectives

Upon completion of this chapter you should be able to:

- understand the structure of a paragraph
- write an effective paragraph
- utilize appropriate vocabulary to write about your daily routine
- use reflexive constructions

De compras por las calles de Buenos Aires, Argentina.

▶ Para hablar del tema

VOCABULARIO ESENCIAL

Estudie las siguientes palabras y expresiones. Le pueden resultar útiles para entender el capítulo y escribir sobre la rutina diaria.

Sustantivos

la agenda	*agenda*
el aseo	*cleaning, cleanliness*
la barbería	*barber shop*
el gimnasio	*gym*
la guardería infantil	*day-care center*
la higiene	*hygiene*
el horario	*schedule*
la iglesia	*church*
la peluquería	*hairstyling salon, barber shop*
el salón de belleza	*beauty shop*
la sinagoga	*synagogue*
el templo	*temple*

Verbos

acostarse (ue)	*to go to bed*
afeitarse / rasurarse	*to shave*
almorzar (ue)	*to have lunch*
bañarse	*to take a bath*
cambiarse de ropa	*to change clothes*
cenar	*to have dinner*
cepillarse los dientes	*to brush one's teeth*
cocinar	*to cook*
cortarse el pelo	*to get a haircut*
desayunar(se)	*to eat breakfast*
descansar	*to rest*
despertarse (ie)	*to wake up*
desvestirse (i, i)	*to undress, get undressed*
divertirse (ie, i)	*to have fun*
ducharse	*to take a shower*
encontrarse (ue) con alguien	*to meet someone, run into someone*
hacer los mandados	*to run errands*
ir al banco	*to go to the bank*
ir de compras	*to go shopping*
lavar la ropa	*to wash clothes*
lavarse el pelo	*to wash one's hair*
levantarse	*to get up*
merendar (ie)	*to snack*
pagar las cuentas	*to pay bills*
pasar la aspiradora	*to vacuum*

peinarse	*to comb one's hair*
poner el despertador	*to set the alarm clock*
tomar una siesta	*to take a nap*
vestirse (i, i)	*to dress, get dressed*

A. Lea el horario de Ernestina Ruiz, estudiante y madre.

martes **24 de mayo de 1999**

A.M.

6:00	
7:00	
8:00	llevar a Joselito a casa de doña Emilia
9:00	
10:00	~~salón de belleza~~ cita con la dentista
11:00	depositar los cheques y hablar con el gerente
12:00	almuerzo con Enrique y Sofía (Hacienda del Viejo)

P.M.

1:00	
2:00	examen de Filosofía 102
3:00	ver Prof. Guardia (traer el borrador)
4:00	primera clase de aeróbicos
5:00	
6:00	
7:00	cena con doña Emilia
8:00	
9:00	
10:00	

B. Ahora, conteste las siguientes preguntas sobre las actividades de Ernestina Ruiz. Use su imaginación cuando sea necesario.

1. ¿Por qué no pudo ir al salón de belleza a las diez de la mañana?

____

____

2. ¿Quién es doña Emilia?

____

____

3. ¿Cuándo va a repasar Ernestina para el examen de Filosofía 102?

____

____

4. ¿Adónde va a las once de la mañana?

____

____

C. Ernestina no especificó las actividades de todo el día. Use su imaginación y diga qué hizo a las...

7:00 A.M. ______________________________

9:00 A.M. ______________________________

5:00 P.M. ______________________________

6:00 P.M. ______________________________

8:00 P.M. ______________________________

10:00 P.M. ______________________________

D. Ahora haga una lista de las palabras en el Ejercicio A que usted no conocía. Añada otras expresiones que considere útiles para escribir sobre las actividades diarias. Si es necesario, busque su significado en el diccionario.

______	______	______
______	______	______
______	______	______
______	______	______
______	______	______
______	______	______
______	______	______
______	______	______
______	______	______
______	______	______

VOCABULARIO CLAVE

Las palabras de esta sección son de uso muy frecuente. Estúdielas y apréndalas. Le ayudarán en sus trabajos de redacción.

al fin y al cabo *in the long run*

Discutimos mucho pero **al fin y al cabo** el que tuvo que pasar la aspiradora fui yo.

así pues, por lo tanto *thus*

Debes levantarte temprano; **así pues**, pon el despertador y no protestes.

apenas *scarcely, hardly*

Apenas hay tiempo para comer y relajarse.

antes que nada *before anything, first and foremost*

Antes que nada usted debe mantener una actitud positiva ante la vida.

Análisis del párrafo y su estructura

En los capítulos 1 y 2 se analizó la oración. Otra unidad más extensa y de mayor importancia es el párrafo. Previamente habíamos definido una oración como un grupo de palabras que expresa una idea o pensamiento. Un párrafo es un grupo de oraciones que expresan una idea o tema. Si no tuviéramos párrafos, una composición apenas sería una larga lista de oraciones inconexas. La buena redacción exige que se desarrolle una idea central o tesis a través de varios pasos o etapas. Cada una de estas etapas representa un párrafo. Las oraciones del párrafo se unen y se expanden para explicar la idea central que se desea comunicar al lector. Cada nuevo párrafo debe representar un cambio marcado de asunto, idea, énfasis, hablante, lugar, tiempo o nivel de generalidad. El párrafo señala las diferentes transiciones en el pensamiento del autor y ayuda a seguir el hilo del argumento.

Los párrafos varían en su tipo y estructura. Muchos contienen una oración que establece la idea central o tema. De ordinario, esta oración se denomina la **oración tópica**. Esta oración encabeza por lo común el párrafo, es la más general y está seguida de otras oraciones **—oraciones subordinadas—** que desarrollan el mensaje o pensamiento central.

Quizá, a través de sus estudios en inglés o en español, haya usted adquirido la falsa idea de que todo párrafo tiene que empezar con una oración tópica. Nada está más alejado (*further*) de la verdad. Si esto fuera cierto, las composiciones serían monótonas y predecibles. En realidad hay párrafos que carecen de (*lack*) oración tópica; otros no tienen oraciones subordinadas. Hay párrafos cuya función es establecer la introducción, otros la conclusión y otros el desarrollo del argumento. Lo esencial es que cada nuevo párrafo cumpla una función lógica dentro de la supraestructura que representa el mensaje del autor. Posibles tipos de oraciones en un párrafo:

1. **Oración tópica:** Representa la idea central del párrafo y debe ser la oración más general.
2. **Oraciones de expansión:** Fortifican, reestablecen, elaboran o proveen información o contexto para algún aspecto de la idea central del párrafo.
3. **Oraciones restrictivas:** Cuando estas oraciones ocurren en un párrafo, su función es restringir (*to restrict*) el tema central o fijarle límites. Sirven para presentar una idea opuesta a la expresada por la oración tópica y son un buen recurso retórico para introducir un pensamiento contradictorio.

Lea el siguiente párrafo y observe la función de las oraciones.
1 = **oración tópica**, 2 = **oración de expansión** y 3 = **oración restrictiva**

Soy esclavo del reloj (1). A las cinco me levanto, me baño, desayuno y salgo para la universidad (2). Al mediodía, si tengo tiempo, almuerzo (2). Por eso de las tres, llego a mi casa (2). Saco a los perros y a las cuatro estoy en el gimnasio (2). A las siete hago la cena y estudio (2). Claro que los fines de semana son muy diferentes (3). Los sábados por la noche son sagrados, mi período de diversión (2). Voy al cine, a un restaurante, a bailar —algo para escaparme de la monotonía (2).

A. Identifique la función de cada una de las oraciones en el siguiente párrafo. Marque con 1 la oración tópica, con 2 las oraciones de expansión y con 3 las restrictivas. Use el párrafo anterior como ejemplo.

A menudo se cae en hábitos insípidos de los cuales es difícil escapar ( ). Las labores monótonas del día, el tráfico de las autopistas y las exigencias del trabajo son en mucho responsables de esta situación ( ). Por falta de imaginación, muchos de nosotros dejamos que la rutina se apodere (*take over*) de nuestra vida ( ). Nos convertimos en robots ( ). Los que sí saben vivir, en cambio, introducen innovaciones y mantienen una actitud positiva ante los retos (*challenges*) cotidianos ( ). Usan el tiempo que pasan atrapados (*trapped*) en el automóvil, por ejemplo, para relajarse escuchando su música preferida ( ). Encuentran la oportunidad de ir al gimnasio o al salón de belleza y siempre saben modificar ligeramente su horario ( ).

Ahora quizá esté usted pensando: «Magnífico, pero, ¿qué debo hacer para escribir buenos párrafos?» La respuesta a esa pregunta no es fácil. La práctica y la observación cuidadosa, con el tiempo, otorgan (*yield*) esas habilidades. Antes que nada, determine el mensaje que desea comunicar al lector. Sin este paso, no existe una buena redacción. Luego, mentalmente o por escrito considere los pasos o divisiones que le llevarán a completar su mensaje. No se preocupe por la introducción ni la conclusión. Los mejores escritores dejan esos detalles para la revisión final.

Hay dos tipos de escritura: una versión espontánea donde dejamos que las ideas fluyan sin preocuparnos de posibles errores y correcciones, y otra refinada que entregamos al lector. Son estos dos procesos los que le permitirán entender y producir buenos párrafos.

Una vez que haya escrito una decena (*ten*) de oraciones, léalas cuidadosamente. ¿Expresan claramente su pensamiento? Ahora bien, ¿presentan solamente un punto de vista o son en realidad material para dos o más párrafos? El proceso de pulimento (*polishing*) debe continuar. Una oración subordinada nunca debe ser más general que la tópica. Si esto sucede, es muy probable que se necesite incluir esa oración en un nuevo párrafo.

¿Ha mantenido el enfoque constante o ha divagado (*digressed*) con información que no es pertinente al caso en discusión? Si hay ideas a favor y en contra, las debe organizar en grupos separados para facilitarle la comprensión al lector.

Cuando el mensaje y la estructura del texto sean claros, se debe continuar con la revisión de la gramática y del vocabulario. Es al releer un trozo que nos damos cuenta de los errores de gramática, de ortografía, de selección léxica, etc. Si usted tiene acceso a una computadora con un procesador de palabras, úsela. Estas máquinas son de gran ayuda para llevar a cabo (*carry out*) los procesos de lectura y autocorrección.

► Para escribir mejor

CÓMO IDENTIFICAR ORACIONES TÓPICAS Y DE EXPANSIÓN

A. Lea el siguiente texto. Busque en el diccionario las palabras que usted no conozca.

La venerable tradición de la siesta

Parece que todo lo que nuestra avanzada y sabia° sociedad moderna desecha° o menosprecia° resulta ser, al fin y al cabo, de transcendental importancia. Hoy presenciamos la vindicación de una de las venerables tradiciones de nuestros abuelos: la siesta.

Se ha comprobado que entre la una y las cuatro de la tarde nuestra energía, actividad mental y facultad de concentración descienden a sus niveles° más bajos. Así pues, es prudente detenerlo todo y darse un descanso de unos treinta minutos como en los buenos tiempos de los trenes a vapor° y los fusiles de chispa°. La muy respetable sociedad japonesa ha sido la promotora de un nuevo movimiento para reinstituir la siesta. Antes de retirarse, el jefe circula por las oficinas para cerciorarse° que su rebaño° va a roncar° en formación de escuadrilla°. Al despertar, milagro° de milagros, la creatividad explota con una ganancia de un veinte por ciento.

La «siestología» será muy pronto una de las ramas° de la medicina y la terapia. El remedio está al alcance° de todos. No hay más que esperar. La hamaca reemplazará la máquina cafetera. La siesta combate la tensión, el temor y la depresión. Reduce los problemas cardiovasculares, el ausentismo, los divorcios y favorece la vitalidad sexual, la memoria y la longevidad.

wise
casts aside/puts down
levels
steam/flintlock rifle/
to make sure/
flock/
snore/
squadron/
miracle/
branches/
reach

Los iniciados hablan de la siesta «acuática» tendidos° sobre un flotador, o la siesta «campestre» bajo la sombra bienhechora° de un corpulento árbol. Hay quien se mete en sus pijamas y sigue un elaborado ritual. Yo me contento con la siesta, punto; ya en el sillón de la oficina, ya en la privacidad de la alcoba°.

stretched
sheltering
bedroom

El pasado tuvo gigantes de la siesta como Napoleón, Edison y Churchill, para nombrar unos pocos. Hoy las generaciones del siglo veintiuno, cansadas y somnolientas°, acogen° a una vieja amiga. ¡Viva la siesta!

sleepy/
welcome

OBSERVE... el uso de la preposición **a** en la expresión "***trenes a vapor***". Note en la última oración de la lectura el uso de la **a personal** en la frase "***acogen a una vieja amiga***".

B. Siga las instrucciones para analizar la organización del texto.

1. Busque la oración tópica del primer párrafo y cópiela.

   ____

   ____

2. Escriba usted en sus propias palabras la idea de la oración tópica del segundo párrafo.

   ____

   ____

3. Busque y copie una de las oraciones de expansión del segundo párrafo.

   ____

   ____

4. ¿Qué tipo de oración es la primera oración del tercer párrafo (tópica, de expansión, restrictiva)? Explique por qué.

   ____

   ____

5. En el cuarto párrafo no hay una oración que se distinga como oración tópica. Escriba su propia oración tópica para este párrafo.

   ____

   ____

C. Lea la siguiente oración tópica.

La productividad de cualquier compañía aumentará considerablemente con una hora de siesta para todos los empleados.

Trabaje con un(a) compañero(a). Juntos escriban tres oraciones restrictivas (oraciones que presentan una idea opuesta a la de la oración tópica) para contrastar con la oración tópica.

1. ______________________________

____

2. ______________________________

____

3. ______________________________

____

D. Escriba usted ahora sobre sus actividades durante un fin de semana especial —romántico tal vez. No olvide incluir una oración tópica y añadir oraciones de expansión y restrictivas. ¡Cuidado! ¡Su profesor(a) indiscreto(a) le puede pedir que lea su trabajo a la clase!

Un fin de semana muy especial

____

____

____

____

____

____

____

____

____

____

► Estructuras en acción

REFLEXIVE PRONOUNS

Reflexive pronouns are often used when writing or speaking in Spanish about one's daily routine. A reflexive pronoun always refers back to the subject. The subject is both the **doer** and the **receiver** of the action.

Examples: Mom bathes them. (not reflexive)
Mamá los baña.

Mom bathes (herself). (reflexive)
Mamá se baña.

Note that English often omits reflexive pronouns when the meaning is clear. (I bathe before going to bed. I shave.) Spanish **always** requires them. (***Me** baño antes de acostar**me**. **Me** afeito.*)

1. Reflexive pronouns in English are easily identifiable because they end in the suffix **-self** / **-selves** (**myself, themselves**, etc.). Spanish reflexive pronouns are identical to the nonreflexive direct or indirect object pronouns in the first and second persons; however, the third person reflexive (both singular and plural) is **se**. Remember, the reflexive pronoun always agrees in person and number with the subject.

Subject	*Reflexive pronoun*
yo	***me*** (myself)
tú	***te*** (yourself)
él, ella, Ud.	***se*** (himself, herself, yourself, itself)
nosotros	***nos*** (ourselves)
vosotros	***os*** (yourselves)
ellos, ellas, Uds.	***se*** (themselves, yourselves)

2. Reflexive pronouns are **always** placed in front of a conjugated verb.

   Examples: *Yo **me** baño.*
   Ella **se** baña.

   They are always **attached** to an **affirmative** command, but must **precede** a **negative** command.

   Examples: *¡Báñe**se**!*
   *¡No **se** bañe!*

   They may either be attached to or precede an infinitive or a present participle (*-ndo*).

   Examples: *Ella va a bañar**se**.*
   (or)
   *Ella **se** va a bañar.*

   *Ella está bañándo**se**.*
   (or)
   *Ella **se** está bañando.*

3. All transitive verbs (verbs that can take a direct object) may be used either reflexively or nonreflexively in Spanish. Remember, when these verbs are used reflexively, the object is the same as the subject. For example: *¿Los niños? Mamá los baña y luego se baña ella.* (The children? Mom bathes them, then she takes a bath.)

Nonreflexive	*Reflexive*
Yo los acuesto. I put them to bed.	*Yo me acuesto.* I go to bed.
El barbero lo afeita. The barber shaves him.	*El barbero se afeita.* The barber shaves (himself).
Nosotros los sentamos. We seat them.	*Nosotros nos sentamos.* We sit down (seat ourselves).
Papá divierte a los niños. Dad amuses the children.	*Pero no se divierte él.* But he's not enjoying himself.

4. Whereas English uses a possessive adjective with articles of clothing and parts of the body (my hair, your teeth, his shirt, her blouse, etc.), Spanish uses the definite article. The possessor is indicated by an indirect object pronoun (either reflexive or nonreflexive).

Examples:

*Yo **me** corté el pelo.*	I cut my hair.
*Ella **me** cortó el pelo.*	She cut my hair.
*Yo **le** corté el pelo.*	I cut her (his) hair.
*Ella **se** cortó el pelo.*	She cut her hair.
*Yo **me** pongo la chaqueta.*	I put on my jacket.
*Ella **me** pone la chaqueta.*	She puts on my jacket (for me).
*Yo **le** pongo la chaqueta.*	I put on her jacket (for her).
*Ella **se** pone la chaqueta.*	She puts on her jacket.

5. The plural reflexive pronouns (*nos, os, se*) are sometimes used to express reciprocal actions, for which English uses **each other** or **one another**.

Examples: *Mamá y papá siempre **se** hablan al desayunar.*
Mom and Dad always talk **to each other** while they eat breakfast.

*Siempre **nos** vemos en la clase de aeróbicos.*
We always see **each other** at aerobics class.

6. A few Spanish verbs assume a different meaning when they are used reflexively.

Reflexive verbs with special meanings

ir	to go	*irse*	to leave, go away
dormir	to sleep	*dormirse*	to fall asleep
quitar	to take away	*quitarse*	to take off (clothing)

7. Some verbs are always used reflexively in Spanish, but they do not necessarily imply a reflexive action. Note the examples below.

Other reflexive verbs

acordarse	to remember
atreverse	to dare
quejarse	to complain

EXERCISES

A. Look at the following text and then complete the items that follow.

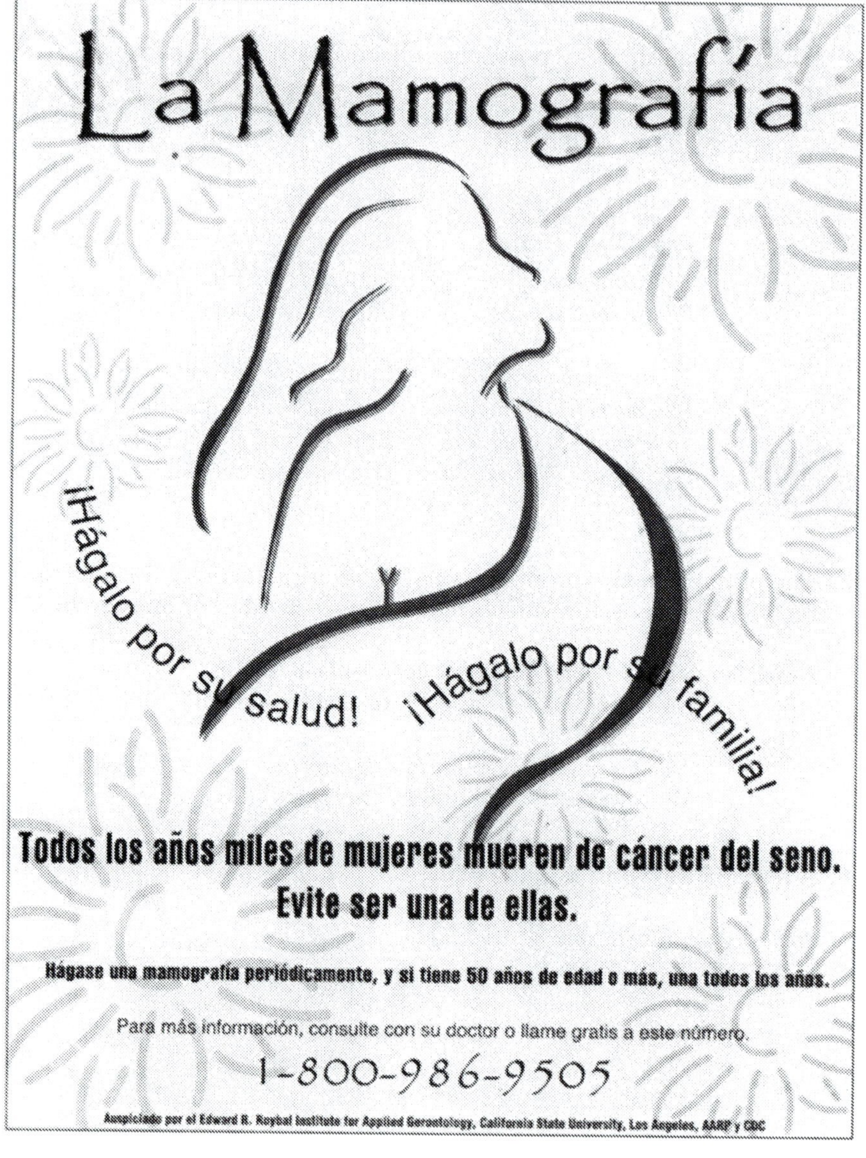

1. Find the reflexive verb construction in the text.

____

2. In this case, *se* is attached. Why?

____

____

____

B. Observe the use of the pronoun *nos* in the following ad.

1. In which sentence is *nos* used nonreflexively?

____

____

2. In which sentence is *nos* used reflexively?

____

____

3. Could the reflexive *nos* be omitted?

   Yes ______________ No ______________

   Why? ____

   ____

C. Give Spanish equivalents of the following sentences.

1. I always brush my teeth before showering.

2. Rosita woke up at 7:00, then she woke up the children.

3. Dad usually puts the children to bed.

4. Get up early and don't complain!

5. Mom dresses the children first, then she gets dressed.

D. Answer the following questions in complete Spanish sentences.

1. ¿Prefiere usted bañarse o ducharse?

2. ¿A qué hora se despertó usted esta mañana?

3. ¿Qué se pone usted cuando hace mucho frío?

4. ¿Cuándo fue la última vez que usted se durmió en clase?

5. ¿Por qué se queja usted tanto de su profesor(a) de español?

____

____

E. Write in Spanish about your morning routine. You may use the following verbs or others you know: *despertarse, levantarse, afeitarse, ducharse, cepillarse los dientes, desayunar, vestirse, peinarse, irse.*

____

____

____

____

____

____

____

____

____

____

____

____

____

► Manos a la obra

A. El nivel de nuestra energía física no es siempre el mismo durante el transcurso del día. Sube a ciertas horas, declina a otras. Averigüe cuáles son sus horas de mayor o menor energía. Obsérvese durante al menos tres días seguidos de acuerdo a la tabla "Medida de energía". La puntuación es la siguiente:

1. sin energía
2. con poca energía
3. con bastante energía
4. con mucha energía
5. con energía extraordinaria

Lleve a cabo sus observaciones desde la hora en que se levanta hasta la hora en que se acuesta. Luego saque un promedio (*average*) de los tres días y anote los resultados en la tabla. Conecte los puntos para obtener una guía de su ritmo biológico.

Medición de energía

	A.M. 6	7	8	9	10	11	12	P.M. 1	2	3	4	5	6	7	8	9	10
1																	
2																	
3																	
4																	
5																	

B. Ahora que usted ha descubierto su ciclo de energía, ¿qué puede hacer para aprovecharse de sus mejores horas del día? Compare su ciclo con el de otros tres compañeros. ¿Existen semejanzas? ¿Se podría hablar de un ciclo universal? Escriba un párrafo en el que explique sus ideas. No se olvide de organizar el párrafo con una oración tópica y de dar detalles con oraciones de expansión y oraciones restrictivas.

C. Según algunos profesores, los resultados de un curso son mejores si los estudiantes lo toman a las ocho de la mañana que si lo siguen a la una de la tarde. ¿Se puede generalizar o las diferencias se deben a (*are due to*) una pura coincidencia? Junto con un(a) compañero(a) de clase escriba un párrafo para comentar esta idea. Luego presenten sus opiniones al resto de la clase.

D. **Transcurre el año 4992. Nuestros descendientes han colonizado el planeta Marte. Hace ya muchos años lograron descongelar (*they were able to defrost*) el agua atrapada en los casquetes polares (*polar ice caps*), y con la vida vegetal traída de la Tierra (*Earth*) crearon una atmósfera similar a la terrestre. Trabaje con dos compañeros más, y con un poco de fantasía escriban en una hoja adicional un párrafo sobre las actividades de Javier Rojas, estudiante de la Universidad Interplanetaria de Marcinia. Las siguientes ideas y expresiones le pueden ayudar en su trabajo.**

enviar mensaje a la colonia en asteroide D5 / programar los robots / revisar la mininave (*mini-ship*) solar / preparar una comida al antiguo sistema terrestre, etc.

PARA LOS INTERNAUTAS

Vaya a **http://www.wiley.com/college/gonzalez,** busque la página que corresponde a este capítulo y haga los ejercicios indicados.

MÁS ALLÁ

Comente los siguientes temas con sus compañeros de clase. Luego escoja uno de ellos y escriba sus opiniones al respecto. Organice sus comentarios en un párrafo completo con oración tópica, oraciones de expansión y oraciones restrictivas.

1. Las mujeres, por lo general, trabajan más que los hombres. Muchas tienen que enfrentarse a (*to face*) todas las labores domésticas y también cumplir con las responsabilidades profesionales de sus campos de trabajo. Además, los hombres no siempre ayudan con el cuidado de los hijos. ¿Están ustedes de acuerdo? Expliquen por qué.

2. No se justifica la división de rutinas entre hombres y mujeres. En nuestra sociedad las labores se deben asignar sin consideración de sexo y es buena idea rotar las responsabilidades. En esta forma habrá verdadera justicia y mejor entendimiento entre los dos sexos. ¿Les parece buena idea? Defiendan sus opiniones.
3. La rutina del mundo moderno llena los consultorios de los psicólogos, psiquiatras y médicos en general. La tensión emocional es muy alta. Casi todos los que viven en las grandes ciudades sufren de trastornos (*disorders*) estomacales, problemas cardíacos y alto colesterol. Apenas hay tiempo para comer y relajarse. ¿Qué se puede hacer para aliviar esta situación tan difícil?

En esta página podrá anotar sus ideas respecto a este capítulo o bien referirse a un episodio de su propia vida.

Mi diario:

Capítulo 4

La comida

¡*Cada uno de estos platillos mexicanos parece más sabroso que el otro!*

Objectives

Upon completion of this chapter you should be able to:

- understand the importance of clarity and precision in your writing
- revise your compositions to make them clearer and more precise
- utilize appropriate vocabulary to write about food, restaurants, eating habits, and nutrition
- use passive voice and appropriate Spanish substitutes for English passive-voice constructions

Para hablar del tema

VOCABULARIO ESENCIAL

Estudie las siguientes palabras y expresiones. Le pueden resultar útiles para entender el capítulo y escribir sobre la comida, los restaurantes y la nutrición.

Sustantivos

el aceite	*oil*
la aceituna	*olive*
el aguacate / la palta (Argentina)	*avocado*
el ajo	*garlic*
la alimentación	*nutrition*
los alimentos	*food, groceries*
el apio	*celery*
el arroz	*rice*
el azúcar	*sugar*
el camarón	*shrimp*
la carne de res	*beef*
la cebolla	*onion*
el cereal	*cereal*
la cereza	*cherry*
el (la) cocinero(a)	*cook*
el colesterol	*cholesterol*
la comida	*food, meal*
los condimentos	*condiments*
la copa	*wine glass*
la cuchara	*spoon*
el cuchillo	*knife*
la ensalada	*salad*
las especias	*spices*
la frambuesa	*raspberry*
los frijoles / las judías (España)	*beans*
la gastronomía	*art of good eating*
el (la) gastrónomo(a)	*gourmet*
la grasa	*fat*
la harina	*flour*
el helado	*ice cream*
el horno	*oven*
el jamón	*ham*
el jarro	*mug*
la langosta	*lobster*
el libro de cocina	*cookbook*
el limón	*lemon*
la manzana	*apple*

los mariscos	*shellfish*
el menú	*menu*
el (la) mesero(a) / el (la) camarero(a)	*waiter, waitress*
la naranja	*orange*
la nuez	*nut*
la olla	*pot*
la papa / la patata (España)	*potato*
la parrilla	*grill*
el pavo	*turkey*
el perejil	*parsley*
el pescado	*fish*
la pimienta	*pepper*
la piña / el ananá (Argentina)	*pineapple*
el plato	*plate, dish*
el pollo	*chicken*
el postre	*dessert*
el puerco	*pork*
la receta de cocina	*cooking recipe*
la sal	*salt*
la sartén	*frying pan*
la taza	*cup*
el tenedor	*fork*
el tomate	*tomato*
el vaso	*glass*
el (la) vegetariano(a)	*vegetarian*
la zanahoria	*carrot*

Verbos

asar	*to roast, broil*
condimentar	*to season*
freír (i, i)	*to fry*
guisar	*to stir-fry, cook*
hervir (ie, i)	*to boil*
hornear	*to bake*
tener apetito	*to have an appetite*
tostar	*to toast*

Adjetivo

apetitoso(a)	*appetizing*

Expresiones

¡Buen apetito! / ¡Buen provecho!	*Enjoy your meal!*

A. Lea el siguiente texto. Busque las palabras que no conozca en su diccionario.

La dieta y el supermercado

Cuando usted se pone a dieta, el saber qué alimentos comprar es muy importante. Para ayudarle, tiene usted aquí tres consejos fundamentales para su viaje al supermercado:

1. Redefina su concepto de lo que es «una comida completa». Un buen sándwich puede contener una alimentación satisfactoria.
2. Nada es prohibido en cantidades limitadas.
3. Lea las etiquetas° con cuidado. Hay platos que se anuncian como de bajas calorías, pero que contienen un alto porcentaje de grasa. labels

Además, tenga presente la siguiente información al pasearse por esos laberintos traicioneros de su tienda de comestibles:

Sección de productos lácteos

1. La leche descremada es buena con el café, el té o los cereales del desayuno.
2. El yogur de dieta es un excelente substituto de los aderezos° para ensalada, y también lo puede agregar a las papas asadas. dresssings
3. Con el queso mozzarella, de bajo contenido graso, puede hacer una exquisita pizza vegetariana.

Sección de frutas y verduras

1. Usted puede usar todas las frutas y verduras frescas en ensaladas o hervidas como plato principal.
2. Añada legumbres congeladas a las sopas y frituras en caldo de pollo, o sírvalas con arroz.

Sección de carnes, aves y mariscos

1. Con dos claras° y una yema° se hace una gran tortilla°, y le puede agregar verduras frescas o congeladas°. Evite el exceso de yemas y reduzca así el contenido de colesterol. **egg whites/ yolk/ omelette/ frozen**
2. Las pechugas de pollo deshuesadas° son excelentes para agregar a ensaladas y verduras cocidas. **boneless**
3. Compre el atún y el salmón enlatados° en agua, no en aceite. Los puede comer en sándwiches para el almuerzo o con arroz y una ensalada para la cena. **canned**

Sección de panes y granos

Ponga en su canasta° pan o galletas de trigo integral, panecillos horneados° sin grasa y pastas frescas. Los supermercados modernos generalmente tienen una sección dietética. Búsquela. Se sorprenderá del buen sabor de estos productos. **basket** **baked**

Sección de condimentos y aderezos

Las principales marcas de aderezos y aliños° tienen toda una gama de productos sin grasa y de bajo contenido calórico. En general, estos sustitutos tienen agradable sabor. **seasonings**

Ya ve, perder esas libras de más y sentirse mejor física y mentalmente no tiene que ser una tortura. Siga usted los consejos básicos cuando vaya al supermercado, y muy pronto tendrá resultados satisfactorios.

B. Conteste las preguntas sobre la información del Ejercicio A.

1. ¿Cuáles son los tres consejos fundamentales para quien visita un supermercado y está a dieta?

____

____

____

____

2. ¿Ha usado usted alguna vez la leche descremada o sin grasa? ¿Cómo podría emplearla una persona que está a dieta?

____

____

3. ¿Qué ingredientes se podrían usar para preparar una perfecta pizza vegetariana?

4. En México y Centroamérica, una tortilla está hecha de maíz o harina. En otras partes de Latinoamérica y en España una tortilla es un platillo diferente. ¿En qué consiste una tortilla española?

5. Usted ha invitado a almorzar a un(a) amigo(a) que está a dieta. ¿Qué le podría ofrecer?

C. Ahora haga una lista de las palabras del Ejercicio A que usted no conocía. Añada otras expresiones que considere útiles para escribir sobre la comida, los restaurantes y la nutrición en general. Si es necesario, busque su significado en el diccionario.

VOCABULARIO CLAVE

Las palabras de esta sección son de uso muy frecuente. Estúdielas y apréndalas. Le ayudarán en sus trabajos de redacción.

es decir *that is to say*

Su gracia consiste en la anfibología, **es decir**, el doble sentido.

ambos(as) *both*

Ambas ideas son buenas.

estar de acuerdo *to agree*

Estoy de acuerdo con la expresión: «Usted es lo que come».

► Análisis de la claridad en la composición

Lea la siguiente adivinanza (*riddle*) y trate de descubrir la solución.

Oro no es.
Plata no es.
Si lees con cuidado,
sabrás qué es.
¿Qué es? ______________________ (solución al final de la página)

La anterior es una adivinanza bien conocida por muchos latinoamericanos. Su gracia consiste en la anfibología, es decir, el doble sentido.

Cuando se escribe, es de gran importancia revisar el trabajo para que éste no sea una adivinanza que el lector tenga que descifrar. Como se dijo en el capítulo anterior, hay dos tipos de escritura: una vaga y confusa que se hace para uno mismo y otra clara y lógica que se presenta a un lector. Ambas juegan un papel importante en el proceso de la composición. Muchas veces se debe dejar que las ideas fluyan de la mente sin prestar gran atención a la forma. Sin embargo, una vez completada la sección o párrafo, es indispensable volver a lo escrito y corregir fallas (*faults*) lógicas, léxicas, gramaticales u ortográficas. Lea en voz alta su trabajo como si lo hubiera escrito otra persona. Esta es una práctica que le ayudará a mejorar mucho su labor.

Esta sección empezó con una adivinanza. Lea ahora el siguiente párrafo y compare la claridad del párrafo con la de la adivinanza.

Es un utensilio de cocina. Puede estar hecho de hierro° o de aluminio. Es circular, más ancho que hondo°, de fondo° plano y con un mango° largo. A veces la superficie interna está recubierta de una capa de teflón. Sirve para freír, tostar o guisar los alimentos.
¿Qué es? ______________________ (solución al final de la página)

iron
deep/
bottom/
handle

(Solución #1: el plátano, Solución #2: la sartén)

La claridad de una composición depende en mucho de una estructura lógica y de una forma léxica y gramatical correcta. Es posible que algunos escritores con mucha experiencia produzcan prosa clara sin necesidad de mucho esfuerzo. El neófito, por lo contrario, debe adherirse a la práctica de revisar su trabajo y de establecer un plan que le permita seguir un desarrollo lógico.

Esto no implica que el estudiante se vea obligado a preparar un bosquejo (*outline*) formal **antes** de empezar a escribir. Recuerde que se había hablado de una prosa íntima en la cual se vierten (*spill out*) las ideas sin preocupaciones formales. Este es el primer paso.

En el segundo, se debe establecer el plan para desarrollar con claridad las ideas de la composición. No espere que su profesor o profesora le haga las correcciones. Descubra usted mismo los problemas. Aquí tiene una lista que le ayudará en sus trabajos de redacción (*editing*). Consúltela siempre antes de entregar la copia final.

LISTA DE REVISIÓN

Fallas lógicas

	Sí	*No*
1. ¿Tiene el párrafo más de una idea principal?	_____	_____
2. ¿Está la idea central claramente expresada?	_____	_____
3. ¿Desarrollan las oraciones del párrafo la idea principal?	_____	_____
4. ¿Hay oraciones que introducen información no relacionada con la idea principal?	_____	_____
5. ¿Ha dado usted suficientes detalles y ejemplos para ilustrar la idea central del párrafo?	_____	_____
6. ¿Hay repetición innecesaria de ideas, información o ejemplos?	_____	_____

Fallas gramaticales

	Sí	*No*
1. ¿Hay cambios innecesarios de tiempos verbales?	_____	_____
2. ¿Hay cambios injustificados de persona?	_____	_____
3. ¿Hay errores de concordancia (*agreement*)? (sustantivo / adjetivo, sujeto / verbo)	_____	_____
4. ¿Hay errores en el uso de:		
a. los pronombres?	_____	_____
b. el subjuntivo y el indicativo?	_____	_____
c. el pretérito y el imperfecto?	_____	_____
d. la voz pasiva?	_____	_____

Fallas léxicas

	Sí	*No*
1. ¿Escogió usted la palabra que mejor expresa su idea? ¿La buscó en el diccionario de lengua española?	_____	_____

		Sí	No
2.	¿Repitió sin necesidad la misma palabra?	_____	_____
	¿Buscó un sinónimo?	_____	_____
3.	¿Hizo una traducción literal de expresiones idiomáticas del inglés?	_____	_____
4.	¿Se ajusta el vocabulario al tono y al nivel de la composición? (uso injustificado de coloquialismos, clichés, etc.)	_____	_____

Fallas ortográficas y de puntuación

		Sí	*No*
1.	¿Revisó la ortografía?	_____	_____
2.	¿Revisó el uso de las tildes (los acentos escritos)?	_____	_____
3.	¿Revisó la puntuación de cada oración?	_____	_____

Para escribir mejor

CÓMO REVISAR UN PÁRRAFO

A. Lea cuidadosamente el siguiente texto. Busque en el diccionario las palabras que usted no conozca.

El horario de las comidas

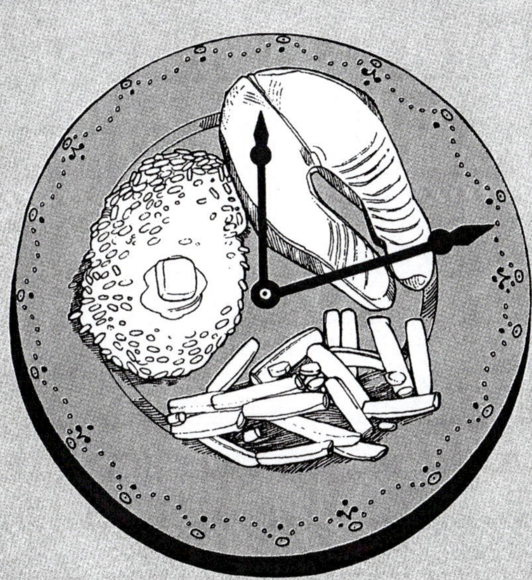

No todos los pueblos tienen las mismas tradiciones culinarias, ni el mismo horario de comidas. Lo que le parece obvio a un estadounidense promedio puede resultarle extraño o absurdo a un habitante de otra sección del planeta.

México es un caso interesante. Allí se funden° las costumbres de una sociedad rural mestiza con las exigencias° de un mundo moderno en constante agitación. En el campo el desayuno es una comida ligera que se toma en las primeras horas del día. Consiste básicamente en un trozo de pan y una bebida, generalmente café. A mitad de la mañana viene el almuerzo —una comida más fortificante de huevos, tortillas y frijoles, por ejemplo. Es, en verdad, una excelente fuente de energía para las arduas labores agrícolas. Como en muchas otras zonas rurales del mundo, la comida principal del día se hace entre las dos y las tres de la tarde. Se le denomina «comida», y consiste en una serie variada de platos. En las últimas horas de la tarde, algunos mexicanos meriendan. La merienda es ligera. Finalmente, después de la puesta del sol°, se sirve la cena, también ligera.

Hoy en las ciudades, las costumbres han variado. Los oficinistas no siempre tienen tiempo para almorzar y se contentan con una taza de café. La «comida» es más liviana° y sin siesta, y muchos mexicanos se ven obligados a cenar en restaurantes después del trabajo. El progreso, para bien o para mal, universaliza hasta la forma de comer.

combine (funden)
demands (exigencias)
sunset (puesta del sol)
light (liviana)

OBSERVE... el uso de la preposición **en** en la expresión "*...y consiste* ***en*** *una serie variada de platos.*"

B. Escriba usted ahora un párrafo semejante que describa sus propias comidas y el horario de las mismas.

___

___

___

___

___

___

___

___

___

___

___

___

___

___

___

C. Ahora relea lo que escribió. ¿Hay fallas lógicas, gramaticales, léxicas, de ortografía o de puntuación? Use la lista de revisión de las páginas 80–81 y haga las correciones necesarias.

D. Después de revisar su trabajo, intercámbielo con un(a) compañero(a). ¿Qué ideas tiene para mejorar el trabajo de su compañero(a)?

Estructuras en acción

PASSIVE VOICE VERSUS ACTIVE VOICE

In active voice constructions, the subject is the **doer** of the action. In the passive voice the subject **receives** the action (is acted upon). Observe the difference:

active: Fernando **prepared** the meal.
*Fernando **preparó** la comida.*

passive: The meal **was prepared** by Fernando.
*La comida **fue preparada** por Fernando.*

True passive voice in Spanish uses the verb *ser* plus the past participle (*-do*), which must agree with the subject in gender and number. The agent of the action (almost always mentioned or implied) is normally introduced by *por.*

Although the true passive (***ser*** **+ past participle + agent introduced by *por***) does exist in Spanish, it is used far less frequently than in English. Often seen in written Spanish (in journalism and formal pieces), it is usually replaced in everyday conversation by the active voice or by a passive voice substitute.

PASSIVE VOICE SUBSTITUTES

1. When the agent of an action is not expressed, is unknown, or is simply considered unimportant, a Spanish *se* construction often replaces the English passive voice. The verb agrees with the subject.

Examples: Dessert **was served** in the garden.
***Se sirvió** el postre en el jardín.*

Where **was** the bread **bought**?
*¿Dónde **se compró** el pan?*

The vegetables **were prepared** ahead of time.
***Se prepararon** las verduras de antemano.*

Jaime **was named** "chef of the year."
***Se nombró** a Jaime «cocinero del año».*

2. The indefinite third-person plural frequently substitutes for the passive voice when the agent is not indicated. The subject (they) is **impersonal**, and does not refer to anyone in particular.

Examples: Dessert **was served** in the garden.
***Sirvieron** el postre en el jardín.*

Where **was** the bread **bought**?
*¿Dónde **compraron** el pan?*

The vegetables **were prepared** ahead of time.
***Prepararon** las verduras de antemano.*

Jaime **was named** "chef of the year."
***Nombraron** a Jaime «cocinero del año».*

3. Some English passive voice constructions would be considered especially awkward (sometimes ungrammatical) rendered into the Spanish passive voice, even when the agent is mentioned.

Examples: **I was given** milk.
***Me dieron** leche.*
***Se me dio** leche.* (less common)

I was given milk by the waiter.
***Me dio** leche el camarero.*

The girls **were seen** at La Frambuesa.
***Vieron** a las chicas en La Frambuesa.*

The recipe **will be given to me**.
***Me darán** la receta.*

The recipe **will be given to me** by Mom.
*Mamá **me dará** la receta.*

We are served a Spanish omelette.
***Nos sirven** una tortilla española.*

4. When the verb indicates a **state or condition** (rather than an **action**), Spanish does not use passive voice or a passive voice substitute. Instead, the verb ***estar*** is used with the past participle.

Examples: The meal **was prepared** by the cook. (true passive voice)
*La comida **fue preparada** por la cocinera.*

but

The meal **is** well **prepared**. (condition or state)
*La comida **está** bien **preparada**.*

Do not overuse the passive voice in Spanish. Either an equivalent active voice construction or a passive substitute is preferred.

EXERCISES

A. Reread carefully «El horario de las comidas» on pages 81–82. Then find the Spanish passive voice *substitutes* for the following English passive voice constructions and write them below.

1. ...the customs of a rural mestizo society are fused with the demands of a modern world...

____

____

2. ...breakfast is a light meal that is eaten early in the day.

____

____

3. ...the main meal of the day is eaten between 2:00 and 3:00 P.M.

____

____

4. It is called "comida"...

____

____

5. ...after sunset, dinner is served...

____

____

B. Rephrase the sentences, following the examples.

Examples: Se compró el pescado a buen precio.
Compraron el pescado a buen precio.

El pescado fue vendido.
Se vendió el pescado.

Compraron el pescado.
Se compró el pescado.

1. Los entremeses fueron preparados por Enrique, y se sirvieron antes de la comida.

____

____

____

2. En algunos países se almuerza al mediodía; en otros a las dos o a las tres de la tarde.

3. La receta fue creada por un famoso cocinero cubano.

4. Sirvieron la comida rápidamente.

5. Allí hacen un pastel de frambuesa delicioso.

C. Write two Spanish passive voice *substitutes* for each of the following English passive voice constructions.

Examples: Guests are served quickly and courteously.
Se les sirve rápida y cortésmente a los comensales.
Les sirven rápida y cortésmente a los comensales.

Paella is served there.
Allí se sirve paella.
Allí sirven paella.

1. The meat was purchased at the butcher shop.

2. Where are fresh fruits sold?

3. Helia was named "waitress of the month."

____

____

4. Breakfast is sometimes served in the dining room.

____

____

5. That dish is made with beans and cheese.

____

____

D. Your Peruvian friend Matilde has all the ingredients for a Spanish omelette, but she doesn't know how to prepare it. Using a *se* construction, tell her in Spanish that...

1. First, the eggs are beaten. (*batir* – to beat)

____

____

2. Next, the onions and potatoes are sliced. (*rebanar* – to slice)

____

____

3. Then, the skillet is heated. (*calentar (ie)* – to heat)

____

____

4. The onions and potatoes are fried in a little oil.

____

____

5. Now, the eggs are put into the skillet.

____

____

6. Finally, salt and pepper are added. (*agregar* – to add)

____

____

► Manos a la obra

A. Lea la siguiente crítica sobre el restaurante «La Frambuesa». Busque y estudie las palabras que no conozca.

La Frambuesa

Manteles° de color frambuesa, paredes de un rosado encendido°, salsa de frambuesa con el paté y el pato, postres de frambuesa. «La Frambuesa» le hace honor al nombre tanto visual como gastronómicamente.

tablecloths/ hot pink

Aquí se ha creado un ambiente elegante, sofisticado. Grandes espejos, amplios sillones negros, tenues° luces indirectas y palmas en maceteras° de terracota hacen de este restaurante un lugar para escapar del trajín° diario.

Hay que felicitar al cocinero por su creatividad y excelentes dotes°. Los entremeses° incluyen un magnífico paté de la casa y berenjenas° con aderezo de anchoas, aceite, vinagre y albahaca°. Se ofrecen también caracoles° en salsa de ajo y raviolis rellenos con hongos° en una salsa ligera de pimientos morrones° y crema.

El menú tiene cuatro platos de pescado: un delicioso salmón hervido con salsa de mantequilla, hinojo° y albahaca ($17,50); pez espada°; atún; lenguado° con una salsa de vino blanco, crema y alcaparras° ($19,75). Siguiendo el tema del restaurante, el pato asado lleva una sabrosa salsa de frambuesas. Los carnívoros pueden disfrutar del solomillo° de res al coñac y pimienta negra, ternera° en vino tinto con setas° y cordero° asado ($18,75).

La sección de postres ofrece tartas de frambuesa, fresas o manzana, flan y pastel de chocolate. Los amantes del vino tienen una amplia lista de la cual escoger.

El servicio es rápido y el personal cordial. Se aceptan las tarjetas de crédito MasterCard, Visa y Amerocar. «La Frambuesa» está en el número 2134 de la avenida Marvista, entre las calles Primera y Salto. Necesita hacer su reservación al teléfono 2-34-67-95. El restaurante está abierto todos los días de las trece a las quince horas para el almuerzo y de las diecisiete a las veintitrés horas treinta para la cena.

soft
pots
hubbub
gifts
appetizers/
eggplant/
basil/snails/
mushrooms/
sweet red peppers
fennel/
swordfish/
sole/capers
sirloin
veal/type of mushroom/
lamb

OBSERVE... el uso de la preposición **a** en la expresión "*...solomillo de res* ***al*** *coñac...*".

B. Escriba ahora usted una crítica sobre su restaurante preferido. Comience por una descripción del lugar. Luego hable de los platos que se ofrecen y del precio promedio de los mismos. Dé también información sobre dirección, teléfono, horario, tarjetas de crédito que se aceptan, etc. Use sustitutos de la voz pasiva cuando pueda y revise posibles errores de lógica, de gramática y de vocabulario según la lista de las páginas 80–81.

____

____

____

____

____

____

____

____

____

C. La clase de español organiza una comida. Participe con su receta de cocina favorita. Escríbala en una hoja adicional y recuerde que debe ser preciso(a). Primero presente los ingredientes en el orden en que se van a usar bajo el título «Ingredientes». Luego, bajo el título «Preparación», explique el proceso paso por paso. Revise su trabajo y no olvide usar sustitutos de la voz pasiva.

PARA LOS INTERNAUTAS

Vaya a **http://www.wiley.com/college/gonzalez**, busque la página que corresponde a este capítulo y haga los ejercicios indicados.

MÁS ALLÁ

Comente los siguientes temas con sus compañeros de clase. Luego escoja uno de ellos y escriba sus opiniones al respecto. No se olvide de revisar su composición para que sea clara.

1. Los regímenes alimenticios pueden causar serios trastornos somáticos (*physical*) y psicológicos. Hay muchas personas que viven siguiendo dietas sin control médico con la esperanza de alcanzar la figura perfecta. Sin embargo, terminan con más peso, enfermas y deprimidas (*depressed*). ¿Qué tipos de dietas conocen ustedes? ¿Hay alguna que sea mejor? ¿Existe una solución buena para controlar el sobrepeso?
2. A menudo se escucha el refrán: «Usted es lo que come». ¿Cuáles son las implicaciones de este dicho? ¿Están ustedes de acuerdo? ¿Por qué sí o no?
3. La mayoría de los humanos somos omnívoros. Una minoría creciente piensa que una dieta vegetariana es mejor. Hagan dos columnas de pros y contras para ambas posiciones. Luego voten entre ustedes y decidan qué dieta es mejor. Expliquen sus razones.

En esta página podrá anotar sus ideas respecto a este capítulo o bien referirse a un episodio de su propia vida.

Mi diario:

Capítulo 5

¡Un buen anuncio publicitario!

Objectives

Upon completion of this chapter you should be able to:

- read and analyze advertisements
- utilize appropriate vocabulary to write about advertising
- use formal and informal commands
- create advertisements and slogans for various products

Bastan unas pocas palabras bien escogidas para que un anuncio atraiga al lector.

► Para hablar del tema

VOCABULARIO ESENCIAL

Estudie las siguientes palabras y expresiones. Le pueden resultar útiles para entender el capítulo y escribir sobre los anuncios publicitarios.

Sustantivos

el ahorro	*savings*
el anuncio	*ad*
la censura	*censorship*
el concesionario	*franchise*
el descuento	*discount*
la ganga	*bargain*
la gran rebaja	*great sale*
el lema	*slogan*
la marca	*brand name, make, mark*
el nivel	*level*
la oferta especial	*special offer*
la oferta limitada	*limited offer*
el premio	*prize, reward*
la publicidad	*advertising*
el sabor	*flavor*
los seres queridos	*loved ones*
el servicio a domicilio	*home delivery*
el sorteo	*raffle*

Verbos

ahorrar	*to save*
alquilar	*to rent*
confiar	*to entrust, trust*
disfrutar	*to enjoy*
dominar	*to control, dominate*
juzgar	*to judge*
respaldar	*to back*

Adjetivos

confiable	*trustworthy*
grato(a)	*pleasant*
gratuito(a)	*free*
sobresaliente	*outstanding*

Expresiones

en pagos cómodos	*easy financing*
los mejores precios	*the best prices*
los precios más bajos	*the lowest prices*

Satisfacción garantizada o le devolvemos su dinero.	*Satisfaction guaranteed or your money back.*
sin pago inicial, sin enganche	*no down payment*
Usted merece lo mejor.	*You deserve the best.*

A. Lea el siguiente anuncio y haga el ejercicio B.

Grabe ... ***Record***

B. Conteste las siguientes preguntas sobre el anuncio.

1. ¿A quién se dirige el anuncio? ¿A la clase media, a una clase adinerada (*wealthy*), a estudiantes?

____

2. ¿En qué se basa su opinión?

____

____

____

C. Ahora haga una lista de otras palabras del Ejercicio A que usted no conocía. Añada otras expresiones que considere útiles para escribir su propio anuncio o para hablar de la publicidad. Si es necesario, busque esos términos en el diccionario.

_______________ _______________ _______________

_______________ _______________ _______________

VOCABULARIO CLAVE

Las palabras de esta sección son de uso muy frecuente. Estúdielas y apréndalas. Le ayudarán en sus trabajos de readacción.

ahora bien *now then*

Ahora bien, el polo es un deporte practicado por las clases adineradas.

al comienzo *at the beginning*

Al comienzo del anuncio se puede usar un juego de palabras.

luego *then, afterwards*

Luego se pueden mencionar las ventajas del producto.

► Análisis de anuncios

La población hispana de los Estados Unidos y los países de habla española en general adquieren cada día más importancia. Muchas compañías norteamericanas están interesadas en la creación de anuncios para atraer ese mercado. Los mensajes comerciales ya no son una simple copia de los producidos en inglés. Las diferencias culturales y lingüísticas exigen un texto original para el público hispanohablante (*Spanish-speaking*). En un mundo en el que la publicidad es una parte inevitable de la vida profesional y personal, es muy importante saber juzgar y utilizar el lenguaje de un buen anuncio. El tipo de redacción que se presenta en este capítulo ofrece oportunidades para adquirir estas destrezas (*skills*).

Antes de escribir un buen anuncio publicitario es importante contestar cinco preguntas fundamentales:

1. ¿Dónde aparecerá el anuncio? ¿En una revista, una cartelera (*billboard*), un periódico, etc.?

2. ¿A quién se dirige la publicación? ¿A un grupo específico o al público en general?
3. ¿Cuál es el propósito del anuncio?
4. ¿Qué tipo de información se debe incluir?
5. ¿Debe dirigirse a las emociones del lector o a la razón y a la lógica?

Una vez obtenidos estos datos (*facts, data*), el paso siguiente es hacer un bosquejo. Lo esencial es llamar la atención del lector. Las estrategias pueden ser pictóricas o lingüísticas. A veces las leyes gramaticales y la puntuación se rompen para despertar el interés del lector. Los juegos de palabras son también comunes.

Cronos

Para empezar, imagine usted que la compañía Cronos, productora de cronómetros (relojes muy precisos), necesita un anuncio para las revistas en español con circulación nacional e internacional. El anuncio se dirigirá a un público de clase media alta o de clase adinerada. Ahora hay que responder a las cinco preguntas fundamentales. Una vez que se obtiene la información, es necesario pensar cómo introducir el cronómetro al mercado en una forma convincente e interesante.

A. Antes de continuar, haga una lista de adjetivos que, en su opinión, sean apropiados para describir un cronómetro.

____________________ ____________________

____________________ ____________________

____________________ ____________________

Claro, la palabra **precisión**, esencia de un cronómetro, debe incluirse en el anuncio. Ahora bien, el polo, un deporte practicado por una clase adinerada, puede ser un buen medio para promover la venta de los relojes Cronos. Se debe establecer una relación entre el reloj y los campeones del deporte. En la primera línea se puede incluir la palabra **precisión** junto con otras que sugieran esta relación. Tal vez sea buena idea usar sólo mayúsculas (*capital letters*) y poner un punto (*period*) después de cada palabra para obligar al lector a hacer una pausa. Los vocablos **control** y **habilidad** podrían ser agregados también. Las palabras más importantes de la lista son **Cronos** y su característica intrínseca: la **precisión**. En una lista el primer y el último elemento son los más fáciles de recordar. Se escoge, pues, **precisión** como la primera palabra y **Cronos** como la última. Esta elección no es arbitraria. Poner el nombre de la marca (*brand name*) al final de la enumeración también sugiere que este término representa un resumen de las ideas anteriores. Luego se dirá que los campeones del polo requieren precisión, habilidad y dominio del tiempo y que los relojes Cronos ofrecen estas características también. Después de escribir estas ideas, es hora de hacer las últimas correcciones de ortografía, gramática, puntuación y estilo. Vea usted el resultado:

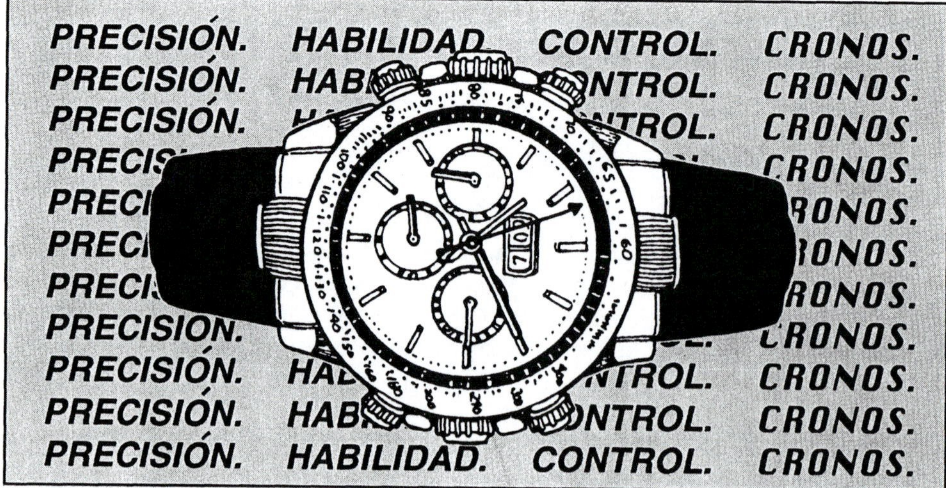

En el mundo del polo, hay ciertas características que distinguen a los auténticos campeones.

Precisión. Habilidad. Dominio del tiempo.

Características compartidas por cada uno de los relojes Cronos.

Por eso, no es de extrañar que tantos líderes del deporte confíen a los expertos el control perfecto del tiempo. Su concesionario Cronos tiene el cronómetro que usted necesita.
Todos nuestros productos vienen respaldados por el sello de Cronos: relojería de gran tradición y solidez.

B. Relea el anuncio de Cronos y luego conteste las siguientes preguntas.

1. ¿Cuáles son las características que distinguen a los campeones del polo?

____

____

2. ¿Por qué confían los deportistas en los relojes Cronos?

____

____

3. ¿Qué simboliza la marca «Cronos»?

____

____

Aerolíneas El Quetzal

El siguiente anuncio va a aparecer en todos los diarios (*newpapers*) del país. El objetivo es convencer al público en general que Aerolíneas El Quetzal es diferente y superior.

C. Mencione usted tres servicios que le debe ofrecer una línea aérea al viajero.

1. ______________________________
2. ______________________________
3. ______________________________

Al comienzo del anuncio, por ejemplo, usted puede usar un juego de palabras. El vocablo **mundo**, con varias interpretaciones, se presta (*lends itself*) a ese objetivo. Lo puede usar dos o tres veces con diferentes significados en la primera parte. Podría decir que El Quetzal es la línea favorita del mundo, luego que es el club más exclusivo del mundo y finalmente que incluye un verdadero mundo —enorme variedad. También podría dedicar un párrafo por completo a enumerar las condiciones que casi todos desean disfrutar durante un viaje.

Se usará un orden cronológico en la presentación del párrafo. Se empezará por el momento del registro del equipaje, se continuará con el tipo de asiento, se podría mencionar luego un periódico, quizá un refresco y posteriormente la comida. Se terminará asegurando al posible viajero que sus más insignificantes caprichos (*whims*) serán obedecidos. La última etapa del trabajo serán las correcciones necesarias. Observe ahora el resultado final:

EL QUETZAL

LA LÍNEA AÉREA FAVORITA DEL MUNDO
EN EL CLUB MÁS EXCLUSIVO DEL MUNDO LOS PRECIOS INCLUYEN «TODO UN MUNDO»

Ninguna otra línea aérea le ofrece una clase como la «Club», con el registro de equipaje más rápido, el asiento más tranquilo, el periódico más reciente, las bebidas mas variadas, una cocina gastronómica y el servicio más atento a los menores caprichos de viajero.

Le ofrecemos vuelos diarios de San Fermín a Islas Blancas a las 13:30 h. (con llegada a las 14:35 h.) y de Islas Biancas a San Fermín a las 9:30 h. (con llegada a las 10:35 h.).

Infórmese en su agencia de viajes o en nuestra oficina más cercana.

D. Relea el anuncio anterior y conteste las siguientes preguntas.

1. ¿Qué le ofrece la clase «Club»?

____

____

2. ¿Dónde puede usted encontrar información sobre vuelos y horarios?

____

____

Estos detalles de redacción, aunque están basados en los anuncios comerciales, son aplicables a todo tipo de composición. El escritor debe escoger las palabras con cuidado para crear un efecto especial, evocar sentimientos o tal vez convencer o divertir al lector.

Para escribir mejor

CÓMO CREAR UN LEMA

Los anuncios intentan persuadir al público por medio de diversas estrategias. Pueden dirigirse a la razón o a las emociones del lector. Pueden dar muchos detalles sobre el producto o crear sólo una imagen general de sus beneficios. Lo importante es comunicar un mensaje breve y específico en pocas palabras, fáciles de recordar. Éste es el **lema**.

A. He aquí algunos ejemplos en español de lemas famosos en los Estados Unidos. ¿Puede usted encontrar el equivalente en inglés?

1. Has avanzado mucho, mujer.

____

2. No salgas de casa sin ella.

____

3. Es la verdadera cosa.

____

4. ¡Está para chuparse los dedos!

____

B. Ahora le toca a usted. Escriba un lema en español para cada uno de los productos que siguen. Recuerde, hay que decidir a quién se va a dirigir el anuncio y presentarle el mensaje a este grupo de forma breve y atractiva.

Frugo

Es un jugo de frutas sin azúcar pero lleno de vitaminas, minerales y fibra. Es bajo en calorías y un poco más caro que los otros jugos de frutas. No es delicioso, pero es excelente para la salud.

1. lema: ____

____

Tócame

Es un radio que es muy barato y que se tira después de usarlo por más de 100 horas. Es tan pequeño que cabe (*fits*) en la oreja.

2. lema: ____

____

Superjefe

Es un reloj que incorpora un «beeper», una calculadora, un televisor, un radio y un teléfono pequeñísimo. Es muy caro y tiene una distribución limitada.

3. lema: ____

____

Tarjeta Esnob

Es una tarjeta de crédito que le permite al dueño o dueña entrar en clubes muy exclusivos, ir al frente de la cola (*line*) y recibir un descuento cada vez que la usa para alquilar una limosina.

4. lema: ____

____

Estructuras en acción

COMMANDS

Since ads generally attempt to persuade an audience, they very often use the command or imperative form of verbs.

Formal Commands

Formal or **polite** (*Ud., Uds.*) COMMANDS, both affirmative and negative, use the **present subjunctive tense**.

comprar	*Compre (Ud.).*	Buy.	*No compre.*	Don't buy.
	Compren (Uds.).	Buy.	*No compren.*	Don't buy.

pensar	*Piense (Ud.).*	Think.	*No piense.*	Don't think.
	Piensen (Uds.).	Think.	*No piensen.*	Don't think.
salir	*Salga (Ud.).*	Leave.	*No salga.*	Don't leave.
	Salgan (Uds.).	Leave.	*No salgan.*	Don't leave.

Informal Commands

Informal or **familiar** (*tú, vosotros*) COMMANDS are formed in the following way:

1. **Affirmative** *tú* commands of most verbs use the third-person singular of the **present indicative tense**.

comprar	*Compra (tú).*	Buy.
escribir	*Escribe (tú).*	Write.

2. **Affirmative** *tú* commands of a few common verbs are **irregular**.

decir	*Di.*	Tell. / Say.	**salir**	*Sal.*	Leave.
hacer	*Haz.*	Do. / Make.	**ser**	*Sé.*	Be.
ir	*Ve.*	Go.	**tener**	*Ten.*	Have.
poner	*Pon.*	Put.	**venir**	*Ven.*	Come.

3. **Negative** *tú* commands always use **the present subjunctive**.

comprar	*No compres.*	Don't buy.
escribir	*No escribas.*	Don't write.
decir	*No digas.*	Don't say / tell.
hacer	*No hagas.*	Don't do / make.
ir	*No vayas.*	Don't go.
tener	*No tengas.*	Don't have.

4. The **familiar plural** (*vosotros*) command is used in Spain but not in most of Latin America. The **affirmative** is formed by changing the final ***-r*** of the infinitive to a ***-d***.

comprar	*Comprad.*	Buy.
comer	*Comed.*	Eat.
escribir	*Escribid.*	Write.

5. The **negative** (*vosotros*) command always uses the **present subjuntive**.

comprar	*No compréis.*	Don't buy.
comer	*No comáis.*	Don't eat.
escribir	*No escribáis.*	Don't write.

Placement of Object Pronouns in Commands

Object pronouns (direct, indirect, and reflexive) are **attached** to **affirmative commands**. Note the use of the written accent.

Dígamelo (Ud.).	Tell it to me.
Dímelo (tú).	Tell it to me.
Decídmelo (vosotros).	Tell it to me.
Siéntese (Ud.).	Sit down.
Siéntate (tú).	Sit down.
Sentaos (vosotros).	Sit down. (The **-d** disappears in the reflexive construction.)

Object pronouns, however, **precede negative commands**.

No me lo diga (Ud.).	Don't tell me (it).
No me lo digas (tú).	Don't tell me (it).
No me lo digáis (vosotros).	Don't tell me (it).
No se sienten (Uds.).	Don't sit down.
No te sientes (tú).	Don't sit down.
No os sentéis (vosotros).	Don't sit down.

Observe the use of **formal commands** in the Handycam ad on page 95 (*Grabe, ¡Guárdelos ...!*) and in the El Quetzal ad on page 99. (*Infórmese.*) The **familiar commands** (*cuídate, haz, come, bebe, no fumes, duerme*) in the following ad lend a more informal, personal tone to the message.

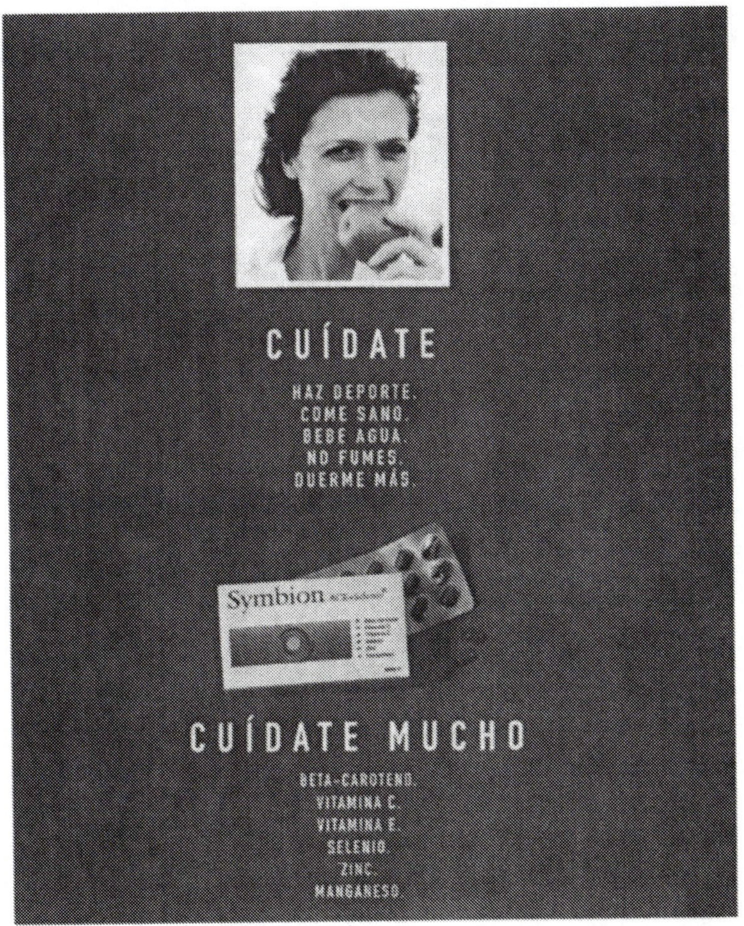

EXERCISES

A. Find four commands in the following ad.

¡Gane un auto nuevo!

Participe en el gran sorteo de

1 Gran Premio
Dodge Daytona Shadow 1991

5 Primeros Premios
Carritos electrónicos para niños

25 Segundos Premios
Carros de pedales para niños

Para más detalles, vea las reglas en la forma de participación.

Ahorre hasta $1.95 con los cupones para productos de Helene Curtis.

1. ______________________ 3. ______________________

2. ______________________ 4. ______________________

Now change them to familiar, less formal commands:

1. ______________________ 3. ______________________

2. ______________________ 4. ______________________

B. Create one negative and one affirmative command related to the following products:

DE ACUERDO

Suaviza la situación con Pert Plus, una fórmula única de shampoo y acondicionador en uno, que deja tu cabello suave y sedoso.

PERT PLUS® LA SUAVIDAD QUE SIEMPRE HAS QUERIDO.

1. ______________________________
2. ______________________________

Sabores exóticos en los helados Goya

1. ______________________________
2. ______________________________

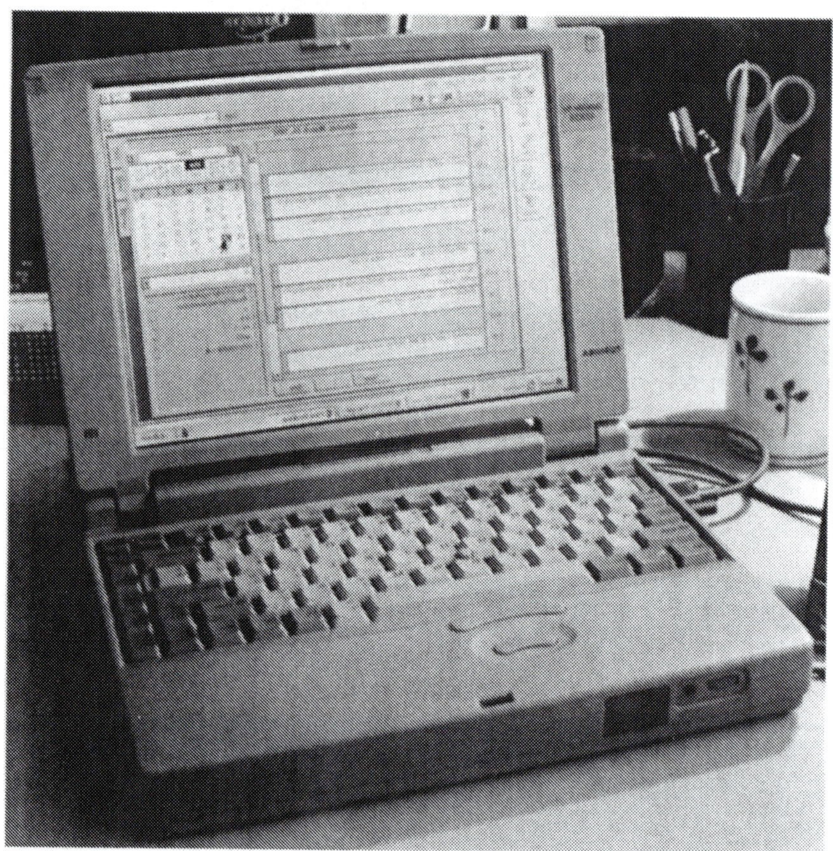

1. ________________________________

2. ________________________________

► Manos a la obra

A. Invente con dos de sus compañeros(as) de clase un producto que quieran vender. Decidan qué beneficios ofrecerá al consumidor, dónde se va a vender (en tiendas, por correo, a domicilio [*door-to-door*], etc.) y cómo se va a llamar. Después, traten de crear un lema o una campaña de publicidad para el producto. ¿Cuál va a ser el mensaje?, ¿a quién estará dirigido?, ¿dónde lo van a anunciar —en periódicos, en revistas, en la radio, en la televisión? Hagan una lista de todas las decisiones.

____

____

____

____

____

B. Ahora escriba individualmente su propio anuncio para el producto del Ejercicio A. Dibuje el producto en el espacio indicado y escriba luego su anuncio.

Ilustración

____

____

____

____

____

____

____

____

C. Reúnase ahora con su grupo. Comparen los anuncios que prepararon y ofrezcan sugerencias de cómo mejorarlos. Escojan el anuncio favorito del grupo y preséntenlo a la clase.

D. Incorporando las sugerencias del grupo, rescriba su propio anuncio en una hoja adicional y entrégueselo a su profesor/a.

PARA LOS INTERNAUTAS

Vaya a **http://www.wiley.com/college/gonzalez,** busque la página que corresponde a este capítulo y haga los ejercicios indicados.

MÁS ALLÁ

Comente los siguientes temas con sus compañeros(as) de clase. Luego escoja uno de ellos y escriba sus opiniones al respecto.

1. ¿Siempre nos dice la publicidad la verdad? ¿Pueden ustedes pensar en algunos ejemplos de anuncios que exageren o tergiversen (*misrepresent*) la verdad? ¿Se debe responsabilizar o enjuiciar (*to sue*) a las televisoras, los periódicos, etc., que publiquen anuncios falsos?
2. La publicidad es a menudo sexista y no presta atención a las diferencias étnico-culturales. Mencionen algunos casos que ustedes hayan observado. ¿Qué se podría hacer para mejorar la calidad de los anuncios en este aspecto?
3. ¿Hasta qué punto es buena la censura en la publicidad? ¿Qué límites fijarían (*would you set*) ustedes? Consideren, entre otras cosas, el tipo de anuncio, la hora en que se pasa (*it is shown*), la publicación en que va a aparecer, el tipo de producto, etc. En una sociedad democrática, ¿piensan ustedes que se debe prohibir la publicidad de ciertos productos? ¿De cuáles? Expliquen sus razones.

En esta página podrá anotar sus ideas respecto a este capítulo o bien referirse a un episodio de su propia vida.

Mi diario:

Capítulo 6

El reportaje a su alcance

Objectives

Upon completion of this chapter you should be able to:

- write a summary
- utilize appropriate vocabulary to interview, report, and write about current events
- use *ser* and *estar* effectively

En quioscos como éste, de Barcelona, España, hay publicaciones para todos los gustos.

▶ Para hablar del tema

VOCABULARIO ESENCIAL

Estudie las siguientes palabras y expresiones. Le pueden resultar útiles para entender el capítulo y para escribir o hablar sobre reportajes.

Sustantivos

el acontecimiento	*happening, event*
la bolsa	*stock exchange, stock market*
el chisme	*gossip, piece of gossip*
el diario	*daily newspaper, journal*
el encabezamiento	*heading, title, caption, headline*
la entrevista	*interview*
el (la) entrevistador(a)	*interviewer*
el (la) entrevistado(a)	*person being interviewed*
la fuente	*source*
el (la) gobernante	*person in charge, head*
el informe	*report*
los medios de comunicación	*media*
el mercado de valores	*stock market*
el noticiario	*newscast, broadcast*
el noticiero	*newscast, broadcast*
el (la) noticiero(a)	*reporter*
el (la) periodista	*journalist*
la polémica	*controversy, polemic*
la política	*policy, politics*
la prensa	*press, newspapers*
el reportaje	*reporting*
el (la) reportero(a)	*reporter*
el resumen	*summary*
la revista	*magazine, journal, review*
el semanario	*weekly publication*
el titular	*headline*

Verbos

contar (ue)	*to tell, relate*
encabezar	*to head, lead, put a heading or title to*
entrevistar	*to interview*
suceder	*to happen, occur*

A. Lea el siguiente reportaje.

Charla con Fernando Botero

Ana María Escallón, directora del Museo de Arte de las Américas, entrevistó a Fernando Botero. He aquí parte de la conversación con el célebre artista colombiano. **E** designa a la entrevistadora, **B** a Botero.

E: ¿Cómo supo usted que quería ser artista?

B: Comencé a pintar —ya sabía que quería ser artista— cuando tenía trece o catorce años. Tengo algunas acuarelas° de la época en que pintaba formas volumétricas aún antes de conocer la importancia del volumen en la pintura. Simplemente, era mi inclinación natural.

watercolors

E: ¿Qué ha aprendido del arte colonial?

B: Un componente que existe en todas mis obras es el arte colonial. Mi interés en las superficies planas° proviene° de ese tipo de arte. Parte de mis trabajos es reflejo del arte al cual estuve expuesto cuando era niño: el arte que se encuentra en las iglesias.

flat/comes from

E: ¿Y el arte precolombino?

B: También tomé mucho de él. Es más evidente en mis esculturas° que en mis pinturas, porque prácticamente no existen modelos para la pintura. Mi interés en el arte prehispánico es evidente en todas mis obras.

pieces of sculpture

E: ¿Cómo enfrenta° la historia del arte cuando analiza su propia° historia?

face/own

B: Soy un artista del Tercer Mundo, un artista que no nació entre museos, en una tradición establecida. Eso me permite ver las cosas con una nueva perspectiva. Mis ojos frescos hacen que las cosas aparezcan° simples. Básicamente invento todo desde el principio.

appear

E: ¿Cuál es la función del arte?

B: La función del arte es exaltar la vida a través de la sensualidad y comunicarla a la naturaleza aunque a veces ésta sea árida.

E: ¿Qué es lo importante en una obra de arte?

B: La coherencia es el elemento definitivo en una obra de arte. Es lo que separa el gran artista de los discípulos. El maestro siempre está obsesionado con una idea que ha deformado tanto que todo lo que hace se ve afectado por esa locura°.

madness, craziness

E: ¿Y cómo ve esa locura de estilo?

B: Como una deformación del espíritu. Hay que estar loco para insistir que las cosas no son como son. Cuanto más fuerte° es el estilo, más loco es el artista. Uno debe convertirse en un monstruo total, capaz de sólo hacer lo que se conforma a esa concepción de la realidad.

The stronger ...

B. Conteste las siguientes preguntas sobre la entrevista anterior.

1. ¿ De niño, dónde estuvo expuesto Botero al arte colonial?

   ____
   ____
   ____

2. ¿En cuáles de sus obras se refleja más la influencia del arte precolombino?

   ____
   ____
   ____

3. Según Botero, ¿cómo es generalmente el mundo del artista tercermundista?

   ____
   ____
   ____

4. Explique la función del arte según Botero.

   ____
   ____
   ____

5. ¿Qué separa el gran artista del simple imitador o discípulo, según el entrevistado? ¿Está usted de acuerdo? Explique brevemente.

   ____
   ____
   ____

6. Observe la fotografía de la escultura de Botero que encabeza la entrevista anterior y haga un breve comentario de la obra.

____

____

____

____

____

C. Ahora haga una lista de las palabras del Ejercicio A que usted no conocía. Añada otras expresiones que considere útiles para hablar de las noticias. Si es necesario, busque su significado en el diccionario.

______________ ______________ ______________

______________ ______________ ______________

______________ ______________ ______________

______________ ______________ ______________

______________ ______________ ______________

______________ ______________ ______________

______________ ______________ ______________

______________ ______________ ______________

______________ ______________ ______________

______________ ______________ ______________

VOCABULARIO CLAVE

Las palabras de esta sección son de uso muy frecuente. Estúdielas y apréndalas. Le ayudarán en sus trabajos de redacción.

al igual que *just like*

Al igual que Oprah y Geraldo, Cristina Saralegui recurre a su espontaneidad para hacer confesar al tímido.

así como *as well as*

Cristina recurre a su espontaneidad **así como** a su legendaria habilidad para entrevistar.

no sólo ... sino que *not only but also*

Cristina **no sólo** trata los tópicos prohibidos **sino que** descubre los secretos más profundos.

a la vez *at the same time*

Los programas de Cristina son **a la vez** producto y radar de nuestra cultura.

de inmediato *right away*

Cuando hablamos con Cristina, su personalidad resalta **de inmediato**.

Análisis del resumen

Un resumen es la condensación de los puntos esenciales de un discurso o escrito. En la mayoría de los casos se trata de (*it's a matter of*) expresar en forma sucinta el contenido de un artículo, un informe o un libro. Cuando tomamos notas en una clase o cuando subrayamos (*we underline*) ciertas líneas de un texto para estudiarlas con más atención luego, estamos también elaborando un resumen. En muchas ocasiones tendrá usted que resumir el contenido de un libro, de un artículo o informe, o quizá necesite escribir un resumen para un artículo que usted u otra persona haya preparado. Así pues, los conocimientos que usted adquiera en este capítulo le serán útiles en diversas situaciones.

Elaboración de un resumen

Un procedimiento sistemático reduce en gran parte las dificultades de elaborar un resumen. Los siguientes pasos le ayudarán en su labor.

1. Comience por examinar con cuidado el artículo, capítulo o informe con el que va a trabajar. Póngale especial atención al título, a los subtítulos y a los encabezamientos y cierres (*endings*) de párrafo. Estas secciones proveen claves (*keys*) esenciales para descubrir el mensaje central.
2. Lea varias veces el trabajo que va a resumir hasta que usted haya comprendido el significado del texto y su organización. Si encuentra vocablos difíciles, búsquelos en su diccionario.
3. Busque y subraye la oración tópica de cada párrafo. Si no hay una oración tópica, escriba una que resuma la idea central.
4. Busque ahora las ideas que sustentan (*support*) las oraciones tópicas. Cópielas o subráyelas si usted las considera importantes, pero evite (*avoid*) los detalles superfluos. No se preocupe de su estilo; éste es tan sólo un borrador.
5. Esta es la etapa de refinamiento y condensación. Una (*Join*) las ideas y simplifique la estructura. Compare su trabajo con el original para cerciorarse (*make sure*) de no haber omitido ningún aspecto importante. Corrija la gramática, la puntuación y la ortografía.
6. Para terminar, dele un título al resumen y explique la fuente (*source*) del mismo. La siguiente es una forma de dar crédito al autor:

   Resumido de (nombre del original) por (nombre del autor), (libro o revista) (mes, año), (páginas).

   Ejemplo: Resumido de «Más cerca de Cristina Saralegui» por Diana Montané, *Más* (julio-agosto 1991), ps. 43–50.

Modelo de la elaboración de un resumen

Lea el siguiente reportaje y luego siga los pasos indicados para hacer un resumen de su contenido.

Más cerca de Cristina Saralegui

"Como latinos tendemos a hacer como el avestruz, meter la cabeza bajo tierra y decir: 'Esa no es la realidad, en mi época estas cosas no se hablaban"

Cristina tiene el único show diurno° en la televisión hispana con su propio nombre, como lo tienen Oprah, Geraldo y Sally Jessy Raphael en la televisión norteamericana. Al igual que ellos recurre° a la astucia° y a su espontaneidad como anfitriona°, así como a su legendaria habilidad para hacer «confesar» al tímido o al agresivo.

¿Cómo lo consigue? ¿Cuál es el secreto de Cristina que no sólo trata° los tópicos prohibidos sino que descubre los secretos más ocultos° de los miembros del panel y de la audiencia, haciendo que el televidente° a su vez se cuestione, o hasta se incomode° en su propia casa?

Ella misma tiene las respuestas: no podemos dejar de ver su programa porque éste es a la vez producto y radar de nuestra cultura. «No creo que la razón por la que el programa es tan exitoso° sea solamente el que

daytime
she resorts to/astuteness/hostess
deals with
hidden
viewer
becomes uncomfortable
successful

se traten temas controversiales», nos asegura° en la sala de su casa en Miami. — **she assures us**

De inmediato° se destaca° su personalidad: su autoridad como reportera, la confianza analítica que pone en sus conclusiones, y sobre todo, esa forma de hablar y el ritmo que lleva cada frase a un final explosivo. — **Right away/ stands out**

«Sí, tenemos temas de sexo, pero están hechos de tal manera que no se discuten gráficamente. Además están hechos con la intención de **in-for-mar**, no para vender o explotar y así obtener buena publicidad».

Saralegui fue la directora de la revista *Cosmopólitan en español* en los años setenta, y esto explica en mucho su estilo y la clase de temas que desarrolla en su ya famoso programa.

A. Siga ahora los pasos para la elaboración de un resumen.

Paso 1

1. ¿Qué le sugiere el título? ¿De qué se trata el reportaje?

____

____

Paso 2

2. Relea la información sobre Cristina y ponga atención al vocabulario y la estructura de los párrafos. Escriba aquí las palabras que no reconoce.

__________ __________ __________

__________ __________ __________

__________ __________ __________

__________ __________ __________

__________ __________ __________

Paso 3

3. Subraye la oración tópica de cada párrafo en las páginas 117 y 118 y cópiela abajo. Si el párrafo no tiene una oración tópica, invente una que resuma la idea central del párrafo.

párrafo 1

____

____

____

párrafo 2

párrafo 3

párrafo 4

párrafo 5

párrafo 6

Paso 4

4. Ahora escriba un borrador de su resumen uniendo las ideas expresadas en las seis oraciones tópicas.

Para escribir mejor

CÓMO ORGANIZAR LOS SUCESOS (EVENTS) EN ORDEN CRONOLÓGICO

A. Lea las siguientes noticias del mundo hispano.

SAN JOSÉ.—El presidente de Costa Rica viajó a Colombia en una visita oficial. Se entrevistó con su homólogo° y discutió asuntos comerciales y de colaboración bilateral. Ambos mandatarios° analizaron la situación de Centroamérica. El gobernante costarricense partió° acompañado de su esposa y del Ministro de Comercio Exterior.

counterpart
leaders
left

MADRID.—El tren de alta velocidad (AVE) alcanzó los trescientos kilómetros por hora en un viaje de prueba. Tardó° cincuenta y cinco minutos en recorrer la distancia Madrid-Ciudad Real. Salió de la estación de Atocha al mediodía y llegó a la capital manchega° a la una menos cinco de la tarde.

It took
of La Mancha

MANAGUA.—La directora del semanario «Gente» se vio involucrada° en un grave accidente de tránsito y se encuentra bajo atención médica. El vehículo en que viajaba la periodista fue embestido° por un camión en la Autopista Sur. La policía recogió a la accidentada y la llevó al Hospital Calderón.

involved
struck

OBSERVE... el uso de la preposición **bajo** en la frase "***bajo** atención médica.*"

B. Haga una lista, en orden cronológico, de los sucesos del accidente en Managua.

____
____
____
____
____

C. Usando como modelos las noticias del Ejercicio A, escriba usted un reporte sobre un suceso mundial, nacional o local.

____
____
____
____
____
____
____
____
____
____

Estructuras en acción

SER AND *ESTAR*

Ser and *estar* are the most common equivalents of the English **to be**. In some cases **only** *ser* may be used; other cases **require** *estar*. With most adjectives, on the other hand, the writer must make a choice between the two verbs.

Summary of ser *vs.* estar

You should use *ser:*

- to identify persons, places, or things.
  Cristina es reportera. Santo Domingo es la capital. El Excélsior *es un periódico mexicano.*

You should use *estar:*

- to indicate location of persons, places, or things.
  La joyería está en la calle 2. Los invitados estuvieron en el hotel.

You should use *ser:*

- to indicate nationality or origin.
  Botero es colombiano; es de Colombia.
- to tell time.
  Eran las tres y media.
- to express days or dates.
  Es domingo. Es el tres de junio.
- to indicate material.
  La casa es de madera. La pistola es de plástico.
- to indicate possession.
  La joyería es de la Sra. Jarquín. La estatua es de Botero.
- to tell the time or location of an event or activity.
  La reunión es a las nueve; es en el gran salón.
- in most impersonal expressions.
  Es importante saber hacer una entrevista.
  Es una lástima que no haya tiempo.

You should use *estar:*

- to form progressive tenses
  El presidente está hablando con el ministro.
  Antes estaba / estuvo escribiendo el documento.

You must decide between *ser* and *estar* with most adjectives.

- *Ser* is used to describe physical attributes, personality traits, and characteristic qualities that are considered **inherent** in the noun. It gives an objective view of what kind of person, place, or thing you are writing about.

  Cristina es famosa.
  El periodista es gordo. (He is 4′10″ and weighs 200 pounds.)
  El tren es rápido. (It can go as fast as 300 kilometers per hour.)
  El Hospital Calderón es moderno. (It was built two years ago.)
  El polo norte es frío.

- *Estar* describes a condition or a state. The writer often expresses a more subjective evaluation of the noun—a judgment or a perception—by using *estar.*

  El detective está viejo. (He's only 40, but he's had a hard life and looks much older.)
  Está gorda. (She's not measurably overweight, but her bone structure and the unflattering dress she is wearing today make her look fat; or, we are surprised that she has gained weight recently.)
  Alfonso está elegante. (Because he is wearing a tuxedo tonight, he **appears to be** rather elegant. He **looks** elegant tonight.)
  ¡Qué frío está el aire aquí! (How cold the air feels!)

- Some adjectives change their meaning entirely depending on whether they are used with *ser* or *estar.*

  Amelia es lista. Amelia is clever (sharp).
  Amelia está lista. Amelia is ready (to go).

  Ana es rica. Ana is a rich woman.
  El pastel está rico. The cake tastes great.

  Juan es nervioso. Juan is a nervous person.
  Juan está nervioso. Juan is nervous now.

Felipe es vivo. Felipe is clever.
Felipe está vivo. Felipe is (still) alive.

La fruta es verde. It is a green-colored fruit.
La fruta está verde. The fruit is not ripe.

You must decide between *ser* and *estar* with past participles (*-do*).

The past participle very often is used as an adjective. In such cases, the participle must agree in number and gender with the subject. This use of *ser* and *estar* is complex; however, the following guidelines will help you to determine which verb to use.

- *Estar* is used with the past participle to indicate a **condition** or **state** that results from some act (but **not** the act itself). It can also indicate a state that the subject reaches.

  La carta está firmada. The letter is signed (as opposed to unsigned, because someone signed it).
  Las sillas ya están pintadas. The chairs are already painted (as opposed to unpainted, because someone painted them).
  Los edificios están destruídos. The buildings are destroyed (because something or someone destroyed them).
  La puerta estaba abierta. The door was open (as opposed to closed, because someone or something opened it).
  Los chicos están satisfechos. The boys are satisfied. (They reached the state of satisfaction.)
  El gato está dormido. The cat is asleep. (He reached the state of sleep.)

- *Ser* is used with the past participle to form the passive voice (See Chapter 4).

- Occasionally the past participle functions as a noun rather than an adjective. In such cases, *ser* is used. Observe the difference:

  Está casada. She is married.
  Es casada (*una mujer casada*). She is a married woman.
  Está herido. He's wounded. (a condition, the result of some act)
  Es un herido. He's a wounded man.
  Está aburrido. He is bored.
  Es un aburrido. He's a boring person.

- In general, past participles with *ser* express an **act**; with *estar* they express a **resultant condition** or **state**.

  Las entrevistas fueron grabadas. (an act) The interviews were recorded. (Someone recorded the interviews.)
  Las entrevistas están grabadas. (a condition) The interviews are recorded. (as opposed to not recorded)

EXERCISES

A. Complete the following sentences with the appropriate form of *ser* or *estar*.

1. La dueña de la joyería ______________ en peligro.
2. La reunión ______________ en Colombia.
3. La joyería ______________ de mi hermano.
4. Este diamante no ______________ auténtico; ______________ artificial.

5. La tía Amelia ______________ la hermana de mi madre.
6. ______________ verdad que Amelia ______________ muy simpática.
7. La estación de Atocha ______________ en Madrid.
8. Los detectives ______________ investigando el robo de la joyería.
9. Los periodistas ______________ guatemaltecos.
10. ______________ las dos de la tarde.
11. La conferencia sobre la situación centroamericana ______________ en Managua.
12. Los conferencistas ______________ en Managua.

B. Complete the following paragraph with the appropriate form of *ser* or *estar*.

Gabriela _______1_______ mi compañera de cuarto. _______2_______ muy trabajadora. En este momento _______3_______ en la biblioteca buscando datos para una tarea de periodismo. _______4_______ muy nerviosa porque ya _______5_______ las dos y tiene que entregar el trabajo a las dos y media. La clase _______6_______ en el edificio de ciencias, que _______7_______ bastante lejos de la biblioteca. _______8_______ probable que Gabriela no vaya a llegar a tiempo. _______9_______ una lástima que el profesor _______10_______ tan exigente: no acepta ningún proyecto que se entregue ni un minuto tarde.

C. Explain the difference in meaning between the following pairs of sentences.

1. Marta **es** delgada. / Marta **está** delgada.

____

____

____

____

____

2. Antonio **es** loco. / Antonio **está** loco.

____

____

____

____

____

3. Los científicos **son** listos. / Los científicos **están** listos.

4. El agua **es** fría. / El agua **está** fría.

5. Tu hijo **es** grande. / Tu hijo **está** grande.

6. La casa **fue** pintada. / La casa ya **está** pintada.

7. Las camisas **fueron** planchadas. / Las camisas ya **están** planchadas.

8. El césped **fue** cortado. / El césped ya **está** cortado.

▶ Manos a la obra

A. El siguiente reportaje es típico de la prensa amarilla, es decir, informa sobre algo escandaloso o extraño. Muchas veces el (la) reportero(a) exagera tanto que se llega a lo inverosímil (*improbable, unbelievable*). Se hace además uso del sobrentendido (*innuendo, implication*) y de los juegos de palabras.

Le robó a su esposa

El 3 de marzo se produjo un asalto en la elegante joyería «Recuerdos Eternos» de la calle Independencia de esta ciudad. Entraron en el establecimiento un hombre y una mujer, ambos enmascarados y armados de pistolas. Lograron huir con una cuantiosa° cantidad de joyas y dinero de la caja fuerte° después de haber tomado como rehenes° a dos de los empleados.

substantial
safe/
hostages

La dueña de la joyería, la señora Esmeralda Jarquín, respetada dama de la sociedad de San Rafael, fue golpeada° violentamente por uno de los enmascarados y tuvo que ser trasladada° a la sala de emergencia del Hospital San Juan de Dios. Según afirmó uno de los rehenes, el asaltante que agredió° a la señora Jarquín exclamó: «Espero que esto te sirva de lección» y después añadió: «Ladrón° que roba a ladrón tiene cien años de perdón».

De acuerdo con las investigaciones del detective Núñez, encargado del caso, se trata de una disputa matrimonial. Parece ser que en un litigio de divorcio, el actual° gerente del Banco Nacional, Lic. Eduardo Montero, ex esposo de la señora Jarquín, perdió la joyería y la casa de habitación, una residencia en el muy exclusivo barrio de «Los Pinares del Río» valorada en varios millones de bolívares°. Las autoridades arrestaron ayer en casa de su hermano al señor Montero y encontraron parte del botín°. No se sabe con certeza quién fue el otro asaltante aunque se sospecha de la nueva esposa del Lic. Montero, su antigua secretaria. Por el momento la señora Jarquín se encuentra convaleciendo en el hospital y el Lic. Montero bajo rejas° esperando ser juzgado°.

struck
taken
assaulted
Thief
current
Venezuelan monetary unit/loot
in custody/awaiting trial

B. Siguiendo los pasos que se explican en la página 116, haga un resumen del reportaje escandaloso «Le robó a su esposa». Use una hoja adicional para escribir el borrador y escriba la versión final en las líneas siguientes. Entréguele el borrador y la versión final a su profesor(a).

____

____

____

____

____

____

____

____

____

____

____

____

____

____

____

____

____

C. Al principio de este capítulo, usted leyó un ejemplo de una entrevista. Entreviste ahora a un(a) compañero(a) de clase. Primero, en una hoja adicional, prepare algunas preguntas. Usted podría, por ejemplo, preguntarle dónde nació, algo de la historia de su familia, sus gustos e intereses, la carrera que estudia, por qué escogió esa profesión, sus triunfos, etc. Luego, tome notas de las respuestas y en las líneas siguientes escriba la versión final. Su profesor(a) le puede pedir que lea su trabajo a la clase.

PARA LOS INTERNAUTAS

Vaya a **http://www.wiley.com/college/gonzalez,** busque la página que corresponde a este capítulo y haga los ejercicios indicados.

MÁS ALLÁ

122 páginas
7 secciones y
Guía visual de pintura y arquitectura N° 13

LA NACION

El tiempo
Hoy: con sol y algunas nubes; brumoso y agradable. Máxima: 23°. Mínima: 16°. Más inf. en la página 6, sección 2a.

Precio $ 1,20 – Recargo envío al interior $ 0,20 | Buenos Aires, sábado 9 de mayo de 1998 | Año 129 – Número 45.447

Estudian eliminar el sistema de jubilaciones de reparto

Un proyecto del Gobierno propondrá que todos los afiliados pasen al régimen privado de capitalización

El Gobierno estudia la eliminación del régimen de reparto y la concentración de todos los aportantes en el de capitalización privada mediante un profundo cambio del actual sistema jubilatorio.

Así lo anunció a La Nación la secretaria de Equidad Fiscal de la Jefatura de Gabinete, Carola Pessino, que trabaja en el proyecto junto con funcionarios de los ministerios de Economía y de Trabajo.

El sistema de jubilación de reparto funciona desde 1950.

"Estamos estudiando para tener algún cambio hacia el año que viene", dijo la funcionaria, que llegó al Gobierno cuando Roque Fernández asumió como ministro de Economía.

Pessino señaló que está trabajando para que el actual régimen, que contempla los dos sistemas -reparto y capitalización-, "alguna vez tenga un corte" y todo se concentre en el privado.

Desde agosto de 1994, cuando se reformó el régimen previsional, el sistema de reparto administrado por el Estado fue perdiendo terreno ante las administradoras privadas.

Todavía permanecen en el viejo sistema 3,3 millones de afiliados, mientras que en el de capitalización privada los inscriptos suman algo más de 6,5 millones.

A pesar de la enorme desigualdad en la cantidad de afiliados que acumula cada régimen hay un dato que los iguala. El nivel de morosidad promedio alcanza al 50%, (80% en el caso de los autónomos) según la cámara de las Administradoras de Jubilaciones y Pensiones.

El proyecto oficial forma parte de un cambio mayúsculo que el Gobierno analiza para el régimen jubilatorio.

Contempla un nuevo régimen para autónomos y la unificación de todo el sistema previsional, que incluye el traspaso a la órbita nacional de las cajas jubilatorias que todavía permanecen en manos de las provincias. **Economía, Pág. 2**

El sistema, hoy

- Gasto previsional para 1998: **$ 17.544 millones**
- Déficit previsional para 1998: **$ 3328 millones**
- Afiliados al sistema de capitalización **6.523.374**
- Afiliados al sistema de reparto **2.304.408**
- Morosidad en autónomos: **80 %**

LA NACION

Gestiones secretas con el FMI en EE.UU.

Acercamiento: el secretario de Trabajo viajó a Washington para limar las diferencias por la reforma laboral y preparar el encuentro González-Camdessus.

Las diferencias que se habían generado entre el Gobierno y el Fondo Monetario Internacional (FMI) por la propuesta oficial de reforma laboral comenzaron a desdibujarse.

Una misión secreta del Ministerio de Trabajo fue la encargada de esta tarea. José Uriburu, secretario de la cartera, viajó hace unos días a Washington en representación del sector más duro del Gobierno para iniciar un acercamiento con los técnicos del

Volvieron las ballenas a la península Valdés

Arslanian: la policía protege aún el juego y la prostitución

Por Hernán Cappiello

El ministro de Justicia y Seguridad bonaerense, Carlos Arslanian, dijo ayer a La Nación que la reforma policial en marcha no pudo erradicar aún la vasta red de sobor-

EL PAIS

DIARIO INDEPENDIENTE DE LA MAÑANA

Barrionuevo y Vera serán juzgados por los tres presuntos delitos del 'caso Marey'

DOMINGO

Un chalé en la Luna

El hallazgo de agua reabre la fiebre por colonizar el satélite

ENTREVISTA

Romay: "La última palabra sobre el 'medicamentazo' la tiene Aznar"

Mujeres sin derecho a rostro

Puerto Rico invade Estados Unidos

El crepúsculo erótico de Josep Pla

África de las Heras, la estrella española del KGB

Castro se quejó a Almunia de que la Embajada española aliente a los disidentes

ENTREVISTA

Cándido Méndez: "La oposición no funciona ni en política económica ni en general"

El Barça golea al Madrid

Núñez pasa la moción de censura, pero con la oposición de 14.356 socios

Secundaria El Camino Real gana Decatlón Académico Nacional

Toluca despluma a **Aguilas** 1-0

Angeles Ochoa vuelve al género de la música lírica

La Opinión

LUNES

Los Angeles, California

La Broadway de fiesta

Confiscan un hotel en Tijuana

- Autoridades creen que estaba ligado al cartel de los hermanos Arellano Félix

Proposiciones: el 'cuarto poder' del gobierno estatal

Comente los siguientes temas con sus compañeros de clase. Luego escoja uno de ellos y escriba sus opiniones al respecto.

1. Muchos opinan que las noticias son demasiado sensasionalistas y fatalistas. ¿Está usted de acuerdo? Explique su posición.
2. ¿Tiene la prensa amarilla razón de existir? Considere publicaciones en inglés como *The Star* o *The National Enquirer* y exponga sus ideas al respecto.
3. Hay quienes afirman que el gobierno puede forzar a los reporteros a revelar sus fuentes. ¿Cuáles son sus opiniones sobre este punto de vista?

En esta página podrá anotar sus ideas respecto a este capítulo o bien referirse a un episodio de su propia vida.

Mi diario:

Las diversiones, los pasatiempos y los compromisos sociales

Objectives

Upon completion of this chapter you should be able to:

- write and respond to invitations
- write and respond to personal notes
- utilize appropriate vocabulary to write about entertainment, pastimes, and social obligations
- use conditional forms and the imperfect subjunctive forms to soften requests

En busca del último disco compacto con sabor latino, Austin, Texas.

▶ Para hablar del tema

VOCABULARIO ESENCIAL

Estudie las siguientes palabras y expresiones. Le pueden resultar útiles para entender el capítulo y escribir sobre las diversiones, los pasatiempos y los compromisos sociales.

Sustantivos

el (la) anfitrión(a) — *host, hostess*
el brindis — *toast*
el enlace matrimonial / la boda — *wedding*
la fiesta sorpresa — *surprise party*
el pésame — *expression of condolence*
la renovación — *renewal*
el salón — *party room*
el sepelio / el funeral — *funeral*
la telenovela — *soap opera*
el televisor — *television set*
los votos — *vows*

Verbos

complacerse en — *to have the pleasure of*
contraer nupcias / casarse — *to get married*
dar / hacer una fiesta — *to throw a party*
estar de moda — *to be fashionable*
estrenar — *to wear something new for the first time; to perform a play or show a movie for the first time*
fallecer — *to die*
participar a alguien de / convidar — *to invite*
ponerse de moda — *to become fashionable*
tener el gusto — *to have the pleasure*
tener lugar / efectuarse / llevarse a cabo — *to take place*

Adjetivos

apreciable / respetable — *respectable*
distinguido(a) — *distinguished*
honorable — *illustrious*

Adverbios

afectuosamente / cariñosamente — *affectionately*
atentamente — *sincerely*

A. Lea el siguiente texto. Busque las palabras que no conozca en su diccionario.

Nuevo furor con ritmo latino

La danza se está convirtiendo en un medio de integración para las culturas de América del Norte y sus vecinos del sur. El tango y otras formas de baile latino están adquiriendo cada vez más popularidad entre los aficionados a la danza en los Estados Unidos.

Como cualquier sustancia adictiva, los bailes latinos tienen una cualidad ilícita, una sensualidad, que la naturaleza puritana de los estadounidenses ha rechazado° tradicionalmente. El movimiento de las caderas° del mambo, la rumba y el cha-cha-chá, los más pronunciados giros° del merengue, la salsa y la cumbia y el contacto físico del tango tienen un denominador común: la sensualidad, que es como una hechicera° que incita y halaga°, guiña° e inclina la cabeza. Es como si fuera un gesto con la mano que invita a acercarse. Y para muchos de los que dan el primer paso, ya no hay marcha atrás°.

rejected
hips
gyrations

enchanter, bewitcher/ flatters, allures/ winks/there is no way back

A través de los tiempos, los ritmos latinos han hecho sentir periódicamente su presencia en los salones de baile. A fines de los años 30, llegaron la rumba y la samba, y en los 40 le tocó el turno al mambo. La resurgencia actual se debe en parte a los que bailaban esos ritmos en sus años jóvenes. Muchas de las personas que participan hoy en día tienen más de 60 años, y la nostalgia los lleva a repetir los mismos pasos que practicaban en su juventud.

Para los más jóvenes, el baile es un ejercicio saludable de efecto terapéutico y consecuencias sociales. La danza sirve para olvidarse de las preocupaciones, extender el círculo de conocidos y establecer nuevas amistades.

El fenómeno, aunque simplista, tiene un gran porvenir°. Algunos bailarines, profesionales y aficionados, lo ven como una forma de restablecer el respeto mutuo entre el hombre y la mujer. El baile en pareja en general, y los bailes latinos en particular, permiten el contacto físico y el flirteo en un ambiente seguro. También el baile sirve para aliviar las tensiones de una sociedad moderna acelerada.

future

B. Conteste las siguientes preguntas.

1. ¿Cuáles son cuatro ritmos mencionados en la lectura anterior?

____

____

2. ¿Según la lectura, qué cualidades de los ritmos latinos los han hecho populares en los Estados Unidos?

____

____

3. ¿Cuál(es) de estos ritmos ha bailado o ha visto bailar? ¿Dónde y cuándo los ha bailado? ¿Dónde los ha visto: en persona, en el cine, por televisión, en el teatro?

____

____

4. Según el artículo, ¿ por qué bailan los más viejos? ¿Y los más jóvenes?

____

____

5. ¿ Cree usted en el aspecto terapéutico de la danza? Explique brevemente.

____

____

C. Ahora haga una lista de las palabras del Ejercicio A que usted no conocía. Añada otras expresiones que considere útiles para escribir sobre las diversiones, los pasatiempos y los compromisos sociales. Si es necesario, busque su significado en el diccionario.

______________ ______________ ______________

______________ ______________ ______________

VOCABULARIO CLAVE

Las palabras de esta sección son de uso muy frecuente. Estúdielas y apréndalas. Le ayudarán en sus trabajos de redacción.

cualquier(a) *any*

Como **cualquier** sustancia adictiva, los bailes latinos tienen una condición ilícita.

ni siquiera *not even*

Estuvo aquí una semana y **ni siquiera** nos llamó.

si bien *though*

Si bien no todos están de acuerdo sobre su origen, el bolero puede describirse como una balada.

en la medida que *to the extent that*

En la medida que nuevas grabaciones aparecen, los jóvenes redescubren el bolero.

► Análisis de las notas y las invitaciones

El lenguaje que se usa en las invitaciones está bastante definido por el uso. En esta sección usted encontrará varios ejemplos de invitaciones que le ayudarán a familiarizarse con ese estilo. En la vida real, usted puede seleccionar de un catálogo o en una tienda la invitación que más se aproxime a su gusto y evitar (*avoid*) así el tener que escribirla. No obstante (*Nevertheless*), muchas personas prefieren agregar un matiz (*touch, tone*) personal a las invitaciones que hacen. Usted, quizá, en alguna ocasión quiera crear su propio estilo o modificar el que le ofrezcan. Muchas veces, sin embargo, se verá en la necesidad de responder a una invitación por escrito. En esta sección encontrará ideas para crear su propia invitación, si así lo desea, y responder a las invitaciones que reciba.

Observe ahora los siguientes ejemplos de invitaciones.

El señor Roberto Mena y la señora Ana de Mena
le invitan a usted y a su apreciable familia
al enlace matrimonial de su hija
Esmeralda
con el señor
Efraín Aguirre Morales
hijo del señor Eduardo Aguirre y la señora
Lía Morales de Aguirre

La ceremonia se efectuará el sábado 26 de noviembre de 1999 a las cinco de la tarde en la Iglesia del Sagrado Corazón. Se ruega pasar luego a una recepción en casa de los padres de la novia, 234 Avenida Los Robles, Alajuela.

Se ruega... *You are asked*

Quince Años

Rodrigo Arguedas y Sara M. de Arguedas se complacen en invitarle a usted y a su distinguida familia a la celebración de los quince años

de su hija
MARÍA DEL SOCORRO

La recepción tendrá lugar el 16 de enero de 1999
de 6 p.m. a 8 p.m.; el baile de 8 p.m. a 12 medianoche
en los salones del Club Campestre Los Pinos,
84 Vía de las Rosas,
Pedregal de San Marcos.

A. Como ya se mencionó, el lenguaje de las invitaciones es bastante formal y está codificado por la tradición y la estructura social. ¿Qué adjetivos se usan para referirse a la familia en las dos invitaciones anteriores?

____

Recuerde que la familia juega un papel muy importante en la sociedad hispana y hay que referirse a ésta con adjetivos como **distinguido, honorable, apreciable**, etc.

Las invitaciones reflejan aspectos religiosos o sociales propios de una cultura, y éstos a veces no tienen equivalentes en otra. Tal es, por ejemplo, el caso de la invitación a la fiesta de quince años. En el mundo hispánico ésta es la fecha en que la joven se presenta en sociedad y es una celebración de gran importancia. En cambio, la adolescente en los Estados Unidos, si organiza una fiesta, lo hace para celebrar sus dieciséis años.

B. ¿Puede usted pensar en otras celebraciones típicas de la cultura estadounidense que no tengan equivalente exacto en otras culturas?

____

____

Suponga ahora que usted ha recibido las dos invitaciones anteriores, pero como no puede asistir ni a la boda, ni a la recepción de quince años, envía una nota para excusarse. Observe las dos notas siguientes. La primera es formal, ya que el autor no tiene una amistad íntima con la familia.

Limón, 23 de octubre de 1999

Sr. Roberto Mena y Sra.

Muy estimados don Roberto y doña Ana:

Muchas gracias por la bondad de invitarme al matrimonio de su hija Esmeralda. Desafortunadamente, cuando recibí su cordial invitación, ya había aceptado un compromiso con la compañía PAMA para asistir a una conferencia en la ciudad de Bogotá durante la última semana de noviembre. Mis mejores deseos para Esmeralda y el señor Hidalgo.

Atentamente,
Miriam Arrieta

En la nota siguiente se aprecia un tono familiar, ya que la autora fue vecina y buena amiga de la familia Arguedas.

Monterrey, 2 de enero de 1999

Sr. Rodrigo Arguedas y Sra.

Muy recordados amigos:

Nada me habría dado más gusto que poder asistir a la celebración de los quince años de María del Socorro. ¡Cómo pasa el tiempo! No hace tanto estaba en pañales y ya es toda una señorita. Muy a mi pesar, me encontraré en la Ciudad de México el día de la fiesta. Ustedes saben bien cómo son los compromisos de negocios. Muchas felicidades y un fuerte abrazo para toda la familia y en especial para la quinceañera.

Afectuosamente,
Eva Lobo

pañales... *diapers*; **Muy a mi pesar** ... *Much to my regret*; **abrazo** ... *hug*

Las notas, mensajes cortos, son sin duda uno de los tipos de escritura más usados en la vida diaria. A continuación encontrará más ejemplos de notas. Observe el uso de los dos puntos (*colon*) después del nombre de la persona a quien se dirige la nota. En contraste con el inglés, en español nunca se usa una coma.

Martita:

No voy a poder comprar los pasteles para la fiesta de esta noche. Tengo que quedarme en la oficina hasta las 7, y la pastelería cierra a la 6:30. ¿Podrías ir tú?

Un millón de gracias,
Felipe

6 de mayo de 1999

Queridos Tomás y Laura:

Muchísimas gracias por todo. La pasé a las mil maravillas. Laura, todavía estoy saboreando tu deliciosa paella. Un abrazo bien fuerte para los dos y un beso para la nenita.

Cariñosamente,

Emilia

saboreando... *savoring*; **beso...** *kiss*

San Francisco, 10 de octubre de 1999

Sr. Ramiro Gutiérrez, Sra. e Hijos

Muy apreciados amigos:

Mi más sincero agradecimiento por las atenciones y cuidados de que fui objeto durante mi estadía en su hogar. Ustedes hicieron que mi permanencia en Lima fuera una experiencia inolvidable. Espero tener la oportunidad de corresponder a sus bondades cuando se encuentren de visita en los Estados Unidos.

Sinceramente,

Gregory White

estadía... *stay*

Para escribir mejor

CÓMO ESCRIBIR UNA TARJETA O POSTAL DE FELICITACIÓN

A. Lea la siguiente selección sobre las postales de felicitación.

LAS POSTALES DE FELICITACION

En todo el mundo, las tarjetas antiguas, ya sean las de Navidad o las del día de San Valentín, están subiendo de valor, y existen coleccionistas que las atesoran. Algunos de ellos poseen ejemplares valorados en miles de dólares. Los ejemplos más antiguos de postales de felicitación se remontan a la época entre 1790 y 1830. En ese tiempo, las tarjetas se hacían a mano, con dibujos originales y únicos realizados por quien las enviaba (es decir, no eran impresas) y también los versos eran originales y escritos a mano por la persona que deseaba expresar su felicitación, su amor o su buen deseo. Estas tarjetas en realidad parecían cartas con bonitas ilustraciones y versitos típicos de aficionados. Quien no sabía dibujar, se limitaba a recortar ilustraciones, colorearlas y pegarlas en el papel en forma artística.

La llamada "edad de oro" de las tarjetas se extiende de los años 1870 a 1920, y las más hermosas fueron las producidas en Alemania. El auge de las tarjetas se hizo posible cuando el sistema de impresión por cromolitografía (o sea, la impresión a color) se hizo accesible al mercado masivo. Las tarjetas antiguas están hechas de papel muy elaborado y tienen colores brillantes, como lila, rojo, azul y rosado, con temas de Santa Claus, Cupidos, flores, corazones y jóvenes románticas.

atesoran... *treasure*; **ejemplares**... *samples*; **se remontan**... *date back to*; **impresas**... *printed*; **recortar**... *cut out*; **pegarlas**... *paste them*; **auge**... *boom, heyday*

OBSERVE... el uso de la preposición ***a*** en la frase "*se hacían **a** mano.*"

B. Conteste las siguientes preguntas sobre la lectura del Ejercicio A.

1. ¿Cómo se hacían las tarjetas entre los años 1790 y 1830?

____

____

____

2. ¿Qué promovió el auge de las tarjetas postales?

____

____

____

3. ¿Cuáles son algunos de los temas que aparecían en las tarjetas antiguas?

______

______

______

C. En grupos de cuatro, escojan una buena razón para enviar una tarjeta o postal. A continuación encontrarán algunas ideas.

- La clase va a dar una fiesta.
- Es el Día de los Enamorados.
- Un(a) amigo(a) va a graduarse.
- Se acerca la Navidad.
- El (la) profesor(a) ha estado enfermo(a).
- Usted ha reñido (*argued*) con su novia(o).
- Es el aniversario de boda de sus padres.
- Acaban de ascender en el trabajo a su esposa(o).
- Se sacó (*won*) la lotería un(a) conocido(a).

¿Pueden agregar otras razones?

______

______

______

Una vez escogido el tema, piensen en el diseño. ¿Hay algún artista entre ustedes que pueda ilustrar la tarjeta? Si no, alguien debe encargarse de recortar ilustraciones para pegarlas en la tarjeta. Por supuesto, la tarjeta puede ser tamaño (*size*) gigante para impresionar a quien la reciba. También incluyan un poema o un pensamiento. Y ahora, ¡manos a la obra! La presentan a la clase la próxima vez.

D. ¿Le gusta viajar? ¿Sabe usted algo de las ciudades y la geografía? Tome la siguiente prueba y autoexamínese.

¿QUE SABE DE CIUDADES?

Estas ciudades y sus contornos son famosas en todo el orbe. ¿Las conoce bien?

La Torre Eiffel

Las pirámides de Giza.

1. ¿En qué ciudad está la Torre Eiffel?
a) París - b) Madrid - c) Montreal
2. ¿Cerca de qué ciudad están las cataratas del Niágara?
a) Los Angeles - b) Buffalo - c) Washington
3. ¿Qué capital está más cerca de la pirámide de Giza?
a) Ciudad de México - b) El Cairo - c) Pekín
4. ¿Cuál es la capital de Albania?
a) Turín - b) Trieste - c) Tirana
5. ¿A qué ciudad se le llama "la capital del sol"?
a) Moscú - b) Lima - c) Miami
6. ¿En qué ciudad se encuentra un monumento al "Oso y el Madroño"?
a) Valencia - b) Buenos Aires - c) Madrid
7. ¿En qué ciudad está el Parque de María Luisa?
a) Bogotá - b) Sevilla - c) Cali
8. ¿Cuál es un famoso barrio de Lima?
a) Palermo - b) El Vedado - c) Miraflores
9. ¿Dónde se encuentra el Palacio de Invierno?
a) Caracas - b) Leningrado - c) Budapest
10. ¿En qué continente se encuentra la capital que se llama Ulan Bator?
a) Africa - b) América - c) Asia

Respuestas: 1a/ 2b/ 3b/ 4c/ 5c/ 6c/ 7b/ 8c/ 9b/ 10c.

E. Ahora escoja una de las siguientes ciudades.

Madrid, Los Ángeles, Nueva York, Chicago, Miami,
San Francisco, la Ciudad de México, Lima,
Buenos Aires, Bogotá o su ciudad favorita

Si es necesario, busque información en una enciclopedia. Mencione, por ejemplo, su posición geográfica, su población y algunos de sus atractivos turísticos. Escriba una postal desde esta ciudad a sus compañeros de clase. Describa la ciudad e incluya un poco de su historia. Su trabajo debe tener al menos cinco oraciones.

▶ Estructuras en acción

SOFTENING REQUESTS

In writing and responding to invitations and notes, as well as in oral communication, Spanish speakers often use the conditional tense to soften a request or make it sound more polite. The use of the imperfect (past) subjunctive instead of the conditional makes it even softer and more polite. Notice the difference in tone in the following examples.

Examples: —*¿**Quieres** acompañarme al concierto?*
—*Claro que **quiero** acompañarte.*
This is informal. Use of the present tense can sometimes even be considered somewhat blunt and not especially polite: **(Do you) want** to go to the concert with me? Of course **I want** to go.

—*¿**Querrías** acompañarme al concierto?*
—*Me **encantaría** ir contigo.*
Here the conditional tense softens the request and the reply considerably and makes them more polite: **Would you like** to go to the concert with me? **I'd be delighted** to go with you.

—*¿**Quisieras** acompañarme al concierto?*
—*¿**Quisiera** acompañarte, pero desgraciadamente tengo otro compromiso.*
Here the imperfect subjunctive makes the request and the reply even softer and more polite: **Might you like** to go (**Might you consider** going) to the concert with me? **I should like very much** to go with you, but unfortunately I have another engagement.

Formation of the Conditional Tense

The conditional tense of almost all verbs *(-ar, -er,* and *-ir)* is formed by using the **entire infinitive** as the stem and adding these endings: *-ía, -ías, -ía, -íamos, -íais, -ían.*

convidar:	*convidaría*	***ser:***	*sería*	***ir:***	*iría*
	convidarías		*serías*		*irías*
	convidaría		*sería*		*iría*
	convidaríamos		*seríamos*		*iríamos*
	convidaríais		*seríais*		*iríais*
	convidarían		*serían*		*irían*

A few verbs have irregular stems in the conditional.

caber:	***cabría***	***querer:***	***querría***
decir:	***diría***	***saber:***	***sabría***
haber:	***habría***	**salir:**	***saldría***
hacer:	***haría***	***tener:***	***tendría***
poder:	***podría***	***valer:***	***valdría***
poner:	***pondría***	***venir:***	***vendría***

Remember that compound verbs (verbs with prefixes) have the same irregularity as the base verb from which they are derived. Look at the examples below.

poner:	***pondría***	***anteponer:***	***antepondría***
		componer:	***compondría***
		disponer:	***dispondría***
		posponer:	***pospondría***
		reponer:	***repondría***
		suponer:	***supondría***
		tra(n)sponer:	***tra(n)spondría***

Formation of the Imperfect Subjunctive

The imperfect (past) subjunctive of every Spanish verb (no exceptions) is formed by deleting the *-ron* ending from the **third-person plural** (*ustedes* form) of the **preterite tense** and adding these endings: *-ra, -ras, -ra, -ramos, -rais, -ran.*[1]

[1]A far less frequently used alternative set of endings for the imperfect subjunctive (*-se, -ses, -se, -semos, -seis, -sen*), seen primarily in Spain and in formal literature, will not be studied in this text. However, you should be able to recognize them.

invitar	*invita~~ron~~*	*invitara* *invitaras* *invitara* *invitáramos* *invitarais* *invitaran*
responder	*respondie~~ron~~*	*respondiera* *respondieras* *respondiera* *respondiéramos* *respondierais* *respondieran*
vivir	*vivie~~ron~~*	*viviera* *vivieras* *viviera* *viviéramos* *vivierais* *vivieran*

Note that the *nosotros* form requires a written accent.

Since the imperfect subjunctive is formed from the preterite tense, any verb that is irregular in the *ustedes* form of the preterite will reflect the irregularity in the imperfect subjunctive. Note the examples below.

saber	*supie**ron***	*supiera* *supieras* *supiera* *supiéramos* *supierais* *supieran*
ser	*fue**ron***	*fuera* *fueras* *fuera* *fuéramos* *fuerais* *fueran*
tener	*tuvie**ron***	*tuviera* *tuvieras* *tuviera* *tuviéramos* *tuvierais* *tuvieran*

Because so many verbs are irregular in the preterite, you should review this tense carefully. Below are some frequently used verbs that have irregular preterites.

andar	*anduvieron*	***poner***	*pusieron*
dar	*dieron*	***producir***	*produjeron*
decir	*dijeron*	***querer***	*quisieron*
estar	*estuvieron*	***saber***	*supieron*
haber	*hubieron*	***tener***	*tuvieron*
hacer	*hicieron*	***traer***	*trajeron*
ir / ser	*fueron*	***venir***	*vinieron*
poder	*pudieron*		

Remember, as you saw with the conditional tense, any compound verb will reflect the irregularity of its root verb. For example: *tener (tuve), detener (detuve), mantener (mantuve), obtener (obtuve), sostener (sostuve),* etc. Note also that like *producir,* any verb that ends in *-ducir* will have *-duj-* in its preterite forms: *conducir (conduje), reducir (reduje), traducir (traduje),* etc.

HYPOTHETICAL SITUATIONS

The imperfect subjunctive is also used in subordinate **if** clauses that contain information that **at the present time** is very hypothetical, unlikely to occur, or contrary-to-fact. The main clause is usually in the conditional tense.

Examples: *Si yo* ***supiera*** *bailar tango,* **bailaría** *contigo.*
If I knew how to tango (I do not), I would dance with you.

Si me ***invitaran*** *a la fiesta,* ***asistiría.***
If they were to invite (should invite, invited) me to the party (they probably will not), I'd go.

To express these hypothetical, unlikely to occur, or contrary-to-fact situations **in the past,** Spanish uses the past perfect (also called pluperfect) subjunctive in the **if** clause, and the conditional perfect tense in the main clause. The **past perfect subjunctive** is formed with the **imperfect subjunctive** of *haber* and the **past participle** (*yo hubiera bailado, nosotros hubiéramos hablado,* etc.). The **conditional perfect** is formed with the **conditional** tense of *haber* and the **past participle** (*yo habría hablado, nosotros habríamos hablado,* etc.).

Examples: *Si yo* ***hubiera sabido*** *bailar tango,* ***habría bailado*** *contigo.*
If I had known how to tango (I did not), I would have danced with you.

Si me ***hubieran invitado*** *a la fiesta,* ***habría asistido.***
If they had invited me to the party (they did not), I would have gone.

NOTE: The **indicative,** not the subjunctive, is used in **if** clauses when the information is possible, likely to occur, or not contrary-to-fact.

Examples: *Si me* ***invitan*** *a la fiesta, voy a asistir.*
If they invite me to the party, I'll go.

Si ***baila*** *muy bien el tango, es porque lo aprendió en Buenos Aires.*
If he dances the tango so well, it's because he learned it in Buenos Aires.

EXERCISES

A. Rewrite the following sentences, changing the underlined verbs to the *conditional tense* to make the requests softer and more polite.

1. <u>Quiero</u> invitarte a cenar conmigo esta noche.

____

____

2. ¿<u>Tiene</u> usted la bondad de explicarme las reglas del tenis?

____

____

3. Me <u>debes</u> decir la verdad.

____

____

B. Now rewrite the sentences from exercise A, making them even softer and more polite by changing the underlined verbs to the *imperfect subjunctive.*

1. ____

____

2. ____

____

3. ____

____

C. Underline the Spanish sentence that is most appropriate in the following circumstances.

1. Your best friend Francisco loves the theater, and you just found out that the local playhouse is doing a series of García Lorca plays. You decide to ask Francisco if he wants to go.

¿Quisieras ir al teatro el mes que viene?

¿Quieres ir al teatro el mes que viene?

2. You call the theater box office to reserve tickets for next month's production of *Bodas de sangre.* The clerk informs you that it is customary to come to the theater personally to pick up the tickets. You decide to ask her to mail them to you.

   ¿Pudiera usted mandarme las entradas por correo?

   ¿Me manda las entradas por correo?

3. The night of the performance you are detained at work, and you pick up Francisco a half hour later than planned. On the way to the theater a policeman stops you and cites you for driving 80 miles per hour. While he is writing the ticket, you try to talk him out of it.

   ¿Me perdona usted esta vez?

   ¿Pudiera usted perdonarme esta vez?

   ¿Me perdonaría esta vez?

4. When you finally get to the theater, the play has already begun, and you politely ask the usher to seat you right away.

   ¿Podría usted sentarnos ahora mismo?

   ¿Puede sentarnos ahora mismo?

5. After the performance, Francisco has to use the restroom. You tell him you'll wait for him in the lobby.

   Te espero en el vestíbulo.

   Quisiera esperarte en el vestíbulo.

6. When you get to the parking lot, you discover that you did not bring your wallet. Somewhat embarrassed, you ask Francisco to lend you five dollars to pay for parking.

   ¿Me prestas cinco dólares?

   ¿Me prestarías cinco dólares?

D. Use the present tense, the conditional tense, or the imperfect subjunctive to write Spanish equivalents of the following requests made to the persons indicated in parentheses.

1. I want to leave work early. (to a friendly co-worker)

   ____

   ____

2. I'd like to leave work early. (to your immediate supervisor, with whom you are relatively comfortable)

   ____

   ____

3. I would very much like to leave work early tonight. (said extremely politely to the CEO of the company, who usually frowns on such requests)

____

____

4. Can you recommend a good movie? (to the co-worker)

____

____

5. Could you recommend a good movie? (to your supervisor)

____

____

6. Might you possibly be able to recommend a good movie? (to the CEO)

____

____

7. Will you pass me the salsa? (to your friend and co-worker, in the cafeteria)

____

____

8. Would you please pass me the salsa? (to your supervisor, at the company picnic)

____

____

9. Could you be so kind as to pass me the salsa? (to the CEO, at the annual company awards banquet)

____

____

E. Give Spanish equivalents of the following sentences according to the information given in parentheses.

1. (Marisol writes to me every month.) If Marisol writes to me next month, I'll answer her.

____

____

2. (Marisol refuses to write to me.) If Marisol wrote (were to write) me once in a while, I would answer her.

____

____

3. (Marisol did not write to me.) If Marisol had written to me, I would have answered her.

4. (Pedro and Mercedes plan to marry soon.) If Pedro and Mercedes get married, they will buy a house in the city.

5. (Pedro and Mercedes are not married.) If Pedro and Mercedes were married, they would buy a house in the city.

6. (Pedro and Mercedes did not marry.) If Pedro and Mercedes had married, they would have bought a house in the city.

F. In the spaces provided, write a very brief note to the following people.

1. your good friend Elena, asking her to call you tonight after her date with Luis

2. a new acquaintance of the opposite sex, asking him (her) if he (she) would be able to come to a party at your house next Saturday

3. Professor Araluce, asking her if she could possibly permit you to miss class on Wednesday so that you can attend your brother's wedding in Las Vegas

4. your brother and his girlfriend, begging them to invite Mom and Dad to their wedding

▶ Manos a la obra

A. Imagínese que ha decidido casarse y escriba la invitación perfecta para su boda. Si ya es casado(a), rescriba su invitación. Consulte la invitación de la página 138 si necesita un modelo.

B. Usted necesita que un(a) conocido(a), su profesor(a) o tal vez su asesor(a) le haga un favor. Escriba una nota solicitando ese favor. Use formas del condicional y del imperfecto del subjuntivo.

C. Haga una lista de sus pasatiempos o diversiones favoritas. Luego, escríbale una nota breve a un(a) compañero(a) para invitarlo(la) a hacer una de estas actividades.

D. Lea la siguiente crítica. Use su diccionario si desconoce algunos términos.

El bolero, que durante siglos ha sido la canción de amor del mundo de habla española, se ha difundido ahora más allá de Cuba, captando la imaginación de una vasta audiencia internacional. Si bien los estudiosos no están de acuerdo en cuanto a sus origenes, todos coinciden que esta forma musical puede describirse como una balada en ritmo lento o medio y con una letra romántica.

Hoy día los numerosos encantos del bolero siguen mostrándose tan vigorosos como cuando las estrellas de los años cincuenta como Lucho Gatica y Olga Guillot cantaban canciones como "Solamente una vez" y "Delirio", que se convirtieron en sinónimos de la cultura latinoamericana en el resto del mundo. En la medida en que las multimillonarias empresas grabadoras extraen de sus achivos las interpretaciones de famosos artistas como Beny Moré, Tito Rodriguez y el trio Los Panchos y las lanzan por primera vez en discos compactos para delicia de las nuevas audiencias de aficionados al bolero, cantantes que ni siquiera habían nacido en la época en que el bolero había llegado al apogeo de su popularidad han descubierto el género y se han apropiado de él. El extraordinario interés mundial por los esfuerzos de la nueva generación de intérpretes ha estimulado el resurgimiento del bolero al mayor nivel de popularidad en las últimas cuatro décadas.

Con el lanzamiento de su álbum, Romance, la superestrella de la música pop mexicana, Luis Miguel, izquierda, reavivó la pasión por el bolero en el mundo entero. Maridalia Hernández, arriba, es una de las jóvenes cantantes que evocan en sus grabaciones el ritmo original y elegante de este género musical.

se ha difundido... *has spread*; **coinciden...** *agree*; **grabadoras...** *recording*; **apogeo...** *high point*; **esfuerzos...** *efforts*

E. Escríbale ahora usted una nota a un(a) amigo(a) para invitarlo(la) a un concierto de Luis Miguel. Use todas las razones que pueda para persuadir a su amigo(a) para que lo (la) acompañe. Use una hoja adicional para escribir su nota.

PARA LOS INTERNAUTAS

Vaya a **http://www.wiley.com/college/gonzalez,** busque la página que corresponde a este capítulo y haga los ejercicios indicados.

MÁS ALLÁ

Comente los siguientes temas con sus compañeros de clase. Luego escoja uno de ellos y escriba sus opiniones al respecto.

1. Generalmente no es fácil encontrar tarjetas producidas comercialmente que expresen lo que queremos decir. Las que se venden en las tiendas son impersonales. ¿Están ustedes de acuerdo? ¿Han tenido problemas para encontrar una tarjeta adecuada? ¿Han diseñado una tarjeta por medios eléctronicos o han recurrido al la «personalizacíon» que se ofrece en algunos sitios? Comenten algunas de sus experiencias.
2. Para algunas personas las diversiones y pasatiempos son una necesidad psicológica. Para otras no son más que una pérdida de tiempo. ¿Qué opinan ustedes? ¿Podrían pensar en algunos ejemplos específicos?
3. Se ha dicho que la televisión tiene una influencia negativa en los niños y adolescentes. ¿Qué clase de experiencias han tenido ustedes como telespectadores? Podrían pensar en varios tipos de programa: programas de violencia, comedias, programas educativos, etc.

En esta página podrá anotar sus ideas respecto a este capítulo o bien referirse a un episodio de su propia vida.

Mi diario:

Capítulo 8

La amistad

Divirtiéndose con los amigos, Córdoba, España.

Objectives

Upon completion of this chapter you should be able to:

- write personal letters
- utilize appropriate vocabulary to write about friends and friendship
- use the subjunctive mood in noun clauses to express wishes, emotion, or doubt

Para hablar del tema

VOCABULARIO ESENCIAL

Estudie las siguientes palabras y expresiones. Le pueden resultar útiles para entender el capítulo y escribir sobre la amistad y los amigos.

Sustantivos

el afecto	*affection, fondness*
el (la) amigo(a) de infancia	*childhood friend*
el buzón	*mailbox*
el (la) camarada	*partner, companion*
el cariño	*affection, love*
el (la) compañero(a)	*companion, mate*
la comprensión	*understanding*
el correo aéreo	*airmail*
la despedida	*farewell, closing of letter*
la dirección	*address*
la entrega inmediata	*immediate delivery*
la estampilla / el sello	*postage stamp*
el papel de carta	*stationery*
el saludo	*greeting*
el secreto	*secret*
el sentido del humor	*sense of humor*
las señas	*address*
el sobre	*envelope*
la vicisitud	*ups and downs, vicissitude*

Verbos

compartir	*to share*
disculparse	*to apologize*
echar de menos	*to miss*
hacerle falta	*to miss someone; to lack*

Adjetivos

amistoso(a)	*friendly*
cariñoso(a)	*affectionate*
cómico(a)	*funny, comical*
comprensivo(a)	*understanding*
fiel	*faithful*
íntimo(a)	*close*

A. Lea la siguiente fábula de Esopo. Si no sabe algunos de los términos, búsquelos en su diccionario.

Los dos amigos

Dos amigos viajaban juntos cuando, de pronto, un oso° se cruzó en su camino. Uno de ellos subió rápidamente a un árbol y se escondió en sus ramas°. El otro, menos ágil que el primero, fracasó° en sus intentos y no pudo protegerse en el árbol. Resignado a su mala suerte, se tiró° al suelo, contuvo la respiración y se hizo el muerto° lo mejor que pudo. El oso se acercó, lo olfateó°, le lamió° la oreja y, convencido de que estaba muerto, siguió su camino tranquilamente. (Parece ser que los osos sólo se interesan en presas° vivas.) Una vez que la fiera° desapareció, el amigo que había presenciado la escena desde la seguridad del ramaje descendió del árbol y, con un tono jocoso°, le preguntó al otro:

—¿Qué secreto te susurró° ese oso al oído?

—Me dijo: —contestó el interpelado°— «Nunca viajes con un amigo que te abandona en el peligro».

Moraleja°: El infortunio prueba la sinceridad de los amigos.

bear
branches/ failed/ he threw himself/ played dead/ sniffed/ licked/ prey/ beast
joking
whispered
person questioned
Moral of the story

B. Conteste las siguientes preguntas sobre el texto.

1. Según la fábula, ¿por qué no se interesó el oso en el amigo que fingió (*pretended*) estar muerto?

____

____

2. ¿Está usted de acuerdo con la moraleja de la historia? Explique.

____

____

____

3. ¿Ha tenido usted una situación en su vida en la que un(a) amigo(a) lo (la) haya abandonado en un momento difícil? Brevemente narre su historia.

____

____

____

____

____

____

____

____

____

____

4. ¿Cómo describiría a un(a) buen(a) amigo(a)? Usted podría usar algunas de la siguientes palabras en su respuesta.

   sincero(a) / colaborador(a) / cariñoso(a) / comprensivo(a) / buena compañía / compartir las vicisitudes de la vida / ofrecer consuelo / saber perdonar

____

____

____

____

____

____

____

____

____

____

C. **Ahora haga una lista de las palabras del Ejercicio A que usted no conocía. Añada otras expresiones que considere útiles para escribir sobre los amigos y la amistad. Si es necesario, busque su significado en el diccionario.**

______________	______________	______________
______________	______________	______________
______________	______________	______________
______________	______________	______________
______________	______________	______________
______________	______________	______________
______________	______________	______________
______________	______________	______________
______________	______________	______________
______________	______________	______________

VOCABULARIO CLAVE

Las palabras de esta sección son de uso muy frecuente. Estúdielas y apréndalas. Le ayudarán en sus trabajos de redacción.

en efecto *as a matter of fact*

En efecto, mi cuarto me gusta mucho.

de repente *all of a sudden*

De repente, empezó a llover.

además de *besides*

Además de mal nadador, yo era cobarde.

► Análisis de la carta personal

Para mantener amistades a larga distancia, a veces es necesario escribir cartas personales, ya que no es siempre posible hablar de todo por teléfono. Esta sección le dará la oportunidad de aprender y practicar la redacción de cartas personales.

Puesto que una carta familiar o amistosa es básicamente una conversación por escrito, a veces es útil imaginar que nuestro amigo o familiar se encuentra con nosotros y le estamos narrando una historia o haciéndole preguntas. El tono amistoso surgirá (*will arise*) entonces en forma espontánea. Básicamente su trabajo debe incluir: la fecha, alguna forma de introducción o saludo, el cuerpo de la carta y una despedida.

Estudie las dos cartas que siguen. Observe el saludo, la despedida y especialmente el tono y el lenguaje de cada una.

Los Ángeles, 2 de diciembre de 1999

Recordados Juan Miguel y Gloria:

Sé que no he escrito en casi un año. No me lo tienen que recordar. ¿Qué quieren que haga? Ésa es mi naturaleza: ¡pe-re-zo-so! Bueno, ya basta de disculpas. Pensándolo bien, ustedes tampoco me han escrito, pero eso no importa, ¿verdad? Lo que cuenta es que siempre les recuerdo con afecto.

¿Cómo está la nenita? Tengo muchos deseos de conocerla. Si es tan bonita y simpática como la mamá, va a ser una futura «Srta. Universo». Perdón, esta brocha° está muy vieja. Debo conseguirme otra. (¡ja! ¡ja!) ¿Entendieron mi chiste? En Costa Rica usamos «pasar la brocha» como sinónimo de adular°.

La invitación sigue en pie° para que nos visiten cuando puedan. Apuesto° que no les vendría mal unas vacaciones en California. Hay tanto que ver y hacer aquí.

Mi vida sigue su rutina sin mayores contratiempos°. Este semestre tomo composición, literatura, psicología y matemáticas. Aunque mis clases exigen mucho trabajo, no puedo quejarme. Los profesores son buenos en su mayor parte y estoy aprendiendo mucho.

Me temo que ésta va a ser una de mis lacónicas° cartas, tipo telegrama, mejor conocidas como «notas». Cuando tenga mis vacaciones, les prometo que voy a escribirles con todos los detalles, o aún mejor, voy a visitarlos.

Un abrazo bien fuerte,

Elvira Sotomayor

brocha: brush
adular: flatter
en pie: stands / Apuesto: I bet
contratiempos: inconveniences
lacónicas: short

Chicago, 18 de septiembre de 1999

Muy queridos don Manuel y doña Pilar:

Acabo de volver a Chicago y estoy tratando de acomodarme°. La residencia estudiantil es un edificio viejo; mi cuarto, sin embargo, tiene bastante carácter propio y, en efecto, me gusta mucho. Hay una ventana que da a un jardín y mi estudio está siempre lleno de luz.

La última semana de mi viaje por España fue inolvidable. Después de enviarles la tarjeta desde Madrid, fui con dos compañeros a Granada. Aunque los trenes que van al sur son muy rápidos y cómodos, mis amigos me convencieron que alquiláramos un coche. Yo tenía mis dudas sobre el asunto, pero resultó ser una buena idea. Nos dio la oportunidad de detenernos en pueblitos y así conocer un poco mejor a la encantadora gente andaluza.

Al llegar a Granada, fuimos primero a la catedral. ¡Tenía tantos deseos de ver la tumba de los Reyes Católicos! El resto del tiempo lo pasamos explorando y saboreando la incomparable Alhambra. Nunca creí que los moros° hubieran producido una joya° arquitectónica de tanto esplendor, lujo y refinamiento. Les digo que si pudiera reencarnar, sin duda alguna, sería como califa° árabe granadino° del siglo XV.

Dejamos el coche en Granada y volvimos a Madrid en tren. Al día siguiente salimos para Chicago y aquí estoy, preparándome para el primer día de clases. Después de un viaje tan fantástico es difícil «descender de las nubes°», pero les aseguro que ya he bajado y que voy a concentrar todos mis esfuerzos en mis estudios.

No puedo encontrar palabras para agradecerles todas sus bondades; así que tendrán que bastar°: «mil gracias, mis queridos padres». Abrazos a Martina, Concepción y Joselito.

Con todo el cariño de su hijo americano,
Ricardo

get settled

Moors

jewel

caliph/from Granada

clouds

suffice

A. ¿Es usted buen(a) observador(a)? ¿Qué expresiones crean el tono amistoso de las cartas? Copie algunos ejemplos de las cartas anteriores en las líneas que siguen.

____

____

B. Toda carta incluye un saludo que varía según el grado de amistad. Los siguientes son posibles saludos:

Querido(a) hermano(a):
Recordado(a) amigo(a):
Amor mío:
Mi cielo:

¿Qué otros saludos podría usar? Escríbalos aquí.

C. Una vez completado el texto, viene la despedida. A continuación hay varios ejemplos de despedidas:

Cariñosamente,
Afectuosamente,
Un abrazo bien fuerte de,
Con todo el cariño de tu hija,

¿Qué otras formas de despedirse podría usar? Escríbalas aquí.

Para escribir mejor

CÓMO NARRAR UNA ANÉCDOTA

A. Lea la siguiente historia basada en un cuento corto del costumbrista costarricense Manuel González Zeledón.

Un baño en la presa

Crucé en compañía de mi hermano Chepe la esquina en dirección a la plaza principal, llegué a la tienda de don Maurilio y doblé a la derecha. Íbamos a la escuela una mañana del mes de marzo. Mi equipo° consistía en camisa con sus dos bolsas pecheras°, pantalones cortos y botas. Bajo el brazo llevaba en un bulto° un cuaderno, una regla°, un mango° verde y una botella de limonada. Los mejores propósitos me llevaban a esa hora a mis cotidianas° lecciones. Pellizcaba° de cuando en cuando el mango y saboreaba su cáscara°.

De repente, siento un par de manos olorosas a zumo° de naranja sobre los ojos y oigo una voz vibrante y juvenil que me grita:

—¡Manuelillo, escapémonos de la escuela y vamos a bañarnos a La Presa! Van con nosotros Toño Arguedas, los Pinto y el Cholo Parra.

El que me llamaba con tanta zalamería° era mi amigo íntimo, mi compañero inseparable, mi siempre admirado Alejandro González Soto, quien hoy duerme el sueño eterno en el fondo del océano, digna tumba de tan digno carácter.

Dudé un instante; el deber° me llamaba a la escuela. Veía pasar ante mis ojos, amenazadora° y terrible la figura de mi padre. Hice un débil esfuerzo para alejar° aquella visión importuna° y, como el acero° sigue al imán°, me sentí arrastrado° por el placer de la escapatoria° y el baño y contesté:

—Bueno, vamos.

Deshicimos parte del camino recorrido° y, a saltos y a brincos°, llegamos a La Presa.

El Cholo, Toño y los Pinto eran excelentes nadadores. Se lanzaban al agua y después de estar largo rato zambullidos°, salían airosos°. Alejandro y Chepe también nadaban muy bien de lado y de espalda. Yo era, además de mal nadador, cobarde°. Con estilo de perro cruzaba, ahogándome°, la parte menos profunda.

equipment
front pockets/
sack/ruler/mango (fruit)/daily/I nibbled/
skin
juice

studied flattery

duty
menacing
to push away/disturbing/steel/magnet/dragged/escapade/
We decided to go back/jumping up and down/
submerged/stylishly/coward/almost drowning

Todos los compañeros estaban en el agua; sólo yo tiritaba°, sentado en la orilla°, contemplando envidioso los graciosos movimientos de los nadadores.

—¿No te vas a tirar°? —me gritó Alejandro.

—Ayudémoslo. —vociferaron a coro°. Y me lanzaron a medio río.

Me ahogaba°, tragaba° agua. Estaba perdido. Mis esfuerzos eran impotentes para salvarme. Sentí que me tiraban de una mano y por fin la luz hirió° mis ojos. Eché a llorar en medio de las carcajadas° de mis compañeros y me encaminé cabizbajo° al lugar donde me había desvestido. Traté de ponerme la ropa pero no pude. Mis camaradas habían anudado° las piernas del pantalón con las mangas° de la camisa. Después de mucho trabajo logré deshacer el daño y vestirme. ¡Nuevo tormento! Se habían comido mi mango, se habían tomado mi limonada y se habían llevado mi bulto.

Lloré largo rato, me encaminé a casa con un miedo horrible. Llegué cuando principiaban a servir el almuerzo. Oí la voz airada° de mi papá que preguntaba por mí. Caí junto a la puerta víctima de un desmayo°.

shivered
river bank
Aren't you going to jump in?/in unison/I was drowning/ swallowing/ struck/ hearty laughs/ down-hearted/ knotted/ sleeves
irate
fainting spell

OBSERVE... el uso de la preposición **de** en la frase *"Traté **de** ponerme la ropa"*.

B. Con un(a) compañero(a), haga un resumen del cuento.

____

____

____

____

____

____

____

____

____

____

C. A casi todos nosotros se nos ha instigado a hacer algo indebido (*inappropriate*). Quizá, nosotros mismos hayamos convencido a alguien de que quebrantara (*to break*) la ley o la autoridad. Puede ser también que un(a) compañero(a) nos haya sacado de un lío (*jam, predicament*). En las líneas que siguen escríbale una carta a un(a) amigo(a) y cuéntele una anécdota sobre una de estas situaciones.

____

____

▶ Estructuras en acción

THE SUBJUNCTIVE IN NOUN CLAUSES

Personal letters often express wishes, desires, requests, hopes, doubts, denials, suggestions, or emotional reactions. In Spanish, such expressions may require the use of the subjunctive under certain conditions. The subjunctive is frequently used in the **subordinate** (dependent) clause of a complex sentence when the verb of the main (independent) clause is a verb of the **will**, a verb of **emotion**, a verb of **doubt** or **negation**, or an **impersonal expression.**[1]

In the letter on page 164, for example, Elvira asks Juan Miguel and Gloria "*¿Qué quieren (ustedes) que (yo) haga?*" **(What do you want me to do?)** The verb of the main clause **(you want)** is a verb of the will; therefore, the verb of the subordinate clause **(that I do)** must be in the subjunctive.

When Ricardo writes to don Manuel and doña Pilar, his "adopted" Spanish parents (page 165), he explains to them that his friends talked him into renting a car: "...mis amigos me convencieron que alquiláramos un coche." In the main clause Ricardo's friends imposed their will (. . . my friends convinced me); therefore, the verb of the subordinate clause (. . . that we should rent a car) is subjunctive.

Subjunctive with Verbs of the Will

Whenever the verb of the main clause is a verb of the will, the verb of the subordinate clause is in the subjunctive, provided that there is a subject change.

Examples: *Maruja prefiere que Fernando le escriba.*
Maruja prefers that Fernando write to her.
(subject change: Maruja → Fernando)

Maruja quería que Fernando le escribiera.
Maruja wanted Fernando to write to her.
(subject change: Maruja → Fernando)

[1]An impersonal expression consists of the third-person singular of *ser* (any tense) plus an adjective; for example, *es necesario, es importante, era triste, fue fantástico,* (*no*) *es verdad.* The subject of an impersonal expression is **it** (understood).

If there is no subject change, an infinitive is used instead of a subordinate clause.

Examples: *Maruja prefiere escribirle a Fernando.*
Maruja prefers to write to Fernando.
(no subject change)

Maruja quería escribirle a Fernando.
Maruja wanted to write to Fernando.
(no subject change)

Some commonly used verbs of the will are:

aconsejar	*to advise*
decir	*to tell, order, command (*but not when it means *to say, communicate information, inform)*
dejar	*to allow*
desear	*to wish*
exigir	*to demand*
hacer	*to make someone do something*
impedir (i, i)	*to prevent*
insistir en	*to insist on*
mandar	*to order, command (*but not when it means *to send)*
pedir (i, i)	*to ask, to request*
preferir (ie, i)	*to prefer*
prohibir	*to forbid, prohibit, keep from*
querer (ie)	*to want*
recomendar (ie)	*to recommend*
rogar (ue)	*to beg, implore*
sugerir (ie, i)	*to suggest*

A few verbs have more than one meaning: sometimes they express will (a command, request, or wish), and other times they simply convey information. They are followed by the subjunctive **only** when they express will. Some verbs of this type are *decir, escribir,* and *insistir.*

Examples: *Me **dice** que lo **llame** a menudo.*
He tells (orders) me **to call** him often. (command)

but

*Me **dice** que lo **llama** a menudo.*
He **tells** me that **she calls** him often. (information)

*Me **escribe** que **vuelva**.*
He writes me **to return**. (command)

but

*Me **escribe** que **vuelve**.*
He writes me that **he is returning**. (information)

Subjunctive with Verbs of Emotion

When the main clause expresses an emotion (such as joy, surprise, fear, sadness, sorrow, etc.), the verb of the subordinate clause is in the subjunctive, provided that there is a change of subject.

Examples: ***Me alegré** de que (tú) me **escribieras**.*
I was happy that **you wrote** to me.
(subject change: [*yo*] → *tú*)

Yo **siento** que tú no me **escribas**.
I am sorry that **you don't write** to me.
(subject change: *yo* → *tú*)

If there is no change of subject, an infinitive is used instead of a subordinate clause.

Example: ***Me alegro** de **escribirte**.*
I am happy that **I am writing** to you.

You should know these common verbs and expressions of emotion.

alegrarse (de)	*to be glad, happy*
esperar	*to hope* (not *to wait)*
estar contento(a) (de)	*to be happy, content*
estar furioso(a)	*to be furious*
gustar	*to please*
sentir (ie, i)	*to regret, be sorry*
sorprender	*to surprise*
temer	*to fear*
tener miedo (de)	*to be afraid*

The verb *temer* is usually followed by the indicative when it conveys a degree of certainty, . . .

Example: ***Temo** que **va** a llover.*
I think (I'm afraid) it's going to rain.
(no emotion expressed, degree of certainty)

but it takes the subjunctive when it expresses emotion.

Example: ***Temo** que **vaya** a llover.*
I'm afraid (It makes me afraid) that **it might** rain.
(emotion expressed, degree of uncertainty)

Subjunctive with Verbs of Doubt or Negation

When there is a change of subject, a verb expressing doubt, negation, uncertainty, or denial in the main clause will require the subjunctive in the subordinate clause.

Example: ***Dudo** que **Luis pueda** ir.*
I doubt that **Luis can** go.
(subject change: I → Luis)

An infinitive is used instead of a subjunctive clause if there is no change of subject.

Example: ***Dudo poder*** *ir.*
I doubt that **I can** go.

Here are some commonly used verbs of doubt or negation.

dudar	*to doubt*
negar (ie)	*to deny*
no creer	*to not believe*
no estar seguro(a)	*to be uncertain, unsure*
no pensar, (ie)	*to not think*

Note that in the case of verbs like *dudar* and *negar*, negating the verb makes it **affirmative**. It is then followed by the indicative rather than the subjunctive.

Examples: ***Dudamos*** *que* ***esté*** *contenta.*
We doubt that **she is** happy.

but

No dudamos *que* ***está*** *contenta.*
We don't doubt (We are sure) that **she is** happy.

Subjunctive with Impersonal Expressions

All impersonal expressions, except *es verdad* (or similar expressions of certainty) are followed by the subjunctive when there is a **change of subject**.

Examples: ***Es necesario*** *que Marta* ***escriba*** *una carta.*
It's necessary for Marta **to write** a letter.
(subject change: it → Marta)

Fue imposible *que Marta* ***escribiera*** *ayer.*
It was impossible for Marta **to write** yesterday.

When there is no subject change, an infinitive is used instead of a subordinate clause.

Examples: ***Es necesario escribir*** *una carta.*
It's necessary to write a letter.

Fue imposible escribir *ayer.*
It was impossible to write yesterday.

Here are some frequently used impersonal expressions that require a subjunctive in the following clause.

es importante	*it is important*
es imposible	*it is impossible*
es increíble	*it is incredible*
es interesante	*it is interesting*
es justo	*it is fitting*
es (una) lástima	*it is a shame*
es mejor	*it is better*
es natural	*it is natural*
es necesario	*it is necessary*
es posible	*it is possible*
es preciso	*it is necessary*
es probable	*it is probable*
es ridículo	*it is ridiculous*
es urgente	*it is urgent*

The **indicative** follows *es verdad* and similar expressions that express certainty.

es cierto	*it is certain)*
es claro	*it is clear*
es evidente	*it is obvious*
es indiscutible	*it is beyond discussion*
es indudable	*it is beyond doubt*
es obvio	*it is obvious*
es seguro	*it is certain*
es un hecho	*it is a fact*

Examples: ***Es verdad*** *que Helia* ***tiene*** *muchas amigas;* ***no es verdad*** *que* ***tenga*** *muchos amigos.*

It's true that Helia **has** a lot of girlfriends; **it's not true** that **she has** many boyfriends.

EXERCISES

A. Find the sentence in Ricardo's letter (page 165) in which he uses the subjunctive to express doubt or disbelief.

1. Copy it here.

____

____

2. Now write its English equivalent.

____

____

B. Write Spanish equivalents of the following sentences.

1. Guillermo calls me occasionally, but I want him to call more often.

2. I was happy that Estela visited us, but I was sorry that she couldn't stay longer.

3. It was true that Refugio and I were close friends, but it was a pity we didn't write each other more often.

4. What a jerk! (*¡Qué estúpido!*) First he writes me that he is coming to visit; then he writes me to send him money for the ticket.

5. I insist on being loyal, and I insist that my friends be loyal too.

C. Your best friend, Mayra, who attends college in Madrid, has written that she is very unhappy. Write her back expressing your concern and offering advice. Combine the following fragments to produce complex sentences and make all necessary changes. Follow the example.

Example: yo / alegrarse de // tú / tener oportunidad de conocer Madrid
Me alegro de que tengas la oportunidad de conocer Madrid.

1. yo / sentir // tú / no estar contenta

2. yo / querer // tú / escribir más

____

____

3. yo / saber // tú / echar de menos a tu familia y amigos

____

____

4. yo / sugerir // tú / hacerse amiga de otros estudiantes de la universidad

____

____

5. yo / no pensar // tú / deber abandonar tus estudios

____

____

6. yo / esperar // tú / seguir mis consejos y // todo te ir bien

____

____

D. Con un(a) compañero(a), termine la siguiente carta.

__________, ____ de __________ de 19 ____

__________ Fernando:

Siento haber tardado tanto en contestar tu última carta, pero aquí es necesario ____

____

____

____.

Realmente no hay nada de nuevo por aquí. Este semestre sigo cursos en ____

____,

así que el tiempo se me escapa muy rápidamente. Además de mis estudios, ____

____

____

____.

Como bien puedes imaginar, estoy muy ocupado(a) durante la semana; sin embargo, en los fines de semana ______________

____

____

____

____.

¡Ojalá que te vaya bien en todo! Me alegro de saber que tú

____

____

____.

¡Y qué bueno que ______________________________

____

____!

Pero es una lástima que ______________________________

____

____

____

____.

Cuando vengas a visitarme ______________________________

____

____

____

____

____.

Vamos a divertirnos mucho. Diles a tus padres que ____________

____

____

____.

Llama a Pablo y dile que me escriba.

Se despide tu amigo(a) de siempre,

____

E. In the last line of the letter in Ejercicio D, explain why the writer uses the subjunctive *escriba* rather than the indicative *escribe.*

____

____

____

F. In the first line of the letter in Ejercicio D, a verb of emotion (*Siento...*) is used, but it is not followed by a subjunctive. Why?

____

____

____

► Manos a la obra

A. El siguiente es un fragmento de una carta de Macedonio Fernández a su amigo, el ilustre escritor argentino Jorge Luis Borges. Es una ingeniosa carta con un gran sentido de humor. Prepárese para lo imprevisto (*unexpected*) y lea la carta junto con un(a) compañero(a). Si tienen problemas, consulten con su profesor(a).

> Querido Jorge:
> Iré esta tarde y me quedaré a comer si hay inconveniente y estamos con ganas de trabajar. (Advertirás que las ganas de cenar ya las tengo y sólo falta asegurarme las otras.)
>
> Tienes que disculparme el no haber ido anoche. Soy tan distraído° que iba para allá y en el camino me acuerdo de que me había quedado en casa. Estas distracciones frecuentes son una vergüenza° y hasta me olvido de avergonzarme.
>
> Estoy preocupado con la carta que ayer concluí y estampillé para vos°; como te encontré antes de echarla al buzón° tuve el aturdimiento° de romperle el sobre y ponértela en el bolsillo°: otra carta que por falta de dirección se habrá extraviado°. Muchas de mis cartas no llegan, porque omito el sobre o las señas o el texto. Esto me trae tan contrariado° que te rogaría vinieras a leer ésta a casa.
>
> *Macedonio*

absent-minded

shame

you (informal), Argentina

mail it/ stupidity/ pocket/has probably been lost/ upset

B. El sentido de humor del autor se nota en la forma en que trastoca (*disarranges*) la realidad y se burla (*makes fun*) del universo que conocemos. Por ejemplo, en las dos primeras líneas dice que irá *si hay inconveniente* cuando normalmente se diría *si no hay inconveniente*. ¿Por qué cree usted que las siguientes oraciones introducen un tono cómico a la carta?

1. Soy tan distraído que iba para allá y en el camino me acuerdo de que me había quedado en casa.

____

____

____

____

____

____

____

2. Estas distracciones frecuentes son una vergüenza y hasta me olvido de avergonzarme.

____
____
____
____
____
____
____

3. Muchas de mis cartas no llegan, porque omito el sobre o las señas o el texto.

____
____
____
____
____
____
____

C. En una hoja adicional, escríbale una carta de tono cómico a un(a) amigo(a) y entréguesela a su profesor(a). Aproveche la oportunidad para usar su sentido de humor.

PARA LOS INTERNAUTAS

WWW

Vaya a **http://www.wiley.com/college/gonzalez,** busque la página que corresponde a este capítulo y haga los ejercicios indicados.

MÁS ALLÁ

Comente los siguientes temas con sus compañeros de clase. Luego escoja uno de ellos y escriba sus opiniones al respecto.

1. La amistad, ¿cuáles son sus límites? ¿Cuánto debe sacrificarse un(a) amigo(a) por otro(a)? ¿En qué momento es lo que pide un(a) amigo(a) inaceptable?
2. El perro es el mejor amigo del hombre. ¿Están ustedes de acuerdo? ¿Por qué? ¿Podrían citar algunos ejemplos?
3. ¿Puede la relación entre un hombre y una mujer ser solamente amistad? ¿Creen ustedes que son inevitables las relaciones íntimas? Den algunos ejemplos para ilustrar su posición.

En esta página podrá anotar sus ideas respecto a este capítulo o bien referirse a un episodio de su propia vida.

Mi diario:

Capítulo 9

El mundo de los negocios

La entrevista es un paso muy importante para obtener un trabajo.

Objectives

Upon completion of this chapter you should be able to:

- write memoranda and business letters
- utilize appropriate vocabulary to write about business
- use the subjunctive mood in adjective and adverb clauses that describe unknown entities and events yet to occur

Para hablar del tema

VOCABULARIO ESENCIAL

Estudie las siguientes palabras y expresiones. Le pueden resultar útiles para entender el capítulo y escribir sobre el mundo de los negocios.

Sustantivos

el aviso	*announcement*
la bancarrota	*bankruptcy*
los bienes	*goods*
la carta de recomendación	*reference letter*
la colocación	*position, job*
el (la) destinatario(a)	*recipient*
la empresa	*business, company, firm*
la entrevista	*interview*
el (la) entrevistador(a)	*interviewer*
el facsímil	*fax*
las finanzas	*finances*
la firma	*firm, company, signature*
los fondos	*funds*
la gerencia	*management*
el (la) gerente	*manager*
la hoja de datos / la hoja de vida / el currículum vitae	*résumé*
el impuesto sobre la renta	*income tax*
la inversión	*investment*
el membrete	*letterhead*
la meta	*goal*
la posición	*position, job*
el préstamo	*loan*
el puesto	*job, position*
la referencia	*reference*
el (la) remitente	*sender*
la sociedad anónima (S.A.)	*incorporated business, corporation*
el (la) solicitante	*applicant*
la solicitud	*application*
el (la) subalterno(a)	*subordinate*
la vacante	*job opening*

Verbos

brindar / prestar servicios	*to offer services*
desempeñar un trabajo	*to work; to do one's job*
invertir (ie, i)	*to invest*
realizar estudios	*to study*
rogar (ue) / suplicar	*to request; to beg*

Adjetivo

financiero(a) *financial*

Adverbios

atentamente / sinceramente *sincerely*

A. Lea la siguiente oferta de empleo, la carta de la solicitante y su currículum vitae.

IMPORTANTE INDUSTRIA ALIMENTARIA REQUIERE:

CONTADOR GENERAL

Los aspirantes deben ser contadores privados, preferiblemente graduados, o estudiantes avanzados en contaduría pública, tener una experiencia de tres años como mínimo en el sector industrial y amplios conocimientos de computación.

El candidato ideal debe poseer un desempeño exitoso en materia tributaria, en trámites de importación y exportación, y en contabilidad de costos.

La edad de los aspirantes debe ser de 30 a 35 años, los cuales deben estar dispuestos a iniciar labores de inmediato.

Los interesados por favor envíen su currículum vitae, con sus aspiraciones salariales, a C&C Consultores S.A., apartado 6452-1000 San José, o bien por medio del facsímil No. 25-75-32. Consideraremos las ofertas recibidas hasta el 16 de setiembre, inclusive. Garantizamos el trato confidencial de sus documentos.

C & C Consultores s.a. Coopers & Lybrand | **Soluciones para su negocio**

San José, 10 de septiembre de 1999

C&C Consultores S.A.
Apartado 6452–1000
San José

Muy estimados señores:

Leí con sumo interés el aviso que su empresa° publicó en *La Nación* en el cual se solicitan los servicios de un contador general.

° **business**

Tengo 32 años, soy graduada de la Escuela de Comercio de la Universidad Nacional, he trabajado con la Compañía Constructora Nacional por cuatro años y tengo experiencia en computación, como se explica en mi currículum vitae.

Quedaré muy agradecida° si ustedes tuvieran la bondad de concederme una entrevista para exponer en detalle el tipo de servicio que podría desempeñar en su firma.

grateful

Si desean cartas de recomendación se las enviaré gustosa.

Atentamente,
Julieta Prado Loría
Julieta Prado Loría

CURRÍCULUM VITAE

Julieta Prado Loría
Calle 8, Avenida 12, Moravia, San José
Teléfono 221-53-79

Metas profesionales
Superarme° en el campo de la contaduría pública y de los negocios

To achieve excellence

Educación
1998 –Universidad Estatal de Santo Tomás, seminario en computación para contadores públicos
1993-1997 –Universidad Nacional, título en contaduría
1987-1992 –Colegio Superior de San Blas, bachillerato

Experiencia
1998 al presente, Compañía Constructora Nacional, contaduría pública de la empresa. Encargada del° departamento de finanzas, responsable de la preparación del impuesto sobre la renta
1994-1997 –asistente del gerente, Supermercados Gigante

In charge of the

Habilidades en computación
hoja electrónica de cómputo°, conocimiento de Data Base

computer spreadsheet

B. Conteste las siguientes preguntas sobre el anuncio, la carta y el currículum vitae.

1. ¿Qué condición se pide a los aspirantes en la oferta de empleo que es ilegal en los Estados Unidos?

2. Si usted estuviera a cargo de reclutar candidatos para el puesto de Consultores Coopers & Lybrand S. A., ¿le concedería usted una entrevista a Julieta? Explique sus razones.

3. En el aviso se pide que se envíen, junto con el currículum vitae, las aspiraciones salariales. Julieta omitió ese detalle. ¿Le parece a usted buena o mala táctica? ¿Por qué?

C. Ahora haga una lista de las palabras del Ejercicio A que usted no conocía. Añada otras expresiones que considere útiles para escribir sobre los negocios. Si es necesario, busque su significado en el diccionario.

VOCABULARIO CLAVE

Las palabras de esta sección son de uso muy frecuente. Estúdielas y apréndalas. Le ayudarán en sus trabajos de redacción.

estar dispuesto(a) a *to be ready to*

Los candidatos deben **estar dispuestos a** empezar su trabajo de inmediato.

sumo *extreme*

Leí con **sumo** interés su oferta de trabajo.

como mínimo, al menos *as a minimum, at least*

Como mínimo debe tener tres años de experiencia en el campo de los negocios.

Al menos debe tener tres años de experiencia en el campo de los negocios.

Análisis de los memorandos y las cartas comerciales

LOS MEMORANDOS

Los memorandos o «memos» son mensajes que se envían dentro de una institución. Son comunicados informales y generalmente cortos. De ordinario los jefes usan este tipo de mensaje para dar instrucciones o notificaciones a sus subalternos. Un memorando se caracteriza por su concisión y claridad.

Hay ocho elementos básicos en un memorando:

1. **el membrete**, es decir, la inscripición con el nombre y señas de la compañía o institución que expide el escrito.
2. **la fecha**
3. **el destinatario** (A: ______________)
4. **el origen** (De: ______________)
5. **el asunto** (el tema o el tópico del memo)
6. **el mensaje** (texto del memorando) y
7. **las iniciales o firma**

Observe ahora dos posibles formatos para un memorando:

Membrete
(dos espacios)
Memorando

(de cuatro a seis espacios)

Fecha:
(dos espacios)

A: ____________________

De: ____________________

Asunto: ____________________
(dos espacios)

texto del mensaje

(cuatro espacios)

firma ____________

Membrete
(dos espacios)
Memorando

(de cuatro a seis espacios)

A: ____________________

De: ____________________

Fecha: ____________________

Asunto: ____________________
(dos espacios)

texto del mensaje

Existen variaciones en el formato del memorando. Por ejemplo, después del membrete y la palabra **memorando**, se puede escribir la fecha; también es posible colocarla (*to place it*) antes del asunto. La firma se incluye en algunas ocasiones; en otras, solamente aparecen las iniciales junto al nombre del remitente. La preposición más corriente para señalar el destinatario es **a**; la preposición **para** también se puede usar.

Observe los siguientes ejemplos de memorandos.

```
INA
                    MEMORANDO

A: D. Prog. Especiales     Fecha: 22 de enero de 1999

De: Lic. Raquel Ortiz A.   Asunto: Envío documento
                    RO
_____________________________________________________

Le remito el documento recibido de CINTERFOR,
«Anuario estadístico de la formación profesional
en América Latina».

El ejemplar es para uso de su departamento por lo
cual le ruego notificar a todos los funcionarios
que se encuentren bajo su dirección.
```

```
   UNIVERSIDAD TÉCNICA ESTATAL DE SANTO TOMÁS

                  MEMORANDO

A:        Cuerpo docente° y alumnado
De:       Dimas Molina Alvarado
Fecha:    8 de noviembre de 1999
Asunto:   Nuevas regulaciones de estacionamiento

De acuerdo con las nuevas regulaciones vigentes°
a partir del próximo mes de diciembre, el cuerpo
docente usará los estacionamientos A y B
ubicados° detrás de la biblioteca. Los
estudiantes estacionarán sus vehículos en las
secciones C, D y F. La sección G se reserva para
los visitantes y los minusválidos°.
```

Faculty

in effect

located

handicapped

A. Relea el memorando anterior (de Dimas Molina Alvarado) e identifique sus partes.

1. ¿Quién es el remitente?

____

2. ¿Cuál es el mensaje del memo?

____

3. ¿Cuándo comenzarán a aplicarse las nuevas medidas?

____

LA CARTA COMERCIAL

Si usted tiene la oportunidad de trabajar en una compañía con nexos (*connections*) con el mundo hispano, le será necesario redactar cartas comerciales. En esta sección podrá practicar la escritura de este tipo de cartas.

La carta comercial es un escrito que requiere más cuidado y preparación que la carta personal o el memorando. He aquí algunos pasos que le ayudarán a obtener mejores resultados en la confección de cartas comerciales:

1. Establezca el motivo de la carta y obtenga los datos necesarios para su redacción.
2. Es buena idea hacer un esquema o bosquejo (*outline*) de la carta.
3. Elabore el borrador (*draft*) de la carta.
4. Haga las correcciones necesarias, aplicando su conocimiento de la estructura gramatical y las reglas de puntuación y ortografía.

Una carta comercial debe incluir lo siguiente.

1. **la fecha**
2. **el destinatario**
3. **el saludo**
4. **el cuerpo de la carta**
5. **la despedida**
6. **la firma**

La fecha de la carta generalmente contiene el lugar de origen también. Empiece con la ciudad o pueblo desde donde escribe, luego use una coma y escriba la fecha comenzando con el día, continuando con el mes y terminando con el año.

Ejemplo: San José, 29 de marzo de 1999

El destinatario es la institución o individuo a quien nos dirigimos. Es de suma importancia que el nombre, el rango (*rank*) o cargo (*position*) y los títulos del destinatario estén correctamente escritos.

Ejemplos: Doctor
Miguel Angel Zúñiga O.
Hospital San Juan de Dios
Paseo Colón 489
San Salvador, El Salvador

Señores
Domingo Fuscaldo Hnos.
Calle 7, Avenida 12
Bogotá, Colombia

El saludo debe ser cordial y sencillo. Generalmente se usa la palabra **estimado(a, os, as)** más el título (**doctor**, **profesora**, **señorita**, etc.). Cuando la carta está dirigida a una empresa o institución, **señores** o **estimados señores** es suficiente. Después de la frase de saludo se colocan (*are placed*) dos puntos.

Ejemplos: Señores:
Estimados señores:
Estimada doctora Sáenz:
Muy señor mío:

B. Ahora usted va a enviar una carta a la Lic. Victoria Gaitán, presidenta del Consejo Superior de Educación. Su dirección: Calle 12, No. 77, Ministerio de Educación Pública, Santiago, Chile. Organice el encabezamiento de la carta incluyendo la fecha, la dirección y el saludo.

fecha

____

nombre y dirección

____

____

____

____

____

saludo

____

El cuerpo de la carta es la sección del texto mismo. Continuamos luego con la despedida. En una carta comercial moderna se emplea una de las siguientes:

Atentamente,

Cordialmente,

Sinceramente,

Ahora escriba una despedida para la carta a la Lic. Gaitán.

despedida

____

Por último encontramos la firma del remitente con su título o rango.

Observe los dos estilos de cartas en la página siguiente.

Estilo bloque

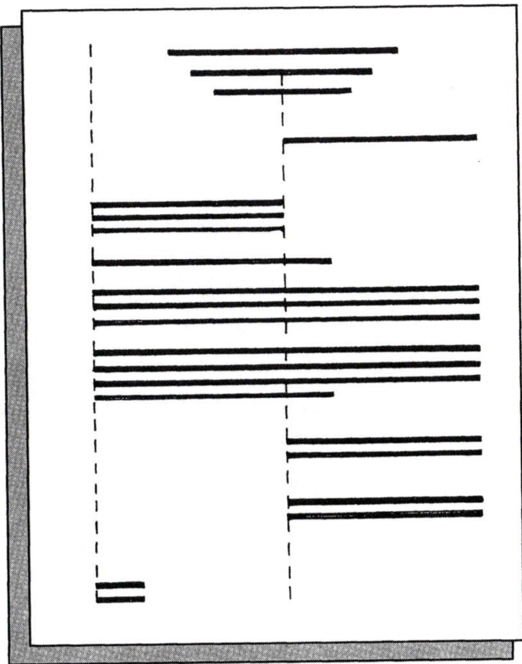

Estilo semibloque

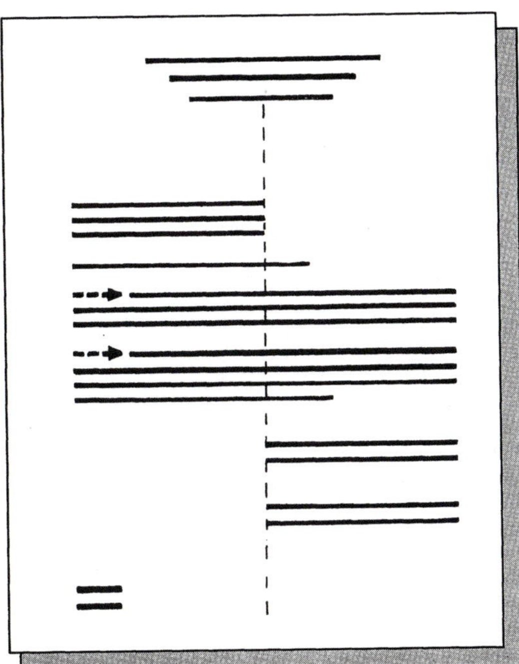

Motivos para una carta comercial

Son muchas las razones para escribir una carta comercial. Entre las más comunes están:

1. solicitar o dar información
2. hacer o cancelar un pedido (*order*) o contrato
3. solicitar u ofrecer empleo
4. dar las gracias por algún servicio
5. presentar quejas (*complaints*) por algún problema
6. dar excusas por un contratiempo

Expresiones y oraciones comunes en las cartas comerciales

Aunque la originalidad siempre es deseable, he aquí unas cuantas oraciones y expresiones que podrían ayudarle para comenzar a redactar cartas comerciales:

Introducciones

1. Leí con gran interés su carta...
2. Muchas gracias por su carta...
3. Muy agradecidos por su interés en...
4. Agradecemos su interés en...
5. Nos es grato (*We are happy, It pleases us*) informarle que...
6. Adjunto (*I enclose*) nuestra última lista de precios...
7. Incluyo nuestro catálogo...
8. Nos complace (*It pleases us*) informarle que...
9. Gracias por la oportunidad que nos brinda (*offer*) para...
10. Es con mucho agrado que...
11. Lamento los problemas que ha tenido...
12. Lamento informarle que...
13. Mis más sinceras disculpas (*apologies*) por...
14. Siento que...
15. Sírvase considerar esta carta como la cancelación de...

Conclusiones

1. Tuvimos sumo agrado en...
2. Esperamos continuar sirviéndole...
3. Ha sido un placer servirle...

El siguiente es un ejemplo de los pasos a seguir en la confección de una carta comercial.

1. motivo: dar información y ofrecer servicios
2. bosquejo:
   - **a.** expresar las gracias
   - **b.** dar información sobre nuestros productos
   - **c.** pedir información y ofrecer servicios
   - **d.** frases de conclusión

3. borrador:

Le agradezco profundamente su interés en los productos de nuestra compañía. El abrir mercados para el público norteamericano de origen hispano nos parece una idea excelente. Por más de tres décadas ha sido nuestra meta complacer el exigente paladar (*palate*) del gastrónomo. Para alcanzar tal meta, ofrecemos hoy al consumidor toda una gama de especias, salsas y encurtidos (*pickles*).

Quizá se podría decir que nuestra especialidad son las salsas y los encurtidos. Producimos dos variedades de encurtido: uno en mostaza y otro en vinagre. En cuanto a las salsas que elaboramos, la «Salsa Inglesa» y la «Salsa Picante» son de inigualable calidad y sabor. Son nuestro orgullo (*pride*). Le agradecería que nos explicara con más detalles las regulaciones con que deberíamos cumplir para un posible envío de nuestros productos a los Estados Unidos. Estamos dispuestos a acomodarnos a sus necesidades y normas. Muchas gracias de nuevo y esperamos tener la oportunidad de servirle en un futuro cercano.

4. copia final:

EL BUEN SABOR, S. A.
225 AV. SAN VALENTÍN
LIMA, PERÚ

26 de julio de 1999

Señor
Luis Marín
La Mirada, California
Estados Unidos

Estimado señor:

Le agradezco profundamente su interés en los productos de nuestra compañía. El abrir mercados para el consumidor norteamericano de origen hispano nos parece una excelente idea. Por más de tres décadas ha sido la meta de la empresa el complacer el exigente paladar del gastrónomo. Para alcanzar tal objetivo, ofrecemos hoy toda una gama de especias, salsas y encurtidos. Las salsas y los encurtidos son, sin embargo, nuestro orgullo. Producimos dos variedades de encurtido: uno en mostaza y otro en vinagre. En cuanto a las salsas que elaboramos, la «Salsa Inglesa» y la «Salsa Picante» son de inigualable calidad y sabor.

Le agradecería que nos explicara con más detalles las regulaciones con las que deberíamos cumplir para hacer un envío a los Estados Unidos. Estamos dispuestos a acomodarnos a sus necesidades y normas. Muchas gracias de nuevo y esperamos tener la oportunidad de servirles en un futuro cercano.

Cordialmente,
Rosalba Perales Ch.
Rosalba Perales Ch.
Gerente de Publicidad

C. Busque y copie de la carta anterior:

1. el membrete

____

____

____

2. el destinatario

____

____

____

3. el remitente

____

____

____

D. Ahora escriba otro posible saludo para la carta.

____

Agregue además otra despedida.

____

Para escribir mejor

CÓMO PREPARAR PREGUNTAS PARA UNA ENTREVISTA

A. Lea la siguiente información sobre las entrevistas.

¿Qué es una entrevista?

La entrevista es el evento más importante en el proceso de obtener un puesto. El patrón ha determinado que las destrezas° del candidato llenan los requisitos de la compañía y ahora quiere medir° personalmente el potencial del solicitante. Muchos factores no se pueden descubrir a través de un currículum vitae u hoja de vida. Es difícil juzgar, sin un contacto personal, las actitudes, la habilidad para comunicarse y los aspectos fuertes o débiles del aspirante. Una entrevista también le ofrece, tanto al entrevistador como al entrevistado, la oportunidad de hacer y contestar preguntas sobre aspectos que aún no estén claros.

skills
to measure

La preparación para la entrevista es esencial. Hay dos áreas que el interesado debe escudriñar° cuidadosamente antes de presentarse a la entrevista: sus aptitudes, valores e intereses y las metas y necesidades de la empresa que busca los servicios. Comience por autoevaluarse. ¿Cuáles son sus habilidades, intereses, cualidades de liderazgo°, conocimientos técnicos, aspiraciones personales, actidudes y esperanzas? Estudie además el tamaño y organización de la firma, su potencial de crecimiento, el tipo de servicio o producto que ofrece, su localización geográfica, las posibles necesidades de la compañía en las que usted puede ser útil y finalmente el prestigio de su futuro trabajo dentro de la empresa. Armado con toda esta información, va a gozar de gran éxito en el competitivo mundo de los negocios.

to scrutinize
leadership

> **OBSERVE...** que la conjunción **o** se convierte en **u** cuando va seguida de **o-, ho-**.

> **OBSERVE...** el uso de la preposición **de** en la expresión **gozar de**.

B. Relea el anuncio de empleo, la carta de solicitud y el currículum vitae de las páginas 183–184 y prepare con otros cuatro compañeros de clase diez preguntas pertinentes para hacerle a Julieta Prado durante la entrevista.

1. ______________________________
2. ______________________________
3. ______________________________
4. ______________________________
5. ______________________________
6. ______________________________
7. ______________________________
8. ______________________________
9. ______________________________
10. ______________________________

C. Ahora intercambien su lista de preguntas con otro grupo y piensen en buenas respuestas para las preguntas de sus compañeros, basándose en la información de la carta y del currículum vitae.

1. ______________________________

2. ____

____

3. ____

____

4. ____

____

5. ____

____

6. ____

____

7. ____

____

8. ____

____

9. ____

____

10. ____

____

► Estructuras en acción

THE SUBJUNCTIVE IN ADJECTIVE CLAUSES

An adjective is a word that describes a person, place, or thing.

Example: *Tengo un puesto* ***interesante.***
(*Interesante* describes *puesto.*)
I have an **interesting** job.

An adjective clause is an entire clause that functions as an adjective.

Example: *Tengo un puesto* ***que es interesante.***
(*Que es interesante* describes *puesto.*)
I have a job **that is interesting**.

If the antecedent (the person, place, or thing being described) is **definite**, **specific**, or **known to exist**, then the verb of the adjective clause is in the **indicative** mood.

Examples: *En nuestra compañía* ***hay*** *muchos empleados que* ***hablan*** *inglés y español.*
In our company **there are** many employees who **speak** English and Spanish.

Tenemos *una contadora que* ***habla*** *inglés y español.*
We have an accountant who **speaks** English and Spanish.

However, if the antecedent is **unknown**, **indefinite**, or **nonexistent**, then the verb of the adjective clause must be in the **subjunctive**.

Examples: *En nuestra compañía* ***no hay ningún*** *empleado que* ***hable*** *inglés y español.*
In our company **there are no** employees who **speak** English and Spanish.

Buscamos *una contadora que* ***hable*** *inglés y español.*
We're looking for an accountant who **speaks** English and Spanish.

NOTE: You may wish to complete exercises A through C on pages 200–201 before beginning the following section.

THE SUBJUNCTIVE IN ADVERB CLAUSES

A word that modifies a verb is an adverb. It gives information such as **when, why, how, under what conditions or circumstances**, etc.

Example: *Escribo el memorando* ***pronto.***
(*Pronto* modifies *Escribo.*)
I'll write the memo **soon**.

An adverb clause is an entire clause that functions as an adverb.

Example: *Escribí el memorando* ***tan pronto como la presidenta me lo pidió.***
(*Tan pronto como la presidenta me lo pidió* modifies *Escribí.*)
I wrote the memo **as soon as the president asked me.**

Adverb clauses are introduced by a conjunction. In Spanish, certain conjunctions are **always** followed by the subjunctive because they contain information that may or may not happen or because they show a cause-and-effect or conditional relationship. They do not express fully realized or accomplished acts; hence there is an **implied uncertainty or doubt**. The following conjunctions always require the subjunctive:

a fin de que	*in order that, so that*
a menos que	*unless*
a no ser que	*unless*
antes (de) que	*before*
con tal (de) que	*provided that*
en caso (de) que	*in case, in the event that*
para que	*so that, in order that*
sin que	*without*

Examples: *Aceptaré el puesto* ***con tal que*** *me* ***ofrezcan*** *un buen sueldo.*
I'll accept the position **provided that they offer** me a good salary.

No debo distribuir el memo ***sin que*** *lo* ***vea*** *el gerente.*
I shouldn't distribute the memo **without** the manager **seeing** it.

Other conjunctions are followed by the **subjunctive** only when they introduce **information that has not yet occurred** or **that is hypothetical**. When they introduce **known facts** or **habitual actions**, then the **indicative** is used.

aunque	*although, even though, even if*
cuando	*when*
después (de) que	*after*
en cuanto	*as soon as*
hasta que	*until*
tan pronto como	*as soon as*

Examples: *Voy a aceptar el puesto,* ***aunque*** *el salario* ***es*** *bajo.*
I'm going to accept the job, **even though** the salary **is** (in fact) low.

but

Voy a aceptar el puesto, ***aunque*** *el salario* ***sea*** *bajo.*
I'm going to accept the job, **even though** the salary **may be** low. (I do not yet know the exact salary.)

Siempre me quedo en la oficina ***hasta que se va*** *el jefe.*
I always stay in the office **until** the boss **leaves**.

Anoche me quedé en la oficina ***hasta que se fue*** *el jefe.*
Last night I stayed in the office **until** the boss **left**.

but

Voy a quedarme en la oficina ***hasta que se vaya*** *el jefe.*
I'm going to stay in the office **until** the boss **leaves**.

When there is no change of subject, a preposition (*antes de, para, sin, después de, hasta,* etc.) plus an infinitive usually replaces the subordinate adverb clause.

Examples: *Revisé el memo* ***antes de que*** *la secretaria lo* ***distribuyera.***
I revised the memo **before** the secretary **distributed** it.
(subject change: *yo* → *la secretaria*)

but

Revisé el memo ***antes de distribuirlo.***
I revised the memo **before I distributed it**.
(no subject change)

Tengo que quedarme ***hasta que*** *el secretario* ***termine*** *la carta.*
I have to stay **until** the secretary **finishes** the letter.
(subject change: *yo* → *el secretario*)

but

Tengo que quedarme ***hasta terminar*** *la carta.*
I have to stay **until I finish** the letter.
(no subject change)

EXERCISES

A. Give Spanish equivalents of the following sentences. Be prepared to justify your choices.

1. We're looking for a bilingual accountant.

____

____

2. We're looking for an accountant who is bilingual.

____

____

3. We have an accountant who is bilingual.

____

____

4. I need an efficient manager.

____

____

5. I need a manager who knows how to write memos.

____

____

6. I have a manager who doesn't know how to write memos.

____

____

B. Use your imagination to complete the following sentences.

1. Tengo un puesto que ______________________________________ ,
pero busco uno que______________________________________ .

2. Hay muchas compañías que____,
pero prefiero trabajar en una compañía que ______________________________
____.

3. En nuestra oficina siempre recibimos memorandos que ____________________
____;
nunca recibimos memos que ____
____.

4. Esa empresa solicita empleados que _____________________________________
____;
ya tiene muchos empleados que ____.

5. Pilar prefiere un gerente que____;
desgraciadamente tiene uno que ____.

C. Reread the C&C Consultores job ad on page 183, then complete the following observations.

C&C Consultores busca un contador...

1. que ______________ (ser) graduado en contaduría pública.
2. que ______________ (tener) bastante experiencia.
3. que ______________ (conocer) de computación.
4. que ______________ (poseer) un desempeño exitoso en contabilidad de costos.
5. que ______________ (tener) de 30 a 35 años.
6. que ______________ (estar) dispuesto a iniciar labores inmediatamente.

D. Doña Esperanza wrote a letter of reference for Rubén Cardona and gave him advice in preparation for his recent job interview. Use either the *indicative* or the *subjunctive* of the verbs in parentheses to complete the following letter in which he thanks her and tells her about the interview.

Guadalajara, 8 de diciembre de 1999

Muy estimada doña Esperanza:

Gracias por su carta de recomendación. Ayer fui a la entrevista con la compañía Pemex. Cuando ______________ (yo/llegar), la secretaria me dijo que el comité entrevistador me vería pronto. Mientras ______________ (yo/esperar), leí mis notas y sus consejos y repasé mis ideas sobre el puesto. La entrevista resultó excelente. Antes de que los miembros de la mesa (*panel*) me _______________ (hacer) preguntas, me explicaron los beneficios de la empresa. Quedé muy impresionado. Después de que _______________ (ellos/terminar) sus explicaciones, hablé yo de mi experiencia y conocimientos.

A menos que _______________ (yo/haber dicho) tonterías sin _______________ (yo/darme) cuenta, creo tener buenas posibilidades de obtener el trabajo. Si me ofrecen el puesto, lo voy a aceptar aunque _______________ (yo/tener) que mudarme (*to move*) a otro estado. Tan pronto como _______________ (yo/recibir) noticias, le escribiré con los detalles. Otra vez, muchas gracias por su ayuda.

Sinceramente,
Rubén Cardona
Rubén Cardona

► Manos a la obra

A. Usted es el (la) gerente de los almacenes Olimpia. Se acerca la Navidad y desea comunicarles a los jefes de departamento el nuevo horario para los días festivos. Escriba un memorando en el que indique que a partir del 23 de noviembre las tiendas estarán abiertas de las nueve de la mañana hasta las diez de la noche y que se trabajará jornada (*shift*) continua con una hora para el almuerzo y otra para la cena. Los turnos de los empleados deben rotar.

____

____

____

____

____

____

____

____

____

B. Su compañía está concursando en una licitación (*bid*) que proveerá un sistema computarizado de contabilidad para una empresa bastante importante. Recientemente sus colegas y usted le hicieron una demostración al posible cliente. En una hoja adicional, escriba una carta en la que reitere las ventajas de su sistema. Incluya las siguientes ideas:

- Dé las gracias por la oportunidad que se le brindó.
- Recuérdeles que el sistema que usted propone es flexible y se ajusta a las necesidades de la compañía.
- Mencione que el costo es razonable.
- Explique que el sistema es de fácil manejo (*easy to manage*).
- Indique que la instalación se puede llevar a cabo (*be accomplished*) en corto tiempo.

PARA LOS INTERNAUTAS

Vaya a **http://www.wiley.com/college/gonzalez,** busque la página que corresponde a este capítulo y haga los ejercicios indicados.

MÁS ALLÁ

Comente los siguientes temas con sus compañeros de clase. Luego escoja uno de ellos y escriba sus opiniones al respecto.

1. Muchas veces surgen conflictos entre los principios morales y los intereses económicos de una empresa. Piensen, por ejemplo, en los dilemas que se presentan en la industria del tabaco, automovilística, de la construcción (*the building industry*), etc. ¿Qué se debe hacer en estas situaciones? Defiendan sus opiniones.
2. ¿Cómo han cambiado las computadoras el mundo de los negocios? Pueden mencionar los efectos de la tecnología en los bancos, las compañías de viaje, los pedidos a través de catálogos, etc. Incluyan todos los cambios que puedan.
3. ¿Cuáles son las cualidades de un(a) buen(a) gerente de empresa? Comenten sobre el trato (*treatment*) que debe mantener con sus subalternos, las habilidades de mando (*leadership skills*), el conocimiento del mercado, etc.

En esta página podrá anotar sus ideas respecto a este capítulo o bien referirse a un episodio de su propia vida.

Mi diario:

Capítulo 10

En busca de tiempos idos

Objectives

Upon completion of this chapter you should be able to:

- understand the narrative process and write short narrations
- utilize appropriate vocabulary to write about your childhood and adolescence
- use the preterite and imperfect correctly

¿No le recuerdan las sonrisas de estos escolares de Costa Rica los días de su niñez?

Para hablar del tema

VOCABULARIO ESENCIAL

Estudie las siguientes palabras y expresiones. Le pueden resultar útiles para entender y escribir narraciones sobre la niñez y la adolescencia.

Sustantivos

el cuento / la historia	*story*
el desarrollo	*development, unfolding*
el desenlace	*unravelling, denouement*
la juventud	*youth*
el (la) maestro(a)	*teacher*
el (la) narrador(a)	*narrator*
la niñez	*childhood*
la trama / el argumento	*plot*

Verbos

aburrirse	*to get bored*
bostezar	*to yawn*
estirarse	*to stretch*
lanzar	*to throw*
molestar	*to bother*
narrar / contar (ue)	*to narrate*
perseguir (i, i)	*to pursue, persecute, harass*
suceder	*to occur, happen*

A. Lea la siguiente narración.

El enfrentamiento° — **confrontation**

De niña, debía caminar a la escuela todos los días. Por el trayecto° siempre tropezaba° con un gordito pelirrojo° y pecoso° que me atormentaba. De fijo tenía algo que lanzarme: piedras pequeñas o insectos muertos. Yo corría hacia la escuela llorando y él me perseguía con gran

Along the way/came across/red-headed/ freckled

estruendo° y risas. Muchas veces la maestra me preguntó: «¿Qué te pasa? ¿Por qué estás llorando?», pero yo tenía demasiado miedo para contarle la verdad.

Pasó mucho tiempo sucediendo lo mismo hasta que un día decidí no huír° más. Fue el día del enfrentamiento. Venía a paso lento hasta que llegué donde estaba el gordito. Me propuse ser valiente y no demostrarle miedo aunque por dentro me moría. Él tomó una piedra para lanzármela, pero al observar que yo permanecía inmóvil°, el brazo se le paralizó. Fue entonces que empecé a avanzar hacia él. La confusión aumentaba en su rostro a cada paso que yo daba. Cuando estuve frente a él, le di un golpe fuerte con mi bolsa del almuerzo en la mitad de su asustada cara. Se fue corriendo hacia la escuela. Desde ese día nunca más me molestó. Luego hasta trató de ser mi amigo. ¡No gracias!

clamor

to run away

motionless

OBSERVE... que en la última línea, la palabra **hasta** (*even*) funciona como un adverbio.

B. Conteste las siguientes preguntas sobre el relato.

1. ¿Qué pasó? Resuma las acciones del relato en las siguientes líneas.

a. ______________________________

____

b. ______________________________

____

c. ______________________________

____

d. ______________________________

____

e. ______________________________

____

2. ¿Qué aprendemos sobre la autora en esta narración?

____

____

____

C. Todos, alguna vez en la vida, hemos sufrido algún tipo de persecución. Brevemente explique quién o quiénes le atormentaban. ¿Por qué recuerda ese episodio?

____

____

____

D. Ahora haga una lista de las palabras del Ejercicio A que usted no conocía. Añada otras expresioness que considere útiles para escribir sobre su niñez y adolescencia. Si es necesario, busque esos términos en el diccionario.

VOCABULARIO CLAVE

Las palabras de esta sección son de uso muy frecuente. Estúdielas y apréndalas. Le ayudarán en sus trabajos de redacción.

de niño(a) *as a child*

De niño, siempre tuve gatos.

de ordinario *regularly, commonly*

Como a mi mamá le encantaban los gatos, **de ordinario** teníamos tres o cuatro en casa. Un gatito que se llamaba Romualdino decidió adoptarme. Le encantaba subirse a mi cama.

al principio *at the beginning*

Al principio yo no quería que el gato durmiera conmigo. Después me acostumbré a encontrarlo en mi cama.

de fijo *surely, without a doubt*

De fijo venía a saludarme con la cola enhiesta *(up)* cuando yo llegaba de la escuela. Por lo general maullaba *(miaowed)* para avisarme su llegada.

entonces, luego *then*

Luego, frotaba *(rubbed)* su cabeza contra la pierna de mi pantalón. Al final siempre lograba lo que quería: que le diera de comer y lo dejara dormir junto a mí.

Análisis de la narración

Narrar quiere decir **contar**. Se puede narrar hechos reales o imaginarios en el presente, en el pasado o en el futuro. Una narración no tiene límites fijos *(fixed, set)*. Su extensión va desde el cuento corto hasta la novela. Aunque la narración se centra en el desarrollo de la acción, el proceso narrativo debe complementarse con la descripción para dar imágenes de los personajes, las cosas que los rodean *(surround)* y los lugares donde se desarrolla la historia.

Aquí tiene una secuencia de eventos. Léala.

entrar en la sala / ver a mi mamá sentada frente al televisor / estar mirando las noticias del día / verme / levantarse / dirigirse a la cocina

Lea ahora los siguientes párrafos y observe especialmente el efecto que tiene el uso del presente, el pasado y el futuro en el tono de la narración.

Entro en la sala. Veo a mi mamá sentada frente al televisor. Está mirando las noticias del día. Cuando me ve, se levanta y se dirige a la cocina.

Entré en la sala. Vi a mi mamá sentada frente al televisor. Estaba mirando las noticias del día. Cuando me vio, se levantó y se dirigió a la cocina.

Entraré en la sala. Veré a mi mamá sentada frente al televisor. Estará mirando las noticias del día. Cuando me vea, se levantará y se dirigirá a la cocina.

A. ¿Qué efecto se logra en la narración con el uso del presente?

____

____

____

¿el pasado?

____

____

____

¿el futuro?

Como usted seguramente observó, el presente le permite al lector descubrir la acción junto con el narrador, el pasado enfatiza *(emphasizes)* la anterioridad de la historia y el futuro es una premonición.

El escritor también puede contar su historia en primera persona (uso de los pronombres **yo** o **nosotros**) o tercera persona (uso de los pronombres **él, ella, ellos o ellas**). Observe la diferencia.

> Era un día caluroso *(hot)*. Me bajé del autobús en Tamarindo. Caminé hasta el hotel y empujé *(I pushed)* la puerta. Una vieja que jugaba solitario sentada detrás del mostrador *(counter)* me miró fijamente *(fixedly)* cuando entré.
>
> Era un día caluroso. El hombre se bajó del autobús en Tamarindo. Caminó hasta el hotel y empujó la puerta. La dueña, una vieja de unos setenta años que jugaba solitario detrás del mostrador, lo miró fijamente y pensó en su hijo muerto.

B. ¿Cuál es la diferencia de efecto entre las dos narraciones?

¿Notó usted que en el primer ejemplo el narrador es el protagonista? La narración se hace únicamente a través de *(through)* los ojos del personaje principal. En el segundo caso, el escritor conoce todos los detalles de la historia y nos los comunica. El narrador tiene la oportunidad de agregar comentarios y de observar objetivamente a sus personajes.

He aquí las partes básicas de una narración.

la introducción

la parte en la que el narrador comienza su relato

el desarrollo

la parte en la que el narrador construye su relato

el clímax

el momento más importante del relato

el desenlace

cómo termina el relato

En «El enfrentamiento», la narradora introduce el relato contándonos que cuando iba a la escuela la atormentaba un niño gordo, pelirrojo y pecoso. El desarrollo nos explica cómo sucede el enfrentamiento. El clímax es el momento del golpe con la bolsa del almuerzo. El desenlace nos narra cómo el niño corre asustado y luego quiere convertirse en amigo de su antigua víctima.

El escritor puede seguir un orden cronológico para construir su obra o puede empezar por el final o en cualquier punto de la trama.

Para escribir mejor

CÓMO UTILIZAR LAS EXPRESIONES DE ENLACE

A. Lea la siguiente historia. Es un poco diferente porque el narrador no es humano.

De cómo encontré mi casa

Era una mañana transparente del mes de julio. El sol quemaba y yo me aburría detrás de aquella valla° blanca. ¿Cómo escapar del ojo vigilante de la vieja? Primero me estiré, luego me rasqué°, después bostecé y de pronto, como caída del cielo, me llegó la inspiración: «¡escarba°!» Encontré un lugar donde la tierra estaba más blanda junto a unas begonias que acababan de regar°. ¡Qué gusto jugar en el barro°! La faena° me tomó más de una hora. Tenía que trabajar sin ser descubierto.

Al fin el hoyo° se hizo lo suficientemente grande y pude deslizarme° debajo del cerco°. ¡En verdad era bueno respirar el aire de la libertad lleno de aromas misteriosos! Tuve que sacudirme° porque todavía tenía tierra pegada° al cuerpo. Empecé a dar pasos nerviosos por la carretera. Desde mi prisión a menudo había visto extrañas criaturas metálicas pasar a gran velocidad, pero ahora me parecían más grandes y amenazantes°. Tendría que obrar con más cautela°.

Corrí y salté° por más de dos horas. El campo era hermoso: altos árboles, flores, insectos, un millar de olores nuevos por descubrir. Me perdía siguiendo una abeja° y luego regresaba al sendero°. Casi se me

fence
scratched
dig
water/mud/task
hole/slip
fence
shake myself off/ stuck
threatening /caution /jumped
bee/path

había olvidado la comida (y eso que a mí me encanta la comida). Ya me empezaba a hacer falta la cocina y todo lo bueno que de seguro allí habría. Pero, ¿cómo regresar? No tenía la menor idea de dónde me encontraba.

De repente, llegué a una bifurcación° del camino. Hice una pausa momentánea y doblé a la derecha. La primera casa que vi no me pareció muy hospitalaria°. Además había un gran perro que me ladró° furioso. La segunda tenía la puerta abierta, y un olor a comida me llegó a las narices°. Un humano se asomó° a la puerta y exclamó: «¡un cachorrito° perdido!» Entré rápidamente en la casa. Había que tomar decisiones rápidas. Adentro me encontré con otro humano. Tuve que hacerme el simpático. Le lamí° la mano y moví la cola°. Los humanos nunca se resisten a mis encantos.

Los primeros días no fueron fáciles. Al principio querían deshacerse° de mí. Luego se les caló entre ceja y ceja° que debía dormir afuera. Me costó un poco que entraran en razón, pero lo logré°. Hoy descanso en la mullida° cama de uno de ellos, y aunque la comida no es siempre excelente, no me puedo quejar°. Me tratan bien, me sacan a correr y me obedecen la mayoría del tiempo.

fork

hospitable/barked

nostrils/appeared/puppy

licked/tail

get rid of/Then they got into their heads/ With some difficulty I got them to see the light./ cushy/complain

B. Usted ya estudió expresiones que le pueden servir para establecer la relación entre varias etapas (*stages*) o sucesos (*events*) de una narración. Revise la siguiente lista.

al principio	después	entonces	luego	de fijo
de ordinario	usualmente	a menudo	de niño(a)	primero
al fin	por último	ahora	de repente	
de pronto	ya	además	finalmente	

¿Cuáles de estas expresiones puede usted encontrar en «De cómo encontré mi casa»?

C. Use las siguientes oraciones y algunas de las palabras de la lista anterior para contar de nuevo lo que le pasó al cachorrito.

El perrito escarbó. Se escapó a la carretera. El cachorrito corrió por el campo. Encontró una casa que le pareció hospitalaria. Vive cómodamente en una casa.

____

____

____

____

____

____

____

____

D. **Ahora, trabajando con otro(a) compañero(a), escriba una versión corta del mismo relato narrado por la señora de cuya casa se escapó el perrito o por los niños que lo hallaron (*found*) en la puerta de su casa. Use algunas de las expresiones del Ejercicio B.**

Estructuras en acción

PRETERITE VS. IMPERFECT

The verb forms most frequently used in narrating past events in Spanish are the preterite and the imperfect.

The **preterite** describes a **completed** act: the writer views it as over and done with, and the reader or listener knows how it turned out. It may focus on either the beginning or the end of an action, but the action or event is seen as complete. The preterite moves the story or plot forward: it narrates what a character actually **did**, or it describes what actually **happened**. Reread "El enfrentamiento" on pages 206–207, and observe how the preterite functions to advance the story line:

> *"...un día* ***decidí*** *no huir más."*
> *"...****llegué*** *donde estaba el gordito."*

"Me ***propuse*** *ser valiente..."*
"Él ***tomó*** *una piedra..."*
"...el brazo se le ***paralizó****."*
*"...****empecé*** *a avanzar hacia él."*
"...le ***di*** *un golpe fuerte..."*
"Se ***fue*** *corriendo..."*

Since the preterite indicates the completion of an act, certain verbs take on a different meaning in this form.

	Present	*Preterite*
conocer	to know (someone)	met (someone)
poder	to be able (can)	could and did (succeeded)
no poder	not to be able	wasn't able and didn't (failed)
querer	to want to (feel like)	wanted to and tried (but didn't)
no querer	not to want to (not feel like)	refused
saber	to know	found out
tener	to have	got, received
tener que	to have to (supposed to)	had to and did

The **imperfect** usually describes conditions, acts already in progress, habitual or ongoing activities, feelings, emotions, and mental or physical states. There is no reference to the beginning or the end of the action. These imperfect verbs frequently create the **background** in which the completed act (preterite verb) occurred. Therefore, focusing on their outcome is not essential to the advancement of the story line. Notice how the following imperfect verbs in "De cómo encontré mi casa" (pages 211–212) function as background information, setting the stage for the action:

*"****Era*** *una mañana transparente..."*
"El sol ***quemaba*** *y yo me* ***aburría****..."*
"...la tierra ***estaba*** *más blanda..."*
"...unas begonias que ***acababan*** *de regar."*
*"****Tenía*** *que trabajar..."*
"El campo ***era*** *hermoso..."*

Formation of the Preterite

1. To form the preterite of all regular verbs (and all *-ar* and *-er* stem-changing verbs), add to the infinitive stem the endings indicated in bold italic in the chart below.

contar:		***aparecer:***		***escribir:***	
	*cont**é***		*aparec**í***		*escrib**í***
	*cont**aste***		*aparec**iste***		*escrib**iste***
	*cont**ó***		*aparec**ió***		*escrib**ió***
	*cont**amos***		*aparec**imos***		*escrib**imos***
	*cont**asteis***		*aparec**isteis***		*escrib**isteis***
	*cont**aron***		*aparec**ieron***		*escrib**ieron***

2. A few regular verbs have a spelling change.

a. verbs that end in *-car, -gar, and -zar* change in the *yo* form:

g → gu	***c → qu***	***z → c***
*llegar: lle**gu**é*	*tocar: to**qu**é*	*empezar: empe**c**é*

b. an unstressed *-i-* between two vowels becomes *-y-:*

creer:	*creyó*	*creyeron*
leer:	*leyó*	*leyeron*
oír:	*oyó*	*oyeron*

3. The commonly used verbs *dar, hacer, ir,* and *ser* are irregular in the preterite. *Ir* and *ser* share the same preterite form.

dar:		***hacer:***		***ir / ser:***	
	di		*hice*		*fui*
	diste		*hiciste*		*fuiste*
	dio		*hizo*		*fue*
	dimos		*hicimos*		*fuimos*
	disteis		*hicisteis*		*fuisteis*
	dieron		*hicieron*		*fueron*

4. The following verbs have irregular stems in the preterite. They are conjugated like *estar.* Note that the first- and third-person singular endings are not stressed.

estar:	
	estuve
	estuviste
	estuvo
	estuvimos
	estuvisteis
	estuvieron

andar	***anduve***	*querer*	***quise***
estar	***estuve***	*saber*	***supe***
haber	***hube***	*tener*	***tuve***
poder	***pude***	*venir*	***vine***
poner	***puse***		

5. A few verbs have a characteristic ***j*** in the preterite stem. They are conjugated like *decir.*

decir:	
	dije
	dijiste
	dijo
	dijimos
	dijisteis
	dijeron

ALSO: *conducir* ***conduje;*** *traducir* ***traduje;*** *traer* ***traje***

Note that most verbs that end in *-ucir (introducir, producir, reducir,* etc.*)* follow the same pattern as *conducir* and *traducir.*

6. Remember that *-ar* and *-er* stem-changing verbs do not change in the preterite. However, *-ir* stem-changing verbs change *e* → *i* and *o* → *u* in the third-person singular and plural.

divertir:	*divertí*	***dormir:***	*dormí*	***sentir:***	*sentí*
	divertiste		*dormiste*		*sentiste*
	divirtió		*durmió*		*sintió*
	divertimos		*dormimos*		*sentimos*
	divertisteis		*dormisteis*		*sentisteis*
	divirtieron		*durmieron*		*sintieron*

Formation of the Imperfect

1. All *-ar* verbs form their imperfect by adding *-aba* endings to the stem.

contar:	*cont**aba***	***narrar:***	*narr**aba***
	*cont**abas***		*narr**abas***
	*cont**aba***		*narr**aba***
	*cont**ábamos***		*narr**ábamos***
	*cont**abais***		*narr**abais***
	*cont**aban***		*narr**aban***

2. All *-er* and *-ir* verbs, except *ir, ser,* and *ver,* form their imperfect by adding *-ía* endings to the stem.

volver:	*volv**ía***	***decir:***	*dec**ía***
	*volv**ías***		*dec**ías***
	*volv**ía***		*dec**ía***
	*volv**íamos***		*dec**íamos***
	*volv**íais***		*dec**íais***
	*volv**ían***		*dec**ían***

3. Only *ir, ser, and ver* are irregular in the imperfect.

ir:	*iba*	***ser:***	*era*	***ver:***	*veía*
	ibas		*eras*		*veías*
	iba		*era*		*veía*
	íbamos		*éramos*		*veíamos*
	ibais		*erais*		*veíais*
	iban		*eran*		*veían*

Summary of Usage: Preterite vs. Imperfect

Use the **preterite** for:

- **an entire completed act.**
  (Ayer comí un buen desayuno.)
- **the beginning of a completed act.**
  (Empecé a desayunar a las seis.)
- **the end of a completed act.**
  (Terminé de desayunar a las seis y quince.)
- **a series of specific completed acts.**
  (Ayer me desperté, me duché, me vestí, desayuné y salí de casa antes de las siete.)

Use the **imperfect** for:

- **ongoing past acts or background conditions that do not focus on the completion, beginning, or end.**
  (Yo era muy joven en esos días. Hacía mucho frío. Sonaba el teléfono. Era de noche.)
- **telling time in the past.**
  (Eran las diez y media)
- **a customary or habitual past act.**
  (Siempre caminaba a la escuela. De ordinario no desayunaba. Me llamabas todos los días.)
- **descriptions of physical and mental conditions or states.**
  (Me sentía muy mal. Era un chico gordo. Estaba nerviosa. No queríamos estudiar.)
- **a series of repeated or habitual acts.**
  (Los sábados siempre salíamos con nuestros amigos, cenábamos en un restaurante modesto y bailábamos hasta la madrugada.)

The preterite and imperfect tenses often occur in the same sentence: the imperfect usually describes the ongoing background action or condition, and the preterite expresses the completed act.

Examples: *Mientras los padres **dormían**, la hija **salió** de la casa.*
While the parents **were sleeping**, the daughter **left** the house.

***Tuve** que sacudirme porque todavía **tenía** tierra pegada al cuerpo.*
I had to shake myself off because I still **had** dirt stuck to my body.

***Mirábamos** la tele cuando alguien **llamó** a la puerta.*
We were watching TV when someone **knocked** at the door.

EXERCISES

A. The author of "El enfrentamiento" (pages 206–207) uses the imperfect to narrate habitual or ongoing background acts and to describe conditions or feelings. Find ten examples of this use of the imperfect in the story and write them on the lines provided.

______________________	______________________
______________________	______________________
______________________	______________________
______________________	______________________
______________________	______________________

B. In "De comó encontré mi casa" (pages 211–212), the writer advances the story line by using the preterite to narrate completed actions. Find ten examples of this use of the preterite in the fourth paragraph of the story and write them on the lines provided.

C. Use the English sentences provided to narrate the following anecdote in Spanish. Use the preterite or imperfect as appropriate.

It was a beautiful spring morning.

Sheila, the most beautiful girl in the ninth grade, was sitting by the pool with the rest of my classmates.

I had to impress *(impresionar)* her.

I got on *(subir a)* the diving board *(el trampolín)* and waited for the moment when Sheila and everybody else were watching.

I dived *(zambullirse)* gracefully *(graciosamente)* and made a perfect entrance.

When I came out of the water Sheila and everybody else were laughing hysterically *(histéricamente)*.

At first, I didn't know what was going on *(suceder)*. Then I turned *(volverse)* and saw my swimming trunks floating *(flotando)* in the middle of the pool.

____

____

____

____

► Manos a la obra

A. Aquí tiene varios temas para una narración:

- La primera vez que salí con...
- Una anécdota de mi clase de...
- Cuando me compraron...
- Mi viaje a...
- Las travesuras *(mischievous antics)* de... (mi perro, gato, etc.)

Escoja uno de los temas anteriores o invente uno si prefiere. Luego escriba unas breves notas sobre la estructura de su trabajo. También anote el vocabulario clave de la historia.

Estructura

introducción

____

____

____

____

____

desarrollo

____

____

____

____

____

____

clímax

desenlace

vocabulario

Usted puede usar una hoja adicional para escribir su **borrador**. En el espacio siguiente escriba **la versión final**. Ponga especial atención a los usos del pretérito y el imperfecto.

PARA LOS INTERNAUTAS

Vaya a **http://www.wiley.com/college/gonzalez,** busque la página que corresponde a este capítulo y haga los ejercicios indicados.

MÁS ALLÁ

Comente los siguientes temas con sus compañeros de clase. Luego escoja uno de ellos y escriba sus opiniones al respecto. Ponga atención especial a los usos del pretérito y el imperfecto.

1. Muchos creen que los años más felices de nuestra existencia son los de la niñez. Piense en su propio caso y encuentre evidencia para justificar o refutar esa idea.
2. Otra creencia *(belief)* es que un adulto es un reflejo de la educación que recibe en la niñez y en la temprana adolescencia. Es decir, los hábitos y las costumbres de los primeros años de vida dejan una huella imborrable *(indelible mark)* en la personalidad del adulto. ¿Está usted de acuerdo con esta idea? ¿Podría mencionar ejemplos?

En esta página podrá anotar sus ideas sobre este capítulo o bien referirse a un episodio de su propia vida.

Mi diario:

Capítulo 11

Dilemas ecológicos

Objectives

Upon completion of this chapter you should be able to:

- describe people, places, and things
- utilize appropriate vocabulary to write about ecological issues
- position adjectives correctly

La Ciudad de México se ve muy afectada por la contaminación del aire.

Para hablar del tema

VOCABULARIO ESENCIAL

Estudie las siguientes palabras y expresiones. Le pueden resultar útiles para entender el capítulo y describir el mundo que le rodea.

Sustantivos

el acuífero	*water table, aquifer*
el bosque	*forest*
la capa de ozono	*ozone layer*
los casquetes polares	*polar ice caps*
los combustibles fósiles	*fossil fuels*
la contaminación	*pollution*
la cuenca	*river basin*
el derrumbe	*landslide*
el efecto invernadero	*greenhouse effect*
el envenenamiento	*poisoning*
el hundimiento	*sinking*
el incendio forestal / la quema	*forest fire*
la inundación	*flood*
el islote	*small barren island*
la lluvia ácida	*acid rain*
la mancha urbana	*urban sprawl*
la margen	*river bank*
el medio ambiente	*environment*
el recalentamiento	*overheating*
el reciclaje	*recycling*
la selva	*jungle*
la sequía	*drought*
el suelo	*ground*
el suministro	*supply*
la tala de árboles	*felling of trees*

Verbos

deforestar	*to deforest*
derretir (i, i)	*to melt*
deshelar (ie)	*to thaw*
erguir	*to raise up straight*
irradiar	*to irradiate*
reciclar	*to recycle*

Adjetivos

altanero(a)	*arrogant, proud*
anárquico(a)	*anarchical, disorderly*
hidrológico(a)	*hydrologic, water-related*

A. Lea la siguiente selección.

El agua y la Ciudad de México

Cuando los aztecas decidieron construir su ciudad en el valle de México sobre el islote de un lago, en lugar de en las márgenes de un río como lo habían hecho otras civilizaciones, no imaginaron que seis siglos después México-Tenochtitlán se convertiría en la ciudad más grande y poblada del mundo. No predijeron° que a lo largo de su historia su ciudad habría de sufrir graves problemas con el agua, grandes inundaciones y hundimiento del suelo.

predicted

Tampoco pensaron que construir su ciudad a más de dos mil doscientos metros sobre el nivel del mar°, en un llano° rodeado por° lagos y montañas, dificultaría siempre el suministro de agua a sus habitantes. Les fue imposible anticipar que la sobrexplotación del acuífero, el crecimiento anárquico y explosivo de la mancha urbana y la acelerada destrucción de los bosques que rodean a la ciudad agravarían el problema.

sea level/ plain/ surrounded by

Los fundadores de la Ciudad de México no habrían creído que a principios del siglo XXI todos esos problemas, junto con el envenenamiento del aire, llevarían al valle de México a una crisis ecológica. La realización de un plan único e integral para restablecer el equilibrio hidrológico y el ecosistema de la cuenca de México es hoy una necesidad imperante°.

compelling

OBSERVE... el uso de la preposición **por** en la frase **rodeado por**.

B. Conteste las siguientes preguntas sobre la lectura del Ejercicio A.

1. ¿Dónde construyeron los aztecas su ciudad capital?

____

____

2. Mencione dos problemas que los fundadores de la Ciudad de México no anticiparon.

____

____

3. ¿A qué altura está la Ciudad de México?

4. ¿Cuál es otra ciudad que tiene problemas ecológicos debido a su posición geográfica? Enumere algunos de esos problemas.

C. Ahora haga una lista de las palabras del Ejercicio A que usted no conocía. Añada otras expresiones que considere útiles para escribir sobre los problemas ecológicos. Si es necesario, busque su significado en el diccionario.

VOCABULARIO CLAVE

Las palabras de esta sección son de uso muy frecuente. Estúdielas y apréndalas. Le ayudarán en sus trabajos de redacción.

a su vez *in turn*

Yo le ayudé, y **a su vez** él también vino a mi ayuda.

a lo largo de *throughout, along*

La Ciudad de México ha visto muchos cambios **a lo largo de** su historia.

Caminamos **a lo largo de** la playa.

tras *after, behind, beyond*

Tras años de mucha dificultad, el problema de la contaminación del agua ha disminuido un poco.

a principios de *at the beginning of*

A principios del próximo año, será obligatorio reciclar el papel usado en la oficina.

junto con *together with*

Los problemas de la contaminación del aire, **junto con** una población siempre creciente, han hecho de la ciudad de México un dilema ecológico.

► Análisis de la descripción

El ojo capta la imagen y nuestro cerebro (*brain*) la interpreta. Ésta es una función rutinaria. El poder verbalizar esas sensaciones visuales, sin embargo, requiere habilidades que sólo se adquieren a través de mucha práctica. Usted experimentará en esta sección con diferentes tipos de descripciones.

Los conocimientos que usted adquiera le pueden ayudar en trabajos técnicos o científicos, si usted se interesa en la ciencia; en la elaboración de biografías y otros escritos para sus cursos de español, si su inclinación es más literaria.

Cuando el autor describe, debe esforzarse (*to strive*) por proveer la información necesaria de tal modo que el lector pueda hacer una reconstrucción mental del objeto, persona o lugar descrito. La descripción ha de variar también de acuerdo con (*according to*) el objetivo que se persiga (*pursues*). Un científico que describe una flor nos dará una versión bastante diferente de la que nos pueda ofrecer un poeta, por ejemplo.

Raramente se encuentra una descripción pura. A menudo es necesario mezclarla (*to mix it*) un poco con la narración. La siguiente es una descripción de un hombre, su medio ambiente y los sentimientos de tristeza que lo invaden al amanecer (*upon the dawning*) de su último día en su tierra.

La tierra expropiada°

°expropriated

El sol apareció sobre las montañas y una figura se recortó° contra la penumbra° del amanecer. El hombre estiró° los brazos desnudos y fuertes para sacudir los últimos recuerdos. Sus pies descalzos° se hundieron en la tierra húmeda que rodeaba su choza°. Sentados junto a él estaban su mujer y cuatro hijos. Sólo el olor a humo y a café quedaban del último desayuno en la finca°. El gobierno quería su tierra para la nueva autopista° transoceánica que traería el progreso y la civilización a su verde tierra tropical. Al principio no le puso atención a la carta con muchos sellos° oficiales que recibió; después se negó° a creer que ya no era dueño° de la tierra que habían labrado° él, sus hijos, sus padres, sus abuelos y sus bisabuelos. Por fin cuando la policía armada llegó a obligarlo a salir, se resignó.

El sol cubría de oro ya todo el campo. El hombre se puso el sombrero, alzó° el saco con sus pertenencias° e inclinó la cabeza hacia un lado para indicarles a su mujer e hijos que lo siguieran. No quería tener que volver a ver la choza. Lágrimas° invisibles brotaron° de sus ojos varoniles°. Sintió un nudo° en la garganta. A lo lejos cantó un gallo°.

was outlined
semidarkness/
stretched/
shoeless/
hut
farm
freeway
stamps/
refused/
owner/tilled
picked up/
belongings
Tears/gushed/
manly/lump/
rooster

OBSERVE... el uso de la preposición **a** en las frases «*olor a humo y a café*».

A. ¿Qué palabras se usan para describir al hombre? Copie algunas en el espacio a continuación.

___

___

___

B. ¿Qué palabras establecen la descripción del paisaje y los alrededores (*surroundings*) del hombre? Copie algunas en el espacio a continuación.

___

___

___

C. Ahora, lea la siguiente descripción corta y conteste las preguntas que la siguen.

La selva

Sobre la tierra sólo quedan troncos calcinados° que se levantan como testigos mudos° de la destrucción. La selva que se erguía altanera e impenetrable se ha visto reducida a ceniza° y silencio. En su lugar aparecerán pastizales° para que coma el ganado°, que a su vez deberá ser sacrificado para que comamos hamburguesas. La selva que nos dio la quinina°, el caucho° y que sin duda encierra° todavía la cura a muchos de nuestros padecimientos°, se quema, se asfixia lentamente.

burned to
ash/mute
witnesses/
ash
pasture
lands/cattle
quinine/
rubber/holds/
suffering

1. Según la descripción, ¿qué está sucediendo en la selva?

2. ¿Qué tipo de palabras (adjetivos, sustantivos, verbos, adverbios, preposiciones, etc.) juegan un papel (*role*) importante en las dos descripciones anteriores? Justifique su respuesta.

► Para escribir mejor

CÓMO PLANTEAR UNA SOLUCIÓN

A. Lea el siguiente artículo.

Calor que empobrece° — **impoverishes**

Hace un año en la región alpina fue encontrado el «hombre de los hielos»: un cadáver de la Edad de Piedra que yacía° en un glaciar tirolés°, cerca de la frontera° austro-italiana y que había permanecido oculto durante miles de años. — **lay buried/ Tyrolean/ border**

El hallazgo°, sin embargo, no fue un golpe de suerte pues «el hielo eterno de los Alpes» ha perdido desde 1850 la mitad de su volumen y hasta el 40 por ciento de su superficie, debido al recalentamiento de la Tierra. — **discovery**

Aunque parezca distante, el avance industrial es la principal causa de este fenómeno, pues juega un papel muy importante en el aumento de la temperatura del planeta, conocido como el efecto invernadero°. — **greenhouse**

La quema de los combustibles fósiles, la deforestación y el uso de aerosoles hacen que gases como el dióxido de carbono se acumulen en la atmósfera e impidan la salida hacia el espacio exterior de la temperatura que irradia el planeta.

B. Trabaje con un(a) compañero(a). Juntos escojan una de las causas del efecto invernadero. Luego hagan una lista de vocabulario pertinente y finalmente describan la causa.

causa ____

vocabulario ____

____

____

descripción ____

____

____

____

____

____

C. Escriban ustedes ahora la solución para el problema que eligieron en el Ejercicio B.

____

____

____

____

____

____

____

____

____

____

► Estructuras en acción

POSITION OF ADJECTIVES

Adjective position is very important when writing descriptions in Spanish. Unlike English adjectives, which are almost always placed before the noun, Spanish adjectives may either precede or follow the noun. The following guidelines will help you to position adjectives correctly.

After the Noun

The great majority of adjectives in Spanish follow the noun. These "descriptive" adjectives point out or describe a quality or characteristic of the noun: they restrict, clarify, and specify. Consider, for example, the general noun *problemas.* By adding the adjective *ecológicos* you can create a subgroup: ecological problems. You can create an even more restrictive subgroup by adding the adjective *mundiales*: *problemas ecológicos mundiales* (worldwide ecological problems).

The following categories of adjectives are used to distinguish the nouns they modify, and therefore they normally are placed after the noun.

1. adjectives that indicate nationality, religion, position, or affiliation

   Examples: *la selva* ***guatemalteca***
   un sacerdote ***católico***
   el partido ***demócrata***
   una familia ***aristócratica***

2. adjectives that express color, form, material, or condition

   Examples: *una tierra* ***negra***
   un edificio ***pentagonal***
   los utensilios ***plásticos***
   una descripción ***clara***

3. adjectives that express technical or scientific concepts

   Examples: *un ataque* ***cardíaco***
   un trabajo ***ecológico***
   un viaje ***espacial***

4. adjectives that are modified by adverbs

   Examples: *el río más* ***grande***
   el lugar más ***conocido***
   un problema muy ***difícil***

Before the Noun

Adjectives are placed before the noun for either grammatical or semantic reasons. Spanish grammar requires that the following kinds of adjectives precede the noun.

1. possessive and demonstrative adjectives

   Examples: ***tu*** *país*
   esta *descripción*
   aquellos *tiempos*

2. ordinal numerals

   Examples: *la* ***primera*** *vez*
   el ***segundo*** *lago*

3. numerical, indefinite, and quantitative adjectives

Examples: ***dos*** *ciudades*
algunas *personas*
varias *opiniones*
otros *conflictos*
muchos *derrumbes*

Sometimes adjectives are placed before the noun in order to express certain meanings.

1. Adjectives that emphasize an inherent quality or characteristic—a quality one normally expects to find in the noun—are placed before the noun. These adjectives do not limit the noun, nor do they add any new characteristics.

   Examples: *la* ***blanca*** *nieve*
   (There is no other color of snow except white.)
   el ***candente*** *sol del desierto del Sahara*
   (One expects the sun in the Sahara to be red hot.)

2. Placing the adjective before the noun sometimes serves to make the characteristic or quality stand out. This effect is accomplished in spoken English by changing the intonation of the voice. Compare:

   Examples: *un* ***buen*** *ecólogo*
   (There is no comparison with other ecologists implied; the point is to make the quality **good** stand out.)
   un ecólogo ***bueno***
   (One can assume that there are other ecologists who are **not** good.)

3. When the adjective describes a quality or characteristic of a **unique** noun, the adjective must be placed before the noun.

   Examples: *la* ***verde*** *selva amazónica*
   la ***alta*** *cordillera de los Andes*

To place the adjective *verde* after the noun phrase *selva amazónica* would imply that there are several Amazon jungles and that not all are green. Likewise, we know that there is only one chain of mountains called the Andes, and that these mountains are very high. Thus the adjective must precede the noun phrase *cordillera de los Andes.*

Adjectives that Change Meaning According to Their Position

The following adjectives change their meaning depending on whether they precede or follow the noun.

Adjective	*Before the noun*	*After the noun*
alguno	some *Tiene algunas ideas.* (He has some ideas.)	any at all (emphatic in negative sentences) *No tiene idea alguna.* (He has no idea whatsoever.)

alto	important, high *Es un alto funcionario.* (He's an important official.)	tall *Es un funcionario alto.* (He's a tall official.)
cierto	certain *Tiene un cierto encanto.* (He has a certain charm.)	true *Es una historia cierta.* (It is a true story.)
diferente	various (plural) *Habla de diferentes temas.* (He talks about various topics.)	different *Es un tema diferente.* (It's a different topic.)
ese	that *Ese hombre nos llamó.* (That man called us.)	(adds a pejorative connotation) *El hombre ese nos llamó.* ("That man" called us.)
grande	famous *Fue una gran mujer.* (She was a great woman.)	big *Fue una mujer grande.* (She was a big / tall woman.)
mismo	same *Hizo el mismo estudio.* (He carried out the same investigation.)	self *Él mismo lo hizo.* (He himself did it.)
nuevo	different *Es un nuevo coche.* (It's a different car.) (It could be a used car I just bought.)	brand-new *Es un coche nuevo.* (It's a brand-new car.)
pobre	unfortunate *El pobre niño se perdió.* (The unfortunate child got lost.)	poor (penniless) *Es un niño pobre.* (He's a poor child. He has no money.)
semejante	such a *No puedo creer semejante historia.* (I can't believe such a story.)	similar *Su historia es semejante a la mía.* (His story is similar to mine.)
simple	mere *Es un simple empleado.* (He's a mere employee.)	easy, simpleminded *Es un problema simple.* (It's an easy problem.)
triste	unimportant *Es un triste burócrata.* (He's an unimportant bureaucrat.)	sad *Es un burócrata triste.* (He's a sad bureaucrat.)

único	only *Es mi única solución.* (It's my only solution.)	unique *Es una solución única.* (It's a unique solution.)
varios	several *Compré varias cosas.* (I bought several things.)	miscellaneous *Hablamos de asuntos varios.* (We talked about miscellaneous topics.)
viejo	dear (referring to persons) *Es una vieja amiga.* (She's a dear friend.)	old *Es una mujer vieja.* (She's an old woman.)

Position of Two or More Adjectives

When two or more adjectives modify a single noun, the following rules determine the position of the adjectives.

1. If both adjectives are descriptive, they follow the noun. The more restrictive adjective comes before the less restrictive.

Examples: *Analiza la política española* ***contemporánea.***
(He's analyzing Spanish politics, focusing on **contemporary** politics.)

Analiza la política contemporánea ***española.***
(He's analyzing contemporary world politics, focusing on **Spanish** politics.)

2. One adjective can precede the noun and the other can follow it. The adjective that denotes a subjective evaluation comes before the noun; the more restrictive and informative adjective follows the noun.

Examples: *la* ***fantástica*** *selva* ***amazónica***

el ***gran*** *pintor* ***argentino***

la ***exquisita*** *poesía* ***romántica*** *española*

3. Adjectives that are equivalent in function are joined by a conjunction or a comma.

Examples: *un informe* ***largo*** *y* ***aburrido***
(Both adjectives emphasize the boring aspect of the report).

una panameña ***alta, atlética*** *y* ***entusiasta***
(All three adjectives describe.)

EXERCISES

A. Position the following adjectives correctly, use a conjunction or comma where necessary, and then explain or justify your choice. In some cases there is more than one correct possibility. Follow the example.

Example: las aguas árticas frías
las frías aguas árticas
Explanation: *"Frías" is an intrinsic quality of the waters of the Arctic; "árticas" is descriptive and limiting (or restrictive).*

1. la guerra sangrienta española civil

   ____

   Explanation: ______________________________

   ____

   ____

   ____

2. grandes cinco ecológicos dilemas

   ____

   Explanation: ______________________________

   ____

   ____

   ____

3. la argentina cosmopolita capital

   ____

   Explanation: ______________________________

   ____

   ____

   ____

4. tierra aquella calcinada y estéril

   ____

   Explanation: ______________________________

   ____

   ____

   ____

5. las andinas montañas altas

____

Explanation: _______________

____

____

____

6. el tratado más simple ecológico

____

Explanation: _______________

____

____

____

B. Express the following phrases in Spanish.

1. two old Inca temples

____

2. a poor (unfortunate) man lost in the big city

____

3. various important details

____

4. an interesting Bolivian university professor

____

5. young Chilean scientists

____

6. a very important contribution

____

7. a famous Argentine painter

____

8. my old (dear) friend

____

9. the clear waters of the Caribbean

____

10. the eternal ice of the Alps

____

▶ Manos a la obra

A. Lea la descripción de la ciudad de Los Ángeles, California.

Los Ángeles

La gran urbe° de acero°, concreto y asfalto se levanta del Océano Pacífico y avanza devorando kilómetro tras kilómetro hasta perderse en el desierto californiano. Cientos de calles se encuentran con autopistas para formar un cerrado laberinto por donde transitan día y noche una multitud de vehículos siempre hambrientos° de combustible, por donde corre una población siempre en marcha, siempre creciente. La colina° de ayer adornada de palmas es hoy la nueva urbanización°, el nuevo supermercado, el nuevo centro comercial. El campo se encoge° y la ciudad se ensancha°. «¿Hasta cuándo podrá la Madre Tierra soportar tanto abuso?» — me pregunto mientras corro a setenta millas por hora hacia mi destino.

metropolis/ steel
hungry
hill
real-estate development/
shrinks/ expands

Los Ángeles es un mosaico de toda nacionalidad, raza y lenguaje humano. Es el prototipo de la ciudad del siglo XXI donde el coreano° vive junto al mexicano y al chino. El árabe es vecino del afroamericano, el australiano y el chileno. El anglosajón trabaja con el hebreo y el tailandés con el vietnamita. Es el escenario donde la violencia y la misericordia°, el amor y el odio, la venganza° y la comprensión, la vida y la muerte se cruzan todos los días.

Korean
compassion/ vengeance

OBSERVE... el uso de la preposión **para** en la frase «**para formar**» y la preposición **por** en la frase «**por donde transitan**».

B. Conteste las siguientes preguntas sobre el texto.

1. ¿Qué describe el primer párrafo?

____

____

____

2. ¿Qué se describe en el segundo párrafo?

____

____

____

C. Escoja usted ahora un pueblo o ciudad que conozca bien.

1. Escriba en las siguientes líneas algunas palabras que describan la apariencia física del lugar.

____

____

____

____

____

2. En el espacio a continuación anote algunas palabras que describan aspectos interesantes del lugar. Usted podría mencionar, por ejemplo, puntos de interés turístico, costumbres famosas, población, etc.

____

____

____

____

____

____

____

____

____

____

3. Usando las ideas de las líneas anteriores, escriba la descripción completa del pueblo o ciudad que usted seleccionó.

D. Ahora le corresponde a usted describir a una persona que admira o que ha influido en su vida. En una hoja adicional, haga una descripción breve de las características físicas o psicológicas de esa persona.

PARA LOS INTERNAUTAS

WWW

Vaya a **http://www.wiley.com/college/gonzalez,** busque la página correspondiente a este capítulo y haga los ejercicios indicados.

MÁS ALLÁ

Comente los siguientes temas con sus compañeros de clase. Luego escoja uno de ellos y escriba sus opiniones al respecto.

1. Los países industrializados quieren prohibirles a los países en desarrollo que exploten sus selvas tropicales, ya que éstas son una de las principales fuentes del oxígeno para nuestro planeta. Describa usted la posición de los países en desarrollo.
2. Algunos grupos que defienden la naturaleza promueven (*advocate*) la desobediencia de la ley para proteger el medio ambiente. ¿Cómo justifican esa posición?
3. Describa usted las responsabilidades que tienen el gobierno, la industria y los ciudadanos en la protección de nuestro planeta.

En esta página podrá anotar sus ideas respecto a este capítulo o bien referirse a un episodio de su propia vida.

Mi diario:

Capítulo 12

Artistas del mundo hispano

Objectives

Upon completion of this chapter you should be able to:

- write an essay
- develop a research paper
- utilize appropriate vocabulary to write about art and artists

"La boda", obra del artista mexicano Alfredo Ramos Martínez.

This chapter is organized differently from previous chapters because its writing task—developing an essay and/or a research paper—synthesizes previous material in order to structure a final more involved composition.

► Para hablar del tema

VOCABULARIO ESENCIAL

Estudie las siguientes palabras y expresiones. Le pueden resultar útiles para entender y escribir sobre arte en general y sobre pintura en especial.

Sustantivos

la acuarela *watercolor*
el autorretrato *self-portrait*
el caballete *easel*
el cuadro *picture, painting*
la escultura *sculpture*
el estudio / el taller *studio*
el hito *landmark, milestone*
la manta / el lienzo / la tela *canvas*
el motivo *motif*
la naturaleza muerta *still life*
el óleo *oil painting*
el paisaje *landscape*
el paisaje marino *seascape*
la permanencia *stay, time spent in a place*
la perspectiva *perspective*
el pincel *artist's brush*
la pintura *paint, painting*
la pintura abstracta *abstract painting*
el retrato *portrait*

Verbos

apartarse de *to put aside*
plasmar *to mould, shape, portray*
provenir *to come from*

Adjetivos

acalorado(a) *heated*
controvertido(a) *controversial*
inusitado(a) *unexpected*
perdurable *lasting*

A. Lea el siguiente artículo.

El mundo de Frida Kahlo

Frida Kahlo, Autorretrato con el pelo suelto.

La pintora mexicana Frida Kahlo se ha convertido en un inusitado fenómeno internacional. En 1990 su obra *Diego y yo* fue la primera pintura latinoamericana vendida por más de un millón de dólares. En mayo de 1991 su autorretrato de 1947, *Autorretrato con el pelo suelto,* rebasó° el precio de esta venta al subastarse° por un millón seiscientos cincuenta mil dólares. La cantante Madonna, que compró *Mi nacimiento* por una canti-

exceeded

to be sold by auction

dad no divulgada°, ha expresado interés en interpretar el papel de Kahlo en el cine. Los autorretratos de Kahlo aparecen en las publicaciones y los lugares más insólitos° del mundo, llevados por las corrientes del consumismo y la promoción comercial. A la pintora mexicana, *in absentia*, se le atribuyen posiciones políticas en los debates de nuestro tiempo que harían arquear° las famosas cejas° de la artista con sorpresa y quién sabe con qué medida de interés. Hoy se habla de Frida como nunca se ha hablado de Pablo Picasso, ni de Diego Rivera, ni de Georgia O'Keefe, con una familiaridad que desconcierta aun el desconcertante mundo del arte contemporáneo.

disclosed
unusual
arch/
eyebrows

Indudablemente, «Frida» es en la actualidad un signo de valor transcultural que significa diversas cosas para diferentes personas, en variados contextos. Ese valor de signo que ha obtenido el nombre de la artista amplifica y difunde su fama y, a la vez, ayuda a crear muchas Fridas imaginarias, tan diferentes como las interpretaciones que provoca su obra. Por otra parte, lo personal de su pintura tiende a explicar la identificación expresa de muchos admiradores de Frida con el dolor y las vicisitudes que marcaron su vida.

La discusión actual de la obra de Frida Kahlo gira° alrededor de dos problemas fundamentales. El primero está relacionado con el dolor personal que Kahlo siempre supo plasmar en su pintura y el cual parece apoyar la idea romántica de que en el arte se conjugan el sufrimiento con la femineidad. De esta insinuación resulta una Frida cuya obra afirma el mito patriarcal de que el ser mujer implica sufrir y ser sufrida. Al adoptar a Kahlo como una figura de culto y veneración, el feminismo tiende a pasar por alto todo un discurso de la victimación femenina que se desprende° de la obra de la artista y que debe ser profundamente cuestionado. Un segundo problema tiene que ver con la apropiación del arte de Kahlo por tendencias extranjeras que le confieren características que no le pertenecen. En 1938 André Breton, el padre del surrealismo, la declaró representativa de su movimiento. Sin embargo, la imaginería de Kahlo tiene más que ver con el folklore mexicano que con la imaginación surrealista. Hoy la crítica afirma sin duda las facetas claramente mexicanas de la pintura de Frida Kahlo.

centers
stems

B. Conteste las siguientes preguntas.

1. Dé algunas razones por las cuales es tan admirada la pintora mexicana Frida Kahlo.

____

____

____

____

____

2. ¿Cuáles son los dos problemas fundamentales que surgen al analizar la obra de la artista?

3. Estudie la pintura de Frida Kahlo *Autorretrato con el pelo suelto* y descríbala brevemente. ¿Le gusta? Explique sus razones. ¿Cree usted que vale $1.650.000?

C. Ahora haga una lista de las palabras del Ejercicio A que usted no conocía. Añada otras expresiones que considere útiles para escribir sobre el arte. Si es necesario, busque su significado en el diccionario.

VOCABULARIO CLAVE

Las palabras de esta sección son de uso muy frecuente. Estúdielas y apréndalas. Le ayudarán en sus trabajos de redacción.

pese a *in spite of*

Pese a que leí el artículo varias veces, aún no lo comprendo bien.

por otra parte *on the other hand*

Además del alto valor artístico de su obra, se debe señalar **por otra parte** su carácter personal.

si bien *although*

Los cuatro pintores, **si bien** diferentes, recibieron todos influencias de sus raíces culturales.

Análisis del ensayo/trabajo de investigación

Muchas veces en la vida profesional se tiene que analizar, interpretar o evaluar un tema por escrito. El tipo de redacción que se ha de usar entonces es **el ensayo**. Un ensayo puede tomar varias formas: puede ser una obra literaria pulida (*polished*) y erudita (este tipo de ensayo es un género literario, al igual que la novela, el cuento, el drama o la poesía), un trabajo de investigación para una de sus clases, un artículo de una revista popular o profesional, un breve artículo de un periódico, o quizá un folleto (*pamphlet, brochure*) comercial o político. Puede, aun, tomar la forma de una carta dirigida a la redacción (*editor*) de un periódico. Otra clase de ensayo, un tipo que muchos estudiantes conocen, es el examen que requiere que el alumno escriba de una manera coherente y organizada una composición que demuestre su conocimiento sobre la materia de un curso.

En el pasado, se insistía en que los estudiantes observaran reglas (*rules*), fórmulas y estructuras bastante rígidas en la elaboración de un ensayo. Se obligaba, por ejemplo, a hacer una distinción entre las diferentes formas técnicas del desarrollo de una tesis de ensayo: el análisis, la definición, la clasificación, la comparación o el contraste. Hoy el interés se centra en la clara y precisa elaboración de un trabajo.

La mayoría de los autores conciben sus escritos siguiendo un cuidadoso plan. Sin embargo, algunos obtienen resultados satisfactorios utilizando solamente unas pocas palabras o frases cortas para guiarse en la redacción de un ensayo. Finalmente, hay quien prefiere que fluyan (*flow*) las ideas sin un plan previo. La experiencia parece demostrar la necesidad, al menos cuando se comienza a escribir, de un bosquejo formal.

Lo más importante para quien desea producir un buen ensayo es seguir tres pasos básicos.

1. Decidir exactamente lo que se quiere enfocar (*to focus on*)—cuál va a ser la tesis de la obra.

2. Desarrollar la tesis lo más específicamente posible, cuidando que lo escrito sea claro, organizado y coherente.
3. Revisar lo escrito.

LA ELECCIÓN DE UN TEMA Y LA DEFINICIÓN DE UNA TESIS

El tema o tópico es el campo general del conocimiento sobre el que se escribe. Por ejemplo, se puede hablar sobre literatura, deportes, pintura, etc. La tesis es una oración que resume la idea principal del ensayo y a la cual se subordina el resto de la composición.

Ejemplo: la pintura (**tema general**)
Diego Rivera revitalizó la pintura mexicana con la inclusión de elementos autóctonos (*indigenous*). (**tesis**)

No siempre es necesario decidir sobre una tesis. Puede suceder que una profesora de historia le dé a la clase un examen tipo ensayo en el cual se requiera escribir sobre un aspecto determinado de un período histórico. Quizá una gerente de una compañía encargue la redacción de un artículo sobre las ventajas de un nuevo tipo de computadora. La mayoría de las veces, sin embargo, es el escritor quien ha de decidir sobre la tesis.

¿Cómo llegar a la decisión? ¿Cómo encontrar esa **tesis**? Antes que nada, lo más recomendable es escribir sobre un asunto conocido que interese al autor. Sería absurdo, por ejemplo, intentar escribir sobre el cine español contemporáneo sin haber visto un razonable número de películas españolas recientes o cuando no se está interesado en el cine. Por supuesto, de vez en cuando es necesario escribir sobre un tema fuera de la especialidad o experiencia personal. En tal caso es absolutamente esencial investigar (*to do research*), leer e informarse hasta lograr un buen dominio de la materia. Cerciórese (*Be sure*) de conocer muy bien la estructura y funcionamiento de su biblioteca, institución clave en sus trabajos de investigación. En la mayoría de las universidades se organizan visitas durante las cuales se dan instrucciones de los varios sistemas disponibles para buscar y obtener préstamos de libros. Los bibliotecarios le pueden aconsejar también sobre cualquier tema o dificultad que se le presente.

Inicialmente se debe escoger un tema o tópico sobre el cual se pueda escribir inteligentemente. Luego hay que delimitar y enfocar ese tópico. Es importante considerar la longitud (*length*) deseada y el tiempo de que se dispone (*available*) para escribir, el límite de páginas o palabras u otros factores semejantes. Sin esta delimitación del tema, el autor puede sobrepasar (*exceed*) el límite de tiempo o de palabras, o aún peor, puede producir un trabajo vago y general, por lo común de poco valor.

Comience por dividir el tema general en aspectos específicos. Subdivida, luego, **uno** de estos aspectos en otro aún más específico. Siguiendo este método encontrará por fin una faceta del tema original lo bastante específica como para poder ser desarrollada en los límites fijados para el ensayo o trabajo asignado. Los ejemplos que siguen ilustran la delimitación y enfoque de temas generales hasta lograr tópicos más específicos.

Ejemplo 1

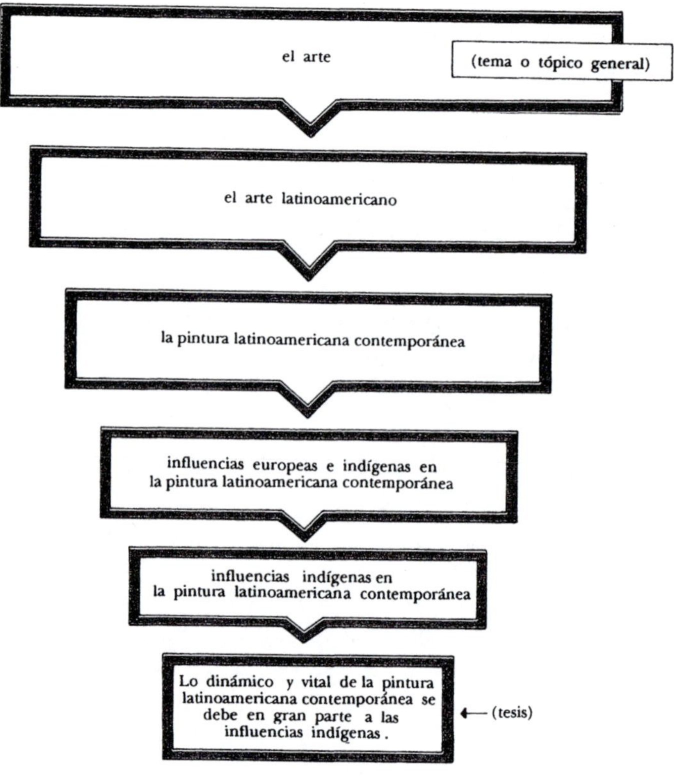

Ejemplo 2

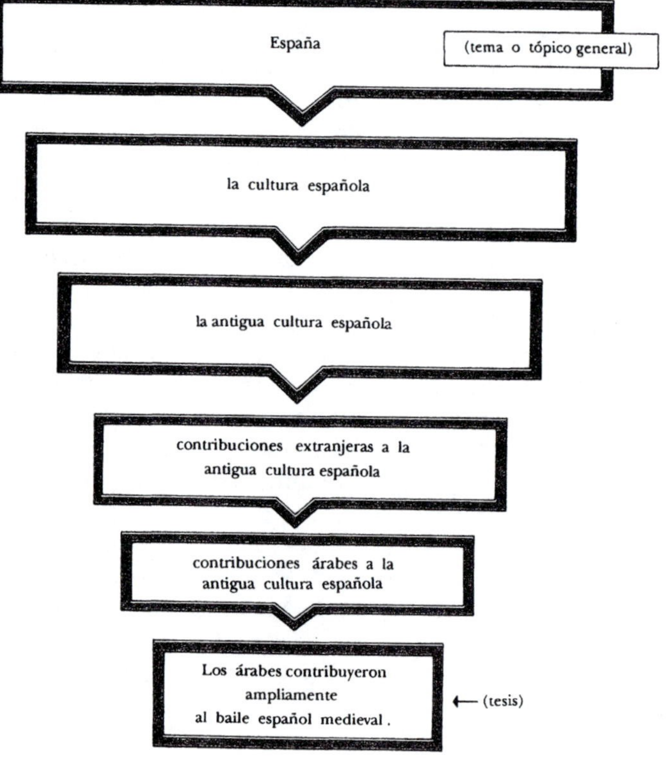

A. Utilice este diagrama para limitar y enfocar el tema general «la música» hasta llegar a una tesis específica que se pueda desarrollar en un ensayo de dos o tres páginas.

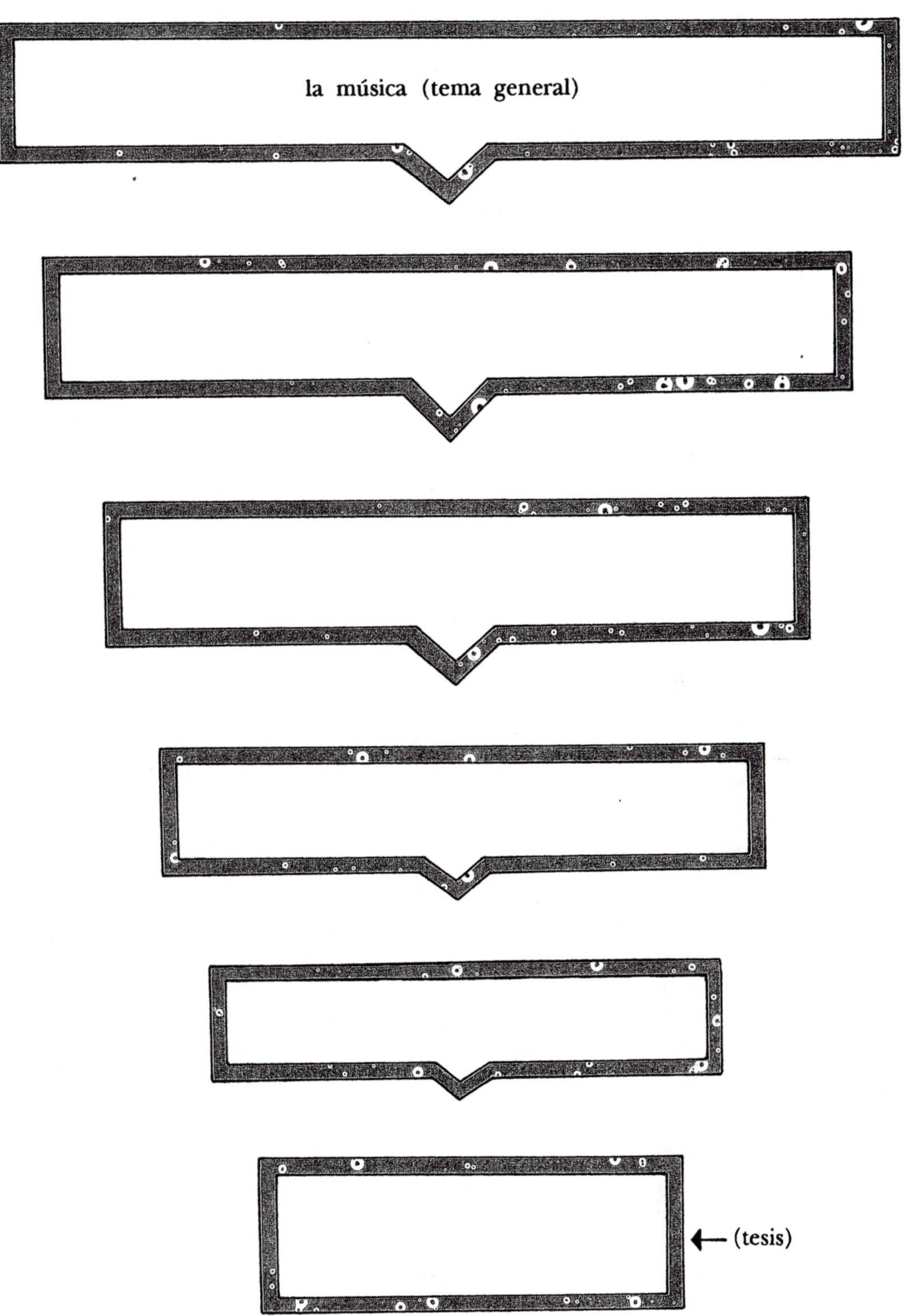

B. Los siguientes temas son demasiado generales para desarrollarse en un ensayo o trabajo de investigación. Escoja usted uno que le interese o pídale a su profesor(a) que le asigne uno. Luego limítelo y enfóquelo en una hoja adicional siguiendo el diagrama del Ejercicio A. Debe obtener la aprobación de su profesor(a); más adelante usted tendrá que desarrollar un esquema basado en el tema escogido.

- la arquitectura
- la escultura
- la religión
- el amor
- Latinoamérica
- la literatura
- las artes plásticas
- España
- el cine
- el canto
- la danza
- los deportes

EL DESARROLLO DE LA TESIS: ORGANIZACIÓN DE SUS IDEAS EN FORMA ESCRITA

La organización

Todo ensayo o trabajo de investigación consta de (*consists of*) varios párrafos o secciones que sirven para desarrollar la tesis. Al principio se hace una introducción que plantea (*states, sets forth*) la tesis de una manera concisa. Es decir, informa al lector sobre cuál es la idea que se va a desarrollar.

También ha de haber alguna clase de conclusión. Esta sección puede resumir (especialmente si el trabajo es extenso) las ideas fundamentales que se han presentado, o plantear una implicación que se deriva de la tesis desarrollada. La conclusión por lo general ocupa un párrafo entero. Entre la introducción y la conclusión se encuentra el desarrollo (*body*) del trabajo. Es una serie de párrafos interrelacionados, cada uno de los cuales elabora o amplía (*develops, enlarges upon*) un único punto o aspecto de la tesis principal.

¿Cuántas páginas o párrafos debe tener el desarrollo de un buen ensayo o trabajo de investigación? La respuesta a esta pregunta es obvia: se deben utilizar cuantas páginas o párrafos sean necesarios para desarrollar la tesis. Hay que enfatizar que la **organización** de cada sección o párrafo es más importante que el **número** de páginas o párrafos que tenga la composición.

Cuando se trató la estructura del párrafo en el capítulo 3, se mencionó la oración tópica o temática. Ésta es generalmente la primera oración del párrafo, aunque, como usted recordará, también puede estar en la mitad o al final, y en algunos casos no existe. La oración tópica menciona un solo aspecto de la tesis del trabajo. Es una síntesis del párrafo en el que se encuentra. El arte de unir esas oraciones en forma coherente es el que produce buenos ensayos y trabajos de investigación. No olvide que en cada párrafo del desarrollo se presenta **un solo aspecto** de la tesis para ampliarla, detallarla (*specify it in detail*), explicarla, corroborarla o reforzarla.

Lea usted el siguiente ensayo y observe cómo cada párrafo del desarrollo plantea con detalles específicos un solo aspecto de la tesis que se presenta en el párrafo introductorio.

Wilfredo Lam, La Jungla.

Los hitos° del modernismo

párrafo 1 Desde la época colonial el arte latinoamericano ha combinado elementos europeos e indígenas, pero durante varios siglos° predominaron los primeros. Las catedrales e iglesias de México y Perú incorporaron motivos decorativos indígenas; no obstante los conceptos, estilos y técnicas eran españoles. Durante los siglos XVIII y XIX, los gustos europeos continuaron influenciando el arte latinoamericano, pero fue a comienzos del siglo XX cuando el equilibrio entre los estilos del Viejo Mundo y los autóctonos cambió radicalmente. **introducción**

párrafo 2 Hoy día el arte latinoamericano es, quizá, el más vital y dinámico del mundo, gracias en buena medida a la visión precursora de cuatro grandes pintores latinomericanos: Diego Rivera, Joaquín Torres-García, Wilfredo Lam y Roberto Matta. Los cuatro estudiaron en Europa, especialmente en París, y se empaparon° de ideas de vanguardia, desde el cubismo al surrealismo automatista; pero se apartaron de estos modelos y buscaron inspiración en las distintas culturas del Nuevo Mundo. El

hitos...*milestones*; **siglos**...*centuries*; **se empaparon**...*absorbed*

resultado fue un arte innovador que, si bien tenía cimientos° europeos, reflejaba una visión singular.

párrafo 3 El mexicano Diego Rivera (1886–1957) se dedicó a la glorificación del hombre común, no simplemente por medio del retrato del trabajador, sino mediante° la incorporación del arte folklórico a su estilo pictórico. En muchos de sus murales reprodujo escenas de la antigua vida mexicana. Rivera transmitió una visión poética, no histórica, de la sociedad mexicana precolombina. Incluyó deidades aztecas y escenas de la mitología azteca con el objeto de captar la totalidad de la visión indígena, y también emuló los gráficos y pinturas precolombinos. En su *Historia de las religiones* (1950–1954), fuentes mayas inspiraron su versión de las prácticas religiosas precolombinas, los sacrificios humanos incluidos.

párrafo 4 De modo similar, el descubrimiento del arte precolombino revolucionó el trabajo del uruguayo Joaquín Torres-García (1874–1949). Anteriormente se había interesado por las formas estilizadas del arte europeo medieval y del arte africano. Alrededor de 1930 abandonó el estructuralismo abstracto puro y pasó a incorporar en sus obras representaciones evocadoras de las figuras creadas por las civilizaciones antiguas. Aunque su obra reflejó la influencia de diversas culturas antiguas, muchos de sus conceptos provinieron directamente del arte precolombino. A diferencia de Rivera, Torres-García no consideró este nuevo estilo como una afirmación de identidad cultural nacional. Debido, quizá, a su propia formación clásica y a su prologada residencia en Europa, percibió la civilización precolombina como un elemento del gran patrimonio° artístico del mundo, no limitado a un determinado país o propio de éste. **desarrollo**

párrafo 5 Mientras que Rivera y Torres-García encontraron inspiración en las culturas indígenas precolombinas, el cubano Wilfredo Lam (1902–1982) se volvió hacia sus raíces africanas. Hijo de padre chino y madre mulata, desde su niñez Lam se vio expuesto° a las influencias de las culturas china, europea y africana; sin embargo se sintió especialmente atraído° por las tradiciones de su madre. En 1938 se trasladó° a París donde Picasso lo puso en contacto con la escultura africana. En sus primeras composiciones es evidente la influencia de Picasso y otros modernistas, pero muy pronto comenzaron a predominar las imágenes nativas. Aunque Lam no practicaba religión alguna, percibió en la santería° y otros cultos una suerte° de fuerza primitiva, de poderío° crudo, que se manifiesta en sus pinturas.

párrafo 6 El chileno Roberto Matta (1911–) es el más joven de los cuatro pintores. Durante su permanencia en México, Matta se interesó en la mitología maya que se basa en una visión cósmica del universo. El hombre y la naturaleza son considerados elementos de una totalidad y el tiempo como algo cíclico. Matta percibió el antiguo sistema como una respuesta creativa al caos fundamental del universo. El pintor también viajó al Perú, donde visitó Machu Picchu y descubrió una profunda afinidad con los artistas precolombinos cuyas obras de belleza perdurable respondían a las exigencias° del majestuoso paisaje peruano.

párrafo 7 Los cuatro artistas, si bien radicalmente diferentes en cuanto a estilo y propósitos, pese a su formación europea, resultaron profundamente influidos por sus raíces y revitalizaron el arte latinoamericano. **conclusión**

cimientos...*bases, foundations*; **mediante**...*by means of*; **patrimonio**...*heritage*; **expuesto**...*exposed*; **atraído**...*drawn to, attracted to*; **se trasladó**...*moved*; **santería**...*African-based religion practiced in the Caribbean*; **suerte**...*kind, type*; **poderío**...*strength*; **exigencias**...*demands*

El ensayo anterior utiliza buenas técnicas expositivas. El primer párrafo es una introducción, y en la última oración la autora plantea su tesis: los estilos indígenas tienen mayor influencia que los europeos en la pintura latinoamericana del siglo XX.

Observe usted cómo la escritora desarrolla su tesis a través de los párrafos del ensayo. En el segundo párrafo menciona a cuatro pintores que, apártandose de modelos europeos e inspirándose en las culturas del Nuevo Mundo, renovaron el arte latinoamericano. Luego cada párrafo que sigue explica con ejemplos y detalles la obra de **uno** de estos artistas. El tercer párrafo, por ejemplo, cita algunos de los temas mexicanos precolombinos que incorpora Diego Rivera en su pintura (dioses aztecas, sacrificios humanos, etc.).

C. Conteste las siguientes preguntas sobre el ensayo.

1. ¿ Qué hace la escritora en el cuarto párrafo?

____

____

____

____

____

2. ¿Qué logra en el quinto párrafo?

____

____

____

____

____

3. ¿Qué muestra el sexto párrafo?

____

____

____

____

____

4. ¿Cuál es la función del séptimo párrafo?

____

____

____

____

____

Note que aunque cada párrafo enfoca un aspecto distinto, todos tienen en común la referencia a la tesis. Observe también el uso de las expresiones de enlace (*linking, connection, transition*) (**hoy día, de modo similar, mientras**) con las cuales se introducen los pá-rrafos 2, 4 y 5. Estas expresiones indican las relaciones entre los diferentes párrafos. La fluidez (*fluidity*) de la composición en gran parte se debe al uso de palabras como éstas que aseguran (*ensure*) la transición y el enlace de las ideas presentadas. En la sección **Vocabulario clave** de cada capítulo usted ya ha estudiado muchas de estas palabras y expresiones.

La organización de datos

En un buen ensayo o trabajo de investigación el escritor recoge (*collects*) y organiza una cantidad de ejemplos, detalles o datos para elaborar o corroborar su tesis. En casos de investigaciones extensas, como se apuntó anteriormente, es imperante consultar obras de autoridades en la materia para justificar o respaldar las ideas propias. Puesto que las bibliotecas y hemerotecas (*periodical section of a library*) prestan libros y revistas por un período relativamente corto, es necesario crear **fichas bibliográficas** donde se conserve toda la información sobre las obras consultadas. Además es también recomendable proveerse de tarjetas donde copiar cualquier información que se considere pertinente. Además de las fuentes obtenidas en una biblioteca, el autor puede utilizar experiencias y observaciones personales para ampliar o sustentar las ideas expuestas. No importa la perspectiva, sea personal o impersonal; lo importante es elaborar la tesis de manera que el lector pueda seguir el hilo (*course, thread*) de la discusión.

Observe los ejemplos de una ficha bibliográfica y de una ficha de anotaciones.

Ficha bibliográfica

PC 4420
G 56 De Anza, Juan Miguel
El españöl de Costa Rica
San José: Editorial Campos,
1997.

Ficha de anotaciones

De Anza, p. 128 velarización de la n dental

«Se observa, sobretodo en la Meseta Central, una velarización de la ŋ en posición final. Este es un fenómeno bastante extendido en Centroamérica. Así pues la palabra camión, normalmente pronunciada [kamión], se convierte en [kamióŋ]»

Buscar más ejemplos y otros posibles casos de este alófono.

Sugerencias para sus fichas

1. Use dos tipos de tarjetas: uno para sus fichas bibliográficas y otro para sus anotaciones.
2. Escriba claramente usando un bolígrafo.
3. Incluya en la ficha bibliográfica la signatura (*call number*) del libro.
4. Use comillas cuando copie textualmente.
5. Copie con cuidado para evitar errores. Revise para verificar que la información esté completa y que no haya faltas de ortografía ni de puntuación.
6. Cuando copie una cita o apunte una anotación, escriba siempre la página donde la encontró.
7. Haga una distinción clara entre sus propios comentarios y las palabras del texto que está usando.
8. Nunca mezcle en una tarjeta información proveniente de varios textos.

D. Vaya a la biblioteca y obtenga toda la información necesaria para escribir un ensayo o trabajo de investigación sobre el tema que usted escogió en el Ejercicio B de la página 250. Siga las recomendaciones dadas para confeccionar fichas. Cuando haya terminado, preséntele todas las fichas a su profesor(a).

¿Cómo empezar?

a) Uso de un esquema

Y ahora bien, ¿qué pasa cuando al sentarse a escribir usted tiene una serie de fichas pero la página y la mente en blanco (*blank*)? No se preocupe. Esta situación es más común de lo que se piensa. Aun los escritores profesionales pasan de vez en cuando por experiencias semejantes. Recuerde que lo mejor en tales momentos es escribir **algo**. Muchas veces lo más difícil es poner la primera palabra en la página. Recuerde también que sus primeros esfuerzos no tienen que ser perfectos. De hecho, sería muy raro si lo fueran. Crear un esquema a través del cual usted pueda desarrollar su tesis es un buen modo de empezar. He aquí un modelo. Adáptelo a las necesidades de su tema.

Esquema
Cambios en la España de Felipe V

I. Introducción
   A. Nacimiento de una nueva era
   B. Los Borbones y el afrancesamiento
II. Desarrollo
   A. Cambios en poder real
      1. el despotismo ilustrado
      2. desaparición de las autonomías municipales y regionales
      3. las secretarías o ministerios aumentan su poder
      4. Felipe V establece la ley Sálica
   B. Cambios en la iglesia
      1. luchas entre el Papado y el poder real
      2. pérdida del poder de la inquisición
   C. Cambios en el arte
      1. cambios de los tonos oscuros a los claros
      2. llegada a España de artistas extranjeros
III. Conclusión
   El deslumbramiento de España por la cultura francesa. Las costumbres españolas se conservan más en el pueblo que en las elites intelectuales.

E. Haga ahora un esquema de su tema. Aunque no sea perfecto y luego tenga que hacerle modificaciones, su elaboración le obligará a organizar los datos y notas recogidos. Deberá entregar el esquema a su profesor(a) para que lo evalúe.

Consulte siempre el esquema para asegurar una exposición armoniosa y lógica. A menudo esta etapa (*step*) del proceso ayuda a reestructurar el esqueleto del trabajo, a generar nuevas ideas o a modificar el enfoque de la tesis.

b) Uso de notas o apuntes

Supongamos, por ejemplo, que usted tiene que escribir un ensayo relativamente corto para el periódico de su universidad sobre el tópico «Un(a) profesor(a) que merece (*deserves*) ser nombrado(a) 'Mejor Profesor(a) del Año'» y tiene dificultad en comenzar. Usted no ha elaborado un esquema preliminar. En esta situación, puede pensar en un(a) profesor(a) y por qué le agrada (*you like him/her*). Anote sus observaciones. Podría escribir:

Está muy bien preparado(a) académicamente.
Aporta (*He/She brings*) ideas innovadoras a sus clases.
Siempre trata de una manera respetuosa y justa a los estudiantes.
Tiene buen sentido (*sense*) de humor.

Ahora usted tiene escrito lo suficiente para elaborar una tesis y la introducción al ensayo: «El (La) profesor(a) ______________ merece ser nombrado(a) 'Mejor Profesor(a) del Año' por su buena preparación académica, por sus técnicas innovadoras, por su trato justo y amable y por su buen sentido del humor».

El próximo paso será usar estos cuatro puntos para desarrollar su ensayo, explicando con detalles y ejemplos cada uno de los puntos del primer párrafo. En el segundo párrafo, puede mencionar las universidades a las cuales asistió el (la) profesor(a), los títulos universitarios que tiene, los honores académicos y profesionales que obtuvo, las organizaciones profesionales a las cuales pertenece, sus viajes de estudio, publicaciones, etc. Siga de la misma manera con el segundo punto (en otro párrafo), el tercer punto (en otro párrafo), etc. Luego finalice el ensayo con una conclusión.

F. Con tres compañeros de clase, utilice la información y las sugerencias anteriores para completar el borrador de un ensayo sobre su profesor(a) ideal. Uds. pueden usar su imaginación o escribir sobre un(a) profesor(a) que conocen. Tengan cuidado de que cada párrafo del desarrollo del ensayo plantee una sola idea o un solo aspecto de la tesis. En esta composición la tesis se encuentra en la primera oración del primer párrafo.

El (La) profesor(a) ______________ merece ser nombrado(a) «Mejor Profesor(a) del Año» por su buena preparación académica, por sus técnicas innovadoras, por su trato justo y amable y su buen sentido del humor. Hay, en efecto, pocos profesores de tan extraordinaria calidad, ya sea en el departamento de ______________, como en toda la universidad.

Graduado(a) en ______________ de la Universidad ________________,

ha realizado estudios de posgrado en ______________________________

____

____

____

También ha ____

____

____

____

Además de sus impresionantes calificaciones académicas, aporta al aula

(*classroom*) ____

____

____

____

____

____

Aunque ____

____

____

____

____

____

____

Obviamente, ____

____

____

____

____

____

____

Después de completar el borrador, hagan **dos** copias para cada miembro del grupo. Las van a necesitar más tarde.

LA REVISIÓN

Ninguna composición se puede considerar realmente completa hasta que el escritor la haya revisado. La revisión es una etapa absolutamente indispensable en la producción de un buen trabajo.

Terminado el borrador, muchos escritores lo leen inmediatamente y hacen los cambios que consideren apropiados. Luego lo dejan. El distanciarse (*Distancing oneself*) del trabajo, ya sea por unas horas o por unos días, los ayuda a contemplar de una manera más objetiva la labor. Otros escritores más experimentados (*experienced*) van revisando el borrador a medida que lo escriben; pero aún así deben distanciarse del trabajo para regresar más tarde a revisarlo.

La revisión final tiene dos etapas: la temática y la formal. Es recomendable corregir estos aspectos en forma separada. Es decir, leer el borrador dos veces.

La revisión temática

La primera lectura del borrador enfoca la organización. Los esfuerzos se concentran en la estructura y la evolución lógica, según el desarrollo de la tesis. Al leer debe preguntarse si el escrito...

- ha presentado claramente la tesis.
- ha ofrecido bastantes detalles o ejemplos para sustentarla (*support it*).
- ha ordenado lógicamente los párrafos del desarrollo de tal modo que cada uno de ellos hable de un solo aspecto de la tesis.

- ha establecido relaciones entre los párrafos y una transición que guíe al lector hacia una conclusión lógica.

La revisión formal

En la segunda lectura, el autor corrige y pule (*polishes*) la gramática, el vocabulario, la puntuación y la ortografía. Para lograr este objetivo le resultarán útiles los apéndices A, B, C y D de ***Composición práctica***. Corrija el uso del acento escrito, las mayúsculas y la puntuación. No olvide a sus viejos amigos, los diccionarios, sin los cuales la labor es casi imposible. Debe también tener en cuenta las convenciones establecidas para el uso de las notas de texto y la bibliografía. Para ayudarle está el Apéndice E en la página 277. Su profesor(a) le puede ayudar también. No deje nunca de reconocer las fuentes de información utilizadas. No hacerlo constituye un serio delito —**el plagio** (*plagarism*). Después de hacer las revisiones necesarias, lo único que le falta es escribir el trabajo «en limpio» y leerlo una vez más en su forma final.

► Manos a la obra

A. Siguiendo las técnicas de revisión que aprendió en este capítulo, utilice un bolígrafo de tinta (*ink*) roja para revisar una de las copias del borrador del Ejercicio F («El (La) profesor(a) ______________ merece ser nombrado(a) 'Mejor Profesor(a) del Año'»). Después de revisar el borrador, escriba usted su propia versión final. Luego entréguele a su profesor(a):

1. la copia del borrador **no** revisada
2. el borrador que usted revisó
3. su versión final «en limpio»

B. Escriba usted (en hojas adicionales) un ensayo o un trabajo de investigación sobre el tema del Ejercicio B de la página 250 que usted escogió y que su profesor(a) evaluó. Use las fichas y el esquema que creó en las páginas 255 y 256. El paso siguiente es escribir el borrador. Consulte el esquema y los apéndices B, C, D y E de *Composición práctica*. Después de revisar su labor, entréguele a su profesor(a) el esquema, el borrador y la versión final del trabajo.

PARA LOS INTERNAUTAS

Vaya a **http://www.wiley.com/college/gonzalez,** busque la página que corresponde a este capítulo y haga los ejercicios indicados.

En esta página podrá anotar sus ideas respecto a este capítulo o bien referirse a un episodio de su propia vida.

Mi diario:

Appendix A

Syllabification and Diphthongs

You must be able to divide a word into syllables in order to determine the position of a written accent. Sometimes it is also necessary to divide a word when it does not fit at the end of a line. Because Spanish syllabification is different from English, you should be aware of the following guidelines.

SYLLABIFICATION

1. The simplest syllable consists of a single vowel.

   a o a-la o-jo i-ra

2. The most common syllable consists of a consonant followed by a vowel.

   ge-ne-ro-so ca-sa pe-ro gé-ne-ro

3. Two consonants are usually divided.

   lis-to al-ta mis-mo al-gu-no im-por-tan-te

   a. A two-consonant combination whose second consonant is *l* or *r* is not separated.[1]

   *a-**pli**-ca-mos de-sa-**gra**-da-**ble** in-**glés***

   b. The letter combinations *ch, ll,* and *rr* are never separated.

   *de-re-**cho** cue-**llo** a-**rran**-car pe-**rro***

4. When there are three consonants together . . .

   a. the first two usually go with the preceding vowel, and the third goes with the vowel that follows.

   ***ins**-ta-lar **trans-cen**-der **ins-pec**-cio-nar*

[1]The combination *s* + *l/r* is an exception: *is-la, des-lin-de, des-ra-ma.*

b. if the third consonant is *l* or *r*, the last two consonants go with the vowel that follows.

*en-**fla**-que-cer* *ex-**tran**-je-ro* *ex-**pli**-car*

5. When there are four consonants together, they are divided between the second and third.

*cons-**crip**-to* *ins-**cri**-bir* *ins-**tru**-men-to*

DIPHTHONGS

In Spanish, a diphthong is the combination of one weak vowel (*i, u*) and one strong vowel (*a, e, o*), or the combination of two weak vowels. A diphthong constitutes **one syllable**, and its vowels are never separated. (See Appendix B, page 263.)

***ai**-re*	**au**-*la*	*c**ui**-dar*
*b**oi**-na*	*d**io**s*	*c**iu**-dad*
*s**ue**-lo*	*c**ie**-lo*	*Ma-r**io***

Some degree of **spoken** stress always goes on the **strong** vowel or on the **second** vowel of a combination of two weak vowels.

NOTE: Two strong vowels do not form a diphthong.
*m**a**-**e**s-tra* *d**e**-s**e**-**o*** *cr**e**-**e**n*

Appendix B

▶ Stress and Written Accent

In every word of two or more syllables, one syllable is stressed (pronounced more intensely than the other[s]). There are three general rules that determine where a word is stressed.

GENERAL RULES

1. Words that end in a vowel or *-n* or *-s* are stressed automatically on the **second-to-the-last syllable**.

   mañana *departamento* *hospitales* *consideran*

2. Words that end in a consonant other than *-n* or *-s* are stressed automatically on the **last syllable**.

   participar *verdad* *hospital* *avestruz*

Most words in Spanish fall into these two categories and therefore do not require a written accent.

3. Any word that follows a different stress pattern than those described above must have a written accent to tell you which syllable to stress.

simpático	*Martínez*	*explicándomelo*	*fácil*
automóvil	*habló*	*José*	*México*
teléfono	*escribirás*	*Mamá*	*Perú*

SPECIAL RULES

1. A diphthong constitutes a single syllable (***seis***, *es-tu-**dia***). However, if the primary stress of the word falls on the weak vowel of a strong-weak vowel combination, a

written accent must be placed over the weak vowel. The diphthong is thereby eliminated. (In the following examples the stressed syllable appears in bold face.)

***Ma**-rio* (diphthong *io*)	*Ma-**rí**-a* (no diphthong)
***dia**-ria* (two diphthongs *ia*)	***dí**-a* (no diphthong)
*con-**ti**-nuo* (diphthong *uo*)	*con-ti-**nú**-o* (no diphthong)
***ha**-cia* (diphthong *ia*)	*ha-**cí**-a* (no diphthong)

2. Interrogative and exclamatory words have a written accent (to distinguish them from **relative pronouns** or **adverbs**). This accent mark has no effect on pronunciation or stress.

¿Cómo?	*¡Cómo!*	*como*
¿Qué?	*¡Qué!*	*que*

3. One-syllable words generally do not have a written accent. However, certain words (many of them one-syllable) have a different meaning when they bear a written accent. They are pronounced and stressed identically with or without the accent.

aun	even (adverb)	*aún*	yet, still (adverb)
de	of, from (preposition)	*dé*	give (subjunctive, command of *dar*)
el	the (definite article)	*él*	he (personal pronoun)
mas	but (conjunction)	*más*	more (adverb or adjective)
mi	my (possessive adjective)	*mí*	me (personal pronoun)
se	himself, herself, itself themselves (reflexive pronoun)	*sé*	I know (present of *saber*), be (imperative of *ser*)
si	if (conjunction)	*sí*	yes (adverb)
		sí	himself, herself, themselves (reflexive prepositional pronoun)
solo	alone (adjective)	*sólo*	only (adverb)
te	you (object pronoun)	*té*	tea (noun)
tu	your (possessive adjective)	*tú*	you (subject pronoun)

4. The demonstratives *este, ese,* and *aquel* (and their feminine and plural forms) have written accents when they function as **pronouns**. When they function as **adjectives** they do not.

   Me gusta ***esta*** (adjective) *foto;*

   a Marta también le gusta ***ésta*** (pronoun).

5. The conjunction ***o*** (or) bears a written accent when it occurs between two numerals (to avoid confusing it with a zero).

   506 (five hundred six)

   5 ***ó*** 6 (five or six)

6. A word that has a written accent in the singular usually retains it in the plural.

   lápiz / lápices *altímetro / altímetros*

   There are two exceptions:

   carácter / caracteres *régimen / regímenes*

7. The first element of a compound word does not retain a written accent.

   décimo + séptimo = decimoséptimo

   así + mismo = asimismo

8. If a compound word is joined by a hyphen, each element of the hyphenated word retains its original written accent.

   histórico-legendario

   político-económico

   hispano-francés

9. Adverbs that end in *-mente* retain the written accent of the original adjective.

   cortés / cortésmente *rápido / rápidamente*

NOTE: Uppercase stressed vowels retain their written accents.

Los Ángeles *Ávila* *Él habla bien.*

Appendix C

► Capitalization

In general, Spanish and English share many similarities in their use of capital letters (*mayúsculas*) and lowercase letters (*minúsculas*). Nevertheless, there are several cases in which the two languages vary. Note, for example, the differences between these two sentences:

I am **S**panish: **I** am from **S**pain and **I** speak **S**panish.

*Soy **e**spañola: soy de **E**spaña y hablo **e**spañol.*

The following guidelines will help you to determine whether to use a capital or a lowercase letter in Spanish.

USE A CAPITAL LETTER FOR . . .

1. the first word of a sentence.

   ***D**ecidieron ir al cine.*

   *¿**A** dónde piensas ir?*

   *¡**Q**ué noche pasamos!*

2. proper nouns, names, and nicknames.

   *Se llama **M**irta **C**ampos.*

   *Nació en **C**aracas, **V**enezuela.*

   ***J**uana la **L**oca*

   *la **F**acultad de **C**iencias y **L**etras*

   la revista **T**iempo

   el periódico **L**a **N**ación

   *el **C**orte **I**nglés* (name of a Spanish department store)

3. **abbreviated** forms of titles and of *usted / ustedes.*

   *¿Conoce **U**d. a **D**. Miguel y a la **S**ra. Lerma?*
   but
   ¿Conoce usted a don Miguel y a la señora Lerma?

4. titles of authorities when referring to a **particular** authority.

   *el **S**enador Marín y los otros senadores*

   *el **P**residente Sarmiento*

   *todos los presidentes, más el **P**residente de Chile*

   *ningún rey como el **R**ey Juan Carlos, **R**ey de España*

5. words that refer to God and to the Virgin Mary.

   *el **S**alvador*

   *el **T**odopoderoso*

   ***N**uestro **S**eñor*

   ***É**l*

   ***N**uestra **S**eñora de **G**uadalupe*

   *la **I**nmaculada*

   *la **M**adre **D**olorosa*

   ***E**lla*

6. the article that accompanies the names of certain **cities.**

   ***L**a Habana*

   ***L**a Paz*

   ***E**l Petén*

   ***L**a Coruña*

USE A LOWERCASE LETTER FOR . . .

1. days of the week.

   *Hoy es **l**unes.*

   *Mañana es **m**artes.*

2. months of the year.

   *el seis de **m**ayo*

   *un día caluroso de **a**gosto*

3. nouns and adjectives of nationality (but **not** the name of the country or city).

Soy ***costarricense****, pero no nací en Costa Rica.*

A los habitantes de Madrid se les llama ***madrileños****.*

los ***mexicanos*** *expulsados de México*

4. languages.

Hablo ***español****,* ***inglés*** *y* ***portugués****.*

Muchos canadienses hablan ***francés****.*

5. the article that accompanies certain **countries**' names.

Es de ***la*** *Argentina, pero vive en* ***el*** *Perú.*

En ***el*** *Canadá se habla francés.*

6. nouns and adjectives that denote political or religious affiliations.

Soy ***demócrata****, pero ella es* ***republicana****.*

Asistieron ***católicos****,* ***judíos*** *y* ***musulmanes****.*

el ***partido liberal***

la ***iglesia mormona***

los ***mormones***

7. titles of books, literary works, articles, artistic works, etc., **with the exception of the first word.**

Mariano Azuela escribío **Los de abajo.**

¿Leyó usted **La familia de Pascual Duarte?**

*El poema se titula «****Canción de otoño en primavera****».*

8. **unabbreviated** titles.

la ***señorita*** *Artino*

el ***señor*** *Gutiérrez*

doña *Elvira y* ***don*** *Fernando*

Appendix D

Punctuation

Proper punctuation is essential to ensure clarity and precision in your writing. With few exceptions, Spanish punctuation is very similar to English. The following guidelines will help you to punctuate your writing effectively.

1. Use a **period** (*punto*) . . .

a. to end a declarative sentence (any sentence that is not interrogative or exclamatory).

Leonora es profesora.

Alberto vive en Murcia.

Quise ir, pero no pude.

Vimos varios animales: alpacas, vicuñas, llamas y guanacos.

b. to end an imperative sentence.

Siéntense aquí, por favor.

No vayas sin avisarme.

c. after abbreviations.

El Sr. Montes trabaja para Soler y Cía., S.A.

La Dra. Roldán compró 20 l. (litros) de gasolina.

NOTE: In writing numbers in Spanish, the period replaces the (English) comma. *5.640.200* (five million, six hundred forty thousand, two hundred)

2. Use a **comma** (*coma*) . . .

a. to separate elements of a series—unless the elements are joined by *y (e)*, *o (u)*, or *ni*.

Hay clase los lunes, miércoles y viernes.

Habla clara, directa e inteligentemente.

No asistieron mexicanos, peruanos, argentinos ni chilenos.

Compró el billete, facturó el equipaje, se despidió y subió al tren.

b. to separate the person(s) spoken to in direct address.

Ven acá, Juanito.

Juanito, ven acá.

Siéntense, señores, por favor.

c. before adversative conjunctions—*pero, mas, sino, sin embargo, al contrario, no obstante, aunque, por lo contrario,* and *a pesar de (que)*—when they connect short sentences.

Le rogué que me ayudara, pero no lo hizo.
Le rogué que me ayudara, mas no lo hizo.

and **before and after** when the conjunction is embedded.

Le rogué que me ayudara; no quiso, sin embargo, hacerlo.

d. before causal conjunctions—*porque, ya que, puesto que, pues,* and *que* when it means **because**.

Escríbalo ahora, que (porque) no se lo voy a repetir.

Preferí no ir, puesto que me sentía muy mal.

e. before consecutive conjunctions—*así que, así es que, por lo tanto, por siguiente, en consecuencia; pues* and *luego* when they mean *por lo tanto* (therefore).

No tenemos el dinero suficiente, por lo tanto no podremos comprarlo.

Me mandaron el boleto equivocado, por consiguiente tendré que devolverlo.

and **before and after** when the conjunction is embedded.

No está interesado en nuestra compañía; no creo, por lo tanto, que haya que entrevistarlo.

f. to set off an explanatory phrase or an element that provides additional or incidental information.

Nos lo dijo Pilar, la hija de don Luis.

El anuncio sobre la fotocopiadora, ya publicado anteriormente, no se usará en nuestra edición.

g. to separate participial phrases from the rest of the sentence.

Firmado el contrato, la ingeniera regresó a su país.

Permaneció de pie, el pelo revuelto por el viento.

Hablando en voz alta, entró en la sala.

h. to set off an embedded subject or any other embedded expression.

En la novela, el asesino, con mucha astucia, entró en el cuarto del enfermo.

La chica, cuyos padres son muy ricos, asiste a una escuela privada.

i. to separate a prepositional phrase when it appears at the beginning of the sentence or when it is embedded.

En la estación de Ubeda, el maquinista hizo su primera parada.

El maquinista hizo, en la estación de Ubeda, su primera parada.

j. after an adverb clause that begins a sentence.

Si tuviera tiempo, iría contigo.

Cuando llegamos al pueblo, ya era de noche.

k. to separate a long, extensive subject.

Los alumnos que habían estudiado diligentemente durante todo el semestre, obtuvieron muy buenas notas.

3. Use a **semicolon** (*punto y coma*) . . .

a. to join the clauses of a compound sentence without a coordinating conjunction.

Los hombres lanzaban sus sombreros al aire; las mujeres zapateaban al ritmo de la música.

b. before adversative conjunctions (*mas, pero, aunque,* etc.) **when the clauses are long**.

En el silencioso pueblo de San Jorge, todo parecía dormir en calma a esas tempranas horas de la mañana; pero la actividad hervía ya en las cocinas de las mujeres que comenzaban las labores del día.

If the clauses are short, a comma is sufficient.

Todo parecía calmado, pero la actividad hervía en las cocinas.

c. instead of a period to separate two sentences when the consecutive or adversative conjunction is embedded in the second sentence.

No vino a verme; me sentí, por lo tanto, desilusionado.
or
No vino a verme. Me sentí, por lo tanto, desilusionado.

Me lo explicó; no pude, sin embargo, entenderlo.
or
Me lo explicó. No pude, sin embargo, entenderlo.

d. to separate similar elements of a series when there is internal punctuation.

Les escribimos al Profesor Martí, jefe del Departamento de Ciencias; a la Sra. Alonso, corresponsal de la revista Más; *y a la Licenciada Ortiz, vicedecana de la Escuela de Derecho.*

4. Use a **colon** (*dos puntos*) . . .

a. before enumerations.

Visité varios países: España, Francia, Italia y Grecia.

Hay tres problemas por resolver: la distancia de la estrella, su composición química y su luminosidad.

b. after the salutation that begins letters, speeches, etc.

Muy estimada doña Luisa:

Muy estimado señor:

Querida Ana:

Señoras y señores:

Muy distinguidos colegas:

c. to introduce quotations.

Me dijeron mis padres: «¡Ojalá que no!»

Explicó el autor: «No tenía la menor idea de lo que me pasaba».

d. to indicate that a second idea or piece of information completes or explains a previous one.

El problema se hizo más complejo: nadie quería participar en el concurso, la directiva se negaba a cooperar y el dinero se acabó.

5. Use **quotation marks** (*comillas*) . . .

a. to mark direct quotes.

Nos dijo: «Tenemos que trabajar más hoy si queremos terminar esta semana».

b. to make a word or phrase stand out.

Estos son los «buenos» del grupo.

c. to indicate nicknames.

Llamábamos a Miguel «El Flaquito» por su apariencia física.

d. to make a comment (affirmation, question, exclamation, etc.) of some sort about a word or phrase.

El poeta utiliza la palabra «agua» para sugerir el transcurso del tiempo.

e. to indicate the titles of movies, poems, plays, stories, articles, and essays.

Acabo de ver la película «Los reyes del mambo».

6. Use **parentheses** (*paréntesis*) or a **dash** (*raya*) . . .

to insert explanatory information.

Varios países (Ecuador, Perú y Chile) participaron.

or

Varios países —Ecuador, Perú y Chile— participaron.

Durante la Edad de Oro (1500–1700) floreció la literatura.

or

Durante la Edad de Oro —1500–1700— floreció la literatura.

7. Use a **dash** to indicate dialogue.

—¿A qué hora quieres ir? —le preguntó ella.

—No me importa. No tengo clases hoy.

8. Use **brackets** (*corchetes*) . . .

a. to insert clarifying or additional information within a quotation.

«Cada miembro [de la iglesia] firmó la carta».

b. to insert information within parentheses.

Participaron varias tribus de la Península (castellanos, leoneses, lusitanos [portugueses], asturianos) en las guerras.

9. Use **ellipsis** points (*puntos suspensivos*) . . .

to indicate the omission of a word or words from a quote. (Some writers enclose the ellipsis in brackets.)

«La cucaracha..., ya no puede caminar».

or

«La cucaracha [...], ya no puede caminar».

NOTE: Remember that Spanish interrogative and exclamatory sentences begin with inverted punctuation marks.

¿Quieres ir conmigo?

¡Claro que sí!

Appendix E

Documentation and Bibliography

The ability to make effective and legitimate use of other people's ideas or statements in your own writing is an essential skill in developing research or term papers, book reviews, and various types of reports. Documentation (within the text) and a list of works cited (at the end of the text) will acknowledge the sources of information and ideas used in your paper and help you avoid plagiarism—the illegitimate use of source materials.

Of the various guides for writing research papers, the following are among the most commonly used in colleges and universities throughout the United States:

Modern Language Association. *MLA Handbook for Writers of Research Papers.* 4th ed. New York: MLA, 1995 (used widely in literature and languages as well as in other fields).

Turabian, Kate L. *A Manual for Writers of Term Papers, Theses, and Dissertations.* 6th ed. Chicago: University of Chicago Press, 1996 (a shortened version of the *Chicago Manual of Style*).

Other guides, such as the *Publication Manual of the American Psychological Association* (used often in the social sciences and in other fields), are preferred by some professors.

Your choice might be governed by the requirements of your university, your academic department, the professor in a particular course, or your own personal taste. The guidelines presented in *Composición práctica* follow the MLA format, and they represent selected aspects of documentation/bibliography that you are most likely to find useful in your writing. For less common situations (sources such as pamphlets, dissertations, interviews, conference proceedings, literary works, etc.) you should consult the *MLA Handbook* or one of the other available resources.

DOCUMENTATION

To document quotations, paraphrases, summaries, etc. in an essay or research paper, MLA format requires parenthetical citations within the body (text) rather than footnotes or endnotes. Each citation should be placed as near the relevant material as possible. It should be short—providing only enough information (usually the author's name and the page number) to allow the reader to locate the full citation in the list of works cited at the end of the paper.

The following guidelines will help you to create and place citations effectively.

1. Very often you can include the author's name in the text itself to introduce the material. In such cases you need only cite the page number(s) in parentheses.

   Bárbara Mujica opinó que "Diego Rivera se dedicó a la glorificación del hombre común" (75).

2. When you do not use the author's name in the body of the text, include his or her last name in the parentheses, followed immediately by the page number(s).

   Varios críticos creen que la obra de Diego Rivera muestra una glorificación del hombre común (Mujica 75).

3. If you cite a work written by two or three authors, include all the authors' last names in the citation.

   González y Farrell señalan la importancia de los diccionarios no sólo en la clase de composición sino en la vida diaria (1).

4. For a work with four or more authors, list all four authors or give the last name of the first author followed by "et al." (*and others*).

   Los autores de *Puntos de partida* explican muy bien el imperfecto del subjuntivo (Knorre, Dorwick, Glass, and Villarreal 466–473).(or) (Knorre et al. 466–473).

   Use the same format (all four names or et al. format) in your list of works cited (or bibliography) at the end of your paper.

5. If your list of works cited has more than one author with the same last name, include each author's first initial in the parenthetical citation in your text (N. Guillén 42) or (J. Guillén 137). If the first initials are identical, spell out the entire first name of each author.

6. When you cite an <u>entire work</u> (either by the author's name alone or by author and title), no parenthetical reference is necessary because the reader will be able to find bibliographical information by looking up the author's name in your list of works cited.

   María de Jorge Isaacs se considera el prototipo de la novela romántica sentimental. (or) La obra maestra de Isaacs se considera el prototipo de la novela romántica sentimental.

7. If your list of works cited has two or more works by the same author, use a shortened version of the title in each citation.

   Darío emplea el símbolo del cisne tanto en sus primeros poemas modernistas (*Azul* 47) como en sus versos posteriores (*Cantos* 94).

8. If you cite two or more sources in the same citation, separate the information with semicolons.

   Algunos críticos mantienen lo contrario (Torres-Ríoseco 76; Loprete 49; Anderson-Imbert 118).

9. For electronic (or other non-print media such as film, television, recordings, etc.) sources, give enough information in the body of your text to enable the reader to locate the complete source in the list of works cited at the end of the paper.

   Manuel Danneman analiza la importancia de varios tipos humanos en la poesía folklórica de Chile.

BIBLIOGRAPHY

A "Works Cited" ("Obras citadas" if your paper is in Spanish) section at the very end of your paper is an alphabetized list of the sources you have referred to in the body of your essay or paper. If your instructor requires you to list everything you have read in preparing the paper, then you should title the list "Works Consulted" ("Obras consultadas").

Start the list on a separate page, and number each page consecutively, continuing the page numbers of the text. Center the heading "Works Cited" one inch from the top of the page, and do not underline it, italicize it, or enclose it in quotation marks. Double-space the entire list. Start each bibliographic entry flush with the left margin, and indent any subsequent lines one-half inch. The list must be alphabetized by authors' (or editors') last names. When a work has no author or editor, alphabetize the first word of the title (disregard *A, An,* or *The*).

The following guidelines will help you organize your "Works Cited" list.

Books

Each entry for a book must include three elements, each followed by a period:

- the author's name(s) (last name first)
- the title (and subtitle when one exists), italicized or underlined, and the edition if other than the first
- publication information: city (followed by a colon), a shortened form of the publisher's name, and the publication date

1. **Single author.**

   Alarcos Llorach, Emilio. *Fonología española.* Madrid: Gredos, 1950.
   Cervantes Saavedra, Miguel de. *Don Quijote de la Mancha.* 20th ed. Madrid: Espasa, 1959.
   Harris, Tracy. *Death of a Language: The History of Judeo-Spanish.* Newark: U of Delaware, 1994.
   Marín, Diego. *La civilización española.* New York: Holt, 1966.

2. **Two or more works by the same author.** List the author's name for the first work; for all subsequent works replace the author's name with three hyphens or a dash, followed by a period.

   Allende, Isabel. *La casa de los espíritus.* Barcelona: Plaza y Janés, 1982.
   ———. *Eva Luna.* Mexico City: Edivisión, 1988.
   ———. *El plan infinito.* Buenos Aires: Sudamericana, 1991.

3. **Two or three authors.**

   Chambers, J. and Peter Trudgill. *Dialectology.* Cambridge: Cambridge U P, 1980.
   González, Trinidad and Joseph Farrell. *Composición práctica.* 2d ed. New York: Wiley, 1999.

4. **Four or more authors.** Either list all the authors' names or give the first author listed on the title page, followed by a comma and "et al." (*and others*).

   Knorre, Marty, Thalia Dorwick, William Glass, and Hildebrando Villarreal. *Puntos de partida.* 4th ed. New York: McGraw-Hill, 1993.

   (or)

   Knorre, Marty et al. *Puntos de partida.* 4th ed. New York: McGraw-Hill, 1993.

5. **Organization as author.**

   Modern Language Association. *MLA Handbook for Writers of Research Papers.* 4th ed. New York: MLA, 1995.

6. **Editor.**

   Osborne, Robert E., ed. *Cuentos del mundo hispánico.* New York, VanNostrand, 1957.

7. **Translation.**

   Cervantes Saavedra, Miguel de. *The Adventures of Don Quixote.* Trans. J. M. Cohen. Harmondsworth, Middlesex, England: Penguin, 1950.

Periodicals

Each entry for a periodical includes the following elements, each followed by a period:

- the author's name(s) (last name first)
- the title of the article, in quotation marks
- publication information: the periodical title (italicized or underlined), the volume and/or issue numbers (if any), the publication date (followed by a colon), and the page number(s) on which the article appears. If there is a volume or issue number, then the year appears in parentheses.

1. **Magazine articles.**

   Canel, Fausto. "Interés, polémica y cine sobre Frida Kahlo." *Más* septiembre-octubre 1991: 86.

   Sheppard, R. Z. "Life, liberty and lustiness: Mario Vargas Llosa." *Time* 29 June 1998: 74.

   Tarragó, Rafael. E. "El legado de la imprenta colonial." *Américas* noviembre-diciembre 1996: 22–27.

2. **Unsigned magazine article.**

   "El mambo, rey del ritmo." *Vanidades continental* noviembre 1992: 26.

3. **Scholarly journal articles.**

   Phillips, June K. "Practical Implications of Recent Research in Reading." *Foreign Language Annals* 17 (1984): 285–96.

   Terrell, T. "Trends in the Teaching of Grammar in Spanish Textbooks." *Hispania* 73 (1990): 201.

4. **Newspaper articles.**

   Murillo, Katiana. "Calor que empobrece." *La Nación* 10 septiembre 1992: B1.

   O'Connor, Anne-Marie. "Carlos Fuentes: The Sum of Unequal Parts." *Los Angeles Times* 24 October 1997: E1–2.

   Poniatowska, Elena. "*Las tierras prometidas* de Rosa Nissán." *La Jornada* 30 marzo 1997: 21–22.

Internet (World Wide Web) Sources

Because the use of Internet and other electronic sources is a relatively new phenomenon, definitive guidelines for documenting such sources have not yet been developed. However, the MLA's Web site suggests that sources accessed from the World Wide Web include all items from the following list that are available and relevant to your paper. A period should follow each item, except the date of access.

- *Author(s),* last name(s) first (or editor, translator, or compiler if applicable).
- *Title of the document or subject line of the posting,* in quotation marks. If the document is a book, give the title, underlined, instead of the document title; if it is part of a book, give both titles.
- *Publication information for any print version of the source.*
- *Title of the scholarly project, database, periodical, or Web site,* underlined. If the site has no title, include a description such as *Home page.*
- *Editor of the scholarly project or database,* in normal order, preceded by *Ed.*
- *Identifying number of the source.* Version number (if not part of the title) or (for a journal) the volume, issue, or other identifying number.
- *Most recent date of electronic publication or posting.*
- *Discussion list information.* The description *Online posting* and the name of the discussion list.
- *Page, paragraph, or section number(s).*
- *Name of organization (if any) sponsoring the site.*
- *Date of access.*
- *Address* (the URL), in angle brackets.

Example:

Danneman, Manuel. "Tipos humanos en la poesía folklórica chilena." Excerpta 1 (1996). Facultad de ciencias sociales, Universidad de Chile 30 junio 1998 ⟨http://www.uchile.cl/facultades/esociales/nuevo/excerpta/excerptO.htm⟩

See Sample "Works Cited" Page on p. 282.

Sample "Works Cited" Page

Works Cited
(or)
Obras citadas

Alarcos Llorach, Emilio. *Fonología española.* Madrid: Gredos, 1950.
Allende, Isabel. *La casa de los espíritus.* Barcelona: Plaza y Janés, 1982.
———. *Eva Luna.* Mexico City: Edivisión, 1988.
———. *El plan infinito.* Buenos Aires: Sudamericana, 1991.
Canel, Fausto. "Interés, polémica y cine sobre Frida Kahlo." *Más* septiembre-octubre 1991: 86.
Cervantes Saavedra, Miguel de. *The Adventures of Don Quixote.* Trans. J. M. Cohen. Harmondsworth, Middlesex, England: Penguin, 1950.
———. *Don Quijote de la Mancha.* 20th ed. Madrid: Espasa, 1959.
Danneman, Manuel. "Tipos humanos en la poesía folklórica chilena." Excerpta 1 (1996). Facultad de ciencias sociales, Universidad de Chile 30 junio 1998 ⟨http://www.uchile.cl/facultades/esociales/nuevo/excerpta/excerptO.htm⟩
González, Trinidad and Joseph Farrell. *Composición práctica.* 2d ed. New York: Wiley, 1999.
Knorre, Marty, Thalia Dorwick, William Glass, and Hildebrando Villarreal. *Puntos de partida.* 4th ed. New York: McGraw-Hill, 1993.
"El mambo, rey del ritmo." *Vanidades continental* noviembre 1992: 26.
Modern Language Association. *MLA Handbook for Writers of Research Papers.* 4th ed. New York: MLA, 1995.
Mujica, Bárbara. "The Life Force of Language." *Américas* noviembre-diciembre 1995: 36–43.
———. "Los hitos del modernismo." *Américas* marzo-abril 1992: 51–52.
O'Connor, Anne-Marie. "Carlos Fuentes: The Sum of Unequal Parts." *Los Angeles Times* 24 October 1997: E1–2.

Appendix F

► Correction Key

Key **Definition and Meaning**

AB *abreviatura*

—incorrect form of abbreviation

—inappropriate use of abbreviation

AP *adjetivo posesivo*

—incorrect use of a possessive adjective when the possessor is obvious (for example, with parts of the body or articles of clothing)

ART *artículo*

—incorrect form of article (definite or indefinite)

—use of article where it should be omitted

—omission of article where it should be used

C *concordancia*

—faulty noun-adjective agreement

—faulty subject-verb agreement

—faulty antecedent-demonstrative agreement

CJ *conjunción*

—incorrect or poor choice of conjunction

—omission of conjunction where one is required

DES *desarrollo*

—problem with or a lack of logical development in a paragraph or in a longer composition (letter, essay, etc.)

G *género*

—incorrect gender (noun, adjective, article, pronoun, demonstrative)

M *mayúscula / minúscula*

—improper capitalization

—improper use of lowercase letter

MC *modismo coloquial*

—an expression used in informal conversation but not appropriate in more formal writing

—incorrect use of idiomatic expression

O *ortografía*

—error in spelling or written accent

P *puntuación*

—incorrect punctuation or lack of punctuation

PC *pronombre complemento*

—incorrect object prounon (direct, indirect, reflexive, object of a preposition)

P/I *pretérito / imperfecto*

—incorrect use of one of these tenses

POS *posición*

—incorrect word position

PR *pronombre relativo*

—incorrect relative pronoun

—omission of relative pronoun

PS *pronombre sujeto*

—unnecessary or inappropriate use of subject pronoun

—omission of subject pronoun where it is needed

REP *repetición*

—excessive repetition of a word or phrase

S *subjuntivo*

—incorrect use of subjuntive

—failure to use subjunctive

S/E *ser / estar*

—one verb used incorrectly in place of the other

T *tiempo*

—incorrect choice of tense

—error in formation of tense

—incorrect sequence of tenses

TR *transición*

—problem in transition

—lack of transition within a sentence, between sentences, between paragraphs

V *verbosidad / verborragia*

—excessive wordiness, lack of conciseness

V/G *vago / general*

—vague, general

—lack of specific details or examples in paragraph or essay development

VOC *vocabulario*

—wrong word or poor choice of words

VP *voz pasiva*

—incorrect form of passive voice construction

—inappropriate use of passive voice

¶ *párrafo*

—problem in paragraphing (sequencing, change of topic, idea development)

Printed in the United States
204607BV00003B/1-68/A

9 780471 405313

AFRICA

FOURTH EDITION

STAFF

Ian A. Nielsen	Publisher
Brenda S. Filley	Production Manager
Lisa M. Clyde	Developmental Editor
Charles Vitelli	Designer
Cheryl Nicholas	Permissions Coordinator
Lisa Holmes-Doebrick	Administrative Coordinator
Shawn Callahan	Graphics
Libra Ann Cusack	Typesetting Coordinator
Juliana Arbo	Typesetter
Diane Barker	Editorial Assistant

AFRICA

FOURTH EDITION

Dr. Jeff Ramsay

The Dushkin Publishing Group, Inc., Sluice Dock, Guilford, Connecticut 06437

BOOKS IN THE GLOBAL STUDIES SERIES

- • Africa
- • China
- • Latin America
- • The Soviet Union and Eastern Europe
- • The Middle East
- • Western Europe
- • Japan and the Pacific Rim

India and South Asia
Southeast Asia

• Currently available

Fourth Edition

Manufactured by The Banta Company, Harrisonburg, Virginia 22801

Library of Congress Catalog Number: 91-71258

ISBN: 1-56134-036-7

Africa

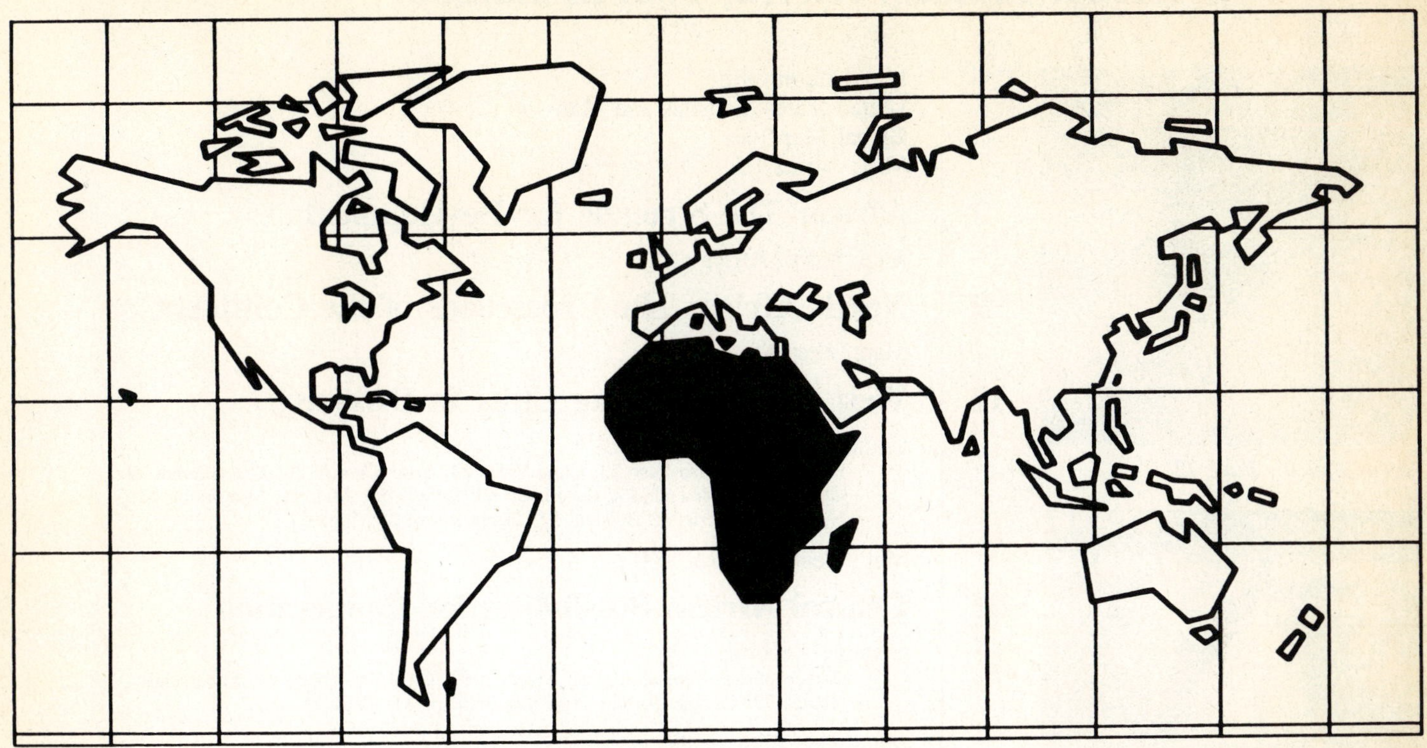

Dr. F. Jeffress Ramsay

Dr. F. Jeffress ("Jeff") Ramsay, the author/editor of *Global Studies: Africa, Fourth Edition,* obtained his Ph.D. in African history from Boston University and has worked closely with the Outreach Program at the African Studies Center, Boston University. He has had extensive experience as an academic and writer in the United States and Botswana, where he is currently resident. He was a Fulbright-Hays/Social Science Research Council Fellow (dual award) affiliated with the National Institute of Research, University of Botswana. Along with Fred Morton and Andrew Murray, he is the coauthor of *Historical Dictionary of Botswana, New Edition* (The Scarecrow Press, 1989), and collaborated with Morton on *The Birth of Botswana, A History of Bechuanaland Protectorate from 1910 to 1966* (Longman Botswana, 1987).

This revised and updated edition draws on essays and country reports written by Dr. Jane Martin, the author/editor for the first edition, and Dr. Jo Sullivan, the past director of the Outreach Program at the African Studies Center and the author/editor for the second and third editions.

SERIES CONSULTANT

H. Thomas Collins
PROJECT LINKS
George Washington University

Contents

Global Studies: Africa, Fourth Edition

North Africa Page 12

West Africa Page 18

Central Africa Page 63

East Africa Page 92

Southern Africa Page 134

Africa: Articles Section

GENERAL

WEST AFRICA

CENTRAL AFRICA

EAST AFRICA

SOUTHERN AFRICA

Introduction

THE GLOBAL AGE

As we approach the end of the twentieth century, it is clear that the future we face will be considerably more international in nature than ever believed possible in the past. Each day, print and broadcast journalists make us aware that our world is becoming increasingly smaller and substantially more interdependent.

The energy crisis, world food shortages, nuclear weaponry, and regional conflicts that threaten to involve us all—all make it clear that the distinctions between domestic and foreign problems are all too often artificial, that many seemingly domestic problems no longer stop at national boundaries. As Rene Dubos, the 1969 Pulitzer Prize recipient, stated: ". . . [I]t becomes obvious that each [of us] has two countries, [our] own and planet earth." As global interdependence has become a reality, it has become vital for the citizens of this world to develop literacy in global matters.

THE GLOBAL STUDIES SERIES

It is the aim of this Global Studies series to help readers acquire a basic knowledge and understanding of the regions and countries in the world. Each volume provides a foundation of information—geographic, cultural, economic, political, historical, artistic, and religious—which will allow readers better to understand the current and future problems within these countries and regions and to comprehend how events there might affect their own well-being. In short, these volumes attempt to provide the background information necessary to respond to the realities of our global age.

Author/Editor

Each of the volumes in the Global Studies series is crafted under the careful direction of an author/editor—an expert in the area under study. The author/editors teach and conduct research and have traveled extensively through the regions about which they are writing.

The author/editor for each volume has written the umbrella essay introducing the area. For the fourth edition of *Global Studies: Africa*, the author/editor has extensively revised and updated the regional essays and country reports. In addition, he has overseen the gathering of statistical information for each country and has been instrumental in the selection of the world press articles that appear at the end of the book.

Contents and Features

The Global Studies volumes are organized to provide concise information and current world press articles on the regions and countries within those areas under study.

Area and Regional Essays

Global Studies: Africa, Fourth Edition, covers North Africa, West Africa, Central Africa, East Africa, and Southern Africa. Each of these regions is discussed in a regional essay focusing on the geographical, cultural, sociopolitical and economic aspects of the countries and people of that area. The purpose of the regional essays is to provide the reader with an effective sense of the diversity of the area as well as an understanding of its common cultural and historical backgrounds. Accompanying each of the regional narratives is a full-page map showing the political boundaries of the countries within the region. In addition to these regional essays, the author/editor has also provided a narrative essay on the African continent as a whole. This area essay examines a number of broad themes in an attempt to define what constitutes "Africa."

A Special Note on the Regions of Africa

The countries of Africa do not fall into clear-cut regions. Many of the political divisions that exist today are the product of Africa's colonial heritage, and often they do not reflect cultural, religious, or historical connections. This has created tensions within nations, and it makes abstract divisions somewhat arbitrary. Nations that share geographical aspects with one group of countries may share a cultural history with a different group. The regional essays provide explanations for the way countries have been grouped in this volume. Readers may encounter different arrangements in other sources. The regional essays should be read carefully to understand why the author/editor chose the divisions made here.

North Africa

North Africa is a special case in relation to the rest of the African continent. Culturally, geopolitically, and economically, the Muslim countries of North Africa are often major players on the Middle Eastern stage as well as on the African scene. For this reason, we have included a regional essay for North Africa in this volume, but the individual country reports and the world press articles for that region appear as part of the expanded coverage of North Africa in *The Middle East* volume of the Global Studies series.

Country Reports

Concise reports on each of the regions with the exception of North Africa follow the regional essays. These reports are the heart of each Global Studies volume. *Global Studies: Africa, Fourth Edition*, contains 47 country reports.

The country reports are comprised of five standard elements. Each report contains a map which positions the country amongst its neighboring states; a summary of statistical information; a current essay providing important historical, geographical, political, cultural, and economic information; a historical timeline offering a convenient visual survey of some key historical events; and, at the end of each report, four graphic indicators with summary statements about the country in terms of development, freedom, health/welfare, and achievements.

A Note on the Statistical Summaries

The statistical information provided for each country has been drawn from a wide range of sources. The most frequently referenced are listed on page 240. Every effort has been made to provide the most current and accurate information available. However, occasionally the information cited by these sources differs significantly; and, all too often, the most current information available for some countries is quite dated. Aside from these difficulties, the statistical summary of each country is generally complete and reasonably current. Care should be taken, however, in using these statistics (or, for that matter, any published statistics) in making hard comparisons among countries.

World Press Articles

Within each Global Studies volume are reprinted a number of articles carefully selected by our editorial staff and the author/editor from a broad range of international periodicals and newspapers. The articles have been chosen for currency, interest, and the differing perspectives they give to a particular region. There are world press articles for each region, with the exception of North Africa. The article section is preceded by a topic guide. The purpose of this guide is to indicate the main theme(s) of the articles. Readers wishing to focus on a particular theme, say, religion, may refer to the topic guide to find those articles.

Spelling

In many instances, articles from foreign sources may use forms of spelling that are different from the American style. Many Third World publications reflect the European usage. In order to retain the flavor of the articles and to make the point that our system is not the only one, spellings have not been altered to conform with the U.S. system.

Glossary, Bibliography, Index

At the back of each Global Studies volume, readers will find a glossary of terms and abbreviations, which provides a quick reference to the specialized vocabulary of the area under study and to the standard abbreviations (IMF, OAU, ANC, etc.) used throughout the volume.

Following the glossary is a bibliography. The bibliography is organized into general-reference volumes, national and regional histories, novels in translation, current events publications, and periodicals that provide regular coverage on Africa.

The index at the end of the volume is an accurate reference to the contents of the volume. Readers seeking specific information and citations should consult this standard index.

Currency and Usefulness

This fourth edition of *Global Studies: Africa*, like other Global Studies volumes, is intended to provide the most current and useful information available necessary to understanding the events that are shaping the cultures of Africa today.

We plan to revise this volume on a continuing basis. The statistics will be updated, regional essays rewritten, country reports revised, and articles completely replaced as new and current information becomes available. In order to accomplish this task, we will turn to our author/editor, and—hopefully—to you, the users of this volume. Your comments are more than welcome. If you have an idea that you think will make the volume more useful, an article or bit of information that will make it more current, or a general comment on its organization, content, or features that you would like to share with us, please send it in for serious consideration for the next edition.

(Oxfam photo)

We must understand the hopes, problems, and cultures of the people of other nations in order to understand our own future.

United States of America

Comparing statistics on the various countries in this volume should not be done without recognizing that the figures are within the timeframe of our publishing date. Nevertheless, comparisons can and will be made, so to enable you to put the statistics of different countries into perspective, we have included comparable statistics on the United States. These statistics are drawn from the same sources that were consulted for developing the statistical information for each country report.

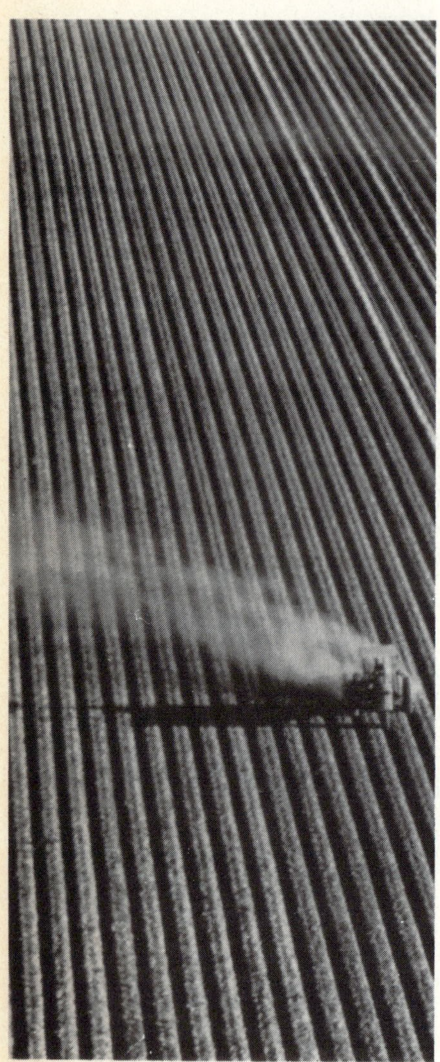

Documerica

The United States is unique. It has some of the most fertile land in the world, which, coupled with a high level of technology, allows the production of an abundance of food products—an abundance that makes possible the export of enormous quantities of basic foodstuffs to many other parts of the world. The use of this technology also permits the manufacture of goods and services that exceed what is possible in a majority of the rest of the world. In the United States are some of the most important urban centers in the world focusing on trade, investment, and commerce as well as art, music, and theater.

GEOGRAPHY

Area in Square Kilometers (Miles): 9,372,614 (3,540,939)
Capital (Population): Washington, DC (638,432)
Climate: temperate

PEOPLE

Population

Total: 255,000,000
Annual Growth Rate: 0.7%
Rural/Urban Population Ratio: 21/79
Ethnic Makeup of Population: 80% white; 11% black; 6.2% Spanish origin; 1.6% Asian and Pacific Islander; 0.7% American Indian, Eskimo, and Aleut

Health

Life Expectancy at Birth: 71.5 years (male); 78.5 years (female)
Infant Death Rate (Ratio): 8.9/1,000
Average Caloric Intake: 138% of FAO minimum
Physicians Available (Ratio): 1/520

Religion(s)

55% Protestant; 36% Roman Catholic; 4% Jewish; 5% others

Education

Adult Literacy Rate: 99.5% (official; estimates vary widely)

COMMUNICATION

Telephones: 182,558,000
Newspapers: 1,676 dailies; approximately 63,000,000 circulation

TRANSPORTATION

Highways—Kilometers (Miles): 6,208,552 (3,866,296); 5,466,612 (3,398,810) paved
Railroads—Kilometers (Miles): 270,312 (167,974)
Usable Airfields: 15,422

GOVERNMENT

Type: federal republic
Independence Date: July 4, 1776
Head of State: President George Bush
Political Parties: Democratic Party; Republican Party; others of minor political significance
Suffrage: universal at 18

MILITARY

Number of Armed Forces: 2,116,800
Military Expenditures (% of Central Government Expenditures): 29.1%
Current Hostilities: currently none

ECONOMY

Per Capita Income: $16,444
Gross National Product (GNP): $4.8 trillion
Inflation Rate: 5%
Natural Resources: metallic and nonmetallic minerals; petroleum; arable land
Agriculture: food grains; feed crops; oilbearing crops; cattle; dairy products
Industry: diversified in both capital- and consumer-goods industries

FOREIGN TRADE

Exports: $250.4 billion
Imports: $424.0 billion

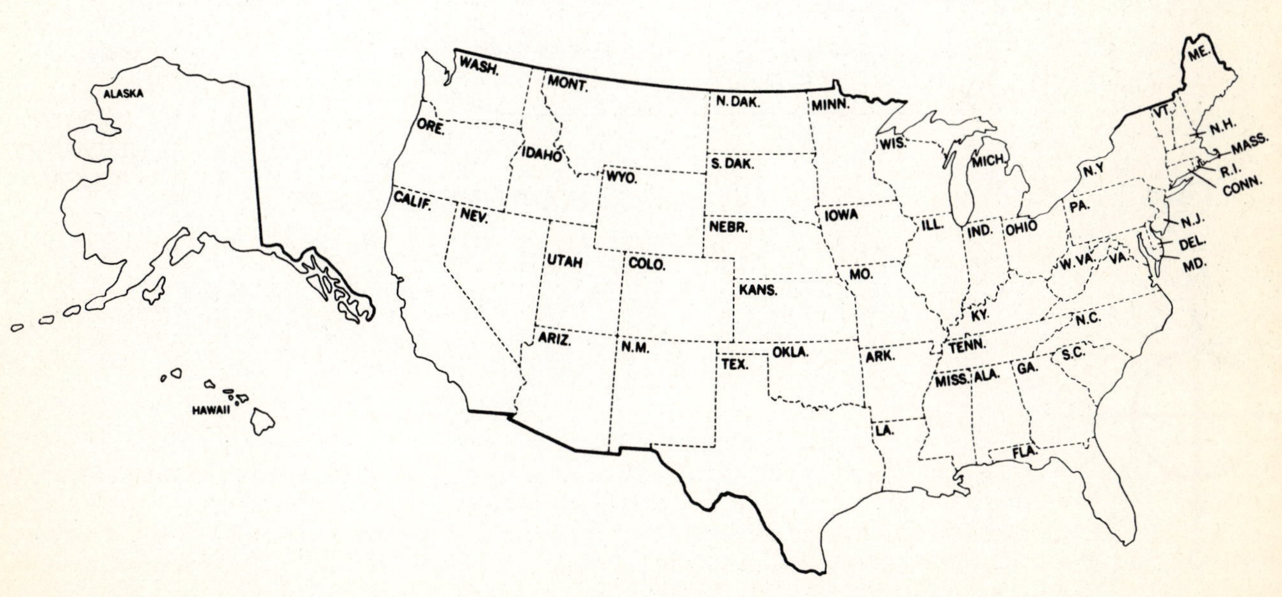

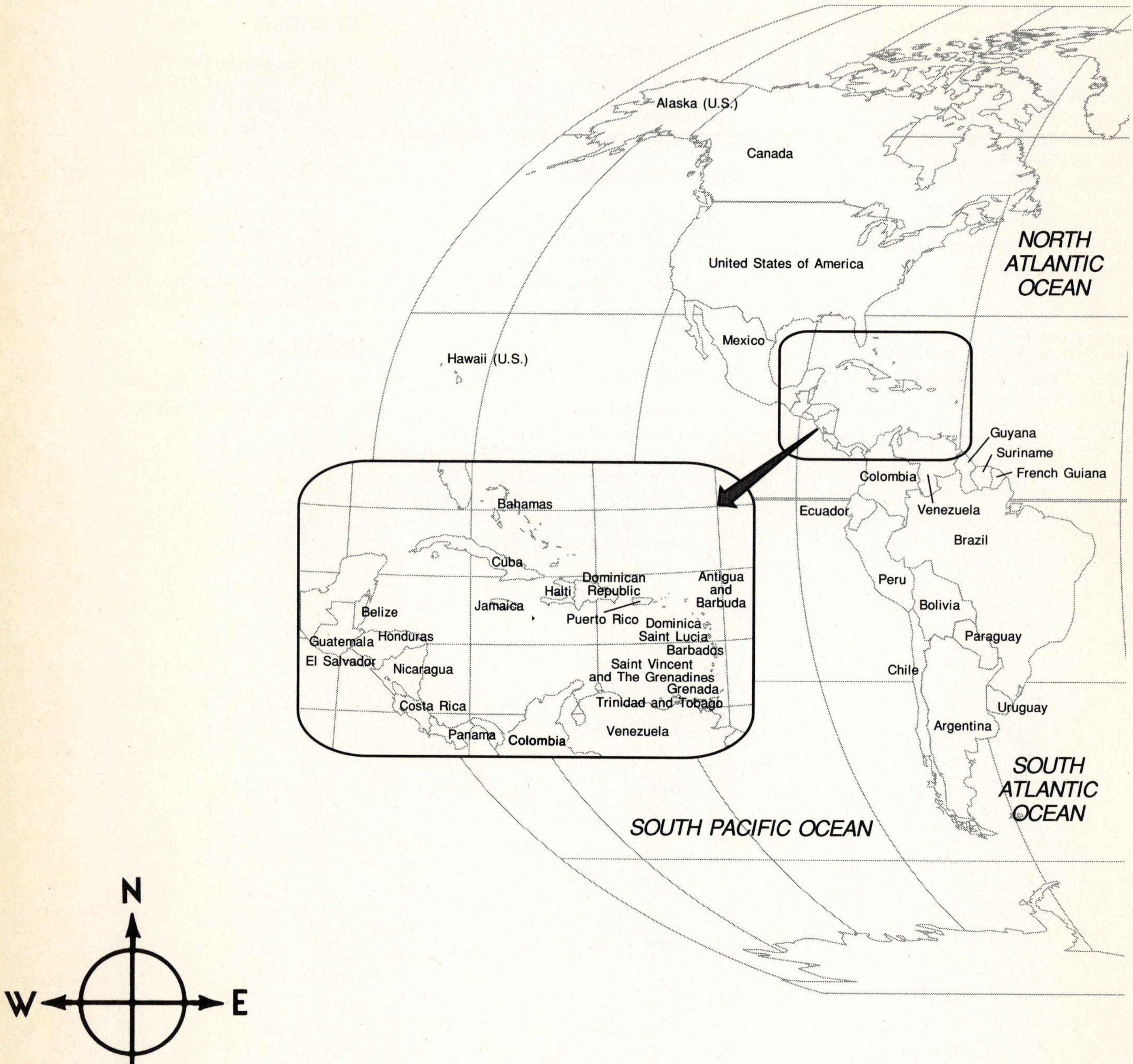

Alaska (U.S.)
Canada
United States of America
NORTH ATLANTIC OCEAN
Mexico
Hawaii (U.S.)
Guyana
Suriname
French Guiana
Colombia
Ecuador
Venezuela
Brazil
Peru
Bolivia
Paraguay
Chile
Uruguay
Argentina
SOUTH ATLANTIC OCEAN
SOUTH PACIFIC OCEAN

Bahamas
Cuba
Haiti
Dominican Republic
Antigua and Barbuda
Jamaica
Puerto Rico
Dominica
Saint Lucia
Barbados
Belize
Honduras
Guatemala
El Salvador
Nicaragua
Saint Vincent and The Grenadines
Grenada
Trinidad and Tobago
Costa Rica
Panama
Colombia
Venezuela

N
W
E
S

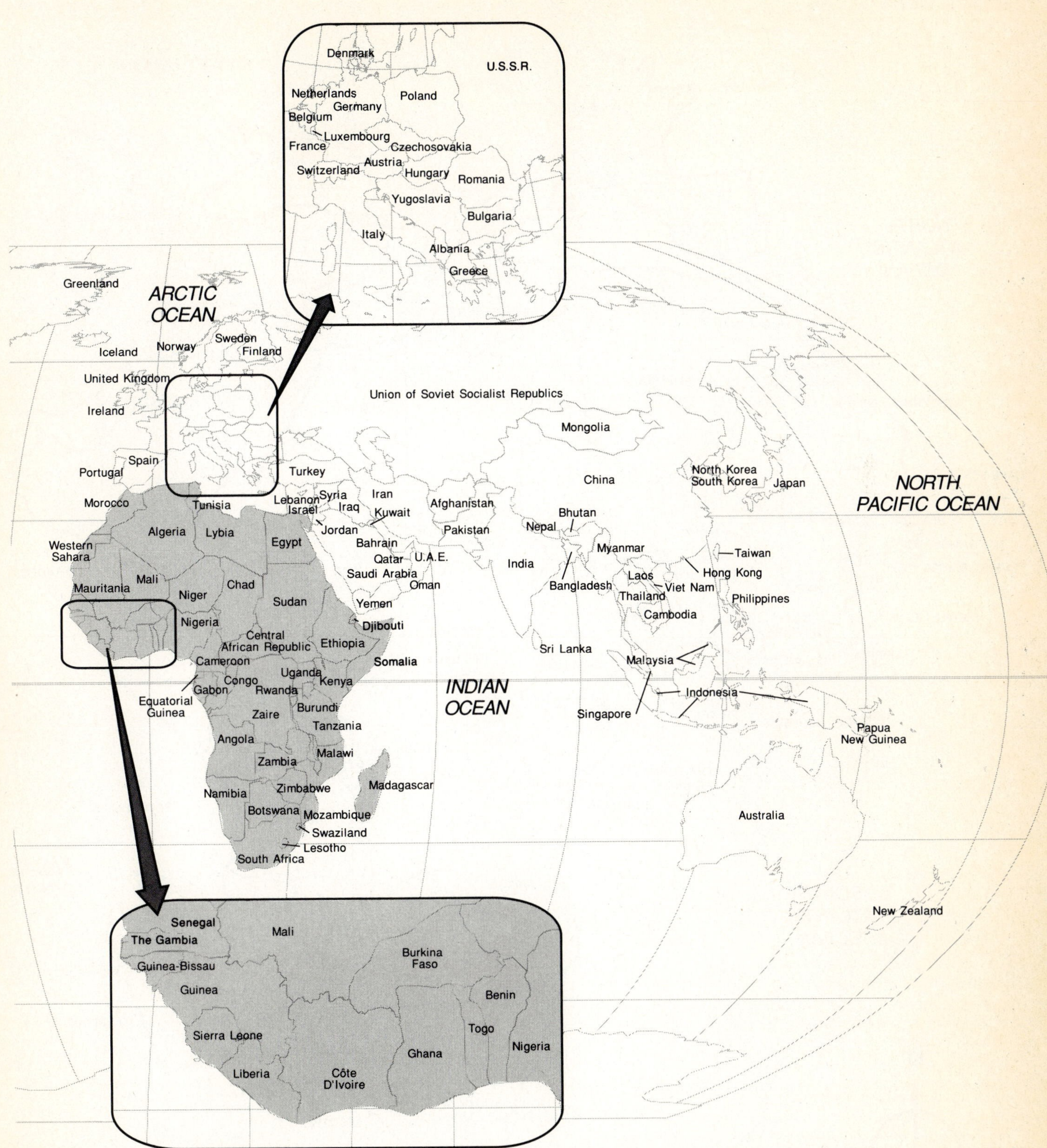

This map of the world highlights the nations of Africa that are discussed in this volume. Regional essays and country reports are written from a cultural perspective in order to give a frame of reference to the current events in that region. All of the essays are designed to present the most current and useful information available today. Other volumes in the Global Studies series cover different areas of the globe and examine the current state of affairs of the countries within those regions.

Africa

We have divided the nations of Africa into five regions (North, West, Central, East, and Southern) for an easier understanding of this diverse continent. See page viii for further discussion of the regions within Africa.

Africa: The Struggle for Development

Seventeen African nations gained their independence in 1960, liberating most of the continent from colonial rule. The times were electric. In country after country, the flags of the United Kingdom, Belgium, France, and the United Nations were replaced by the banners of new states, whose leaders offered idealistic promises to remake the continent—and thus the world. Hopes were high, and even the most ambitious of goals seemed obtainable. Africans and non-Africans alike spoke of the resource-rich continent as being on the verge of a developmental take-off. In the United States and elsewhere, some of the old, racist myths about Africa were at last being questioned.

Today, however, 3 decades after the great freedom year, conditions throughout Africa are sobering rather than euphoric. For most Africans, independence has been more of a desperate struggle for survival rather than an exhilarating path to development. Africa is often described in the global media as "a continent in crisis," "a region in turmoil," "on a precipice," and "suffering"—phrases that echo the sensationalist writings of nineteenth-century missionaries eager to convince others of the continent's need for salvation. Sadly, such modern headlines are more accurate than were the mission tracts of yesteryear. Today millions of Africans are indeed seeking some form of salvation from the grinding poverty, pestilence, and, in many areas, wars which afflict their lives. Perhaps this hunger is why contemporary African evangelists are so much more successful in swelling their congregations than were their brethren in the past. It is certainly not for lack of competition; Africa is a continent of many, often overlapping faiths. In addition to Islam and other spiritual paths, Africans have embraced a myriad of secular ideologies: Marxism, African Socialism, People's Capitalism, Structural Adjustment, Pan-Africanism, Authenticity, Nonracialism, the One-Party State, and the Multiparty State. The list seems endless but salvation ever more distant.

(World Bank photo by Pamela Johnson)

This is an electrical transformer at the Volta Aluminum Company in Tema, Ghana. Modern technology and new sources of power are among the factors spurring economic development.

Africa's current circumstances are indeed difficult, yet the past 30 years have brought progress as well as problems. The goals so optimistically pronounced at independence have, for the most part, not been abandoned. Even when states have faltered, the societies they encompass have remained dynamic and adaptable to shifting opportunities. The support of strong families continues to allow most Africans to overcome enormous adversity. Today there are starving children in Africa, but there are also many more in school uniforms studying to make their future dreams a reality.

A DIVERSE CONTINENT

Africa is a large continent. Indeed, Africa, which is almost four times the size of the United States (excluding Alaska), ranks just under Asia as the world's biggest continent. Well over one-quarter of the membership of the United Nations consists of African states, more than 50 in all. Such facts are worth repeating, for even well-educated outsiders often lose sight of Africa's continental scope when they discuss its problems and prospects.

Not only is the African continent vast but, according to archeologists, it was also the cradle of human civilization. It should therefore not be surprising that the 600 million or so contemporary Africans maintain extraordinarily diverse ways of life. They speak more than a thousand languages and live their lives according to a rich variety of household arrangements, kinship systems, and religious beliefs. The art and music styles of the continent are as varied as its people.

Given its diversity, it is not easy to generalize about Africa. For every statement, there is an exception. However, one aspect that is constant among all African societies is that they have always been changing, and in modern times doing so at an ever-increasing rate. Cities have grown and people have moved back and forth between village and town, giving rise to new social groups, institutions, occupations, religions, and forms of communication, which have made their mark in the countryside as well as in the urban centers. All Africans, whether they be urban computer programmers or hunter-gatherers living in the remote corners of the Kalahari, have taken on new practices, interests, and burdens; yet, they have maintained their African identity. Uniquely African institutions, values, and histories underlie contemporary lifestyles throughout the continent.

Memories of past civilizations are a source of pride and community. The medieval Mali and Ghana empires, the glory of Pharaonic Egypt, the Fulani caliphate of northern Nigeria, the knights of Kanem and Bornu, the great Zimbabwe, and the kingdom of the Kongo, among others, are all remembered. The past is connected to the present through the generations and by ties to the land. In a continent where the majority of peoples are still farmers, land remains "the mother that never dies." It is valued for its fruits and because it is the place to which the ancestors came and were buried.

The art of personal relationships continues to be important. Typically, people live in large families. Children are considered precious, and large families are still desired for social as well as economic reasons. Elders are an important part of a household; nursing homes and retirement communities generally do not exist. People are not supposed to be loners. "I am because we are" remains a valued precept. In this age of nation-states the "we" may refer to one's ethnic community, while obligations to one's extended family often take precedence over other loyalties.

Most Africans, like the majority of Americans or Asians, believe in a spiritual as well as a material world. The African continent contains a rich variety of indigenous belief systems which often coexist with the larger religions of Islam and various Christian sects. Many families believe that their lives are influenced by their ancestors. Africans from all walks of life will seek the services of professional "traditional" healers to explain an illness or suggest remedies for such things as sterility or bad fortune. But this common pattern of behavior does not preclude one from turning to scientific medicine; all African governments face strong popular demand for better access to modern health facilities.

Islam has long been a strong force in Africa. Today the religion rivals Christianity as the fastest-growing faith on the continent. The followers of both religions often accommodate their faiths to local traditions and values. People may also join new religious movements and churches, such as the Brotherhood of the Cross and Star in Nigeria or the Church of Simon Kimbangu in Zaire, that link Christian and indigenous beliefs with new ideas and rituals. As do other institutions in the towns and cities, the churches and mosques provide their followers with social networks.

Like local religion, local art often reflects the interactions of a changing world. An airplane is featured on a Nigerian gelede mask, the Apollo space mission inspires a Burkinabe carver, and an Ndebele dance wand is a beaded electric pole.

THE TROUBLED PRESENT

Some of the crises in Africa today threaten its peoples' traditional resiliency. The facts are grim: in material terms, the average African is poorer today than at independence, and it is predicted that poverty will only increase in the near future. In the 1980s widespread famine occurred in 22 African nations, with 4 countries still suffering from chronic famine and at least 15 others in need of outside aid. Drought conditions have led to food shortages in every African region. The Food and Agricultural Organization (FAO) of the United Nations estimated that 70 percent of all Africans did not have enough to eat in the mid-1980s. An outpouring of assistance and relief efforts, at the time, saved as many as 35 million lives. And although agricultural output rose in most areas during the late 1980s, insufficient food promises to be a long-term crisis. In many areas, marginal advances in agricultural production, through better incentives to farmers, have been counterbalanced by declining commodity prices on world markets, population growth, and infestations of insects. Problems of climate irregularity, transport, obtaining needed inputs, and storage require continued assistance and long-range planning.

Wood, the average person's source of energy, grows scarcer every year; most governments have had to contend with the rising cost of imported fuels. Meanwhile, diseases that were once believed to have been conquered have reappeared: rinderpest has been discovered among cattle and cholera has been found among populations where they have not been seen for generations. The spread of acquired immune deficiency syndrome (AIDS) also threatens lives and long-term productivity.

Armed conflicts have devastated portions of Africa. The current travails of Angola, Ethiopia, Liberia, Mozambique, Somalia, and the Sudan, due to internal strife encouraged to greater or lesser degrees by outside forces, place them in a distinct class of suffering—a class that until recently also included Chad and Uganda. More than a million people have died in these countries during the past 5 years, while millions more have become refugees. Except for scattered enclaves, normal economic activities have been greatly disrupted or have ceased altogether.

Almost all African governments are in debt (as is, it should be noted, the United States). The entire debt of African countries is more than $250 billion. It is smaller in its absolute amount than that of Latin America, but as a percentage of its economic output, the continent's debt is the highest in the world and is rising swiftly. The industrial output of all but a few African countries is lower than that of most other nations of the world. While the majority of Africans are engaged in food production, not enough food is produced in most countries to feed their citizens. The decline of many commodity prices on the world market has reduced national incomes. As a result, the foreign exchange needed to import food, machinery, fuel, and other goods is very limited in most African countries. Excluding South Africa, the continent's economy in 1987 grew by only 0.8 percent, far below its population growth rate. In the same year cereal production declined 8 percent and overall agricultural production grew by only 0.5 percent.

In order to obtain money to meet debts and pay for their running expenses, many African governments have been obliged to accept the stringent terms of global lending agencies, most notably the World Bank and the International Monetary Fund (IMF). These terms have led to great popular hardship, especially in the urban areas, through austerity measures such as the abandonment of price controls on basic foodstuffs and the freezing of wages. African governments and some other observers are questioning both the justice and practicality of these terms: in 1986, for example, 16 African countries transferred 350 percent more money to the IMF than they received from it in 1985.

THE EVOLUTION OF AFRICA'S ECONOMIES

Africa has seldom been rich, although it has vast potential resources and some rulers and elites have become very wealthy. In earlier centuries the slave trade contributed to limiting African material expansion in many regions. During the era of European exploration and colonialism, African involvement in the world economy greatly increased. Policies and practices developed that continue to be of mixed benefit to Africans.

During the 70 or so years of European colonial rule throughout most of Africa, the nations' economies were shaped to the advantage of the imperialists. Cash crops such as cocoa, coffee, and rubber began to be grown for the European market. Some African farmers benefited from these crops, but the cash-crop economy also involved large foreign-run plantations. It also encouraged the trends toward use of migrant labor and the decline in food production. Many people became dependent for their livelihoods on the forces of the world market, which, like the weather, were beyond their immediate control.

Mining also increased during colonial times—again for the benefit of the colonial rulers. The ores were extracted from African soil by European companies. African labor was employed, but the machinery came from abroad. The copper, diamonds, gold, iron ore, and uranium were shipped overseas to be processed and marketed in the Western economies. Upon independence African governments received a varying percentage of the take through taxation and consortium agreements. But mining remained an "enclave" industry, sometimes described as "a state within a state" because such industries were run by outsiders who established communities that used imported machinery and technicians and exported the products to industrialized countries.

Inflationary conditions in other parts of the world have had myriad adverse effects. Today the raw materials that Africans produce often receive low prices on the world market, while the manufactured goods that African countries import are expensive. Local African industries lack spare parts and machinery, and farmers frequently cannot afford to transport crops to market. As a result, the whole economy slows down. Thus, Africa, because of the policies of former colonial powers and current independent governments, is tied into the world economy in ways that do not always serve its best interests.

THE PROBLEMS OF GOVERNMENT

Outside forces are not the only cause of Africa's current crises. In general, Africa is a misgoverned continent. During the past 30 years the idealism that has characterized various nationalist movements, with their promises of popular self-determination, have given way in most states to cynical authoritarian regimes. In 1989 only Botswana, Mauritius, soon-to-be-independent Namibia, and arguably The Gambia and Senegal could reasonably claim that their governments were elected in genuinely free and fair elections.

The government of Robert Mugabe in Zimbabwe undoubtedly enjoyed majority support, but political life in that state has been seriously marred by violence and intimidation aimed mostly at the opposition. Past multiparty contests in the North African nations of Egypt, Morocco, and Tunisia, as well as West Africa's Liberia, were manipulated to assure that the ruling establishments would remain unchallenged. Elsewhere the continent was divided between military and/or one-party regimes, which often combined the seemingly contradictory characteristics of weakness and absolutism at the top. While a few of the single-party states, most notably Tanzania, have offered people genuine—if limited—choices of leadership, most have been, to a greater or lesser degree, simply vehicles of personal rule.

Just as 1989 was a year of democratic upheaval in Europe, so too has 1990 been a year of unparalleled democratic reawakening in Africa, which has toppled the political status quo in a few areas and threatened its survival in many more. Single-party monopolies of power have been replaced by multiparty systems in Algeria and the island nations of Cape Verde, Comoros, and São Tomé and Príncipe. There has also been significant movement toward reform in a dozen or other countries, but it is too early to know if truly democratic systems of government will ultimately prevail.

Events have most closely paralleled the changes of Eastern Europe in Benin. There the self-proclaimed, military-based, Marxist-Leninist regime of Mathieu Kérékou was pressured into relinquishing power to a transitional civilian government made up of technocrats and former dissidents. Television broadcasts of this "civilian coup" have enjoyed large audiences in neighboring countries. In several other countries, such as the Côte d'Ivoire, Gabon, Somalia, and Zaire, mounting opposition has resulted in promises of free elections by long-ruling autocrats. But there remains deep skepticism as to whether these pledges will be fulfilled, especially since human-rights abuses have continued.

With a handful of exceptions, such as Malawi, where the police state continues to assure public silence, all of the single-party states are experiencing some form of public debate over the merits of a transition to a multiparty system. In places like the Congo and Tanzania, well-entrenched ruling orders have so far largely confined the issue to party organs. Elsewhere, prodemocracy agitators have taken to the streets. Protesters in Zambia have forced the government to put the issue to a public referendum, although how this concession will be implemented remains to be seen. The Kenyan government, however, has steadfastly refused to give any ground and has met mounting opposition with increased repression.

Military regimes have not been immune to the winds of change sweeping the continent. In Nigeria, Africa's most populous country, General Ibrahim Babangida has long been committed to a transition back to civilian control. His

(Oxfam photo)

"There is no wealth where there are no children" is an African saying.

administration's hope to move the nation smoothly to a guided democracy in which only two government-created, and -defined, parties will be allowed to compete for power remains on target, but rising dissent and a recent coup attempt have called the process into question.

Why have most postcolonial African governments taken autocratic forms? And why is this fact being so widely challenged now? There are no definitive answers to either of these questions. One common explanation for authoritarianism in Africa has been the weakness of the states themselves. Most African governments face the difficult task of maintaining national unity with diverse, ethnically divided citizenries. Although the states of Africa may overlay and overlap historic kingdoms, most are products of colonialism. Their boundaries were fashioned during the late-nineteenth-century European partition of the continent, which divided and joined ethnic groups by lines drawn in Europe. The successful leaders of African independence movements worked within the colonial boundaries, and when they joined together in the Organization of African Unity (OAU), they agreed to respect the territorial status quo.

While the need to stem interethnic and regional conflict has been one justification for placing limits on popular self-determination, another explanation can be found in the administrative systems that the nationalist leaderships inherited. All of the European colonies in Africa functioned as police states. Not only were various forms of opposition curtailed, but relatively intrusive security establishments were created to watch over and control the indigenous populations. Although headed by Europeans, most colonial security services employed local staff members who were prepared to assume leadership roles at independence. A wave of military coups swept across West Africa during the 1960s; elsewhere, aspiring dictators like Hastings Kamazu Banda in Malawi were quick to appreciate the value of the inherited instruments of control.

Africa's economic difficulties have also frequently been cited as contributing to its political underdevelopment. On the one hand, Nigeria's last civilian government, for example, was certainly undermined in part by the economic crisis that engulfed it due to falling oil revenues. On the other hand, in a pattern reminiscent of recent changes in Latin America, current economic difficulties resulting in high rates of inflation and indebtedness seem to be tempting some African militaries, such as Benin's, to retreat to the barracks and allow civilian politicians to assume responsibility for the implementation of inevitably harsh austerity programs.

External powers have long sustained African dictatorships, through grants of military and economic aid and, on occasion, direct intervention. For example, a local attempt to restore constitutional rule in Gabon, in 1964, was thwarted by French paratroopers, while Sese Seko Mobutu's kleptocratic hold over Zaire has from the very beginning relied on overt and covert assistance from the United States and other Western states. The Soviet Bloc and China have in the past also helped to support their share of unsavory

African allies, in places like Ethiopia, Equatorial Guinea, and Burundi.

There are signs that the end of the Cold War may lead to a reduced desire on the part of outsiders to continue to maintain their unpopular African allies. At the same time, the major international lending agencies have increasingly concerned themselves with the perceived need to adjust the political as well as economic structures of debtor nations. This new emphasis is justified in part by the alleged linkage between political unaccountability and economic corruption and mismanagement.

The on-going decline of socialism on the continent is also having a significant political effect. Some regimes have professed a Marxist orientation, while others have believed that a special African Socialism could be built on the communal and cooperative traditions of their societies. In countries such as Guinea-Bissau and Mozambique, a revolutionary socialist orientation was introduced at the grass-roots level during the struggles for independence, within areas liberated from colonialism. The various socialist governments have not been free from personality cults, nor from corruption and oppressive measures. Yet many governments that have eschewed the socialist label have, nonetheless, developed public corporations and central-planning methods, similar to those that openly professed Marxism. In recent years virtually all of Africa's governments, partly in line with IMF and World Bank requirements but also because of the inefficiency and losses of many of their public corporations, have placed greater emphasis on private-sector development.

REASONS FOR OPTIMISM

Although the problems facing African countries have grown since independence, so have their achievements. The number of persons who can read and write in local languages as well as English, French, or Portuguese has increased enormously. More people can peruse newspapers, follow instructions for fertilizers, and read the labels on medicine bottles. Professionals trained in modern technology who, for example, plan electrification schemes, organize large office staffs, and develop medical facilities are more available because of the many African universities that have developed in the past 3 decades. Health care has also expanded and improved in most areas. Outside of the areas that have been ravaged by war, life expectancy has generally increased and infant-mortality rates have declined.

Despite the terrible wars that are being waged in a few nations, mostly in the form of civil wars, postcolonial African governments have been notably successful in avoiding armed conflict with one another. The principal exception to this rule has been the apartheid regime in South Africa, which has launched numerous acts of aggression against neighboring Southern African states. Even here, however, there is reason for hope that the South African government's recent withdrawal from Namibia and opening of a dialogue with its internal opponents will bring its campaign of regional destabilization to a lasting end.

Another positive development is the increasing attention that African governments and intra-African agencies are giving to women. The pivotal role of women in agriculture and other activities is being recognized and supported. In many countries, prenatal care and hospital care for mothers and their babies have increased, conditions for women workers in factories have improved, and new cooperatives for women's activities have been developed. Women have also played an increasingly prominent role in the political life of many countries.

The advances that have been made in Africa are important ones, but they could be undercut by continued economic decline. Africa needs debt relief and outside aid simply to maintain the gains that have been made. Yet as the African proverb observes, "someone else's legs will do you no good in traveling." African-conceived and -implemented measures will be vital.

Africa, as the individual country reports in this volume reveal, is a continent of many and varied resources. There are mineral riches and a vast agricultural potential. However, the continent's people, the youths who make up more than half of the population and the elders whose wisdom is revered, are its greatest resource. The rest of the world, which has benefited from the continent's material resources, can also learn from the social strengths of African families and communities.

North Africa

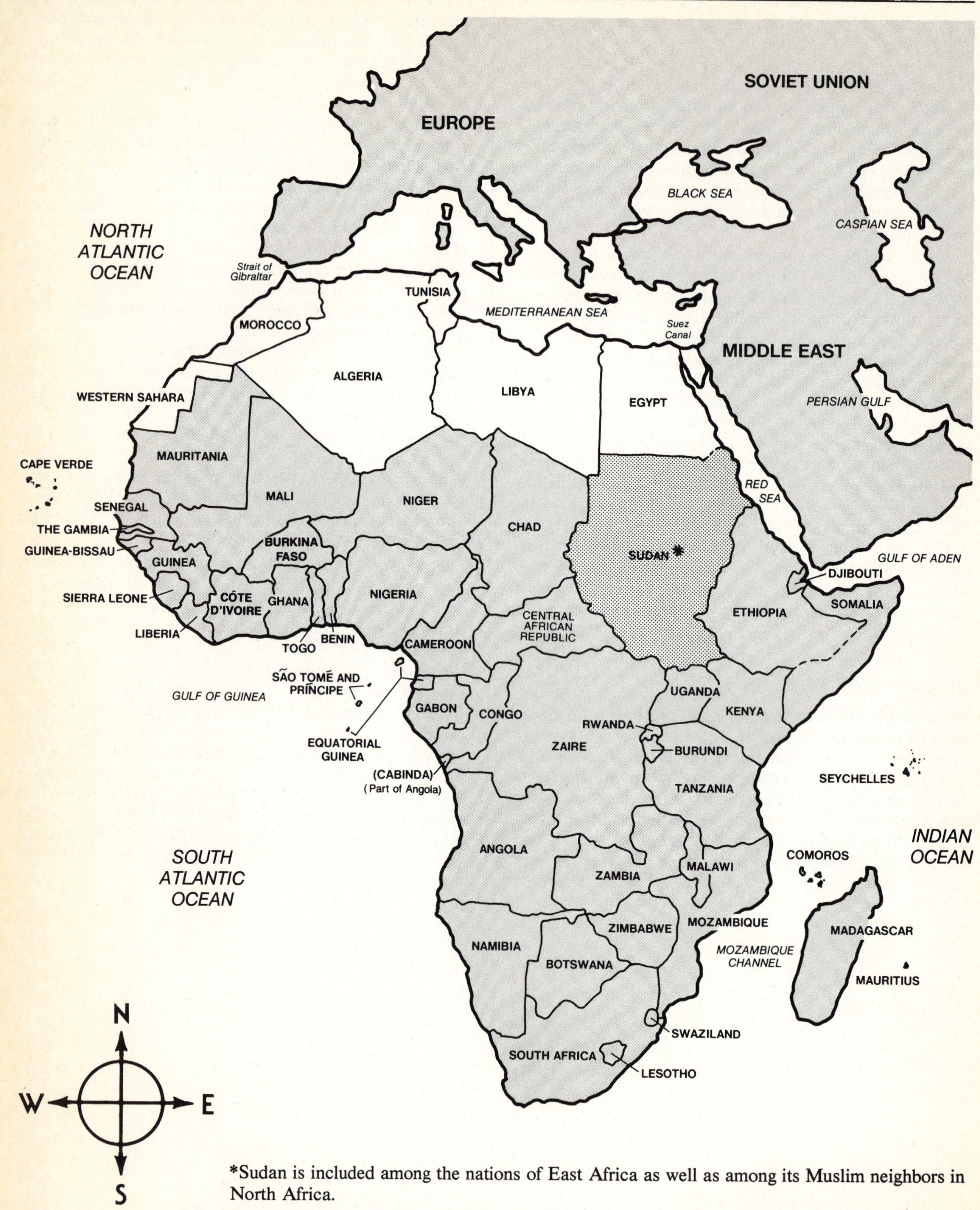

*Sudan is included among the nations of East Africa as well as among its Muslim neighbors in North Africa.

North Africa: The Crossroads of the Continent

Located at the geographical and cultural crossroads between Europe, Asia, and the rest of Africa, since ancient times North Africa has served as a link between the civilizations of sub-Saharan Africa and the rest of the world. Traders historically carried the continent's products northward, either across the Sahara or up the Nile River and Red Sea, to the great port cities of the region's Mediterranean coast. Goods flowed southward as well.

The trade networks also carried ideas. From coastal North Africa, Islam spread across much of the rest of the continent to become the religion of at least one out of three Africans.

North Africa's role as the continent's principal window to the world gradually declined after 1500 A.D., as trans-Atlantic trade increased (the history of East Africa's participation in Indian Ocean trade goes back much further). However, the countries of North Africa have continued to play an important role in the greater continent's development.

The countries of North Africa—Morocco, Algeria, Tunisia, Libya, and Egypt—and their millions of people differ from one another, but they share a predominant, overarching Arab-Islamic culture that both distinguishes them from the rest of Africa and unites them with the Arabic-speaking nations of the Middle (or Near) East.

To understand the societies of North Africa and their role in the rest of the continent, it is helpful to examine the area's geography. The region's diverse environment has long encouraged its inhabitants to engage in a broad variety of economic activities: pastoralism, agriculture, trading, crafts, and later, industries.

GEOGRAPHY AND POPULATION

Except for Tunisia, which is relatively small, the countries of North Africa are sprawling nations. Algeria, Libya, and Egypt are among the biggest countries on the continent, and Morocco is not far behind. Their sizes can be misleading, however, for much of their territories are encompassed by the largely barren Sahara Desert.

The populations of the five states today range from Egypt's 55 million people to Libya's 4 million; Morocco has 25 million, Algeria 23 million, and Tunisia 8 million citizens. All of these figures are increasing at a rapid rate; indeed, well over half of the region's citizens are under age 21.

Due to its scarcity, water is the region's most precious resource. Because of this, most people live either in valleys near the Mediterranean coast or along the Nile River. The Nile courses through the desert for thousands of miles, creating a narrow green ribbon, which is the home of 95 percent of Egypt's population who live within 12 miles of its banks. More than 90 percent of the people of Algeria, Libya, Morocco, and Tunisia live within 200 miles of either the Mediterranean (and, in the case of Morocco, the Atlantic coast as well).

Besides determining where people live, the temperate, if

(United Nations photo)

Land has been less of a barrier to regional cohesiveness in North Africa than have politics and ideology.

often too dry, climate of North Africa has always influenced local economies and lifestyles. There is intensive agriculture along the coasts and rivers. Algeria, Morocco, and Tunisia are well known for their tree and vine crops, notably citrus fruits, olives, and wine grapes. The intensively irrigated Nile Valley has, since the time of the American Civil War—which temporarily removed U.S.-produced fiber from the world market—been a leading source of high-quality cotton, as well as locally consumed foodstuffs. In the oases that dot the Sahara Desert, date palms are grown for their sweet fruits, which are almost a regional staple. Throughout the steppelands, between the fertile coasts and the desert, pastoralists follow flocks of sheep and goats or herds of cattle and camels in constant search of pasture. It was such nomads who, in the past, developed the trans-Saharan trade. As paved roads and airports have replaced their caravan routes, long-distance nomadism has declined. But the traditions the lifestyle bred, including a love of independence, remain an important part of North Africa's cultural heritage.

(United Nations photo by Y. Nagata)

Oil and gas discoveries in North Africa produced wide-ranging economic effects.

Urban culture has flourished in North Africa since the ancient times of the Egyptian pharaohs and the mercantilist rulers of Carthage. Supported by trade and local industries, the region's medieval cities, such as Cairo, Fez, and Kairouan, were the administrative centers of great Islamic empires whose civilizations shined during Europe's dark ages. In the modern era, the urban areas have remained bustling industrial centers, ports, and political capitals.

Geography—or, more precisely, geology—has helped to fuel economic growth in recent decades. Although agriculture continues to provide employment in Algeria and Libya for as much as a third of each country's labor force, discoveries of oil and natural gas in the 1950s dramatically altered these two nations' economic structures. Between 1960 and 1980 Libya's annual per capita income jumped from \$50 to almost \$10,000, transforming it from among the poorest to among the richest countries in the world. Although less dramatically than Libya, Algeria has also greatly benefited from the exploitation of hydrocarbons. Egypt and Tunisia have developed much smaller oil industries which, nonetheless, provide for their domestic energy needs and generate much-needed foreign exchange. While it has no oil, Morocco profits from its possession of much of the world's phosphate production. The decline in oil prices during the 1980s reduced revenues, increased unemployment, and contributed to unrest, especially in Algeria. The effects on oil revenues of the Iraqi invasion of Kuwait cannot yet be predicted for the long term.

CULTURAL AND POLITICAL HERITAGES

The vast majority of the inhabitants of North Africa are Arabic-speaking Muslims. Islam and Arabic both became established in the region between the sixth and eleventh centuries. Thus, by the time of the Crusades in the eastern Mediterranean, the societies of North Africa were thoroughly incorporated into the Muslim world even though the area had earlier been the home of many early Christian scholars, such as St. Augustine. Except for Egypt, where about 6 percent of the population remain loyal to the Coptic Church, there is virtually no Christianity among modern North Africans. Until recently, important Jewish communities have existed in all of the region's countries, but their numbers have dwindled, due to mass immigration to Israel.

With Islam came Arabic, the language of the Koran. Today Egypt and Libya are almost exclusively Arabic speaking. In Algeria, Morocco, and Tunisia, Arabic coexists with various local minority languages, which are collectively known as Berber (from which the term "Barbary" was derived). As many as a third of Moroccans speak a form of Berber as their first language. Centuries of interaction between the Arabs and Berbers, as well as their common adherence to Islam, have promoted a sense of cultural unity between the two communities, although ethnic disputes have developed in Algeria and Morocco over demands that Berber be included in local school curricula. As is the case almost everywhere else on the continent, the linguistic situation in North Africa was further complicated by the introduction of

European languages during the colonial era. Today French is particularly important as a language of technology and administration in Algeria, Morocco, and Tunisia.

At the beginning of the nineteenth century all of the countries of North Africa except Morocco were autonomous provinces of the Ottoman Empire, which was based in present-day Turkey and also incorporated most of the Middle East. Morocco was an independent state; indeed, it was one of the earliest to recognize the independence of the United States from England. From 1830 the European powers gradually encroached upon the Ottoman's North African realm. Thus, like most of their sub-Saharan counterparts, all of the states of North Africa fell under European imperial control. Algeria's conquest by the French began in 1830, but due to fierce local resistance, it took decades to accomplish. France also seized Tunisia in 1881 and, along with Spain, partitioned Morocco in 1912. Britain occupied Egypt in 1882. Italy invaded Libya in 1911, although anti-Italian resistance continued until World War II, when the area was liberated by Allied troops.

The differing natures of their European occupations have influenced the political and social characters of each of the North African states. Algeria, which was directly incorporated into France as a province for 120 years, did not win its independence until 1962, after a protracted and violent revolution. Morocco, by contrast, was accorded independence in 1956 after only 44 years of Franco-Spanish administration, during which period the local monarchy continued to reign. Tunisia's 75 years of French rule also ended in 1956, as a strong nationalist party took the reins of power. Egypt, although formally independent of Britain, did not win genuine self-determination until 1952, when a group of nationalist army officers came to power by overthrowing the British-supported monarchy. Libya became a temporary ward of the United Nations after Italy was deprived of its colonial empire during World War II. The nation was granted independence by the new world body in 1951, under a monarch whose religious followers had led much of the anti-Italian resistance.

NATIONAL POLITICS

Egypt

Egypt reemerged as an important actor in the world stage soon after Gamal Abdel Nasser came to power in the aftermath of the overthrow of the monarchy. One of the major figures in the post-World War II Non-Aligned Movement, Nasser gave voice to the aspirations of millions in the Arab world and Africa, through his championing of pan-Arab and pan-African anti-imperialist sentiments.

Faced with the problems of a burgeoning population at home and his nation's limited natural resources, Nasser nonetheless refused to let his government become dependent on a single foreign power. Domestically, he adopted a policy of developmental socialism. Because of mounting debts, which were spurred by enormous military spending, and increasing economic problems, many Egyptians had already begun to reassess some aspects of Nasser's policies by the time of his death in 1970. His successor, Anwar al-Sadat, reopened Egypt to foreign investment in hopes of attracting much-needed capital and technology. In 1979 Sadat also drew Egypt closer to the United States by signing the Camp David Accords, which ended more than 3 decades of war with Israel. Egypt has since been one of the largest recipients of American economic and military aid.

Sadat's increasingly authoritarian rule, as well as his abandonment of socialism and foreign policy initiatives, made him a target of domestic discontent. In 1981 he was assassinated. His successor, Hosni Mubarak, has since modestly liberalized Egyptian politics and pursued what are essentially moderate internal and external policies. While maintaining peace with Israel, Mubarak has succeeded in

(United Nations photo by Y. Nagata)

The Egyptian president, Hosni Mubarak, continues the legacy of his predecessor, Anwar al-Sadat.

reconciling Egypt with other Arab countries, which had strongly objected to the Camp David Agreement. In 1990 he took a leading role among the majority of Arab leaders opposed to Iraq's seizure of Kuwait. However, rapid urbanization, declining per capita revenues, debt, and unemployment—all linked to explosive population growth—have continued to strain the Egyptian economy and fuel popular discontent.

Libya

For years Libya was ruled by a pious, autocratic king whose domestic legitimacy was always in question. After 1963 the nation came under the heavy influence of foreign oil companies, which discovered and produced the country's only substantial resource. In 1969 members of the military, led by Colonel Muammar al-Qadhafi, overthrew the monarchy. Believed to be about age 27 at the time of the coup, Qadhafi was an ardent admirer of Nasser's vision of pan-Arab nationalism and anti-imperialism.

Qadhafi invested billions of dollars, earned from oil, in ambitious domestic-development projects, successfully ensuring universal health care, housing, and education for his people by the end of the 1970s. He spent billions more on military equipment and aid to what he deemed nationalist movements throughout the world. Considered a maverick, he has come into conflict with many of his fellow African and Arab rulers, as well as with outside powers like the

(United Nations photo by Bill Graham)

Nomadic traditions including loyalty to family and love of independence are still important to the cultural inheritance of North Africa.

United States. Despite Qadhafi's persistent efforts to forge regional alliances, political differences and the expulsion of expatriate workers, due to declining oil revenues, have increased tensions between Libya and its neighbors, as well as among the country's own military and middle class.

Strained relations between Libya and the United States over Qadhafi's activist foreign policy and support for international terrorists culminated in a U.S. air raid on the Libyan capital of Tripoli in 1986. The United States has also required American businesses and citizens to leave Libya and has sought other ways to undermine Qadhafi's ambitions. With the support of the United States and other powers, the Hissène Habré government of Chad was able to expel the Libyan military from its northern provinces in 1987.

Tunisia

Although having the fewest natural resources of the North African countries, Tunisia enjoyed a high degree of political stability and economic development during the 3 decades that immediately followed the restoration of its independence in 1956. Habib Bourguiba, leader of the nationalist party, the Neo-Destour, led the country to independence while retaining cordial economic and political ties with France and other Western countries. Bourguiba's government was a model of pragmatic approaches to both economic growth and foreign policy. A mixed economy was developed, and education's contribution to development was emphasized. The nation's Mediterranean coast was transformed into a vacation spot for European tourists.

However, in the 1980s, amidst economic recession and after 30 years of single-party rule, Tunisians became increasingly impatient with their aging leader's refusal to recognize opposition political parties. Strikes, demonstrations, and opposition from Muslim fundamentalists, as well as underground secular movements, were the context for Bourguiba's forced retirement in 1987. He was succeeded by his prime minister, Zine al-Abidine ben Ali, whose efforts in 1988 to release jailed Muslim activists and to open political dialogue led to a period of optimism and widespread support. By the middle of that year he had replaced most of the Cabinet ministers who had served under Bourguiba. But while multiparty elections were held in 1989, they were marred by opposition charges of fraud. There is growing unemployment among Tunisia's youthful, rapidly expanding, population.

Algeria

Algeria, wracked by the long and destructive revolution that preceded independence in 1962, has been ruled by a coalition of military and civilian leaders who rose to power as revolutionary partisans of the National Liberation Front (FNL) during the war. Although FNL leaders have differed over what policies and programs to emphasize, in the past they were able to forge a governing consensus in favor of secularism (but with respect for Islam's special status), a socialist domestic economy, and a foreign policy based on nonalignment. The country's substantial oil and gas revenues were invested in large-scale industrial projects, which were carried out by the state sector. But by the end of the 1970s serious declines in agricultural productivity and growing urban unemployment, partially due to the country's high overall rate of population growth, had sent hundreds of thousands of Algerian workers to France in search of jobs. In 1988 rising bread prices led to severe rioting, which left more than 100 people dead.

In the aftermath of the 1988 unrest, the FNL's long period of one-party rule appears to be coming to a close. The government has legalized opposition parties. In local elections held in 1990, the Islamic Salvation Front, a coalition group of Muslim fundamentalists, triumphed, possibly presaging a future political realignment at the national level. Meanwhile, increased encouragement is now being given to private-sector development.

Internationally, Algeria has been known for its troubleshooting role in difficult diplomatic negotiations. In 1980 it mediated the release of the U.S. hostages held in Iran. After years of tension, largely over the war in Western Sahara, Algeria resumed diplomatic relations with its western neighbor, Morocco, in 1988.

(United Nations photo by M. Jimenex)

Morocco's King Hassan II is a leader whose influence is often pivotal in North African regional planning.

Morocco

Morocco is ruled by King Hassan II, who came to power in 1961 when his highly respected father, King Muhammad V, died. The political parties that developed during the struggle against French rule have continued to contest elections. However, Hassan has rarely permitted them to have a genuine influence in policymaking, preferring to reserve the role for himself and his advisors. As in Tunisia, Moroccan agricultural development has been based on technological innovations rather than on land reform. The latter, while it could raise productivity, would likely anger the propertied supporters of the king. Elites also oppose business-tax reforms, yet the government needs revenues to repay its multi-billion-dollar debt. Much of the country's economic development has been left to the private sector. High birth rates and unemployment have led many Moroccans to join the Algerians and Tunisians in seeking employment in Europe.

Morocco's 15-year war to retain control of phosphate-rich Western Sahara, a former Spanish colony whose independence is being fought for by a local nationalist movement known as Polisario, has been a persistent drain on the country's treasury (it costs about $1 billion a year to wage). Despite major military and economic assistance from the United States, France, and Saudi Arabia, Morocco has been unable to crush Polisario resistance, though its defensive tactics in recent years have proved effective in frustrating guerrilla infiltration throughout most of the territory. A United Nations peace plan calling for a referendum over the territory's future has been tentatively agreed to by both sides, but it remains to be implemented.

REGIONAL AND CONTINENTAL LINKS

Since the 1950s there have been many calls for greater regional integration in North Africa. Under Nasser, Egypt was the leader of the pan-Arab movement and even joined Syria in a brief political union from 1958 to 1961. Others have attempted to create a union of the countries of the Maghrib (Arabic for "west") region, that is Algeria, Morocco, and Tunisia. Recently these three countries, along with the adjacent states of Libya and Mauritania, have agreed to work toward an economic community. However, they continue to be politically divided. At one time or another Qadhafi has been accused of subverting all of the region's governments; Algeria and Morocco have disagreed over the disposition of the Western Sahara; and each country has, at some point, closed its borders to its neighbors' citizens. Still, the logic of closer political and economic links, and the example of increasing European unity on the other side of the Mediterranean, will keep the issue of regional unity alive.

(United Nations photo by J. Slaughter)

Creating an economic and political integration of North African countries has been a goal for a number of years. Economic unification has solid reasons and benefits of wider markets, diversified products, and resultant expanded employment; political unification, however, is much more complex, due to the historical and cultural diversity of the area. The Moroccan port of Casablanca, above, is an obvious economic asset to the whole area.

Both as members of the Organization of African Unity (OAU) and as individual states, the North African countries have had strong diplomatic and political ties with the rest of the continent. In addition, they are deeply involved in regional affairs outside Africa, particularly those of the Arab and Mediterranean worlds. There have been some modest tensions across the Sahara. Requests by the North African nations that other OAU countries break diplomatic relations with Israel were promptly met in the aftermath of the 1974 Arab-Israeli War. Many sub-Saharan countries hoped that in return for their solidarity the Arab nations would extend development aid to help them, in particular to cope with rising oil prices. Although some aid was forthcoming (mostly from the Persian Gulf countries, rather than from the North African oil producers), it was less generous than many expected. During the 1980s a number of sub-Saharan countries resumed diplomatic relations with Israel.

Border disputes, ideological differences, and internal conflicts have caused additional tensions. The Polisario cause in Western Sahara, for example, has badly divided the OAU. When the organization recognized the Polisario's exiled government, in 1984, Morocco, along with Zaire, withdrew from membership in the body. However, the OAU has also had its regional successes. In 1974, for example, its mediation led to a settlement of a long-standing border dispute between Algeria and Morocco.

West Africa

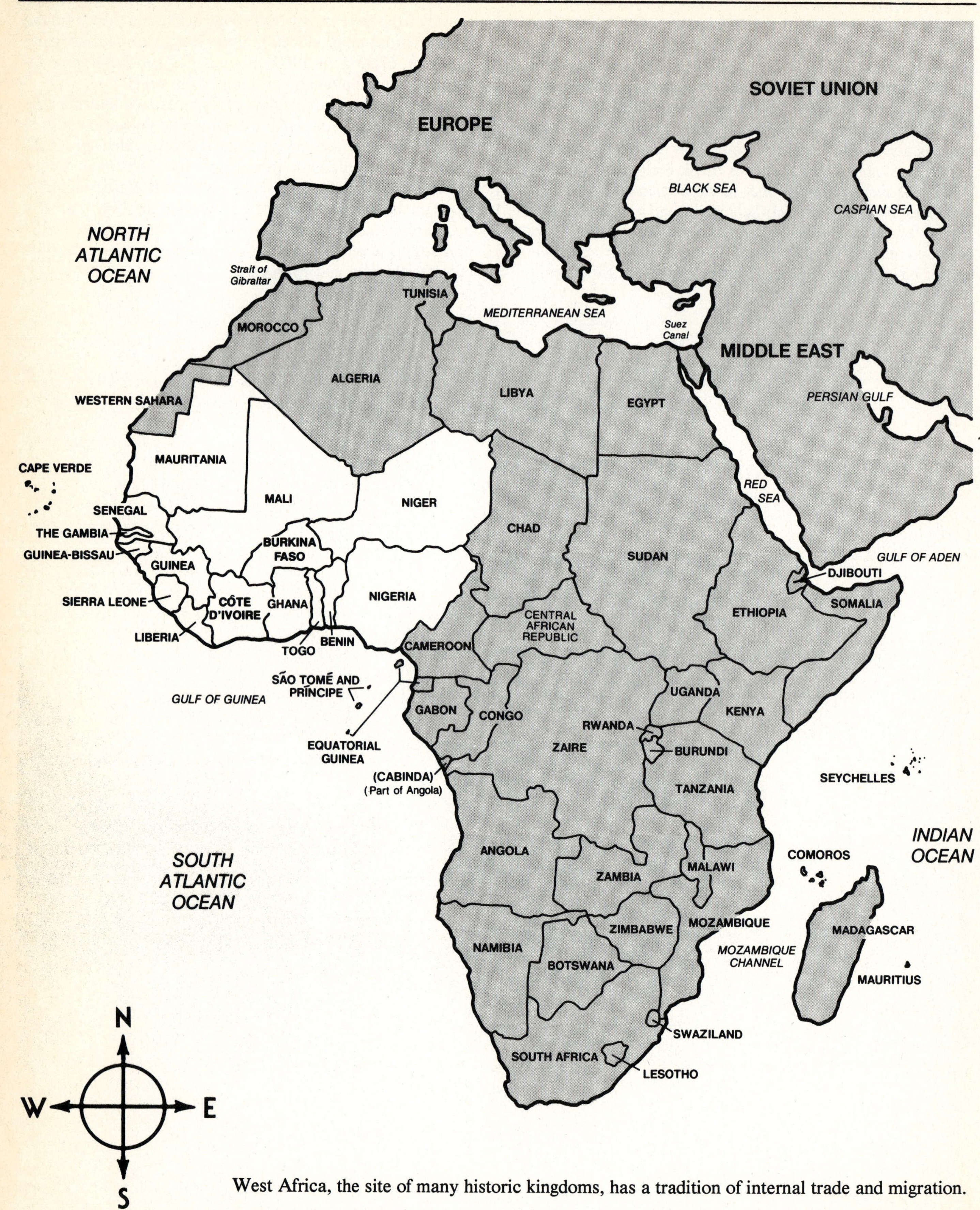

West Africa, the site of many historic kingdoms, has a tradition of internal trade and migration.

West Africa: Seeking Unity in Diversity

Anyone looking at a map of Africa will identify West Africa as the great bulge on the western coast of the continent. It is a region bound by the Sahara Desert to the north, the Atlantic Ocean to the south and west and, in part, by the Cameroonian Mountains to the east. Historically, each of these boundaries has been a bridge rather than a barrier, in that the region has long been linked through trade to the rest of the world.

At first glance, West Africa's great variety is more striking than any of its unifying features. It contains, for example, the environmental extremes of desert and rain forest. While most of its people rely on agriculture, every type of occupation can be found, from herders to factory workers. Hundreds of different languages are spoken; some are as different from one another as English is from Arabic or Japanese. Local cultural traditions and the societies that practice them are also myriad.

Yet the more one examines West Africa, the more one is impressed with the features that give the nations of the region a degree of coherence and unity. Some of the common characteristics and cross-cutting features of West Africa as a whole include the vegetation belts that stretch across the region from west to east, creating a similar environmental mix among the region's polities; the constant movement of peoples across local and national boundaries; and efforts being made by West African governments toward greater integration in the region, primarily through economic organizations. West Africans also share elements of a common history.

With the exception of Liberia, all of the contemporary states of West Africa were the creations of competing European colonial powers—France, Germany, Britain, and Portugal—who divided most of the area during the late nineteenth century. Before this partition, however, much of the region was interlinked by the spread of Islam and patterns of trade, including the sad legacy of intensive involvement, between the sixteenth and nineteenth centuries, in the trans-Atlantic slave trade. From ancient times great kingdoms expanded and contracted across the West African savanna and forest, giving rise to sophisticated civilizations.

WEST AFRICAN VEGETATION AND CLIMATE ZONES

Traveling north from the coastlines of such states as Nigeria, Ghana, or the Côte d'Ivoire, one first encounters tropical rain forests, which give way to woodland savanna and, later, to drier, more open plains. In Mali, Niger, and other landlocked countries to the north, the savanna gives way to the still drier Sahel environment, between the savanna and the Sahara Desert, and finally to the desert itself.

Whatever their ethnicity or nationality, the peoples living within each of the above vegetation zones generally share the benefits and problems of similar livelihoods. For instance, cocoa, coffee, yams, and cassava are among the cash and food crops planted in the cleared forest and woodland zones which stretch from Guinea to Nigeria. Groundnuts, sorghum, and millet are commonly harvested in the savanna belt that runs from Senegal to northern Nigeria. Herders in the Sahel, who historically could not go too far south with their cattle because of the presence of the tsetse fly in the forest, which are deadly to cattle, continue to cross state boundaries in search of pasture.

People throughout West African periodically have suffered from drought, whose effects, in recent years, have often been aggravated by greater population pressures on the land. These factors have contributed to environmental changes. In particular, the condition of the Sahel has deteriorated through a process of desertification, leading to large-scale relocations among many of its inhabitants. To address the problem, the eight Sahelian countries—Cape Verde, The Gambia, Burkina Faso, Mali, Senegal, Niger, Chad (in Central Africa), and Mauritania—have formed a coordinating Committee for Struggle Against Drought in the Sahel (CILSS).

Farther to the south, large areas of woodland savanna have turned into grasslands as their forests have been cut down by land-hungry farmers. Drought has also resulted in widespread brush fires in Ghana, the Côte d'Ivoire, Togo, and Benin, which have transformed forests into savannas and savannas into deserts. Due to the depletion of forest, the Harmattan, a dry wind that blows in from the Sahara in January and February, now reaches many parts of the coast that in the recent past did not feel its breadth. Its dust and haze have become a sign of the new year, and of new agricultural problems, throughout much of West Africa.

The great rivers of West Africa, such as the Gambia, Niger, Senegal, and Volta, along with their tributaries, have become increasingly important, both as avenues of travel and trade and for the water they provide. Countries have joined together in large-scale projects, designed to harness their waters for irrigation and hydroelectric power, through regional organizations like the Mano river grouping of Guinea, Liberia, and Sierra Leone, and the Organization for the Development of the Senegal River, which is comprised of Mali, Mauritania, and Senegal.

THE LINKS OF HISTORY AND TRADE

The peoples of West Africa have never been united as members of a single political unit. Yet some of the precolonial kingdoms that expanded across the region have great symbolic importance for those seeking to enhance interstate cooperation. The Mali empire of the thirteenth to fifteenth centuries, the Songhai empire of the sixteenth century, and the nineteenth-century Fulani caliphate of Sokoto, all based in the savanna, are widely remembered as examples of past supranational glory. The kingdoms of the southern forests, such as the Asante Confederation, the Dahomey kingdom, and the Yoruba city-states, were smaller than the great savanna empires to their north. Although generally later in origin and different in character from the northern states, the forest kingdoms are, nonetheless, also sources of greater regional identity.

The precolonial states of West Africa gave rise to great urban centers, which were interlinked through extensive trade networks. This development was probably the result of the area's agricultural productivity, which supported a relatively high population density from early times. Many modern settlements have long histories. Present-day Timbuctu and Gao, in Mali, were important centers of learning and commerce in medieval times. Some other examples include Ouagadougou, Ibadan, Benin, and Kumasi, all in the forest zone. These southern centers prospered in the past by sending gold, kola, leather goods, cloth, and slaves to the northern savanna and southern coast.

The cities of the savannas linked West Africa to North Africa. From the eleventh century, the ruling groups of the savanna increasingly turned to the universal vision of Islam. While Islam also spread to the forests, the southernmost areas were ultimately more strongly influenced by Christianity, which was introduced by Europeans who became active along the West African coast during the fifteenth century. For centuries the major commercial link between Europe, the Americas, and West Africa was the trans-Atlantic slave trade, but during the nineteenth century so-called legitimate commerce in palm oil and other tropical products replaced it. New cities such as Dakar, Freetown, and Lagos developed rapidly as centers of the Atlantic trade.

THE MOVEMENT OF PEOPLES

Despite the false view of many who see Africa as being a continent made up of isolated groups, one constant characteristic of West Africa has been the transregional migration of its people. Herders have moved east and west across the savanna and south into the forests. Since colonial times many professionals, as well as laborers, have sought employment outside their home areas.

Some peoples of West Africa, such as the Malinke, Fulani, Hausa, and Mossi, have developed especially well-established heritages of mobility. In the past the Malinke journeyed from their early center in Mali to coastal areas in Guinea, Senegal, and The Gambia. Other Malinke traders also made their way to Burkina Faso, Liberia, and Sierra Leone, where they came to be known as Mandingoes.

The Fulani have developed their own patterns of seasonal movement. They herd their cattle south across the savanna during the dry season and return to the north during the rainy season. Urbanized Fulani groups have historically journeyed from west to east, often serving as agents of Islamization as well as promoters of trade. More recently many Fulani have been forced to move southward as a result of the deterioration of their grazing lands. The Hausa, who mostly live in northern Nigeria and Niger, are also found throughout much of West Africa. Indeed, their trading presence is so widespread that some have suggested that the Hausa language be promoted as a common *lingua franca* for West Africa.

Millions of migrant laborers are regularly attracted to the Côte d'Ivoire and Ghana from the poorer inland states of Burkina Faso, Mali, and Niger, thus promoting economic interdependence among these states. Similar large-scale migrations also occur elsewhere. The drastic expulsion of aliens by the Nigerian government in 1983 was startling to the outside world in part because few had realized that so many Ghanaians, Nigeriens, Togolese, Beninois, and Cam-

(IFC/World Bank photo by Ray Witkin)

A worker cuts cloth at a textile mill in Côte d'Ivoire. The patterns are similar to traditional patterns. Most of the cloth will be exported.

eroonians had taken up residence in Nigeria. But such immigration is not new, though its scale into Nigeria was greatly increased by that country's oil boom. Peoples such as the Yoruba, Ewe, and Vai, who were divided by colonialism, have often ignored modern state boundaries in order to maintain their ethnic ties. Other migrations also have roots in the colonial past. Sierra Leonians worked as clerks and craftspeople throughout the coastal areas of British West Africa, while Igbo were recruited to serve in northern Nigeria. Similarly, Beninois became the assistants of French administrators in other parts of French West Africa, while Cape Verdians occupied intermediate positions in Portugal's mainland colonies.

THE PROGRESS OF WEST AFRICAN INTEGRATION

Many West Africans recognize the weaknesses inherent in the region's national divisions. The peoples of the region would benefit from greater multilateral political cooperation and economic integration. Yet there are many obstacles blocking the growth of pan-regional development. National identity is probably even stronger today than it was in the days when Kwame Nkrumah, the charismatic Ghanaian leader, pushed for African unity but was frustrated by parochial interests. The larger and more prosperous states, such as Nigeria and the Côte d'Ivoire, are reluctant to share their wealth with smaller countries, which, in turn, fear being swallowed.

While the political status quo is currently being challenged throughout West Africa, for the moment the region is divided, between those states that are seeking to develop constitutional systems of government and those under single-party and/or military control, often dominated by a single autocrat. Overlapping ethnicity is also sometimes more a source of suspicion rather than of unity between states. Because the countries were under the rule of different colonial powers, French, English, and Portuguese serve as official languages of the different nations, which also inherited different administrative traditions. Moreover, during colonial times independent infrastructures were developed in each country; these continue to orient economic activities toward the coast and toward Europe rather than to encourage links between West African countries.

Political changes also affect regional cooperation and domestic development. Senegambia, the now-defunct confederation of Senegal and The Gambia, was dominated by Senegal and resented by many Gambians. The civil war in Liberia has also led to division between the supporters and opponents of the intervention there of a multinational regional peacekeeping force. The situation has been further aggravated by threats by various Liberian factions against expatriates from other West African states.

Despite the many roadblocks to unity, multinational organizations have developed in West Africa, stimulated in large part by the severity of the common problems that the countries face. The West African countries have a good record of cooperating in the avoidance of armed conflict and the settlement of their occasional border disputes. In addition to the multilateral agencies, previously cited, that are coordinating the struggle against drought and the development of various river basins, there are also a number of regional commodity cartels such as the five-member Groundnut Council. The West African Examinations Council standardizes secondary-school examinations in most of the countries where English is an official language, while most of the Francophonic states share a common currency.

The most ambitious and encompassing organization in the region is the Economic Organization of West African States (ECOWAS), which includes all of the states incorporated in the West African section of this text. Established in 1975 by the Treaty of Lagos, ECOWAS aims to promote trade, cooperation, and self-reliance. Thus far, the progress of the organization in these areas has been limited. But ECOWAS can point to some achievements: several joint ventures have been developed; steps toward tariff reduction are being taken; competition between ECOWAS and the Economic Community of West Africa (CEAO), an economic organization of former French colonies, has been lessened by limiting CEAO; and ECOWAS members have agreed in principle to establish a common currency. Some members of ECOWAS sought to have the organization play a political role in settling the bloody Liberian conflict, but the success of this effort, along with that of the already dispatched West African peacekeeping force, remains uncertain. There is hope that ECOWAS will become more effective in developing West African solutions to the problems of the region's economies.

Benin (People's Republic of Benin)

GEOGRAPHY

Area in Square Kilometers (Miles): 112,620 (43,483) (slightly smaller than Pennsylvania)
Capital (Population): Porto-Novo (330,000)
Climate: tropical

PEOPLE

Population
Total: 4,551,000
Annual Growth Rate: 3.1%
Rural/Urban Population Ratio: 80/20
Languages: official: French; others spoken: Fon; Yoruba; Adja; Bariba; others

Health
Life Expectancy at Birth: 47 years (male); 51 years (female)
Infant Death Rate (Ratio): 143/1,000
Average Caloric Intake: 100% of FAO minimum
Physicians Available (Ratio): 1/20,343

Religion(s)
80% traditional indigenous; 12% Muslim; 8% Christian

THE DAHOMEY KINGDOM

The Dahomey kingdom, established in the early eighteenth century by the Fon people, was a highly organized state. The kings had a standing army, which included women; a centralized administration, whose officers kept census and tax records and organized the slave trade and, later, the oil trade; and a sophisticated artistic tradition. Benin, like Togo, has important links with Brazil which date back to the time of the Dahomey kingdom. Current Beninois families—such as the da Souzas, the da Silvas, and the Rodriguezes—are descendants of Brazilians who settled on the coast in the mid-nineteenth century. Some were descended from former slaves, who may have been taken from Dahomey long before. They became the first teachers in Western-oriented public schools and continued in higher education themselves. In Brazil, Yoruba religious cults, which developed from those of the Yoruba in Benin and Nigeria, have become increasingly popular in recent years.

Education
Adult Literacy Rate: 28%

COMMUNICATION

Telephones: 8,650
Newspapers: 1

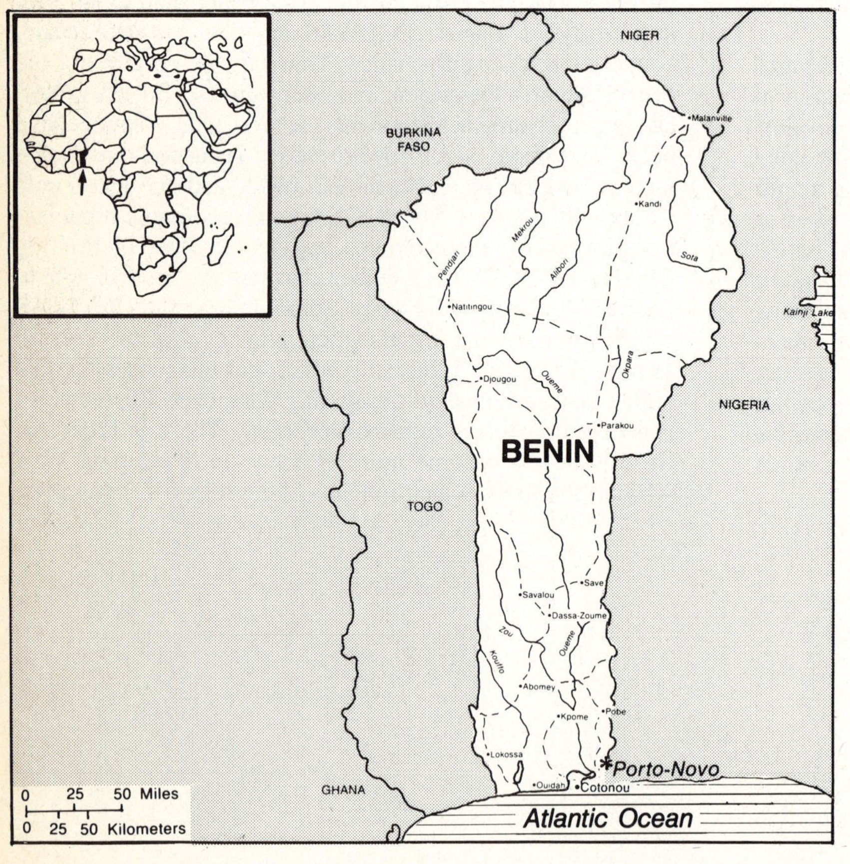

TRANSPORTATION

Highways—Kilometers (Miles): 8,400 (5,208)
Railroads—Kilometers (Miles): 579 (360)
Commercial Airports: 1 international

GOVERNMENT

Type: Transitional
Independence Date: August 1, 1960
Head of State: President Ahmed Mathieu Kérékou
Political Parties: Coalition of Democratic Forces; Communist Party of Benin; People's Revolutionary Party of Benin; others
Suffrage: universal for adults

MILITARY

Number of Armed Forces: 6,350
Military Expenditures (% of Central Government Expenditures): 17.2%
Current Hostilities: none

ECONOMY

Currency ($ U.S. Equivalent): 319 CFA francs = $1
Per Capita Income/GNP: $374/$1.4 billion
Inflation Rate: n/a
Natural Resources: none known in commercial quantities
Agriculture: palm products; cotton; corn; yams; cassava; cocoa; coffee; groundnuts
Industry: shoes; beer; textiles; cement; processed palm oil

FOREIGN TRADE

Exports: $172 million
Imports: $225 million

The kingdom of Dahomey is established **1625**

The French conquer the Dahomey kingdom and declare a French protectorate **1892**

Dahomey becomes independent **1960**

Kérékou comes to power in the sixth attempted military coup since independence **1972**

The name of Dahomey is changed to Benin **1975**

An attempted coup involves exiles, mercenaries, and implicates Gabon, Morocco, and France **1977**

1980s–1990s

The government acknowledges that the Soviet Union dumped radioactive waste in Benin

Kérékou announces the abandonment of Marxism-Leninism as Benin's guiding ideology

Unrest, strikes, and escapes by political prisoners lead to the promise of multiparty elections

BENIN

For 10 days in February 1990 the citizens of Benin gathered around television sets and radios for live broadcasts of the National Conference of Active Forces of the Nation. The conference, which, in the aftermath of weeks of civil unrest, President Ahmed Mathieu Kérékou had convened to discuss Benin's future, turned into a trial of his 17-year rule. With the eyes and ears of the nation tuned in, critics of the regime were able to pressure Kérékou into handing over effective power to a transitional government.

The major task of the new, civilian administration is to oversee Benin's political transformation, from a one-party Marxist-Leninist state, in which ultimate control was exercised by the military, into a multiparty democracy. Benin's "civilian coup d'etat" and the subsequent approval of a new Constitution have placed the nation in the forefront of the democratization process currently sweeping Africa. Should a freely elected government come to power in the elections promised for 1991, it will inherit a nearly bankrupt state and a mostly impoverished population.

A COUNTRY OF MIGRANTS

Benin numbers among the least developed countries in the world. It had for decades experienced only limited economic growth; during the last 5 years the nation's real gross domestic product has actually declined. As a result, emigration has become a way of life for many.

The migration of Beninois in search of economic opportunities in neighboring states is not a new phenomenon. Before 1960 educated citizens from the then French colony of Dahomey (as Benin was called until 1975) had become prominent in junior-administrative positions throughout other parts of French West Africa. But as the region's newly independent states began to localize their civil-service staffs, most of the Beninois expatriates lost their jobs. Their return home increased bureaucratic competition within Benin. This, in turn, led to heightened political rivalry among various ethnic regional groups. Such local antagonisms contributed to a series of military coups between 1963 and 1972, which culminated in Kérékou's seizure of power.

THE ECONOMY

Nigeria's urban areas have provided major markets for food, encouraging Beninois farmers to switch from cash crops to growing yams, cassava, and other food crops, which are smuggled across the border. The emergence of this parallel export economy was largely driven by the Kérékou regime's practice of paying its farmers among the lowest official produce prices in the region. Given that agriculture, in terms of both employment and income generation, forms the largest sector of the Benin economy, the rise in smuggling activities has greatly contributed to the growth of graft and corruption.

Benin's small industrial sector is primarily geared to processing primary products, such as palm oil and cotton, for export. It has thus been adversely affected by the shift away from producing cash crops for the local market. Small-scale manufacturing has centered around the production of basic consumer goods and construction materials. The biggest enterprises are state-owned cement plants. Employment activities—both legal and illegal—related to transport and trade are also important.

Due to the relative absence of rain forest, an impediment to travel, Benin's territory has historically served as a trade corridor between the coast and inland, savanna, regions of West Africa. Today the nation's roads are comparatively well developed, and the railroad carries goods from the port at Cotonou to northern areas of the country. An extension of the railroad will reach Niamey, the capital of Niger.

While many Beninois have come to attribute their nation's poor economy to the failure of "Marxist-Beninism," there also exists substantial support for the Stalinist (pro-Albanian) Communist Party of Dahomey (PDC), which, along with other political parties, has now been unbanned. During the Kérékou years the PDC was active as an underground movement. The party played a leading role in organizing mass antigovernment demonstrations in December 1989 but subsequently boycotted February 1990's conference. The PDC is expected to put up strong opposition to the newly formed Coalition of Democratic Forces (RFD), which represents most of the elements taking part in the current transitional government.

DEVELOPMENT

Palm-oil plantations were established in Benin in the mid-nineteenth century by Africans. They have continued to be African-owned and capitalist-oriented in a society that is proclaimed socialist. Today there are some 30 million trees, and palm-oil products are a major export used for cooking, lighting, soap, margarine, and lubricants.

FREEDOM

In 1990 Jean Florentin Fehilo, a leading human-rights activist, was appointed as the acting minister of the Interior. Political restrictions have been lifted and prisoners of conscience freed.

HEALTH/WELFARE

One-third of the national budget of Benin goes to education, and the number of students receiving primary education has risen to 50% of the school-age population. College graduates serve as temporary teachers through the National Service System, but more teachers and higher salaries are needed.

ACHIEVEMENTS

Fon appliqued cloths have been described as "one of the gayest and liveliest of the contemporary African art forms." Formerly these cloths were made and used by the Dahomeyan kings. Now they are sold to tourists, but they still portray the motifs and symbols of past rulers and the society they ruled.

Burkina Faso

GEOGRAPHY

Area in Square Kilometers (Miles): 274,500 (106,000) (about the size of Colorado)
Capital (Population): Ouagadougou (442,000)
Climate: tropical to arid

PEOPLE

Population

Total: 8,530,000
Annual Growth Rate: 1.7%
Rural/Urban Population Ratio: 92/8
Languages: official: French; others spoken: Mossi, Senufo, Fula, Bobo, Mande, Gurunsi, Lobi, others

Health

Life Expectancy at Birth: 47 years
Infant Death Rate (Ratio): 176/1,000
Average Caloric Intake: 95% of FAO minimum
Physicians Available (Ratio): 1/70,033

Religion(s)

45% traditional indigenous; 43% Muslim; 12% Christian

DR. OUEDRAOGO AND THE NAAM MOVEMENT

In 1989 Dr. Bernard Ledea Ouedraogo was awarded the Hunger Project's third annual Africa Prize for Leadership for the Sustainable End of Hunger, an honor bestowed in recognition of his important contribution in raising rural living standards throughout West Africa. During the 1960s Dr. Ouedraogo became disillusioned with the top-down methods then employed by the Burkinabe government and international aid groups when trying to mobilize local peasants for development projects. His response was to organize the Naam movement, originally as a support network for the *naam,* the traditional Burkinabe village cooperatives. The movement assisted the naam in establishing their own development projects. Naam has since grown to become the largest peasant movement in Africa, with more than 4,000 affiliated grass-roots groups in Chad, The Gambia, Guinea-Bissau, Mali, Mauritania, Niger, Senegal, and Togo, as well as in Burkina Faso.

Education

Adult Literacy Rate: 8%

COMMUNICATION

Telephones: 16,000
Newspapers: 4

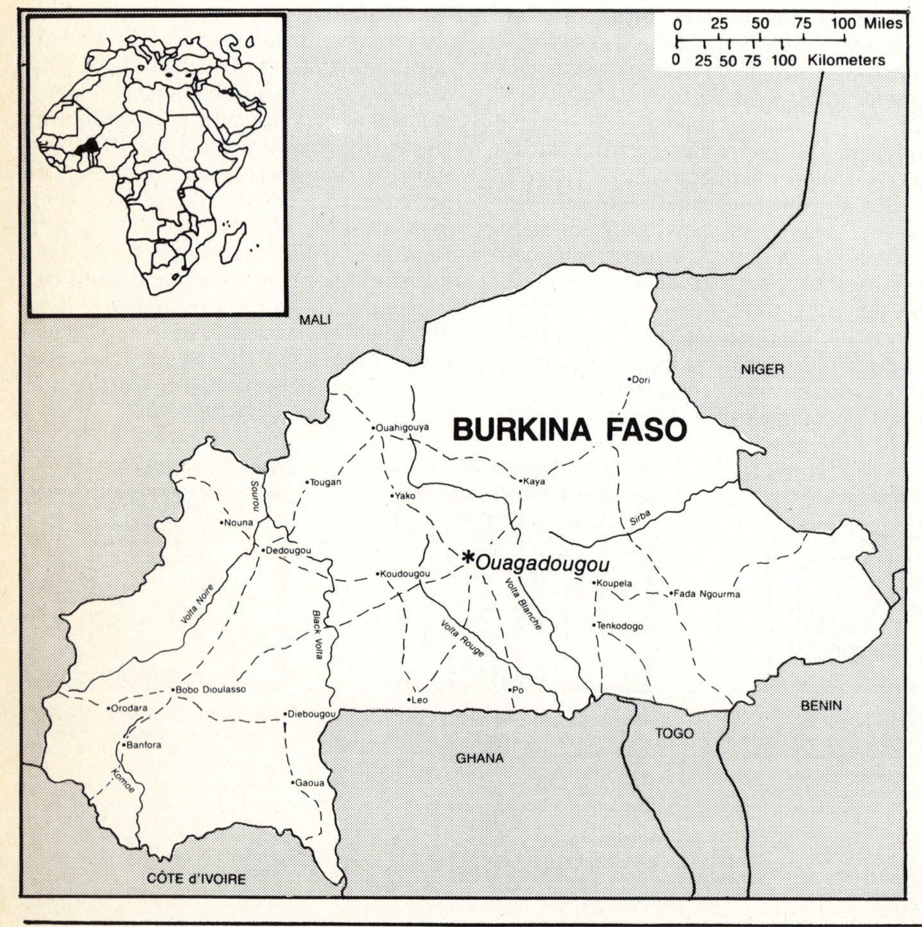

TRANSPORTATION

Highways—Kilometers (Miles): 13,134 (8,143)
Railroads—Kilometers (Miles): 517 (320)
Commercial Airports: 2 international

GOVERNMENT

Type: republic under control of a military council
Independence Date: August 5, 1960
Head of State: Blaise Compaore
Political Parties: banned following the 1980 coup
Suffrage: universal for adults

MILITARY

Number of Armed Forces: 8,750
Military Expenditures (% of Central Government Expenditures): 20%
Current Hostilities: none

ECONOMY

Currency ($ U.S. Equivalent): 319 CFA francs = $1
Per Capita Income/GNP: $150/$1.2 billion
Inflation Rate: 8.4%
Natural Resources: manganese; limestone; marble; gold; uranium; bauxite; copper
Agriculture: millet; sorghum; corn; rice; livestock; peanuts; shea nuts; sugar cane; cotton; sesame
Industry: agricultural processing; brewing; light industry

FOREIGN TRADE

Exports: $310 million
Imports: $434 million

The first Mossi kingdom is founded
1313

The French finally overcome Mossi resistance and claim Upper Volta
1896

Upper Volta is divided among adjoining French colonies
1932

Upper Volta is reconstituted as a colony
1947

Independence under President Maurice Yameogo
1960

Lieutenant Colonel Laminzana succeeds Yameogo, who resigns after rioting in the country
1966

1980s–1990s

After several military coups, Captain Thomas Sankara comes to power

The country's name is changed to Burkina (Mossi for "land of honest men") Faso (Dioula for "democratic republic")

Sankara is assassinated; Blaise Compaore succeeds as head of state

BURKINA FASO

Having suffered through four successful military coups and many more bloody power struggles during the past decade, Burkina Faso's government has become chronically unstable. The last coup resulted in the overthrow and assassination of the charismatic and controversial Thomas Sankara, whose radical leadership had become the focus of much support and opposition, both within and outside the country. Successive military and civilian regimes have for decades faced a daunting task in trying to cope with the challenge of developing the nation's fragile economy.

DEBILITATING DROUGHTS

At the time of its independence from France, in 1960, as the Republic of Upper Volta, the landlocked country inherited little in the way of colonial infrastructure. In the ensuing decades progress has been hampered by prolonged periods of severe drought. Efforts have been made to integrate foreign relief donations into local development schemes. Of particular note have been projects instituted by the traditional rural cooperatives known as *naam,* which have been responsible for such small-scale, but often invaluable, local improvements as new wells and pumps, better grinding mills, and the distribution of tools and medical supplies. Despite such community action, the effects of drought have been devastating. Hard hit has been pastoral production, which has long been a mainstay of the local economy, especially in the north. It is estimated that the most recent drought destroyed about 90 percent of the livestock.

Although most Burkinabe continue to survive as agriculturalists and herders, many are dependent on wage labor. In the urban centers, there exists a significant working-class population, who support the nation's politically powerful trade-union movement. The division between this urban community and the rural population is not absolute, for it is common for individuals to combine wage labor with farming activities. Another category, whose numbers exceed those of the local wage-labor force, are those individuals who seek employment outside the country. At least a million work as migrant laborers in other parts of West Africa, a pattern that dates back to the early twentieth century.

UNIONS FORCE CHANGES

As is the case in much of Africa, it is the salaried urban population who, at least next to the army, have exercised the greatest influence over successive Burkinabe regimes. Trade-union leaders representing these workers have been instrumental in forcing changes in government. Although many unionists have championed various shades of Marxist-Leninist ideology, they, along with their natural allies in the civil service, arguably constitute a conservative element within the local society. During the mid-1980s they became increasingly concerned about the dynamic Sankara's efforts to promote a nationwide network of grass-roots Committees for the Defense of the Revolution (CDRs) as vehicles for empowering the nation's largely rural masses.

To many unionists, the mobilization and arming of the CDRs was perceived as a direct challenge to their own status. This threat seemed all the more apparent when Sankara began to cut urban salaries, in the name of a more equitable flow of revenue to the rural areas. When several union leaders challenged this move, they were arrested on charges of sedition. Sankara's subsequent overthrow thus had strong backing from within organized labor and the civil service, which, along with the military, have remained the principal supporters of the new Popular Front regime of Blaise Compaore and its policy of "national rectification."

Beyond its core of support, the Popular Front government has generally been met with sentiments ranging from hostility to indifference. While Compaore claimed with some justification that Sankara's rule had become too arbitrary and that he had resisted forming a party with a set of rules, many people mourned the fallen leader's death.

To stabilize his position at home and abroad, Compaore has talked of future elections while trying to ally various independent groups to the Front through a broader coalition, the Popular Democratic Organization-Labor Movement (ODP-MT). But having recently declared that "Burkina's development cannot at present occur in a one-party system nor in anarchic multipartyism, which breeds national division," Compaore's vision of democratization remains ambiguous.

DEVELOPMENT

Despite the political turbulence of recent years, Burkina Faso's economy has recorded positive, albeit modest, annual growth rates for more than a decade. Most of the growth has been in agriculture.

FREEDOM

There is a surprisingly strong tradition of pluralism in Burkina Faso, despite the circumscribed nature of human rights under successive military regimes. Freedom of speech and association are curtailed, and political detentions are common.

HEALTH/WELFARE

The inadequacy of public health is reflected in the Burkinabe life expectancy of 47 years. Mass immunization campaigns have been successfully carried out, but in an era of Structural Adjustment, the prospects for a dramatic improvement in health appear bleak.

ACHIEVEMENTS

The biannual Pan-African Film Festival is held in Ouagadougou. This festival has contributed significantly to the development of the film industry in Africa. Burkina Faso has nationalized its movie houses, and the government has encouraged the showing of films by African filmmakers.

Cape Verde (Republic of Cape Verde)

GEOGRAPHY

Area in Square Kilometers (Miles): 4,033 (1,557) (a bit larger than Rhode Island)
Capital (Population): Praia (50,000)
Climate: temperate

PEOPLE

Population
Total: 359,000
Annual Growth Rate: 1.4%
Rural/Urban Population Ratio: 74/26
Languages: official: Portuguese and Kriolu

Health
Life Expectancy at Birth: 60 years (male); 64 years (female)
Infant Death Rate (Ratio): 89/1,000
Average Caloric Intake: 133% of FAO minimum
Physicians Available (Ratio): 1/6,862

Religion(s)
80% Catholic; 20% traditional indigenous

Education
Adult Literacy Rate: 37%

CAPE VERDEANS IN THE UNITED STATES

Large-scale immigration of Cape Verdeans to the United States began in the nineteenth century. Today the Cape Verdean-American community is larger than the population of Cape Verde itself; it is concentrated in southern New England. Most early immigrants arrived in the region aboard whaling and packet ships. The 1980 United States census was the first to count Cape Verdeans as a separate ethnic group.

The community has, on the whole, prospered, and is currently better educated than the U.S. national norm. Cape Verdeans in the United States maintain close ties with their homeland, assisting in local development projects.

COMMUNICATION

Telephones: 4,300
Newspapers: 7 weeklies

TRANSPORTATION

Highways—Kilometers (Miles): 2,250 (1,395)
Railroads—Kilometers (Miles): none
Commercial Airports: 1 international

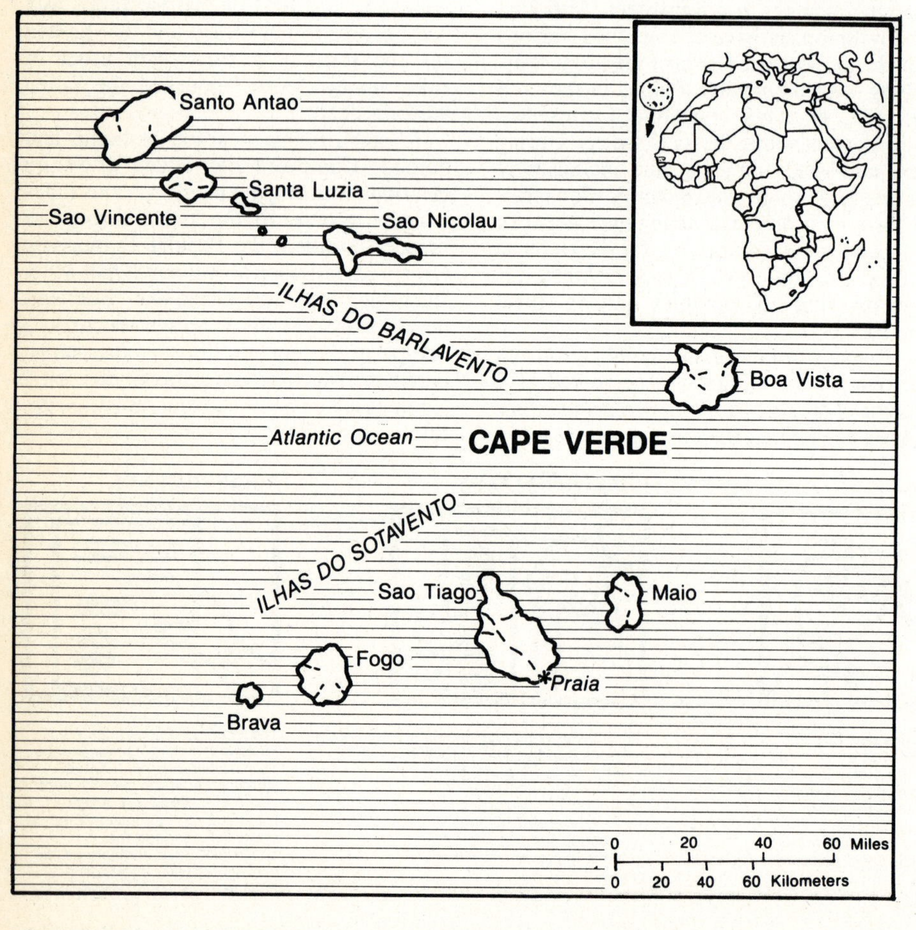

GOVERNMENT

Type: republic
Independence Date: July 5, 1975
Head of State: President Aristides Maria Pereira; Prime Minister (General) Pedro Verona Rodrigues Pires
Political Parties: African Party for the Independence of Cape Verde; Movement for Democracy
Suffrage: universal over 18

MILITARY

Number of Armed Forces: 1,300
Military Expenditures (% of Central Government Expenditures): n/a
Current Hostilities: none

ECONOMY

Currency ($ U.S. Equivalent): 77 escudos = $1
Per Capita Income/GNP: $350/$140 million
Inflation Rate: 12%
Natural Resources: fish; agricultural land; salt deposits
Agriculture: corn; beans; manioc; sweet potatoes; bananas
Industry: fishing; flour mills; salt

FOREIGN TRADE

Exports: $8.9 million
Imports: $124 million

Cape Verdean settlement begins
1462

Slavery is abolished
1869

Thousands of Cape Verdeans die of starvation during World War II
1940s

The PAIGC is founded
1956

Warfare begins in Guinea-Bissau; Amilcar Cabral is assassinated
1973

A coup in Lisbon initiates the Portuguese decolonization process
1974

Independence
1975

1980s–1990s

The 2nd PAICV Party Congress endorses moves toward private-sector development

The PAICV renounces its political monopoly; opposition groups emerge

Local elections are postponed to coincide with national multiparty elections, set for 1991

THE REPUBLIC OF CAPE VERDE

The Republic of Cape Verde is an archipelago located about 400 miles west of the Senegalese Cape Verde, or "Green Cape," after which it is named. Unfortunately, green is a color that is often absent in the lives of the islands' citizens. Throughout its history Cape Verde has suffered from periods of prolonged drought (the last such period lasted from 1968 to 1984).

When the country gained independence in 1975 there was little in the way of nonagricultural production. As a result, for its survival the new nation had to rely on foreign aid and the remittances of Cape Verdeans working abroad. Despite the continuance of this pattern of dependence, the years of independence have brought about a genuine improvement in the lives of most Cape Verdeans.

For nearly 500 years Cape Verde was ruled by Portugal. Most of the islanders are the descendants of Portuguese colonists (many of whom came as convicts) and African slaves who began to settle on the islands shortly after their discovery by Portuguese mariners in 1456. The merging of these two groups gave rise to the distinct Cape Verdean Kriolu language (which is also spoken in Guinea-Bissau).

Under Portuguese rule, Cape Verdeans were generally treated as second-class citizens, although a few rose to positions of prominence in other parts of the Portuguese empire. Economic stagnation, exacerbated by cycles of severe drought, drove many islanders to emigrate.

THE LIBERATION STRUGGLE

In 1956 the African Party for the Independence of Guinea-Bissau and Cape Verde (PAIGC) was formed under the dynamic leadership of Amilcar Cabral, a Cape Verdian revolutionary who, with his followers, hoped to see the two Portuguese colonies form a united nation. Between 1963 and 1974, the PAIGC waged a successful war of liberation in Guinea-Bissau, which led ultimately to the independence of both territories.

Cabral was assassinated by the Portuguese in 1973, but during the late 1970s his successors, while ruling the two countries separately, maintained the unity of the PAIGC. This arrangement began to break down in the aftermath of a 1980 coup in Guinea-Bissau, which resulted in the party's division along national lines. In 1981 the Cape Verdean PAIGC formally renounced its Guinean links and became the African Party for the Independence of Cape Verde (PAICV).

THE ECONOMY

Since independence the PAIGC/CV governments challenged the colonial legacy of economic underdevelopment, exacerbated by drought. Lack of rainfall in the past occasionally resulted in the deaths of up to 50 percent of the islands' population. In contemporary times famine has been warded off through a reliance on imported foodstuffs, mostly received as aid.

The government has attempted to strengthen local food production by assisting the 70 percent of the population engaged in subsistence agriculture, by drilling for underground water, by terracing, by irrigating, and by building a water-desalinization plant (with U.S. assistance). Major efforts have also been devoted to tree-planting programs as a way to cut back on erosion and eventually to make the country self-sufficient in wood fuel. But with no more than 15 percent of the islands' territory potentially suitable for cultivation, the prospect of Cape Verde developing self-sufficiency in food appears to be remote. The one hopeful area is fishing.

The few factories that exist on Cape Verde are small-scale operations catering to local needs. Only textile industries have enjoyed modest success in exporting.

Notwithstanding the overall grim economic picture, past PAICV governments oversaw an impressive expansion in social services, particularly in the areas of health and education. Despite this record of achievement, the PAICV was voted out of office in Cape Verde's first multiparty elections. For many years the PAICV, a small vanguard organization of no more than 6,000, had maintained a formal monopoly of power. But in 1990 rising agitation led to the legalization of opposition groups, most of which coalesced as the Movement for Democracy (MPD). In February 1991 the MPD won a landslide victory, gaining about 65 percent of the vote, and more than two-thirds of the seats in the National Assembly. The MPD plans to amend the Constitution to further Cape Verde's shift to a multiparty system.

DEVELOPMENT

In a move designed to attract greater investment from overseas, especially from Cape Verdean-Americans, the country has recently joined the International Finance Corporation.

FREEDOM

Dissent is limited, but tolerated, in Cape Verde's one-party system. Government decision-makers are answerable to elected bodies. A new Constitution should entrench Cape Verde's ongoing transition into a multiparty liberal democracy. Articles in the *Terra Nova* have occasionally led to political prosecutions.

HEALTH/WELFARE

Greater access to health facilities has resulted in a sharp drop in infant mortality and a rise in life expectancy. Clinics have begun to encourage family planning. Since independence great progress has taken place in social services, particularly education.

ACHIEVEMENTS

Cape Verdean Kriolu culture is renowned for its artistic creativity, particularly in music and poetry. Popular Cape Verdean music groups, such as Balinundo, have enjoyed an increasing international audience. Local drama and other forms of artistic expression are showcased on national television.

Côte d'Ivoire (Republic of Côte d'Ivoire)

GEOGRAPHY

Area in Square Kilometers (Miles): 323,750 (124,503) (slightly larger than New Mexico)
Capital (Population): Abidjan (economic) (1,850,000); Yamoussoukro (political) (120,000)
Climate: tropical

PEOPLE

Population

Total: 11,798,000
Annual Growth Rate: 5%
Rural/Urban Population Ratio: 53/47
Languages: official: French; others spoken: Dioula, Agni, Baoulé, Kru, Senufo, Mandinka, others

Health

Life Expectancy at Birth: 47 years (male); 50 years (female)
Infant Death Rate (Ratio): 121/1,000
Average Caloric Intake: 112% of FAO minimum
Physicians Available (Ratio): 1/24,696

THE ARTS OF CÔTE d'IVOIRE

The arts of Côte d'Ivoire, including music, weaving, dance, and sculpture, have flourished. The wood carvings of the Senufo, Dan, and Baoulé peoples are famous the world over for their beauty and intricate design. Masks are particularly valued and admired by outsiders, but many collectors have never met the Ivoirian people for whom the art has social and religious significance. The Dan mask, for example, is not only beautiful—it also performs a spiritual function. When worn as part of a masquerade performance, it represents religious authority, settling of disputes, enforcing the laws of the community, and respect for tradition.

Religion(s)

66% traditional indigenous; 22% Muslim; 12% Christian

Education

Adult Literacy Rate: 35%

COMMUNICATION

Telephones: 88,000
Newspapers: 1

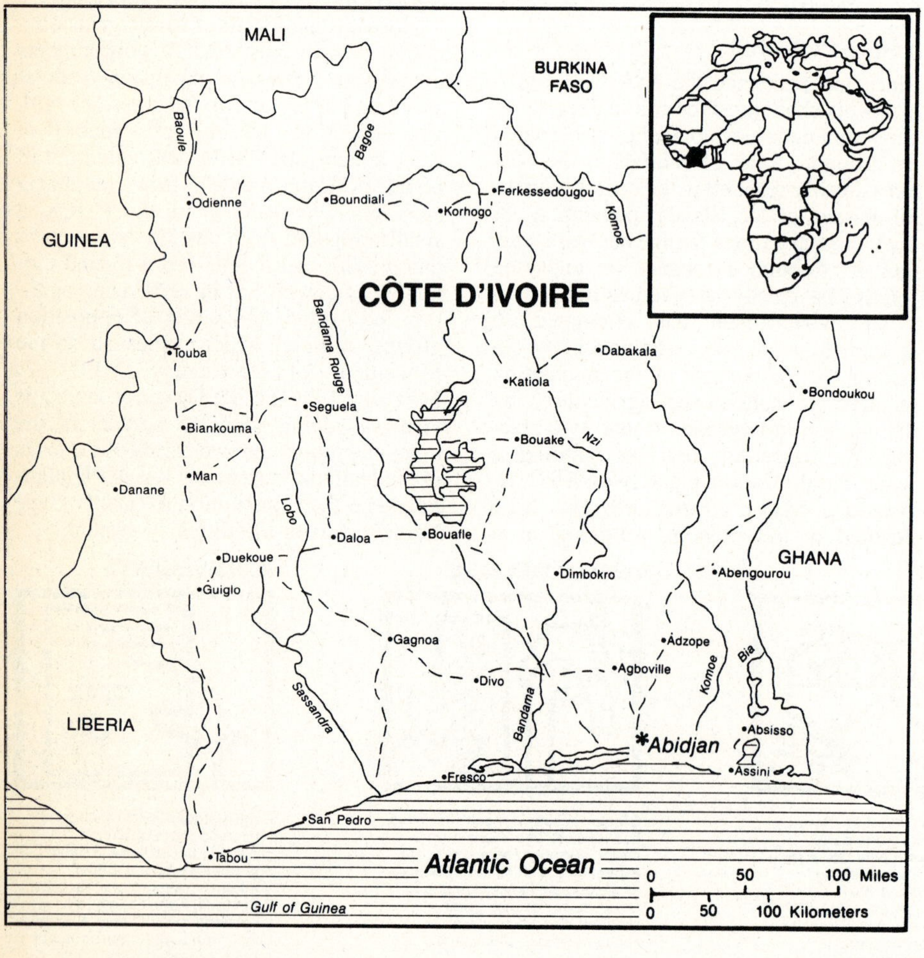

TRANSPORTATION

Highways—Kilometers (Miles): 53,736 (33,316)
Railroads—Kilometers (Miles): 657 (408)
Commercial Airports: 1 international

GOVERNMENT

Type: republic
Independence Date: August 7, 1960
Head of State: President Félix Houphouët-Boigny
Political Parties: Democratic Party of Côte d'Ivoire
Suffrage: universal over 21

MILITARY

Number of Armed Forces: 14,900
Military Expenditures (% of Central Government Expenditures): n/a
Current Hostilities: none

ECONOMY

Currency ($ U.S. Equivalent): 319 CFA francs = $1
Per Capita Income/GNP: $921/$9.3 billion
Inflation Rate: 4.3%
Natural Resources: agricultural lands; timber
Agriculture: coffee; cocoa; bananas; pineapples; palm oil; corn; millet; cotton; rubber
Industry: food and lumber processing; oil refinery; textiles; soap; automobile assembly

FOREIGN TRADE

Exports: $6.2 billion
Imports: $4.6 billion

THE COTE d'IVOIRE

After 3 decades of rule by its paternalistic first president, Felix Houphouët-Boigny, 1990 marked the opening of a new phase in the political life of the Côte d'Ivoire. Months of mounting prodemocracy protests and labor unrest have led to the legalization of opposition parties, previously banned under the country's one-party system of government, and the prospect that the 85- (official age) to 90-year-old president will soon be stepping down, despite his reelection in a bitterly disputed October 1990 ballot. These changes are taking place against a backdrop of a prolonged deterioration of the nation's once-vibrant economy. A primary explanation for this downturn is the decline in revenue from cocoa and coffee, long the state's principal export earners. This circumstance has led to mounting state debt, which in turn has pressured the government to impose unpopular austerity measures on its citizenry. The Côte d'Ivoire's current problems and potential are better understood in the context of its economy's overall performance under Le Vieux ("The Old Man"), as Houphouët-Boigny is called.

During its first 2 decades of independence the Côte d'Ivoire (French for "Ivory Coast") had one of the highest economic growth rates in the world. This growth was all the more notable in that, in contrast to most other Third World "success stories" during the same period, it was fueled by the expansion of commercial agriculture. The nation became the world's leading producer of cocoa and the third-largest producer of coffee. Although prosperity gave way to recession during the 1980s, the average per capita income of the country remains one of the highest in Africa. Statistics also indicate that, on average, Ivoirians live longer and better than do the citizens of most neighboring states. But the creation of a productive, market-oriented economy has not eliminated the reality of widespread poverty, leading some to question whether the majority of Ivoirians have derived reasonable benefit from their nation's wealth.

PROSPERITY FOR WHOM?

To the dismay of many young Ivoirians struggling to enter the country's tight job market, much of the political and economic life of the Côte d'Ivoire is controlled by its large expatriate population, which is mostly made up of French and Lebanese. These communities have grown tremendously since independence. Many of the foreigners are now quasi-permanent residents who have thrived by managing plantations, factories, and commercial enterprises. Others can be found in prominent positions in the civil service.

A group to have prospered in the past consists of commercial farmers, many of whom are medium- or small-scale producers, who number in the millions. About two-thirds of the workforce are employed in agriculture, with coffee alone being the principal source of income for some 2.5 million people, including those who provide services for the industry. In addition to cocoa and coffee, Ivoirian planters grow bananas, pineapples, sugar, cotton, palm oil, and other cash crops for export. Some of these farmers, including the nation's so-called No. 1 Peasant, Houphouët-Boigny, are quite wealthy, but most have only modest incomes.

In recent years the circumstance of Ivoirian coffee and cocoa planters has become much more precarious, due to fluctuations in the prices paid for their commodities on the world market. In this respect, the growers, along with their colleagues elsewhere, are to some extent victims of their own success. Their productivity, in response to international demand, has been a factor in depressing prices through increased supply. In 1988 President Houphouët-Boigny held cocoa in storage in an attempt to force a price rise, but the effort failed, aggravating the nation's economic downturn. As a result, the government has since taken a new approach, scrapping plans for future expansion in cocoa production in favor of promoting food crops such as yams, corn, and plantain, for which there is a broad West African as well as domestic Ivoirian market.

Ivoirian planters often hire low-paid laborers from other West African countries. There are about 2 million migrant laborers in the Côte d'Ivoire, who are employed throughout the economy. Their presence is not a new phenomenon but goes back to colonial times. Burkina Faso, where many laborers come from, was actually once a part of Côte d'Ivoire. Today Burkinabe as well as the citizens of other former colonies of French West Africa have the advantage of being paid in a regional currency, the CFA franc. A good road system and the Ivoirian railroad, which extends to the Burkinabe capital of Ouagadougou, facilitates the travel of migrant workers to the rural as well as urban areas.

Other factors help to determine how much individual Ivoirians benefit from the country's development. Residents of Abidjan, the capital, and its environs near the coast receive more services than do the citizens of interior areas. Professionals in the cities make better salaries than do laborers on farms or in small industries. Yet inflation and world recession have made daily life difficult for the middle class as well as for poorer peasants and workers. This has led to rising discontent. In 1983 teachers went on strike to protest the discontinuance of their housing subsidies. The government refused to yield and banned the teachers' union; the teachers went back to work. The ban has since been lifted, but the causes of discontent remain, for no teacher can afford the

(United Nations photo)

Some question whether all Ivoirians have benefited fairly from the country's wealth.

Agni and Baoulé peoples migrate to the Ivory Coast from the East
1700s

The Ivory Coast officially becomes a French colony
1893

Samori Touré, a Malinke Muslim leader and an empire builder, is defeated by the French
1898

The final French pacification of the country takes place
1915

The Ivory Coast becomes independent under Felix Houphouët-Boigny's leadership
1960

1980s–1990s

The PDCI approves a plan to move the capital from Abidjan to Yamoussoukro

Police attack prodemocracy demonstrations, leading to a further upsurge in unrest

The pope agrees to consecrate the controversial Yamoussoukro basilica

high rents in the cities. Moreover, teachers deeply resent the fact that other civil servants, ministers, and French cooperants (helpers on the Peace Corps model) did not have their subsidies cut, and they demand a more even "distribution of sacrifices." In 1987 teachers' leaders were detained by the government.

For most Ivoirians, conditions are likely to become worse before they improve. The nonagricultural sectors of the national economy have also been experiencing difficulties. For example, many state industries are unable to make a profit, due to their heavy indebtedness. Serious brush fires, mismanagement, and the clearing of forests for cash-crop plantations have put the nation's sizable timber industry in jeopardy. And plans for expansion of offshore oil production have not been implemented, because the billions of dollars needed for investment have not been raised.

Côte d'Ivoire's inability to raise capital for its oil industry is a reflection of the debt crisis which has plagued the country since the collapse of its cocoa and coffee earnings. Finding itself in the desperate situation of being forced to borrow to pay interest on its previous loans, the government suspended most debt repayments in 1987. Subsequent rescheduling negotiations with international creditors has resulted in an IMF- and World Bank-approved Structural Adjustment Plan (SAP). If fully implemented, this plan will result in a sharp reduction in the prices paid to Ivoirian farmers and a drastic curtailment in public spending, which is expected to lead to severe salary cuts for public and parastatal workers. Recent pressure by the lending agencies for the Ivoirian government to cut back on its commitment to cash crops is particularly ironic, given the praise that they have bestowed on the same policies in the past.

POLITICAL STABILITY

The government's ability to gain popular acceptance for its austerity measures is compromised by instances of corruption and extravagance at the top. A notorious example of the latter is a basilica that has recently been constructed at Yamoussoukro, the home village of Houphouët-Boigny, which is to become the nation's new capital city. This air-conditioned structure, patterned after the papal seat of St. Peter's Cathedral in Rome, is the largest Christian church building in the world. Supposedly a personal gift of Houphouët-Boigny to the Vatican (a most reluctant recipient), its 3-year construction is believed to have cost hundreds of millions of dollars.

The Côte d'Ivoire's current political upheaval comes after years of stability under President Houphouët-Boigny's mildly authoritarian one-party regime. To his credit, Le Vieux has in the past proved himself to be adept at striking a balance among the country's various regional and ethnic groups. He has also generally preferred to deal with internal opponents by emphasizing the carrot rather than the stick. While popular opinion seems to favor new leadership, it may not be easy for any successor to emerge from the shadow of Houphouët-Boigny's personal rule. The next leader is likely to come from the ruling Democratic Party of the Côte d'Ivoire (PDCI), which demonstrated its continued control over the electoral process in the nationwide elections held in 1990. One possible successor is Henri Konan Bedie, who is currently serving as the speaker of the National Assembly. New opposition parties have only begun to organize themselves openly and are clearly skeptical of the PDCI's commitment to multipartyism. In a joint news conference, the leaders of four of the largest parties charged the government with creating "numerous impediments to the effective implementation of pluralist democracy" and threatened "to send their militants into the streets" if their concerns were not addressed.

The course of domestic conflict in the Côte d'Ivoire will be keenly watched elsewhere. For decades Houphouët-Boigny has acted as the doyen of the more conservative, pro-Western leaders in Africa. Hostile to Libya and receptive to both Israel and to "dialogue" with South Africa, the Côte d'Ivoire has remained especially close to France, which maintains a military presence in the country. Rumors that the French have informed Houphouët-Boigny (as well as his Gabonese ally Omar Bongo) that they are no longer willing to commit their troops to his regime's survival have led to talk of an ongoing process of "Paristroika."

DEVELOPMENT

It has been said that the Côte d'Ivoire is "power hungry." The Soubre Dam, being developed on the Sassandra River, is the sixth and largest hydroelectric project in the Côte d'Ivoire. It will serve the eastern area of the country. Another dam is planned on the Cavalla River, between the Côte d'Ivoire and Liberia.

FREEDOM

The first Congress of the Ivoirian League of Human Rights met in July 1990 and called upon the government to establish "real democracy" in the country based on a respect for fundamental rights, including education and health services for all.

HEALTH/WELFARE

The Côte d'Ivoire has one of the lowest soldier-to-teacher ratios in Africa. Education absorbs about 40% of the national budget. Training of Ivoirians has reduced the country's reliance on French technicians in recent years.

ACHIEVEMENTS

Ivoirian textiles are varied and prized. Block printing and dyeing produce brilliant designs; woven cloths made strip by strip and sewn together include the white Korhogo tapestries, covered with Ivoirian figures, birds, and symbols drawn in black. Manufactured cloths often copy handmade prints.

The Gambia (Republic of The Gambia)

GEOGRAPHY

Area in Square Kilometers (Miles): 11,295 (4,361) (smaller than Connecticut)
Capital (Population): Banjul (49,200)
Climate: subtropical

PEOPLE

Population
Total: 840,000
Annual Growth Rate: 3.2%
Rural/Urban Population Ratio: 79/21
Languages: official: English; others spoken: Mandinka, Wolof, Fula, Sarakola, Diula, others

Health
Life Expectancy at Birth: 41 years (male); 44 years (female)
Infant Death Rate (Ratio): 217/1,000
Average Caloric Intake: 97% of FAO minimum
Physicians Available (Ratio): 1/10,588

Religion(s)
85% Muslim; 14% Christian; 1% traditional indigenous

Education
Adult Literacy Rate: 12%

HALEY'S *ROOTS*

"Kambay Bolong" and "Kunte Kinte" were two of the unfamiliar terms that Alex Haley's grandmother repeated as she told him of their "furthest back" ancestor, the African. When Haley started the search for his roots, he consulted linguists as well as Africans about these words. "Kambay Bolong" was identified as the Gambia River and "Kinte" as one of the major Mandinka lineages or large families. Thus began Haley's association with The Gambia, which culminated in his visit to the town of Juffure in Gambia's interior. There Haley heard the history of the Kinte clan from a *griot,* or bard, and identified his past ancestor. Today many Americans and others who have read or heard of Haley's story are among the tourists who visit The Gambia.

COMMUNICATION

Telephones: 3,500
Newspapers: 6

TRANSPORTATION

Highways—Kilometers (Miles): 2,990 (1,853)
Railroads—Kilometers (Miles): none
Commercial Airports: 1 international

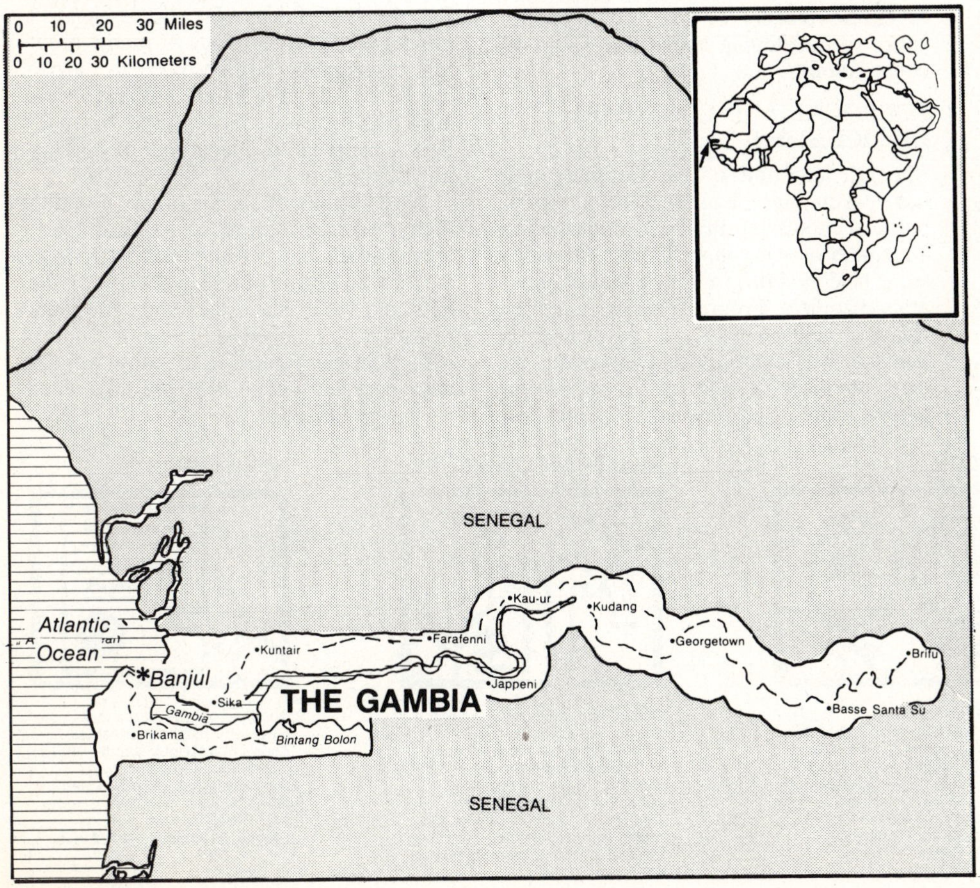

GOVERNMENT

Type: republic
Independence Date: February 18, 1965
Head of State: President (Sir) Alhaji Dawda Kairaba Jawara
Political Parties: Progressive People's Party; National Convention Party; Gambia People's Party
Suffrage: universal for adults

MILITARY

Number of Armed Forces: 550
Military Expenditures (% of Central Government Expenditures): n/a
Current Hostilities: internal conflicts

ECONOMY

Currency ($ U.S. Equivalent): 6.53 dalasis = $1
Per Capita Income/GNP: $255/$180 million
Inflation Rate: 22%
Natural Resources: fish; ilmenite; zircon; rutile
Agriculture: peanuts; rice; cotton; millet; sorghum; fish; palm kernels; livestock; rutile
Industry: peanuts; brewing; soft drinks; agricultural-machinery assembly; wood and metal working; clothing; tourism

FOREIGN TRADE

Exports: $35 million
Imports: $99 million

The British build Fort James at the current site of Banjul, on the Gambia River
1618

The Gambia is ruled by the United Kingdom through Sierra Leone
1807

Independence
1965

1980s–1990s

An attempted coup against President Dawda Jawara leads to Senegalese intervention

The rise and fall of the Senegambia Confederation

An era of political rebuilding and the Economic Recovery Program

THE GAMBIA

"The Gambia is a banana in the teeth of Senegal" goes an African saying. Indeed, except for its small seacoast, The Gambia, Africa's smallest noninsular nation, is entirely surrounded by its much larger neighbor. The nation's separate existence is rooted in the activities of British slave traders who in 1618 established a fort at the mouth of the Gambia River, from which they gradually spread their commercial and, later, political dominance upstream.

Notwithstanding their separate colonial experiences, the Gambians have much in common with the Senegalese. The Gambia's three major ethnolinguistic groups —the Mandinka, Wolof, and Fula or Peul—maintain links with their relatives in Senegal. The Wolof language serves as a *lingua franca* in the Gambian capital of Banjul as well as in urban areas of Senegal. Islam is the major religion in both countries (both also have substantial Christian and animist minorities). Gambian Muslims share with their Senegalese coreligionists a tradition of belonging to "Brotherhoods" organized around a common leader, or marabout. The economies of the countries are similar, with each, since the colonial period, being heavily reliant on the cultivation of groundnuts as a cash crop. Since independence both The Gambia and Senegal have also struggled to establish themselves politically as multiparty democracies.

THE SENEGAMBIAN CONFEDERATION

In 1981 the Gambian and Senegalese governments were drawn closer together by an attempted coup in Banjul. While Gambian President Dawda Jawara was absent in London, dissident elements within his Paramilitary Field Force joined with members of two small, self-styled, revolutionary socialist parties to depose him. Jawara, based on a 1965 mutual-defense agreement, was able to enlist the aid of some 3,000 Senegalese troops against his rebel compatriots. Constitutional rule was quickly restored, but the killings of 400 to 500 persons during the attempt, and subsequent mass arrests of suspected accomplices, left Gambians bitter and divided.

In the immediate aftermath of the uprising The Gambia agreed to merge with Senegal in a loose confederation, which some envisioned might eventually lead to a full political union. However, the Senegambia Confederation was marred by the circumstances of its formation. Other squabbles have also divided the two nations. Mutual frustration over the failure to resolve such questions led to the Confederation's formal demise in 1989. At the time, the leaders of the two countries spoke of developing alternative forms of cooperation.

POLITICAL AND ECONOMIC DIFFICULTIES

The rise and fall of the Confederation have taken place against a backdrop of political rebuilding in The Gambia in the aftermath of the coup attempt. Elections were held in 1982 in which Dawda Jawara's People's Progressive Party (PPP) was returned to power. The government's mandate was compromised, however, by the detention of the main opposition party's leader, Sherif Mustapha Dibba, on charges—later dismissed—of complicity in the revolt. Dibba's National Convention Party (NCP) nonetheless managed to attract a quarter of the vote. In 1987 the NCP and two smaller, recently formed, opposition parties increased their share of the vote. However, the government maintained a respectable 59 percent of the electorate, while actually increasing its representation in the Parliament. The result was seen as a mandate for the government to proceed with its Economic Recovery Program (ERP).

Since the introduction of ERP austerity measures, overall economic performance has improved, with gross domestic product growth of about 5 percent per year. But the ERP has so far had a negative impact on the livelihoods of many, proving especially burdensome to urban dwellers, and the harsh effects of the austerity measures have raised the public's sensitivity to allegations of corruption at the top.

Most Gambians are justifiably proud of their country's record of political tolerance, which has recently been strengthened by an easing of tensions between the PPP and NCP. Since the 1950s President Jawara has remained as the nation's dominant political figure, and many wonder what course local politics will take when he leaves the stage.

DEVELOPMENT

Since independence The Gambia has developed a tourist industry. Whereas in 1966 only 300 individuals were recorded as having visited the country, the figure for 1988–1989 was over 112,000. Tourism is now the second biggest sector of the economy, accounting for 10% of the gross domestic product.

FREEDOM

Despite the imposition of martial law in the aftermath of the 1982 coup, The Gambia has a strong record of respect for individual liberty and human rights. Banjul is the headquarters of the Organization of African Unity's Commission for Human and People's Rights.

HEALTH/WELFARE

School enrollment has expanded greatly since The Gambia's achievement of independence, but 40% of Gambian children remain outside the primary school setup. The Economic Recovery Program austerity has made it harder for the government to achieve its goal of education for all.

ACHIEVEMENTS

Gambian *griots*—hereditary bards and musicians such as Banna and Dembo Kanute—have maintained a traditional art. Formerly, griots were attached to ruling families; now they perform over Radio Gambia and are popular throughout West Africa.

Ghana (Republic of Ghana)

GEOGRAPHY

Area in Square Kilometers (Miles): 238,538 (92,100) (slightly smaller than Oregon)
Capital (Population): Accra (965,000)
Climate: tropical to semi-arid

PEOPLE

Population

Total: 13,754,000
Annual Growth Rate: 3.1%
Rural/Urban Population Ratio: 69/31
Languages: official: English; others spoken: Akan (including Fanti, Asante, Twi), Ewe, Ga, Hausa, others

Health

Life Expectancy at Birth: 50 years (male); 54 years (female)
Infant Death Rate (Ratio): 98/1,000
Average Caloric Intake: 85% of FAO minimum
Physicians Available (Ratio): 1/9,422

Religion(s)

45% traditional indigenous; 43% Christian; 12% Muslim

NKRUMAH

Kwame Nkrumah is a name remembered by peoples all over the world. Nkrumah developed ideas and institutions for peacefully but actively resisting British domination of Ghana, and he founded the Convention People's Party (CCP), which involved peoples of all walks of life in that struggle. Nkrumah believed that none of Africa was free until all of Africa was free. His efforts to develop a united Africa and his exploration of and warnings about neo-colonialism in Africa remain influential. Although his government was overthrown by a military coup, later regimes that criticized him nevertheless recognized his greatness and importance.

Education

Adult Literacy Rate: 30%

COMMUNICATION

Telephones: 74,930
Newspapers: 5

TRANSPORTATION

Highways—Kilometers (Miles): 54,196 (33,676)
Railroads—Kilometers (Miles): 953 (592)
Commercial Airports: 2 international

GOVERNMENT

Type: military; governed by the Provisional National Defense Council
Independence Date: March 6, 1957
Head of State: Flight Lieutenant Jerry Rawlings (chairman of the Provisional National Defense Council)
Political Parties: banned after the 1981 coup
Suffrage: universal over 18

MILITARY

Number of Armed Forces: 10,700
Military Expenditures (% of Central Government Expenditures): n/a
Current Hostilities: internal conflicts

ECONOMY

Currency ($ U.S. Equivalent): 262 cedis = $1
Per Capita Income/GNP: $420/$5.1 billion
Inflation Rate: 44%
Natural Resources: gold; diamonds; bauxite; manganese; fish; timber; oil
Agriculture: cocoa; coconuts; coffee; subsistence crops; rubber
Industry: mining, lumber; light manufacturing; fishing; aluminum

FOREIGN TRADE

Exports: $977 million
Imports: $988 million

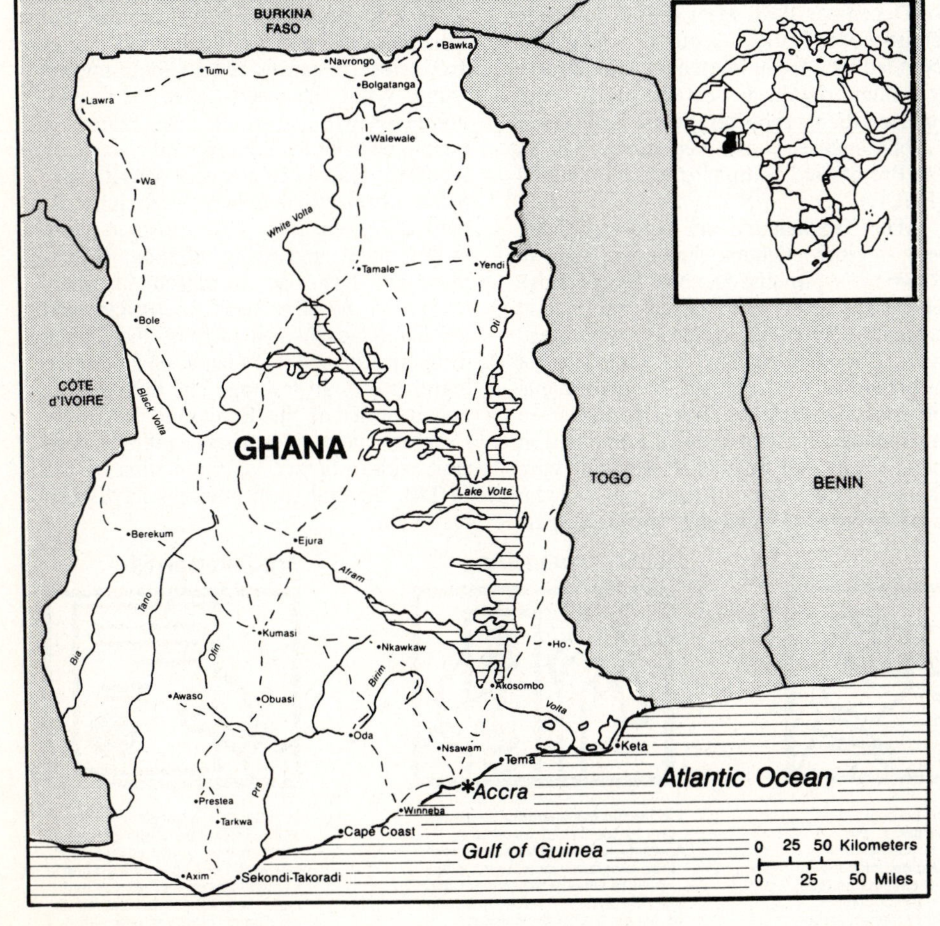

A Portuguese fort is built at Elmina **1482**

The establishment of the Asante Confederation under Osei Tutu **1690s**

The "Bonds" of 1844 signed by British officials and Fante chiefs as equals **1844**

The British finally conquer the Asante, a final step in British control of the region **1901**

Ghana is the first of the colonial territories in sub-Saharan Africa to become independent **1957**

Nkrumah is overthrown by a military coup **1966**

The first coup of Flight Lieutenant Rawlings **1979**

1980s–1990s

The second coup by Rawlings, the PNDC is formed

Rawlings accepts World Bank and IMF austerity measures

An alleged coup attempt and prodemocracy agitation lead to heightened political tension

GHANA'S POLITICAL HERITAGE

At its independence, in 1957, Ghana assumed a leadership role in the struggle against colonial rule elsewhere on the African continent. At the time, both its citizens and many outside observers were optimistic about the country's future. As compared to many other former colonies, the country seemed to have a strong infrastructure for future development. Unfortunately, the years since Ghana's hopeful beginning have been filled with disappointment.

Successive Ghanaian governments have pursued shifting strategies of development. Kwame Nkrumah, the nation's first president, attempted to implement an ambitious policy of industrial development. When substantial overseas investment failed to materialize, he turned to socialism. His efforts led to a modest rise in local manufacturing, but the sector's productivity was compromised by inefficient planning, limited resources, the expense of technological inputs, and mounting government corruption. The new state enterprises were financed largely from the export earnings of cocoa, which had emerged as the principal cash crop during the colonial period. Following colonial precedent, Nkrumah adopted a policy of paying local cocoa farmers well below the world-market price for their output, in order to expand state revenues.

In 1966 Nkrumah, who had transformed Ghana into a one-party state in which power was increasingly concentrated in his office, was overthrown by the military. Since then the army has been the dominant political institution in the country, although there have been short periods of a formal return to civilian control. Although the officers abandoned much of Nkrumah's socialist commitment, they continued his policy of squeezing the cocoa farmers, with the long-term result of encouraging planters both to cut back on their production and to attempt to circumvent the official prices through smuggling. This trend, coupled with falling cocoa prices on the world market and rising import costs, helped push Ghana into a state of severe economic depression during the 1970s; it is estimated that during that period real wages fell by some 80 percent. Ghana's crisis was aggravated by an unwillingness on the government's part to devalue the local currency, the cedi, which encouraged black-market trading.

REVOLUTION OR REGIMENTATION?

In December 1981, after a brief return to constitutional rule, a group of young officers led by a flight lieutenant named Jerry Rawlings regained power. Along with their civilian supporters, these self-styled revolutionaries constituted themselves as the Provisional National Defense Council (PNDC).

Many Ghanaians were skeptical of the new regime. Others, however, saw in Rawlings's populist rhetoric the promise of change after years of corruption and stagnation. People's Defense Committees were formed throughout the country to act as both official watchdogs and instruments of mass mobilization. For a period these institutions, motivated by a combination of idealism and popular frustration with the status quo, seemed to be pushing the country toward anarchy, through their penchant for revolutionary vigilantism, but by 1983 they had been reined in. During that same year the country faced a new crisis, when the Nigerian government suddenly expelled nearly a million Ghanaian expatriates, who had to be resettled quickly.

Faced with an increasingly desperate situation, the PNDC, in a move that surprised many, given its seemingly leftist leanings, began to implement a comprehensive, International Monetary Fund-supported program of reducing the state's size and economic role. As a result of this Economic Recovery Program (ERP), some 45,000 civil servants were fired, the cedi was progressively devalued, and wages and prices began to reflect their market value. While these steps have led to economic growth, since the late 1980s the human costs of the government's austerity measures have been a source of criticism. Many ordinary Ghanaians, especially urban salary earners, have suffered from falling wages and rising inflation. Unemployment has also increased in many areas. On the other hand, the prices paid to Ghana's cash-crop farmers have risen dramatically, and there has been a boom in legitimate retail trading. The mixed costs and benefits of the Economic Recovery Program have given rise to political tension within as well as opposition to the PNDC. Several coup attempts have been reported.

DEVELOPMENT

To reduce dependence on oil imports, Ghana aims to expand the use of solar energy for telecommunications and for water pumps and irrigation projects.

FREEDOM

Curfews, closed borders, pressure on the press, and courts that do not allow for appeal are measures imposed by the government. Executions take place. Students, union leaders, and others have protested these restrictions, but many have been imprisoned or exiled. Authorities closed universities in 1987 and 1988.

HEALTH/WELFARE

To lessen the austerity measures and to counteract years of decline, Ghana plans to support food programs for workers, give credit to small-scale farmers and market sellers, promote self-help projects, and finance water supply, sanitation, health care, and housing.

ACHIEVEMENTS

In 1988 Ghana celebrated the 25th anniversary of the School of the Performing Arts at the University of Legon. Integrating the world of dance, drama, and music, the school has trained a generation of artists committed to Ghanaian, African, and international traditions in the arts.

Guinea (Republic of Guinea)

GEOGRAPHY

Area in Square Kilometers (Miles): 246,048 (95,000) (slightly larger than Oregon)
Capital (Population): Conakry (656,000)
Climate: tropical

PEOPLE

Population
Total: 6,147,000
Annual Growth Rate: 2.8%
Rural/Urban Population Ratio: 74/26
Languages: official: French; others spoken: Fula, Mandinka, Susu, Malinke, others

Health
Life Expectancy at Birth: 44 years
Infant Death Rate (Ratio): 159/1,000
Average Caloric Intake: 78% of FAO minimum
Physicians Available (Ratio): 1/22,884

Religion(s)
85% Muslim; 10% Christian; 5% indigenous

SAMORI TOURÉ

In the late nineteenth century Malinke leader Samori Touré established a powerful state in the interior of Guinea and Côte d'Ivoire. Samori, called "the Napoleon of the Sudan," was a Muslim, and he converted many of the areas that he conquered, but he was not a jihadist. His state was based on modern military organization and tactics; this enabled him to resist the European conquest longer and more effectively than any other West African leader. Through alliances, sieges, control of arms trade, and, ultimately, manufacture of guns and ammunition, Samori fought the French and resisted conquest throughout the 1890s. Manipulating African competition and people's fear of Samori, the French allied with African leaders and prevented a unified resistance to their rule.

Education
Adult Literacy Rate: 48%

COMMUNICATION

Telephones: 10,000
Newspapers: 1

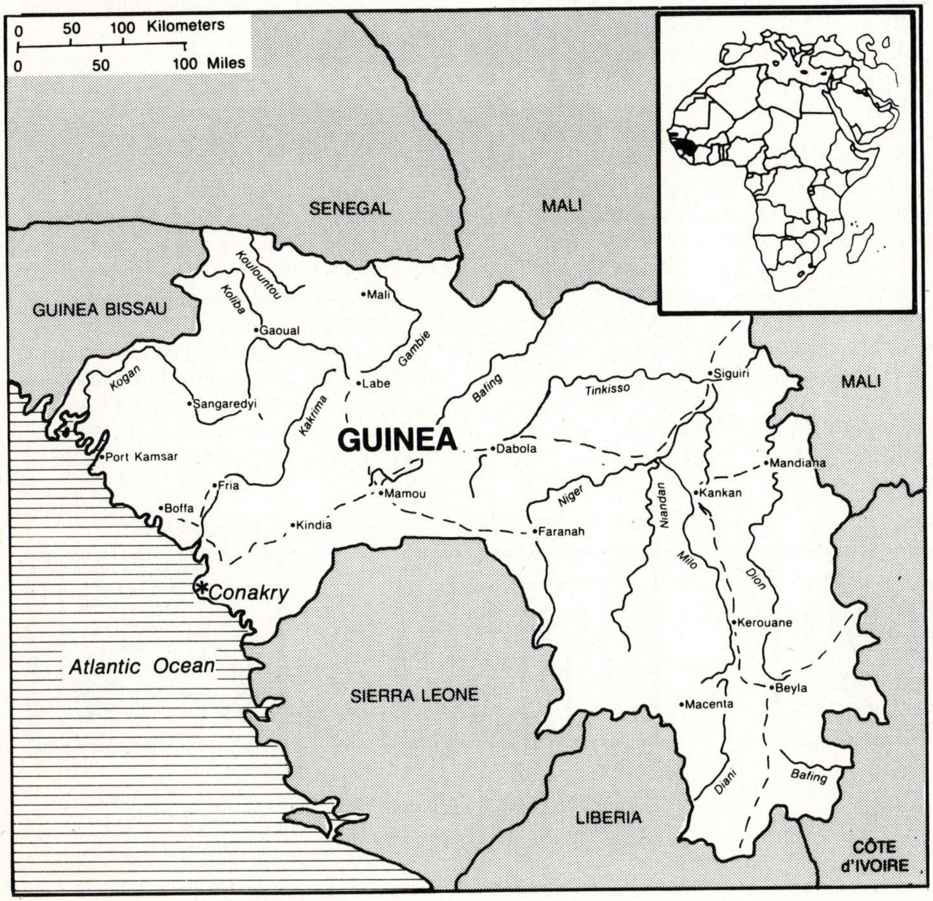

TRANSPORTATION

Highways—Kilometers (Miles): 28,400 (13,608)
Railroads—Kilometers (Miles): 940 (582)
Commercial Airports: 2 international

GOVERNMENT

Type: republic, under military regime
Independence Date: October 2, 1958
Head of State: President (General) Lansana Conté
Political Parties: none
Suffrage: universal over 18

MILITARY

Number of Armed Forces: 11,000
Military Expenditures (% of Central Government Expenditures): n/a
Current Hostilities: none

ECONOMY

Currency ($ U.S. Equivalent): 301 francs = $1
Per Capita Income/GNP: $305/$1.9 billion
Inflation Rate: 6%
Natural Resources: bauxite; iron ore; diamonds; gold; water power
Agriculture: rice; cassava; millet; corn; coffee; bananas; palm products; pineapples
Industry: bauxite; alumina; light manufacturing and processing

FOREIGN TRADE

Exports: $537 million
Imports: $403 million

A major Islamic kingdom is established in the Futa Djalon
1700s

Samori Touré, the leader of a state in the Guinea and Ivory Coast interior, is defeated by the French
1898

French President Giscard d'Estaing visits Guinea: the beginning of a reconciliation between France and Guinea
1978

Led by Sekou Touré, Guineans reject continued membership in the French Community; an independent republic is formed
1958

1980s–1990s

Sekou Touré's death is followed by a military coup

The introduction of the severe Structural Adjustment Program leads to urban unrest and widespread hardship

President Lansana Conté grants amnesty to political prisoners and suggests dialogue with Guinean exiles over a new constitution

GUINEA

Nineteen eighty-eight marked the 30th anniversary of Guinea's independence from France. Sixty years earlier, France had overcome stiff local resistance to conquer the country.

In a 1958 referendum, Guineans voted to leave the community of self-governing West African states which France had established. At the time Guinea was the only member of the French Community to opt for immediate independence. The French reacted spitefully, withdrawing all aid, personnel, and equipment from the new government.

France's response has had an influence on the nation's postindependence development. The prompt arrival of assistance from the Soviet Bloc, along with the ability of the locally dominant Democratic Party of Guinea (PDG) to provide an institutional basis for a new administrative framework, gave impetus to the early establishment of a one-party socialist state, the first such regime on the African continent. The major figure behind this transformation was Sekou Touré, the country's first president.

SEKOU TOURÉ AND HIS SUCCESSORS

From his early years as a radical trade-union activist during the late 1940s until his death in office in 1984, Sekou Touré remained the dominant personality within Guinea. A descendent of the nineteenth-century Malinke hero Samori Touré, he proved to be a charismatic but repressive leader. Touré's rule was characterized by economic mismanagement and the widespread abuse of human rights. It is estimated that some 2 million people, about 1 out of every 4 Guineans, fled the country during his rule. At least 2,900 individuals disappeared under detention.

By the late 1970s Touré, pressured by rising discontent and his own apparent realization of the country's poor economic performance, began to modify both his domestic and foreign policies. This shift led to better relations with Western countries but resulted in little improvement in the lives of his people. In 1982 Amnesty International launched a campaign to publicize the Touré regime's dismal record of political killings, detentions, and torture, but the world remained largely indifferent.

On April 3, 1984, a week after Touré's death, the army stepped in, claiming that it wished to end all vestiges of the late president's dictatorial regime. The coup was accomplished without a shot and was well received by Guineans. Hundreds of political prisoners were released, and the once-powerful PDG was disbanded. A new government was formed, under the leadership of Colonel Lansana Conté.

The Conté government survived a 1985 coup attempt and has since promised to hand over power to an elected civilian government in 1994, by which time it hopes to have succeeded in its program to restructure the local economy.

The government has committed itself to a severe Structural Adjustment Program (SAP), which has proved painful to many Guineans. Adoption of the free-market philosophy of the World Bank and International Monetary Fund has led to a dismantling of many socialist structures. Other steps have included a radical devaluation of the nation's currency, a sharp reduction in the civil service, and removal of the food and fuel subsidies enjoyed by urban dwellers. While international financiers have generally praised each of these steps, a trebling of food prices led in 1988 to campus and urban riots. This challenge to Conté's rule and discontent among the military led the president to postpone some price increases and reshuffle his Cabinet, but the government has proceeded with the introduction of the second phase of its SAP.

Despite its status as one of the world's 25 poorest countries, Guinea is well blessed with natural resources, which hold out the prospect for a more prosperous future. Guinea's greatest economic failing has been the poor performance of its agricultural sector. Unlike many of its neighbors, the country enjoys a favorable climate and soils. But although some 80 percent of the population engage in subsistence farming, only 3 percent of the land is cultivated; foodstuffs remain a major import. The blame for this situation largely falls on the Touré regime's legacy of an inefficient state-controlled system of marketing and distribution.

DEVELOPMENT

Recent economic growth in Guinea is reflected in the rising traffic in Conakry harbor, whose volume between 1983 and 1987 rose 415%. Plans are being made to improve the port's infrastructure.

FREEDOM

Although committed to a gradual program of democratization, the Conté government rules by decree and limits dissent through its control over media.

HEALTH/WELFARE

The life expectancy of Guineans, 44 years, is among the lowest in the world, reflecting the actual stagnation of the nation's health service during the Touré years.

ACHIEVEMENTS

More than 80% of the programming broadcast by Guinea's television service is locally produced. This output has included more than 3,000 movies. A network of rural radio stations is currently being installed.

Guinea-Bissau (Republic of Guinea-Bissau)

GEOGRAPHY

Area in Square Kilometers (Miles): 36,125 (13,948) (about the size of Indiana)
Capital (Population): Bissau (125,000)
Climate: tropical

AMILCAR CABRAL

Amilcar Cabral (1924–1973), born in Cape Verde and raised in Guinea-Bissau, was an idealist who developed plans for his country's liberation and an activist who worked to put these plans into action. He was a friend of Agostinho Neto of Angola, a founding member of Angola's present ruling party MPLA, and he worked in Angola. Cabral worked for an African system of government, a change in structures that would mean "a reorganization of the country on new lines." He believed that a revolution could not result from leadership alone; everyone must fight a mental battle and know their goals before taking arms. Cabral's work with peasants from 1952 to 1954, while carrying out an agricultural census, helped him to understand and reach rural peoples who were to be the crucial force in the development of Guinea-Bissau's independence from Portugal.

PEOPLE

Population

Total: 932,000
Annual Growth Rate: 2.2%
Rural/Urban Population Ratio: n/a
Languages: official: Portuguese; others spoken: Kriolo, Fula, Mandinka, Manjara, Balante, others

Health

Life Expectancy at Birth: 42 years
Infant Death Rate (Ratio): 137/1,000
Average Caloric Intake: 74% of FAO minimum
Physicians Available (Ratio): 1/8,657

Religion(s)

65% traditional indigenous; 32% Muslim; 3% Christian

Education

Adult Literacy Rate: 19%

COMMUNICATION

Telephones: 3,000
Newspapers: 1

TRANSPORTATION

Highways—Kilometers (Miles): 5,058 (3,135)
Railroads—Kilometers (Miles): none
Commercial Airports: 1 international

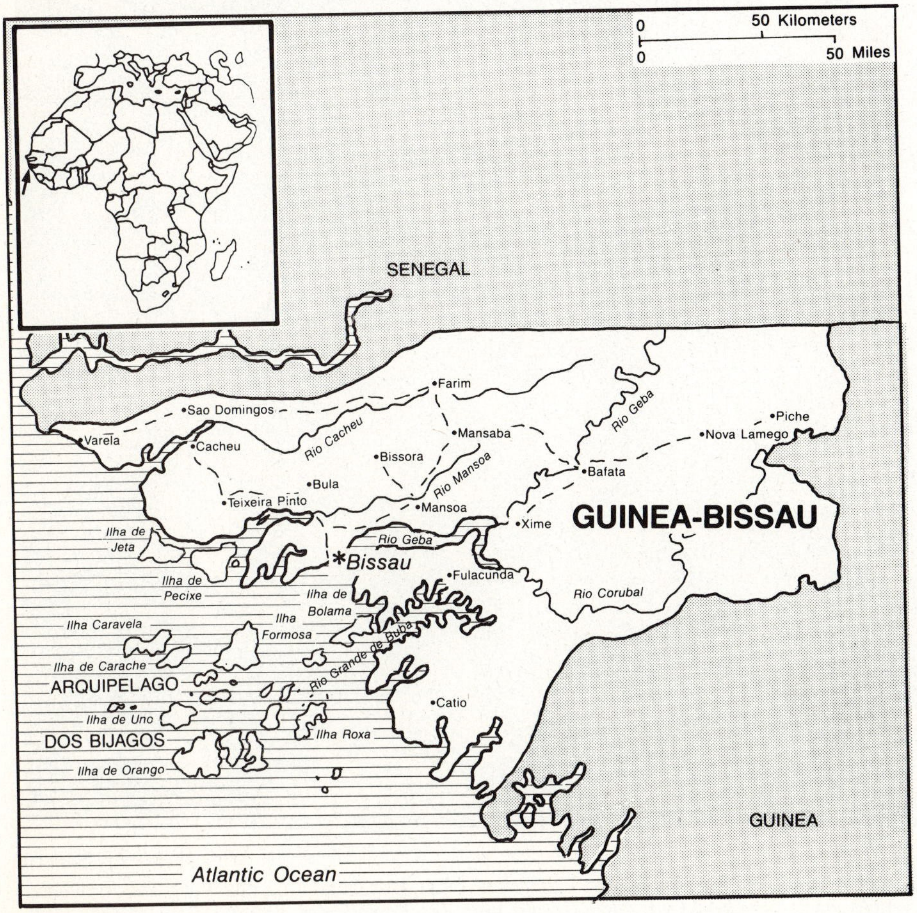

GOVERNMENT

Type: republic; overseen by Revolutionary Council
Independence Date: September 24, 1973
Head of State: President (Major) João Bernardo Vieira
Political Parties: African Party for the Independence of Guinea-Bissau and Cape Verde (PAIGC)
Suffrage: universal over 15

MILITARY

Number of Armed Forces: 7,200
Military Expenditures (% of Central Government Expenditures): n/a
Current Hostilities: recent border clashes with Senegal

ECONOMY

Currency ($ U.S. Equivalent): 652 pesos = $1
Per Capita Income/GNP: $185/$150 million
Inflation Rate: 30%
Natural Resources: bauxite; timber; shrimp; fish
Agriculture: peanuts; rice; palm kernels; groundnuts
Industry: agricultural processing; hides and skins; beer; soft drinks

FOREIGN TRADE

Exports: $16 million
Imports: $63 million

GUINEA-BISSAU

Guinea-Bissau, wedged between Senegal and Guinea on the west coast of Africa, has an unenviable claim to being the poorest country in the world. To many outsiders, the nation is better known for the liberation struggle which was waged by its people between 1962 and 1974 against Portuguese colonial rule. Mobilized through the African Party for the Independence of Guinea-Bissau and Cape Verde (PAIGC), the people of Guinea-Bissau, who then numbered fewer than 1 million, played a major role in the overthrow of fascist rule within Portugal and the liberation of its other African colonies. The movement's effectiveness has led many to view its struggle as a model of anti-imperialist resistance.

The origins of Portuguese rule in Guinea-Bissau go back to the late 1400s. For centuries the area was raided as a source of slaves, who were shipped to Portugal and its colonies of Cape Verde and Brazil. With the nineteenth-century abolition of slave trading, the Portuguese began to impose forced labor within Guinea-Bissau itself. During the twentieth century the fascist New State government in Portugal rationalized its repression by extending limited civil rights only to those educated Africans who were officially judged to have assimilated Portuguese culture—the so-called *assimilados.* In Guinea-Bissau, only 0.3 percent of the local population were ever recognized as assimilados. Many within this select group were migrants from Cape Verde who, in contrast to mainland Africans, automatically enjoyed the status.

THE INDEPENDENCE MOVEMENT

In 1956 six assimilados, led by Amilcar Cabral, founded the PAIGC as a vehicle for the liberation of Cape Verde as well as Guinea-Bissau. From the beginning many Cape Verdeans, such as Cabral, played a prominent role within the PAIGC. But the group's largest following and main center of activity was in Guinea-Bissau. In 1963 the PAIGC turned to armed resistance and began organizing itself as an alternative government. By the end of the decade the movement had gained a mass following

(FAO photo by F. Mattioli)

With the implementation of the 200-mile Exclusive Economic Zones (EEZs), the fishing industry of West African nations has increased in overall terms. Previously a large majority of the region's fish stocks were harvested by foreign vessels from the Soviet Union, Poland, Spain, Korea, and France; today the EEZ has effectively given countries like Guinea-Bissau a much-needed boost in food production.

Portuguese ships arrive; claimed as Portuguese Guinea; slave trading develops
1446

Portugal gains effective control over most of the region
1915

The African Party for the Independence of Guinea-Bissau and Cape Verde (PAIGC) is formed
1956

Liberation struggle in Guinea-Bissau under the leadership of the PAIGC and Amilcar Cabral
1963–1973

Cabral is assassinated; the PAIGC declares Guinea-Bissau independent
1973

Revolution in Portugal leads to Portugal's recognition of Guinea-Bissau's independence and the end of war
1974

1980s–1990s

Vieira comes to power through a military coup

Guinea-Bissau refuses to accept the International Court decision awarding the potentially oil-rich ocean bed to Senegal

Senegalese and Guinea-Bissau forces are involved in border clashes

and was in control of two-thirds of the countryside.

In its liberated areas, the PAIGC was notably successful in establishing its own marketing, judicial, and educational, as well as political, institutions. Widespread participation throughout Guinea-Bissau in the 1973 election of a National Assembly encouraged a number of countries formally to recognize the PAIGC declaration of state sovereignty during the same year. This development helped to convince leading Portuguese officers that the fight to maintain their African empire was futile. By that time many within the colonial army's ranks had begun to sympathize with their "enemy," in part through their clandestine exposure to the writings of Cabral and other revolutionaries. In 1974 the military seized power in Portugal and moved quickly to recognize Guinea-Bissau's independence.

THE CHALLENGES OF INDEPENDENCE

Since 1974 the leaders of Guinea-Bissau have tried to confront the problems of independence while maintaining the idealism of their liberation struggle. The nation's weak economy has limited their success. Guinea-Bissau has little in the way of manufacturing or mining, although explorations have revealed potentially exploitable reserves of oil, bauxite, and phosphates. (Many of the enterprises that do exist in the capital city of Bissau were created to serve the large garrison of Portuguese troops who occupied the city during the liberation struggle.) Although more than 80 percent of the population are engaged in agriculture, the urban population is dependent on imported foodstuffs. This situation has been generally attributed to a poor communications infrastructure and a lack of incentives for farmers to grow surpluses. Only 8 percent of the small country is currently cultivated. Efforts to improve the rural economy during the early years of independence were further marred by severe drought.

MILITARY COUP AND A NEW CONSTITUTION

Amilcar Cabral was assassinated in 1973. His brother, Luis Cabral, succeeded him as the leader of the PAIGC and thereafter became Guinea-Bissau's first president. Before 1980 both Guinea-Bissau and Cape Verde were separately governed by a united PAIGC, which had as its goal the forging of a political union between the two territories. But in 1980 Luis Cabral was overthrown by members of his military, who accused him of governing through a "Cape Verdean clique." João Vieira, a popular military commander during the liberation war who had also served as prime minister, was appointed as the new head of state. As a result, relations between Cape Verde and Guinea-Bissau deteriorated, leading to a breakup in the political links between the two nations.

Under Vieira, the PAIGC has continued to rule Guinea-Bissau as a single-party state. Over the years grass-roots democracy, which the party had fostered in its liberated zones during the war, has been compromised by a centralization of power around Vieira and other members of the military-dominated Council of State. Several coup attempts since 1980, most notably in 1985, resulted in increased authoritarianism. During the 1984 elections the voters' choices were limited to candidates appearing on party-prepared lists.

In 1987, in an effort to revive its bankrupt economy, the government adopted a Structural Adjustment Program (SAP). The peso was devalued, civil servants were dismissed, and various subsidies were reduced. The effects of these reforms on urban workers have been cushioned somewhat by foreign aid.

In a desperate move, the government in 1988 signed an agreement with the Intercontract Company which would have allowed the firm to use Guinea-Bissau territory for 5 years as a major dumping site for toxic waste from the United Kingdom, Switzerland, and the United States. In return, the government would have earned up to $800 million, a figure some 50 times greater than the current annual value of the nation's exports. The government was forced to revoke the agreement, however, after the deal was exposed by members of the country's exiled opposition. It is believed that a major environmental catastrophe would have resulted had the plan gone through. This incident underscores the vulnerability of Guinea-Bissau's underdeveloped economy.

DEVELOPMENT

Two joint-venture fishing companies, the Soviet-Guinean Estrela do Mar and the Franco-Guinean SEMPESCA, have exploited Guinea-Bissau's rich fishing reserves, and local fishermen are supported by international funding. Fishing is a top priority, but production and consumption are still far behind that of other West African countries.

FREEDOM

PAIGC leadership controls all organizations as well as the government. PAIGC nominated one-third of the candidates for elections to regional councils. Vieira commuted the death sentences of 6 of 12 coup plotters. Forty-four others received jail terms; 5 of the accused died in police custody.

HEALTH/WELFARE

Despite genuine efforts on the part of the government and international aid agencies to improve the situation, Guinea-Bissau's health statistics remain appalling: an overall 42-year life expectancy, 20% infant mortality, and more than 90% of the population infected with malaria.

ACHIEVEMENTS

A major agricultural-industrial complex at Cumeré was completed in 1981 through the support of Saudi Arabia, Italy, and the Islamic Development Bank. Groundnuts and cereals produced by farmers or rural-development projects are processed by Cumeré.

Liberia (Republic of Liberia)

GEOGRAPHY

Area in Square Kilometers (Miles): 111,370 (43,000) (somewhat larger than Pennsylvania)
Capital (Population): Monrovia (425,000)
Climate: tropical

PEOPLE

Population

Total: 2,640,000
Annual Growth Rate: 3.4%
Rural/Urban Population Ratio: 60/40
Languages: official: English; others spoken: Kpelle, Bassa, Dan, Vai, Wee, Loma, Kru, Glebo, Mano, Gola, Mandinka

Health

Life Expectancy at Birth: 54 years (male); 58 years (female)
Infant Death Rate (Ratio): 127/1,000
Average Caloric Intake: 114% of FAO minimum
Physicians Available (Ratio): 1/11,185

Religion(s)

60% Christian; 25% traditional indigenous; 15% Muslim

KRU MARINERS

For 400 years Kru-speaking peoples from the southeast of Liberia have worked on European ships as sailors, navigators, and stevedores. They have guided ships to shore, unloaded cargo, and provided food supplies to passing traders. Many have sold goods from their canoes on their return trips to the Liberian coast, while others have established Kru communities in port cities such as Freetown, Accra, and Calabar. Their trading activities, acquaintance with European culture, and mobility enabled them to resist Liberian settler control throughout the nineteenth century. In 1915 their revolt against the Liberian government ended when U.S. troops bombarded the Kru Coast.

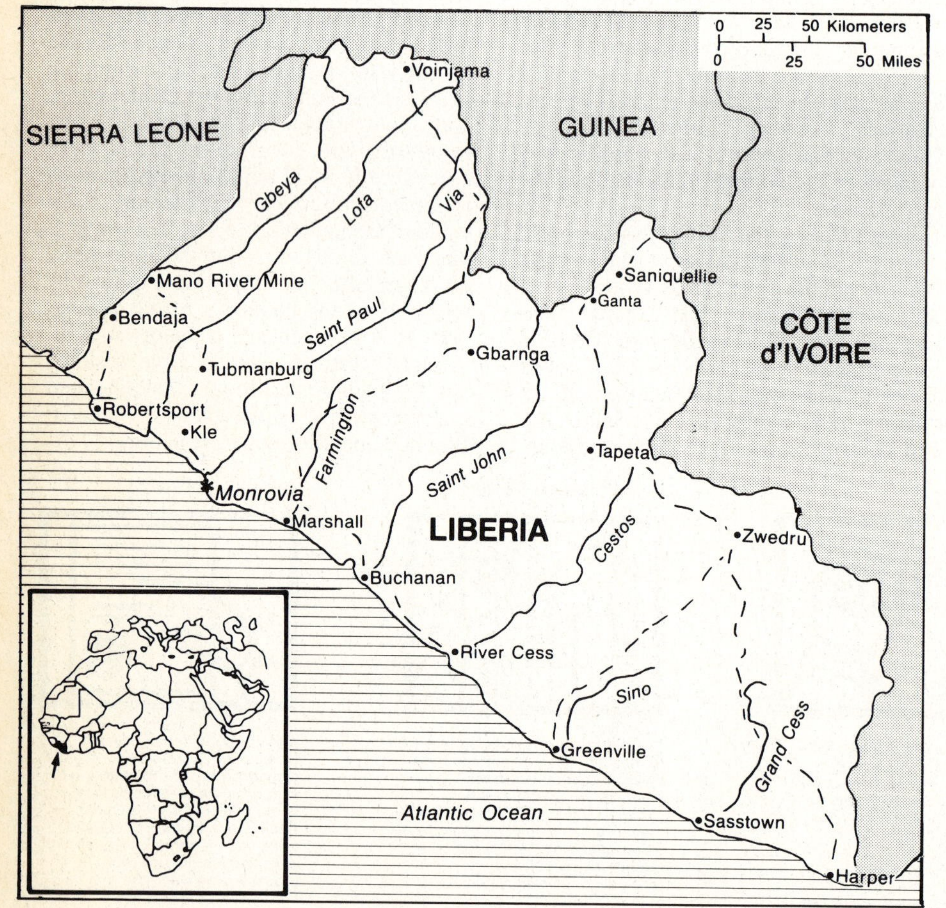

Education

Adult Literacy Rate: 35%

COMMUNICATION

Telephones: 8,510
Newspapers: 4

TRANSPORTATION

Highways—Kilometers (Miles): 10,087 (6,254)
Railroads—Kilometers (Miles): 480 (298)
Commercial Airports: 1 international

GOVERNMENT

Type: republic
Independence Date: July 26, 1847
Head of State: President—none at this writing due to internal political turmoil
Political Parties: National Democratic Party of Liberia; Liberian Action Party; Liberian People's Party (banned); Liberian Unification Party; Unity Party; United People's Party
Suffrage: universal over 18

MILITARY

Number of Armed Forces: 6,050
Military Expenditures (% of Central Government Expenditures): 2.4%
Current Hostilities: internal hostilities

ECONOMY

Currency ($ U.S. Equivalent): 1 Liberian dollar = $1
Per Capita Income/GNP: $395/$988 million
Inflation Rate: 12%
Natural Resources: iro ore; rubber; timber; diamonds
Agriculture: rubber; rice; palm oil; cassava; coffee; cocoa; sugar
Industry: iron and diamond mining; rubber processing; food processing; lumber milling

FOREIGN TRADE

Exports: $550 million
Imports: $335 million

LIBERIA

In August 1980 Sergeant Samuel Doe and 17 other noncommissioned officers and enlisted men entered the Executive Mansion and assassinated Liberia's President William Tolbert. Doe proceeded to take power as leader of a ruling body, the People's Redemption Council (PRC), made up of civilian and military ministers. To most Liberians, the coup held out the promise of a new Liberia, based on greater national unity, social justice, and democracy. Unfortunately, such optimism went unrealized. A decade later the nation was reduced to near anarchy by a bloody civil war. The presidency of Doe, like that of Tolbert, had collapsed due to its authoritarianism, corruption, ethnic chauvinism, and inability to meet the needs of Liberia's impoverished masses.

LIBERIA BEFORE 1980

The Republic of Liberia has a unique history. Among the African states, it shares with Ethiopia the distinction of having avoided European rule. Between 1847 and 1980 the republic was governed by an elite made up primarily of descendants of African-Americans who had begun settling the Liberian coast 2 decades earlier. These so-called Americo-Liberians only made up about 3 percent of the population, but for decades they controlled the country's political life through their dominance of the governing True Whig Party (TWP). Although the republic's constitution was ostensibly democratic, the TWP controlled the electoral process to its own advantage.

Most Liberians belong to groups who were already established in the country when the black settlers arrived. The largest of these indigenous ethnolinguistic groups are the Kpelle, Bassa, Gio, Kru, Krahn, and Vai. These communities have been organized into local village democracies and loose regional confederations. Historically, they resisted the domination of the Americo-Liberians. However, through superior weaponry, the Liberian state expanded into the interior.

Members of the indigenous groups gradually gained positions within the Liberian state by accepting Americo-Liberian norms. Yet book learning, Christianity, and an ability to speak English helped an indigenous person to advance within the state only if he or she accepted its status quo, which included becoming a client of an Americo-Liberian patron. In a special category were the important interior "chiefs" who were able to maintain their local authority as long as they accepted their subordination to the republic.

During the twentieth century Liberian society began to be changed by the emergence of forces such as the vast Firestone rubber plantations, iron-ore mining, and urbanization. President William Tubman (1944–1971) proclaimed a Unification Policy, to promote national integration, and an Open-Door Policy, to encourage outside investment. However, most of the profits that resulted from the investments that did occur left the country, while the wealth that remained was concentrated in the hands of the TWP elite.

In the decade after Tubman's death, during William Tolbert's administration, many Liberians became more conscious of the inequities of society and the ineffectiveness of the TWP in addressing them. Young educated people, from all ethnic backgrounds, refused to join the regime's patronage system. Dissident associations, such as the Movement for African Justice and the Progressive Alliance of Liberia, were formed.

Meanwhile, economic conditions worsened. Four percent of the population controlled 60 percent of the wealth, while the masses grew relatively more impoverished. Rural stagnation drove many to the capital city of Monrovia, where many remained unemployed and, during the 1970s, burdened by high inflation. The inevitable explosion occurred in 1979, when the government announced a 50-percent price increase for rice, the national staple. Police fired on demonstrators, killing as many as 140 persons and wounding hundreds more. Chaos and rioting resulted in great property damage and led the government to appeal to neighboring Guinea for troops. It was clear that the True Whig Party was losing its grip. When the 1980 coup finally occurred it had widespread support.

(FAO photo by John Isaac)

The chaos that has inflicted Liberia in recent times has left the country destitute. Virtual political anarchy has destroyed the infrastructure, economy, cities, and culture of the land.

The Vai move onto the Liberian coast from the interior
1500s

The first Afro-American settlers arrive from the United States
1822

The first coup changes one Americo-Liberian government for another
1871

The League of Nations investigates forced labor charges
1931

President William Tubman comes to office
1944

William Tolbert becomes president
1972

The first riots in contemporary Liberian history occur when the price of rice is raised
1979

1980s–1990s

The assassination of Tolbert; a military coup brings Samuel Doe to power

Doe is elected president amidst accusations of election fraud

Civil war leads to the death of Doe, anarchy, and foreign intervention

"SAME TAXI, DIFFERENT DRIVER"

Doe came to power as Liberia's first indigenous president, a symbolically important event that many believed would herald substantive changes. Some major institutions of the old order, such as the TWP and the Masonic Temple (looked upon as Liberia's secret government) were disbanded. The House and Senate were suspended. Offices changed hands, but the old administrative system persisted. Many of those who came to power were members of Doe's own ethnic group, the Krahn, who had long been prominent in the lower ranks of the army.

The PRC promised to return Liberia to civilian rule in 1986. A new Constitution was approved, which, like the old one, was based on that of the United States. The 4-year ban on politics was lifted in 1984, but the PRC prevented two parties from organizing and banned several opposition leaders. Doe ran for president.

In spite of harassment, thousands of Liberians went to the polls in October 1985. Doe was declared the winner, but there was much evidence of ballot tampering. One month later, exiled General Thomas Quiwonkpa led an abortive coup attempt. During and after the uprising up to 11,500 people were killed, including many belonging to Quiwonkpa's Gio group, who were the victims of reprisals by loyalist (largely Krahn) troops. Doe was inaugurated but several opposition-party members refused to take their seats in the National Assembly, while others, fearing for their lives, went into exile.

During the late 1980s Doe presided over an authoritarian regime. Many locals called on the U.S. government, in particular, to withhold aid until detainees were freed and new elections held. The U.S. Congress criticized the regime, but by 1988 more than half a billion dollars in American financial and military support had been delivered. Meanwhile Liberia suffered from a shrinking economy and a growing foreign debt, which by 1987 had reached $1.6 billion. The Doe government was not entirely to blame for Liberia's financial condition. The treasury was already in the red, in large part due to the vast expenditures incurred by the previous administration in hosting the 1979 conference of the Organization of African Unity (OAU). The rising cost of oil, and declines in world prices for natural rubber, iron ore, and sugar further crippled the local economy. Government corruption and instability under Doe simply made a bad economic situation worse.

CIVIL WAR

In December 1989 a small force, calling itself the National Patriotic Front of Liberia (NPFL), invaded Liberia's Nimba county. The rebellion, which was led by Charles Taylor, a former member of Doe's government who had fled the country amidst corruption charges, grew rapidly. Many NPFL recruits were members of the local Gio and Mano communities, whose civilian populations were victimized by government forces. Like Doe's army, Taylor's recruits were an undisciplined mob who soon degenerated into murderous reprisals against their perceived political and ethnic rivals, especially the Krahn. The fighting reached the outskirts of Monrovia in July 1990, by which time it was estimated that more than 5,000 had been killed and another 150,000 (about 7 percent of the national population) had fled the country.

Initially, many people believed that the NPFL forces would quickly capture Monrovia, but the Doe loyalists held out; and a third force under Prince Johnson, a former army officer, emerged to complicate the picture. As Monrovia was plunged into bloody anarchy, there were calls in some quarters for U.S. military intervention. But Washington limited itself to the evacuation of foreigners (the troops of Doe, Johnson, and Taylor had killed and kidnapped expatriates and violated diplomatic immunity). Instead, in September a joint West African peacekeeping force, made up of personnel from The Gambia, Ghana, Guinea, Nigeria, and Sierra Leone, was landed to try to restore order and create an interim government. Shortly thereafter units loyal to Johnson wounded and captured Doe in an ambush at the peacekeeper's headquarters. By the next day Doe was dead. The nature of Doe's demise underscored the uncertain task facing the peacekeepers, who have since spent much of their time fighting the NPFL. The West African intervention, nonetheless, appears to represent Liberia's best hope for breaking its slide toward national disintegration.

DEVELOPMENT

Liberia is a major exporter of iron ore, and iron ore has been the main source of government revenue—superceding rubber—since the 1960s. The first iron-ore mine at Bomi Hills has mined out the profitable ore, and its decline is an ominous illustration of the limited value of mineral exploitation.

FREEDOM

From 1986 Doe presided over a "shamocracy"—that is, a repressive dictatorial regime thinly disguised as a constitutionally elected government. Since the outbreak of civil war in 1989 all competing forces have engaged in widespread violence and violations of human rights.

HEALTH/WELFARE

Among the important educational institutions in Liberia are the University of Liberia and Cuttington College, one of the only private higher educational institutions in Africa, funded by the Protestant Episcopal Church and the government. But education suffered greatly under the economic strains of the 1980s.

ACHIEVEMENTS

Through a shrewd policy of diplomacy, Liberia managed to maintain its independence when the United Kingdom and France conquered neighboring areas during the late nineteenth century. It espoused African causes during the colonial period; for instance, Liberia brought the case of Namibia to the World Court in the 1950s.

Mali (Republic of Mali)

GEOGRAPHY

Area in Square Kilometers (Miles): 1,240,142 (478,819) (about the size of Texas and California combined)
Capital (Population): Bamako (800,000)
Climate: tropical to arid

PEOPLE

Population
Total: 8,460,000
Annual Growth Rate: 2.7%
Rural/Urban Population Ratio: 79/21
Languages: official: French; others spoken: Bamanankan, Mandinka, Voltaic, Tamacheg (Tuareg), Dogon, Fulde, Songhai, Malinké

Health
Life Expectancy at Birth: 41 years (male); 44 years (female)
Infant Death Rate (Ratio): 173/1,000
Average Caloric Intake: 83% of FAO minimum
Physicians Available (Ratio): 1/12,652

DOGON COSMOLOGY

The Dogon, a people numbering about one-quarter million, share religious beliefs that govern their daily lives and their art and that are based on careful astronomical observances. A most significant aspect is the Grand Mask, which represents the creation myth and divine order. About every 60 years a new mask is carved to represent the ancestor of the Dogon who first knew Death. The rituals surrounding the carving and creation of a new mask recall Dogon origins and unite all the Dogon people. The dance performances of this mask determine planting seasons, celebrate new generations of Dogon men, and commemorate at the funerals of initiates. The Grand Mask brings together myth, ritual, and the community; it is "the soul of the Dogon."

Religion(s)
90% Muslim; 9% traditional indigenous; 1% Christian

Education
Adult Literacy Rate: 10%

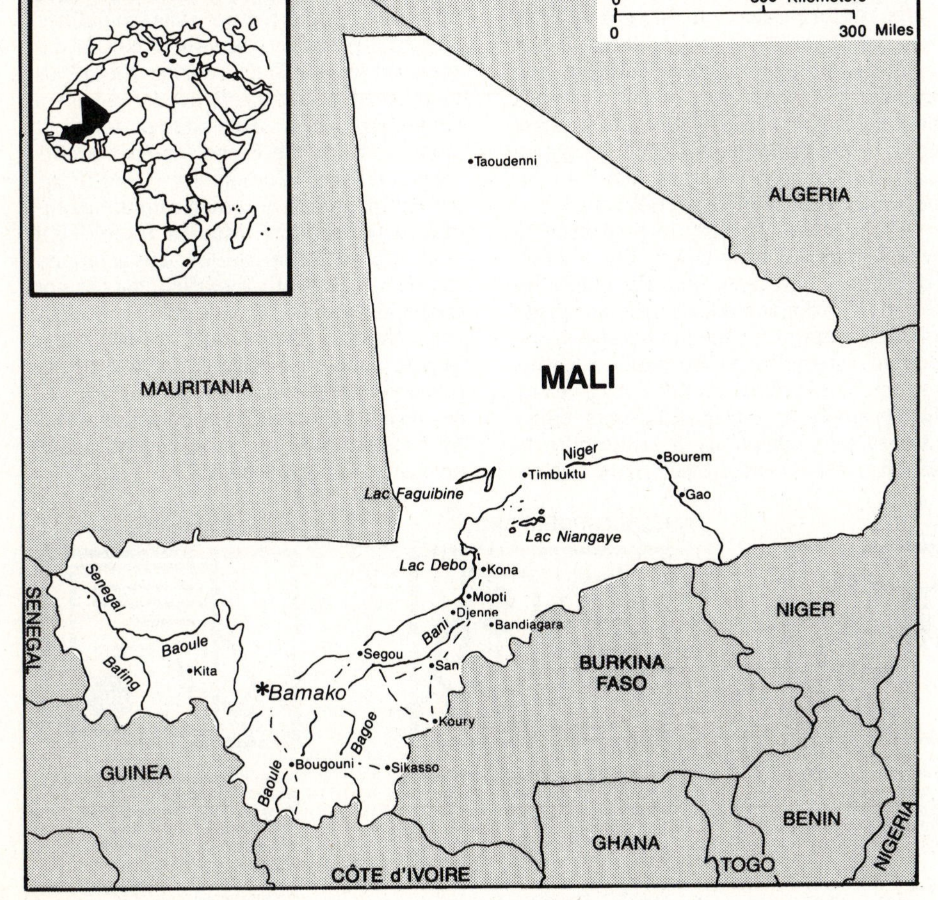

COMMUNICATION

Telephones: 9,537
Newspapers: 2

TRANSPORTATION

Highways—Kilometers (Miles): 15,700 (9,756)
Railroads—Kilometers (Miles): 642 (400)
Commercial Airports: 3 international

GOVERNMENT

Type: military republic
Independence Date: June 20, 1960
Head of State: President (General) Moussa Traoré
Political Parties: Democratic Union of Malian People
Suffrage: universal over 21

MILITARY

Number of Armed Forces: 6,400
Military Expenditures (% of Central Government Expenditures): 17%
Current Hostilities: none

ECONOMY

Currency ($ U.S. Equivalent): 319 CFA francs = $1
Per Capita Income/GNP: $190/$1.3 billion
Inflation Rate: 9%
Natural Resources: bauxite; iron ore; manganese; lithium; phosphate; kaolin; salt; limestone; gold
Agriculture: millet; sorghum; corn; rice; sugar; cotton; peanuts; livestock
Industry: food processing; textiles; cigarettes; fishing

FOREIGN TRADE

Exports: $260 million
Imports: $493 million

The Mali empire extends over much of the upper regions of West Africa **1250–1400s**

The Songhai empire controls the region **late 1400s–late 1500s**

The French establish control over Mali **1890**

Mali gains independence as part of the Mali Confederation; Senegal secedes from the confederation months later **1960**

A military coup brings Traoré and the Military Committee for National Liberation to power **1968**

The Democratic Union of the Malian People (UDPM) is the single ruling party; Traoré is the secretary general **1979**

School strikes and demonstrations; teachers and students are detained **1979–1980**

1980s–1990s

The ruling party rejects calls for an end to its political monopoly

Pope John Paul II, while visiting Bamako, calls for increased tolerance between Christians and Muslims

Representatives from Mali, Niger, and Algeria meet to examine the "serious security problem" caused by the movement of nomadic Tuareg communities across their borders

MALI

The published epic of Sundiata Keita, the thirteenth-century founder of the great Mali empire, is recognized throughout the world as a masterpiece of classical African literature. In Mali itself, the story of the Malinke hero-king can still be heard from the lips of the *griots,* or traditional bards, who sing at special gatherings and on radio programs of Sundiata's great deeds. For Malians, the epic is a living source of national pride and unity.

AN IMPERIAL PAST

Sundiata's state was one of three great West African empires whose centers lay in modern-day Mali. Between the fourth and thirteenth centuries A.D. the area was the site of ancient Ghana, which prospered through its export of gold to Asia, Europe, and the rest of Africa. (The modern state of Ghana, whose territory was never part of the earlier empire, adopted its name at independence as a symbol of Pan-African rather than local grandeur.) The Mali empire was superseded by that of Songhai, which was conquered by the Moroccans at the end of the sixteenth century. These empires were in fact confederations.

From the 1890s until 1960 another form of imperial unity was imposed over Mali (then called the French Sudan) and the adjacent territories that made up French West Africa. The legacy of broader colonial and precolonial unity, as well as its landlocked position, has since independence inspired modern Malian leaders in their search for closer ties with neighboring countries.

In the transition period to independence Mali formed a brief confederation with Senegal. This union broke down after only a few months of existence, but since then the two countries have cooperated through the Organization for the Development of the Senegal River and through other regional groupings. Mali has also strengthened its ties with nearby Guinea.

ENVIRONMENTAL CHALLENGES

In terms of its per capita gross national product, Mali is one of the 10 poorest countries in the world. More than 85 percent of the people are employed in agriculture—mostly subsistence—but during most years the government has had to rely on international aid to make up for local food deficits. Most of the country lies within either the expanding Sahara Desert or the semiarid region known as the Sahel, which has become drier as a result of recurrent drought. Much of the best land lies along the Senegal and Niger Rivers, which support most of Mali's agropastoral production. In earlier centuries the Niger River was able to sustain great trading cities such as Timbuctu and Djenne, but today most of the riverbank does not support crops. Efforts to increase cultivation, through expanded irrigation and various crop schemes, have so far been met with limited overall success.

While Mali's inability to feed itself in recent years has been largely due to environmental constraints, namely locust infestation, drought, and desertification, the inefficient state-run marketing and distribution systems have also had a negative impact. Low official produce prices have, furthermore, encouraged farmers either to engage in subsistence agriculture or to sell their crops on the black market. New policy commitments to liberalize agricultural trading, as part of an International Monetary Fund-approved Structural Adjustment Program, have yet to prove themselves, although a modest surplus was reported for the 1989–1990 cereal harvest. In contrast to agriculture, Mali's mining sector has experienced promising growth.

GOVERNMENT

Until recently, Malian governments were officially committed to state socialism. The first president, Modibo Keita, a descendant of Sundiata, during the 1960s established a command economy and a single-party state. His attempt to go it alone—outside the French-sponsored African Financial Community (CFA Franc Zone)—proved to be a major failure. General (now President) Moussa Traoré led a coup against Keita in 1968. His administration has gradually modified, but has not totally abandoned, Keita's policies. Politically, Traoré's Democratic Union of the Malian people has refused to give up its monopoly of power, in the face of renewed calls for multiparty democracy and the restoration of independent trade unions within the society.

DEVELOPMENT

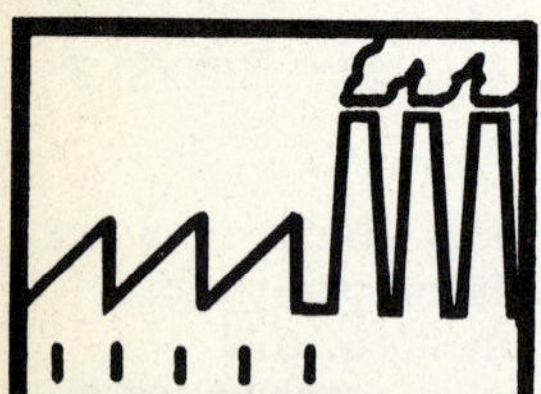

In 1989 the government received international financial backing for ongoing efforts to overhaul its energy infrastructure. A new oil-storage depot is to be built, and the country's hydroelectric capacity is to be expanded.

FREEDOM

Government control of the media and one-party rule limit freedom of expression and association. There have been occurrences of political detention.

HEALTH/WELFARE

About a third of Mali's budget is devoted to education. A special literacy program in Mali teaches rural people how to read and write and helps them with the practical problems of daily life by using booklets that concern fertilizers, measles, and measuring fields.

ACHIEVEMENTS

A carefully planned agricultural project, Isle de Paix (Island of Peace), along the Niger River has produced substantial harvests in spite of severe drought. Rice yields were almost 3 times as productive as other, more expensive projects.

Mauritania (Islamic Republic of Mauritania)

GEOGRAPHY

Area in Square Kilometers (Miles): 1,030,700 (398,000) (about the size of Texas and California combined)
Capital (Population): Nouakchott (500,000)
Climate: arid to semi-arid

PEOPLE

Population

Total: 1,804,000
Annual Growth Rate: 2%
Rural/Urban Population Ratio: 60/40
Languages: official: Arabic, French; others: Hasanya, Bamanankan, Fulde, Sarakole, Wolof, Berber languages

Health

Life Expectancy at Birth: 44 years (male); 47 years (female)
Infant Death Rate (Ratio): 138/1,000
Average Caloric Intake: 94% of FAO minimum
Physicians Available (Ratio): 1/19,563

Religion(s)

More than 99% Sunni Muslim

SLAVERY IN MAURITANIA

Mauritania has been one of the few regions in the world where the widespread practice of slavery has continued. In 1980 slavery was formally abolished, but there have been several reports of its persistence. A 1984 United Nations report, like the reports of past French colonial administrators, noted that slavery had still to be eliminated in isolated areas. However, the human-rights organization Africa Watch has recently accused successive Mauritanian regimes of passing anti-slavery legislation to appease world opinion while pursuing policies that ensure the institution's survival. Africa Watch estimates that there are at least 100,000 black slaves (5 percent of the nation's population) serving Maurish masters in the country.

Education

Adult Literacy Rate: 17%

COMMUNICATION

Telephones: 3,161
Newspapers: 1

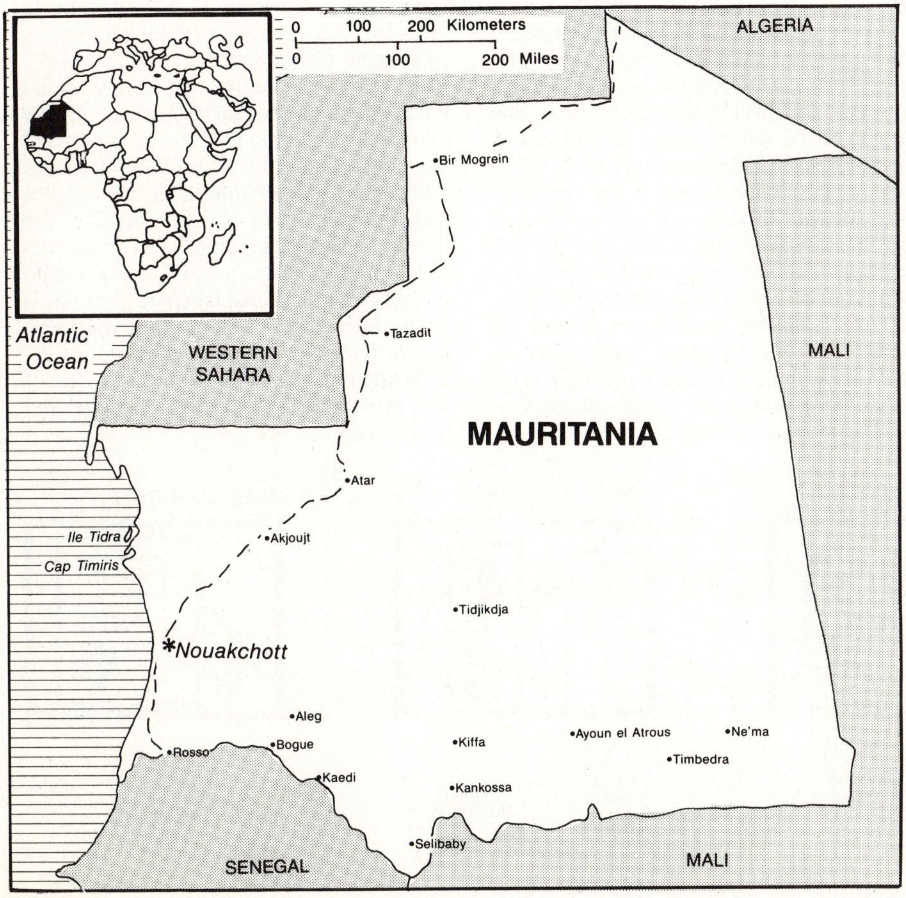

TRANSPORTATION

Highways—Kilometers (Miles): 8,900 (5,530)
Railroads—Kilometers (Miles): 650 (404)
Commercial Airports: 3 international

GOVERNMENT

Type: military republic
Independence Date: November 28, 1960
Head of State: Colonel Moauia Ould Sidi Mohamed Taya, prime minister and chairman of the Military Committee for National Recovery
Political Parties: none
Suffrage: none

MILITARY

Number of Armed Forces: 10,950
Military Expenditures (% of Central Government Expenditures): n/a
Current Hostilities: internal conflicts

ECONOMY

Currency ($ U.S. Equivalent): 78 ouguiyas = $1
Per Capita Income/GNP: $450/$600 million
Inflation Rate: 10%
Natural Resources: iron ore; gypsum; fish; copper
Agriculture: livestock; millet; corn; wheat; dates; rice; peanuts
Industry: iron-ore mining; fish processing

FOREIGN TRADE

Exports: $428 million
Imports: $235 million

The Almoravids spread Islam in the Western Sahara areas through conquest
1035–1055

The Mauritanian area becomes a French colony
1920

Mauritania becomes independent under President Moktar Ould Daddah
1960

A military coup brings Khouma Ould Haidalla and the Military Committee for National Recovery to power
1978

The Algiers Agreement: Mauritania makes peace with Polisario and abandons claims to Western Sahara
1979

1980s–1990s

Mauritania abolishes slavery in 1980, but reports indicate that it has not been eradicated

Supporters of the Front for the Liberation of Africans in Mauritania are arrested

Race riots touch off, leading to population exchanges between Mauritania and Senegal

MAURITANIA

For decades Mauritania has grown progressively drier. Today three-quarters of the country is desert sand; less than 1 percent of the land is suitable for cultivation, and only 10 percent for grazing. To make matters worse, the surviving arable and pastoral areas have been plagued by grasshoppers and locusts. Although more than 80 percent of Mauritanians are engaged in subsistence agriculture and/or pastoralism, persistent ecological crisis has resulted in Mauritania's failure to meet its need locally for cereals (since the 1950s) and meat (since the 1970s).

In the face of such natural disasters, people have moved. Since the mid-1960s the percentage of urban dwellers has swelled, from less than 10 percent to about 40 percent, while the nomadic population during the same period has dropped, from more than 80 percent to about 20 percent.

LIMITED OPPORTUNITIES

As the capital has grown from a few thousand to half a million in a single generation, its poverty—and that of the nation as a whole—has become more obvious. People seek new ways to make a living away from the land, but there are few jobs. Only about 15 percent of Mauritanians are able to obtain wage labor. The largest employer, after the army, is the iron mines at Kedia (nearly depleted) and Gueb-el-Rhein in the northern desert. During the first 2 decades of independence, which took place in 1960, the export earnings from Kedia were considerable, leading many to believe that the country had exceptionally bright prospects. It was such misplaced optimism that motivated the country's first president, Ould Daddah, to pull Mauritania out of the Franc Zone in 1973 by adopting the ouguiya as a national currency.

DIVISION AND UNITY

Mauritania's faltering economy has coincided with an increase in racial and ethnic tensions. Since independence the government has been dominated by the Maurs (or Moors), who speak Hassaniya Arabic. Historically, this community has been divided between the aristocrats and commoners, of Arab and Berber origin, and their black African slaves, who have been assimilated into Maurish culture but remain socially segregated. Together, the Maurs account for anywhere from 30 to 60 percent of the citizenry, although the refusal of the government to release its data from the last two censuses suggests that the smaller estimates are more accurate.

The other half of Mauritania's population is composed of the blacks, who are mostly Pulaar (Toucouleur and Peul), Soninke, and Wolof speakers. Like the Maurs, all of these groups are Muslim. For this reason, Mauritania's rulers have stressed Islam as a source of national unity. Muslim brotherhood has not, however, been able to overcome the divisions between the northern Maurs and the southern blacks. One major source of friction has been the Arabization efforts of successive Mauritanian governments, which have been opposed by most southerners. In recent years the country's desertification has created new sources of tension. As their pastures have turned to sand, many of the Maurish nomads who have not found refuge in the urban areas have moved southward. There, with state support, they began in the 1980s to deprive southerners of their land.

Growing oppression of blacks has been met with resistance. An underground movement, the Front for the Liberation of Africans in Mauritania (FLAM), has emerged. Black grievances were also linked to an unsuccessful coup attempt in 1987. Interethnic hostility exploded in 1989 when a border dispute with Senegal led to race riots which left several hundred Senegalese dead in Nouakchott. In response, the Moorish trading community in Senegal became the target of reprisals. Mauritania has claimed that 10,000 Maurs were killed in Senegal, but this figure is extremely exaggerated (other sources put the number at about 70). Following this bloodshed, tens of thousands of refugees were repatriated across both sides of the border. Mass deportations of "Mauritanians of Senegalese origin" have fueled charges that the Nouakchott regime is trying to eliminate its non-Maurish population. Despite international mediation efforts and fall-off in deportations, a state of belligerence persists between Senegal and Mauritania.

DEVELOPMENT

Mauritania's coastal waters are among the richest in the world. During the 1980s the local fishing industry grew at an average annual rate of more than 10%. Many now believe that the annual catch has reached the upper levels of its sustainable potential.

FREEDOM

Most freedoms are restricted, and there have been reports of the perpetuation of chattel slavery. Mauritania's prison at Oualata, where many black activists have been detained, is notorious for its particularly brutal conditions of incarceration.

HEALTH/WELFARE

There have been modest improvements in the areas of health and education since independence, but conditions remain poor. The 1990 *Human Development Report* gave Mauritania low marks regarding its commitment to human development.

ACHIEVEMENTS

There is a current project to restore ancient Mauritanian cities, such as Chinguette, which are located on traditional routes from North Africa to Sudan. These centers of trade and Islamic learning were points of origin for the pilgrimage to Mecca and were well known in the Middle East.

Niger (Republic of Niger)

GEOGRAPHY

Area in Square Kilometers (Miles): 1,267,000 (489,191) (almost 3 times the size of California)
Capital (Population): Niamey (300,000)
Climate: arid to semiarid

PEOPLE

Population

Total: 7,440,000
Annual Growth Rate: 3%
Rural/Urban Population Ratio: 79/21
Languages: official: French; others spoken: Hausa, Zarma/Songhai, Kanuri, Fulde, Tamacheg (Tuareg), others

Health

Life Expectancy at Birth: 44 years
Infant Death Rate (Ratio): 145/1,000
Average Caloric Intake: 91% of FAO minimum
Physicians Available (Ratio): 1/38,500

Religion(s)

97% Muslim; 3% traditional indigenous

MATERNAL-LANGUAGE SCHOOLS

In Niger, more and more primary-school pupils are attending classes conducted in their maternal languages. These maternal-language schools, as they are called, have been developed over a number of years through careful planning and experimentation and are based on the idea that the mastery of basic concepts is most successfully achieved in one's first language. These schools also work to foster and reinforce values of the community through a curriculum that reflects the cultural heritage of the pupils. Niger's maternal-language schools are dedicated to providing students with strong foundations in reading, writing, and arithmetic as well as to encouraging individuals' strong sense of their own cultural identities.

Education

Adult Literacy Rate: 13%

COMMUNICATION

Telephones: 11,842
Newspapers: 1

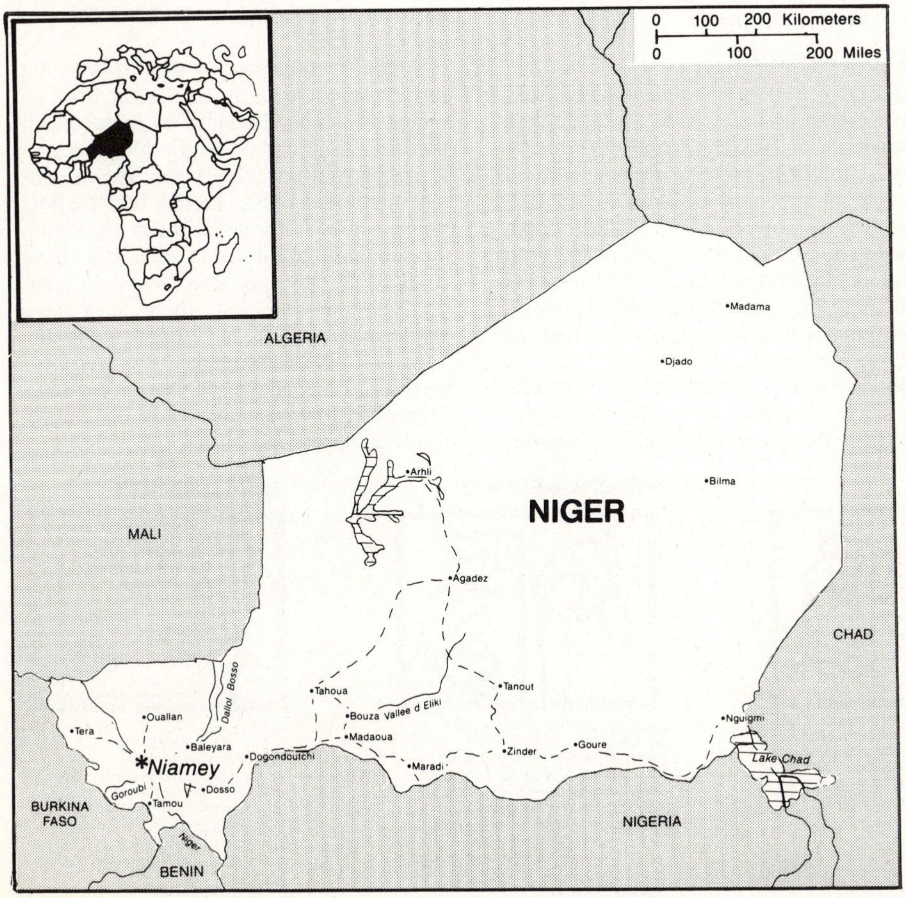

TRANSPORTATION

Highways—Kilometers (Miles): 19,137 (11,891)
Railroads—Kilometers (Miles): none
Commercial Airports: 2 international

GOVERNMENT

Type: republic, administered by Supreme Military Council
Independence Date: August 3, 1960
Head of State: President (Brigadier General) Ali Saibou
Political Parties: National Movement for the Development of Society
Suffrage: universal over 16

MILITARY

Number of Armed Forces: 7,800
Military Expenditures (% of Central Government Expenditures): n/a
Current Hostilities: none

ECONOMY

Currency ($ U.S. Equivalent): 319 CFA francs = $1
Per Capita Income/GNP: $200/$1.6 billion
Inflation Rate: 22%
Natural Resources: uranium; coal; iron; tin; phosphates
Agriculture: millet; sorghum; peanuts; beans; cotton
Industry: mining; textiles; cement; agricultrual products; construction

FOREIGN TRADE

Exports: $251 million
Imports: $354 million

The Mali empire includes territories and peoples of current Niger areas
1200s–1400s

Hausa states develop in the south of present-day Niger
1400s

The area is influenced by the Fulani empire centered at Sokoto, now in Nigeria
1800s

France consolidates rule over Niger
1906

Niger becomes independent
1960

A military coup brings Colonel Seyni Kountché and a Supreme Military Council to power
1974

1980s–1990s

President Kountché dies and is replaced by Saibou

A French DC-10 on a flight between Brazzaville and Paris crashes over Niger, killing 172; terrorism is suspected

The Nigerien Army massacres Tuaregs

DROUGHT AND DESERTIFICATION

It was a good year in 1989: Niger's farmers produced a substantial surplus in cereals. As a result,the government was for the first time in years able to forgo any request for emergency food aid from the international community. Although boosted by unusually good rains, the good harvest was primarily an outgrowth of efforts to promote local agricultural productivity.

Farming is especially difficult in Niger. Less than 3 percent of the nation's vast territory is suitable for cultivation even during the best of times. Unfortunately, much of the last 2 decades have been the worst of times for Nigeriens. Recurrent drought and ongoing desertification have posed a constant challenge to their livelihoods.

Drought had an especially catastrophic effect during the late 1970s. Most Nigeriens were reduced to dependency on foreign food aid, while about 60 percent of their livestock perished. Some people believe that this ecological disaster afflicting Africa's Sahel region, which includes southern Niger, was of such severity as to disrupt the delicate long-term balance between desert and savanna. However, a growing number of other observers have concluded that the intensified desertification of recent years is primarily rooted in human, rather than natural, causes. Many attribute environmental degradation to introduction of inappropriate forms of cultivation, overgrazing, deforestation, and new patterns of human settlement. Much of the debate on humans' negative impact on the Sahel environment has been focused on some of the agricultural-development schemes which were once conceived as the region's salvation.

In recent years the Nigerien government has placed a greater emphasis on helping its farmers help themselves, through the extension of credit, higher guaranteed minimum prices, and better communications. Vigorous efforts have been made in certain regions to halt the spread of desert sands by supporting village tree-planting campaigns. Given the inevitability of drought, the government has also increased its commitment to stockpiling of food in granaries. However, for social and political reasons as much as for economic ones, government policy has discouraged the flexible nomadic pattern of life which is characteristic of many Nigerien communities.

The Nigerien government's emphasis on agriculture has, in part, been motivated by the realization that the nation cannot rely on its immense uranium deposits for its future development. Depressed demand throughout the 1980s resulted in substantially reduced prices and output.

MILITARY RULE

For nearly half of its independent existence Niger was governed by a civilian administration under President Hamani Diori. In 1974, during the height of drought, Lieutenant Colonel Seyni Kountché took power in a bloodless coup. Since then political power has rested with the Supreme Military Council. Ministerial portfolios, appointed by the president, have been filled by civilians as well as military personnel.

In 1987 Kountché died of natural causes and was succeeded as president by Colonel (now Brigadier General) Ali Saibou. Under Saibou, a National Movement for the Development of Society (MNSD) was established in 1989 as the country's sole political party. However, the subsequent charade of single-party elections has coincided with growing calls for a return to multiparty democracy. Within Niger, prodemocracy agitation has the backing of the nation's labor confederation. The government has also been challenged by student unrest. Saibou has hinted that a move to political pluralism is possible but currently "premature." Three underground opposition movements—the Muslim Integrist Party, the United Democratic Front, and the Revolutionary Socialist Party—are now active.

Another challenge to the government has emerged recently in the form of an increase in armed attacks by members of the largely nomadic Tuareg ethnic group. A major raid on Tahoua resulted in considerable casualties. In the raid's aftermath, reprisals by government troops on Tuareg communities are reported to have resulted in the massacre of untold hundreds. As in the past, there have been suggestions of Libyan support for the Tuaregs. Others maintain that Niger's interethnic violence is rooted in the regime's favoritism toward members of the Zarma (or Djerma) ethnic group.

DEVELOPMENT

Village cooperatives, especially marketing cooperatives, pre-date independence and have grown in size and importance in recent years. They have successfully competed with well-to-do private traders for control of the grain market.

FREEDOM

Human rights are circumscribed by Niger's authoritarian regime. The government has not, however, been able to quell growing agitation for multiparty democracy.

HEALTH/WELFARE

A national conference on educational reform in Zinder stimulated a program to use Nigerien languages in primary education and integrated the adult-literacy program into the rural-development efforts. The National Training Center for Literacy Agents is crucial to literacy efforts.

ACHIEVEMENTS

Niger has consistently demonstrated a strong commitment to the preservation and development of its national cultures through its media and educational institutions, the National Museum, and events such as the annual youth festival at Agades.

Nigeria (Federal Republic of Nigeria)

GEOGRAPHY

Area in Square Kilometers (Miles): 923,768 (356,669) (twice the size of California)
Capital (Population): Lagos (5,000,000 est.)
Climate: tropical to arid

PEOPLE

Population
Total: 118,819,000 est.
Annual Growth Rate: 3.3%
Rural/Urban Population Ratio: 77/23
Languages: official: English; others spoken: Hausa, Yoruba, Igbo, Efik, Idoma, Ibibio, others (250 languages are recognized by the Nigerian government)

Health
Life Expectancy at Birth: 48 years (male); 49 years (female)
Infant Death Rate (Ratio): 119/1,000 est.
Average Caloric Intake: 91% of FAO minimum
Physicians Available (Ratio): 1/11,347

AFRICA'S NOBEL LAUREATE

Nigerian writer Wole Soyinka received the Nobel Prize for Literature in 1986. Soyinka is noted for his many works, ranging from plays such as *The Trials of Brother Jero* to novels such as *The Interpretors*, many poems, and nonfiction writings. The son of a Yoruba pastor and an active Christian mother, Soyinka grew up in the western Nigerian town of Abeokuta. Warm and vivid scenes of his childhood are recalled in detail in his autobiography, *Ake: The Years of Childhood*. An outspoken critic of the federal government during the Nigerian Civil War, Soyinka was jailed from 1967 to 1969. His plays are produced all over the world, and he continues to speak out on the arts and politics.

Religion(s)
50% Muslim; 40% Christian; 10% traditional indigenous

Education
Adult Literacy Rate: 42%

COMMUNICATION

Telephones: 708,390
Newspapers: 48

TRANSPORTATION

Highways—Kilometers (Miles): 107,990 (67,104)
Railroads—Kilometers (Miles): 3,505 (2,178)
Commercial Airports: 4 international

GOVERNMENT

Type: federal republic; under control of military government
Independence Date: October 1, 1960
Head of State: President Ibrahim Babangida
Political Parties: Social Democratic Party; National Republican Convention
Suffrage: universal for adults

MILITARY

Number of Armed Forces: 94,500
Military Expenditures (% of Central Government Expenditures): 1%
Current Hostilities: occasional border incidents over Lake Chad

ECONOMY

Currency ($ U.S. Equivalent): 7.62 naira = $1
Per Capita Income/GNP: $300/$30 billion
Inflation Rate: 47%
Natural Resources: oil; minerals; timber
Agriculture: cotton; cocoa; rubber; yams; cassava; sorghum; palm kernels; millet; corn; rice; livestock
Industry: mining; crude oil; natural gas; coal; tin; columbite; processing: oil, palm, cotton, rubber, petroleum; manufacturing: textiles, cement, building materials, chemicals, beer brewing

FOREIGN TRADE

Exports: $8.4 billion
Imports: $5.7 billion

NIGERIA

Nigeria is sometimes referred to as "the giant of Africa." It is the continent's most populous country, although the actual number of Nigerians remains a source of speculation, with estimates ranging from 80 million to 120 million (it is likely that the higher figure is more accurate). This lack of an agreed-upon figure is due to the fact that all attempts to conduct an accepted postcolonial census have failed, as a result of interethnic competition (a new attempt is scheduled for 1991). Nigeria's hard-working population has also given the country Africa's largest economy, as measured by gross domestic product (GDP). But per capita income is estimated at about $300 per year, about average for the continent.

It is common to equate Nigeria's wealth with its status as Africa's leading oil producer. However, while about 90 percent of the country's export earnings and 75 percent of its government revenue are derived from hydrocarbons, the oil sector's contribution to total GDP is a more modest 20 percent.

Unfortunately, neither Nigeria's size nor its oil has yet resulted in a sustained pattern of economic growth and political development. For Nigerians, the 3 decades of independence have been an emotional and material roller coaster ride. On the one hand, it has been a period marred by interethnic violence, economic downturns, and, for 2 decades, military rule. On the other, independence has also coincided with times of economic growth, cultural achievement, and human development. To some, this great land of great extremes has thus typified both the hopes and frustrations of the continent as a whole.

NIGERIA'S ROOTS

For centuries the river Niger, which cuts across much of Nigeria, has facilitated long-distance communication between various communities of the forest and savanna regions of West Africa. This fact helps to account for the rich variety of cultures which have emerged within the territory of modern Nigeria over the past millennium. Archaeologists and historians have revealed the rise and fall of many states whose cultural legacies continue to define Nigeria. A notable artistic example of this heritage is the bronze sculptures of ancient Benin, whose humanistic grace is unique but comparable to the greatest of classic statuary. Other important states included the Oyo empire and the Sokoto caliphate, which helped to consolidate and spread Islam across much of Nigeria during the early nineteenth century. Many Nigerians have historically also been organized into smaller polities, such as independent villages and family-based commonwealths.

Precolonial Nigeria produced a wide range of craft goods, including leather, glass, and metalware. The cultivation of cotton and indigo supported the growth of a local textiles industry. During the mid-nineteenth century southern Nigeria prospered through palm-oil exports, which lubricated the wheels of Europe's Industrial Revolution. Earlier much of the same country was disrupted through its participation in the slave trade. Most African-Americans are of Nigerian descent.

Today more than 250 languages are spoken in Nigeria. Pidgin English, which is based on African grammar, is widely used as a *lingua franca* in the cities and towns. Roughly two-thirds of Nigerians speak either Hausa, Yoruba, or Igbo. During and after the colonial era the leaders of these three major cultural groups clashed politically from their separate regional bases.

The British, who conquered Nigeria in the late nineteenth and early twentieth centuries, administered the country through a policy of divide-and-rule. In the predominately Muslim, Hausa-speaking north, the British co-opted the old ruling class, virtually excluding Christian missionaries. But in the south, the missionaries, along with their schools, were encouraged, and Christianity and education spread rapidly. Many Yoruba farmers of the southwest profited through their cultivation of cocoa. Although most remained as farmers, many of the Igbo of the southeast became prominent as nonagricultural workers, such as state employees, artisans, wage workers, and traders. As a result, the Igbo tended to migrate in relatively large numbers to other parts of the colony.

REGIONAL CONFLICTS

At independence, in 1960, the Federal Republic of Nigeria was composed of three states: the Northern Region, dominated by Hausa speakers; the Western Region of the Yoruba; and the predominately Igbo Eastern Region. Politics quickly deteriorated into conflict among the three major ethnic groups. At one time or another each of the regions threatened to secede from the Federal Republic. This strained situation turned into a crisis following the military's overthrow of the civilian government in 1966.

In the coup's aftermath the army itself divided along ethnic lines, and its ranks soon became embroiled in an increasingly violent power struggle. This situation led to the massacre of some 10,000 Igbos living in the north. In response, the Eastern Region declared its independence as the Republic of Biafra. The ensuing civil war between the Biafran partisans and federal forces lasted for 3 years. During this time much of the outside world's attention became focused on the conflict through visual images of the mass starvation which was occurring in rebel-controlled areas under federal blockade.

Despite the extent of the war's tragedy, the collapse of Biafran resistance was followed by a largely successful process of national reconciliation. During this time the military government of Yakubu Gowon (1966–1975) succeeded in diffusing ethnic politics through a restructured federal system, based on the creation of new states. The oil boom, which began soon after the conflict, helped the nation-building process by concentrating vast resources in the hands of the federal government in Lagos.

Thirteen years of military rule ended in 1979. A new Constitution was implemented, which abandoned the British parliamentary model and adopted a modified version of the American balance-of-powers system. In order to encourage a national outlook, Nigerian presidential candidates needed to win a plurality that included at least one-fourth of the vote in two-thirds of the states.

CIVILIAN POLITICS

Five political parties competed in the 1979 elections. Each had similar platforms, promising social welfare for the masses, support for Nigerian business, and a foreign policy based on nonalignment. Ideological differences tended to exist within the parties as much as among them, although the People's Redemption Party (PRP) of Aminu Kano became the political home for many socialists. The most successful party was the somewhat right-of-center National Party of Nigeria (NPN), whose candidate, Shehu Shagari, won the presidency.

New national elections took place in August and September 1983, in which Shagari received just over 12 million of 25.5 million votes. However, the newly reelected government did not survive long. On December 31, 1983 there was a military coup, led by Major General Muhammad Buhari, a former petroleum commissioner in the Gowon government. The 1979 Constitution was suspended, Shagari and others were arrested, and a federal military government was reestablished.

Although no referendum was ever taken on the matter, it is clear that many Nigerians initially welcomed the coup. Their response was a reflection of widespread disillusionment with the Second (civilian) Republic. Superficially, the political picture had seemed very bright in the early 1980s. A commitment to national unity was well established. Although marred by incidents of political violence, two elections had successfully taken place. Due process of law, judicial independence, and press freedom—never entirely eliminated under previous military rulers—were extended and seemingly entrenched.

At the time, however, many were also beginning to speak of the state as a "republic of the privileged and rich," in which the poor masses held little stake. To such critics, the electoral system, while balancing the interests of the power elites in different sections of the country, was not seen as empowering ordinary people. A major reason for this failing was the endemic corruption that pervaded government. People lost confidence as certain officials and their cronies became millionaires overnight. Such transparent abuses of power had also occurred under the previous military regime. But whereas conspicuous corruption had been tolerated during the oil-boom years of the 1970s, it became the focus of public and institutional anger as Nigeria's economy contracted during the 1980s.

OIL BOOM AND BUST

Nigeria, as a leading member of the Organization of Petroleum Exporting Countries (OPEC), experienced a period of rapid social and economic change during the 1970s. The recovery of oil production after the civil war and the subsequent hike in prices led to a massive increase in revenue and attracted considerable amounts of outside investment. This growth was accompanied by a rapid expansion of certain types of social services. Universal primary education was introduced and the number of universities grew, from 5 in 1970 to 21 in 1983. A few Nigerians became very wealthy, and a growing middle class emerged. Rising public consumption and runaway government spending fueled high rates of inflation, which ultimately undercut the economics of internal production.

Oil revenues had already begun to fall off when the NPN government embarked upon expensive new projects, such as the construction of a new federal capital at Abuja, in the center of the country. Such forms of expenditure seemed prestigious and provided many opportunities for Nigerian businesspeople and politicians, but they extended nonproductive sectors of the economy while intensifying import dependence.

Nigerian agriculture, unable to afford the higher wages spawned by inflation, entered a period of crisis, and the rapidly growing cities became dependent on foreign food products to feed their populations. Meanwhile, nonpetroleum exports, once the mainstay of the economy, either virtually disappeared (as was the case with peanuts, which had been the staple of the colonial north) or declined drastically (as did cocoa, tin, rubber, and palm oil).

While gross indicators appeared to report impressive industrial growth in Nigeria, most of the new industry depended heavily on foreign inputs and was geared toward direct consumption rather than the production of machines or spare parts. Selective import bans merely led to the growth of smuggling.

ADJUSTMENTS NECESSARY

The golden years of the middle and late 1970s were also banner years for inappropriate expenditure, corruption, and waste. At the time, given the scale of

(United Nations photo)

Nigeria experienced a tremendous influx of money when its oil industry took advantage of the 1970s' worldwide oil panics. The huge increase in cash resources led to the growth of a middle class, and a flurry of expensive new projects. One such project is the Kainji Dam, which will supply a significant amount of energy to agriculture, industry, and the populace.

incoming revenue, it looked as if these were manageable problems. However, with world-trade recession and the decline of oil revenues, it became apparent that Nigeria would be forced to make painful and unprecedented adjustments. Gross domestic product fell drastically in the 1980s with the collapse of oil prices, reducing foreign exchange and the availability of imports.

The entire social and political system owed its stability to the effective distribution of the oil wealth to many groups of Nigerians. As the economy worsened, there were signs of increasing populist resentment against the new wealthy class. In 1980 an Islamic movement condemning corruption, wealth, and private property defied authorities in the northern metropolis of Kano. The army was called in and killed nearly 4,000. Similar riots subsequently occurred in the cities of Maiduguri, Yola, and Gombe. Attempts by the government to control organized labor through reorganizing the union movement into one legal, centralized federation met with unofficial strikes (including a general strike in 1981) and illicit breakaways. In an attempt to placate the growing number of unemployed Nigerians, more than 1 million West Africans, mostly Ghanaians, were quickly expelled, a locally popular but futile gesture.

REFORM OR RETRIBUTION?

Major General Muhammed Buhari justified the military's return to power on the basis of a need to take drastic steps to solve the economic problems of the nation, which were blamed almost exclusively on official corruption. A "war against indiscipline" was declared, which initially resulted in the trial of a number of political leaders whose economic crimes were at times staggering. The discovery of private caches of millions of naira, the local currency, and foreign exchange fueled public outrage and added modestly to the treasury. Tribunals sentenced former politicians to long jail terms. In its zeal, the government looked for more and more culprits while jailing journalists and others who questioned aspects of its program. In 1985 Major General Ibrahim Babangida led a successful military coup, charging Buhari with abuse of human rights, keeping power within a small group in the military, and mismanagement of the economy.

Babangida released detained journalists and former politicians who were not yet charged with crimes. In a clever strategy, he also encouraged all Nigerians to participate in national forums on the benefits of an International Monetary Fund loan and a Structural Adjustment. The government turned down the loan but used this popular step as a political opportunity to implement many of the austerity measures rec-

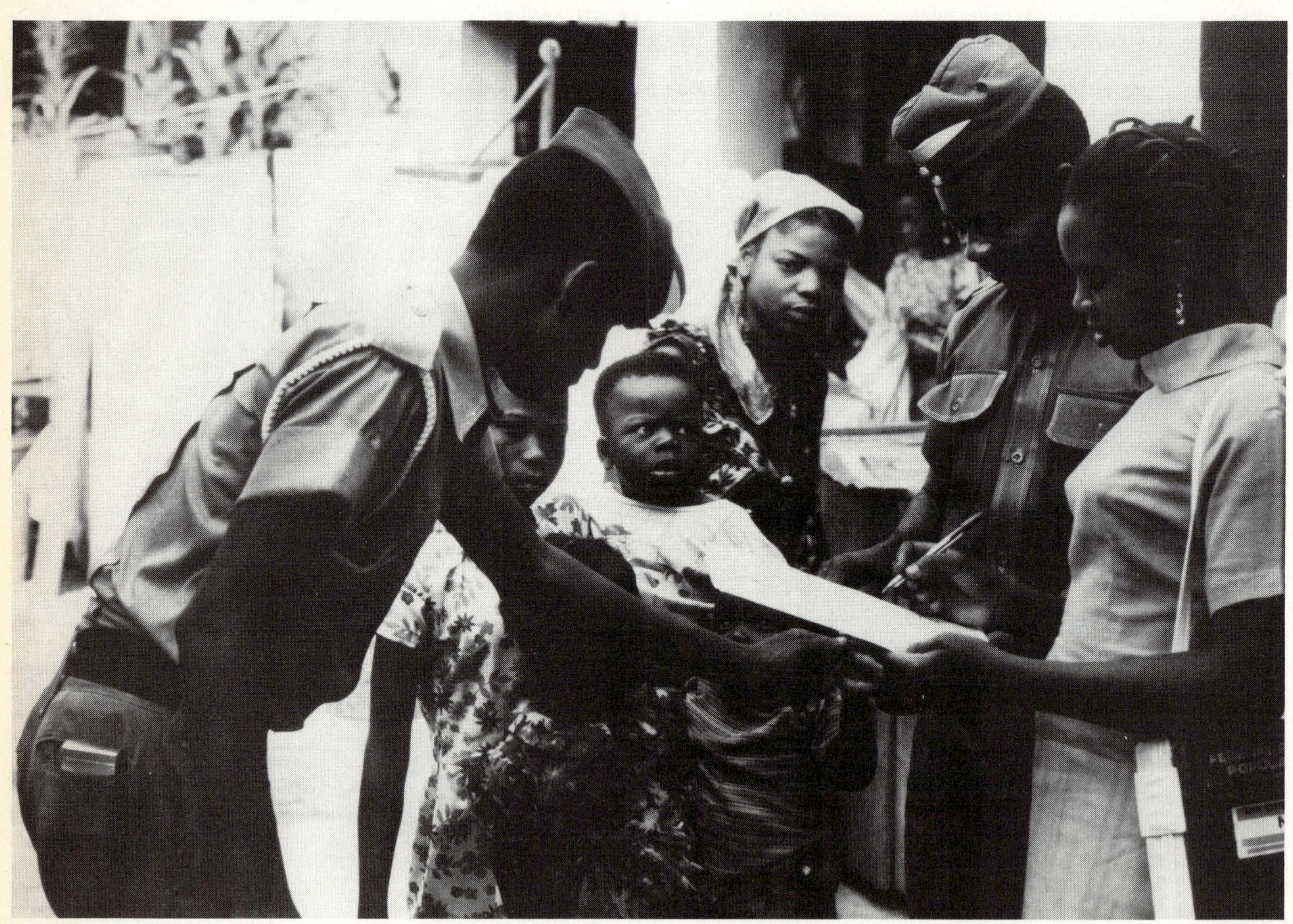

(United Nations photo)

Nigeria has the largest population of any African state, but the controversial nature of recent censuses has caused governments to postpone the process repeatedly. A new census currently is planned for 1991.

Ancient life flourishes
1100–1400

The beginning of Usuman dan Fodio's Islamic jihad (struggle)
1804

The first British protectorate is established at Lagos
1851

A protectorate is proclaimed over the north
1900

Nigeria becomes independent as a unified federal state
1960

Military seizure of power; proclamation of Biafra; civil war
1966–1970

An oil-price hike inaugurates the oil boom
1973

Elections restore civilian government
1979

1980s–1990s

Muhammed Buhari's military coup ends the Second Republic; later Buhari is toppled by Ibrahim Babangida

Wole Soyinka is awarded the Nobel Prize for Literature

Lean times; austerity measures provoke protests and strikes

ommended by the IMF and World Bank.

The 1986 budget signaled the beginning of a government-initiated Structual Adjustment Program (SAP). The naira was devalued, budgets restricted, and plans made for privatizing state-run industries. Because salaries remained the same while prices rose, the cost of basic goods rose dramatically, with painful consequences for middle- and working-class Nigerians as well as the poor.

Although the price of oil on the world market has improved, the economy has continued to be tight, causing many to see the SAP as a burden. As part of its SAP, the government in 1988 began gradually to reduce local fuel subsidies. To pre-empt strikes over fuel prices, the government appointed an administrator to watch over the Nigerian Labor Congress. Nonetheless, when some transport owners raised fares 50 to 100 percent, students and workers protested; bank staff and other workers went on strike. When students and others protested in Jos, police killed demonstrators.

The Babangida government has faced additional internal challenges while seeking to project an image of stability to foreign investors. A coup attempt was foiled in 1985; university unrest was put down with force in both 1986 and 1988, closing campuses for months at a time. Religious riots between Christians and Muslims in northern cities in 1987 led to many deaths. Several people implicated in these disturbances were sentenced to jail, but religious tensions continued to simmer.

Despite official statements supporting press freedom, restrictions on the media resurfaced under Babangida. Dele Giwa, the outspoken editor of *Newswatch* magazine, was killed by a parcel bomb in 1986. His killers have yet to be found. The remaining editors of the magazine were arrested in 1986, and the magazine was banned for several months in 1987. In 1988 the government banned satellite monitoring of foreign broadcasts.

Babangida has promised to return Nigeria to full civilian control gradually, by 1992, but many Nigerians have become suspicious of and/or indifferent to his Transitional Program for the restoration of democracy. Local nonparty elections were held in 1987, and a mostly elected Constituent Assembly subsequently met and approved modifications to Nigeria's 1979 Constitution. Despite the trappings of electoral involvement, the Transitional Program has been tightly controlled. Former politicians are banned from participation in the process, and a two-party model has been imposed on what traditionally has been a multiparty political culture. When none of 13 potential parties gained Babangida's approval, the general decided to create two new parties of his own, one "a little to the left" and another "a little to the right." Neither party is to be allowed to challenge the nation's most controversial policy: the SAP.

The rise of prodemocracy protests throughout West Africa, including the dramatic capitulation of the military rulers in neighboring Benin, has raised questions about Babangida's ability to impose democracy his way. After 20 years of military rule, it has become difficult for ordinary Nigerians to see the army as their savior from the venal politicians.

Doubts about the military in general, and Babangida's grasp on power in particular, were raised in April 1990, when a group of dissident officers launched yet another coup attempt to "stop intrigues, domination, and internal colonization of the Nigerian state by the so-called chosen few." In their radio broadcasts, the insurrectionists announced the expulsion of five northern states from the Federal Republic, thus raising the specter of a return to interethnic civil war. The uprising was crushed, but confidence in the Babangida regime and the Transitional Program was badly shaken.

Despite Nigeria's troubles, there are grounds for optimism about its future. Rising oil prices and the SAP have led to stability and modest growth in the economy. After years of little accomplishment, there are also signs that the Economic Community of West African States (ECOWAS) will begin to play a greater role in promoting economic cooperation throughout the region. Such a development should prove especially beneficial to Nigeria, whose size and infrastructure make it the natural leader of the Community. Furthermore, Nigeria's strong civil society bolsters the chances of political pluralism taking root, which is the ultimate check on economic and political abuses of power.

DEVELOPMENT

Nigeria hopes to mobilize its human and natural resources to encourage labor-intensive production and self-sufficient agriculture. Recent bans on food imports such as rice and maize will increase local production, and restrictions on imported raw materials should encourage research and local input for industry.

FREEDOM

Although the Babangida government freed journalists and critics jailed by Buhari, student protests have been dealt with harshly, and journalists and trade-union officials have been arrested. Convicted criminals and drug dealers are executed.

HEALTH/WELFARE

Nigeria's infant mortality rate is now believed to be about 119 per 1,000. (Some estimate it to be as high as 150 per 1,000.) While social services grew rapidly during the 1970s, Nigeria's strained economy since then has led to cutbacks in health and education.

ACHIEVEMENTS

Nigeria has a long tradition of an outspoken and lively press, under both civilian and military governments. Private and state-sponsored newspapers abound in all the large cities and are eagerly read by Nigerian citizens. Recently, national and international magazines specializing in investigative journalism have expanded their readership.

Senegal (Republic of Senegal)

GEOGRAPHY

Area in Square Kilometers (Miles): 196,840 (76,000) (about the size of South Dakota)
Capital (Population): Dakar (1,300,000)
Climate: tropical

PEOPLE

Population
Total: 7,704,000
Annual Growth Rate: 2.6%
Rural/Urban Population Ratio: 62/38
Languages: official: French; others spoken: Wolof, Fulde, Oyola, Mandinka, Sarakole, Serer

Health
Life Expectancy at Birth: 45 years (male); 48 years (female)
Infant Death Rate (Ratio): 112/1,000
Average Caloric Intake: 100% of FAO minimum
Physicians Available (Ratio): 1/10,441

Religion(s)
75% Muslim; 20% traditional indigenous; 5% Christian

Education
Adult Literacy Rate: 10%

GORÉE ISLAND

The tiny, rocky island of Gorée, opposite Dakar on the mainland, has a tragic history. Beginning in the seventeenth century Gorée was occupied by European traders as an easily defensible slave entrepôt. For more than 200 years the French, Dutch, and English used Gorée as a collection and distribution center for the Atlantic slave trade. Slaves from the Senegalese interior and many other parts of West Africa were housed and examined in cramped slave quarters before walking the narrow passageway to the sea and transport to the Americas. The Senegalese government has preserved the site as a reminder of the slave trade's horrors. Gorée attracts visitors from around the world, including many African-Americans.

COMMUNICATION

Telephones: 33,000
Newspapers: 3

TRANSPORTATION

Highways—Kilometers (Miles): 14,700 (9,114)
Railroads—Kilometers (Miles): 905 (561)
Commercial Airports: 4 international

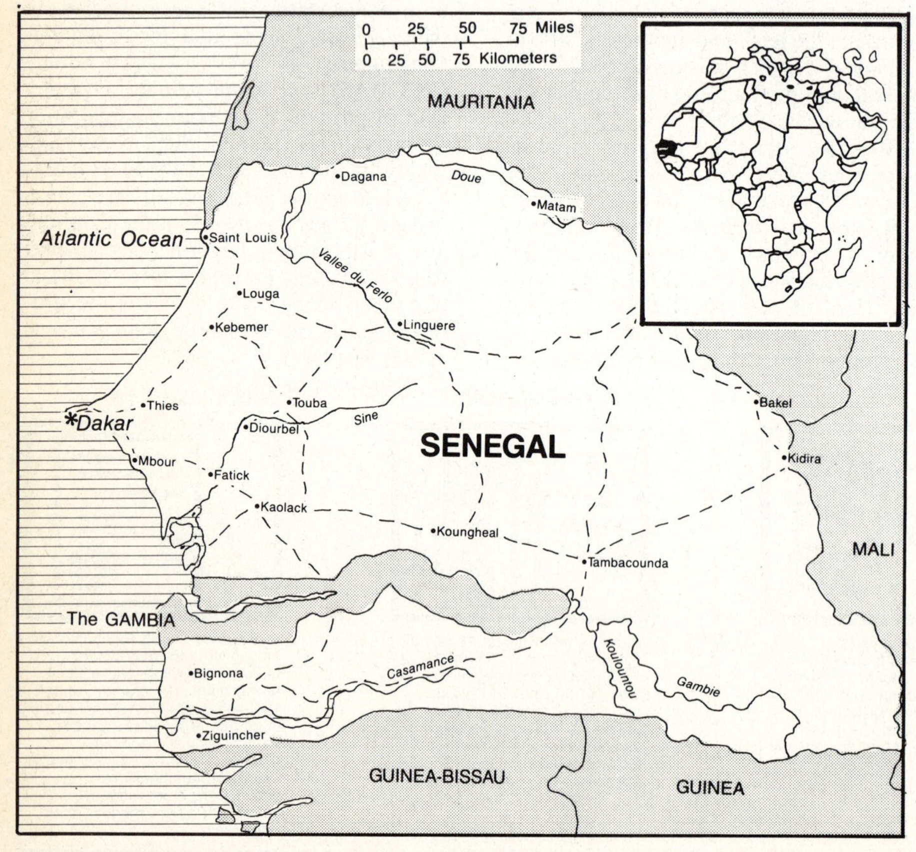

GOVERNMENT

Type: republic
Independence Date: April 4, 1960
Head of State: President Abdou Diouf
Political Parties: Socialist Party; Democratic Party; African Independence Party; Republican Movement; National Democratic Alliance; others
Suffrage: universal for adults

MILITARY

Number of Armed Forces: 9,700
Military Expenditures (% of Central Government Expenditures): 2.3%
Current Hostilities: none

ECONOMY

Currency ($ U.S. Equivalent): 319 CFA francs = $1
Per Capita Income/GNP: $380/$3.8 billion
Inflation Rate: 12%
Natural Resources: fish; phosphates
Agriculture: millet; sorghum; manioc; rice; cotton; groundnuts
Industry: fishing; food processing; light manufacturing

FOREIGN TRADE

Exports: $483 million
Imports: $705 million

SENEGAL

The story of Ibrahima Dieng is typical of the tribulations faced by many Senegalese. A Muslim, Dieng lives with his two wives in a compound in the capital city, Dakar. When he receives a money order from his nephew in Paris, he cannot cash it, because he lacks the connections and skills to overcome the bureaucratic obstacles that stand in his way. The lawyer he enlists to help him steals the money. "In a country like ours, only the scoundrels live well," says Dieng.

The story is fictional, the plot of a bittersweet and thought-provoking film entitled "Mandabi," by Senegal's best-known filmmaker, Ousmane Sembene. Like many of Sembene's films, it illustrates the complex and sometimes frustrating ways in which local African customs, Islamic practices, and European influences have come to define modern Senegalese society.

THE IMPACT OF ISLAM

The majority of the Senegalese are Muslim. Islam was introduced into the region as early as the eleventh century and was spread through trade, evangelism, and the establishment of a series of theocratic Islamic states during the seventeenth, eighteenth, and nineteenth centuries.

Today most Muslims are associated with one of the Brotherhoods, or "ways," of Islam. The leaders of these Brotherhoods, who are usually referred to as *marabouts,* often act as the "spokesmen for the rural areas" as well as "spiritual directors" of their followers. Abdou Diouf, the current president of Senegal, has relied on the political support of the principal marabouts in his election campaigns. The Brotherhoods have also played an important economic role. For example, members of the Mouride Brotherhood, who number about 700,000, have become prosperous by growing groundnuts, the nation's principal exported cash crop.

FRENCH INFLUENCE

While Islamic influences entered Senegal from the north and east, European ways spread from the coast. During the seventeenth century French merchants established bases to facilitate their trade in slaves and gum. More and more territory gradually fell under the political control of

The potential of drought is an ongoing concern in the Sahel zone of Senegal. It is an ever present factor in any agricultural program. The young herder above with his starving cattle is an all too familiar image.

The French occupy present-day St. Louis and, later, Gorée Island
1659

The Jolof kingdom controls much of the region
1700s

All Africans in 4 towns of the coast vote for a representative to the French Parliament
1848

Interior areas are added to the French colonial territory
1889

Senegal becomes independent as part of the Mali Confederation; shortly afterwards, it breaks from the confederation
1960

1980s–1990s

President Senghor retires and is replaced by Diouf

Senegalese political leaders unite in the face of threats from Mauritania

Senegalese troops, part of the Allied efforts in the Persian Gulf War, die in a plane crash in Saudi Arabia

the French. As a result, many coastal communities have been influenced by France for generations.

Although Wolof is used by many as a lingua franca, French continues to be the common language as well as the language of the country. The educational system, too, maintains a French character. Many Senegalese, like the fictional Dieng's nephew, migrate to France, either to attend school or (more often) to work as low-paid laborers. The French maintain a military force near Dakar and are major investors in the Senegalese economy. The government and judiciary of Senegal are modeled after those of France, and the bureaucracy that plagues Dieng has its roots in the old French colonial system.

POLITICS

Under President Diouf, Senegal has strengthened its commitment to a multiparty system of democracy. After succeeding the nation's renowned first president, Leopold Senghor, Diouf liberalized the political process by allowing an increased number of opposition parties effectively to compete against his own ruling Socialist Party. He also restructured his administration in ways that were credited with making it less corrupt and more efficient. Some have said that these moves have not gone far enough, while others have suggested that the reformist Diouf has had to struggle hard against his party's old guard.

In national elections in 1988, Diouf won 77 percent of the vote, while his Socialist Party won 103 out of 120 seats. Although many outside observers believed that the election had been plagued by fewer irregularities than in the past, opposition protests against alleged fraud touched off serious rioting in Dakar. As a result, the city was placed under a 3-month state of emergency. Diouf's principal opponent, Maitre Abdoulaye Wade of the Democratic Party, who in the official returns won a quarter of the presidential vote, was among those arrested and tried for incitement. Subsequent meetings between Diouf, Wade, and others have, however, eased tensions.

THE ECONOMY

Many believe that the *Sopi* (Wolof for "change") riots of 1988 were primarily motivated by popular frustration with Senegal's weak economy, especially among its youth (about half of the population are under age 21), who face an uncertain future. Senegal's relatively large (38 percent) urban population has suffered from rising rates of unemployment and inflation, which have been aggravated by the country's attempt to implement an International Monetary Fund-approved program of structural adjustment (SAP). In recent years the economy has grown modestly but so far has failed to attract the new investments needed to meet the ambitious privatization goals of the SAP. Among rural dwellers, drought and locusts have made life difficult. Fluctuating world-market prices and local diseases as well as drought have undermined groundnut exports.

FOREIGN RELATIONS

Senegal has also been beset by difficulties in its relations with neighboring states. The Senegambia Confederation, which many hoped would lead to greater cooperation with The Gambia, was dissolved in September 1989. Relations with Guinea-Bissau also became strained as a result of that nation's failure to recognize the result of international arbitration over disputed, potentially oil-rich, waters. Senegalese have also suspected that individuals in Bissau may be linked with separatist agitation in Senegal's southern province of Casamance.

For Senegal, the major source of cross-border tension has been Mauritania. In 1989 longstanding border disputes between the two countries led to a massacre of Senegalese in Mauritania, which set off widespread revenge attacks against Mauritanians in Senegal. In the aftermath of the killings, tens of thousands of Senegalese and Mauritanians were repatriated. The situation between the two countries has remained tense, in large part due to the persecution of Mauritania's "black" (Pulaar, Soninke, and Wolof) communities by its military government, which as championed the interests of that country's "Moors," Hassaniya Arabic speakers. Many Mauritanians belonging to the persecuted groups have been pushed into Senegal, leading to calls for war. However, mediation efforts have been welcomed by both sides.

DEVELOPMENT

The newly built Diama and Manantali Dams will allow for the irrigation of many thousands of acres for domestic rice production. At the moment large amounts of rice are imported, mostly to feed the urban population.

FREEDOM

Senegal's reputation has continued to be tarnished by charges of vote rigging, but the trend appears to favor the continued strengthening of multiparty democracy. Following the 1988 state of emergency, a general amnesty was declared for politically motivated crimes.

HEALTH/WELFARE

Like other Sahel countries, Senegal has a relatively high infant-mortality rate and a low life-expectancy rate. Health facilities are considered to be below average, even for a country of Senegal's modest income, but recent child-immunization campaigns have been fairly successful.

ACHIEVEMENTS

Dakar, sometimes described as the "Paris of West Africa," has long been a major cultural center for the region. Senegalese writers such as former President Leopold Senghor were founders of the Francophonic African tradition of Negritude. The University of Dakar is renamed after Cheikh Anta Diop, a world-renowned scholar.

Sierra Leone (Republic of Sierra Leone)

FOURAH BAY COLLEGE

Fourah Bay College, a significant educational institution for all of West Africa, was founded in Sierra Leone in 1814 as a Christian school. By 1827 it was a training institution for teachers and missionaries, and in 1876 it was affiliated with the University of Durham in the United Kingdom. As the only option for higher education for Africans on the continent before 1918, Fourah Bay College trained many early nationalists and coastal elites during the colonial period. These graduates formed a network of Western-educated African leaders throughout West Africa.

GEOGRAPHY

Area in Square Kilometers (Miles): 72,325 (27,925) (slightly smaller than South Carolina)
Capital (Population): Freetown (470,000)
Climate: tropical

PEOPLE

Population

Total: 4,318,000
Annual Growth Rate: 2.3%
Rural/Urban Population Ratio: 78/22
Languages: official: English; others spoken: Krio, Temne, Mende, Vai, Kru, Fulde, Mandinka, others

Health

Life Expectancy at Birth: 46 years
Infant Death Rate (Ratio): 195/1,000
Average Caloric Intake: 85% of FAO minimum
Physicians Available (Ratio): 1/18,609

Religion(s)

52% traditional indigenous; 36% Muslim; 12% Christian

Education

Adult Literacy Rate: 15%

COMMUNICATION

Telephones: 15,000
Newspapers: 1

TRANSPORTATION

Highways—Kilometers (Miles): 7,460 (4,635)
Railroads—Kilometers (Miles): 84 (54)
Commercial Airports: 1 international

GOVERNMENT

Type: republic
Independence Date: April 27, 1961
Head of State: President Joseph Saidu Momoh
Political Parties: All People's Congress; others in exile
Suffrage: universal over 21

MILITARY

Number of Armed Forces: 3,180
Military Expenditures (% of Central Government Expenditures): 7.4%
Current Hostilities: none

ECONOMY

Currency ($ U.S. Equivalent): 41 leones = $1
Per Capita Income/GNP: $320/$1.1 billion
Inflation Rate: 77%
Natural Resources: diamonds; bauxite; rutile; chromite; iron ore
Agriculture: coffee; cocoa; ginger; rice; piassava
Industry: mining; beverages; cigarettes; construction materials

FOREIGN TRADE

Exports: $129 million
Imports: $137 million

Early inhabitants arrive from Africa's interior **1400–1750**

Settlement by people from the New World and recaptured slave ships **1787**

Sierra Leone is a Crown colony **1801**

Mende peoples unsuccessfully resist the British in the Hut Tax War **1898**

Independence **1961**

The new Constitution makes Sierra Leone a one-party state **1978**

1980s–1990s

President Siaka Stevens steps down; Joseph Momoh, as the sole candidate, is elected in the first nationwide presidential election

Debt-servicing cost mounts

Following countrywide unrest, a coup attempt by police fails

SIERRA LEONE

The modern nation of Sierra Leone is the product of a unique colonial history. Its capital city and main urban center, Freetown, was founded by waves of black settlers who were sent there by Britain, which governed the colony. The first to arrive were the so-called Black Poor, a group of 400 who were sent out from England in 1787. Shortly thereafter they were joined by former slaves from Jamaica and Nova Scotia. The latter group had gained their freedom by fighting with the British, against their American masters, in the U.S. War of Independence. About 40,000 Africans who were released by the British and others from slave ships captured on the West African coast were also settled in Freetown and the surrounding areas in the first half of the nineteenth century. (At the time, the West African slave trade had been declared illegal and was being suppressed by the major European powers.) The descendants of Sierra Leone's various black settlers blended African and British ways into a distinctive Creole culture. Besides speaking English, they developed their own language, Krio, which has become the nation's *lingua franca*. The Creoles today make up only a small percentage—about 5 percent—of Sierra Leone's multiethnic population.

NATIONAL POLITICS

In the 1950s, as more and more people were given the vote, interior peoples—rather than Creoles—became dominant in local politics. The first party to win broad national support was the Sierra Leone People's Party (SLPP), under Sir Milton Margai, which led the country to independence in 1961. During the 1967 national elections the SLPP was narrowly defeated by the All People's Congress (APC), led by Siaka Stevens, who, however, was prevented by the nation's military from assuming power until 1968. Between 1968 and 1985 Stevens presided over a steady erosion of civil liberties.

Sierra Leone's last multiparty election, held in 1977, was marred by violence and allegations of fraud. The following year, in a blatantly rigged referendum, supposedly 97 percent of the population agreed to the APC's elevation as the sole political party. Under Stevens, authority has steadily shifted from Parliament and the judiciary to the executive branch. In 1985 the then 80-year-old Stevens stepped down in favor of his chosen successor, Major General Joseph Momoh, whose promotion underscored the military's stake in the regime.

A CORRUPTED ECONOMY

Authoritarian rule in Sierra Leone has emerged in the context of, and perhaps to some extent has been motivated by, the country's declining economy. Today Sierra Leone is poor, having recently been added to the United Nation's list of Least Developed Countries (LDCs). Revenues from diamonds, which formed the basis for prosperity during the 1950s, and gold have steadily fallen, due to the depletion of old diggings and massive smuggling. Efforts to open new mines have been hampered by the government's chronic inability to curtail the rampant corruption that plagues the society.

The two-thirds of Sierra Leone's labor force employed in agriculture are those who have suffered the most from the nation's faltering economy. Poor producer prices, coupled with an international slump in demand for cocoa and robusta coffee, have cut into rural incomes. In 1986 the government promised to improve its prices, as part of its Green Revolution Program, but this has largely failed to happen. In addition, much of Sierra Leone's agricultural production, like its minerals, has stayed out of official markets through smuggling.

The cost of servicing Sierra Leone's debt is estimated to have amounted in 1989 to 130 percent of the total value of its exports. This grim figure may lead to the introduction of an International Monetary Fund-supported Structural Adjustment Program (SAP). Should austerity measures be imposed, they would have a particularly severe effect on the urban population, who for the past decade have been devastated by hyperinflation. But the ACP/Momoh regime's ability to carry out such painful measures is compromised by emerging agitation for a return to multiparty government. In 1990 the prestige of Sierra Leone's government was further tarnished by British press reports that hundreds, possibly thousands, of Sierra Leone children have been exported, mostly to Lebanon, on what amount to slave contracts.

DEVELOPMENT

The recently relaunched Bumbuna hydroelectric project should reduce Sierra Leone's dependence on foreign oil, which has accounted for nearly a third of its imports. In response to threats of boycotting, the country's Lungi International Airport has been upgraded.

FREEDOM

Many members of Sierra Leone's press have bravely reported on official corruption and abuses of power. This has led in some cases to the banning of papers and detention of journalists. Recent government harassment has been focused on *The New Shaft* and *The Chronicle*.

HEALTH/WELFARE

Average life expectancy in Sierra Leone is 46 years. The country's infant mortality rate is one of highest in the world.

ACHIEVEMENTS

The Sande Society, a women's organization that trains Mende young women for adult responsibilities and regulates women's behavior, has contributed positively to life in Sierra Leone. Beautifully carved wooden helmet masks are worn by women leaders in the society's rituals. Ninety-five percent of Mende women of all classes and education join the society.

Togo (Republic of Togo)

GEOGRAPHY

Area in Square Kilometers (Miles): 56,600 (21,853) (slightly smaller than West Virginia)
Capital (Population): Lomé (366,000)
Climate: tropical

PEOPLE

Population

Total: 3,246,000
Annual Growth Rate: 2.9%
Rural/Urban Population Ratio: 85/15
Languages: official: French; others spoken: Ewe, Mina, Dagomba, Kabye, others

Health

Life Expectancy at Birth: 47 years
Infant Death Rate (Ratio): 107/1,000
Average Caloric Intake: 92% of FAO minimum
Physicians Available (Ratio): 1/22,727

Religion(s)

58% traditional indigenous; 22% Christian; 20% Muslim

Education

Adult Literacy Rate: 45% male; 20% female

TOURISM IN TOGO

Often described as "the Switzerland of Africa" (a description frequently used for Lesotho and Malawi as well), Togo has encouraged the development of numerous fashionable hotels in Lomé, the capital on the coast, and inland. Two national game parks have been publicized, as have dance and music groups. There are quite a few foreign tourists. Africans from Ghana, Benin, and Nigeria, and Europeans and North Americans vacation in Togo. The government employed a public-relations firm from the United States to help in the development of its tourist industry and in making contacts with various corporations that might do business in Togo.

COMMUNICATION

Telephones: 11,105
Newspapers: 1

TRANSPORTATION

Highways—Kilometers (Miles): 7,850 (4,867)
Railroads—Kilometers (Miles): 525 (326)
Commercial Airports: 2 international

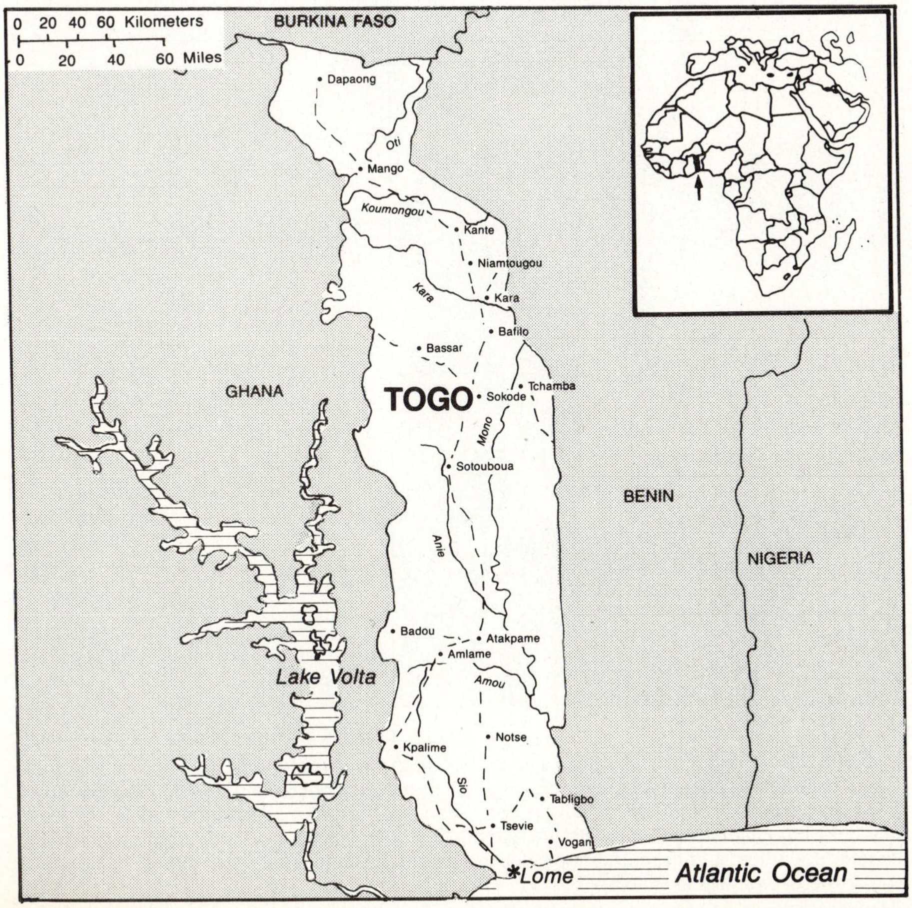

GOVERNMENT

Type: republic; under military rule
Independence Date: April 27, 1960
Head of State: President (General) Gnassingbé Eyadéma
Political Parties: Rally of the Togolese People
Suffrage: universal for adults

MILITARY

Number of Armed Forces: 5,910
Military Expenditures (% of Central Government Expenditures): n/a
Current Hostilities: none

ECONOMY

Currency ($ U.S. Equivalent): 319 CFA francs = $1
Per Capita Income/GNP: $240/$780 million
Inflation Rate: 8%
Natural Resources: phosphates; limestone
Agriculture: yams; manioc; millet; sorghum; cocoa; coffee; rice
Industry: phosphates; textiles; agricultural products; tourism

FOREIGN TRADE

Exports: $242 million
Imports: $262 million

TOGO

In 1979 Togo adopted an economic-recovery strategy that many consider to have been a forerunner of the Structural Adjustment Programs (SAPs) introduced in much of the rest of Africa. Faced with mounting debts as a result of falling export revenues, the government of Togo's long-ruling strongman, Gnassingbé Eyadéma, began to loosen the state's grip over the local economy. This initial step was followed up, beginning in 1982, with a more rigorous International Monetary Fund/World Bank-supported program of privatization and other market-oriented reforms. Given this chronology, Togo's economic prospects have become a focus of attention for those looking for lessons about the possible effects of SAPs elsewhere. The fact that progress has been mixed gives both proponents and opponents of economic liberalization grounds for debate.

ADJUSTING STATISTICS

Supporters of Togo's SAP point out that since 1985 the country has enjoyed an average growth in gross domestic product of 3.3 percent per year, which is modestly above its figures for population growth. While this statistic is an improvement over the 1.7 percent rate recorded between 1973 and 1980, it is well below the 7.2 percent rate of growth that prevailed from 1965 to 1972. Since the late 1980s there has also been a rise in private consumption—7.6 percent per annum—and a drop in inflation—from about 13 percent in 1980 to an estimated 2 percent in 1989.

The livelihoods of certain segments of the Togolese population have materially improved during the past decade. Some of these beneficiaries are among the more than two-thirds of the workforce employed in agriculture. Encouraged by the government's increased purchase prices, cash-crop farmers have expanded their outputs of cotton and coffee. This is especially true in the case of cotton production, which tripled between 1983 and 1989. Nearly half of the nation's smallholders now grow the crop.

Balanced against the growth of cotton has been a decline in cocoa, which emerged during the colonial period as Togo's principal cash crop. Despite better producer prices during the mid-1980s, output fell as a result of past decisions not to plant new trees. Given the continuing collapse of cocoa prices on the world market, this earlier shift may actually prove to have been opportune. The long-term prospects of coffee are also in doubt, due to a growing global preference for the arabica beans of Latin America over the robusta beans which thrive throughout much of Africa. As a result, the government since 1988 has had to reverse course by drastically reducing its prices for both coffee and cocoa, a move it hopes will prove to be only temporary.

In terms of food production, the nation has been able to provide for most of its needs, although critics cite Togo's importation of large quantities of rice and a malnutrition rate of 4.3 percent (other figures show malnutrition affecting one out of three children) to challenge official claims of food self-sufficiency. A closer look reveals that the country's food situation is complicated by an imbalance between the drought-prone northern areas and the more productive south. Studies

(United Nations photo by Anthony Fisher)

Water is of extreme importance to the livelihood of Togo. In recent years, cash-crops such as cotton and coffee have increased in production at the sacrifice of cocoa, the traditional exportable crop. The positive world market for cotton has given Togo much needed income. While food production in Togo is officially adequate, the situation is complicated by the drought-prone north and its need for support from the more productive southern areas. The water these children are drawing is not universally available.

Germany occupies Togo **1884**

Togo is mandated to the United Kingdom and France by the League of Nations following Germany's defeat in World War I **1919**

UN plebicites result in the independence of French Togo and incorporation of British Togo into Ghana **1956–1957**

Independence is achieved **1960**

Murder of President Sylvanus Olympio; a new civilian government is organized after the coup **1963**

The coup of Colonel Etienne Eyadéma, now President Gnassingbé Eyadéma **1967**

The Rally of the Togolese People (RPT) becomes the only legal party in Togo **1969**

1980s–1990s

A coup attempt leads to French military intervention

Togo's debts are rescheduled

Eyadéma begins a consultation campaign with his subjects but rejects calls for a restoration of multiparty elections

have also shown a potentially ominous decline in food production in the cotton-growing regions.

In other areas, Togo's government can cite improvements in transport and telecommunications. The national highway system, built largely by the European Development Fund, has allowed the port of Lomé to develop as a transshipment center for exports from neighboring states as well as for the nation's own interior. At the same time, the government has been able to claim modest progress in cutting its budget deficit. But it is in precisely this area that the cost of Togo's adjustment is most apparent, for public expenditures in health and education declined by about 50 percent between 1982 and 1985. Whereas school enrollment rose from 40 percent to more than 70 percent during the 1970s, it has slipped back below 60 percent in recent years.

The ultimate justification for the Togolese SAP has been a desire to attract overseas capital investment. In addition to sweeping privatization, a Free Trade Zone has been established. But so far the inflow of overseas investment has been modest. There have also been complaints that many foreign investors have simply bought former state industries on the cheap, rather than starting up new enterprises. Privatization along with austerity measures are also blamed for unemployment and wage cuts among urban workers. One-third of the state-divested enterprises have been liquidated.

Whatever the long-term merits of the SAP, it is clear that it has so far resulted in neither a clear pattern of sustainable growth nor an improved standard of living for most Togolese. For the foreseeable future, the health of Togo's economy will continue to be tied to export earnings derived from three commodities—phosphates, coffee, and cocoa—whose price fluctuations were responsible for the nation's past cycle of boom, during the 1960s, followed by bust, during the 1970s.

GNASSINGBÉ EYADÉMA

In 1963 the Togolese Army set a sad precedent for much of West Africa by assassinating the nation's first president, Sylvanus Olympio. After a subsequent period of instability, power was seized by one of the murderers, then Colonel Etienne Eyadéma, who has ruled the country ever since. (He is now known as Gnassingbé Eyadéma.) In 1969 Eyadéma institutionalized his regime as a one-party state. All Togolese are obligated to belong to his party, the Rally of the Togolese People (RPT). Under the Constitution, all power is effectively concentrated in the hands of President Eyadéma. The supposedly elected National Assembly (all candidates are approved from the top) exists solely as a consultative body.

A cult of personality is officially encouraged around the figure of Eyadéma, whose representation, sometimes enhanced with such features as angel wings, has become omnipresent as a public icon. In the last election it was claimed that Eyadéma received a 99.7 percent "yes" vote. Borrowing from his friend President Mobutu Sese Seko of Zaire, Eyadéma has bestowed upon himself the public title of "The Guide" and has abolished the use of European personal names as part of his campaign for "an authentic model of national development." This policy as well as the need for a one-party state have been justified by the need to encourage national unity among the more than 40 ethnic groups that inhabit the country. However, some 90 percent of Togo's military and security forces are said to belong to Eyadéma's own ethnic group, the Kabre.

Eyadéma's personal rule has not gone unchallenged. A failed assassination attempt during his first year in power is annually commemorated as the "Feast of Victory over Forces of Evil." Eyadéma's ability to remain in power has rested upon the goodwill of France as well as the climate of fear created by his own security apparatus. A coup attempt in 1986 led to the intervention of French troops, who have since remained in the country. It is the French as well as the Togolese who will probably determine whether the Eyadéma regime will survive the wave of prodemocracy agitation currently sweeping Africa.

DEVELOPMENT

Much hope for the future of Togo is riding on the recently created Free Trade Zone at Lomé. Firms within the zone are promised a 10-year tax holiday if they export at least three-quarters of their output. The project is backed by the U.S. Overseas Private Investment Corporation.

FREEDOM

Eyadéma has tried to improve his image in recent years through the creation of a Human Rights Commission. The commission's president, Me Yawo Agboyibor, is widely respected for his efforts, which are credited with an improvement in the treatment accorded to citizens by their army and police.

HEALTH/WELFARE

The nation's health service has declined as a result of austerity measures. Juvenile mortality is 15%. Self-induced abortion now causes 17% of the deaths among Togolese women of child-bearing age.

ACHIEVEMENTS

The name of Togo's capital, Lomé, is well known in international circles for its association with the Lomé Convention, a periodically renegotiated accord through which products from various African, Caribbean, and Pacific countries are given favorable access to European markets.

Central Africa

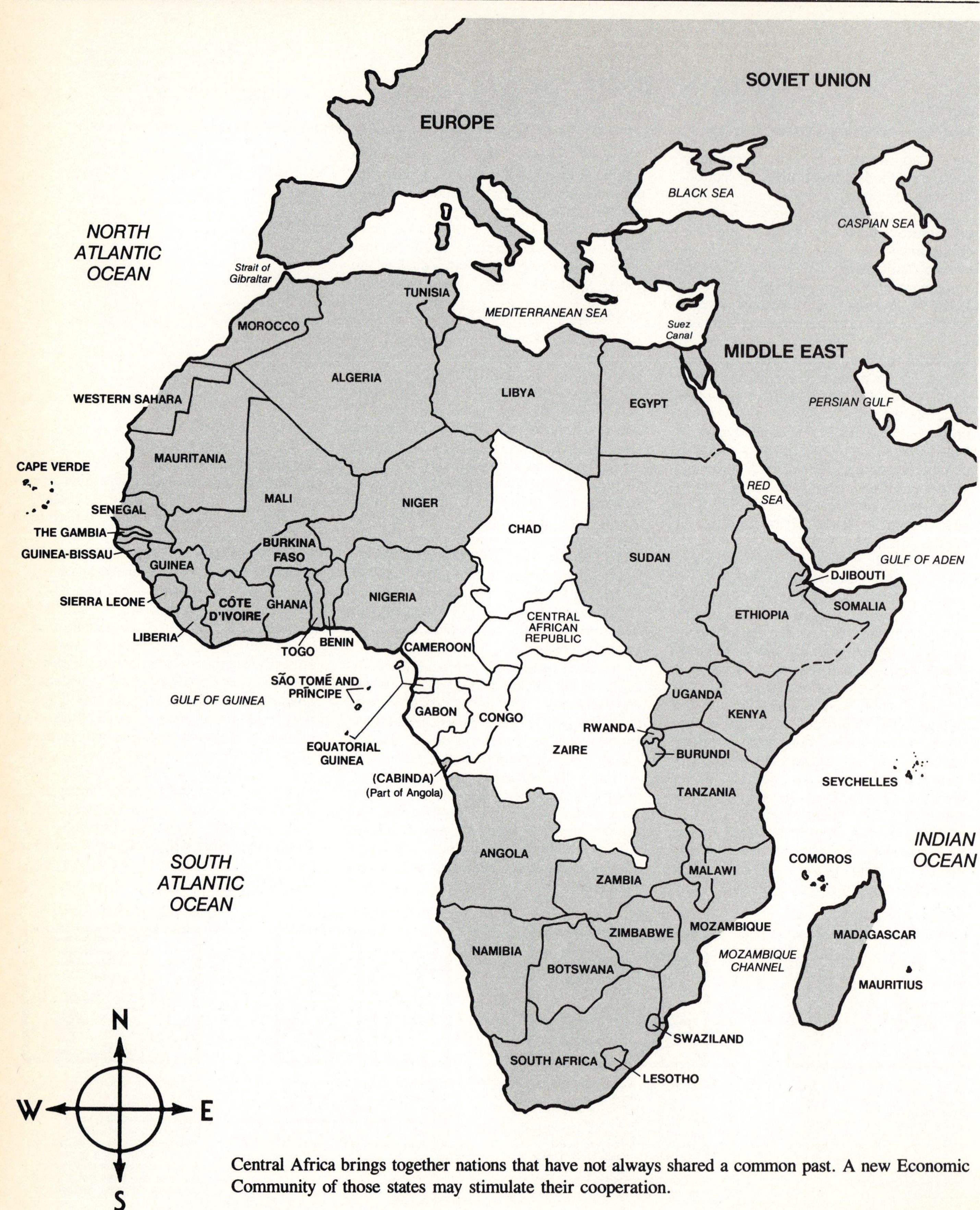

Central Africa brings together nations that have not always shared a common past. A new Economic Community of those states may stimulate their cooperation.

Central Africa: Possibilities for Cooperation

(United Nations photo)

In Africa, cooperative work groups often take on jobs that would be done by machinery in industrialized countries.

The Central African region, as defined in this book, brings together countries that have not always shared a common past, nor do they necessarily seem destined for a common future. Cameroon, Chad, the Central African Republic, Congo, Equatorial Guinea, Gabon, São Tomé and Príncipe, and Zaire are not always grouped together as one region. Indeed, users of this volume who are familiar with the continent may also associate the label "Central Africa" with other states, such as Angola and Zambia, rather than some of the states mentioned here. Geographically, Chad is more closely associated with the Sahelian nations of West Africa than with the heavily forested regions of Central Africa to its south. Similarly, southern Zaire has long-standing cultural and economic links with Angola and Zambia, which in this text are associated with the states of Southern Africa, largely because of their political involvements.

Yet despite its seemingly arbitrary nature, the eight states that are defined here as belonging to Central Africa have much in common. French is a predominant language in each of the states, except for Equatorial Guinea, and São Tomé and Príncipe. All of the states, except for São Tomé and Príncipe and Zaire, share a common currency. While Chad's current economic prospects appear to be exceptionally poor, the natural wealth found throughout the rest of Central Africa makes the region as a whole one of enormous potential. In the postcolonial era the eight Central African governments have made some progress in realizing their developmental possibilities through greater regional cooperation.

The countries of Central Africa incorporate a variety of peoples and cultures, resources, environments, systems of government, and national goals. Most of the modern nations overlay both societies that were village-based and localized and others that were once part of extensive state formations. Islam has had little influence in the region, outside of Chad and northern Cameroon. In most areas, Christianity coexists with indigenous systems of belief.

Sophisticated wooden sculptures are one of the great cultural achievements associated with most Central African societies. To many, the carvings are only material manifestations of the spiritual potential of complex local cosmologies. However, the art forms are myriad and distinctive, and their diversity is as striking as the common features they possess.

At a surface level, the postcolonial political orders of Central Africa have ranged from the conservative regimes in Gabon and Zaire to the self-designated Marxist-Leninist states of the Congo and São Tomé and Príncipe. More fundamentally, all of the states have fallen under the rule of unelected autocracies, whose continued existence has been dependent on (sometimes external) military force. However, this authoritarian status quo is being challenged. São Tomé and Príncipe has recently turned toward multiparty democracy, and considerable agitation currently exists in the other states for democratization. In Cameroon, Gabon, and Zaire, the existence of opposition parties was formally recognized in 1990, but the old regimes are still in power.

(Peace Corps photo)

The manufacture and sale of traditional crafts are important to many Central African economies. The Traditional Handicrafts Cooperative Society in Cameroon facilitates trade in these local items.

GEOGRAPHICAL DISTINCTIVENESS

All of the states of the Central African region, except Chad, encompass equatorial rain forests. Citizens who live in these regions must cope with a climate that is hot and moist, while facing the challenges of utilizing the great equatorial forests. The problems of living in these heavily forested areas account in part for the relatively low, albeit growing, population densities of most of the Central African states. The difficulty of establishing roads and railroads impedes communication and thus development. The peoples of the rainforest areas tend to cluster along riverbanks and existing rail lines. In modern times, largely because of the extensive development of minerals, many inhabitants have moved to the cities, which accounts for the comparatively high urban population ratios in all of the states.

Central Africa's rivers have long been its lifelines. The watershed in Cameroon between the Niger and Zaire Rivers provides a natural divide between the West and Central African regions. The Congo, or Zaire, River is the largest in the region, but the Oubangi, Chari, and Ogooue, as well as others, are also important for the communication and trading opportunities they offer. The rivers flow to the Atlantic Ocean, a fact that has encouraged the orientation of Central Africa's external trade toward Europe and the Americas.

Many of the countries of the region share similar sources of wealth. The rivers are capable of generating enormous amounts of hydroelectric power. The rain forests are also rich in lumber, which is a major export of every country, except Chad and São Tomé and Príncipe. Other forest products such as rubber and palm oil are widely marketed. Lumbering and clearing activities for agriculture have led to environmentalist concerns about the depletion of the rain forests. As a result, in recent years there have been some organized boycotts in Europe of the region's hardwood exports, although far more trees are felled to process plywood.

As one might expect, Central Africa as a whole is one of the areas least affected by the drought conditions that periodically plague much of Africa. However, serious drought is a well-known visitor in Chad, the Central African Republic, and the northern regions of Cameroon, where it contributes to local food shortages. Savanna lands are found to the north and the south (in southern Zaire) of the forests. Whereas rain forests have often inhibited travel, the savannas have long been transitional areas, great avenues of migration linking the regions of Africa while providing agricultural and pastoral opportunities for their residents.

Besides the products of the forest, the Central African countries share other resources. Cameroon, Congo, and Gabon derive considerable revenues from their petroleum reserves. Other important minerals include diamonds, copper, gold, manganese, and uranium. The processes involved in the exploitation of these commodities, as well as the

(WFP photo by F. Mattioli)

Women in Chad winnow sesame seed. Cash crops such as sesame seed and cotton can encourage an economy, but they also can divert labor from food production.

demand for them in the world market, are issues of common concern among the producing nations. Many of the states also share an interest in exported cash crops, such as coffee, cocoa, and cotton, whose international prices are subject to sharp fluctuations. The similarity of their environments and products provides an economic incentive for Central African cooperation.

THE LINKS TO FRANCE

Many of the different ethnic groups in Central Africa overlap national boundaries. Examples include the Fang, who are found in Cameroon, Equatorial Guinea, and Gabon; the Bateke of Congo and Gabon; and the Kongo, who are concentrated in Angola as well as in Congo and Zaire. Such cross-border ethnic ties are less important as sources of regional unity than are the European colonial systems that the countries inherited. While Equatorial Guinea was controlled by Spain, São Tomé and Príncipe by Portugal, and Zaire by Belgium, the predominant external power in the region remains France. The Central African Republic, Chad, Congo, and Gabon were all once part of French Equatorial Africa. Most of Cameroon was also governed by the French, who were awarded the bulk of the former German colony of the Kamerun as a "trust territory" in the aftermath of World War I. French administration provided the five states with similar colonial experiences.

Early colonial development in the former French colonies and Zaire was affected by European *concessions companies,* institutions that were sold extensive rights (often 99-year leases granting political as well as economic powers) to exploit such local products as ivory and rubber. At the beginning of this century 41 companies controlled 70 percent of the territory of contemporary Central African Republic, Congo, and Gabon. Mining operations as well as large plantations were established, which often relied on forced labor. Individual production by Africans was also encouraged, again often through coercion rather than through economic incentives. While the colonial companies encouraged production and trade, they did little to aid the growth of infrastructure or long-term development. Only in Zaire was industry promoted to any great extent.

In general, French colonial rule, along with that of the Belgians, Portuguese, and Spanish, and the activities of the companies, offered few opportunities for Africans to gain training and education. There was also little encouragement of local entrepreneurship. An important exception to this pattern was the policies pursued by Felix Eboue. A Blackman from French Guiana who served as a senior administrator in the Free French administration of French Equatorial Africa during the 1940s, he increased opportunities for the urban elite in the Central African Republic, Congo, and Gabon. Eboue also played an important role in the Brazzaville Conference of 1944 which, recognizing the important role that the people of the French colonies had played in World War II, abolished forced labor and granted citizenship to all. Yet political progress toward self-government was uneven. Because of the lack of local manpower development, at independence there were too few people who were qualified to shoulder the bureaucratic and administrative tasks of the regimes that took power. People who could handle the economic institutions for the countries' benefit were equally scarce; and, in any case, the nations' economies remained, for the most part, securely in outside, largely French, hands.

The Spanish on the Equatorial Guinea island of Fernando Po and the Portuguese of São Tomé and Príncipe also profited from the exploitation of forced labor on their plantations. Political opportunities in these territories were even more limited than on the mainland. Neither country gained independence until fairly recently: Equatorial Guinea in 1968, and São Tomé and Príncipe in 1975.

In the years since independence most of the countries of Central Africa have been influenced, pressured, and supported by France and the other former colonial powers. French firms in the Central African Republic, Congo, and Gabon continue to be predominant in the exploitation of local resources. Most of these companies are only slightly encumbered by the regulations of the independent states in which they operate, and all are geared toward European markets and needs. Financial institutions are generally branches of French institutions, and all of the former French colonies, as well as Equatorial Guinea, are members of the Central African Franc Zone. French expatriates occupy senior positions in local civil-service establishments as well as in companies; there are many more of them resident in the region today than there were 30 years ago. In addition, French troops are stationed in the Central African Republic, Chad, and Gabon, regimes that owe their very existence to past French military interventions. Besides being a major trading partner, France has contributed significantly to the budgets of its former possessions, especially the poorer states of the Central African Republic and Chad.

(World Bank/CIRC photo by Alain Prott)

Timber from the rain forests is one of the major resources of Central Africa. Environmentalists are very concerned about ecological effects of the exploitation of this resource.

Despite having been under Belgian rule, Zaire is an active member of the Francophonic bloc in Africa. In 1977 French troops put down a rebellion in southeastern Zaire. Zaire, in turn, has sent its troops to serve beside those of France in Chad and Togo. Since playing a role in the 1979 coup which brought the current regime to power, France has also had a predominant influence in Equatorial Guinea.

EFFORTS AT COOPERATION

Although many Africans in Central Africa recognize that closer links among their countries would be beneficial, there have been fewer initiatives toward political unity or economic integration in this region than in East, West, or Southern Africa. In the years before independence Barthelemy Boganda, of what is now the Central African Republic, espoused and publicized the idea of a "United States of Latin Africa," which was to include contemporary Angola and Zaire as well as the territories of French Equatorial Africa. However, he was frustrated by Paris as well as by other, local, politicians. When France offered

(World Bank photo by Ivan Albert Andrews)

This palm oil processing mill was financed by the World Bank as part of a development project in Cameroon.

independence to its colonies in 1960, soon after Boganda's death, the possibility of forming a federation was discussed. But Gabon, which was wealthier than the other countries, declined to participate. The Central African Republic, Chad, and Congo drafted an agreement that would have created a federal legislature and executive branch governing all three countries, but local jealousies defeated this plan.

There have been some formal efforts at economic integration among the former French states. A Customs and Economic Union of the Central African States (UDEAC) was established in 1964, but its membership has been unstable. Chad and the Central African Republic withdrew to join Zaire in an alternate organization. (The Central African Republic later returned, bringing the number of members to six.) The East and Central African states together planned an economic community in 1967, but this did not materialize.

Only recently have there been new and hopeful signs of progress toward greater economic cooperation. Urged on by the UN Economic Commission on Africa, and with the stimulus of the 1980 Lagos Plan of Action, the Central African states met in 1982 to prepare for a new economic grouping. In 1983 all of the Central African states, as well as Rwanda and Burundi in East Africa, signed a treaty establishing the Economic Community of Central African States (ECCA) to promote economic and industrial cooperation.

Some have criticized the ECCA as a duplicate of UDEAC, but its goals are broader than a customs union (although it does urge cooperation in that area also). Members hoped that the union would stimulate industrial activity, increase markets, and reduce the dependence on France and other countries for trade and capital. But with dues often unpaid and meetings postponed, the ECCA has so far failed to meet its potential.

Central African states, while sharing a rich environment, have suffered more than other regions in Africa from the neglect and exploitation of their former colonial powers. They have not found common ways to develop mineral and forest resources and to deal with outside companies. Little implementation has resulted from former unions. As the Swahili proverb goes, "the toughness of the hoe is tested in the garden." Many hope that the ECCA will lead to a pragmatic Central African market, thus fulfilling the need for a harmonization of trade and industrial policies, and, perhaps, become a building block for greater continental as well as Central African unity.

Cameroon (United Republic of Cameroon)

GEOGRAPHY

Area in Square Kilometers (Miles): 475,400 (183,568) (somewhat larger than California)
Capital (Population): Yaoundé (852,000)
Climate: tropical to semi-arid

PEOPLE

Population

Total: 11,093,000
Annual Growth Rate: 2.7%
Rural/Urban Population Ratio: 60/40
Languages: official: English, French; others spoken: Fulde, Ewondo, Duala, Bamilike, Bassa, Bali, others

Health

Life Expectancy at Birth: 49 years (male); 53 years (female)
Infant Death Rate (Ratio): 120/1,000
Average Caloric Intake: 106% of FAO minimum
Physicians Available (Ratio): 1/18,365

Religion(s)

35% Roman Catholic; 25% traditional indigenous; 22% Muslim; 18% Protestant

THE KORUP FOREST

"Do not call the forest that shelters you a jungle" is an African proverb. The primary rain forests in Cameroon and other parts of Central Africa are the homes of plants and animals that have developed in this environment over thousands of years and that serve humanity. Korup is one Cameroon rain forest that is to be designated a national park. A recent survey discovered more than 42,000 trees and climbers in Korup, including 17 tree species never described before. An international campaign has been launched to preserve such rain forests, under the auspices of the World Wildlife Fund and the International Union for the Conservation of Nature and Natural Resources. Korup is the subject of a film that is being shown to raise funds for its preservation and that of other rain forests.

Education

Adult Literacy Rate: 76%

COMMUNICATION

Telephones: 47,200
Newspapers: 1

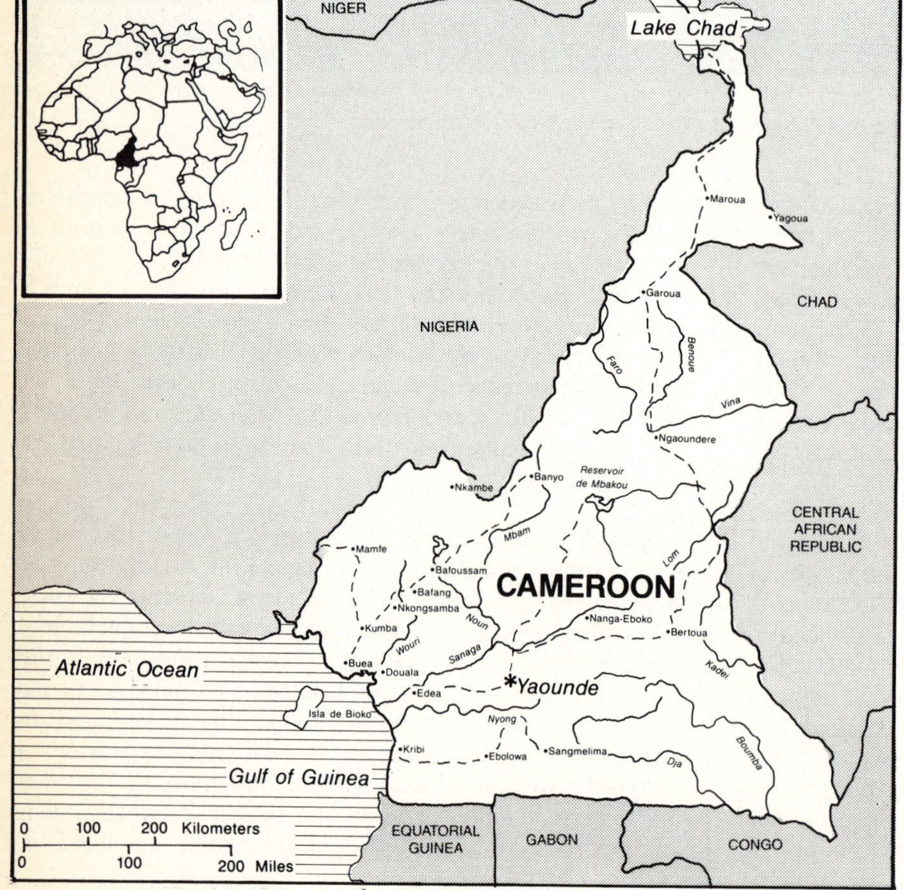

TRANSPORTATION

Highways—Kilometers (Miles): 65,000 (40,300)
Railroads—Kilometers (Miles): 1,003 (622)
Commercial Airports: 4 international

GOVERNMENT

Type: republic
Independence Date: January 1, 1960
Head of State: President Paul Biya
Political Parties: Cameroon People's Democratic Movement
Suffrage: universal over 21

MILITARY

Number of Armed Forces: 11,600
Military Expenditures (% of Central Government Expenditures): $219 million (1.7%)
Current Hostilities: none

ECONOMY

Currency ($ U.S. Equivalent): 286 CFA francs = $1
Per Capita Income/GNP: $955/$12.9 billion
Inflation Rate: 8.6%
Natural Resources: timber; oil; bauxite; iron ore; rubber
Agriculture: coffee; cocoa; food crops; cotton; bananas; peanuts; tobacco; tea
Industry: small manufacturing; consumer goods; aluminum

FOREIGN TRADE

Exports: $2 billion
Imports: $2.3 billion

CAMEROON

Frequently called "the hinge of Africa," Cameroon is a nation of variety. Geographically, the land is divided between the tropical forests in the south, the drier savanna of the northcentral region, and the mountainous country along its western border, which forms a natural division between West and Central Africa. In terms of religion, the country is roughly balanced among Christians, Muslims, and local animists. Cameroon has an ethnically diverse population, with more than a dozen major languages and some 230 subgroups. Many of the languages spoken in southern Cameroon are classified by linguists as Bantu. The "Bantu line" that runs across the country, roughly following the course of the Sanaga River, forms a boundary between the Bantu languages of Central, East, and Southern Africa and the non-Bantu tongues of North and West Africa. Many scholars believe that the roots of the Bantu language tree are buried in Cameroonian soil. Cameroon is also unique among the continental African states in sharing two European languages, English and French, as its official mediums. This circumstance is a product of the country's unique colonial heritage.

Three European powers have ruled over Cameroon. The Germans were the first to occupy the territory. From 1884 to 1916 they laid the foundation of much of the country's communications infrastructure and, primarily through the establishment of European-run plantations, export agriculture. Although Cameroon's experience under the Germans was harsh, the period nonetheless would later be invoked as the basis for modern Cameroonian nationalism. During World War I the area was divided between the British and French, who subsequently ruled their respective zones as League of Nations (later United Nations) mandates. The French received the larger eastern share of the former German colony, while British Cameroon consisted of two narrow strips of territory which were administratively integrated into its Nigerian territory.

During the 1950s Cameroonians in both the British and French zones began to agitate for unity and independence. At the core of their nationalist vision was the "Kamerun Idea," a belief that the period of German rule had given rise to a pan-Cameroonian identity. The largest and most radical of the nationalist movements in the French zone was the Union of the Cameroonian People (UPC). In the face of colonial hostility, it turned to armed struggle. Between 1955 and 1963, when most of the UPC guerrillas had been defeated, some 10,000 to 15,000 people were killed. Most of the victims belonged to the Bamileke and Bassa ethnic groups, of southwestern Cameroon, who largely supported the UPC struggle (for this reason, some texts refer to the war as the Bamileke Rebellion).

In the face of the UPC revolt, the French proceeded with a dual policy of repression against the guerrilla supporters and the devolution of political power to local non-UPC politicians. Most of these "moderate" leaders, who enjoyed core followings both in the heavily Christianized southeast and the Muslim north, coalesced as the Cameroonian Union,

(United Nations photo by Shaw McCutcheon)

In recent years Cameroon has experienced political unrest as various factions have moved to establish a stable form of government. At the base of this political turmoil, however, is a need to raise the living standards of the population through an increase in agricultural production. These farmers with their cattle herds are really the image of this essential agricultural element, and they represent the common denominator of a successful Cameroonian future.

The establishment of the German Kamerun Protectorate
1884

The partition of Cameroon; separate British and French mandates are established under the League of Nations
1916

The UPC is formed
1948

The UPC is outlawed for launching revolts in the cities
1955

The Independent Cameroon Republic is established with Ahmadou Ahidjo as the first president
1960

The Cameroon Federal Republic reunites French Cameroon with British Cameroon after a UN-supervised referendum
1961

The new Constitution creates a unitary state
1972

1980s–1990s

Ahidjo resigns and is replaced by Biya

Lake Nyos releases lethal volcanic gases, killing an estimated 2,000 people

Nationwide agitation for a restoration of multiparty democracy

whose leader was Ahmadou Ahidjo, a northerner. In pre-independence elections, Ahidjo's party won just over half—51—of the 100 seats. Ahidjo thus led a divided, war-torn nation to independence in 1960.

THE QUEST FOR UNITY

In 1961 the southern section of British Cameroon voted in a plebiscite to join Ahidjo's republic, while the northern section opted to remain part of Nigeria. The principal party in the south was the Kamerun National Democratic Party, whose leader, John Foncha, became the vice president of the Cameroon Federal Republic, while Ahidjo served as president. Initially, the former British and French zones maintained their separate local parliaments, but Ahidjo spearheaded a move toward a unified form of government. By 1966 all of the nation's legal political groups were incorporated into a single party, the Cameroon National Union (CNU), thus creating a de facto one-party state. Trade unions and other mass organizations were also gradually absorbed into the CNU. In 1972 Ahidjo pressed for the abolition of the federation as well as a constitution for a unified Cameroon. These proposals were approved, by a suspiciously overwhelming majority of 3,217,058 to 158. In the decade that followed Ahidjo was able to rule in an authoritarian manner.

THE TRANSFER OF POWER

In 1982 Ahidjo, apparently believing that he was in worse health than was actually the case, suddenly resigned, after 22 years in office. His hand-picked successor was Paul Biya. To the surprise of many, the heretofore self-effacing Biya quickly proved to be his own person. He brought young technocrats into the ministries and initially called for a more open and democratic society. But as Biya pressed forward, he came into increasing conflict with Ahidjo, who tried to reassert his authority through his position as CNU chair. The ensuing power struggle took on overtones of an ethnic conflict, between Biya's largely southern Christian supporters and Ahidjo's core following of northern Muslims.

In 1983 Ahidjo lost and went into exile. The next year he was tried and convicted, in absentia, for allegedly plotting Biya's overthrow. In April 1984, 2 months after Ahidjo's conviction, his supporters in the Presidential Guard attempted to overthrow Biya. The revolt was put down, but an estimated 500 to 1,000 people died, mostly in the vicinity of the capital, Yaoundé. More than 1,000 persons were arrested, many of whom are still thought to be in detention despite government amnesties.

Since the coup Biya has ruled through repression, while restructuring the ruling apparatus. In 1985 the CNU was overhauled and its name changed to the Cameroon People's Democratic Movement (CPDM). Perhaps out of a persisting fear of Ahidjo's northern Muslim base, Biya has continued to rely upon a core of southern Christian support, centered among his own Beti group. In addition to the north, opposition to President Biya has been especially strong in the Anglophonic west, but has been growing in other regions as well.

NEW OPPOSITION

As in many parts of Africa, 1990 witnessed an upsurge in prodemocracy agitation in Cameroon. In March an opposition party, the Social Democratic Front (SDF), was formed in Bamenda, the main town in the west, over government objections. In May as many as 40,000 people from the vicinity of Bamenda, out of a total population of about 100,000, attended a SDF rally. Government troops opened fire on school children returning from the demonstration. This action led to a wave of unrest, which spread to Yaoundé. The government media tried to portray the SDF as a subversive movement of "English speakers," but the party has significant support in other areas.

In the aftermath of the "Bamenda massacre," the political situation within Cameroon has remained tense. Biya has suggested the possibility of an opening to multipartyism, but the future remains uncertain. In addition to the SDF, a number of other opposition groups are active, including the long-banned UPC, which is believed to have sympathizers within as well as outside Biya's ruling CPDM. The Roman Catholic Church has also taken a strong stand in favor of liberalization and respect for human rights, while labor unrest is growing.

DEVELOPMENT

The Cameroon Development Corporation (CDC) coordinates more than half of the agricultural exports and, after the government, employs the most people. Cocoa and coffee comprise more than 50% of Cameroon's exports. Lower prices for these commodities have reduced the country's income.

FREEDOM

Since independence, de jure rights to freedom of association and speech have been progressively restricted in practice. Detention without trial, torture, secret executions, and increasingly pervasive censorship have occurred in recent years. There is general religious tolerance in the country, but Jehovah's Witnesses are targets of state persecution.

HEALTH/WELFARE

The literacy rate in Cameroon, 76%, is among the highest in Africa. There exists, however, great divergences in regional figures. In addition to public schools, the government devotes a large proportion of its budget to subsidizing private schools.

ACHIEVEMENTS

The strong showing by Cameroon's national soccer team, The Indomitable Lions, in the 1990 World Cup Competition is a source of pride for sports fans throughout Africa. Their success, along with the record number of medals won by African athletes in the 1988 Olympics, is symbolic of the continent's coming of age in international sports competitions.

Central African Republic

GEOGRAPHY

Area in Square Kilometers (Miles): 622,436 (240,324) (slighty smaller than Texas)
Capital (Population): Bangui (473,000)
Climate: tropical to semi-arid

PEOPLE

Population
Total: 2,877,000
Annual Growth Rate: 2.6%
Rural/Urban Population Ratio: 56/44
Languages: official: French; others spoken: Songo, Banda, Baya, Mangia, M'Baka

Health
Life Expectancy at Birth: 45 years (male); 48 years (female)
Infant Death Rate (Ratio): 141/1,000
Average Caloric Intake: 92% of FAO minimum
Physicians Available (Ratio): 1/25,690

Religion(s)
25% traditional indigenous; 25% Protestant; 25% Roman Catholic; 15% Muslim; 10% others

THE BREAKUP OF FRENCH EQUATORIAL AFRICA

As the Central African Republic moved toward independence in 1959, Barthelemy Boganda, the leader of the territory's nationalist movement, did not share the sense of euphoria exhibited by many of his colleagues. To him, the French path to independence had become a trap. Where there once had been a united French Equatorial Africa (A.E.F.) there were now five separate states, each struggling toward its own nationhood. Boganda, as president of the Grand Council of the A.E.F., had led the struggle to transform the territory into a true Central African Republic. But in 1958 French President Charles De Gaulle overruled all objections in forcing the breakup of the A.E.F. Boganda believed that thus balkanized, the Central African states would each be too weak to achieve true independence, but he still hoped that A.E.F. reunification might prove possible after independence.

Education
Adult Literacy Rate: 40%

COMMUNICATION

Telephones: 3,320
Newspapers: 1

TRANSPORTATION

Highways—Kilometers (Miles): 22,560 (13,987)
Railroads—Kilometers (Miles): none
Commercial Airports: 1 international

GOVERNMENT

Type: republic; under military rule
Independence Date: August 13, 1960
Head of State: General André-Dieudonné Kolingba (chief of state)
Political Parties: C.A.R. Democratic Rally
Suffrage: suspended

MILITARY

Number of Armed Forces: 10,385 paramilitary personnel
Military Expenditures (% of Central Government Expenditures): 1.8%
Current Hostilities: none

ECONOMY

Currency ($ U.S. Equivalent): 288 CFA francs = $1
Per Capita Income/GNP: $453/$1.21 billion
Inflation Rate: 4.2%
Natural Resources: diamonds; uranium; timber
Agriculture: coffee; cotton; peanuts; food crops; livestock
Industry: timber; textiles; soap; cigarettes; processed food; diamond mining

FOREIGN TRADE

Exports: $138 million
Imports: $285 million

Separate French administration of the Oubangui-Chàri colony is established **1904**

Gold and diamonds are discovered **1912–1913**

Barthelemy Boganda sets up MESAN, which gains wide support **1949**

Boganda dies; David Dacko, his successor, becomes president at the time of independence **1960**

Jean-Bedel Bokassa takes power after the first general strike **1966**

Bokassa becomes emperor **1976**

Bokassa is involved in the massacre of students; Dacko returns as head of state **1979**

1980s–1990s

André-Dieudonné Kolingba takes power

Bokassa is tried for murder, embezzlement, and other abuses

Kolingba rejects calls for multiparty democracy

CENTRAL AFRICAN REPUBLIC

Jean-Bedel Bokassa, who ruled the Central African Republic (C.A.R.) from 1966 until 1979, is reported once to have said: "Everything around here is financed by the French government. We ask the French for money, get it and waste it." Sadly, the statement conveys much about the nature of governance over the past 3 decades in this large, but in most parts thinly inhabited, country. Since independence from France in 1960, the political, economic, and military presence of the French has remained pervasive. At the same time, Central Africa's resources, as well as French largess, have been dissipated. It is a history made more lamentable by the fact that despite its geographic isolation and relative lack of infrastructural development during the colonial era, the C.A.R. remains a land of considerable potential. With diamond wealth, timber, and plenty of arable land, the country is better endowed than many of its neighbors. What the C.A.R. has clearly lacked is a leadership firmly committed to national development rather than corruption and internationally sanctioned waste.

POSTINDEPENDENCE

In 1960 the Central African Republic's population was just over 1 million. Up to 50,000 people were employed on projects managed by Europeans. The movement for independence was led by Barthelemy Boganda, a former priest who in 1949 founded the Popular Movement for the Social Evolution of Black Africa (MESAN). Boganda was a pragmatist willing to use moderate means in his struggle. His vision, however, was quite radical, for he hoped to unite French, Belgian, and Portuguese territories into his independent "Central African Republic." Locally, his movement succeeded in gaining a following among the peasantry as well as among intellectuals. In 1958 Boganda became the first prime minister of the then self-governing Oubangui-Chàri, but he died in a mysterious plane crash just before independence.

Boganda's successors failed to live up to his stature. At independence the country was led by David Dacko, a nephew of Boganda's, who succeeded to the leadership of MESAN but also cultivated the political support of the local French settlers, who had seen Boganda as an agitator. MESAN itself was transformed from an idealistic mass movement into a ruling-party apparatus, which, when challenged by dissident former members who formed a rival organization, lost little time in proclaiming its monopoly of power. Dacko's MESAN was the vehicle for an increasingly wealthy elite of the politically connected. Services for the masses were neglected, while corruption and abuses of power grew. A general strike in December 1965 was followed by a military coup on New Year's Eve, which put Dacko's cousin and Army Commander Jean-Bedel Bokassa in power. Dacko's overthrow was justified by the very real need to launch political and economic reforms. However, a more likely explanation for the move was external concerns about the former leader's increasingly friendly relationship with the Chinese, and Bokassa's own budding megalomania.

The country suffered greatly under Bokassa's increasingly eccentric rule. During the 1970s he was often portrayed, alongside Idi Amin of Uganda, as an archetype of African leadership at its worst. It was, however, more the sensational nature, such as public torture and dismemberment of prisoners, rather than the scale of his brutality, that captured headlines.

In 1979 global attention was focused on the Bokassa regime when reports surfaced that Bokassa had personally participated in the beating to death of between 80 and 100 school children. The students had protested his decree that they purchase and wear new uniforms bearing his imperial portrait. In the wake of this incident the French government decided that their ally had become a liability. While Bokassa was away on a state visit to Libya, French paratroopers returned Dacko to power.

Dacko was toppled for the second time in 1981 in a bloodless military coup, in which the nation's current leader, General André-Dieudonné Kolingba, was installed. Kolingba's provisional military regime was transformed into a new one-party state in 1985.

During the 1980s rising indebtedness and falling exports led to financial intervention on the part of the World Bank and the International Monetary Fund. The agencies, along with the French, have supported a program of Structural Adjustment reforms. This has resulted in the privatization of some state industries as well as budgetary cutbacks.

DEVELOPMENT

Production of cotton, one of the country's most important exports, fell seriously in the 1970s, and the nation had one of the lowest yields per growing unit of all African producers. In the 1980s increases in cotton production were accompanied by lower prices, thus hindering economic recovery.

FREEDOM

Human rights continue to be restricted. There have been allegations of forced labor in the form of corvee and enforced cultivation. Political prisoners have included Thomas Kwazo, a journalist who in 1986 reported on an alleged meeting between Kolingba and Bokassa.

HEALTH/WELFARE

The literacy rate is very low in the Central African Republic. Teacher training is currently being emphasized, especially for primary-school teachers.

ACHIEVEMENTS

Commodity prices fluctuate, with cotton prices down and coffee prices up. To increase production and transport of crops, France plans assistance in repairing a hydroelectric plant and improvements in river and road transportation.

Chad (Republic of Chad)

GEOGRAPHY

Area in Square Kilometers (Miles): 1,284,634 (496,000) (four-fifths the size of Alaska)
Capital (Population): N'Djamena (511,700)
Climate: arid to semi-arid

PEOPLE

Population
Total: 5,018,000
Annual Growth Rate: 2.1%
Rural/Urban Population Ratio: 77/23
Languages: official: French; others spoken: Chadian Arabic, Fulde, Hausa, Kotoko, Kanembou, Sara Maba, others

Health
Life Expectancy at Birth: 38 years (male); 40 years (female)
Infant Death Rate (Ratio): 136/1,000
Average Caloric Intake: 72% of FAO minimum
Physicians Available (Ratio): 1/53,376

Religion(s)
44% Muslim; 33% Christian; 23% traditional indigenous

THE KNIGHTS OF KANEM-BORNU

Between the ninth and nineteenth centuries A.D. much of modern Chad prospered under the rulers of Kanem and Bornu. The sultans of these two states, which were usually united, established great trading empires, linking the Mediterranean coast of North Africa with the Central African interior. As in the cases of medieval Europe and Japan, the leading element in the sultans' armies was heavily armored cavalry. Despite the local introduction of firearms by the sixteenth century, the tradition of armored knighthood survived until the arrival of the French colonialists. Kanem-Bornu armored costume is distinctive, being designed for the hot Sahelien climate.

Education
Adult Literacy Rate: 25%

COMMUNICATION

Telephones: 5,000
Newspapers: 4

TRANSPORTATION

Highways—Kilometers (Miles): 31,322 (19,420)
Railroads—Kilometers (Miles): none
Commercial Airports: 2 international

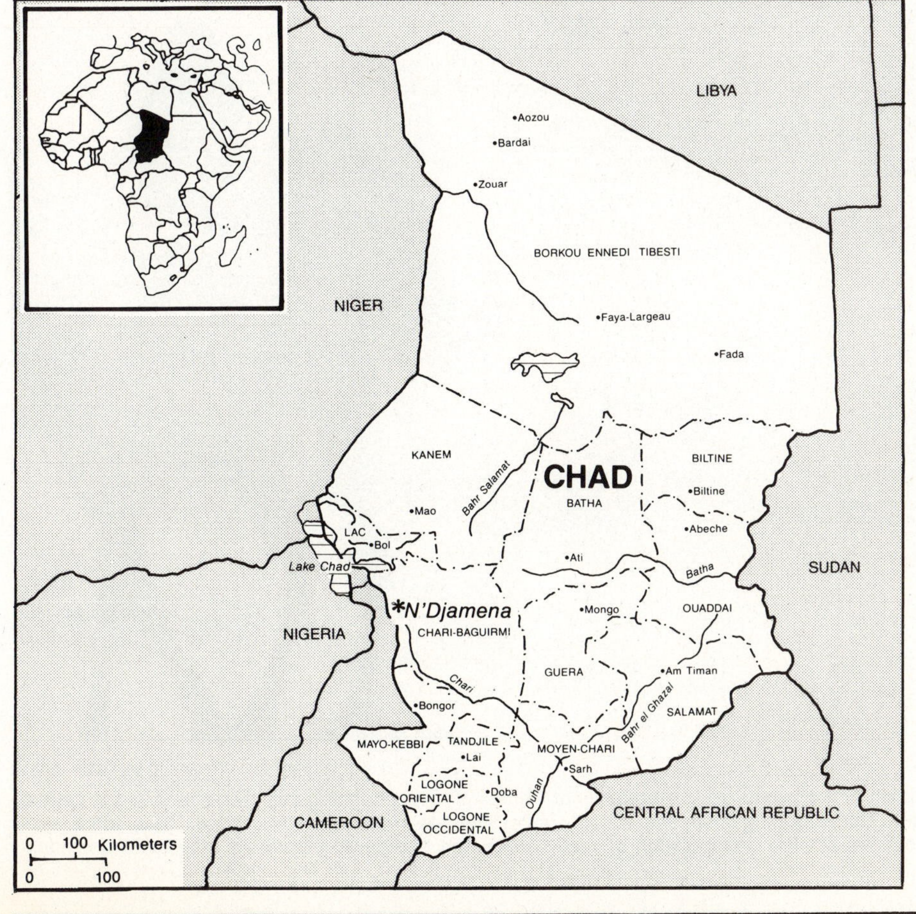

GOVERNMENT

Type: republic
Independence Date: August 11, 1960
Head of State: President Indriss Deby
Political Parties: National Union for Independence and Revolution
Suffrage: universal over 18

MILITARY

Number of Armed Forces: 22,900
Military Expenditures (% of Central Government Expenditures): n/a
Current Hostilities: none

ECONOMY

Currency ($ U.S. Equivalent): 288 CFA francs = $1
Per Capita Income/GNP: $190/$902 million
Inflation Rate: 8.3%
Natural Resources: petroleum; uranium; natron; kaolin
Agriculture: subsistence crops; cotton; cattle; fish; sugar
Industry: livestock products; beer; bicycle and radio assembly; textiles; cigarettes

FOREIGN TRADE

Exports: $432 million
Imports: $214 million

CHAD

During the 1980s Chad was the focus of global media interest as a result of the internationalization of its long-running civil war. Until the emergence of a national government under Hissène Habré, in 1987, the country seemed hopelessly divided by its varied armed factions, which sought and received the support of outside powers. Habré's recent overthrow by his former army chief, Idriss Deby, has revived fears that Chad may once more become "the Lebanon of Africa."

CIVIL WAR

Chad's modern conflicts are, in part, rooted in the country's ethnic and religious divisions. It has been common for outsiders to speak of the struggle as being between Arab-oriented Muslim northerners and black Christian southerners. In reality, however, Chad's regional and ethnic allegiances are much more complex. Geographically, the country is more accurately divided into three zones: the northern Sahara, a middle Sahel region, and the southern savanna. Within each of these ecological areas live peoples who speak different languages and engage in a variety of economic activities. The majority of peoples in the supposedly Christian south are in fact local animists. Throughout the civil war there have emerged greater ethnoregional and religious loyalties, but such aggregates have tended to be fragile and their allegiances shifting.

At independence, in 1960, France turned over power to François Tombalbaye, a Christian Sara speaker from the south. Tombalbaye ruled through a combination of repression, ethnic favoritism, and incompetence, which quickly alienated his government from broad sectors of the Chadian population. A northern-based coalition of armed groups, the National Liberation Front of Chad (Frolinat), was increasingly successful in its insurgency aimed at overthrowing the Tombalbaye regime. The success of the Frolinat alliance led to French military intervention, beginning in 1968, but failed to stem the rebellion. In 1975 officers in Tombalbaye's army, tired of the war and upset by the president's increasingly conspicuous brutality, overthrew the government and established a military regime, headed by Felix Malloum.

Yet Malloum's government proved itself unable to defeat Frolinat. Thus, in 1978 it agreed to share power with the largest of the Frolinat groups, the Armed Forces of the North (FAN), led by Hissène Habré. This agreement broke down in 1979, resulting in fighting in the capital city of N'Djamena. FAN came out ahead, while Malloum's men withdrew to the south. The triumph of the "northerners" immediately led to further fighting among factions allied to Habré and others loyal to his rival within the Frolinat movement, Goukouni Oueddi. Habré had earlier split from Oueddi, whom he accused of indifference toward Libya's unilateral annexation in 1976 of the Aouzou Strip, along

(United Nations photo by John Isaac)

The long-running civil war of the 1980s caused the death of thousands upon thousands of Chadians. Compounding this civil strife was the severe drought, which caused a great deal of internal migration. This migrating family was the rule rather than the exception of this period. Today, more rains and more peaceful conditions have expanded agriculture, but the depopulation of many areas has hampered potentially significant additional agricultural advancements.

Independence is achieved under President Tombalbaye
1960

Revolt breaks out among peasant groups; FROLINAT is formed
1965–1966

Establishment of a Transitional Government of National Unity (GUNT) includes both Hissène Habré and Goukouni Oueddi
1978

1980s–1990s

Qadhafi recognizes Habré's government

Habré comes to power through conquest; Oueddi and others continue the war

Habré's regime overthrown by Indriss Deby

Chad's northern frontier. At the time, Libya was the principal foreign backer of Frolinat.

In 1980, shortly after the last French forces withdrew from Chad, the Libyan Army invaded the country, at the invitation of Oueddi. Oueddi was then proclaimed the leader in a Transitional Government of National Unity (GUNT), which was established in N'Djamena. In the aftermath of this development, Nigeria and other neighboring states, joined by France and the United States, pushed for the withdrawal of Libyan forces. This pressure grew in 1981, after Libyan leader Maummar Al-Qadhafi announced the merger of Chad and Libya. Following a period of intense negotiations the Libyans began to pull back, at Oueddi's request.

The removal of the Libyan forces from most of Chad was accompanied by revived fighting between GUNT and the FAN forces, who now enjoyed substantial covert American support via Egypt and Sudan. A peacekeeping force assembled by the Organization of African Unity (OAU) proved ineffectual. The internal collapse of GUNT, in 1982, led to a second major Libyan invasion. The Libyan offensive was countered by the return of French forces, assisted by Zairian troops and smaller contingents from several other Francophonic African countries. Between 1983 and 1987 the country was virtually partitioned along the 16th Parallel, with Habré's French-backed coalition in the south and the Libyan-backed remnants of GUNT in the north.

Finally in 1987, a political and military breakthrough occurred. Habré's effort to unite the country led to a reconciliation with Malloum's followers and elements within GUNT. Oueddi himself was apparently placed under house arrest in Libya. Emboldened, Habré launched a major offensive north of the 16th Parallel, which, to the surprise of many, rolled back the better-equipped Libyan forces, who by now included a substantial number of Lebanese mercenaries. A factor in the Libyan defeat was the supply of American Stinger missiles to Habré's forces, who used them to neutralize Libya's powerful air force (Habré's government lacked significant airpower of its own). A ceasefire was declared after the Libyans had been driven out of all of northern Chad, with the exception of a portion of the disputed Aouzou Strip. In 1988 Qadhafi announced that he would recognize the Habré government and pay compensation to Chad. The announcement was welcomed—with some skepticism—by Chadian and other African leaders, though no mention was made of the conflicting claims to the Aouzou Strip.

The long-running struggle for Chad took another turn in November 1990 with the sudden collapse of Habré's government in the face of a three week offensive by guerrillas loyal to Deby. In his first months in office Deby, who came to power with Libyan and Sudanese support, has sought to gain legitimacy by promising a new national government based on multi-party politics.

A BETTER FUTURE?

The suffering caused by the long, drawn-out conflict in Chad has been immense. It is estimated that between 200,000 and 400,000 people perished as a direct result of the warfare. Many died during the drought that afflicted the country during the mid-1980s, when fighting further reduced food production and hampered relief efforts. Better rains and the return of relatively peaceful conditions have already resulted in a major expansion in agriculture, but the conflict has left as one of its legacies the depopulation of rural areas. Many Chadians have fled to the cities for security but have found little in the way of employment.

If peace can be maintained the livelihood of Chad's population will obviously benefit. Unfortunately the country's overall prospects for development are bleak under current conditions. The country has some potential mineral wealth, but its geographic isolation as well as current world prices are a disincentive to investors. Local food self-sufficiency should be obtainable, although the country faces recurrent drought, and their geography limits the potential of earning revenue by exporting crops. Chad thus appears to be an extreme case of the more general African need for a radical transformation of prevailing regional and global economic interrelationships. Had outside powers devoted half the resources to Chad's development over the past decades as they did to its civil conflicts perhaps the country's future would appear somewhat brighter.

DEVELOPMENT

The cotton crop, one of the mainstays of the economy, suffered during the war. The problems of the war were compounded by the recurring droughts of the 1970s and 1980s. Rains in the mid-1980s brought some relief but also fostered locust infestation.

FREEDOM

The civil war led to a breakdown in law and order. Not only were there battle casualties, but disappearances and arbitrary killings of civilians can be documented. Former refugees and families of opponents have been detained without trial.

HEALTH/WELFARE

The Medecins Sans Frontieres (composed of French, Belgian, and Swiss medical personnel) began a $5-million project to build and reorganize Chad's health-care system.

ACHIEVEMENTS

Achievements are difficult to ascertain in a time of such dislocation. There have been some signs of recovery in textile, sugar, and other enterprises, and state salaries are paid more regularly (although they have been cut). Food production increased after rains in 1985, but aid is needed to fight locusts.

Congo (People's Republic of the Congo)

GEOGRAPHY

Area in Square Kilometers (Miles): 349,650 (132,000) (slightly smaller than Montana)
Capital (Population): Brazzaville (595,100)
Climate: tropical

PEOPLE

Population

Total: 2,242,000
Annual Growth Rate: 3%
Rural/Urban Population Ratio: 49/51
Languages: official: French; others spoken: Lingala, Kikongo, Teke, Sangha, M'Bochi, others

Health

Life Expectancy at Birth: 52 years (male); 55 years (female)
Infant Death Rate (Ratio): 110/1,000
Average Caloric Intake: 99% of FAO minimum
Physicians Available (Ratio): 1/8,065

Religion(s)

50% Christian; 48% traditional indigenous; 2% Muslim

RELIGIOUS LIFE

Many different religions have gained followings among peoples of Congo in recent times. There is even a Tenrikyo Shinto center from Japan in the country. Many people claim affiliation with Christian faiths, and one-third are Roman Catholic. Swedish evangelical missionaries came to Congo in the early twentieth century, and the Salvation Army and the Jehovah's Witnesses gained followers in the pre-independence period. Many new religious movements developed after World War I, often centered around figures who were considered messiahs, such as Simon Kimbangu, who founded a Christian church that is now a member of the World Council of Churches, and André Matsoua, an early nationalist. Until the 1950s the only secondary schools in the country were the two seminaries preparing priests for the Roman Catholic Church.

Education

Adult Literacy Rate: 63%

COMMUNICATION

Telephones: 18,100
Newspapers: 3

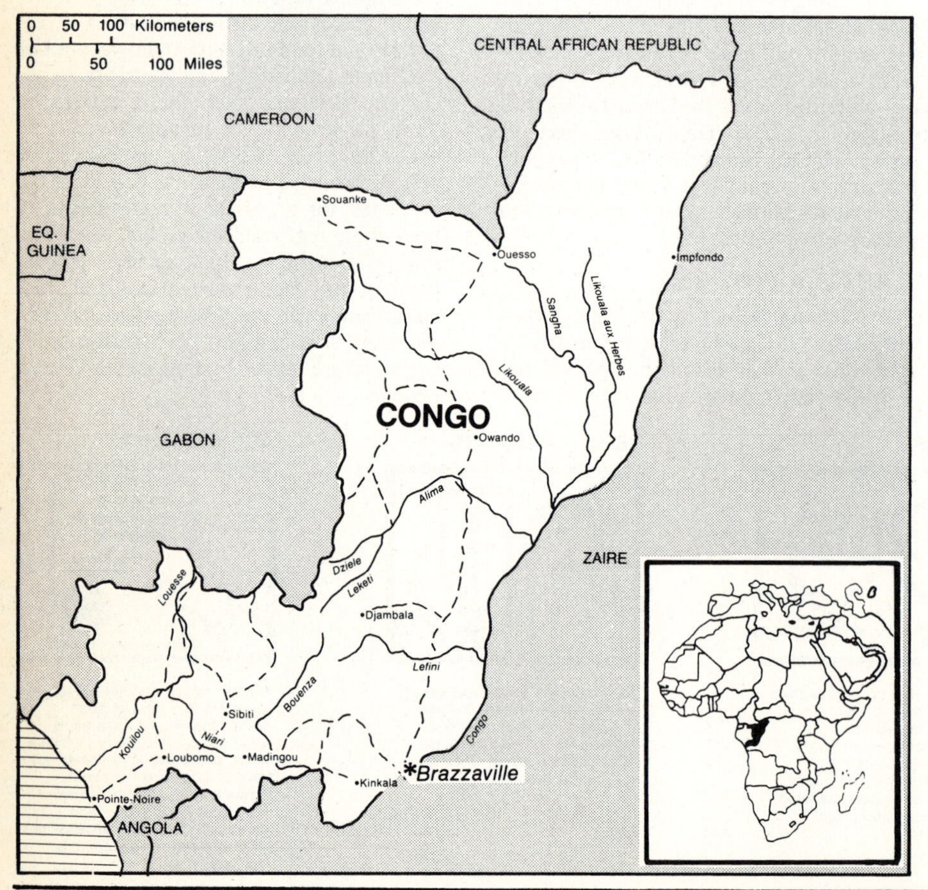

TRANSPORTATION

Highways—Kilometers (Miles): 12,000 (7,440)
Railroads—Kilometers (Miles): 797 (494)
Commercial Airports: 2 international

GOVERNMENT

Type: people's republic
Independence Date: August 15, 1960
Head of State: President (Colonel) Denis Sassou-Nguesso
Political Parties: Congolese Labor Party
Suffrage: universal over 18

MILITARY

Number of Armed Forces: 8,800
Military Expenditures (% of Central Government Expenditures): 4.6%
Current Hostilities: none

ECONOMY

Currency ($ U.S. Equivalent): 319 CFA francs = $1
Per Capita Income/GNP: $1,000/$2.6 billion
Inflation Rate: 1.5%
Natural Resources: wood; potash; petroleum; natural gas
Agriculture: cocoa; coffee; tobacco; palm kernels; sugarcane; rice; peanuts
Industry: processed agricultural and forestry goods; cement; textiles

FOREIGN TRADE

Exports: $912 million
Imports: $494 million

THE CONGO

The People's Republic of the Congo takes its name from the river that forms the country's southeastern border, with Zaire. Because Zaire, prior to 1971, also called itself the Congo, the two countries are sometimes confused. Close historical and ethnic ties do in fact exist between the two nations.

The largest ethnolinguistic group in the Congo and western Zaire, as well as northern Angola, are the (Ki)Konga speakers. During the fifteenth and sixteenth centuries their ancestors united to form the powerful kingdom of the Kongo. The Konga kings then ruled over much of Central Africa, while establishing commercial and diplomatic ties with Europe. But the kingdom had virtually disappeared by the late nineteenth century, when the territory along the northwest bank of the Congo River, the modern republic, was annexed by France, while the southeast bank, modern-day Zaire, was placed under the rule of King Leopold of Belgium.

Despite the establishment of this political division, cultural ties between the Congo and Zaire—the former French and Belgium Congos—remain strong. Brazzaville, the Congolese capital, sits across the river from the Zairian capital of Kinshasha. The metropolitan region formed by these two centers has, through such figures as the late Congolese artist Franco, given rise to *souskous,* a musical style that has gained an international following. Nightclubs featuring the souskous sound have only recently appeared in the United States but enjoy great popularity in such places as Tokyo and Paris as well as throughout much of Africa.

ECONOMIC DEVELOPMENT

Brazzaville, which today houses more than one-quarter of the Congo's population, was established during the colonial era as the administrative headquarters of French Equatorial Africa, a vast territory that included the modern states of Chad, Central African Republic, and Gabon as well as the Congo. As a result, the city expanded and the area around it developed as an imperial crossroads. However, the Congolese paid a heavy price for its growth. Thousands died while working under brutal conditions to build the Congo-Ocean Railroad linking Brazzaville to Pointe-Noire on the coast. Many more suffered as forced laborers for foreign concessionaires during the early decades of the twentieth century.

As the economies of most African states declined or stagnated during the late 1970s and 1980s, the Congo generally experienced growth as a result of its oil wealth. Hydrocarbons now account for 90 percent of the total value of the nation's exports. The danger of such dependence

(United Nations photo by Sean Sprague)

Since the People's Republic of the Congo achieved its independence in 1960, it has made enormous educational strides. Almost all children in the country now attend school, and this has had a tremendous effect on helping to realize the potential of the country's natural resources.

Middle Congo becomes part of French Equatorial Africa **1910**

Conference establishes French Union; Felix Eboue establishes positive policies for African advancement **1944**

Independence is achieved, with Abbe Fulbert Youlou as the first president **1960**

A general strike brings the army and a more radical government (National Revolutionary Movement) to power **1963**

A new military government under Marien Ngouabi takes over; Congolese Workers' Party is formed **1968–1969**

Ngouabi is assassinated; Colonel Yhombi-Opango rules **1977**

Denis Sassou-Nguesso becomes president **1979**

1980s–1990s

A crisis budget is adopted to cope with the debt

The arrest of 20 army officers, all belonging to the Kouyou ethnic group, leads to a rebellion in the north

Sassou-Nguesso tours the United States, building closer ties

was underscored in 1986–1987, when falling oil prices led to a sharp (12 percent) decline in gross domestic product. Another major threat to the economic health of the Congo is its mounting debt. As a result of heavy borrowing during the oil-boom years, by 1989 the total debt was estimated to be 50 percent greater than the value of the country's annual economic output, while the annual cost of servicing the debt is almost equal to the government's domestic expenditures.

The debt has led to International Monetary Fund (IMF) pressure on the Congolese government to introduce austerity measures as part of a Structural Adjustment Program (SAP). The Congolese government has proved eager to move away from its previous policy emphasis on central planning, in favor of a greater reliance on market economics. During the mid-1980s severe budgetary cutbacks were also carried out. However, the government is reluctant to reduce further its spending on such things as food subsidies and state-sector employment. With more than half of the Congolese now urbanized, there is deep concern about the social, and no doubt political, effects of more austerity measures. Many urbanites are already either unemployed or underemployed; even those with steady formal-sector jobs have been squeezed by wages that fail to keep up with the inflation rate. A new accord with the IMF is, nonetheless, considered imminent.

Although most Congolese appear to be facing tough times in the immediate future, the country's overall economic and social picture is hopeful. Oil prices are rising. The country is also endowed with a wide variety of mineral reserves which, even if developed on a modest scale, will aid in its efforts to diversify the economy. Timber has long been a major industry. The Congolese forests, along with those of neighboring Gabon, are the world's main source of okoume logs, which are a preferred material for manufacturing plywood. In addition, after years of neglect, the agricultural sector is also growing. The goal of a return to food self-sufficiency is reachable. And despite their currently low commodity prices, cocoa, coffee, tobacco, and sugar are major cash crops, and palm-oil estates are being rehabilitated.

The currently small, though well-established, Congolese manufacturing sector also has much potential. The Congo's urbanized population is relatively skilled, thanks to the enormous educational strides that have been made since independence. Almost all children now attend school. The infrastructure serving Brazzaville and Pointe-Noire, coupled with the government's emphasis on private-sector growth, should prove attractive to outside investors and encouraging to local entrepreneurs. Despite the ruling party's commitment to "scientific socialism," which was followed until recently, some three-quarters of industrial turnover takes place in the private sector.

POLITICAL DEVELOPMENT

A series of military coups in the 1960s resulted in the adoption of Marxist-Leninism as the official state ideology. During the past 2 decades the Congolese Labor Party (PCT) has enjoyed a monopoly of power, even though it has remained a small vanguard organization of only a few thousand members. Leadership at the top is in the hands of the senior ranks of the military; the current president, Denis Sassou-Nguesso, was a colonel when he assumed office. Although the PCT has always allowed for a mixed economy and has pursued a nonaligned foreign policy, its commitment to state socialism was for many years quite strong. While the PCT government has not formally abandoned this commitment, it has begun its own process of perestroika, or restructuring, favoring a shift toward market economics.

The ruling party's changing economic focus has been accompanied by talk in some quarters of a need for political renewal. In 1990 the government responded to the collapse of marxist-Leninist regimes elsewhere by appointing a special PCT commission to conisder possible reforms. To the surprise of many the PTC subsequently agreed to relinquish its monopoly of power by returning the Congo to a multiparty system of government. Prior to this surprising development the government had continued to argue that any restoration of a multiparty system would lead to ethnic conflict. But evidence from past coup attempts and other public manifestations of competition within the PCT suggests that intra-ethnic conflict between and among northern and southern groups has long been a significant factor in local politics.

DEVELOPMENT

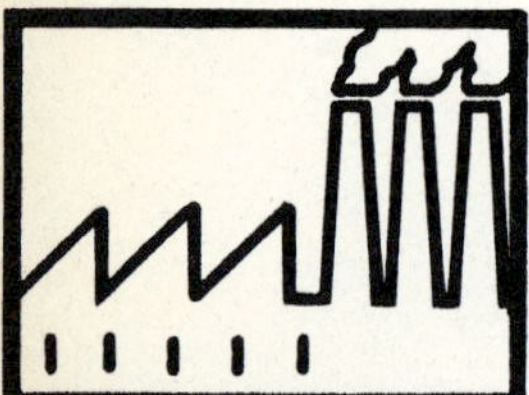

The Congo's Niari Valley has become the nation's leading agricultural area, due to its rich alluvial soils. The government has been encouraging food-processing plants to locate in the region.

FREEDOM

Amnesty International has accused the Congolese government of political detentions and torture. Freedom of speech and association are denied. Jehovah's Witnesses are banned, while the activities of certain other religious sects are restricted.

HEALTH/WELFARE

Almost all Congolese between ages 6 and 16 currently attend school. Adult-literacy programs have also proved successful, giving the country one of the highest literacy rates in Africa. However, 30% of Congolese children under age 5 are reported to suffer from chronic malnutrition.

ACHIEVEMENTS

There are a number of Congolese poets and novelists who combine their creative efforts with teaching and public service. Tchicaya U'Tam'si, who died in 1988, wrote poetry and novels and worked for many years for UNESCO in Geneva.

Equatorial Guinea (Republic of Equatorial Guinea)

GEOGRAPHY

Area in Square Kilometers (Miles): 28,023 (10,820) (about the size of Maryland)
Capital (Population): Malabo (38,000)
Climate: equatorial

PEOPLE

Population
Total: 369,000
Annual Growth Rate: 2.5%
Rural/Urban Population Ratio: n/a
Languages: official: Spanish; others spoken: Fang, Benge, Combe, Bujeba, Balengue, Fernandino, Bubi

Health
Life Expectancy at Birth: 47 years (male); 52 years (female)
Infant Death Rate (Ratio): 118/1,000
Average Caloric Intake: n/a
Physicians Available (Ratio): 1/76,800

Religion(s)
60% Catholic; 40% Protestant or traditional indigenous

RELATIONS WITH SOUTH AFRICA

Equatorial Guinea has a controversial relationship with South Africa. This erupted in 1988, when Equatorial Guinea signed an agreement with South Africa and a conservative West German institute to allow South Africa to build a satellite-tracking station in Equatorial Guinea and to rebuild the airport for South African flights. Neighboring Nigeria, fearing a nearby South African military base, protested loudly. Equatorial Guinea agreed to expel seven South Africans. An unsuccessful invasion of São Tomé and Príncipe in March 1988 is believed to have been backed by South Africa and launched from bases in Equatorial Guinea. Therefore, amid reports that South Africans were still there, relations between Nigeria and Equatorial Guinea remained strained.

Education
Adult Literacy Rate: 40%

COMMUNICATION

Telephones: 2,000
Newspapers: 2

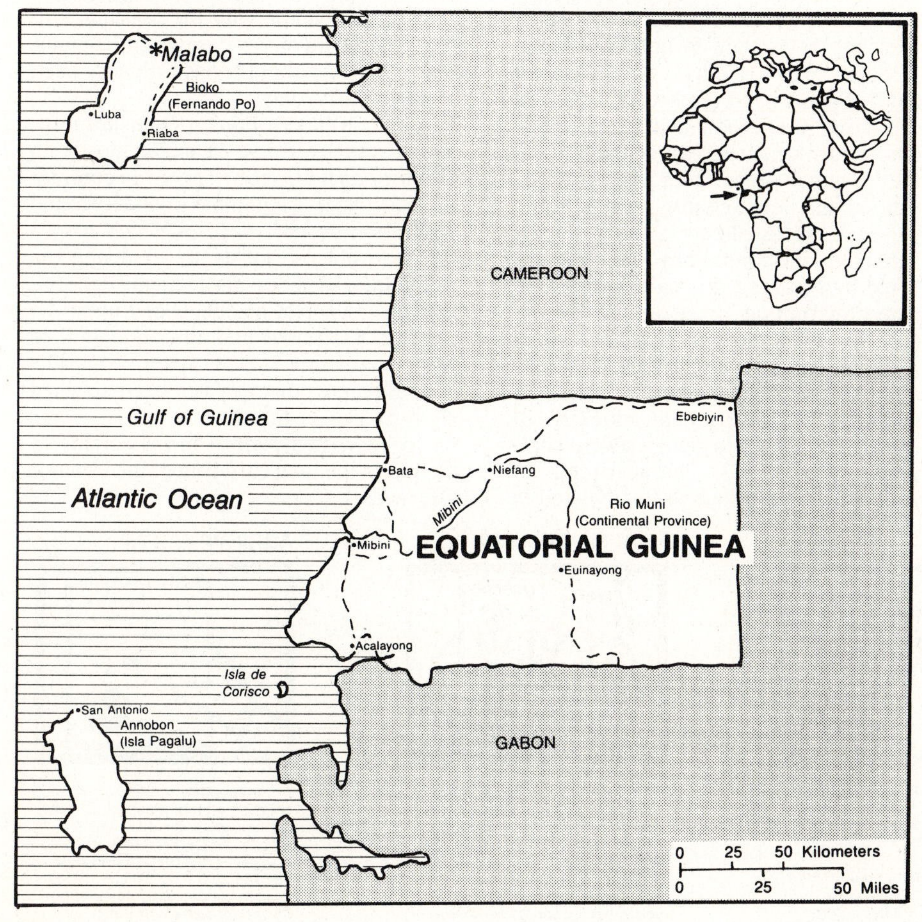

TRANSPORTATION

Highways—Kilometers (Miles): 1,240 (769)
Railroads—Kilometers (Miles): none
Commercial Airports: 2 international

GOVERNMENT

Type: unitary republic; governed by Supreme Military Council
Independence Date: October 12, 1968
Head of State: Brigadier General Teodoro Obiang Ngeuma Mbasogo
Political Parties: Democratic Party of Equatorial Guinea
Suffrage: universal for adults

MILITARY

Number of Armed Forces: 3,100
Military Expenditures (% of Central Government Expenditures): 11%
Current Hostilities: internal conflicts

ECONOMY

Currency ($ U.S. Equivalent): 319 CFA francs = $1
Per Capita Income/GNP: $293/$103 million
Inflation Rate: 33%
Natural Resources: wood
Agriculture: cocoa; coffee; timber; rice; yams; bananas
Industry: fishing; sawmilling; palm-oil processing

FOREIGN TRADE

Exports: $30 million
Imports: $50 million

Europeans explore modern Equatorial Guinea
1500s

The Dutch establish slave-trading stations
1641

Spain claims the area of Equatorial Guinea; the process of establishing de facto control is not completed until 1926
1778

The League of Nations investigates charges of slavery on Fernando Po
1930

The murder of nationalist leader Acacio Mane leads to the founding of political parties
1958

Local autonomy is granted
1963

Independence; Macias Nguema begins his reign
1968

A coup ends the dictatorial regime of Macias Nguema; Obiang Nguema becomes the new ruler
1979

1980s–1990s

Equatorial Guinea joins the Franc Zone

Obiang institutionalizes his regime as a one-party state

The South African presence on Bioko (Fernando Po) leads to tensions with Nigeria

EQUATORIAL GUINEA

Since 1979 the citizens of Equatorial Guinea have been trying to recover from the nightmare of their first decade of independence. Under the deranged misrule of Macias Nguema (1968–1979), virtually all public and private enterprise collapsed; indeed, between 1974 and 1979 the country stopped having a budget. During this period one-third of the nation's population went into exile, while tens of thousands of others were either murdered or allowed to die of disease and starvation. Many of those people who survived were put to forced labor, and the rest were left to subsist off the land. This reign of terror and decay finally ended when Macias was overthrown by his nephew and chief aide, Obiang Nguema.

The modern descent of Equatorial Guinea contrasts with the mood of optimism that characterized the county when it gained its independence from Spain in 1968. At that time the new republic was buoyed by the prospects of a growing gross domestic product, potential mineral riches, and exceptionally good soils. The major responsibility for the decline must lie with the sadistic brutality of Macias Nguema and his senior accomplices, who were mostly drawn from among his own Esangui clan within the larger Fang ethnic community. However, the uneven pattern of colonial development among the nation's diverse regions contributed to its internal weakness at independence.

The republic is comprised of two small islands, Fernando Po (now officially known as Bioko) and Annobon, and the relatively larger and more populous coastal enclave of Rio Muni. Before the two islands and the enclave were united during the nineteenth century as Spain's only colony in sub-Saharan Africa, all three areas were victimized by their intense involvement in the slave trade. Under colonial rule, however, they suffered along separate paths.

CHARGES OF SLAVERY

Spain's major colonial concern was the prosperity of the large cocoa and coffee plantations that were established on the islands, particularly on Fernando Po. Because of resistance from the local Bubi, labor for these estates was imported from elsewhere in West Africa. Coercive recruitment and poor working conditions led to frequent charges of slavery.

Despite early evidence of its potential riches, Rio Muni was largely neglected by the Spanish, who only occupied its interior in 1926. During the 1930s and 1940s much of the enclave was under the political control of the Elar-ayong, a nationalist movement that sought to unite the Fang, Rio Muni's principal ethnic group, against both the Spanish and the French rulers in neighboring Cameroon and Gabon. The territory has remained one of the world's least developed areas, with poor communications and few schools, hospitals, or other basic infrastructure.

Although no community was left unscarred by Macias Nguema's tyranny, the greatest disruption occurred on the islands. By 1976 the entire resident-alien population had left, along with most surviving members of the educated class. On Annobon, the government blocked all international efforts to stem a severe cholera epidemic in 1973. The near-total depopulation of the island was completed in 1976, when all able-bodied men on Annobon, along with another 20,000 from Rio Muni, were drafted for forced labor on Fernando Po. Annobon subsequently served as a depot for the Soviet Navy.

OPPOSITION

If Equatorial Guinea's first decade of independence was hell, the second has been purgatory. The current government is merely a more respectable, less abusive, version of the old regime. Obiang Nguema rules as a dictator with the assistance of other members of the entrenched Esangui. Since 1987 the country has officially been a single-party state.

About 100,000 Equato-Guinean refugees continue to live in exile, mostly in Cameroon and Gabon. This exile community has fostered a number of underground opposition groups, none of which has so far been able seriously to challenge the status quo. Besides his Esangui cohorts, Obiang's survival has depended upon the financial assistance and other goodwill of Morocco, France, and Spain. Madrid's commitment, however, has been strained by criticism in the Spanish press, which has been virtually alone in publicizing to the world the long suffering of the Equato-Guineans.

DEVELOPMENT

The cocoa, coffee, and plywood industries are reviving. Prospecting for a number of minerals is underway in Rio Muni. Trade with France increased during the 1980s.

FREEDOM

The human-rights situation, while vastly improved from the horror of the Macias years, remains quite grim. Jehovah's Witnesses and several Pentecostal churches are banned, and their memberships are subject to arrest and forced labor. "Illegal aliens" are also subject to forced labor. Non-Esangui are discriminated against.

HEALTH/WELFARE

At independence, Equatorial Guinea had one of the best doctor-to-population ratios in Africa, but Macias's rule left it with the lowest. Health care is gradually reviving, with major assistance coming from public and private Spanish sources. China and Cuba have also contributed skilled personnel.

ACHIEVEMENTS

At independence, 90% of all children attended school, but the schools were closed under Macias. Since 1979 primary education has revived and now incorporates most children. Major assistance currently comes from the World Bank and from Spanish missionaries.

Gabon (Gabonese Republic)

GEOGRAPHY

Area in Square Kilometers (Miles): 264,180 (102,317) (about the size of Colorado)
Capital (Population): Libreville (350,000)
Climate: tropical

PEOPLE

Population

Total: 1,068,000
Annual Growth Rate: 0.8%
Rural/Urban Population Ratio: 65/35
Languages: official: French; others spoken: Fang, Eshira, Bopounou, Bateke, Okande, others

Health

Life Expectancy at Birth: 50 years (male); 56 years (female)
Infant Death Rate (Ratio): 106/1,000
Average Caloric Intake: 102% of FAO minimum
Physicians Available (Ratio): 1/4,031

Religion(s)

55%–75% Christian; less than 1% Muslim; remainder traditional indigenous

ALBERT SCHWEITZER AT LAMBARENE

Lambarene, a town of about 7,000 residents on the Ogooue River in Gabon's interior, is the site of the mission hospital that Albert Schweitzer built and in which he practiced medicine. Schweitzer, born in Alsace-Lorraine, then a part of Germany, was a philosopher, theologian, organist, and specialist on Bach as well as a medical missionary. At age 38 he came to Lambarene, where he lived and worked for 52 years. The hospital that he built was like an African village, consisting of many simple dwellings. It accommodated many patients and their relatives and operated without all of the necessities of hospitals in Europe. In later times innovative changes were not always accepted by the authoritarian Schweitzer or his staff. The work at Lambarene saved lives and cured thousands. Schweitzer was awarded the Nobel Peace Prize for his efforts for "the Brotherhood of Nations." Yet he shared the distorted images of Africans so deeply ingrained among Westerners, and he did not believe that Africans could advance in Western ways.

Education

Adult Literacy Rate: 62%

COMMUNICATION

Telephones: 13,800
Newspapers: 2

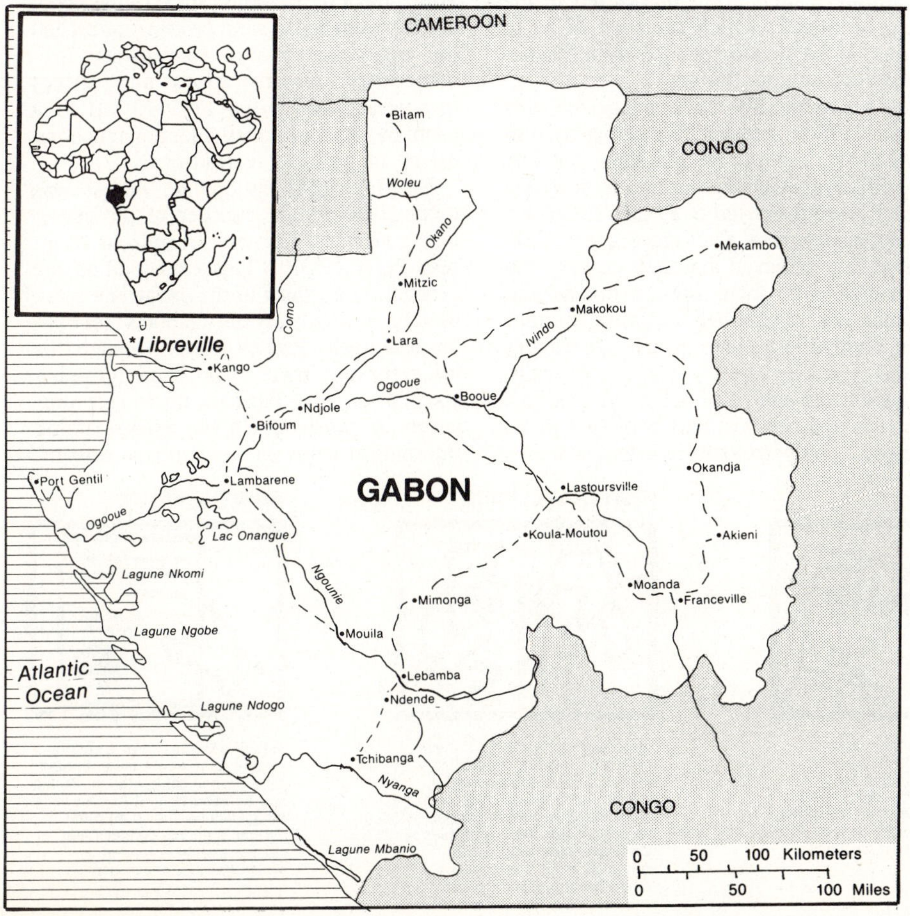

TRANSPORTATION

Highways—Kilometers (Miles): 7,500 (4,650)
Railroads—Kilometers (Miles): 649 (402)
Commercial Airports: 3 international

GOVERNMENT

Type: republic; one-party presidential regime
Independence Date: August 17, 1960
Head of State: President Omar Bongo
Political Parties: Gabonese Democratic Party
Suffrage: universal over 18

MILITARY

Number of Armed Forces: 4,550
Military Expenditures (% of Central Government Expenditures): 3.2%
Current Hostilities: none

ECONOMY

Currency ($ U.S. Equivalent): 319 CFA francs = $1
Per Capita Income/GNP: $3,500/$3.2 billion
Inflation Rate: 3%
Natural Resources: timber; petroleum; iron ore; manganese; uranium; gold; zinc
Agriculture: cocoa; coffee; palm oil
Industry: petroleum; lumber; minerals

FOREIGN TRADE

Exports: $1.1 billion
Imports: $760 million

Libreville is founded by the French as a settlement for freed slaves **1849**

Gabon becomes a colony within French Equatorial Africa **1910**

The Free French in Brazzaville seize Gabon from the pro-Vichy government **1940**

Independence is gained; Leon M'ba becomes president **1960**

Bongo becomes Gabon's second president after M'ba's death **1967**

The Gabonese Democratic Party (PDG) becomes the only party of the state **1968**

1980s–1990s

The French undermine the Morena attempt to form a government-in-exile

In the face of escalating unrest, Bongo agrees to multiparty elections

Riots in Port Gentil lead to French military intervention

GABON

Since independence, in 1960, Gabon has achieved the second-highest gross domestic product per capita in Africa, after Libya. Exploitation of the country's natural riches, especially its oil, has given the "average Gabonese" an annual income of about $3,500. Unfortunately, there is a wide gap between such statistical wealth and the real poverty that still shapes the lives of most Gabonese.

At the top of the governing elite is President Omar Bongo, whose main palace, built at a reported cost of $300 million, symbolizes his penchant for grandeur. Shortly after taking office, in 1967, Bongo institutionalized his personal rule as the head of a one-party state. Until recently his Democratic Party (PDG) had an absolute monopoly of power. But it is Gabon's former colonial master, France, not the ruling party's by-laws, that has upheld the regime.

FRENCH PRESENCE

The French colonial presence in Gabon dates back to 1843. Between 1898 and 1930 many Gabonese were subject to forced labor, cutting timber for French concessions companies. World War II coincided with a period of significant political liberalization in the territory. During the 1950s two major political parties emerged to compete in local politics: the Social Democratic Union of Gabon (UDSG), led by Jean-Hilaire Aubame; and the Gabonese Democratic Bloc (BDG) of Indjenjet Grondjout and Leon M'ba.

In the 1957 elections the UDSG received 60 percent of the popular vote, but gained only 19 seats in the 40-seat Assembly. M'ba, who had the support of French logging interests, was elected by 21 BDG and independent deputies as leader. As a result, it was M'ba who was at the helm when Gabon gained its independence in November 1960. This birth coincided with M'ba's declaration of emergency powers as part of an effort to create a strong presidency around himself. His action provoked a period of prolonged constitutional crisis.

In January 1964 M'ba dissolved the Assembly because of its members' continued refusal to accept a one-party state under his leadership. The following month the president himself was forced to resign, by a group of army officers. Power was transferred to a civilian Provisional Government, headed by Aubame, which also included BDG politicians such as Grondjout as well as several prominent unaffiliated citizens. However, no sooner had the Provisional Government been installed than Gabon was invaded by French troops. Local military units were massacred in the surprise attack, which returned M'ba to office. M'ba was succeeded by his handpicked successor, Bongo.

It has generally been suggested that France's 1964 invasion was primarily motivated by a desire to maintain absolute control over Gabon's uranium deposits, which were then vital to France's nuclear-weapons program. Ever since, many Gabonese have believed that their country has remained a de facto French possession. France has maintained a strong military and civilian presence. France dominates Gabon's resource-rich economy. Typically, France is the source of half of the nation's imports and the destination of half of its exports. The petroleum industry, which is the third largest in sub-Saharan Africa, is 70 percent controlled by the French-owned company Elf-Gabon.

Gabon's political and economic status quo is being challenged by its increasingly urbanized population. Although Bongo was able to co-opt or exile many of the figures who had once opposed M'ba, a new generation of opposition has emerged, both at home and in exile. The leading opposition group during the past decade has been the underground Movement for National Recovery (Morena). In 1989 Bongo began talks with some elements within Morena, which has led to a division within its ranks. But Bongo's efforts to restructure his government by including some of the opposition have failed to stem growing unrest and the emergence of new movements. Prodemocracy demonstrations and strikes throughout the spring of 1990 led to a promise of multiparty elections and an easing of political restrictions.

In May 1990 nationwide unrest was touched off by the murder of the secretary-general of the newly legalized Progress Party (PGP). This event led to the evacuation of much of the expatriate community at Port-Gentil, Gabon's second-largest city, by French forces. Despite this intervention, there has been growing speculation that Paris is no longer prepared to prop up Bongo against rising internal pressure for fundamental reform.

DEVELOPMENT

The Trans-Gabonais Railway is one of the largest construction projects in Africa. Work began in 1974 and, after some delays, most of the line is now complete. The railway has opened up much of Gabon's interior to commercial development.

FREEDOM

Since 1967 President Omar Bongo has maintained power through a combination of repression and the deft use of patronage. The current transition to a multiparty process may lead to a greater respect for human rights.

HEALTH/WELFARE

The government claims to have instituted universal, compulsory education for Gabonese up to age 16. Independent observers doubt the government's claim but concur that major progress has been made, with recent estimates of 70% attendance within the age group. Health services have also expanded greatly.

ACHIEVEMENTS

Gabon will soon have a second private television station, funded by a French cable station. Profits will be used to fund African films which will be shown on other African stations. Gabon's first private station is funded by Swiss and Gabonese capital.

São Tomé and Príncipe (Democratic Republic of São Tomé and Príncipe)

GEOGRAPHY

Area in Square Kilometers (Miles): 1,001 (387) (slightly larger than New York City)
Capital (Population): São Tomé (40,000)
Climate: tropical

PEOPLE

Population
Total: 125,000
Annual Growth Rate: 3%
Rural/Urban Population Ratio: n/a
Languages: official: Portuguese; other spoken: Fang; Kriolu

Health
Life Expectancy at Birth: 64 years (male); 67 years (female)
Infant Death Rate (Ratio): 70/1,000
Average Caloric Intake: 78% of FAO minimum
Physicians Available (Ratio): 1/2,354

Religion(s)
80% Christian; 20% traditional indigenous

THE PEOPLE OF THE ISLANDS

The current inhabitants of São Tomé and Príncipe are mostly of mixed African and European descent. During the colonial period the society was stratified along racial lines. At the top were the Europeans—mostly Portuguese. Just below them were the *mesticos* or *filhos da terra*, the mixed-blood descendants of slaves. Descendants of slaves who arrived later were known as *forros*. Contract workers were labeled as *servicais*, while their children became known as *tongas*. Still another category was the *angolares*, who reportedly were the descendants of shipwrecked slaves. All of these colonial categories were used to divide and rule the local population; the distinctions have begun to diminish as an important sociological factor on the islands.

Education
Adult Literacy Rate: 50%

COMMUNICATION

Telephones: 2,200
Newspapers: 2 weeklies

TRANSPORTATION

Highways—Kilometers (Miles): 300 (186)
Railroads—Kilometers (Miles): none
Commercial Airports: 1 international

GOVERNMENT

Type: republic
Independence Date: July 12, 1975
Head of State: President Manuel Pinto da Costa
Political Parties: the ruling Movement for the Liberation of São Tomé and Príncipe; parties associated with the Democratic Coalition of the Opposition
Suffrage: universal over 18

MILITARY

Number of Armed Forces: n/a
Military Expenditures (% of Central Government Expenditures): 1.6%
Current Hostilities: none

ECONOMY

Currency ($ U.S. Equivalent): 77 dobras = $1
Per Capita Income/GNP: $340/$37.9 million
Inflation Rate: 4.2%
Natural Resources: fish
Agriculture: cacao; coconut palms; coffee; bananas; palm kernels
Industry: beer; soft drinks; palm oil; copra; tourism; manufacturing; construction

FOREIGN TRADE

Exports: $9.1 million
Imports: $17.3 million

The Portuguese settle São Tomé and Príncipe
1500s

Slavery is abolished, but forced labor continues
1876

The Portuguese massacre hundreds of islanders
1953

Factions within the liberation movement unite to form the MLSTP in Gabon
1972

Independence
1975

Manuel Pinto da Costa deposes and exiles Miguel Trovoada, the premier and former number-two man in the MLSTP
1979

1980s–1990s

New policy of economic and political liberalization

The attempted invasion by the FRNSTP and mercenaries (a 42-man force trained by South Africans in Namibia) is foiled

The new Constitution, allowing for multiparty democracy, is adopted

SÃO TOMÉ AND PRÍNCIPE

On July 12, 1975, after a half-millennium of Portuguese rule, the islands of São Tomé and Príncipe took their place as one of Africa's smallest and poorest nations. Before 1975 the islands' economic life centered around the interests of a few thousand white settlers—particularly a handful of large-plantation owners who together controlled more than 80 percent of the land. After independence most of the whites fled, taking their skills and capital and leaving the economy in disarray. Under government management, however, production on the plantations has been revived.

FORCED LABOR

The Portuguese began the first permanent settlement of São Tomé and Príncipe in the late fifteenth century. Through the intensive use of slave labor, the islands developed rapidly as one of the world's leading exporters of sugar. Only a small fraction of the profits was consumed locally; and high mortality rates, caused by brutal working conditions, led to an almost insatiable demand for more slaves. After the mid-sixteenth century profits from sugar declined, due to competition from Brazil and the Caribbean. A prolonged economic depression set in.

In the early nineteenth century a second economic boom swept the islands, when they became leading exporters of coffee and, more importantly, cocoa. São Tomé and Príncipe's position in the world market has since declined, yet both cash crops, along with copra, have continued to be economic mainstays. Although slavery was officially abolished during the nineteenth century, forced labor was maintained by the Portuguese into modern times. Involuntary contract workers, *servicais,* were imported to labor on the islands' plantations, which still had notoriously high mortality rates. Sporadic labor unrest and occasional incidents of international outrage led to some improvement in working conditions, but fundamental reforms came about only after independence. A historical turning point for the islands was the Batepa Massacre in 1953, when several hundred African laborers were killed following local resistance to labor conditions.

POLITICS

Since independence São Tomé and Príncipe has been ruled as a one-party state by the Movement for the Liberation of São Tomé and Príncipe (MLSTP), which emerged in exile as the islands' anticolonial movement. In 1990 the country's process of *abertura,* or political and economic opening, reached a new stage with the legalization of opposition parties and the introduction of direct elections with secret balloting. Press restrictions have also been lifted, and the nation's security police have been purged.

The previously exiled Sãotoméan opposition groups have welcomed the democratization process, although their suspicions of the government have not entirely disappeared. Despite complaints about the inadequate time for preparation, most of the opposition movements are likely to compete in upcoming national elections. Since 1986 some movements have been loosely associated as the Democratic Coalition of the Opposition. In April 1990 the changed political climate was also reflected in a series of strikes, the first since independence, involving telecommunications workers and laborers on some of the state plantations.

ECONOMIC DEVELOPMENT

The move to a multiparty system has been accompanied by a pledge on the part of President Manuel Pinto da Costa to move to a full market economy. This development is a continuation of the economic reforms introduced since 1985 by the once avowedly Marxist-Leninist president, who, along with most of his party, now styles himself as a market-oriented social democrat. Other steps have included the establishment of a Free Trade Zone, the privatization of state farms, and the encouragement of private capital to build up the islands' tourist industry. These moves have been accompanied by a major expansion of Western loans and assistance to the islands, an inflow of capital that now accounts for nearly half of the gross domestic product (GDP). Besides tourism, the government has focused its development efforts on fishing. In 1978 a 200-mile maritime zone was declared over the tuna-rich waters around the islands. With the recent influx of foreign aid and investment, the islands' overall economic picture appears to be heading for immediate improvement.

DEVELOPMENT

Local food production has been significantly boosted by a French-funded scheme. In recent years France has overtaken Portugal as the biggest European presence in the islands.

FREEDOM

Prior to 1987 human rights were circumscribed in São Tomé and Príncipe. Gradual liberalization has now given way to a commitment to pluralism.

HEALTH/WELFARE

The government since independence has had enormous progress in expanding health care and education. The Sãotoméan infant mortality rate, 70 per 1,000, is now among the lowest in Africa and average life expectancy, 65 years, among the highest. Sixty-three percent of the population between 6 and 19 years are now in school.

ACHIEVEMENTS

São Tomé and Príncipe shares in a rich Luso-African artistic tradition. The country is particularly renowned for poets such as Jose de Almeida and Francisco Tenriero, who were among the first to express in the Portuguese language the experiences and pride of Africans.

Zaire (Republic of Zaire)

GEOGRAPHY

Area in Square Kilometers (Miles): 2,300,000 (905,063) (one-quarter the size of the United States)
Capital (Population): Kinshasa (3,000,000)
Climate: equatorial

PEOPLE

Population
Total: 36,589,000
Annual Growth Rate: 3.3%
Rural/Urban Population Ratio: 56/44
Languages: official: French; others spoken: Kiswahili, Lingala, Azande, Luba, Chokwe, Songo, Kongo, Kuba, Lunda, Bemba, Alur, many others

Health
Life Expectancy at Birth: 51 years (male); 55 years (female)
Infant Death Rate (Ratio): 103/1,000
Average Caloric Intake: 94% of FAO minimum
Physicians Available (Ratio): 1/18,294

Religion(s)
70% Christian; 20% traditional indigenous; 10% Muslim

A SCENE FROM LEOPOLD'S GENOCIDES

The following is an excerpt from E. D. Morel's *Red Rubber,* p. 97.

> Look inside the hostage house, staggering back as you enter from odours which belch forth in poisonous fumes. As your eyes get accustomed to the half-light, they will not rest on those skeleton-like forms—bones held together by black skin—but upon the faces. The faces turn upward in mute appeal for pity; the hollow cheeks, the misery and terror in their eyes, the drawn parched lips emitting inarticulate sounds. A woman, her pendulous, pear shaped breasts hanging like withered parchment against her sides, where ribs seem bursting from its covering, holds in her emaciated arms a small object more pink than black. You stoop to touch it—a new born babe, twenty-four hours hold, assuredly not more. It is dead but the mother clasps it still. She herself is almost past speech, and will soon join her babe in the great Unknown. The horror of it the unspeakable horror of it.

Education
Adult Literacy Rate: 55% (male); 37% (female)

COMMUNICATION

Telephones: 31,200
Newspapers: 4

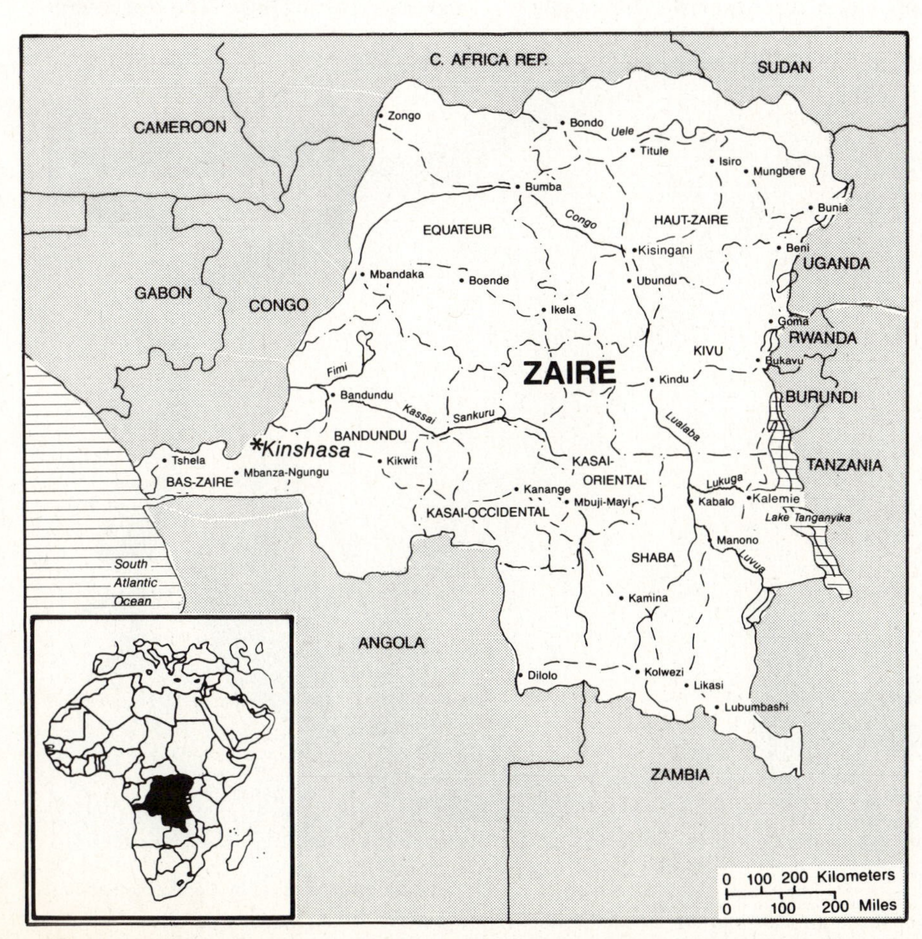

TRANSPORTATION

Highways—Kilometers (Miles): 146,500 (90,830)
Railroads—Kilometers (Miles): 5,254 (3,257)
Commercial Airports: 4 international

GOVERNMENT

Type: republic; strong presidential authority
Independence Date: June 30, 1960
Head of State: President Marshal Mobutu Sese Seko
Political Parties: Popular Movement of the Revolutionary Party
Suffrage: universal over 18

MILITARY

Number of Armed Forces: 52,000
Military Expenditures (% of Central Government Expenditures): n/a
Current Hostilities: low-intensity insurgency

ECONOMY

Currency ($ U.S. Equivalent): 465 Zaires = $1
Per Capita Income/GNP: $195/$6.5 billion
Inflation Rate: 82%
Natural Resources: copper; cobalt; zinc; diamonds; manganese; tin; gold; rare metals; bauxite; iron; coal; hydroelectric potential; timber
Agriculture: coffee; palm oil; rubber; tea; cotton; cocoa; manioc; bananas; plantains; corn; rice; sugar
Industry: mineral mining; consumer products; food processing; cement

FOREIGN TRADE

Exports: $2.2 billion
Imports: $1.9 billion

ZAIRE

"Together, my brothers, we are going to start a new struggle which will lead our country to peace, prosperity and greatness. . . . [W]e are going to make the Congo the hub of all Africa." So spoke Patrice Lumumba, the country's first prime minister, on June 30, 1960, the day when Zaire (then the Democratic Republic of the Congo) became an independent nation. Zaire had then, and still has, the potential to become the hub of all Africa, and yet "peace, prosperity and greatness" are far from being achieved.

THE HUB OF AFRICA

In geographic terms, Zaire is certainly the hub of Africa. Located at the continent's center, it encompasses the entire Zaire River Basin. Although the tropical climate has impeded development, the country encompasses a great variety of land forms and has good agricultural possibilities. It contains a vast range of rich resources, some of which (such as cobalt, copper, and diamonds) have been intensively exploited for several decades. The river itself is the potential source of 13 percent of the world's hydroelectric power.

Zaire links Africa from west to east. The country faces the Atlantic, with a very narrow coast on that ocean. Eastern Zaire has been influenced by forces from East Africa. In the mid-nineteenth century Swahili, Arab, and Nyamwezi traders from Tanzania established their hegemony over much of southeastern Zaire, pillaging the countryside for ivory and slaves. While the nineteenth-century slave trade has left bitter memories, the Swahili language has spread to become a *lingua franca* throughout much of the eastern third of the country.

A DIVERSE HERITAGE

Zaire's 36 million people belong to about 250 different ethnic groups, speak nearly 700 different languages and dialects, and have many varied lifestyles. Boundaries established in the late nineteenth century hemmed in portions of the Azande, Kongo, Chokwe, and Songye peoples within present-day Zaire. However, they maintain contacts with their kin in other countries.

Many important precolonial kingdoms were centered in Zaire, including the Luba, Kuba, and Lunda kingdoms—the latter in earlier centuries exploited the salt and copper of southeast Zaire, in present-day Shaba Province. The kingdom of Kongo, located at the mouth of the Congo River, flourished during the fifteenth and sixteenth centuries, establishing important diplomatic and commercial relations with Portugal. The elaborate political systems of these kingdoms are an important heritage for Zaire.

KING LEOPOLD'S GENOCIDE

The European impact, like the Swahili and Arab influences from the east, had profoundly destructive results for Zaire's peoples. The Congo Basin was explored and exploited by private individuals before it came under Belgian domination. King Leopold of Belgium, in his capacity as a private citizen, sponsored H. M. Stanley's expeditions to explore the Congo River Basin. In 1879 Leopold used Stanley's "treaties" as a justification for setting up a so-called Congo Independent State over the whole region. This state was actually his private proprietary colony. To turn a profit on his vast enterprise, Leopold acted on the assumption that the people and resources in the territory were his personal property. His own state company and other concessionaires to which he leased portions of his colony began brutally to coerce the local African population into providing ivory, wild rubber, and other commodities. The armed mili-

(United Naitons photo by Caracciolo/Banoun)

Zaire is the hub of Africa. On the west the Zaire River Basin empties into the South Atlantic, where a small fishing industry survives.

tias sent out to collect quotas of goods committed numerous atrocities, sometimes destroying whole villages.

No one knows for sure how many Africans perished in the Congo Independent State as a result of the brutalities of Leopold's agents. At the time, some critics estimated that the territory's population was reduced by 10 million over a period of 20 years. Many were starved to death as forced laborers. Others were massacred in order to induce survivors to produce more rubber. Women and children suffocated in "hostage houses" while men did their masters' bidding. Thousands fled to neighboring territories. For years the Congo regime was able to keep information of its crimes from leaking overseas, but eventually tales from missionaries and others emerged. Accounts such as E. D. Morel's "Red Rubber" and Mark Twain's caustic "King Leopold's Soliloquy" as well as gruesome pictures of men, women, and children whose hands had been severed by troops, stirred public opinion. Eventually even the European imperialists, during the era when their racial arrogance was at its height, could no longer stomach "the King with Ten Million Murders on his Soul."

During the years of Belgian administration, control became somewhat more benign, but a tradition of abuse had been established. The colonial authorities used armed forces for "pacification" campaigns, tax collection, and labor recruitment. New individuals were made into colonial chiefs and given arbitrary powers that they would not have had under indigenous political systems. Concessionary companies continued to use force to recruit labor for their plantations and mines. The most famous companies that gained immense profits from the exploitation of the Belgian Congo were Lever Brothers and the Union Minière, which exploited the minerals of Shaba Province.

The Belgian colonial regime encouraged the presence and work of Roman Catholic missions. Health facilities as well as a paternalistic system of education were developed. A strong elementary-school system was part of the colonial program, but the Belgians never instituted a major secondary-school system, and there was no institution of higher learning. A small group of high-school-educated Congolese, known as *évolués* ("evolved ones"), served the needs of an administration that never intended nor planned for Zaire's independence.

THE COMING OF INDEPENDENCE

In the 1950s independence movements developed in the countries surrounding Belgian Congo and throughout the African continent. The Congolese—especially those in the towns—were affected by these forces of change. The Belgians themselves began to recognize the need to prepare for a different future. Small initiatives began to be allowed; nationalist associations were first permitted in 1955. In the same year a publication proposed a 30-year timetable for independence. Some évolués as well as Belgians agreed with the proposals. Other Congolese, including the members of the Alliance of the Ba-Kongo (ABAKO), an ethnic association in Kinshasa, and the National Congolese Movement (MNC), led by Patrice Lumumba, reacted against it.

A serious clash at an ABAKO demonstration in 1959 resulted in some 50 deaths. In the face of mounting unrest, and further encouraged by the imminent independence of the French Congo (the modern Republic of the Congo), the Belgians conceded a rapid transition to independence. A constitutional conference in January 1960 established a federal-government system for the future independent state. There was, however, no real preparation for such a drastic political change. Belgian colonial civil servants expected that they would stay on to work with each new Congolese government minister or administrator; they were to be disappointed.

THE CONGO CRISIS

The Democratic Republic of the Congo became independent on June 30, 1960, under the leadership of President Joseph Kasavubu and Prime Minister Patrice Lumumba. Before a week had passed an

(United Nations photo by Milton Grant)

The eastern area of Zaire is confronted by many of the same challenges as East Africa; while the land supports agriculture, drought is a constant threat.

army mutiny had stimulated widespread disorder. The scars of the Congo's uniquely bitter colonial experience showed. Unlike all of the other postcolonial states in Africa, in the Congo, hatred toward the white former masters turned to violence, resulting in the hurried flight of the majority of the nation's large European community. Ethnic and regional bloodshed took a much greater toll among the African population. The wealthy Katanga Province (now Shaba) and South Kasai seceded. Lumumba called upon the United Nations for assistance, and troops came from a variety of countries to serve in the UN force. Later, as a result of a dispute between President Kasavubu and himself, Lumumba sought Soviet aid. Congo could have become a Cold War battlefield, but the army, under Lumumba's former confidant, Joseph Desiré Mobutu, intervened. Lumumba was arrested and turned over to the Katanga rebels; he was later assassinated. Western interests and, in particular, the U.S. Central Intelligence Agency (CIA) played a substantial if not fully measurable role in the downfall of the idealistic Lumumba and the rise of his cynical successor, Mobutu. Rebellions by Lumumbists in the northeast and Katanga secessionists, supported by foreign mercenaries, continued through 1967.

MOBUTU'S GOVERNMENT

Mobutu seized full power in 1965, ousting Kasavubu in a military coup. With ruthless energy, he eliminated the rival political factions within the central government and crushed the rebel forces. Mobutu banned party politics. In 1971 he established the Second Republic as a one-party state in which all power was centralized around the "Founding President."

Every citizen at birth is legally expected to be a disciplined member of Mobutu's Popular Revolutionary Movement (MPR). With the exception of some religious organizations, virtually all social institutions in Zairian society function as party organs. In running the MPR, Mobutu is assisted by a Central Committee, whose 148 members are appointed by himself.

The official ideology of the MPR republic is Mobutuism—the words, deeds, and decrees of "the Guide," first-citizen Mobutu. All citizens are supposed to sing his praises daily at the workplace, in schools, and at social gatherings. In hymns and prayers, the name Mobutu is often substituted for that of Jesus. A principal slogan of Mobutuism is "authenticity." Supposedly this has meant a rejection of European for African values and norms. It is Mobutu alone, however, who is entitled to define what is authentic. Mobutu changed his own name to Mobutu Sese Seko, "the all powerful," and declared all European personal names illegal. He also established a national dress code in which ties were outlawed and men were expected to wear his "abacost" suit, while women were obliged to wear the *paigne*, or wrapper. The name of the country was changed from Congo to Zaire, a named derived from sixteenth-century Portuguese mispronunciation of the (Ki)Konga word for river.

Outside Zaire, some have taken Mobutu's protestations of authenticity at face value, while a few other African dictators, such as Togo's Gnassingbé Eyadéma, saw the value in emulating aspects of Mobutu's fascist methodology. But the majority of Zairians have grown to loathe the "cultural revolution." Zaire is perhaps the only place in the world where the necktie has become a symbol of resistance. On a more substantial level, authenticity was briefly accompanied by a program of nationalization. Union Minière and other corporations were placed under government control. In 1973–1974 plantations, commercial institutions, and other businesses were also taken over, in a "radicalizing of the Zairian Revolution."

However, the expropriated industries and businesses have enriched a small elite, rather than benefiting the nation. In many cases, they were given away by Mobutu to his cronies, who often simply sold off their assets. Consequently, the economy has suffered. Industries and businesses have been mismanaged or ravaged. Some individuals have become extraordinarily wealthy, while the population as a whole has become progressively poorer with each passing year. Mobutu is said to be the wealthiest person in Africa, with a fortune estimated in excess of $5 billion (about equal to Zaire's national debt), most of it invested and spent outside Africa.

Mobutu has allowed virtually no opposition. Those who are critical of his government often face imprisonment, torture, or death. Student demonstrations have resulted in the closure of the university and forced conscription into the army for students. In May 1990 anti-Mobutu activity at the University of Lumumbashi led to the storming of the campus by troops of the Special Presidential Division, who bayoneted to death at least 100 in an all-night rampage. Workers' strikes are not allowed. Revolts in the Shaba Province in 1977 and 1978 were suppressed through Moroccan, French, and Belgian interventions, which were backed by the United States. A number of small-scale rural insurrections are ongoing. The Roman Catholic Church and the Kimbanguist Church of Jesus Christ Upon This Earth are the only institutions that have been able to speak out.

ECONOMIC DISASTER

Zaire's economic potential was developed by and for the Belgians, but by 1960 that development had gone further than in many other African colonial territories. While Zaire started with a good economic base, the chaos of the early 1960s brought development to a standstill. The Mobutu years have been marked by regression. Development projects have been initiated, but often without careful planning. World economic conditions, including the falling prices of copper and cobalt, have contributed to Zaire's difficulties.

However, the main obstacle to any sort of economic progress is the rampant corruption of Mobutu and those around him. The governing system in Zaire has often been characterized as a kleptocracy, or rule by thieves. An organized system of exploitation transfers wealth from ordinary citizens to officials and the elite. With Mobutu stealing billions and those closest to him stealing millions, the entire society operates on an "invisible" tax system, whereby citizens must, for example, bribe nurses for medical care, bureaucrats for documents, principals for school admission, and police to stay out of jail.

Accepting bribes is a necessary function for most civil servants, for they are generally paid little or nothing. This fundamental fact applies to the soldiers in most army units, who thus survive by living off the civilian population. Recently the American military learned this lesson first hand when it conducted joint military exercises with Zairian paratroopers. When a number of American troops' parachutes got caught in trees, they were robbed of their possessions by the Zairian troops, who then deserted into the forest.

Ordinary people suffer. Real wages of urban workers in Zaire are only 2 percent of what they were in 1960. Rural incomes have also deteriorated. The official price paid to coffee farmers, for example, is only one-fifth what it was in 1954 under the exploitative Belgian regime. Much of the nation's coffee and other cash crops are smuggled, more often than not through the connivance of senior government officials. Thus, although Zaire's agriculture has great economic potential, the returns from this sector continue to shrink. Despite its immense size and plentiful rainfall, Zaire must now import 60 percent of its food requirements. Rural people move to the city or, for lack of employment, move back to the country and take up subsistence agriculture, rather than cash-crop farming, in order to ensure their own survival. The deterioration of roads and bridges has led to the decline of all trade.

Since 1983 the government has imple-

Leopold sets up the Congo Independent State as his private kingdom
1879

Congo becomes a Belgian colony
1906

Congo gains independence; civil war begins; a UN force is involved; Patrice Lumumba is murdered
1960

Mobutu takes command in a bloodless coup
1965

The name of the state is changed to Zaire
1971

1980s–1990s

Mobutu announces a ceasefire in the Angolan conflict, but no agreement is signed or observed

Mobutu proclaims the Third Republic; students are massacred at Lumumbashi

Supplies are funneled through Kinshasa in support of the UNITA offensive in northern Angola

mented International Monetary Fund (IMF) austerity measures, but this has only cut public expenditures. It has had no effect on corruption, nor has it increased taxes on the rich. More than 30 percent of Zaire's budget goes for debt servicing.

U.S. SUPPORT FOR MOBUTU

The Mobutu regime has been able to sidestep its financial crises and maintain power through the support of foreign powers, especially Belgium, France, Germany, and the United States. A U.S. intelligence report prepared in the mid-1950s concluded that the then Belgian Congo was indeed the hub of Africa and thus vital to American strategic interests. Since then U.S. policy has been first to promote and perpetuate Mobutu as a pro-Western source of stability in the region. Mobutu himself has skillfully cultivated this image.

Since the early 1960s Mobutu has collaborated with the United States in opposing the Marxist-oriented Popular movement for the Liberation of Angola (MPLA). By so doing, Mobutu has not only set himself up as an important U.S. ally but has also been able to pursue regional objectives of his own. The National Front for the Liberation of Angola (FNLA), long championed by the CIA as a counterforce to the MPLA, is led by Mobutu's in-law Holden Roberto. Mobutu has also long coveted Angola's oil-rich enclave of Cabinda and has thus sought CIA and South African assistance for the "independence" movement there. In recent years millions of American dollars have been spent upgrading the airstrip at Kamina in Shaba Province, which has reportedly been used by the CIA to supply the guerrillas of the National Union for the Total Independence of Angola (UNITA), another faction opposed to the MPLA government. In 1989 Mobutu tried to set himself up as a mediator between the government and the UNITA rebels, but even the latter have grown to distrust him.

The United States has clear evidence of Mobutu's human-rights violations and of the oppression and corruption that characterize the Zaire government. Defectors from the highest levels of government in Zaire have revealed many of the evils of the regime. Since 1987 Mobutu has responded with heavily financed public-relations efforts and lobbying of American legislators for continued support. In 1988, however, 58 members of the U.S. Congress signed a letter protesting the house arrest of critic Tshisekedi wa Mulumba, and legislation has been introduced to stop U.S. aid to Zaire until the human-rights situation improves. The continued U.S. support of Mobutu reflects Washington's cynical perception that there is no satisfactory alternative to his rule.

Mobutu has also allied himself with other conservative forces in Africa and the Middle East. Moroccan troops came to his aid during the revolts in Shaba Province in 1977 and 1978. For his part, Mobutu has been a leading African supporter of Morocco's stand with regard to the Western Sahara dispute. Zaire has been an active member of the Francophonic African bloc. In 1983 Mobutu dispatched 2,000 Zairian troops to Chad in support of the government of Hissène Habré, then under attack from Libya, while in 1986 his men again joined French forces in propping up the Eyadéma regime in Togo. He has also maintained and strengthened his ties with South Africa; today Zaire imports almost half of its food from the apartheid state.

In 1982 Zaire renewed diplomatic ties with Israel, after the break in relations following the Arab-Israeli War of 1973. Since then Israelis have joined French and Belgians as senior advisors and trainers working with the Zairian Army. About 50,000 refugees from conflicts in Zaire are in neighboring countries; Zaire itself hosts more than 300,000, many of whom are Angolans fleeing warfare there.

Despite Mobutu's cultivation of foreign assistance to prop up his dictatorship, internal opposition has been growing. In 1990 he tried to head off his critics both at home and abroad by promising to set up a new Third Republic, based on multiparty democracy. Despite this step, repression in Zaire, as evidenced by the massacre at the University of Lumumbashi, has intensified in response to growing protests and resistance throughout Zairian society. Mobutu's apparent ambition to windowdress his authoritarianism by having two new parties, dedicated to shades of Mobutuism, join the MPR in his rubberstamp assembly is being challenged. However, his besieged regime continues to be bolstered by American support.

DEVELOPMENT

The United States and Western European countries continue to aid development projects for transportation, health, and education. However, mismanagement, corruption, and lack of maintenance have resulted in little improvement for Zaire's citizens.

FREEDOM

Zaire has shown little respect for human rights. One Amnesty International report concluded that all political prisoners are tortured. Death squads are active.

HEALTH/WELFARE

In 1978 more than 5 million students were registered for primary schools and 35,000 for college. However, the level of education is declining. Many teachers were laid off in the 1980s, though nonexistent "ghost teachers" remained on the payroll. The few innovative educational programs are outside the state system.

ACHIEVEMENTS

Kinshasa is a musical center, the home of creative popular styles of vocal music and new dance bands. Souskous is one style, and Pablo Lubadika of the group Le Peuple is one of the most popular singers. Rochereau and Franco are vocalists with longstanding reputations. Zaire music is popular and sets styles throughout Africa as well as in Europe and America.

East Africa

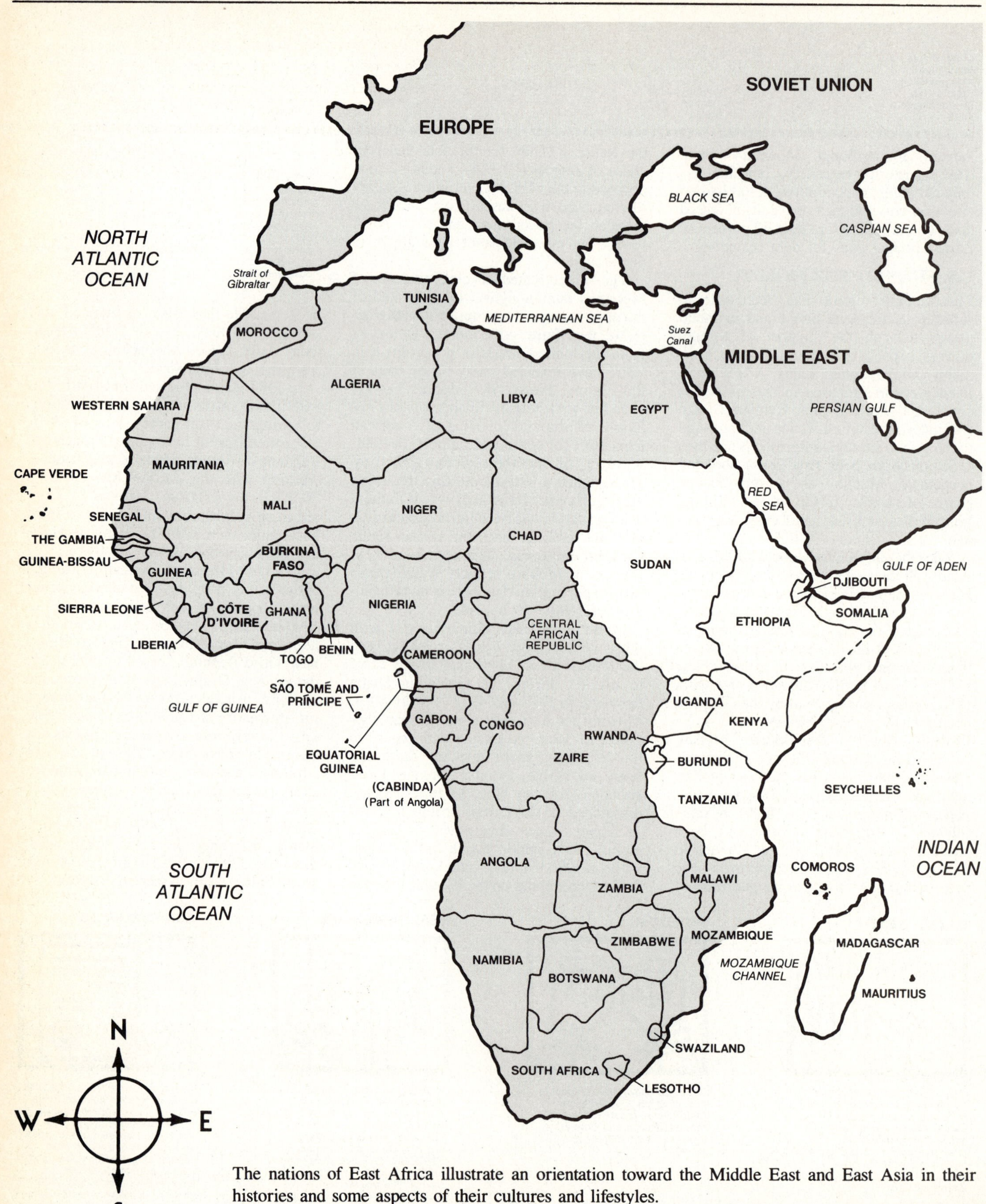

The nations of East Africa illustrate an orientation toward the Middle East and East Asia in their histories and some aspects of their cultures and lifestyles.

East Africa: A Mixed Inheritance

The vast East African region, ranging from Sudan in the north to Tanzania and the Indian Ocean islands in the south, is an area of great diversity. Although the islands are the homes of distinctive civilizations with ties to Asia, their interactions with the African mainland give their inclusion here validity. Ecological features such as the Great Rift Valley, the prevalence of cattle-herding lifestyles, and long-standing participation in the Indian Ocean trading networks are some of the region's unifying aspects.

CATTLE-HERDING SOCIETIES

A long-horned cow would be an appropriate symbol for East Africa. Most of the region's rural inhabitants, who make up the majority of people from the Horn to Lake Malawi to Madagascar, value cattle for their social as well as economic importance. The Nuer of Sudan, the Somali near the Red Sea (who, like many other peoples of the Horn, herd camels as well as cattle, goats, and sheep), and the Maasai of Tanzania and Kenya are among the pastoral peoples whose herds are their livelihoods. Farming communities such as the Kikuyu of Kenya, the Baganda of Uganda, and the Malagasey of Madagascar also prize cattle.

Much of the East African landmass is well suited for herding. Whereas the rain forests of West and Central Africa are generally infested with tsetse flies, whose bite is fatal to livestock, most of East Africa is made up of belts of tropical and temperate savanna, which are ideal for grazing. Thus pastoralism has long been predominant in the savanna zones of West and Southern, as well as East, Africa. Tropical rain forests are almost nonexistent, being found only on the east coast of Madagascar and scattered along the mainland's coast. Much of the East African interior is dominated by the Great Rift Valley, which stretches from the Red Sea as far south as Malawi. This geological formation is characterized by mountains as well as valleys and features the region's Great Lakes, including Lake Albert, Lake Tanganyika, and Lake Malawi.

(World Bank photo by Kay Muldoon)

Lively and extensive trade and migration patterns have characterized East Africa throughout much of its history.

People have been moving into and through the East African region since the existence of humankind; indeed, most of the earliest human fossils have been unearthed in the region. Today almost all of the mainland inhabitants speak languages that belong to either the Bantu or Nilotic linguistic families. There has been much historical speculation about the past migrations of these peoples, but current archaeology indicates that both linguistic groups have probably been established in the area for a long time, although oral traditions and other forms of historical evidence indicate locally important shifts in settlement patterns into the contemporary period. Ironworking and, in at least a few cases, small-scale steel production, have long been a part of the regional economy. Long-distance trade and the production of various crafts have also existed since ancient times. As is the case today, in the past the inhabitants of the region had to confront insufficient and unreliable rainfall. Drought and famine in the Horn and in areas of Kenya and Tanzania have in recent years caused suffering, changed lifestyles, and dislocated many.

ISLAMIC INFLUENCE

Many of the areas of East Africa have been influenced, since at least as far back as Roman times and perhaps much further, by the Middle East and other parts of Asia. Over the past thousand years most parts of East Africa, including the Christian highlands of Ethiopia and the inland inter-lakes states, such as Buganda, Burundi, and Rwanda, became familiar to the Muslim Arab traders of the Swahili and Red Sea coasts and the Sudanese interior. Somalia, Djibouti, and Sudan, which border the Red Sea and are in close proximity to the Arabian Peninsula, have been the most influenced by Arab Islamic culture. Mogadishu, the capital of Somalia, began as an Islamic trading post in the tenth century. The Islamic faith, its various sects or brotherhoods, the Koran, and the Sharia (the Islamic legal code) are predominant throughout the Horn, except in the Ethiopian interior and southern Sudan. Today many Somali, Sudanese and others migrate to the oil-rich states of Arabia to work; the August 1990 Iraqi invasion of Kuwait has caused thousands of them to become refugees.

Farther south, in the communities and cultures on the perimeters of the east coast, Arabs and local Bantu-speaking Africans combined—from as early as the ninth century but especially during the 1200s to 1400s—to form the culture and the language that we now call Swahili. In the first half of the nineteenth century the sultan of Oman, Seyyid Said, transferred his capital to Zanzibar, in recognition of the outpost's economic importance. Motivated by the rapid expansion of trade in ivory and slaves, many Arab-Swahili traders began to establish themselves and build settlements as far inland as the forests of eastern Zaire. As a result, some of the noncoastal peoples also adopted Islam, while Swahili developed into a regional *lingua franca.*

The whole region from the Horn to Tanzania continued to be affected by the slave trade through much of the nineteenth century. Slaves were sent from Uganda and southern Sudan north to Egypt and the Middle East, and from Ethiopia across the Red Sea. Others were taken to the coast by Arab, Swahili, or African traders either to work on the plantations in Zanzibar or to be shipped to the Persian Gulf and the Indian Ocean islands.

In the late nineteenth and early twentieth centuries South Asian laborers from what was then British India were brought in by the British to build the East African Railroad. South Asian traders already resided in Zanzibar; others came and settled in Kenya and Tanzania, becoming shopkeepers and bankers in inland centers, such as Kampala and Nairobi, as well as on the coast, in Mombasa and Dar es Salaam, or in smaller stops along the railroad. South Asian laborers were also sent in large numbers to work on the sugar plantations of Mauritius; their descendants now make up about two-thirds of that island's population.

The subregions of East Africa include the following: the countries of the Horn, East Africa proper, and the islands. The Horn includes Djibouti, Ethiopia, Somalia, and Sudan, which are here associated with one another not so much because of a common heritage, or on account of any compatibility of their governments (for, indeed, they are often hostile to one another), but because of the movements of peoples across borders in recent times. East Africa proper is comprised of Kenya, Tanzania, and Uganda, which do have underlying cultural ties and a history of economic relations in which Rwanda and Burundi have also shared. The Indian Ocean islands include the Comoros, Madagascar, Mauritius, and the Seychelles, which, notwithstanding the expanses of ocean that separate them, have certain cultural aspects and current interests in common.

THE HORN

Traditionally, Ethiopia has had a distinct, semi-isolated history that has separated the nation from its neighbors. This early Christian civilization, which was periodically united by a strong dynasty but at other times was disunited, was centered in the highlands of the interior, surrounded by often hostile lowland peoples. Before the nineteenth century it was in infrequent contact with other Christian societies. During the 1800s, however, a series of strong rulers reunified the highlands and went on to conquer surrounding peoples such as the Afar, Oromo, and Somali. In the process, the state (with the exception of Eritrea, which was incorporated after World War II) expanded to its current boundaries. While the empire's expansion helped it to preserve its independence during Africa's colonial partition, today sectarian and ethnic divisions, which are a legacy of the imperial state-building process, threaten to tear the polity apart.

Ethiopia and the other contemporary nations of the Horn have been influenced by outside powers, whose interests in the region have been primarily rooted in its strategic location. In the nineteenth century both Britain and France became interested in the Horn, because the Red Sea was the link between their countries and the markets of Asia. This was especially true after the completion of the Suez Canal in 1869. Both of the imperial powers occupied ports on the Red Sea at the time. They then began to compete over the upper Nile in modern Sudan. In the 1890s French forces literally

(United Nations photo by Ray Witlin)

In the drought-affected areas of East Africa, people must devote considerable time and energy to the search for water.

raced from the present-day area of the Congo to reach the center of Sudan before the arrival of a larger British expeditionary force, which had invaded the region from Egypt. Ultimately the British were able to consolidate their control over the entire Sudan.

Italian ambitions in the Horn were initially encouraged by the British, in order to counter the French. Italy's defeat by the Ethiopians at the Battle of Adowa in 1896 did not deter its efforts to dominate the coastal areas of Eritrea and southeastern Somalia. Later Italy, under Benito Mussolini, briefly (1936–1942) occupied Ethiopia itself.

During the Cold War, great-power competition for control of the Red Sea and the Gulf of Aden, which are strategically located near the oilfields of the Middle East as well as along the course of Suez shipping, continued between the United States and the Soviet Union. Local events led to shifts in alignments. Before 1977, for instance, the United States was closely allied with Ethiopia and the Soviet Union with Somalia. However, in 1977–1978 Ethiopia, under a self-proclaimed Marxist-Leninist government, allied itself with the Soviet Union, receiving in return the support of Cuban troops and billions of dollars worth of socialist-bloc military aid, on loan, for use in its battles against Eritrean and Somali rebels. The latter group, living in Ethiopia's Ogaden region, were seeking to become part of a greater Somalia. In this irredentist adventure, they had the direct support of invading Somalian troops. Although the United States refused to counter the Soviets by in turn backing the irredentists, it subsequently established relations with the Somali government at a level that allowed it virtually to take over the former Soviet military facility at Berbera.

Discord and Drought

The countries of the Horn, unlike the East African states farther south or the island states, are alienated from one another, and there are no prospects for a regional community among them in the foreseeable future. Although the end of the Cold War has greatly reduced superpower competition, local animosities continue to wreak havoc in the region. Today the Horn is both bound together and torn apart by its millions of refugees, who continue to flee civil wars in Ethiopia, Somalia, and Sudan. All three states currently suffer under vicious authoritarian regimes, which in recent years have engaged in genocide against dissident segments of their populations (see the individual country reports). The horrible effects of these wars have been magnified by recurrent droughts. As a result, hundreds of thousands of people have starved to death in the last decade, while many more have barely survived due to international aid efforts.

Ethiopians have left their homes for Djibouti, Somalia, and Sudan for relief from war and famine. Sudanese and Somali have fled to Ethiopia for the same reasons. Today every country harbors not only refugees but also dissidents from neighboring lands and has a citizenry related to those who live in adjoining countries. Peoples such as the Afar minority in Djibouti often seek support from their kin in Ethiopia. Somali liberation fighters have fled to Ethiopia to

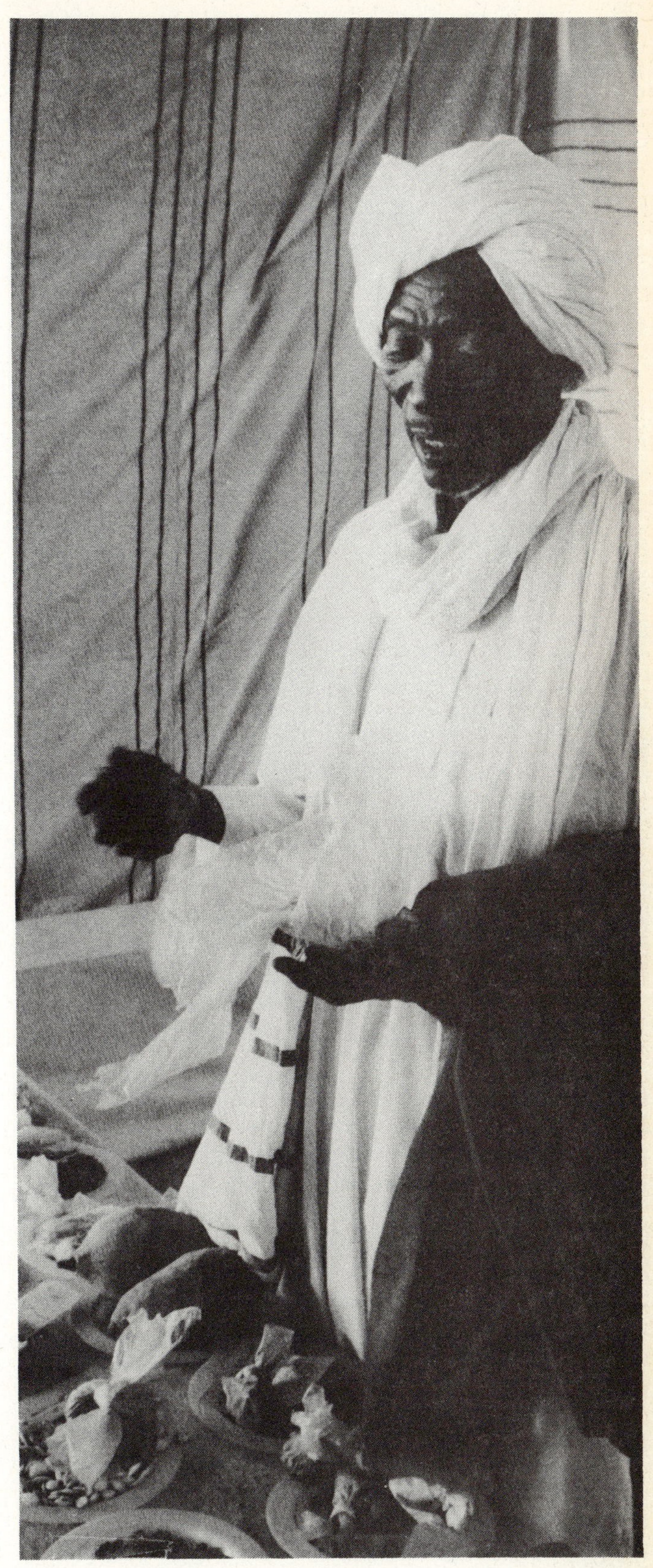

(WHO photo)

East African peoples, especially along the coast, blend heritages from Asia, the Middle East, and Africa.

(United Nations photo by Y. Müller)

Of the millions of refugees, displaced by civil wars in Ethiopia, Somalia, and Sudan, fully 60 percent are children.

organize against the Somalian government, while Somalia has continued to give aid and comfort to Ethiopia's Ogaden population. Ethiopia allegedly assists southern rebels against the government of Sudan, and Sudan in turn supports the Tigray and Eritrean rebel movements against Ethiopia. At times, the states of the region have reached agreements among themselves to curb their interference in one another's affairs. However, they have made almost no progress in the more fundamental task of establishing peace with their own rebels, thus assuring that the region's violent downward spiral continues.

EAST AFRICA PROPER

The peoples of Kenya, Tanzania, and Uganda, as well as Burundi and Rwanda, have underlying connections rooted in the past. The kingdoms of the Lakes region of Uganda, Rwanda, and Burundi, though they have been politically superseded in the postcolonial era, have left their legacies. For example, myths about a heroic dynasty of rulers, the Chwezi, who ruled over an early Uganda-based kingdom, are widespread. Archaeological evidence attests to the actual existence of the Chwezi, probably in the sixteenth century. Peoples in western Kenya and Tanzania, who have lived under less centralized systems of governance, but nonetheless have rituals similar to those of the Ugandan kingdoms, also share the traditions of the Chwezi dynasty, which have become associated with a spirit cult.

The precolonial kingdoms of Rwanda and Burundi, both of which came under German and later Belgian control during the colonial era, were socially divided between a ruling warrior class, the Tutsi, and a much larger peasant class, the Hutu. Although both states are now independent republics, their societies remain bitterly divided along these ethnoclass lines. In Rwanda, the feudal hegemony of the Tutsi was overthrown, but in Burundi it has been maintained through a repressive police state, which in 1972 and 1988 resorted to the mass murder of Hutu. Both countries also share the burden of being predominantly agricultural countries with little land to support their large populations.

Kenya and Uganda were taken over by the British in the late nineteenth century, while Tanzania, originally conquered by Germany, became a British colony after World War I. In Kenya, the British encouraged the growth of a settler community. Although never much more than 1 percent of the colony's resident population, the settlers were given the best agricultural lands in the rich highlands region around Nairobi and, throughout most of the colonial era, were allowed to exert their political and economic hegemony over the local Africans. The settler populations in Tanzania and Uganda were smaller and less powerful. While the settler presence in Kenya led to land alienation and consequent misery for many Africans, it also fostered a fair amount of colonial investment in infrastructure. As a result, Kenya had a relatively sophisticated economy at the time of its independence, a fact that was to complicate proposals for its economic integration with Tanzania and Uganda.

During the 1950s the British established the East African Common Services Organization to promote greater economic cooperation between its Kenyan, Tanganyikan (Tanzanian), and Ugandan territories. By the early 1960s the links between the states were so close that President Julius Nyerere of Tanzania proposed that his country delay its independence until Kenya also gained its freedom in hopes that the two countries would then join together. This did not occur.

In 1967 the Common Services Organization was transformed by its three, now independent, members into a full-fledged common market known as the East African Community (EAC). The EAC collectively managed the railway system, development of harbors, and international air, postal, and telecommunications facilities. It also maintained a common currency, a development bank, and other economic, cultural, and scientific services. Peoples moved freely across the borders of the three EAC states. However, the EAC soon began to unravel, as conflicts over its operations grew. It finally collapsed in 1977. The countries disputed the benefits of the association, which seemed to have been garnered primarily by Kenya. The ideologies and personalities of its leaders at the time—Nyerere, Jomo Kenyatta of Kenya, and Idi Amin of Uganda—differed greatly. Relations between Kenya and Tanzania deteriorated to the point that the border between them was closed for several years.

In 1983 Kenya, Tanzania, and Uganda agreed on the division of the assets of the old Community; Kenya experienced the largest losses. Tanzania and Kenya opened their borders and began rebuilding their relationship. The economic strains that all three countries face in their dealings with the world economy make clear the value of the defunct EAC. But political factors continue to complicate the quest for greater regional cooperation. Kenyatta was succeeded by his vice president, Daniel arap Moi, whose regime over the past decade has become increasingly repressive in the face of mounting opposition. Uganda still suffers from years of warfare and instability, which were the legacies of the brutal regimes of Amin and Milton Obote, whose second administration was overthrown in a 1985 coup. Uganda's current president, Yoweri Museveni, maintains an uneasy control over a country still plagued by violence. Although the governments of Kenya, Rwanda, Sudan, Tanzania, and Zaire pledged in 1986 to prevent exiles from using asylum to destabilize their homelands, tensions in the region continue. Relations between Uganda and Kenya have been strained over allegations that each has harbored the other's dissidents. However, the two governments agreed to ease tensions after trade and transport disputes led to border clashes in 1987–1988.

A number of joint projects may contribute to the rebirth of some form of East African community. A Preferential Trade Area of 19 East and Southern African nations was established in 1981. Burundi, Rwanda, Tanzania and Uganda are sharing in the construction of a hydroelectric project on the Kagera River. Uganda has established cooperative military links with both Kenya and Tanzania. In addition, the governments of Burundi, Rwanda, Tanzania, and Zaire have met to discuss security, trade, and cultural exchange in the region. Rwanda and Burundi are members of the Economic Community of Central African States (ECCA), but their economic ties with East African states have led the UN Economic Commission on Africa, as well as other multinational organizations, to include them in the East African regional groupings.

There has been much talk of improving relations. "Think East Africa," the *Standard* of Kenya wrote, commenting on the cultural links that existed in the area before colonialism. Salim Salim, a Tanzanian statesman, noted, "You can choose a friend, but you cannot choose a brother. . . . In this case, Kenyans and Ugandans are our brothers."

THE ISLANDS

The Comoros, Madagascar, Mauritius, and the Seychelles each have their own special characteristics. Nonetheless, they also have some common traits. All four island nations have been strongly influenced by historic contacts with Asia as well as with mainland Africa and Europe. Madagascar and the Comoros have populations that originated in Indonesia and the Middle East as well as in Africa; the Malagasey language is related to Indonesian Malay. The citizens of Mauritius and the Seychelles are of European as well as African and Asian origin.

All four island groups have also been influenced by France. Mauritius and the Seychelles were not permanently inhabited until the 1770s, when French settlers arrived with their African slaves. The British subsequently took control of these two island groups and, during the 1830s, abolished slavery. Thereafter the British encouraged migration from South Asia and, to a lesser extent, from China, to make up for labor shortages on the islands' plantations. Local French-based Creoles remain the major languages on the islands.

In 1978 all of the islands, along with opposition groups from the French possession of Réunion, formed the Indian Ocean Commission. Originally a body with a socialist orientation, the commission campaigned for independence for Réunion and the return of the island of Diego Garcia by Britain to Mauritius, as well as for the dismantling of the U.S. naval base located there. By the end of the 1980s, however, the export-oriented growth of Mauritius and the continuing prosperity of the Seychelles' tourist-based economy were helping to push all four nations toward a greater emphasis on market economics in their multilateral, as well as internal, policy initiatives. Madagascar has recently offered investment incentives for Mauritius-based private firms, and the Comoros is moving to follow suit. Mauritians have already played prominent roles in the development of tourism in the Comoros.

In addition to their growing economic ties with one another, the Comoros and Mauritius, and to a somewhat lesser extent Madagascar and the Seychelles as well, have developed economic ties with South Africa, despite their opposition to its racist policies. Should South Africa succeed in dismantling apartheid, its links with the islands would undoubtedly grow and become less ambiguous.

Burundi (Republic of Burundi)

GEOGRAPHY

Area in Square Kilometers (Miles): 27,834 (10,759) (about the size of Maryland)
Capital (Population): Bujumbura (272,000)
Climate: tropical to temperate

PEOPLE

Population
Total: 5,645,000
Annual Growth Rate: 3.2%
Rural/Urban Population Ratio: 92/8
Languages: official: Kirundi, French; others spoken: Kiswahili, others

Health
Life Expectancy at Birth: 50 years (male); 54 years (female)
Infant Death Rate (Ratio): 111/1,000
Average Caloric Intake: 99% of FAO minimum
Physicians Available (Ratio): 1/31,713

Religion(s)
67% Christian; 32% traditional indigenous; 1% Muslim

THE BUTLER-OBIOZOR REPORT

"The Burundian Affair," a report drafted by William Butler and George Obiozor and issued in 1972 by the International Commission of Jurists and the International League of the Rights of Man, was an early indictment of the role of the Burundi government in its ongoing atrocities against the Hutu population. It concluded that the government was guilty of genocidal acts, defining genocide as "a denial of the right of existence of entire human groups" and/or the "systematic killing of people based on their race or ethnic origin, creed or color." The report served as the major evidence for introducing the situation in Burundi as a case for consideration by the UN Commission on Human Rights. However, the Commission dropped the case in 1975, without having undertaken any action.

Education
Adult Literacy Rate: 34%

COMMUNICATION

Telephones: 8,000
Newspapers: 1 daily

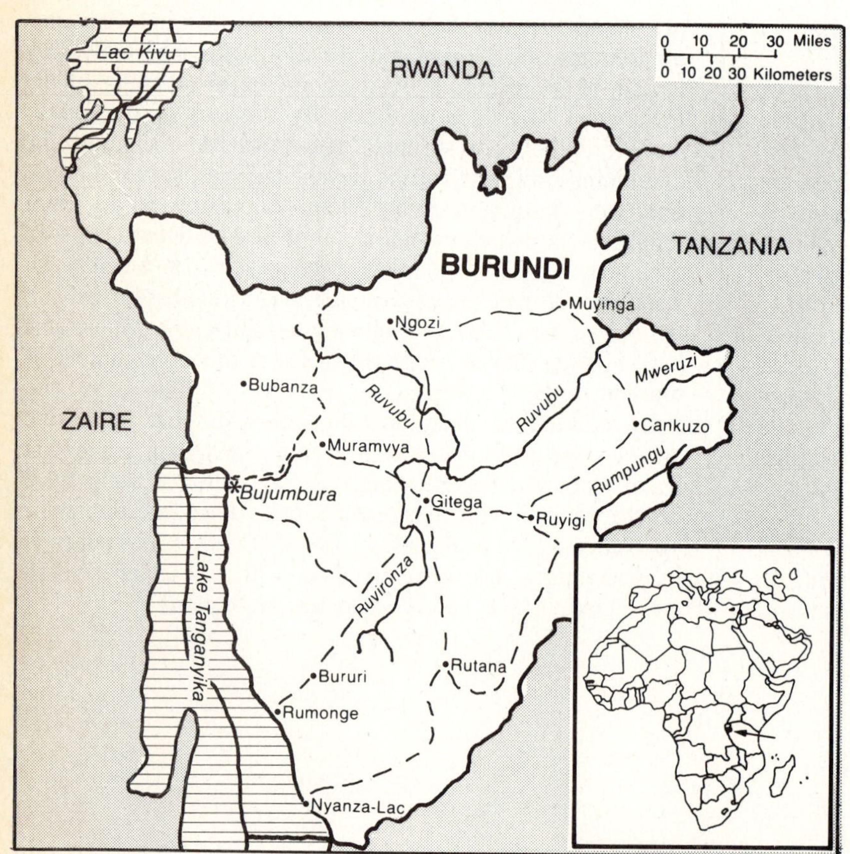

TRANSPORTATION

Highways—Kilometers (Miles): 7,800 (4,846)
Railroads—Kilometers (Miles): none
Commercial Airports: 1 international

GOVERNMENT

Type: republic
Independence Date: July 1, 1962
Head of State: President (Major) Pierre Buyoya
Political Parties: Union for National Progress
Suffrage: universal over 19

MILITARY

Number of Armed Forces: 7,200
Military Expenditures (% of Central Government Expenditures): 3.1%
Current Hostilities: internal ethnic violence

ECONOMY

Currency ($ U.S. Equivalent): 176 Burundi francs = $1
Per Capita Income/GNP: $255/$1.3 billion
Inflation Rate: 4.4%
Natural Resources: nickel; uranium; cobalt; copper; platinum
Agriculture: coffee; tea; cotton; food crops
Industry: light consumer goods; beer brewing

FOREIGN TRADE

Exports: $128 million
Imports: $204 million

BURUNDI

Burundi is a small, beautiful, and crowded country whose peoples are deeply divided. Those in power have resorted to mass murder to maintain a system of domination based on ethnicity and class. In 1972 and again in 1988 tens of thousands perished in the "killing fields" of Burundi. The general response of the outside world, both official and nonofficial, to these tragedies was characterized by opportunistic support for the oppressor and near total indifference to the plight of the oppressed.

ETHNIC GROUPS

Burundi's population is ethnically divided into three distinctive groups. At the bottom of the social hierarchy are the Twa, who are commonly stereotyped as "pygmies." Believed to be the earliest inhabitants of the country, the Twa today account for only about 1 percent of the population. The largest group, 83 percent, are the Hutu, who largely subsist as peasant farmers. The dominant group are the Tutsi, who constitute some 15 percent of the population. Among the Tutsi, who are subdivided into clans, status has long been associated with cattle keeping. Leading Tutsi continue to form an aristocratic ruling class over the whole of Burundi society. Until 1966 the leader of Burundi's Tutsi aristocracy was the Mwangi, or king.

The history of the Burundi kingdom goes back at least as far as the sixteenth century. By the late nineteenth century, when the kingdom was incorporated into German East Africa, the Tutsi had subordinated the Hutu, who became clients of local Tutsi aristocrats, herding their cattle and rendering other services. The Germans and subsequently the Belgians, who assumed paramount authority over the kingdom after World War I, were content to rule through Burundi's established social hierarchy. However, many Hutu as well as Tutsi were educated by Christian missionaries.

NATIONALIST MOVEMENT

In the late 1950s the Tutsi Prince Louis Rwagasore tried to accommodate Hutu as well as Tutsi aspirations by establishing a nationalist reform movement known as the Union for National Progress (Uprona). Rwagasore was assassinated before independence, but Uprona led the country to independence in 1962, with the Mwami, Mwambutsa IV, retaining considerable power as head of state. The Tutsi elite remained dominant, but the Uprona Cabinets contained representation from the two major groups. This attempt to balance the interests of the Tutsi and Hutu broke down in 1965, when Hutu politicians within both Uprona and the rival People's Party won 80 percent of the vote and the majority of the seats in both houses of the bicameral legislature. In response, the Mwami abolished the legislature before it could convene. A group of Hutu army officers then attempted to overthrow the government. Mwambutsa fled the country, but the re-

(United Nations photo by Derek Lovejoy)

Burundi remains one of the poorest countries in the world, and any money saved in energy needs is an essential goal. By using solar energy to preserve the fish caught in Lake Tanganyika these fish-drying nets are an important element in assuring an inexpensive food product.

Mwami Ntare Rugaamba expands the boundaries of the Nkoma kingdom **1795**

The area is mandated to Belgium by the League of Nations after the Germans lose World War I **1919**

Prince Louis Rwagasore leads a nationalist movement and founds Uprona **1958–1961**

Rwagasore is assassinated; independence is achieved **1961**

A failed coup results in purges of Hutu in the government and army; Michel Micombero seizes power **1965–1966**

Government forces massacre 200,000 Hutu **1972**

Jean-Baptiste Bagaza comes to power in a military coup **1976**

1980s–1990s

Buyoyo rules out multiparty democracy

Ethnic violence leaves 5,000 to 25,000 dead, mostly Hutu

Bagaza is overthrown in military coup led by Peirre Buyoyo

volt was crushed in a countercoup by Tutsi officers led by Michel Micombero.

In the aftermath of the uprising Micombero took power amidst a campaign of reprisals in which it is estimated that some 5,000 Hutu were killed. At the end of 1966 he deposed Mwambutsa's son, Ntare V, from kingship and set up a "Government of Public Safety," which set about purging Hutu members from the government and the army. At the time, political struggle involved interclan competition among the Tutsi as well as the maintenance of their hegemony over the Hutu.

CHALLENGES TO THE GOVERNMENT

Under Micombero, Burundi continued to be marred by interethnic violence, occasional coup attempts, and promonarchist agitation. A major purge of influential Hutu was carried out in 1969. In 1972 Ntare V was lured to Uganda by Idi Amin, who turned over the former king to Micombero. Ntare was placed under arrest upon his arrival and subsequently was murdered by his guards. A declaration of martial law then set off an explosion of violence. In response to an alleged uprising involving the deaths of up to 2,000 Tutsi, government supporters began to massacre large numbers of Hutu. Educated Hutu were especially targeted in a 2-month campaign of selective genocide, which is generally believed to have claimed some 200,000 victims (estimates range from 80,000 to 500,000 deaths for the entire period, with additional atrocities being reported through 1973). More than 100,000 Hutu fled to Uganda, Rwanda, Zaire, and Tanzania; most still reside in those countries. Among the governments of the world, only Tanzania and Rwanda showed any deep concern for the course of events. China, France, and Libya, in particular, used the crisis as an opportunity to upgrade significantly their military aid to the Burundi regime.

In 1974 Micombero formally transformed Burundi into a one-party state under Uprona. Although Micombero was replaced 2 years later in a military coup by Colonel Jean-Baptiste Bagaza, power remained effectively in the hands of members of the Tutsi elite, who controlled Uprona, the civil service, and the army. In 1985 Bagaza widened existing state persecution of the Seventh Day Adventists and Jehovah's Witnesses to include the Roman Catholic Church (to which two-thirds of Burundi's population belongs), accusing it of fostering seditious—that is, pro-Hutu—sympathies. However, the overthrow of Bagaza by Pierre Buyoyo, in a 1987 military coup, led to a lifting of the anti-Catholic campaign.

Ethnic violence erupted again in 1988. Apparently some Tutsi were killed by Hutu in northern Burundi, in response to rumors of another massacre of Hutu. In retaliation, the army massacred between 5,000 and 25,000 Hutu. Another 60,000 Hutu took temporary refuge in Rwanda, while more than 100,000 were left homeless.

LAND ISSUES

Burundi remains one of the poorest countries in the world, despite its rich volcanic soils and generous international development assistance (it has consistently been one of the highest per capita aid recipients on the continent). In addition to the dislocations caused by cycles of interethnic violence, the nation's development prospects are seriously compromised by geographic isolation and population pressure on the land. About 25 percent of Burundi is under cultivation, generally by individual farmers trying to subsist on plots of usually no more than 3 acres. Another 60 percent of the country is devoted to pasture for, mostly Tutsi, livestock. Hutu farmers continue to be tied by patron-client relationships to Tutsi overlords. In recent years the government has introduced a villagization scheme, which it has tied to its agricultural-improvement efforts. Despite the promise of access to fertilizers and new agricultural equipment, many peasants have resisted the effort.

Before the 1988 killings, President Buyoyo had begun cautiously to increase Hutu participation in his government. These efforts have continued. The current Cabinet boasts a Hutu majority, but ultimate power remains in the hands of the Tutsi-controlled Military Committee of National Salvation. A National Unity Commission, appointed by the president, may recommend further reforms. However, in a March 1990 speech, Buyoyo rejected calls for a restoration of multiparty politics, claiming that it would encourage tribalism.

DEVELOPMENT

Burundi's sources of wealth are limited. There is no active development of mineral resources, although sources of nickel have been located and may be mined soon. There is little industry, and the coffee crop, which contributes 75% to 90% of export earnings, has declined.

FREEDOM

Burundi remains in the hands of a repressive military regime supported by the Tutsi elite. The government has in the past imposed internal travel restrictions aimed at the Hutu majority. Religious organizations continue to be subject to restrictions.

HEALTH/WELFARE

Much of the educational system has been in private hands, especially the Roman Catholic Church. Burundi lost many educated and trained personnel because of the Hutu massacres in the 1970s and 1980s.

ACHIEVEMENTS

Burundi's plans for future economic development show consideration of regional possibilities. Sugar, cheese, cooking oil, and soft-drink and beer factories are expected to benefit from demand throughout the area. Transportation will be improved through regional cooperation with East African rail networks.

Comoros (Comoros Federal Islamic Republic)

GEOGRAPHY

Area in Square Kilometers (Miles): 2,171 (838) (about the size of Delaware)
Capital (Population): Moroni (28,000)
Climate: tropical; marine

PEOPLE

Population

Total: 460,000
Annual Growth Rate: 3.5%
Rural/Urban Population Ratio: n/a
Languages: official: Shaafi-Islam; others spoken: French, Swahili, Arabic

Health

Life Expectancy at Birth: 54 years (male); 58 years (female)
Infant Death Rate (Ratio): 89/1,000
Average Caloric Intake: 102% of FAO minimum
Physicians Available (Ratio): 1/23,009

Religion(s)

86% Sunni Muslim; 14% Roman Catholic

MAYOTTE ISLAND

In 1974, when the other Comoran islands voted overwhelmingly for independence, Mayotte opted to remain French by a two-to-one margin. Since then the French have continued to administer the island with the support of the local population—more than 95 percent of whom have, in recent years, voted in favor of becoming an overseas department of France. Unlike the other islands, Mayotte is predominately Christian. Historically, it has been greatly influenced by Malagasy and French culture. Comoran claims to the island are supported by the Organization of African Unity, and in the United Nations only France voted against a resolution calling for their inclusion in the Comoros. Despite the location of its naval base on the island, France may be eager to withdraw from Mayotte, but is reluctant to do so against the wishes of Mayotte and domestic opinion.

Education

Adult Literacy Rate: 15%

COMMUNICATION

Telephones: 1,800
Newspapers: n/a

TRANSPORTATION

Highways—Kilometers (Miles): 750 (465)
Railroads—Kilometers (Miles): none
Commercial Airports: 1 international

GOVERNMENT

Type: Islamic republic
Independence Date: July 6, 1975
Head of State: President Said Mohamed Djohar
Political Parties: Comoran Union for Progress
Suffrage: universal for adults

MILITARY

Number of Armed Forces: 700
Military Expenditures (% of Central Government Expenditures): 3%
Current Hostilities: none

ECONOMY

Currency ($ U.S. Equivalent): 288 Comoran francs = $1
Per Capita Income/GNP: $475/$207 million
Inflation Rate: n/a
Natural Resources: agricultural land
Agriculture: perfume essences; copra; coconuts; cloves; vanilla; cinnamon; yams; rice
Industry: perfume distillation; tourism

FOREIGN TRADE

Exports: $12 million
Imports: $52 million

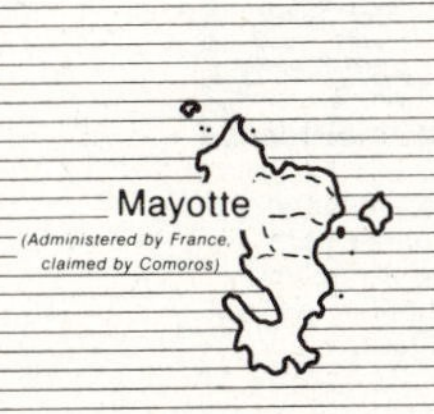

Various groups settle in the islands, which become part of a Swahili trading network
1500s

French rule over Mayotte is established
1843

A French protectorate over the remaining Comoro islands is proclaimed
1886

The islands are ruled as part of the French colony of Madagascar
1914–1946

Independence is followed by a mercenary coup, which installs Ali Soilih
1975

Ali Soilih is overthrown by mercenaries; Ahmed Abdullah is restored
1978

1980s–1990s

Abdullah proclaims a one-party state; real power remains in the hands of mercenary leader Bob Denard

Comoros is linked to South African supply of Renamo rebels in Mozambique

The assassination of Abdullah leads to removal of Denard and multiparty elections

COMOROS

At the time of its unilateral declaration of independence from France, in 1975, the Comoros was one of the world's least developed nations. The subsequent years have not been kind to the Comorans; their lives have been made difficult by natural disaster, eccentric and authoritarian leadership, and external intervention. However, the recent restoration of a multiparty democratic process has raised hopes for a better future.

HISTORY AND POLITICS

The Comoros archipelago was populated by a number of Indian Ocean peoples, who—by the time of the arrival of the first Europeans during the early sixteenth century—had already combined to form the predominately Muslim, Swahili-speaking society found on the islands today. In 1886 the French proclaimed a protectorate over the three main islands that currently constitute the Federal Islamic Republic of the Comoros. Throughout the colonial period the Comoros were especially valued by the French for strategic reasons.

A month after independence the first Comoran government, led by the wealthy Ahmed Abdullah Abderemane, was overthrown by mercenaries, who installed Ali Soilih in power. The new leader promised a socialist transformation of the nation and began to implement land reform. This program was never completed, however, because Soilih rapidly lost support both at home and abroad. Under his leadership, gangs of undisciplined youths terrorized society and the basic institutions and services of government all but disappeared. The situation was made even worse by a major volcanic eruption, which left 20,000 people homeless, and by the arrival of 16,000 Comoran refugees after a massacre of Comorans in neighboring Madagascar.

In 1978 another band of mercenaries—this time led by the notorious Bob Denard, whose exploits in Zaire, Togo, and elsewhere had made his name infamous throughout Africa—overthrew Soilih and restored Abdullah to power. Denard, however, remained the true power behind the throne.

The Denard-Abdullah government enjoyed close ties with influential right-wing elements in France and South Africa. Connections with Pretoria were manifested through the use of the Comoros as a major conduit for South African supplies to the Renamo rebels in Mozambique. Economic ties with South Africa, especially in tourism and, it is alleged, sanctions busting, also grew. Besides France, the government established good relations with Saudi Arabia and other conservative Arab governments, while attracting significant aid from international agencies.

In 1982 the country legally become a one-party state. Attempted coups in 1985 and 1987 aggravated political tensions. Many Comorans particularly resented the overbearing influence of Denard and his men. By November 1989 this group had come to include President Abdullah himself. With the backing of France and South Africa, Abdullah moved to replace Denard's mercenaries with a French-approved security unit. However, before this move could be implemented, Abdullah was murdered following a meeting with Denard.

The head of the Supreme Court, Said Djohar, was appointed as interim president. After a period of some confusion, during which popular protests against Denard swelled, Djohar quietly sought French intervention to oust the mercenaries. With both Paris and Pretoria united against him, Denard agreed to relinquish power in exchange for safe passage to South Africa.

The removal of Denard and the temporary stationing of a French peacekeeping force was accompanied by lifting of political restrictions in preparation for presidential elections. In March 1990 a run-off resulted in a 55-percent electoral mandate for Djohar.

THE ECONOMY

The Comoran economy experienced modest growth during the 1980s. But with a large and rapidly growing population, the nation suffers from severe land and job shortages.

Lately there has been a significant expansion of tourism, largely due to local investment and promotion by the South African-based Sun International Group. What little industry exists on the islands consists almost entirely of agricultural processing. Hopes for future growth are currently tied to attracting low-wage manufactures from Mauritius, where labor shortages exist as a result of the success of that country's Free Trade Zone.

DEVELOPMENT

One of the major projects undertaken since independence has been the on-going expansion of the port at Mutsamundu, which will allow large ships to visit the islands. Vessels of up to 25,000 tons can now dock at the harbor.

FREEDOM

Since independence, freedom has been abridged under both Ahmed Abdullah and Ali Soilih. The new government (elected in 1990) has ended abuses.

HEALTH/WELFARE

Health statistics improved during the 1980s. A recent World Health Organization survey estimated that 10% of children ages 3 to 6 years are seriously malnourished and another 37% are moderately malnourished.

ACHIEVEMENTS

Since ancient times the Comoros has been famous for its high-quality ylang-ylang essence, which is used in the finest of perfumes.

Djibouti (Republic of Djibouti)

GEOGRAPHY

Area in Square Kilometers (Miles): 23,200 (8,960) (about the size of New Hampshire)
Capital (Population): Djibouti (400,000) (est.)
Climate: arid to semi-arid

PEOPLE

Population

Total: 500,000 (est.)
Annual Growth Rate: 2.6%
Rural/Urban Population Ratio: 25/75
Languages: official: French, Arabic; others spoken: Somali, Saho-Afar

Health

Life Expectancy at Birth: 46 years (male); 49 years (female)
Infant Death Rate (Ratio): 119/1,000
Average Caloric Intake: n/a
Physicians Available (Ratio): 1/3,790

Religion(s)

94% Muslim; 4% Christian

Education

Adult Literacy Rate: 20%

DJIBOUTI POLITICS

Local politics in Djibouti has been dominated since independence by the aging President Hassan Gouled Aptidon. No clear-cut successor currently exists. Since the creation of a one-party state, a number of underground movements have emerged in opposition to the continued domination of the president's Popular Rally for Progress. One group that surfaced in 1989, the Movement for Unity and Democracy, poses a potential threat through its alleged association with the Somali National Movement, which is currently waging an armed struggle in northern Somalia against that country's government. In 1990 two other dissident movements, one Afar-oriented and the other Issa-oriented, combined forces as the Union of Movements for Democracy. Another major, nonparty, political force is the Ugaz, or sultan, of the Issa Somali, who is based in the Ethiopian town of Dire Diwa. It is said that the Ugaz and his council confirmed Gouled Aptidon as the political leader of Djibouti's Issa in 1975. Other Afar and Somali clan heads, living on both sides of the border, are also influential.

COMMUNICATION

Telephones: 7,300
Newspapers: 3 weeklies

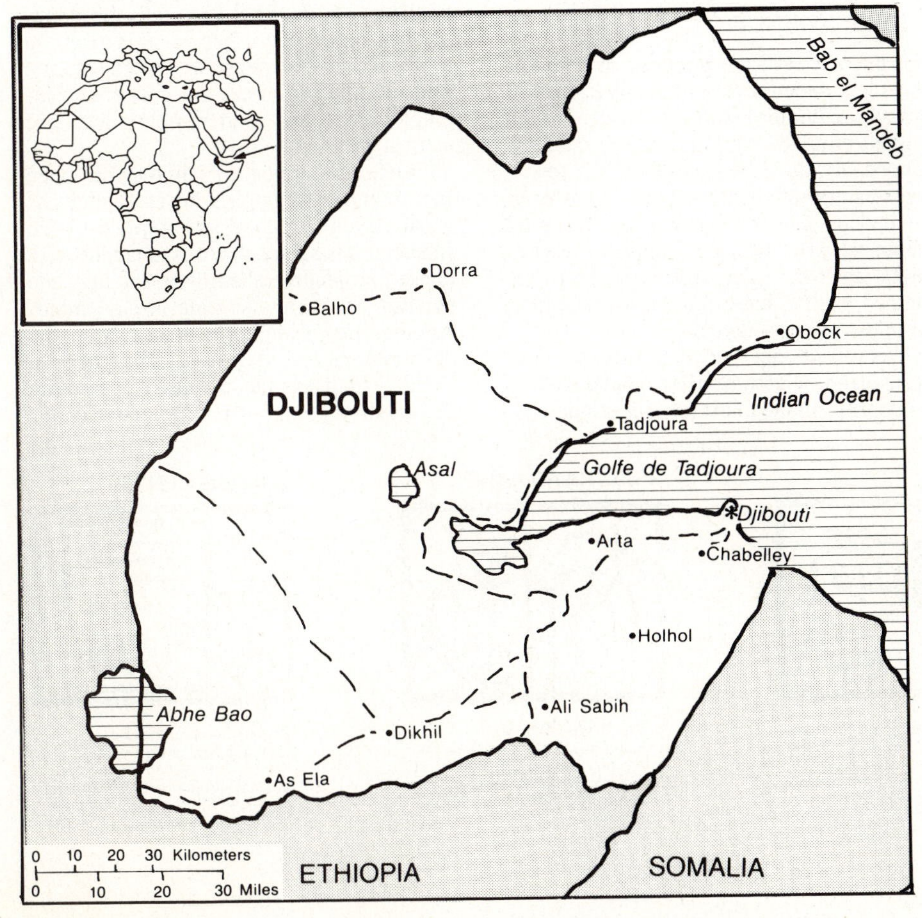

TRANSPORTATION

Highways—Kilometers (Miles): 2,906 (1,801)
Railroads—Kilometers (Miles): 97 (60)
Commercial Airports: 1 international

GOVERNMENT

Type: republic
Independence Date: June 27, 1977
Head of State: President Hassan Gouled Aptidon
Political Parties: People's Progress Assembly
Suffrage: universal for adults

MILITARY

Number of Armed Forces: 4,330
Military Expenditures (% of Central Government Expenditures): n/a
Current Hostilities: none

ECONOMY

Currency ($ U.S. Equivalent): 177 Djibouti francs = $1
Per Capita Income/GNP: $1,070/$333 million
Inflation Rate: 8%
Natural Resources: none
Agriculture: goats; sheep; camels; cattle; coffee
Industry: port and maritime support; construction

FOREIGN TRADE

Exports: $128 million
Imports: $198 million

France buys the port of Obock
1862

France acquires the port of Djibouti
1888

The Addis Ababa-Djibouti Railroad is completed
1917

Djibouti votes to remain part of Overseas France
1958

Independence; the Ogaden War
1977

1980s–1990s

Drought and warfare lead to a major influx of refugees

President Hassan Gouled Aptidon visits France and reaffirms Franco-Djibouti political and military ties

The underground Union of Movements for Democracy is formed as an interethnic antigovernment coalition

DJIBOUTI

Djibouti is a small city-state, situated between Ethiopia and Somalia at the southern mouth of the Red Sea. Since achieving its independence from France, in 1977, the country has had to strike a cautious balance between the competing interests of its two larger neighbors. Most of the nation's people are either Afar or Somali speakers. In the past Somalia has claimed ownership of the territory, based on the numerical preponderance of its Somali population, variously estimated at 50 to 70 percent. However, local Somali, as well as Afars, also have strong ties to communities in Ethiopia.

Djibouti's deepwater harbor regularly handles half of Ethiopia's trade. The port's location at the crossroads of Africa and Eurasia has also made it a focus of continuing strategic concern by nonregional powers, particularly France, which maintains a large military presence in the country.

Modern Djibouti's colonial genesis was a product of mid-nineteenth-century European rivalry over control of the Red Sea. In 1862 France occupied the town of Obock, across the harbor from the city of Djibouti. This move was taken in anticipation of the opening of the Suez Canal, in 1869, which transformed the Red Sea into the major shipping route between Asia, East Africa, and Europe. At the time Britain and Italy also established bases in the region. In 1888 France, having acquired Djibouti city and its hinterland, proclaimed its authority over French Somaliland, the modern territory of Djibouti.

In the late 1960s French Somaliland, after years of pro-independence agitation, was transformed into the autonomous Territory of Afars and Issas. The name reflected a continuing colonial policy of divide and rule; members of the Issas clan constitute just over half of the area's Somali speakers. A new territorial government was introduced and given broad responsibility over local affairs, but most of the Somali politicians, in protest over what they considered to have been a rigged referendum, initially boycotted its proceedings.

By the 1970s neither Ethiopia nor France was opposed to Djibouti's independence. However, both, for their own strategic reasons, backed the Afar community in its desire for assurances that the territory would not be incorporated into Somalia. An ethnic power-sharing arrangement was established, which in effect acknowledged local Somali preponderance. The empowerment of local Somali, in particular the Issa, was accompanied by a diminishing of pan-Somali sentiment.

INDEPENDENCE

On June 27, 1977 the Republic of Djibouti became independent, with the blessings of France, Ethiopia, and Somalia. French troops remained stationed in the country, supposedly as a guarantee of its sovereignty. Internally, political power has been divided by means of ethnically balanced Cabinets, with the prime minister always being an Afar. The presidency has remained in the hands of Hassan Gouled Aptidon, an Issa-Somali.

War broke out between Ethiopia and Somalia a few months after independence. Djibouti remained neutral, but ethnic tensions mounted as Somali refugees from the fighting arrived. In 1981 the Afar-dominated Djiboutian Popular Movement was outlawed. The Issa-dominated Popular Rally for Progress (RPP) then became the country's sole legal party.

PROSPECTS

Throughout the last decade refugees have continued to pour into Djibouti, fleeing the continuing conflicts and famines within both Ethiopia and Somalia. As a result, the country's population has swelled by about one-third, to an estimated 550,000. This influx has increased Djibouti's dependence on external food aid; the country has never been able to feed itself in modern times. At least 95 percent of current food requirements are imported. Unemployment and underemployment are critical problems.

Traffic in the port of Djibouti has been increasing, in large part due to its status as a safe haven from regional conflicts. With financial assistance from Arab donors, a phased project to rehabilitate and upgrade maritime facilities is being implemented. Another promising project has been the development of the Assal Geothermal Field, which has the potential of making the country an exporter of electricity.

DEVELOPMENT

Recent discoveries of gas reserves could result in a surplus for export. A number of small-scale irrigation schemes have been established. There is also a growing, though still quite small, fishing industry.

FREEDOM

Freedom of speech, association, and other rights are restricted by Djibouti's single-party system. However, the government has not been associated with acts of arbitrary repression or gross violations of human rights.

HEALTH/WELFARE

Progress has been made in reducing infant mortality, but health services are strained. School enrollment has expanded by nearly one-third since 1987.

ACHIEVEMENTS

Besides feeding its own refugees, the government of Djibouti has played a major role in assisting international efforts to relieve the recurrent famines in Ethiopia, Somalia, and Sudan.

Ethiopia (People's Democratic Republic of Ethiopia)

GEOGRAPHY

Area in Square Kilometers (Miles): 1,221,900 (471,800) (about four-fifths the size of Alaska)
Capital (Population): Addis Ababa (1,412,000)
Climate: temperate in highlands; arid to semiarid in lowlands

PEOPLE

Population
Total: 51,667,000
Annual Growth Rate: 3.5%
Rural/Urban Population Ratio: 89/11
Languages: official: Amharic; others spoken: Tigrinya, Oromo, Somali, Arabic, Italian, English, others

Health
Life Expectancy at Birth: 49 years (male); 52 years (female)
Infant Death Rate (Ratio): 116/1,000
Average Caloric Intake: 78% of FAO minimum in areas not severely affected by drought
Physicians Available (Ratio): 1/95,856

KING LABILA

During the twelfth and thirteenth centuries the Ethiopian state, having declined since the days of the Axumites, was revived under the Zagwe dynasty. The best known of the Zagwe rulers is Labila, who is remembered for his architectural legacy. At his capital of Roha, he built an impressive palace which survives to this day. More famous, however, are the churches which he had carved out of solid rock, supposedly to fulfill a heavenly injunction which he received in his sleep. The churches survive as centers of worship, attracting pilgrims from throughout Coptic Ethiopia.

Religion(s)
40%–45% Muslim; 35%–40% Ethiopian Orthodox Christian; 15%–25% traditional indigenous and others

Education
Adult Literacy Rate: 55%

COMMUNICATION

Telephones: 162,000
Newspapers: 3

TRANSPORTATION

Highways—Kilometers (Miles): 44,300 (27,466)
Railroads—Kilometers (Miles): 988 (612)
Commercial Airports: 4 international

GOVERNMENT

Type: provisional military government
Independence Date: none
Head of State: President Mengistu Haile Mariam
Political Parties: Democratic Unity Party
Suffrage: universal over 21

MILITARY

Number of Armed Forces: 318,800
Military Expenditures (% of Central Government Expenditures): n/a
Current Hostilities: internal conflicts with liberation groups in several provinces; border disputes with Somalia

ECONOMY

Currency ($ U.S. Equivalent): 2.07 birrs = $1
Per Capita Income/GNP: $130/$6.6 billion
Inflation Rate: 9.6%
Natural Resources: potash; salt; gold; copper; platinum
Agriculture: cereals; coffee; pulses; oil seeds; livestock
Industry: processed food; textiles; cement; building materials; hydroelectric power

FOREIGN TRADE

Exports: $418 million
Imports: $1.1 billion

ETHIOPIA

In the early months of 1990 international famine-relief agencies reported that, for the third time in 2 decades, millions of northern Ethiopians faced potential starvation, due to drought. This news coincided with the daily bombing and strafing of the northern provincial center of Mekele by the Ethiopian Air Force. The latter incident underscores the broader reality: starvation in contemporary Ethiopia is not so much an act of nature as an outcome of the nation's troubled politics. It is also politics, more than anything else, that is responsible for the fact that Ethiopia, often spoken of as a potential breadbasket of the African continent, is now the poorest country in the world. Such is the sad fate that has befallen this proud civilization whose roots go back at least as far as the time of the Roman Empire.

AN IMPERIAL PAST

Ethiopia rivals Egypt as Africa's oldest country. For centuries its kings claimed direct descent from the biblical King Solomon and the Queen of Sheba. Whether Ethiopia was the site of Sheba is uncertain. The history of the country is better established from the time of the Axum kingdom, which prospered from the first century A.D. During the fourth century the Axumite court adopted the Coptic Christian faith, which has remained central to the culture of Ethiopia's highland region. Today some 40 percent of the population are Coptic. To this day the Church uses the Geez, the ancient Auxmite tongue from which the modern Ethiopian languages of Amharic and Tigrinya are derived, in its services.

From the eighth century much of the area surrounding the highlands fell under Muslim control, thus all but cutting off the Copts from their European coreligionists. Today about 45 percent of the Ethiopians are Muslim, most of whom live in the lowlands. For many centuries Ethiopia's history was characterized by struggles among the groups inhabiting these two regions and religions. At times a powerful ruler would succeed in making himself truly "King of Kings," by uniting the Christian highlands and expanding into the lowlands. At other times the mountains would be divided into weak polities, which were vulnerable to the raids of Muslim and non-Muslim lowlanders.

Modern Ethiopian history began in the nineteenth century, when the highlands became politically reunited by a series of kings, culminating in Menilik II, who built up their power by importing European armaments. Once the Coptic core of his kingdom was intact, Menilik began to spread his authority across the lowlands, thus uniting most of contemporary Ethiopia. In 1889 and 1896 Menilik also defeated invading Italian armies, thereby preserving his empire's independence during the European partition of Africa.

From 1916 to 1974 Ethiopia was ruled by Ras Tafari (from which is derived the term Rasta, or Rastafarian) who, in 1930, was crowned as the Emperor Haile Selassie. Selassie was a controversial figure. For many decades he was seen both at home and abroad as a reformer who was modernizing his state. In 1936, after his kingdom had been occupied by Italy's Benito Mussolini, he made a memorable speech before the League of Nations warning the world of the price it would inevitably pay for appeasing fascist aggression. At the time many African-Americans and Africans outside of Ethiopia saw him as a great hero in the struggle of black peoples everywhere for dignity and empowerment. Selassie returned to his throne in 1941 and thereafter served as an elder statesman to the African nationalists of the 1950s and 1960s. However, by the latter decade his own domestic authority was being increasingly questioned.

In his later years Selassie could not or would not move against the forces that were undermining his empire. Despite its trappings of progress, the Ethiopian state remained quasi-feudal in its character. Many of the best lands were controlled by the nobility and Church, whose leading members lived privileged lives at the expense of the peasantry. Many educated people grew disenchanted with what they perceived as a reactionary monarchy and social order. Urban workers resented being paid low wages by often foreign owners. Within the junior ranks of the army and civil service, there was also great dissatisfaction at the way in which their superiors were able to siphon off state revenues for their personal enrichment. But the empire's greatest weakness was its inability to accommodate the aspirations of the various ethnic, regional, and sectarian groupings living with its borders.

Ethiopia is a multiethnic state. Since the

(United Nations photo by Muldoon)

From 1916 to 1974 Ethiopia was ruled by Ras Tafari (from which today's term Rastafarian is derived); in 1930 he was crowned Emperor Haile Selassie. He is pictured above on the left shaking hands with the infamous Idi Amin, past president of Uganda. The year of this photo was 1973; in 1974 Selassie was overthrown by the military.

time of Menilik the dominant group has been the Coptic Amhara speakers. In recent years movements fighting for ethnoregional autonomy have emerged among the Tigrinya of Tigre, the Oromo, and, to a lesser extent, the Afars, while many Somali in Ethiopia's Ogaden region have long struggled for union with neighboring Somalia. Somali irredentism led to open warfare between the two principal Horn of Africa states in 1963–1964 and 1977–1978.

The northern coastal province of Eritrea is a special case. From the late nineteenth century until World War II it was an Italian colony. After the war it was federated with Selassie's empire. After a questionable 1962 referendum, Eritrea's autonomy was abrogated and the territory was fully annexed as an Ethiopian province. Since then a local independence movement, now largely united as the Eritrean People's Liberation Front (EPLF), has waged an armed struggle. Eritrea is itself a multiethnic and bisectarian area, with the greatest support for the EPLF coming from local Tigrinya, while the government maintains some support among southern Afars.

In 1974 Haile Selassie was overthrown by the military, after months of mounting unrest throughout the country. A major factor in triggering the coup was the government's inaction in 1972–1974, when famine swept across the northern provinces, claiming some 200,000 lives. Some accused the Amhara government of using the famine as a way of weakening the predominately Tigrinya areas of the empire. Others simply saw the tragedy as proof of the venal incompetence of Selassie's administration.

REVOLUTION AND REPRESSION

The overthrow of the old order was welcomed by most Ethiopians. Unfortunately, what began as a promising revolutionary transformation quickly degenerated into a repressive dictatorship, which has pushed the nation into chronic instability and distress. From the beginning a Provisional Military Administrative Council, or Dergue (Amharic for "committee"), took command. By the end of 1974, after the first in a series of bloody purges within its ranks, the Dergue had embraced Marxism as its guiding philosophy. Revolutionary measures followed. Companies and lands were nationalized. Students were sent into the countryside to assist in land reforms and to teach literacy. Peasants and workers were organized into cooperative associations called *kebeles*. Initial steps were also taken to end Amhara hegemony within the state.

Progressive aspects of the Ethiopian revolution were offset by the murderous nature of the regime. Power struggles within the Dergue, as well as its determination to eliminate all alternatives to its authority, contributed to periods of "red terror," during which thousands of supporters of the revolution as well as those associated with the old regime were killed. Out of this worst of times emerged the dictatorship of Ethiopia's current leader, Colonel Mengistu Haile Mariam, who shot his way to the top in 1977.

Until recently Mengistu sought to legitimize his rule through a commitment to turn Ethiopia into a Marxist-Leninist state. He formally presided over a Commission for Organizing the Party of the Working People of Ethiopia, which, in 1984, announced the formation of a single-party state, led by the new Workers' Party. In reality, power remained concentrated in the hands of Mengistu and his Dergue.

CIVIL WAR

Since 1974 Ethiopia has remained a land at war with itself. In the face of oppressive central authority, ethnic-based resistance movements have become increasingly effective in their struggles throughout much of the country. In the late 1970s the Mengistu regime began to receive massive military aid from the Soviet Bloc in its campaigns against the Eritreans and Somali. Some 17,000 Cuban troops, and thousands of other military personnel from the Warsaw Pact countries, allowed the government temporarily to gain the upper hand in the fighting. For its own part, the Ethiopian Army grew to more

(United Nations photo by John Isaac)

Ethiopia has been in a civil war since 1974; this continuous fighting has displaced millions of people. The problem of this forced migration has been compounded by drought and starvation. These drought victims are gathered at one of the many relief camps.

Emperor Tewodros begins the conquest and development of modern Ethiopia **1855**

Ethiopia defeats Italian invaders at the Battle of Adowa **1896**

Fascist Italy invades Ethiopia and rules until 1941 **1936**

The Eritrean liberation struggle begins **1961**

Famines in Tigray and Welo provinces result in up to 200,000 deaths **1972–1973**

Emperor Haile Selassie is overthrown; the PMAC is established **1974**

Diplomatic realignment and a new arms agreement with the Soviet Union **1977**

1980s–1990s

Massive famine, resulting from drought and warfare

Tigray and Eritrean struggles intensify; many are killed; cities are captured and recaptured

The Ethiopian government formally abandons its commitment to Marxist-Leninism

than 300,000 men under arms at any given time, the largest military force on the continent. Throughout the 1980s military expenditures claimed more than half of the national budget.

Despite the massive domestic and international commitment on the side of the Mengistu regime, the rebels have been gradually gaining the upper hand. Almost all of northern Eritrea, except its besieged capital city of Asmara, has fallen to the EPLF, which has built up its own powerful arsenal, largely from captured government equipment. Local rebels have also liberated the province of Tigray and, as part of a broader coalition, pushed south toward Ethiopia's capital city of Addis Ababa. Although Ethiopia and Somalia reached an agreement not to assist each other's rebels in 1988, the Ogaden region remains unsettled. There has also been resistance to Mengistu from within the ranks of the national army. A major rebellion against his authority in 1989 was crushed, devastating military morale in the process.

Ethiopians continue to pay a terrible price for their nation's conflicts. Tens of thousands have been killed in combat, but many more have perished from the side effects of war. In 1984–1985 the conscience of much of the world was moved by the images of mass starvation in the northern war zone. At the time, the global media and concerned groups like Band Aid paid relatively little attention to the nonenvironmental factors that contributed to the crisis. Up to 1 million lives were lost before adequate relief supplies reached the famine areas.

The human crisis in Ethiopia persists. It is true that food production continues to suffer from drought and other environmental factors, such as soil erosion. However, the fact that people continue to starve despite the availability of international relief can only be attributed to the use of food as a weapon of war. There have been constraints on local crop production. Having seized the lands of the old ruling class, the Mengistu regime, in accordance with its Marxist-Leninist precepts, has invested most of its agricultural inputs in large state farms, whose productivity has been abysmal. Meanwhile, peasant production has also fallen in non-drought areas, due to insecure tenure, poor producer prices, lack of credit, and an absence of consumer goods.

Ethiopia's rural areas are further disrupted by the government's heavy-handed villagization and relocation schemes. The latter measure aims to move $1^1/_2$ million people to "more fertile" regions in the southwest. Some 600,000 were moved in 1984–1985, when the program was suspended as a result of international protests at forced participation, resulting in thousands of deaths. The program has since been restarted. Many consider the scheme to be part of the central government's war effort against local communities resistant to its authority. By the same token, villagization has long been associated with counterinsurgency efforts; concentrated settlements allow occupying armies to exert greater control over potentially hostile populations.

BLEAK PROSPECTS

As of this writing, the eventual collapse of the Mengistu regime seems certain, but not an end to the long suffering of the Ethiopian people. The war continues to take a terrible toll, with armies on all sides becoming increasingly reliant on young boys to fight their battles. Throughout the 1980s the Cuban military presence was scaled back. Now, in the aftermath of the collapse of the Soviet Bloc, Mengistu has lost his Warsaw Pact support. To make up for the winding down of the Soviet commitment, Mengistu is searching for new allies. Marxist-Leninism has been formally abandoned as the state ideology. The Workers' Party has become the Democratic Unity Party, which is supposedly open to the participation of all political factions. Such reforms have been treated with domestic and international skepticism. While Israel has begun to assist the Ethiopian military, which it has long seen as a counterforce to Arab hegemony in the Red Sea, most other states are unwilling to commit themselves to Mengistu's survival. Negotiations are on-going, but little progress has been made.

Unfortunately, while the fall of Mengistu would undoubtedly be welcomed by many, it is not clear whether any succeeding authority will be able to unify what has become a bitterly divided country. But the possible alternative of Ethiopia's breakup would most likely only contribute to greater dislocation and decline.

DEVELOPMENT

There has been some progress in the country's industrial sector over the past decade, after sharp decline during the 1970s. Soviet Bloc investment resulted in the establishment of new enterprises in such areas as cement, textiles, and farm machinery.

FREEDOM

The Ethiopian government rules through repression. Many of the movements seeking its overthrow also display authoritarian tendencies.

HEALTH/WELFARE

Progress in spreading literacy during the 1970s was undermined by the dislocations of the 1980s. Ethiopia today has some 500 government soldiers for every teacher.

ACHIEVEMENTS

With a history spanning 2 millennia, the cultural achievements of Ethiopia are vast. Addis Ababa is the headquarters of the Organization of African Unity. Ethiopia's Kefe Province is the home of the coffee plant, from whence it takes its name.

Kenya (Republic of Kenya)

GEOGRAPHY
Area in Square Kilometers (Miles): 582,488 (224,900) (slightly smaller than Texas)
Capital (Population): Nairobi (959,000)
Climate: tropical to arid

PEOPLE

Population
Total: 24,639,000
Annual Growth Rate: 3.8%
Rural/Urban Population Ratio: 80/20
Languages: official: English, Kiswahili; others spoken: Kikuyu Luo, Kamba, Kipsigi, Maasai, Luhya, Gusii, Nandi, Somali, others

Health
Life Expectancy at Birth: 62 years (male); 67 years (female)
Infant Death Rate (Ratio): 60/1,000
Average Caloric Intake: 88% of FAO minimum
Physicians Available (Ratio): 1/8,953

Religion(s)
38% Protestant; 28% traditional indigenous; 28% Catholic; 6% Muslim

CULTURE AND POLITICS

In the past as well as today, cultural activities in Kenya have been closely connected with politics, encouraging nationalism and revealing inequities. Events occurring at the Kamriitha Community Educational and Cultural Center illustrate this statement. The center was built by community efforts in Kamriithu, a Kenyan town of 10,000 people. The villagers developed a program at the center and operated it. The literacy committee organized a literacy study course, and the community organized dramas that illustrated the people's experiences and ideas. Ngugi wa Thiong'o was commissioned to write the first play—about the townspeople's own lives—and they discussed and criticized it as well as performed it in a theater that the town had built. The production was highly successful, but was banned, because the authorities felt it encouraged class conflict. Its potential for organizing peasants was a threat to the government. Ngugi was detained (he is now in exile). Later the center was closed and the theater destroyed.

Education
Adult Literacy Rate: 60%

COMMUNICATION

Telephones: 260,000
Newspapers: 4

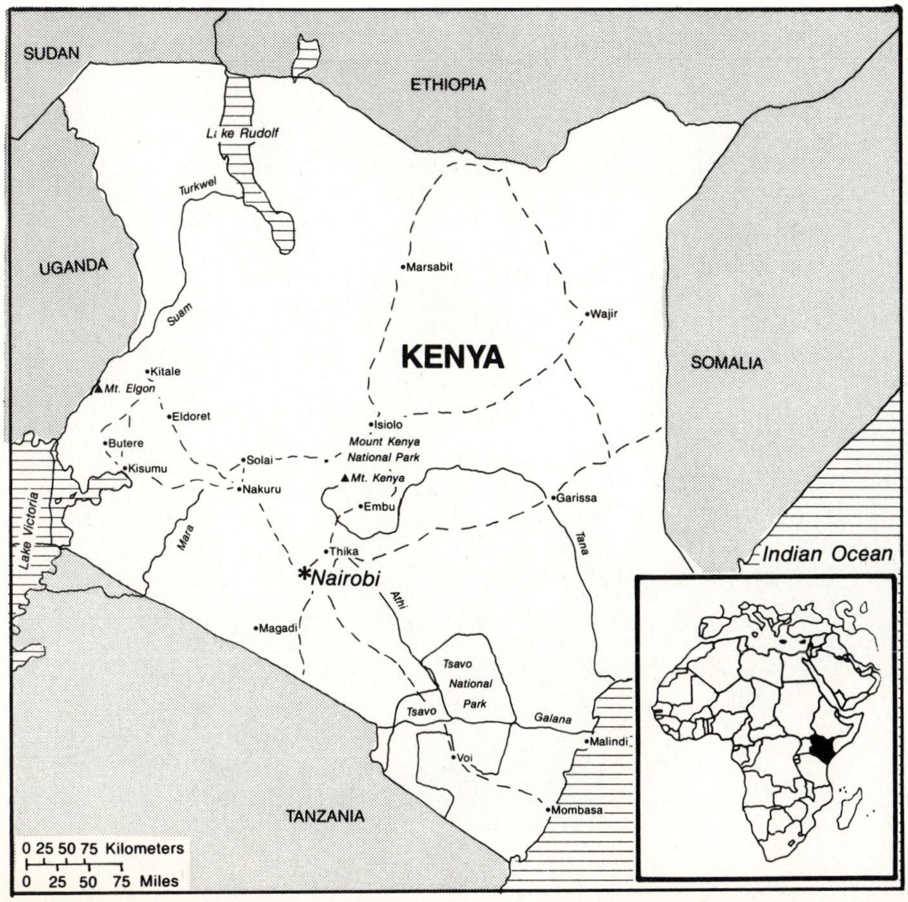

TRANSPORTATION

Highways—Kilometers (Miles): 64,590 (40,046)
Railroads—Kilometers (Miles): 2,040 (1,265)
Commercial Airports: 2 international

GOVERNMENT
Type: republic; one-party state
Independence Date: December 12, 1963
Head of State: President Daniel arap Moi
Political Parties: Kenya African National Union
Suffrage: universal over 21

MILITARY
Number of Armed Forces: 23,000
Military Expenditures (% of Central Government Expenditures): 1%
Current Hostilities: border conflict with Uganda

ECONOMY
Currency ($ U.S. Equivalent): 21.7 Kenya shillings = $1
Per Capita Income/GNP: $360/$8.5 billion
Inflation Rate: 8.3%
Natural Resources: wildlife; land; soda ash; wattle
Agriculture: corn; wheat; rice; sugarcane; coffee; tea; sisal; pyrethrum; livestock
Industry: petroleum products; cement; beer; automobile assembly; food processing; tourism

FOREIGN TRADE
Exports: $1.0 billion
Imports: $1.8 billion

KENYA

A few months before his assassination in 1969, Tom Mboya, Kenya's Minister of Economic Development and Planning, wrote the following in a *New York Times* essay:

> We suffered during our struggle for independence, but in many ways it was a simpler period than today. The present period is less dramatic. Nationalist sentiment must remain powerful, but it can no longer be sustained by slogans and the excitement of independence. Rather, it must itself sustain the population during the long process of development. For development will not come immediately. It is a process that requires time, planning, sacrifice, and work.

Mboya's words are still relevant more than 2 decades later. Despite its deep historic roots and postindependence economic growth, Kenya is still a state struggling to develop as a nation.

HISTORY

In the precolonial past the African communities of Kenya belonged to relatively small-scale, but economically interlinked, societies. Predominately pastoral groups, such as the Maasai, exchanged cattle for the crops of farming communities of the Kikuyu, Kamba, and others. Organized Swahili city-states developed on the coast. In the nineteenth century caravans of Swahili and Arab traders stimulated economic and political changes. However, the outsiders who had the greatest impact on the Kenyan interior were European settlers, who began to arrive in the first decade of the twentieth century.

By the 1930s much of the temperate hill country around Nairobi, Kenya's capital city, had become the "White Highlands." More than 6 million acres of land—Maasai pasture and Kikuyu and Kamba farms—were stolen. African communities were often removed to increasingly overcrowded reserves. Laborers, mostly Kikuyu migrants from the reserves, worked for the new European owners, sometimes on lands that they had once farmed for themselves.

By the 1950s African grievances had been heightened by increased European settlement and the growing removal of African "squatters" from European estates. There were also growing class and ideological differences among Africans, which led to tensions between educated Christians with middle-class aspirations and displaced members of the rural underclass. Many members of the latter group, in particular, began to mobilize themselves in largely Kikuyu oathing societies, which coalesced into the Mau Mau movement.

Armed resistance by Mau Mau guerrillas began in 1951 with isolated attacks on settlers. In response, the British proclaimed a state of emergency, which lasted for 10 years. Without any outside support, the Mau Mau held out for years by making effective use of the highland forests as sanctuaries. Nonetheless, by 1955 the uprising had largely been crushed. Although at the time the name "Mau Mau" became for many Americans, through sensational press reports, synonymous with antiwhite terrorism, only 32 European civilians actually lost their lives during the rebellion. By contrast, at least 13,000 Kikuyu were killed. Another 80,000 Africans were detained by the colonial authorities, and more than 1 million persons were resettled in controlled villages. While the Mau Mau were overwhelmed by often ruthless counterinsurgency measures, they achieved an im-

(UN photo by Nagata)

Historically Kenya was predominated by pastoral groups, and this Maasai tribesman is a member of that substantial portion of the population.

portant victory: the British realized that the preservation of Kenya as a white-settler-dominated colony was militarily and politically untenable.

In the aftermath of the emergency, the person who emerged as the leader of Kenya's nationalist movement was Jomo Kenyatta, who had been detained and accused by the British—without any evidence—of leading the resistance movement. Kenyatta, a charismatic leader, became prime minister and later president after Kenya gained independence in 1963. He continued to lead the country until his death in 1978.

The situation in Kenya looked promising during the early years of Kenyatta's leadership. His government encouraged racial harmony, and the slogan "Harambee" (Swahili for "Pull Together") became a call for people of all ethnic groups and races to work together for development. Land reforms provided plots to $1^1/_2$ million farmers. A policy of Africanization created business opportunities for Kenyan entrepreneurs, and industry grew. Although the ruling Kenya African National Union (KANU) was supposedly guided by a policy of "African Socialism," Kenya was seen by many as a showcase of capitalist development.

POLITICAL DEVELOPMENT

Under Kenyatta, Kenya became a de facto one-party state. The principal opposition party, the Kenya People's Union (KPU), was ultimately suppressed and its leadership harassed and jailed. KANU became the focus of political competition. But politics was marred by political violence, including the assassinations of prominent critics within government, most notably Mboya and, in 1975, then Foreign Affairs Minister J. M. Kariuki. Constraints on freedom of association were justified in the interest of preventing ethnic conflict—much of the KPU support came from the Luo group. However, ethnicity has been important in shaping intraparty struggles within KANU.

Under Daniel arap Moi, Kenyatta's successor, the political climate has grown steadily more repressive. In 1982 his government was badly shaken by an attempted military coup. It did not succeed, but there was much violence in Nairobi. About 250 persons died; approximately 1,500 were detained. The air force was disbanded and the university, whose students came out in support of the coup participants, was temporarily closed.

In the aftermath of the coup attempt all parties other than KANU were formally outlawed. Moi followed up this step by declaring, in 1986, that KANU was above the government, the Parliament, and the judiciary. Press restrictions, detentions, and blatant acts of intimidation, including public death threats toward sitting parliamentary members (MPs), have since become common. Those MPs brave enough to be critical of Moi's imperial presidency are removed from KANU and thus the Parliament. Political tensions are blamed on local agents of an ever-growing list of outside forces, including Christian missionaries and Muslim fundamentalists, foreign academics and the news media, and Libya and the United States.

A number of underground opposition

(United Nations photo by Y. Nagata)

Since its independence Kenya has experienced an encouraging level of economic growth. Today it is the most industrialized country in Eastern Africa, and manufacturing is becoming an important factor in the well-being of the country.

The British East African Protectorate is proclaimed
1895

British colonists begin to settle in the Highlands area
1900–1910

Mau Mau, a predominately Kikuyu movement, resists colonial rule
1952

Kenya gains independence under the leadership of Jomo Kenyatta
1963

Tom Mboya, a leading trade unionist and government minister, is assassinated
1969

Daniel arap Moi becomes president upon the death of Kenyatta
1978

1980s–1990s

A coup by members of the Kenyan Air Force is crushed; political repression increases

Dissident activity by the Mwakenya movement; there are reports of a Mau Mau revival

Prodemocracy agitation leads to serious unrest

groups have emerged since 1982. Particularly prominent in the mid-1980s was the socialist-oriented Mwakenya movement, whose ranks include such prominent exiles as the writer Ngugi wa Thiong'o. In 1987 Mwakenya merged with a number of other dissident groups to form the United Movement for Democracy, or UMOJA (Swahili for "unity"). The early months of 1990 witnessed an upsurge in antigovernment unrest. In February the suspicious murder of Foreign Minister Robert Ouko touched off rioting in Nairobi and his home city of Kisumu. Another riot occurred when squatters were forcibly evicted from the Nairobi shantytown of Muoroto. Growing calls for the restoration of multiparty democracy led to further unrest. The detention in July of two ex-Cabinet ministers, Kenneth Matiba and Charles Rubia, for their part in the democracy agitation, sparked nationwide rioting, which left at least 28 people dead and 1,000 arrested.

As with earlier KANU-KPU conflicts, the current polarization of Kenyan politics has ethnic dimensions. The presence of members of Moi's own Kalenjin community in the upper echelons of the security establishment has become pervasive. At the same time, many who have been demoted or purged by Moi, as well as those active in dissident circles, are Kikuyu, who were favored under Kenyatta. However, class as well as ethnicity continue to be an important factor; the top 10 percent of the population owns an estimated 40 percent of the wealth, while the bottom 30 percent own 10 percent. The failure of the Kenyan economy to stem the growth of poverty among the latter group has given rise to social tension. In addition, Kenya's relatively large middle class has grown resentful of increased repression and the evident corruption at the very top.

ECONOMIC DEVELOPMENT

Although its rate of growth declined during much of the 1980s, the Kenyan economy has consistently expanded since independence. Kenya is the most industrialized country of East Africa. Manufacturing, which accounts for 13 percent of the gross domestic product, is mostly concentrated in import substitution and the processing of domestic products. Foreign capital has played an important role in industrial development, but the largest share of investment has come from the government and the local private sector. The government has recognized the need to move toward more export-oriented industries, but global competition and the economic balkanization of the potential African market are major constraints.

The bulk of Kenya's foreign-exchange earnings have come from agriculture. A wide variety of cash crops are exported, including coffee, cotton, horticulture, pyrethrum, sisal, sugar, tobacco, and tea. This diversity has buffered the nation's economy to some degree from the uncertainties associated with single-commodity dependence. While large plantations, now often owned by wealthy Kenyans, have survived from the colonial era, much of the commercial production is carried out by smallholders.

Tourism accounts for about 20 percent of Kenya's foreign-exchange earnings, but its immediate prospects for major growth are not good. The sector has suffered from a combination of increased competition by other African countries, widely publicized attacks on visitors, political unrest, the AIDS epidemic, and a declining wildlife population.

While external problems associated with Kenya's vulnerability to global-market forces and internal tensions arising out of its pattern of wealth distribution are both critical concerns, perhaps the greatest danger to the nation's well-being is its rapidly expanding population. Kenya has the highest population growth rate in Africa, in excess of 4 percent per year. More than half of its population are under age 14. Good arable conditions prevail in only about 20 percent of Kenya. As a consequence, pressure on the land is enormous and is aggravated by the existence of large estates. The prospects of creating nonagricultural employment for the burgeoning workforce, even in the context of an "economic miracle," are not very promising. This creates a potentially vicious circle, for the experience of other societies indicates that the population will continue to climb rapidly until the standard of living for most Kenyans substantially improves. In the meantime, ethnic competition as well as the opposition by certain religious groups greatly complicate official population-control measures.

DEVELOPMENT

To counteract stagnating tourist revenues, the Kenyan government has placed itself at the forefront of the movement to ban ivory trading. Besides reducing the elephant population, poachers in Kenya have threatened tourist traffic by creating lawless conditions in their areas of operation.

FREEDOM

Kenya under Daniel arap Moi has retained something of the form but little of the substance of a democracy. With the press heavily censored, many Kenyans have turned to anonymous music cassettes for news and opinions.

HEALTH/WELFARE

Individual Kenyan communities have raised considerable amounts of money for self-help projects; politicians compete in pledging large amounts for the building of schools, clinics, and other developments. Other members of the community contribute what they can afford, and local citizens provide free labor for construction and maintenance.

ACHIEVEMENTS

Kenya annually devotes about half of its government expenditures to education. Most Kenyan students can now expect 12 years of schooling. Tertiary education is also expanding.

Madagascar (Democratic Republic of Madagascar)

GEOGRAPHY

Area in Square Kilometers (Miles): 587,041 (226,658) (slightly smaller than Texas)
Capital (Population): Antananarivo (650,000)
Climate: tropical and moderate

PEOPLE

Population

Total: 11,800,000
Annual Growth Rate: 3.2%
Rural/Urban Population Ratio: 78/22
Languages: official: Malagasy; others spoken: French, others

Health

Life Expectancy at Birth: 50 years (male); 54 years (female)
Infant Death Rate (Ratio): 97/1,000
Average Caloric Intake: 111% of FAO minimum
Physicians Available (Ratio): 1/12,553

Religion(s)

52% traditional indigenous; 41% Christian; 7% Muslim

Education

Adult Literacy Rate: 67%

MALAGASY POETS

What invisible rat
comes from the walls of night
gnaws at the milky cake of the moon?

Thus begins one of the poems of Jean-Joseph Rabearivelo (1901–1937), one of Madagascar's greatest twentieth-century poets. Like the poets who followed him, such as Jean Jacques Rebemananjara and Jacques Flavien Ranaivo, Rabearivelo wrote in French and was deeply affected by French poets, literature, and culture. Yet all of these poets were attached to local Malagasy forms and rhythms and were inspired by the *hainteny* form, which was so characteristic of the popular songs of the island. Several of the poems of Rabearivelo and Rananivo are reprinted in *A Book of African Verse*, edited by J. Reed and C. Wake (London, 1964).

COMMUNICATION

Telephones: 38,200
Newspapers: 7

TRANSPORTATION

Highways—Kilometers (Miles): 40,000 (24,800)
Railroads—Kilometers (Miles): 1,020 (632)
Commercial Airports: 3 international

GOVERNMENT

Type: republic; authority held by Supreme Revolutionary Council
Independence Date: June 26, 1960
Head of State: President (Colonel) Didier Ratsiraka
Political Parties: Advance Guard of Malagasy Revolution; Congress Party for Malagasy Independence; Movement for National Unity; Malagasy Christian Democratic Union; Militants for the Establishment of a Proletarian Regime; National Movement for Independence of Madagascar
Suffrage: universal over 18

MILITARY

Number of Armed Forces: 28,500
Military Expenditures (% of Central Government Expenditures): 2.2%
Current Hostilities: none

ECONOMY

Currency ($ U.S. Equivalent): 1,531 Malagasy francs = $1
Per Capita Income/GNP: $155/$1.7 billion
Inflation Rate: 17%
Natural Resources: graphite; chrome; coal; bauxite; ilmenite; tar sands; semiprecious stones; timber; mica; nickel
Agriculture: rice; livestock; coffee; vanilla; sugar; cloves; cotton; sisal; peanuts; tobacco
Industry: food processing; textiles; mining; paper; petroleum refining; automobile assembly; construction; cement; farming

FOREIGN TRADE

Exports: $284 million
Imports: $319 million

MADAGASCAR

Madagascar has been called "the smallest continent"; indeed, many geologists believe that it once did form the core of a larger landmass whose other principal remnants are the Indian subcontinent and Australia. In other ways, the world's fourth-largest island remains a world unto itself. Botanists and zoologists know it as the home of flora and fauna not found elsewhere. The island's culture is also distinctive. The Malagasy language, which with dialectical variations is spoken throughout the island, is related to the Malay tongues of Indonesia. But despite their geographic separation and Asiatic roots, the Malagasy are conscious of their African identity.

While the early history of Madagascar is the subject of much scholarly debate, it is clear that by the year A.D. 500 the island had begun to be settled by Malay-speaking peoples, who may have migrated via the East African coast rather than directly from Indonesia. The cultural imprint of Southeast Asia is evident in such things as local architecture, music, cosmology, and agricultural practices. African influences are equally apparent. During the precolonial period the peoples of Madagascar were in communication with communities on the mainland. Waves of migration across the Mozambique Channel contributed to the island's modern ethnic diversity.

THE MERINA KINGDOM

During the early nineteenth century most of Madagascar was united by the rulers of Merina. In seeking to build up their realm and preserve its independence, the kings and queens of Merina welcomed European, mostly English, missionaries who helped introduce new ideas and technologies. As a result, many Malagasy, including the royalty, adopted Christianity. The kingdom had established diplomatic relations with the United States and various European powers and was thus a recognized member of the international community. Internally, foreign businesspeople were attracted to invest in the island's growing economy, while the rapid spread of schools and medical services, increasingly staffed by Malagasy, brought profound changes to the society.

The Merina court hoped that their "Christian civilization" and modernizing army would deter European aggression. However, the French were determined to establish a protectorate over the island. An 1884–1885 Franco-Malagasy War ended in a stalemate, but an 1895 French invasion led to the kingdom's destruction. It was not an easy conquest. The Malagasy Army, with its artillery and modern fortifications, held out for many months, but eventually it was outgunned by the invaders. French sovereignty was proclaimed in 1896, but "pacification" campaigns continued for another decade.

French rule reduced what had been a prospering state into a colonial backwater. The pace of development slowed as the local economy was restructured to serve the interests of French settlers, whose numbers had swelled to 60,000 by the time of World War II. Probably the most important French contribution to Madagascar was the encouragement their misrule gave to the growth of local nationalism.

(United Nations photo by L. Rajaonina)

Madagascar has a unique ethnic diversity influenced by migrations from the African mainland and many countries of Southeast Asia. The varied cultural makeup of the population can be easily seen on the faces of these school children.

Merina rulers gain sovereignty over other peoples of the island
1828

The French complete the conquest of the island
1904

A revolt is suppressed by the French, with great loss of life
1947–1948

Independence from France is achieved without armed struggle; Philbert Tsiranana becomes the first president
1960

A coup leads to the fall of the First Malagasy Republic
1972

Didier Ratsiraka becomes president by military appointment
1975

1980s–1990s

The government begins to reverse its socialist policies

Dissidents organized as Kung Fu societies engage in violent clashes with AREMA

Elections in 1989–1990 seem to confirm the commitment to multiparty democracy

By the 1940s a strong sense of Malagasy identity had been forged, through common hatred of the colonialists.

The local overthrow of Vichy power by the British in 1943 created an opening for Malagasy nationalists to organize themselves into mass parties, the most prominent of which was the Malagasy Movement for Democratic Renewal (MRDM). In 1946 the MRDM elected two overseas deputies to the French National Assembly on the basis of its call for immediate independence. Paris responded by instructing its administrators to "fight the MRDM by every means." Arrests led to resistance.

In March 1947 a general insurrection began. Peasant rebels using whatever weapons they could find liberated large areas from French control. French troops countered by destroying crops and blockading rebel areas in an effort to starve the insurrectionists into surrendering. Thousands of Malagasy were massacred. By the end of the year the rebellion had been largely crushed, although a state of siege was maintained until 1956. No one knows for sure how many Malagasy lost their lives in the uprising, but contemporary estimates ranged from 80,000 to 90,000.

INDEPENDENCE AND REVOLUTION

Madagascar gained its independence in 1960. However, many viewed the new government, led by Philibert Tsiranana of the Social Democratic Party (PSD), as a vehicle for continuing French influence; memories of 1947 were still strong. Lack of economic and social reform led to a peasant uprising in 1971. The Maoist-inspired rebellion was suppressed, but the government was left weakened. In 1972 new unrest, this time spearheaded by students and workers in the towns, led to Tsiranana's overthrow by the military. After a period of confusion, radical forces consolidated power around the figure of then Lieutenant Commander Didier Ratsiraka, who in 1975 assumed the presidency.

Under Ratsiraka, a new Constitution was adopted that allowed for a controlled process of multiparty competition in which all parties were grouped within the National Front. Within this framework, the largest party has remained Ratsiraka's Vanguard of the Malagasy Revolution (AREMA). Initially, all parties were expected to support the president's Charter of the Malagasy Revolution, which called for a Marxist-oriented socialist transformation.

In accordance with the charter, foreign-owned banks and financial institutions were nationalized. A series of state enterprises were also established to promote industrial development, but few of them proved viable.

Although 80 percent of the Malagasy were employed in agriculture, rural investment was modest. The government attempted to work through *fokonolas,* indigenous village-managed bodies. State farms and collectives were also established on land expropriated from French settlers. While these efforts led to some improvements, such as increased mechanization, state marketing monopolies and planning constraints contributed to shortfalls. Efforts to keep consumer prices low were blamed for a drop in rice production, the Malagasy staple, while cash-crop production, primarily coffee, vanilla, and cloves, suffered from falling world prices.

As in many other parts of Africa, the 1980s were for Madagascar a period of economic difficulty. Food shortages sparked rioting. Some critics blamed the government for not going far enough in promoting revolutionary change. However, Ratsiraka's administration, with varying degrees of support from the factions grouped within it, has gradually embraced economic liberalization.

It is too early to judge the success of recent shifts in economic policy, but the moves have gained domestic political approval. A period of increased political restriction culminated in 1985 in an unsuccessful attempt by the president to establish a one-party state. Since then politics has become increasingly open. There was general acceptance of the legitimacy of 1989–1990 elections, in which AREMA triumphed over a fractured opposition. The two largest opposition parties, the once-Marxist MFM, which emerged from the 1972 unrest, and Vonjy, which was formed by supporters of the late Tsiranana, both favor liberalization. In February 1990 most remaining restrictions on freedom of association were dropped, a move that has led to the open revival of the PSD.

DEVELOPMENT

In 1989 Export Processing Zones were established in order to attract foreign investment through tax and currency incentives. The government especially hopes to attract business from neighboring Mauritius, whose success with such zones has led to labor shortages and a shift toward more value-added production.

FREEDOM

After a period of repression against its critics of both the left and right, the government has lifted most legal restrictions. Power remains concentrated in the hands of Didier Ratsiraka and the Supreme Revolutionary Council.

HEALTH/WELFARE

Primary-school enrollment is now universal. Thirty-six percent of the appropriate age group attend secondary school, while 5% ages 20–24 are in tertiary institutions. Malaria remains a major health challenge.

ACHIEVEMENTS

A new wildlife preserve will allow the unique animals of Madagascar to survive and develop. Sixty-six species of land animals are found nowhere else on earth, including the aye-aye, a nocturnal lemur which has bat ears, beaver teeth, and an elongated clawed finger, all of which serve the aye-aye in finding food.

Mauritius

GEOGRAPHY

Area in Square Kilometers (Miles): 1,865 (720) (about the size of Rhode Island)
Capital (Population): Port Louis (155,000)
Climate: subtropical; marine

PEOPLE

Population
Total: 1,070,000
Annual Growth Rate: 1.8%
Rural/Urban Population Ratio: 59/41
Languages: official: English and French; others spoken: Creole, Hindi, Urdu

Health
Life Expectancy at Birth: 66 years (male); 73 years (female)
Infant Death Rate (Ratio): 20/1,000
Average Caloric Intake: 122% of FAO minimum
Physicians Available (Ratio): 1/1,408

Religion(s)
51% Hindu; 30% Chrisitan; 16% Muslim; 3% other

DIEGO GARCIA

On the eve of the nation's independence, secret negotiations between British and Mauritian representatives resulted in Mauritius's sale of the island of Diego Garcia and neighboring atolls to the British for the small sum of $7 million. The inhabitants of Diego Garcia were completely ignored; moreover, they were subsequently moved to Mauritius in order to make room for a U.S. military base (which increased the militarization of the Indian Ocean). The people of Mauritius, through their government, have demanded the island's return. The United Kingdom and the United States have offered more money to former inhabitants of the island and have agreed to their eventual return in an unspecified, but distant, future. The first National Congress of the ruling Socialist Militant Movement in 1986 called for the restoration of Mauritian sovereignty over Diego Garcia, "currently occupied by the American Army." Mauritian claims enjoy widespread support from the international community, but the issue remains unresolved.

Education
Adult Literacy Rate: 83%

COMMUNICATION

Telephones: 48,460
Newspapers: 7

TRANSPORTATION

Highways—Kilometers (Miles): 1,801 (1,116)
Railroads—Kilometers (Miles): none
Commercial Airports: 1 international

GOVERNMENT

Type: independent state; recognizes the British monarch as chief of state
Independence Date: March 12, 1968
Head of State: Prime Minister Aneerood Jugnauth; President Veerasamy Ringadoo
Political Parties: Mauritian Labor Party; Mauritian Militant Movement; Mauritian Socialist Party; others
Suffrage: universal over 18

MILITARY

Number of Armed Forces: no standing defense force
Military Expenditures (% of Central Government Expenditures): n/a
Current Hostilities: none

ECONOMY

Currency ($ U.S. Equivalent): 15.0 rupees = $1
Per Capita Income/GNP: $1,910/$1.9 billion
Inflation Rate: 9.2%
Natural Resources: agricultural land
Agriculture: sugar; tea; tobacco
Industry: sugar production; consumer goods; labor-intensive goods for export; tourism

FOREIGN TRADE

Exports: $1.0 billion
Imports: $1.3 billion

The Dutch claim, but abandon, Mauritius
1600s

French settlers and slaves arrive
1722

The Treaty of Paris formally cedes Mauritius to the British
1814

Slavery is abolished; South Asians arrive
1835

Rioting on sugar estates shakes the political control of the Franco-Mauritian elite
1937

An expanded franchise allows greater democracy
1948

Independence
1968

Labor unrest leads to the detention of MMM leaders
1971

A cyclone destroys homes as well as much of the sugar crop
1979

1980s–1990s

A Socialist-led coalition government is formed; Libyan diplomats are expelled

Social Democratic Party leader Gaetan Duval is charged with conspiracy to murder; Duval claims political harassment

Mauritius and Madagascar sign trade and investment agreements

A DIVERSE SOCIETY

Although it was not permanently settled until 1722, Mauritius is today the home of more than a million people of South Asian, Euro-African, Chinese, and other origins. Out of this human diversity has emerged a society that in recent decades has become a model of democratic stability, economic growth, and ethnic, racial, and sectarian tolerance.

Mauritius was first settled by the French, some of whom achieved great wealth by setting up sugar plantations. The plantations prospered through their exploitation of slave labor imported from the African mainland. Over time the European and African communities merged into a common Creole culture, whose membership currently accounts for one-quarter of the Mauritian population. A small number also claim pure French descent; for decades members of this group have formed an economic and social elite. More than half of the sugar acreage remains the property of 21 large Franco-Mauritian plantations, while the rest is divided between nearly 28,000 small landholdings. French cultural influence remains strong.

In 1810 Mauritius was occupied by the British, who ruled the island until 1968. When the British abolished slavery, in 1835, the plantation owners turned to large-scale use of indentured labor from what was then British India. Today nearly two-thirds of the population are of South Asian descent.

POLITICS

Although the majority of Mauritians gained suffrage only after World War II, the island has maintained an uninterrupted record of parliamentary rule since 1886. Ethnic divisions, as reflected in voting patterns, have long been important in shaping political allegiance. However, ethnic constituency-building has not led, in recent years, to communal polarization. Other factors—such as class, ideology, and opportunism—have also been influential. All postindependence governments have been coalitions with multiethnic representation.

The current Socialist prime minister, Aneerood Jugnauth, once served as a member of the Marxist-oriented Mauritian Militant Movement (MMM). Although electoral victories by the MMM in 1985 and scandals within the Socialist coalition threatened Jugnauth's government, it won a majority in the last general election, held in 1987.

ECONOMIC DEVELOPMENT

Until the 1970s the Mauritian economy remained almost entirely dependent on sugar. Sugar now ranks below textiles in its contribution to export earnings and gross domestic product. A third major pillar of the economy is tourism.

The transformation of Mauritius over the past 2 decades from mono-crop dependency into a fledgling industrial state with a strong service sector has made it one of the major economic success stories of the developing world. Mauritian growth has been built on a foundation of export-oriented manufacturing. At the core of the Mauritian take-off is its island-wide Export Processing Zone (EPZ), which has attracted industrial investment through a combination of low wages, tax breaks, and other financial incentives. The Mauritian boom has occurred in the context of continued adherence to its liberal-democratic tradition of governance. The constitutional rights of the citizenry have been upheld. This has notably included a respect for the right of workers to organize and bargain collectively. The Mauritian labor movement is one of the strongest in Africa.

The success of the Mauritian economy is relative. Mauritius is still considered a middle-income country. In reality, there are, as with most developing societies, great disparities in the distribution of wealth. Nonetheless, quality-of-life indicators, such as the United Nations' human-development index, confirm a rising standard of living for the population as a whole. While great progress has been made toward eliminating poverty and disease, concern has also grown about the environmental capacity of the small, crowded island to sustain its current rate of development. There is also a general recognition that Mauritian prosperity is, and will for the foreseeable future remain, extremely vulnerable to global-market forces.

DEVELOPMENT

The success of the Mauritian EPZ along with the export-led growth of various Asian economies have encouraged a growing number of other African countries, such as Botswana, Cape Verde, and Madagascar, to launch their own export zones.

FREEDOM

Political pluralism and human rights are respected on Mauritius. The nation has more than 30 political parties, of which about a half-dozen are important at any given time.

HEALTH/WELFARE

Medical and most educational expenses are free. Food prices are heavily subsidized. Rising government deficits, however, threaten future social spending.

ACHIEVEMENTS

Perhaps Mauritius's most important modern achievement has been its successful efforts to reduce its birth rate. This has been brought about by government-backed family planning as well as by increased economic opportunities for women.

Rwanda (Republic of Rwanda)

GEOGRAPHY

Area in Square Kilometers (Miles): 26,338 (10,169) (about the size of Maryland)
Capital (Population): Kigali (300,000)
Climate: temperate

PEOPLE

Population

Total: 7,609,000
Annual Growth Rate: 3.8%
Rural/Urban Population Ratio: 95/5
Languages: official: French; Kinyarwanda; other spoken: Kiswahili

Health

Life Expectancy at Birth: 50 years (male); 54 years (female)
Infant Death Rate (Ratio): 113/1,000
Average Caloric Intake: 94% of FAO minimum
Physicians Available (Ratio): 1/42,989

Religion(s)

65% Roman Catholic; 25% traditional indigenous; 9% Protestant; 1% Muslim

Education

Adult Literacy Rate: 47%

RWANDA'S HISTORIANS

A number of specialists were attached to the ruling dynasty of the traditional kingdom of Rwanda, including several categories of official historians. Each group was responsible for preserving particular materials. Some were genealogists who told the lists of kings and queens; some told *ibisigo*, dynastic poems that glorified the rulers; and others preserved secrets of the dynasty. This traditional knowledge was all passed down orally, since the language was not written. Particular families were responsible for passing this knowledge from one generation to another; it was memorized exactly. Such historical information is different from the written sources upon which Western historians have relied, but it is valid data that can be used in the reconstruction of Rwanda's past.

COMMUNICATION

Telephones: 6,600
Newspapers: 1

TRANSPORTATION

Highways—Kilometers (Miles): 4,885 (3,069)
Railroads—Kilometers (Miles): none
Commercial Airports: 1 international

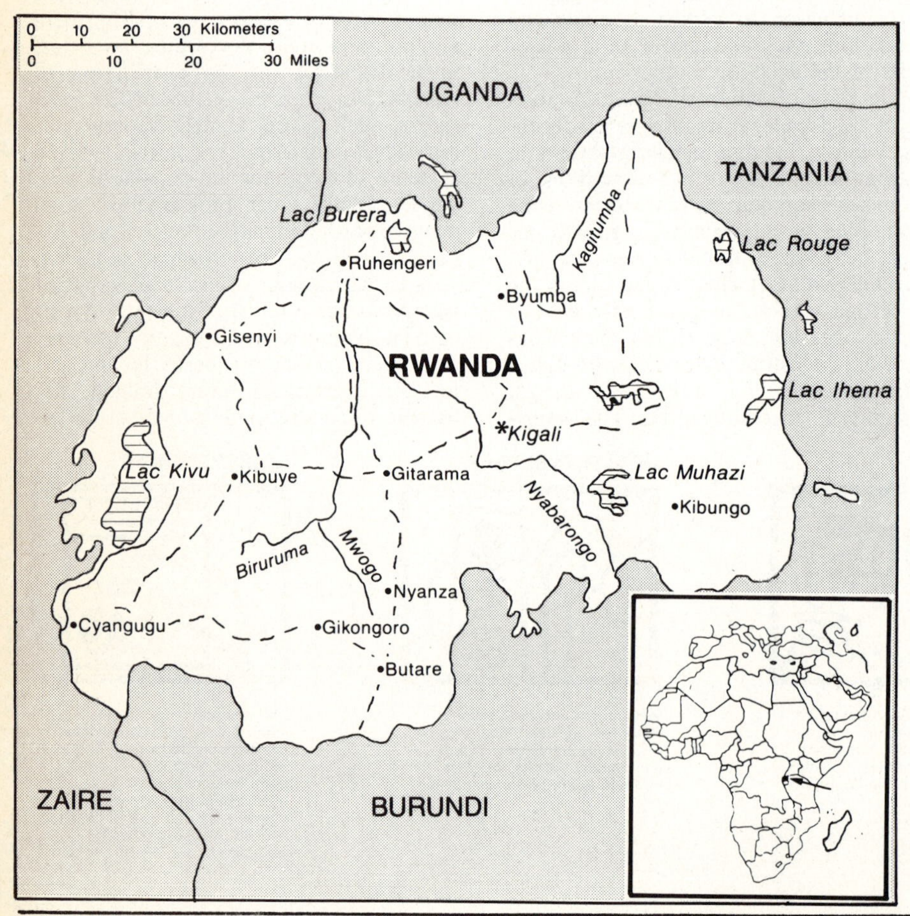

GOVERNMENT

Type: republic
Independence Date: July 1, 1962
Head of State: President (Major General) Juvenal Habyarimana
Political Parties: National Revolutionary Movement for Development
Suffrage: universal for adults

MILITARY

Number of Armed Forces: 5,200
Military Expenditures (% of Central Government Expenditures): 2.1%
Current Hostilities: none

ECONOMY

Currency ($ U.S. Equivalent): 78 Rwanda francs = $1
Per Capita Income/GNP: $325/$2.3 billion
Inflation Rate: 3%
Natural Resources: tungsten; tin; cassiterite
Agriculture: coffee; tea; pyrethrum; beans; potatoes
Industry: food processing; mining; light consumer goods

FOREIGN TRADE

Exports: $118 million
Imports: $278 million

Mwami Kigeri Rwabugiri expands and consolidates the kingdom **1860–1895**

Belguim rules Rwanda as a mandate of the League of Nations **1916**

The Hutu rebellion **1959**

Rwanda becomes independent; Gregoire Kayibana is president **1962**

Juvenal Habyarimana seizes power **1973**

The National Revolutionary Movement for Development is formed **1975**

A new Constitution is approved in a nationwide referendum; Habyarimana is reelected president **1978**

1980s–1990s

Unsuccessful coup attempt

Election for 50 members of Parliament and for president; Habyarimana is the sole presidential candidate

Refugees from Burundi mass along the border

RWANDA

In the beginning, according to a dynastic poem of Rwanda, the godlike ruler, Kigwa, fashioned a test by which to choose his successor. He gave each of his sons a bowl of milk to guard during the night. His son Gatwa drank his milk. Yahutu slept and spilled the milk. Only Gatutsi guarded it well.

The myth reflects a reality that Rwandans (or Banyarwanda, as the inhabitants are sometimes called) have adhered to throughout their history; the Twa, commonly stereotyped as "pygmies" (1 percent of the population), have been the outcasts; the Hutu (89 percent) have been the servants; and the Tutsi (10 percent) have been the aristocrats. Hutu and Tutsi were linked through cattle contracts, by which Hutu serfs were given users' rights to cattle and "protection" from their Tutsi masters, who, in turn, were entitled to receive various services. There were many other ties between these groups, whose members are still evenly distributed throughout the country. All of the people were subjects of the *Mwami*, or king, who headed a royal family that had a special status in Rwanda.

RADICAL CHANGES

This feudal society no longer exists in its historical form—and the changes have been revolutionary. During the colonial era, when first the Germans and later the Belgians ruled through few administrators, primarily using the existing political system, traditional caste distinctions and royal prerogatives were maintained. New ideas and practices were introduced through Roman Catholic missions and schools and through the encouragement of growing cash crops, especially coffee. Discontent was evident even before the colonial era, due to the pressure of people and herds on already crowded lands.

The most radical developments occurred in the late 1950s and the early 1960s. Gradually, in the late 1950s, because of pressure from the United Nations (UN), Belgium began to introduce political opportunities to Rwandans. In 1959, after the death of the Mwami, continued oppression by former advisors, who took power, led to bloody Hutu uprisings against the Tutsi. In 1961 Hutu leaders and the Hutu majority party, Parmehutu (the Hutu Emancipation Movement), gained support, won victories at the polls, and became the governors of Rwanda. The uprisings and later Tutsi attacks and Hutu reactions in 1963–1964 caused thousands of deaths and the flight of tens of thousands to neighboring countries.

HABYARIMANA TAKES POWER

Major General Juvenal Habyarimana, a Hutu from the north, took power in a coup in 1973 and initiated the National Revolutionary Movement for Development (MRND) to bring together the hostile elements in the country. Habyarimana has maintained tight control over Rwanda, although a few opportunities for popular initiative have been evident. Voters have been given a limited choice of electoral candidates; union activity is allowed within a single, officially sponsored labor federation; and some church publications are allowed to criticize the government.

Hostility between Hutu and Tutsi remains. Many Tutsi left Rwanda during the upheavals of the late 1950s and 1960s and took up residence in the neighboring countries of Burundi, Uganda, and Tanzania. They now number more than 200,000. In October of 1990 a large number of armed refugees from Uganda invaded northern Rwanda, which has since remained in a state of civil war. The extreme population pressure in Rwanda, which is Africa's most densely populated country, has been used as a justification by the government to effectively bar the return of the refugees, but the new crisis has increased international pressure for the refugees' resettlement.

Rwanda is also the host for refugees fleeing oppression or conflict in neighboring Burundi and Uganda. About 18,000 Hutu from Burundi were integrated into Rwandan society, although not given citizenship. New massacres of Hutu in 1988 caused an influx of more than 50,000 additional refugees from Burundi, overloading Rwanda's already strained economy; most returned to Burundi.

Rwanda's main export is coffee. Unlike many African coffee producers, Rwanda has benefited from the growing demand for arabica over robusta coffee beans on the world market. The country is hoping to capitalize on the publicity surrounding the American film *Gorillas in the Mist* (1988) to build up its tourist industry; the film chronicles the life of American naturalist Dian Fossey, who championed the protection of Rwanda's gorilla population.

DEVELOPMENT

With the help of the European Economic Community, Rwanda is attempting to increase the variety of crops grown for export so it may become less dependent on coffee. Tea, tobacco, and pyrethrum are among the products whose growth is being encouraged.

FREEDOM

Freedom of speech and association is restricted in Rwanda. De facto policy of discrimination against Tutsi prevails. Jehovah's Witnesses and several smaller sectarian groups are persecuted.

HEALTH/WELFARE

The government recognizes that the high rate of population growth can eat up economic gains as well as increasing already severe pressures on land. A national population office was created, and resources committed to family planning were increased. Some question the reservation of large game reserves for European hunters, when farmland is scarce.

ACHIEVEMENTS

Abbé Alexis Kagame, a Rwandan Roman Catholic churchman and scholar, has written studies of traditional Rwanda poetry and has written poetry about many of the traditions and rituals. Some of his works have been composed in Kinyarwanda, the official language of Rwanda, and translated into French. He has gained an international reputation among scholars.

Seychelles (Republic of Seychelles)

GEOGRAPHY

Area in Square Kilometers (Miles): 435 (175) (about twice the size of Washington, DC)
Capital (Population): Port Victoria (23,012)
Climate: subtropical; marine

PEOPLE

Population
Total: 68,000
Annual Growth Rate: 0.9%
Rural/Urban Population Ratio: 50/50
Languages: official: English, French; other spoken: Creole

Health
Life Expectancy at Birth: 65 years (male); 75 years (female)
Infant Death Rate (Ratio): 15/1,000
Average Caloric Intake: n/a
Physicians Available (Ratio): 1/1,847

Religion(s)
98% Christian; 2% other

Education
Adult Literacy Rate: 60%

COCO DE MER

To botanists around the world, the Seychelles has long been famous as the home of the exotic coco de mer palm. The fruit of this tree, the *coco de mer,* or "sea coconut," is both the largest and heaviest of all seeds, taking 7 years to mature and weighing between 30 to 40 pounds. For centuries these nuts, which were carried by Indian Ocean currents to distant shores, were worth more than their weight in gold. Their sensual shape, like that of a female pelvis, made them highly valued as an aphrodisiac; indeed, ancient legend held that the coco de mer was the forbidden fruit of the biblical Garden of Eden. The source of the nuts remained a mystery until 1768, when a Frenchman discovered the palms.

COMMUNICATION

Telephones: 13,000
Newspapers: 1

TRANSPORTATION

Highways—Kilometers (Miles): 259 (160)
Railroads—Kilometers (Miles): none
Commercial Airports: 1 international

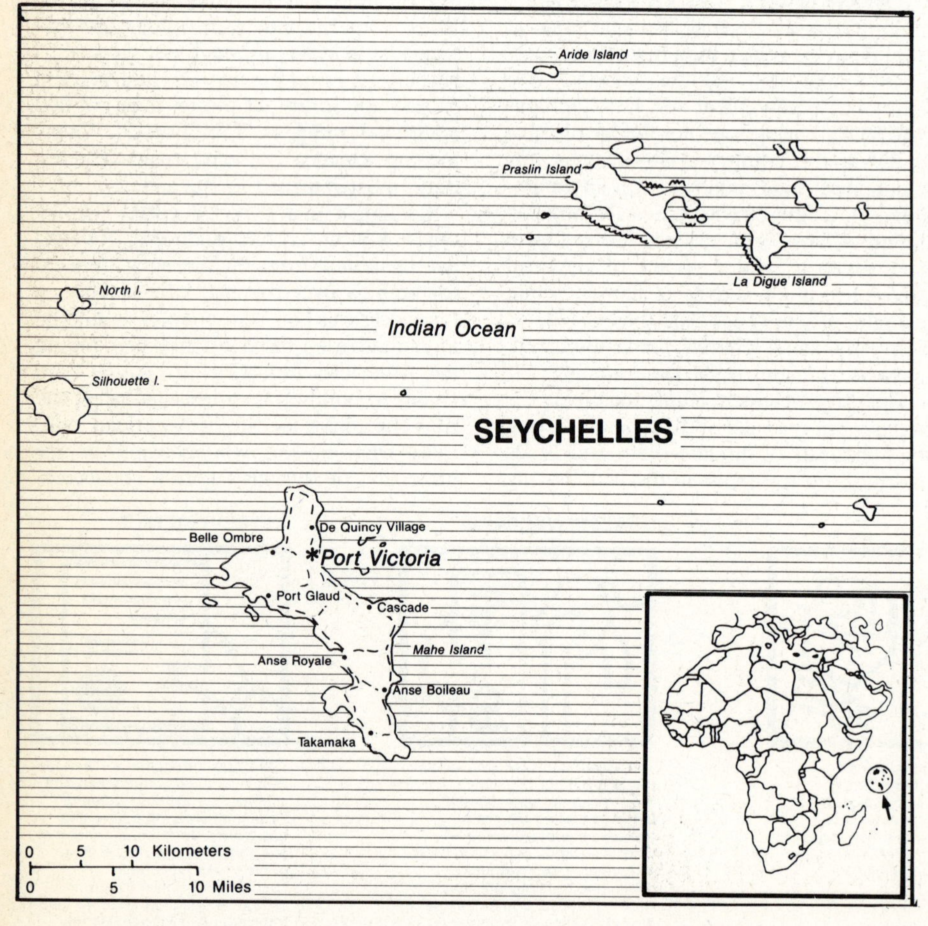

GOVERNMENT

Type: republic
Independence Date: June 29, 1976
Head of State: President France Albert René
Political Parties: Seychelles People's Progressive Front
Suffrage: universal for adults

MILITARY

Number of Armed Forces: 1,500
Military Expenditures (% of Central Government Expenditures): 6%
Current Hostilities: none

ECONOMY

Currency ($ U.S. Equivalent): 5.48 rupees = $1
Per Capita Income/GNP: $3,720/$255 million
Inflation Rate: 2.3%
Natural Resources: agricultural land; fish
Agriculture: vanilla; coconuts; cinnamon
Industry: tourism; copra and vanilla processing; coconut oil; construction

FOREIGN TRADE

Exports: $17 million
Imports: $116 million

French settlement begins 1771
British rule is established 1814
The British end slavery 1830
Seychelles is detached from Mauritius by the British and made a Crown colony 1903
Legislative Council with qualified suffrage is introduced 1948
Universal suffrage 1967
Independence 1976
Coup of Albert René against James Mancham 1977
1980s–1990s
A mercenary coup attempt fails
A 1988 Amnesty International report alleges government fabrication of drug-possession cases for political reasons
René rejects renewed calls for a multiparty system

REPUBLIC OF SEYCHELLES

The Republic of Seychelles consists of a series of widely scattered archipelagos off the coast of East Africa. Over the last 2 decades the lives of the Seychellois have been dramatically altered by rapid economic growth, political independence, and the establishment of a self-styled revolutionary socialist state. Behind this transformation has been the political rivalry of two very different, but equally controversial, leaders—James Mancham and Albert René—who together have guided their micro-state from a relatively isolated French and British colonial past into its current prosperity.

THE ROOTS OF CONFLICT

The roots of contemporary Seychellois politics and economics go back to 1963, when Mancham's Democratic Party and René's People's United Party were established. The former favored private enterprise and the retention of the British imperial connection, while the latter advocated an independent socialist state. Electoral victories in 1970 and 1974 allowed Mancham, as chief minister, to pursue his dream of turning the Seychelles into a tourist paradise and a financial and trading center. Mancham was notably successful in his promotion of tourism, which, following the opening of an international airport on the main island of Mahe in 1971, fueled an economic boom. Between 1970 and 1980 per capita income rose, from about $150 to $1,700. At the same time, however, Mancham gained a reputation in many quarters as a freewheeling jetsetter who was indifferent to government detail.

In 1974 Mancham, in an about-face, joined René in advocating the islands' independence. The following year the Democratic Party set up a coalition government with the People's United Party. On June 29, 1976 the Seychelles became independent, with Mancham as president and René as prime minister.

A COUP BY RENÉ

On June 5, 1977, when Mancham was out of the country, René's supporters, with Tanzanian assistance, staged a successful coup in which several people were killed. Thereafter René assumed the presidency and suspended the Constitution. A period of rule by decree gave way in 1979, without the benefit of referendum, to a new constitutional framework in which the People's Progressive Front, successor to the People's United Party, was recognized as the nation's sole political voice.

The first years of one-party government were characterized by continued economic growth, which allowed for an impressive expansion of social welfare programs. Despite the government's efforts to diversify the economy, tourism has continued to be the predominant economic sector.

Political power since the coup has remained largely concentrated in the hands of René. The first years of his regime were marked by unrest. In 1978 the first in a series of unsuccessful countercoups took place. It was followed, several months later, by violent protests against the government's attempts to impose a compulsory National Youth Service, which would have removed the nation's 16- and 17-year-olds from their families in order to foster their sociopolitical indoctrination in accordance with the government's socialist ideals. Another major incident occurred in 1981, when a group of international mercenaries, who had the backing of authorities in Kenya and South Africa as well as exiled Seychellois, were forced to flee in a hijacked jet after an airport shootout with local security forces. Following this attempt Tanzanian troops were sent to the islands. A year later the Tanzanians were instrumental in crushing a mutiny of Seychellois soldiers, which resulted in a number of deaths and the detention of one-fifth of the local army. Since then a number of other alleged plots have been uncovered.

Despite its success in creating a model welfare state, which has undoubtedly strengthened its popular acceptance, the René regime has continued to govern in a repressive manner. Internal opposition is not tolerated, and exiled activists have been largely neutralized. In February 1990 President René reiterated his position that the Seychelles would remain a one-party state, in the face of moves toward multipartyism elsewhere in Africa and in Eastern Europe. Despite the regime's espousal of socialism as a legitimizing ideology, the government has recently loosened its grip over the local economy, while seeking to stimulate private-sector investment from overseas.

DEVELOPMENT

The government continues to pursue a flexible economic program designed to encourage healthy outside investment while promoting the growth of local government-owned companies. Some have expressed concern that foreign investors will use Seychelles to avoid sanctions against South Africa.

FREEDOM

Since the 1977 coup, press censorship, mail openings, preventive detention, forced exile, and political indoctrination of the youth have become a part of life. Disappearances of political opponents have been reported.

HEALTH/WELFARE

Under the new government, a national health program has been established; private practice has been abolished. Free-lunch programs have raised nutritional levels among the young. Education is also free up to age 14.

ACHIEVEMENTS

Under its current government, Seychelles has become a world leader in wildlife preservation. An important aspect of the nation's conservation efforts has been the designation of Aldrabra Island as an international wildlife refuge.

Somalia (Somali Democratic Republic)

GEOGRAPHY

Area in Square Kilometers (Miles): 638,000 (246,331) (slightly smaller than Texas)
Capital (Population): Mogadishu (1,000,000 est.)
Climate: arid to semi-arid

PEOPLE

Population
Total: 8,424,000
Annual Growth Rate: 0.8%
Rural/Urban Population Ratio: 75/25
Languages: official: Somali; other spoken: Arabic, Oromo, Italian, English, others

Health
Life Expectancy at Birth: 53 years (male); 54 years (female)
Infant Death Rate (Ratio): 125/1,000
Average Caloric Intake: 100% of FAO minimum
Physicians Available (Ratio): 1/26,243

Religion(s)
99% Sunni Muslim; 1% other

Education
Adult Literacy Rate: 12%

REFUGEES IN SOMALIA

Life in Somalia has been disrupted in recent decades by large influxes of refugees. Drought in 1974–1975 led to the relocation of some 150,000 nomadic people into the arable regions of the country. War in the Ogaden region during the late 1970s led to the migration of at least 700,000 Ethiopian Somalis. Although some returned to Ethiopia, drought and warfare there have led to new influxes since 1986. Today there are at least 400,000 people living in refugee camps, and the government puts the total number of displaced people at 1.2 million to 1.6 million. Warfare within Somalia has also led to a reverse flow; an estimated 300,000 have fled to the Ogaden from northern Somalia.

The refugee situation has been responsible for a massive injection of outside aid, constituting up to a third of the national budget. There have been allegations that Somali officials have inflated their refugee figures in order to divert aid to the military and black market.

COMMUNICATION

Telephones: 6,000
Newspapers: 2

TRANSPORTATION

Highways—Kilometers (Miles): 15,215 (9,433)
Railroads—Kilometers (Miles): n/a
Commercial Airports: 1 international

GOVERNMENT

Type: republic; under military regime
Independence Date: July 1, 1960
Head of State: President Ali Mahdi Mohamed (acting)
Political Parties: Somali Revolutionary Socialist Party
Suffrage: universal for adults

MILITARY

Number of Armed Forces: 65,000
Military Expenditures (% of Central Government Expenditures): n/a
Current Hostilities: border disputes with Ethiopia; conflicts with Ethiopian-backed Somali rebels

ECONOMY

Currency ($ U.S. Equivalent): 644 Somali shillings = $1
Per Capita Income/GNP: $210/$1.7 billion
Inflation Rate: 82%
Natural Resources: uranium; timber; fish
Agriculture: livestock; bananas; sugarcane; cotton; cereals
Industry: sugar refining; tuna and beef canning; textiles; iron-rod plants; petroleum refining

FOREIGN TRADE

Exports: $58 million
Imports: $354 million

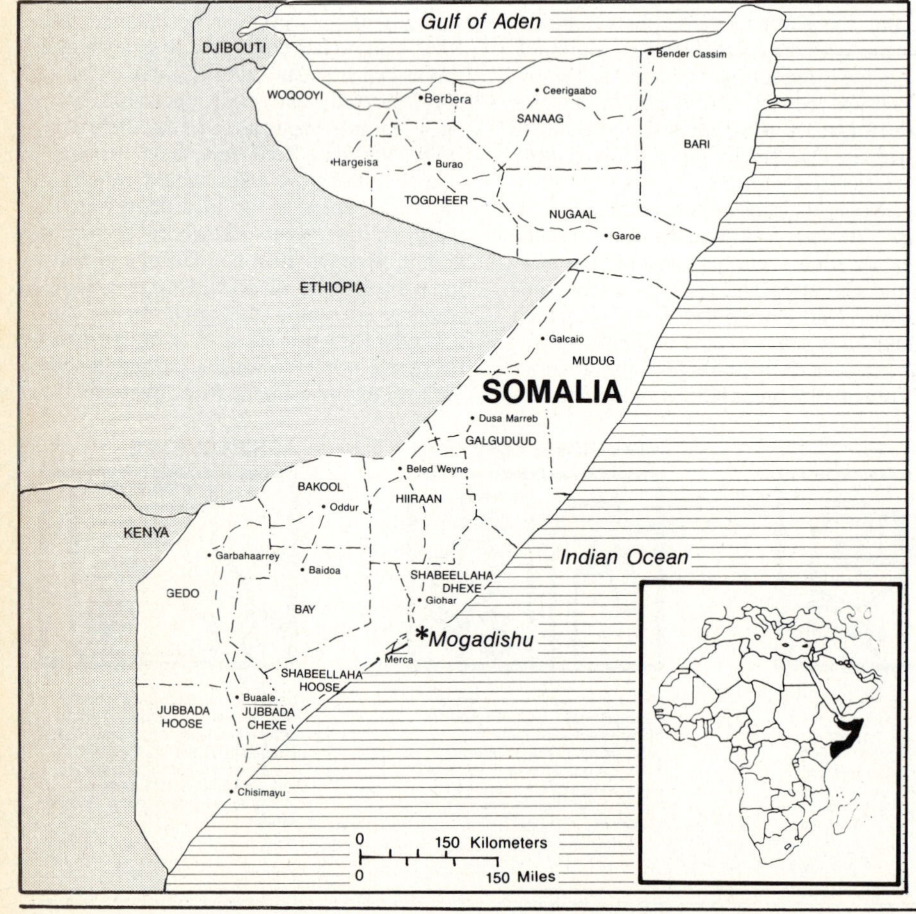

The British take control of northern regions of present-day Somalia
1886–1887

Italy establishes a protectorate in the eastern areas of present-day Somalia
1889

The Somalia Youth League is founded; it becomes a nationalist party
1943

THE SOMALI

"Abundance and scarcity are never far apart; the rich and poor frequent the same house."

(Quoted by I. M. Lewis in *The Somali Democracy*)

This popular Somali proverb testifies to the delicate balance between subsistence and famine in a dry land. Although their numbers have been declining, about half of Somalia's people are still nomadic pastoralists. Their herds are generally quite large. (In the early 1980s more than a million animals, mostly goats and sheep, were exported annually.) Large numbers of cattle and camels are also kept. But drought and disease are perennial problems. Hundreds of thousands of animals were lost due to lack of rain during the mid-1980s, while reports of rinderpest have, since 1983, led to a sharp drop in exports due to the closing of the once-lucrative Saudi Arabia market to African animals. Besides leading to a drop in incomes, this ban has aggravated the already serious problem of overgrazing.

Another quarter of the Somali population combine livestock keeping with agriculture. Cultivation is possible in the area between the Juba and Shebelle Rivers and in a portion of the north. Although up to 15 percent of the country is potentially arable, only about 1 percent of the land is put to plow at any given time. Bananas, cotton, and frankincense are major cash crops, and maize and sorghum are subsistence cereal crops. Like their pastoralist cousins, Somali farmers walk a thin line between abundance and scarcity, for locusts as well as drought are common visitors.

The delicate nature of Somali agriculture helps to explain the country's burgeoning urbanization. Today one in four Somali lives in the large towns and cities. The largest center is Mogadishu, the capital city, which houses more than a million people. Unfortunately, as Somali flow in from the countryside, they generally find little employment. The country's manufacturing and service sectors are small. As a result, more than 100,000 Somali have become migrant workers in the Persian Gulf states.

Unlike the populations of many African countries, Somali share a common language and sense of cultural identity. Islam, the state religion, is also a binding feature.

(UN photo by Rice)

Approximately half of the population of Somalia are nomadic pastoralists. The perennial problems of drought and disease have made such an existence difficult indeed.

Thus Somalia has presented an image of having a greater degree of national coherence than many other African states. However, competing clan allegiances play a divisive political role in the society. The appeal of greater Somali nationalism has also been a source of conflict by encouraging irredentist sentiments.

THE RISE OF SIAD BARRE

During the colonial era the territory that constitutes modern Somalia was divided. For about 75 years the northern region was governed by the British; the southeastern portion was subject to Italian rule. The different colonial legacies have continued to complicate efforts at nation-building. Some northerners believe that their region has been neglected and would benefit from greater political autonomy. Such feelings have recently been intensified by civil war.

Somalia became independent on July 1, 1960, when the new national flag, a white five-pointed star on a blue field, was raised in the former British and Italian territories. The star symbolized the five branches of the Somali nation—that is, the now-united peoples of British and Italian Somalilands and the unredeemed Somali still living in French Somaliland (modern Djibouti), Ethiopia, and Kenya.

In 1969 Siad Barre, president until 1991, came to power through a coup which promised radical change. As chairman of the military's Supreme Revolutionary Council, Barre combined Somali nationalism and Islam with a commitment to "scientific socialism." Some genuine efforts were made to restructure society through the development of new local councils and worker management committees. New civil and labor codes were written. The Somali Revolutionary Socialist Party

Somalia is formed through a merger of former British and Italian colonies under UN Trusteeship
1960

Siad Barre comes to power through an army coup; the Supreme Revolutionary Council is established
1969

The Ogaden war in Ethiopia results in Somalia's defeat
1977–1978

1980s–1990s

Barre is injured in an auto accident; General Ali Samatar assumes greater authority as prime minister

The SNM escalates its campaign in the north; government forces respond with attacks on the local Issaq population

Barre flees Mogadishu, USC forms a provisional government Ali Mahdi Mohamed takes over as interim president

(SRSP) was developed as the sole legal political party.

Initially, the new order seemed to be making progress. The Somali language was alphabetized in a modified form of Roman script, which allowed the government to launch mass-literacy campaigns. A number of rural-development projects were also implemented. In particular, roads were built, breaking down isolation between regions. The theme was "Tribalism divides, socialism unites." Tribalism in this case stood for clan divisions.

The promise of Barre's early years in office gradually faded. Little was done to follow through the developments of the early 1970s. Barre increasingly bypassed the participatory institutions he had helped to create. His government became one of personal rule: he took on emergency powers, relieved members of the governing council of their duties, surrounded himself with members of his own Marehan Darod clan, and isolated himself from the public.

IRREDENTISM AND RESISTANCE

Barre has also isolated Somalia in Africa by pursuing irredentism, policies that would unite the other points of the Somali star under his rule. To accomplish this task, he began to encourage local guerrilla movements among the ethnic Somali living in Kenya and Ethiopia. Bad relations between Somalia and Kenya were eased in 1982, but the war in the Ogaden region of Ethiopia has been less easy to resolve.

In 1977 Barre sent his forces into the Ogaden region to assist the local rebels of the Western Somali Liberation Front. The invaders initially achieved military success against the Ethiopians, whose forces had been weakened by revolutionary strife and battles with Eritrean rebels. However, the intervention of some 17,000 Cuban troops and other Soviet Bloc personnel on the side of the Ethiopians quickly turned the tide of battle. At the same time, the Somali incursion was roundly condemned by all members of the Organization of African Unity (OAU). Ground and air attacks across the borders of Ethiopia and Somalia continued in the 1980s.

The intervention of the Soviet Bloc on the side of the Ethiopians was a bitter disappointment to Barre, who had enjoyed Soviet support for his military buildup. In exchange, he had allowed the Soviet Union to establish a secret base at the strategic northern port of Berbera. However, in 1977 the Soviets decided to shift their allegiance to the new revolutionary government in Ethiopia during its times of need. Barre then tried to attract U.S. support with offers of basing rights at Berbera, but the Carter administration was unwilling to jeopardize American interests in either Ethiopia or Kenya by backing Barre's irredentist adventure. U.S.–Somali relations became closer during the Reagan administration, which signed a 10-year pact giving U.S. forces access to air and naval facilities at Berbera. The United States increased its aid to Somalia in return, but it refused to become a major arms supplier.

In 1988 Barre met with Ethiopian leader Mengistu Mariam. Together they pledged to respect their mutual border. This understanding came about in the context of growing internal resistance to the Barre regime. By 1990 three guerrilla movements—the Somalia National Movement (SNM) in the north, the Somalia Patriotic Movement in the center, and the United Somalia Congress (USC) in the south of the country, were each enjoying growing success against government forces. Initially the greatest threat to the government came from the SNM rebels who captured a number of population centers including Hargeisa, Somalia's second-largest city.

Growing resistance resulted in massive atrocities on the part of government forces. Human-rights concerns were cited by the Bush administration in ending most U.S. assistance to Somalia. The American cutbacks were probably a reflection of the growing international consensus that Barre would soon fall. In March 1990 Barre called for a national dialogue and spoke of a possible end to one-party rule. But continuing atrocities, including the killing of more than 100 protesters at the national stadium, fueled further armed resistance. In January 1991 the USC besieged Mogadishu, causing Barre to flee the city. Barre's downfall has been accompanied by attempts to create a government of national unity.

DEVELOPMENT

Somalia has the longest coastline in Africa. In the mid-1970s the government pressed some formerly nomadic communities into adopting fishing. After initial resistance, the program has led to growing catches in recent years.

FREEDOM

The human-rights group Africa Watch accused the Barre regime of direct responsibility for the deaths of more than 50,000 citizens in 1988–1989. Amnesty International and the U.S. State Department have also been especially critical of Somalia's human-rights record since 1988.

HEALTH/WELFARE

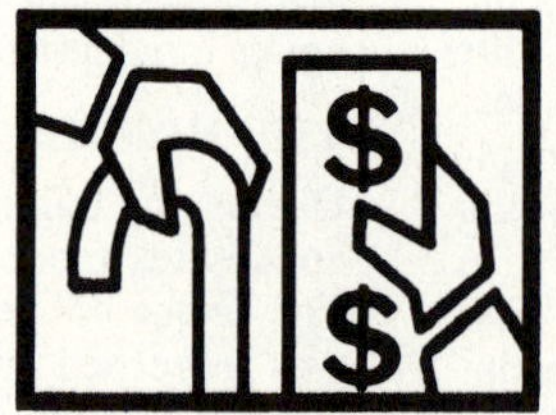

Three-quarters of the Somali people are without access to any form of health care. By 1986 education's share of the Somali budget had fallen to 2%. At 525 troops per teacher, Somalia has the highest such ratio in Africa.

ACHIEVEMENTS

Somalia has been described as "a nation of poets." Many scholars attribute the strength of the Somali poetic tradition not only to their nomadic way of life, which encourages oral arts, but to the local role of poetry as a social and political medium.

Sudan (Democratic Republic of the Sudan)

GEOGRAPHY

Area in Square Kilometers (Miles): 2,504,530 (967,500) (about one-fourth the size of the United States)
Capital (Population): Khartoum (476,000)
Climate: desert in north to tropical in south

PEOPLE

Population
Total: 24,972,000
Annual Growth Rate: 2.9%
Rural/Urban Population Ratio: 65/35
Languages: official: Arabic; others spoken: Nuer, Dinka, Shilluki, Masalatis, Fur, Nubian, English, others

Health
Life Expectancy at Birth: 57 years (male); 55 years (female)
Infant Death Rate (Ratio): 107/1,000
Average Caloric Intake: 99% of FAO minimum
Physicians Available (Ratio): 1/11,513

THE OPPRESSION OF WOMEN IN SUDAN

Since coming to power in 1989 the Sudanese government has instituted a sweeping policy aimed at radically redefining the role of women in society. Traditionally, both Muslim and non-Muslim women in Sudan have enjoyed such basic freedoms as access to higher education, professional employment, the right to engage in trade, and freedom of movement. All of these freedoms are currently being curtailed in the name of Islamic propriety. Women are being systematically removed from the Sudanese civil service and many fields of tertiary education. It has been suggested that in the future women will be free to be nurses and primary-school teachers. Women are now no longer free to travel without a male escort. Thousands of, mostly non-Muslim, women are the principal victims of enslavement by Arab militias.

Religion(s)
60% Sunni Muslim in north; 25% traditional indigenous; 15% Christian

Education
Adult Literacy Rate: 31%

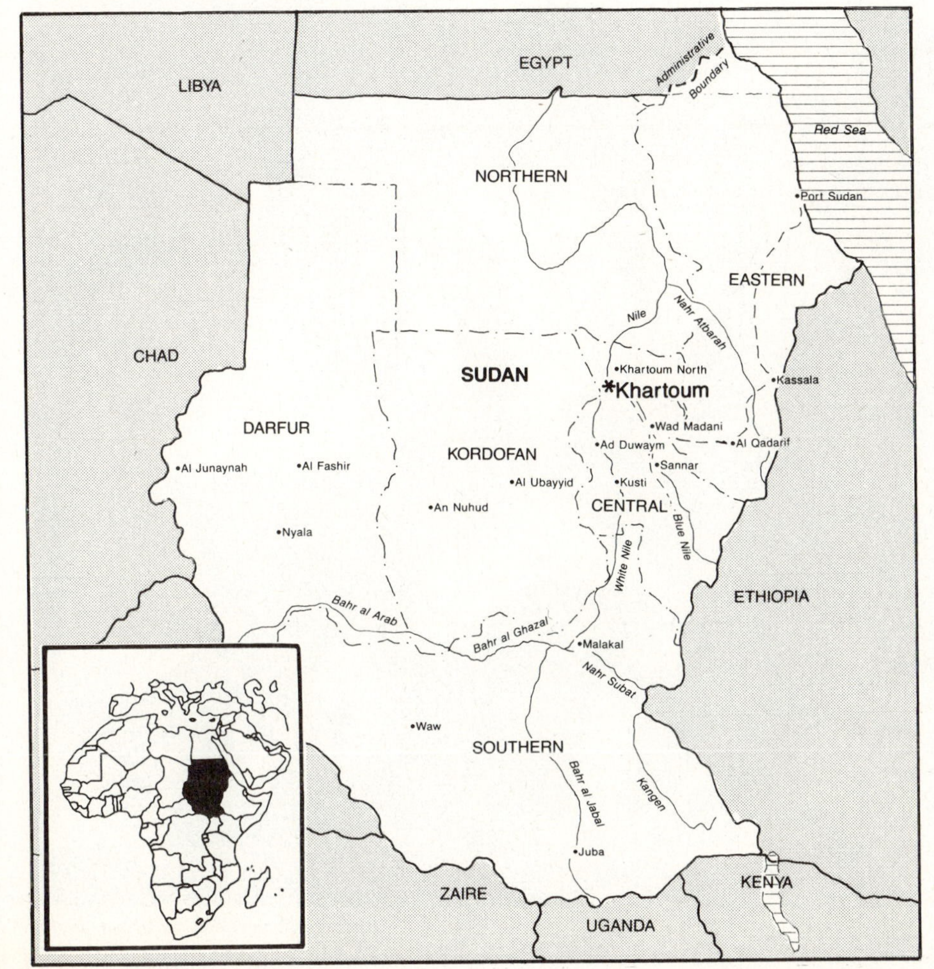

COMMUNICATION

Telephones: 73,400
Newspapers: 2

TRANSPORTATION

Highways—Kilometers (Miles): 20,000 (12,400)
Railroads—Kilometers (Miles): 5,500 (3,410)
Commercial Airports: 5 international

GOVERNMENT

Type: republic
Independence Date: January 1, 1956
Head of State: Prime Minister Umar Hasan al-Bashir
Political Parties: banned
Suffrage: universal for adults

MILITARY

Number of Armed Forces: 71,750
Military Expenditures (% of Central Government Expenditures): 7.2%
Current Hostilities: civil war

ECONOMY

Currency ($ U.S. Equivalent): 4.5 Sudanese pounds = $1 (fixed rate)
Per Capita Income/GNP: $340/$8.5 billion
Inflation Rate: 70%
Natural Resources: oil; iron ore; copper; chrome; other industrial metals
Agriculture: cotton; peanuts; sesame; gum arabic; sorghum; wheat
Industry: textiles; cement; cotton ginning; edible oils; distilling; pharmaceuticals

FOREIGN TRADE

Exports: $550 million
Imports: $1.2 billion

SUDAN

Sudan is Africa's largest country. Its size as well as ethnic and religious diversity have frustrated the efforts of successive postindependence governments to build a lasting sense of national unity. Since the takeover of the state in 1989 by a repressive military clique allied to the fundamentalist National Islamic Front (NIF), the polarization of Sudanese society has deepened to an unprecedented extent. If there is any hope for unity and reconciliation in this vast land of enormous potential, it now lies in the broad-based coalition opposed to the current regime.

HISTORY

Sudan, like its northern neighbor Egypt, is a gift of the Nile. The river and its various branches snake across the country, providing water to most of the 80 percent of the Sudanese who survive by farming. From ancient times the upper Nile region of northern Sudan has been the site of a series of civilizations whose histories are closely intertwined with those of Egypt. There has been constant human interaction between the two zones. Some groups, such as the Nubians, expanded northward into the Egyptian lower Nile.

The last ruler to unite the Nile valley politically was the nineteenth-century Turko-Egyptian ruler Muhammad Ali. After absorbing the (by then predominately Arabized Muslim) northern Sudan into his Egyptian state, Ali gradually expanded his authority to the south and west over non-Arabic and in many cases non-Muslim groups. This process, largely motivated by a desire for slave labor, for the first time united the diverse regions that today make up Sudan. In the 1880s much of the Sudan fell under the theocratic rule of the Mahdists, a local anti-Egyptian Islamic movement. The Mahdists were defeated by an Anglo-Egyptian force in 1898. Thereafter the United Kingdom dominated Sudan until its independence in 1956.

INTERNAL PROBLEMS

Sudanese society has remained divided since independence. In the north there has been strong Pan-Arab sentiment, but some 60 percent of the Sudanese, concentrated in the south and west, are non-Arab. Forty percent of the Sudanese, especially in the south, are also non-Muslim. Despite this fact, many, but by no means all, Sudanese Muslims have favored the creation of an Islamic state. Ideological divisions among various socialist- and nonsocialist-oriented factions have also been important. Sudan has long had a strong communist party, drawing on support of organized labor, and an influential middle class.

The division between northern and southern Sudan has been especially deep. A mutiny by southern soldiers prior to independence escalated into a 17-year rebellion by southerners against what they perceived to be the hegemony of Muslim Arabs. Some 500,000 southerners perished before the Anya Nya rebels and the government reached a compromise settlement recognizing southern autonomy in 1972.

In the north, the first 14 years of independence saw the rule of 7 different civil-

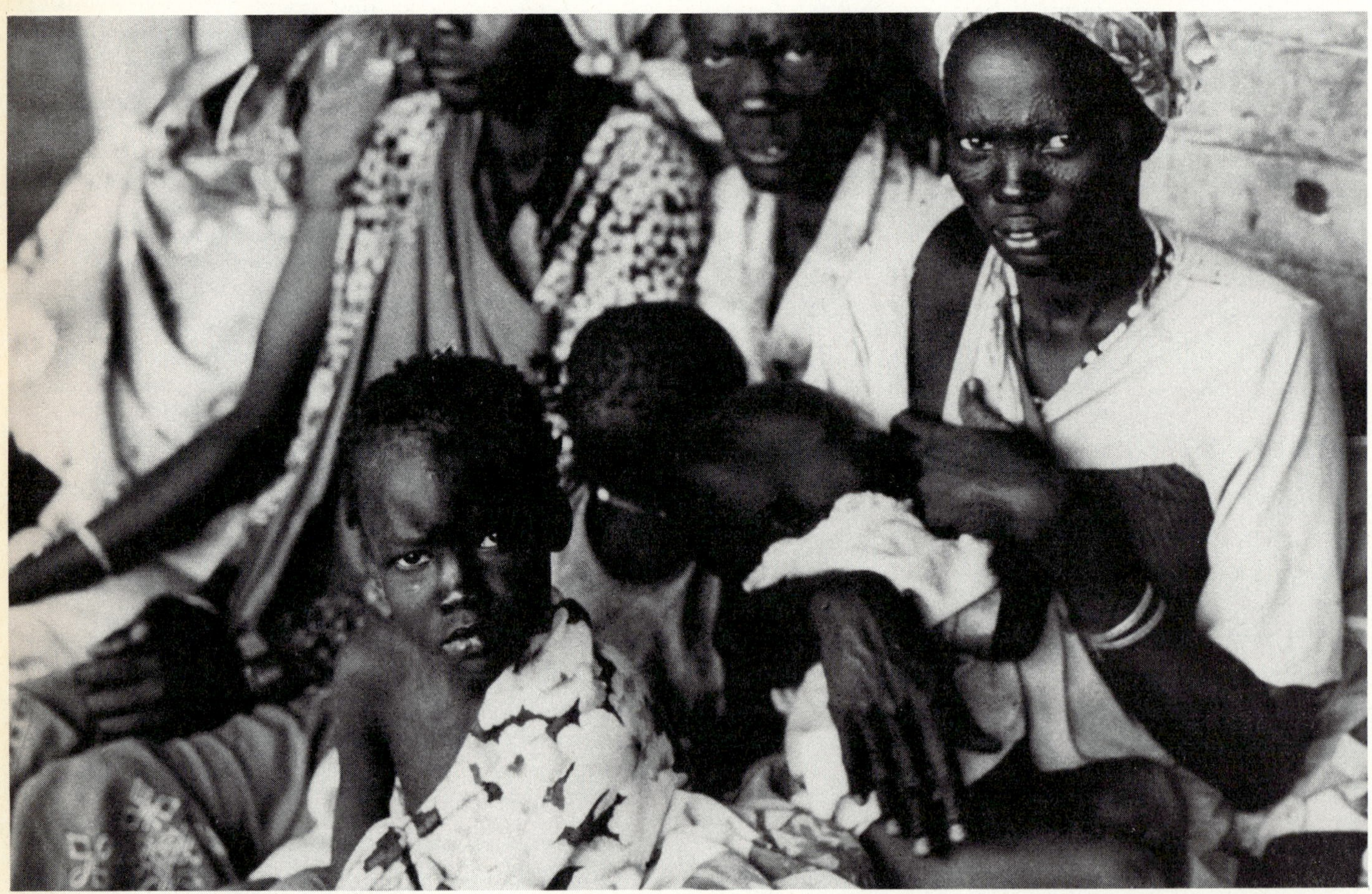

(United Nations photo by Milton Grant)

Nearly 30 percent of the Sudanese population have been displaced by warfare and drought. The effect on the people has been devastating, and even the best efforts of the international community have met with limited success.

Egypt invades northern Sudan **1820**

The Mahdist Revolt begins **1881**

The Anglo-Egyptian Condominium begins **1899**

Independence **1956**

Jaafar Nimeiri comes to power **1969**

Hostilities end in southern Sudan **1972**

1980s–1990s

Islamic law replaces the former penal code; renewed civil war in the south

Nimeiri is overthrown in a popular coup; an elected government is installed

A military coup installs a hard-line Islamic fundamentalist regime

ian coalitions as well as 6 years of military rule. Despite this chronic instability, a tradition of liberal tolerance among political factions was generally maintained. Government became increasingly authoritarian during the administration of Jaafar Nimeiri, who came to power in a 1969 military coup.

Nimeiri quickly moved to consolidate his power by eliminating challenges to his government from the Islamic right and the communist left. His greatest success was ending the Anya Nya revolt, but his subsequent tampering with the provisions of the peace agreement led to renewed resistance. In 1983 Nimeiri decided to impose Islamic law throughout Sudanese society. This led to the growth of the Sudanese People's Liberation Army (SPLA), which quickly seized control of much of the southern Sudanese countryside. Opposition to Nimeiri had also been growing in the north, as more people became alienated by the regime's increasingly heavy-handed ways and inability to manage the declining economy. Finally, in 1985, he was toppled in a coup.

The holding of multiparty elections in 1986 seemed to presage a restoration of Sudan's tradition of pluralism. With the SPLA preventing voting in much of the south, the two largest parties were the northern-based Umma and the Democratic Union Party (DUP). The third-largest vote-getter was the National Islamic Front (NIF), with eight other parties plus a number of independents gaining parliamentary seats. The major challenge facing the new coalition government led by Umma was reconciliation with the SPLA. Because the SPLA, unlike the earlier Anya Nya, was committed to national unity, the task did not appear insurmountable. However, arguments within the government over meeting key SPLA demands such as the repeal of Islamic law caused the war to drag on. A hard-line faction within Umma and the NIF sought to resist a return to secularism. In March 1989 a new government made up of Umma and DUP committed itself to accommodating the SPLA, but a month later, on the day that the Cabinet was to ratify an agreement with the rebels, there was a coup by pro-NIF officers.

Besides leading to a breakdown in all efforts to end the SPLA rebellion, the NIF/military regime has been responsible for establishing the most intolerant, repressive government in Sudan's modern history. Extrajudicial executions have become common. Instances of pillaging and enslavement of non-Muslim communities by Arab militias have increased. NIF-affiliated security groups have become a law unto themselves, striking out at their perceived enemies and intimidating Muslims and non-Muslims alike to conform to their fundamentalist norms. Supposedly Islamic norms are also being invoked to justify the radical campaign to undermine the status of women. The climate of fear has become pervasive.

The extreme tactics of the new government have led to growing resistance. Most of the now-banned political parties, including Umma, DUP, and the Communists, have aligned themselves with the SPLA as the National Democratic Forces Forum. In response, the government has become increasingly ruthless. In April 1990, 28 officers were summarily executed as part of a continuing purge of the armed forces.

ECONOMIC PROSPECTS

Although it has great potential, political conflict has left Sudan as one of the poorest nations in the world. The country's underutilized water resources have led to talk of creating "the breadbasket of the Arab world," and untapped oil reserves in the south could transform the country from an energy importer to exporter. However, warfare and lack of financing is blocking needed infrastructural improvements. Sudan's foreign debt exceeds $13 billion, of which more than $3 billion is in arrears.

Figures for 1988 show that nearly 7 million Sudanese (out of a total population of 22.8 million) have been displaced—more than 4 million by warfare, with drought and desertification contributing to the remainder. There has also been a substantial influx of refugees from neighboring states. Sudan is a major recipient of international emergency food aid, but in 1988 an estimated 250,000 starved to death, due to the effect of war in blocking aid from reaching famine victims. Human-rights concerns, as well as the war and financial mismanagement, have led to a recent fall-off in development assistance.

DEVELOPMENT

Since independence, many ambitious development plans have been launched, but progress has been limited by political instability. The periodic introduction and redefinition of "Islamic" financial procedures has complicated long-term planning.

FREEDOM

Prior to the 1989 coup Sudan's human-rights record in areas unaffected by civil strife was fairly good. In the war zone, raids by Arab militias on non-Arab communities are responsible for numerous atrocities and a revival of slavery. The current regime rules through massive repression.

HEALTH/WELFARE

Civil strife and declining government expenditure have resulted in rising rates of infant mortality. Warfare has also prevented famine relief from reaching needy populations, resulting in instances of mass starvation.

ACHIEVEMENTS

The United Nations-sponsored program Operation Lifeline is currently feeding some 4 million Sudanese. International pressure has resulted in recent government and SPLA cooperation with UN personnel in the relief effort.

Tanzania (United Republic of Tanzania)

GEOGRAPHY

Area in Square Kilometers (Miles): 939,652 (363,950) (more than twice the size of California)
Capital (Population): Dar es Salaam (1,400,000); Dodoma (political)
Climate: tropical; arid; temperate

PEOPLE

Population

Total: 25,971,000
Annual Growth Rate: 3.4%
Rural/Urban Population Ratio: 82/18
Languages: official: Kiswahili; others spoken: Chagga, Gogo, Ha, Haya, Luo, Maasai, Hindu, Arabic, English, others

Health

Life Expectancy at Birth: 49 years (male); 54 years (female)
Infant Death Rate (Ratio): 107/1,000
Average Caloric Intake: 87% of FAO minimum
Physicians Available (Ratio): 1/24,385

Religion(s)

34% traditional indigenous; 33% Muslim; 33% Christian

THE SWAHILI COAST

A trading coastal culture, African-based with Arabian influence, developed over hundreds of years on the East African coast. For 2,000 years merchants from the Mediterranean and the Middle East traded along the coast of East Africa. Eventually, the mingling of Bantu-speaking peoples with Arab culture created the Swahili, an Afro-Arab people with their own African-based language. Based in cities on islands and along the coast, they traded with Arabia, Persia, India, and China, and eventually with the interior of what are now known as Kenya and Tanzania. Converted to Islam and also Arabic speaking, these cosmopolitan peoples traded interior produce for porcelain, spices, and textiles from all over the world and created an impressive written and oral literature. They still play an important role in the political and commercial life of Tanzania.

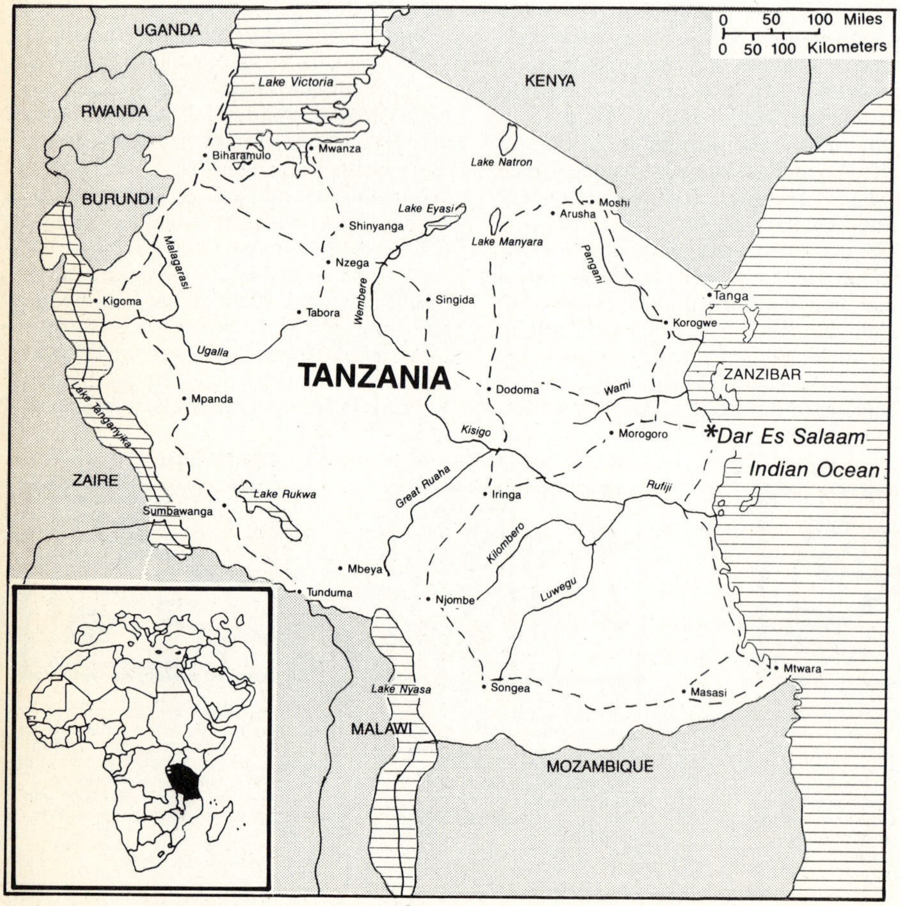

Education

Adult Literacy Rate: 79%

COMMUNICATION

Telephones: 63,000
Newspapers: 5

TRANSPORTATION

Highways—Kilometers (Miles): 81,900 (50,778)
Railroads—Kilometers (Miles): 3,569 (2,212)
Commercial Airports: 3 international

GOVERNMENT

Type: republic
Independence Date: December 9, 1961
Head of State: President Ali Hassan Mwinyi
Political Parties: Chama Cha Mapinduzi (Revolutionary Party)
Suffrage: universal over 18

MILITARY

Number of Armed Forces: 46,700
Military Expenditures (% of Central Government Expenditures): 3.3%
Current Hostilities: none

ECONOMY

Currency ($ U.S. Equivalent): 193 Tanzanian shillings = $1
Per Capita Income/GNP: $235/$5.9 billion
Inflation Rate: 29%
Natural Resources: hydroelectric potential; unexploited iron and coal; gem stones; gold; natural gas
Agriculture: cotton; coffee; sisal; tea; tobacco; wheat; cashews; livestock; cloves
Industry: agricultural processing; diamond mining; oil refining; shoes; cement; textiles; wood products

FOREIGN TRADE

Exports: $394 million
Imports: $1.3 billion

TANZANIA

After a period of first German rule and then British trusteeship, the Tanzanian mainland gained its independence, as Tanganyika, in 1961. In 1964 it merged with the small island state of Zanzibar, which had been a self-governing British protectorate, to form the new nation of Tanzania. Three years later the new union committed itself to a path of socialism, self-reliance, and democracy, through its adoption of a governing program called the Arusha Declaration.

At the time Tanzania was one of the least developed countries in the world. It has remained so. Beyond this fundamental fact there is much controversy over the degree to which the goals of the Arusha Declaration have been achieved. To some critics, the Tanzanian experiment has reduced a country of great potential wealth to ruin. Supporters often counter that it has led to a stable society in which major strides have been made toward participatory governance, equality, and human development. Both sides exaggerate.

THE ECONOMY

Like many nations in Africa, Tanzania has a primarily agrarian economy that is constrained by a less than optimal environment. Although some 90 percent of the population are employed in agriculture, only 8 percent of the land is under cultivation. Rainfall for most of the country is low and erratic, and soil erosion and deforestation are critical problems in many areas. However, environment has been only one factor in Tanzania's generally poor agricultural performance. There has been instability in world-market demand for the nation's principal cash crops: coffee, cotton, cloves, sisal, and tobacco. At the same time, the costs of imported fuel, fertilizers, and other inputs have risen.

Government policies have also led to underdevelopment. Perhaps the greatest policy disaster was the program of villagization. Tanzania hoped to relocate its entire rural and unemployed urban populations into so-called *ujaama* (Swahili for "familyhood") villages, which were to become the basis for agrarian progress. During the early 1970s coercive measures were adopted to force the pace of resettlement. Agricultural production is estimated to have fallen by as much as 50 percent as a result of ujaama dislocation, transforming the nation from being a grain exporter to a grain importer; overall per capita decline for the decade was 7 percent.

Another policy constraint was the exceedingly low official produce prices paid to farmers. Many peasants simply withdrew from the market, while others turned to black-market sales. Since 1985 the official market has been liberalized and prices have risen. While this has been

(UN photo by Ray Witlin)

The economy of Tanzania is primarily agrarian; however, rainfall for most of the country is sporadic. This, coupled with wide swings in world-market demand for their cash crops has led to economic pressures affecting food crops. These men in the village of Lumeji are receiving seed grains needed to develop Tanzania's food production.

The sultan of Oman transfers the capital to Zanzibar as Arab commercial activity increases **1820**

Germany declares a protectorate over the area **1885**

The Maji Maji rebellion unites many ethnic groups against German rule **1905–1906**

Tanganyika becomes a League of Nations mandate under the United Kingdom **1919**

Tanganyika becomes independent; Julius Nyerere is the leader **1961**

Tanzania is formed of Tanganyika and Zanzibar **1964**

The Arusha Declaration establishes a Tanzanian socialist program for development **1967**

A Tanzanian invasion force enters Uganda **1979**

1980s–1990s

Nyerere retires; Ali Hassan Mwinyi succeeds as president

Tanzania accepts IMF conditions and loans

Tensions with the CCM over unrest in Zanzibar

accompanied by a modest rise in production, the lack of consumer goods in the rural areas is widely seen as disincentive to greater progress.

All sectors of the Tanzanian economy have suffered from deteriorating infrastructure. Here again there are both external and internal causes. Balanced against rising imported energy and equipment costs have been inefficiencies caused by poor planning, barriers to capital investment, and a relative neglect of communications and transport. Even when crops or goods are available, they often cannot reach their destination. Tanzania's few bituminized roads are in a chronic state of disrepair, and there have been frequent shutdowns of its railways. Much of the southern third of the country, in particular, is isolated from access to even inferior transport services.

Between 1980 and 1987 manufacturing declined from 10 to 4 percent of gross domestic product (GDP), with most sectors operating at less than half of their capacity. Inefficiencies have also increased in the nation's mining sector. Diamonds, gold, iron, coal, and other minerals are currently exploited, but production has been falling and now accounts for less than 1 percent of GDP. Lack of investment capital has led to a deterioration of existing operations and an inability to open new deposits.

As with agriculture, the Tanzanian government has, in recent years, increasingly abandoned socialism in favor of free-market incentives, in its efforts to rehabilitate and expand the industrial and service sectors of the economy. A number of state enterprises are being privatized, and better opportunities are being offered to outside investors. Tourism is being promoted after decades of neglect.

SOCIAL AND POLITICAL DEVELOPMENT

Although the statistical evidence is inadequate, it is nonetheless clear that Tanzania has made real progress in extending health, education, and other social services to its population. But past claims of achieving universal primary literacy are seemingly contradicted by the 1986 primary-school enrollment figure of 69 percent, (slightly above the African average of 66 percent). Fewer than 1 percent of the population receives tertiary education.

Some 1,700 health centers and dispensaries have been built since 1961. However, these centers frequently lack medicines, equipment, and even basic supplies such as bandages and syringes. Although the country has a national health service, patients often end up paying for the material costs of their care. In 1987 the overall life expectancy rate was estimated at 53 years, as compared to 51 for the continent as a whole.

Much of the progress that has been made in human services is a function of outside donations. Despite the Arusha Declaration's emphasis on self-reliance, for decades Tanzania has been either at or near the top of the list of African countries in its per capita receipt of international aid. By 1987, aid, primarily from Western countries, accounted for more than a third of the total GNP.

Tanzania is a one-party state. Political activity is restricted to the ruling Chama Cha Mapinduzi (CCM) Party, whose platform remains the Declaration. Membership in the party is restricted, with actual power being concentrated in the hands of a small elite, who make up the party's Central Committee. The party attempts to control most social activity through its network of community and workplace cells, by which all Tanzanians have at least one CCM member responsible for monitoring their affairs. In elections, voters are allowed to choose between two CCM-selected candidates for 75 percent of the seats in the Parliament. Outside of religion, the party controls most social organizations and, with the government, the local media.

Tanzania's politics is in a state of transition. Since the 1950s political life has been dominated by Julius Nyerere, who has been the driving force behind the Arusha experiment. However, in 1985 he gave up the presidency in favor of Ali Hassan Mwinyi and, in 1990, he resigned as chairman of the CCM. Within the CCM, Mwinyi must now balance himself between those who wish to accelerate current moves toward political and/or economic liberalization and those who wish to maintain the older order. Although Tanzania is relatively free of ethnic conflict, there exist sectarian tensions between Christians and Muslims. A Zanzibari separatist movement exists. There has also been modest agitation in favor of establishing multiparty democracy.

DEVELOPMENT

In April 1990 the World Bank approved a $200 million loan to assist Tanzania in the radical restructuring of its agricultural marketing system. Unprofitable state farms are to be sold off, the cereal marketing board is to be abolished, and the role of cash-crop marketing boards will be reduced.

FREEDOM

Freedom of speech and association remain restricted by the CCM's leading role in society. Nyerere has recently encouraged debate within the CCM on the merits of multipartyism. Outside of the party, prodemocracy activist James Mapalala has formed an unauthorized Civil and Legal Rights Movement.

HEALTH/WELFARE

The 1990–1991 Development Plan calls for the government to give priority to health and education in its expenditures. This reflects a recognition that early progress in these areas has been undermined to some extent in recent years. Malnutrition remains a critical problem.

ACHIEVEMENTS

Since independence, the government has had enormous success in its program of promoting the use of Swahili as the national language throughout society. Mass literacy in Swahili has facilitated the rise of a national culture, helping to make Tanzania one of the more cohesive African states.

Uganda (Republic of Uganda)

GEOGRAPHY

Area in Square Kilometers (Miles): 235,885 (91,076) (slightly smaller than Oregon)
Capital (Population): Kampala (331,000)
Climate: tropical to semi-arid

PEOPLE

Population

Total: 17,960,000
Annual Growth Rate: 3.5%
Rural/Urban Population Ratio: 86/14
Languages: official: English; others spoken: Kiswahili, Luganda, Iteso, Soga, Acholi, Lugbara, Nyakole Nyoro, others

Health

Life Expectancy at Birth: 48 years (male); 50 years (female)
Infant Death Rate (Ratio): 107/1,000
Average Caloric Intake: 83% of FAO minimum
Physicians Available (Ratio): 1/27,420

Religion(s)

66% Christian; 18% traditional indigenous; 16% Muslim

SONG OF LAWINO

Song of Lawino, a "poetic novel" by Ugandan poet and novelist Okot p'Bitek, has been popular in the Western world as well as in Africa. First written in the Acholi language, it has been translated into English by the author and depicts a "modern" Ugandan man who has assumed Western values. The story is told through the eyes of his African wife, who is not Western-educated but is wiser than he. The views she presents illustrate how sensible many traditional African ways are. For example, in one passage, the wife says: "Listen/My husband,/In the wisdom of the Acoli/Time is not stupidly split up/Into seconds and minutes, . . ./It does not resemble/A loaf of millet bread/Surrounded by hungry youths/From a hunt./It does not get finished/Like vegetables in the dish. . . ."

Education

Adult Literacy Rate: 57%

COMMUNICATION

Telephones: 61,600
Newspapers: 5

TRANSPORTATION

Highways—Kilometers (Miles): 26,200 (16,244)
Railroads—Kilometers (Miles): 1,286 (797)
Commercial Airports: 1 international

GOVERNMENT

Type: republic; under control of the National Resistance Council
Independence Date: October 9, 1962
Head of State: President Yoweri Kaguta Museveni
Political Parties: National Resistance Movement; Nationalist Liberal Party; Democratic Party; Conservative Party; Uganda People's Congress
Suffrage: universal for adults

MILITARY

Number of Armed Forces: 70,000
Military Expenditures (% of Central Government Expenditures): 1.4%
Current Hostilities: internal conflicts

ECONOMY

Currency ($ U.S. Equivalent): 370 Uganda shillings = $1
Per Capita Income/GNP: $300/$4.9 billion
Inflation Rate: 72%
Natural Resources: copper; other minerals
Agriculture: coffee; tea; cotton
Industry: processed agricultural coods; copper; cement; shoes; fertilizer; steel; beverages

FOREIGN TRADE

Exports: $272 million
Imports: $626 million

Establishment of the oldest Ugandan kingdom, Bunyoro, followed by the formation of Baganda and other kingdoms
1500

Kabaka Metesa I of Baganda welcomes British explorer H.M. Stanley
1870s

A British protectorate over Uganda is proclaimed
1893

An agreement gives Baganda special status in the British protectorate
1900

UGANDA

After a decade and a half of repressive rule accompanied by massive interethnic violence, Uganda is still struggling for peace and reconciliation. A land rich in natural and human resources, Uganda suffered dreadfully during the despotic regimes of Milton Obote (1962–1971, 1980–1985) and Idi Amin (1971–1979). Under these two dictators, hundreds of thousands of Ugandans were murdered by the state.

The country had reached a state of general social and economic collapse by 1986, when the forces of the National Resistance Movement (NRM) established the current administration, led by Yoweri Museveni. The new government has made considerable progress in restoring a sense of normalcy throughout most of the country, but it faces overwhelming challenges in its attempts to rebuild the nation.

HISTORIC GEOGRAPHY

The breakdown of Uganda is an extreme example of the disruptive role of ethnic and sectarian competition, which was fostered by policies of both its colonial and postcolonial governments. Uganda consists of two major zones: the plains of the northeast and the southern highlands. It has been said that you can drop anything into the rich volcanic soils of the well-watered south and it will grow. Until the 1960s the area was divided into four kingdoms—the Buganda, Bunyoro, Ankole, and Toro—whose peoples speak related Bantu languages. The histories of each of these states stretches back to the fifteenth century A.D. European visitors of the nineteenth century were impressed by their sophisticated social orders, which they equated with the feudal monarchies of medieval Europe. When the British took over, they integrated the ruling class of the southern highlands into a system of "indirect rule." By then missionaries had already succeeded in converting many southerners to Christianity; indeed, civil war between Protestants, Catholics, and Muslims within Buganda had been the British pretext for establishing their overrule.

(UN photo by T. Chen)

Uganda is a land rich in natural and human resources with tremendous potential for economic growth and the well-being of its population. A major problem has been Uganda's despotic regimes, which have infested the politics in recent decades. Idi Amin, above, was dictator from 1971 to 1979, and under his repressive rule hundreds of thousands of Ugandans were murdered by the state.

The Acholi, Lanig, Karamojang, Teso, Madi, and Kakwa peoples who are predominant in the northeast lack the political heritage of hierarchical state-building found in the south. Linguistically, these groups are also separate, speaking either Nilotic or Nilo-Hametic languages. The two regions were united by the British as the Uganda protectorate during the 1890s (the name Uganda, which is a corruption of Buganda, has since become the accepted term for the larger entity). However, under colonial rule, the zones developed separately.

Cash-crop farming, especially of cotton, by local peasants spurred an economic boom in the south. The Bugandan ruling class particularly benefited. Growing levels of education and wealth led to the European stereotype of the "pro-

Kabaka of Baganda is exiled to the United Kingdom by the British for espousing Bagandan independence **1953**

Uganda becomes independent **1962**

Milton Obote introduces a new unitary Constitution and forces Bagandan compliance **1966**

Idi Amin seizes power **1971**

Amin invades Tanzania **1978**

Tanzania invades Uganda and overturns Amin's government **1979**

1980s–1990s

The rise and fall of the second Obote regime leaves 300,000 dead

The NRM takes power under Yoweri Museveni

Recovery produces slow gains; unrest continues in the northeast

gressive" Bugandans as "the Japanese-of-Africa." A growing class of Asian entrepreneurs also played an important role in the local economy, although its prosperity, as well as that of the Bugandan elite, suffered from subordination to resident British interests. The growing economy of the south contrasted with the relative neglect of the northeast. Forced to earn money to pay taxes, many northeasterners became migrant workers in the south. They were also recruited, almost exclusively, to serve in the colonial security forces.

As independence approached, many Bugandans feared that their interests would be compromised by other groups. Under the leadership of their king, Mutesa II, they sought to uphold their separate status. Other groups feared that Bugandan wealth and educational levels could lead to their dominance. A compromise federal structure was agreed to for the new state. At independence, the southern kingdoms retained their autonomous status within the United Kingdom of Uganda. The first government was made up of Mutesa's royalist party and the United People's Congress, a largely non-Bugandan coalition, led by Milton Obote, a Langi. Mutesa was elected as president and Obote as prime minister.

THE REIGN OF TERROR

In 1966 the delicate balance of ethnic interests was upset when Obote used the army, still dominated by fellow northeasterners, to overthrow Mutesa and the Constitution. In the name of abolishing "tribalism," Obote established a one-party state and ruled in an increasingly dictatorial fashion. In 1971 he was overthrown by his army chief, Idi Amin. Amin began his regime with widespread public support but alienated himself by favoring fellow Muslims and Kakwa. He expelled the 40,000-member Asian community and distributed their property to his cronies. The Langi, suspected of being pro-Obote, were also early targets of his persecution, but his attacks soon spread to other members of Uganda's Christian community—that is, about 80 percent of the total Ugandan population. Educated people in particular were purged. The number of Ugandans murdered by Amin's death squads is unknown; the most common figure is 300,000, but estimates range from 50,000 to 1 million. Many others went into exile.

A Ugandan military incursion into Tanzania led to war between the two countries in 1979. Many Ugandans joined with the Tanzanians in defeating Amin's army and its Libyan allies. Unfortunately, the overthrow of Amin, who fled into exile, did not lead to better times. In 1980 Obote was returned to power through a fraudulent vote count.

The second Obote administration was characterized by a continuation of the violence of the Amin years. An estimated 300,000 people, mostly southerners, were massacred by Obote's security forces, while an equal number fled the country. Much of the killing occurred in the Bugandan area known as the Luwero triangle, which was completely depopulated; today its fields are still full of skeletons. As the killings escalated, so did the resistance of Museveni's NRM guerrillas, who had taken to the bush in the aftermath of the failed election. In 1985 a split between Ancholi and Langi officers led to Obote's overthrow and yet another pattern of interethnic recrimination. Finally, in 1986, the NRM gained the upper hand.

THE STRUGGLE CONTINUES

Museveni's NRM administration has faced enormous challenges in trying to bring about national reconstruction. Their task has been complicated by continued warfare in the northeast by armed factions representing elements of the former regimes, independent Karamojong communities, and followers of prophetic religious movements. In 1987 an uprising of the Holy Spirit rebels of Alice Lakwena was crushed, at the cost of 15,000 lives.

Museveni's inability so far to end completely Uganda's cycle of violence is largely a legacy of the bitterness and social breakdown brought about by his predecessors. Currently in Uganda there is cause for both hope and despair. A sense of civil society has been returning to much of the country. With peace has come economic growth, which has made up for some of the past decline. However, the northeast remains unsettled. Whereas NRM troops enjoyed a good reputation when fighting Obote, their discipline has been breaking down. Voting for local Revolutionary Councils took place in 1989, but there are as yet no firm plans for national elections.

DEVELOPMENT

Food production has improved in many areas, but insecurity and violence have obstructed the recovery of agriculture, preventing harvesting and impeding transportation.

FREEDOM

The human-rights situation has improved greatly under Uganda's NRM government, but detentions without trial, massacres of civilians, and other abuses have been carried out by the government as well as its opponents. Freedom of speech and association are curtailed.

HEALTH/WELFARE

Uganda's traditionally strong school system was not completely destroyed under Amin and Obote. In 1986 some 70% of primary-school children attended classes. The killing and exiling of teachers have resulted in a serious drop of standards at all levels of the education system, but progress is under way.

ACHIEVEMENTS

The Ugandan government was one of the first countries in Africa (or the world) to acknowledge the seriousness of the AIDS epidemic within its borders. It has instituted public-information campaigns and has welcomed outside support. The sero-positive rate in urban areas is 15%.

Southern Africa

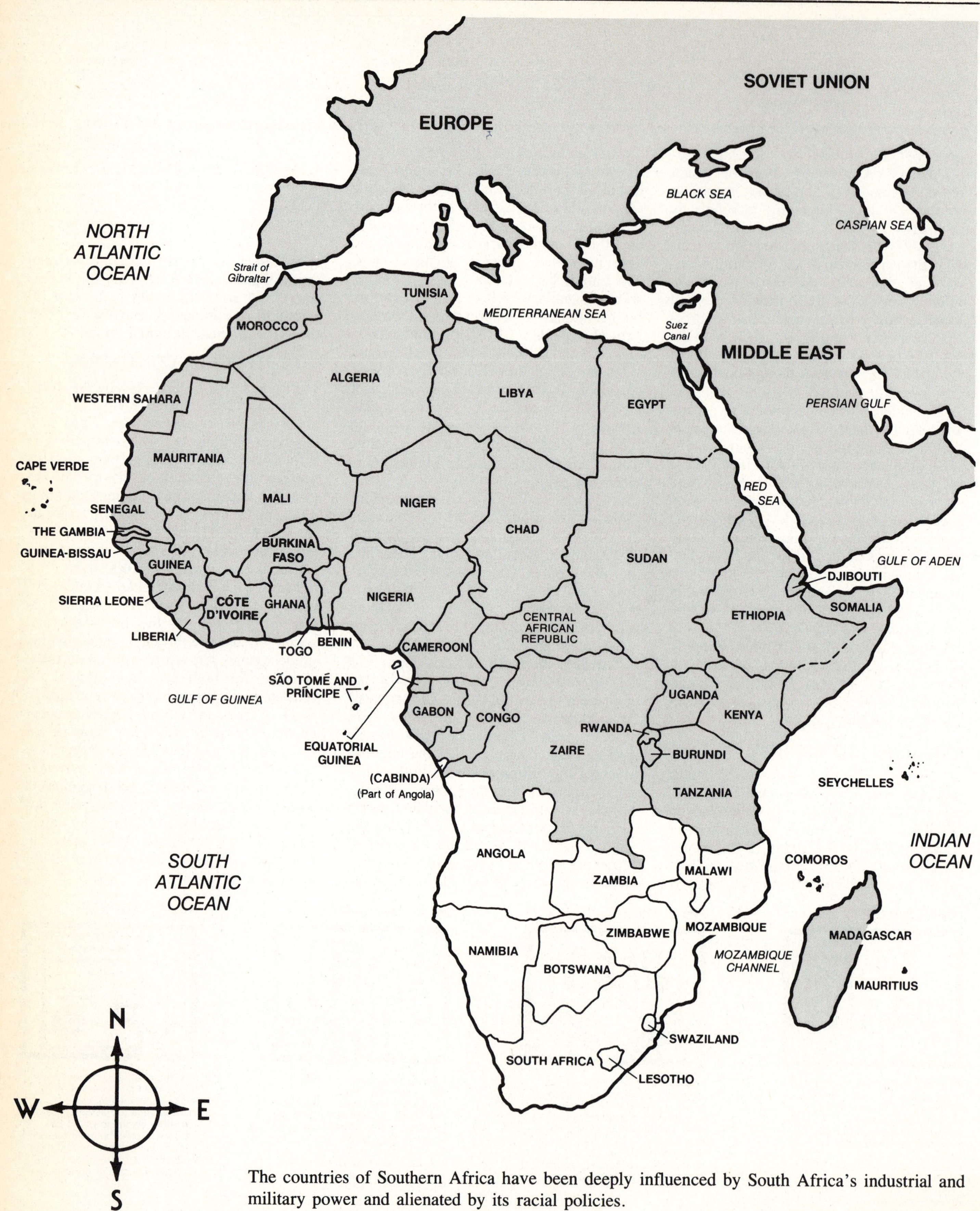

The countries of Southern Africa have been deeply influenced by South Africa's industrial and military power and alienated by its racial policies.

Southern Africa: The Continuing Struggle for Self-Determination

Southern Africa, which includes the nations of Angola, Botswana, Lesotho, Malawi, Mozambique, Namibia, South Africa, Swaziland, Zambia, and Zimbabwe, is a diverse region made up of savannas and forest, snow-topped mountains and desert, and areas of temperate Mediterranean and torrid tropical climates. Southern African identity, however, is defined as much by the region's peoples and their past and present interactions as by its geographic features. An appreciation of local history is crucial to understanding the forces that both divide and unite the region today.

EUROPEAN MIGRATION AND DOMINANCE

A dominant theme in the modern history of Southern Africa has been the evolving struggle of the region's indigenous black African majority to free itself of the racial hegemony of white settlers from Europe and their descendants. By the twelfth century A.D., but probably earlier, the southernmost regions of the continent were populated by a variety of black African ethnic groups who spoke languages belonging to the Bantu as well as Khoisan linguistic classifications. Members of these two groupings practiced both agriculture and pastoralism; archaeological evidence indicates that cattle keeping goes back at least as far as the fifth century. Some, such as the Kongo of northern Angola and the Shona peoples of the Zimbabwean plateaux had, by the fifteenth century, organized strong states; while others, like most of the Nguni speakers, prior to the early nineteenth century, lived in smaller communities. Trade networks existed throughout the region, linking various local peoples not only to one another but also to the markets of the Indian Ocean and beyond. Indeed, in the grounds of the Great Zimbabwe, a stone-walled settlement that flourished in the fifteenth century, porcelains from China have been unearthed.

During the sixteenth century small numbers of Portuguese began settling along the coasts of Angola and Mozambique. A century later, in 1652, the Dutch established a settlement at Africa's southernmost tip, the Cape of Good Hope. While the Portuguese flag remained generally confined to coastal enclaves until the late nineteenth century, throughout the eighteenth century the Dutch colony expanded steadily into the interior, seizing the land of local Khoisan communities. Unlike the colonial footholds of the Portuguese and other Europeans on the continent, which prior to the nineteenth century were mostly centers for the export of slaves, the Dutch Cape Colony imported slaves from Asia as well as elsewhere in Africa. Although not legally enslaved, conquered Khoisan were also reduced to servitude. In the process, a new society evolved at the Cape, which, much like the antebellum American South, was racially divided between free white settlers and subordinated peoples of mixed African and Afro-Asian descent.

During the Napoleonic Wars, Britain took over the Cape Colony. Shortly thereafter, in 1820, significant numbers of English-speaking colonists began arriving in the region. The arrival of the British coincided with a period of political realignment throughout much of Southern Africa, which is commonly referred to as the *Mfecane*. Until recently the

(United Nations photo by Ray Witlin)

Countries throughout Southern Africa are developing projects to employ laborers who might otherwise migrate to urban centers in South Africa—a pattern established in colonial times. These workers are building a highway in Lesotho.

historical literature has generally attributed this upheaval to dislocations caused by the rise of the Zulu state under the great warrior Prince Shaka. However, more recent scholarship has focused on the disruptive effects of increased traffic in contraband slaves from the interior to the Cape and the Portuguese stations of Mozambique, following the international ban on slavetrading.

During the 1830s the British abolished slavery throughout their empire and extended limited civil rights to nonwhites at the Cape. In response, a large number of white Dutch-descended Boers, or Afrikaners, moved in to the interior, where they founded two republics which were free of British control. This migration, called the Great Trek, did not lead the white settlers into an empty land; many African groups lost their farms and pastures to the superior firepower of the early Afrikaners, who often coerced local communities into supplying corvee labor for their farms and public works. But a few African polities, like the kingdom of Lesotho, were able to preserve their independence by acquiring their own firearms.

During the second half of the nineteenth century white migration and dominance spread throughout the rest of Southern Africa. The discovery of diamonds and gold in northeastern South Africa encouraged white exploration and subsequent occupation farther north. During the 1890s Cecil Rhode's British South Africa Company occupied modern Zambia and Zimbabwe, which then became known as the Rhodesias. British traders, missionaries, and settlers also invaded the area now known as Malawi. Meanwhile, the Germans seized Namibia, while the Portuguese began to expand inland from their coastal enclaves. Thus by 1900 the entire region had fallen under white colonial control.

With the exception of Lesotho, now a British protectorate, all of the European colonies in Southern Africa had significant populations of white settlers, who in each case played a predominant political and economic role in their respective territories. Throughout the region, this white supremacy was fostered and maintained through racially discriminatory policies of land alienation, labor regulation, and the denial of full civil rights to nonwhites. In South Africa, where the

(United Nations photo by J. P. Laffont)

Angolan youths celebrated when the nation became independent in 1974.

largest and longest-settled white population resided, the Afrikaners and English-speaking settlers were granted full self-government in 1910, with a Constitution that left that country's black majority virtually powerless.

BLACK NATIONALISM AND SOUTH AFRICAN DESTABILIZATION

After World War II new movements advocating black self-determination gradually gained ascendancy throughout the region. However, the progress of these struggles for majority rule and independence was gradual. By 1968 the countries of Botswana, Lesotho, Malawi, Swaziland, and Zambia had gained their independence. The area was then polarized between liberated and nonliberated nations. In 1974 a military uprising in Portugal brought statehood to Angola and Mozambique, after long armed struggles by liberation forces within the two territories. Wars of liberation also led to the overthrow of white-settler rule in Zimbabwe (formerly Rhodesia), in 1980, and the independence of Namibia, in 1990.

Today South Africa stands alone on the continent as an area of continued white minority rule. This fact has continued to have serious implications for the entire Southern African region, as well as for the oppressed masses inside of South Africa itself. Since the late nineteenth century South Africa has developed into the region's dominant economic and military power. Most of the subcontinent's roads and rails run through South Africa. For generations South Africa has also recruited expatriate as well as local black African workers for its industries and mines. Today the country is the most economically developed country on the continent, with manufactured goods and agricultural surpluses that are in high demand elsewhere. Thus, in addition to the dependent economies of its own region, countries farther to the north trade with South Africa and use its infrastructure. Altogether some 46 countries in Africa import South African goods and crops.

To reduce their economic dependency on South Africa, while cooperating on mutually beneficial development projects, all of the black-ruled countries of Southern Africa, plus the East African nation of Tanzania, joined together to form the Southern African Development Coordination Conference (SADCC). Founded in 1980, this organization is working to exploit the vast potential of its member countries, which have a large share of the continent's resources as well as a combined population of some 65 million. Each SADCC government has assumed responsibility for research and planning in a specific developmental area—that is, Angola for energy, Mozambique for transport and communication, Tanzania for industry, and so on. Over the past decade SADCC has succeeded in attracting considerable outside aid for building and rehabilitating its member states' infrastructures. The organization's greatest success so far has been the Beira corridor project, which has enabled said Mozambican port to serve once more as a major regional transit point. Other successes include total telecommunications independence from South Africa, new regional power grids, and the upgrading of Tanzanian roads to carry Malawian goods to the port of Dar es Salaam.

(United Nations photo)

Followers of Stephen Biko left South Africa after the Soweto riots and his death. They added to the numbers and spirit of the South African liberation movement.

The violent destabilizing policies of the South African military over the last decade have complicated SADCC's task. The independent black-ruled states, especially the so-called Frontline States (Angola, Botswana, Mozambique, Tanzania, Zambia, and Zimbabwe), are hostile to South Africa's racial policies and, to varying degrees, have long provided havens for those oppressed by them. South Africa has responded by striking out against its exiled opponents through overt and covert military operations, while encouraging insurgent movements among some of its neighbors, most notably in Angola and Mozambique.

In Angola, South Africa (along with the United States) has backed the rebel movement Unita, while in Mozambique it has assisted Renamo. Both of these movements have resorted to the sabotaging of railways and roads in their operational areas, a tactic that has greatly increased the dependence of the landlocked states of Botswana, Malawi, Zambia, and Zimbabwe on South African communications. It is estimated that during the 1980s the overall monetary cost to the Frontline States of the destabilization campaign by South Africa and its proxies' forces was $60 billion (the same countries' combined annual gross national product was only about $25 billion in 1989). The human costs have been even greater. Hundreds of thousands of people have been killed and at least equal numbers maimed, while more than 1 million in Mozambique alone have become refugees.

In the context of its region, South Africa has been a military superpower. Despite the imposition of a mandatory United Nations arms embargo on it in 1977, the country's military establishment has been able to secure both the arms and the sophisticated technology needed to develop its own military/industrial complex. South Africa today is nearly self-sufficient in basic munitions, with a vast and advanced arsenal of weapons and a possible nuclear-arms capacity. Whereas in 1978 it imported 75 percent of its weapons, today the figure is only about 5 percent. However, the embargo has been effective. While South African industry produces many sophisticated weapons systems, some of which have been quietly sold abroad, it has faced increasing difficulties in maintaining its regional superiority in such high-technology components as fighter aircraft. By 1989 the increasing edge of Angolan pilots and air-defense systems was a significant factor in South Africa's decision to disengage from that country's civil war. The economic costs of South African militarization have also been steep. In addition to draining some 20 percent of its total budget outlays, the destabilization campaign has contributed to increased international economic sanctions, which since 1985 have cost its economy at least $20 billion.

South Africa sought to justify its acts of aggression by claiming that it was simply engaged in counterinsurgency operations against guerrillas of the African National Congress (ANC) and Pan Africanist Congress (PAC), which have been struggling for the regime's overthrow. In fact, the various Frontline States have all taken a cautious attitude toward the South African political refugees they harbor, specifically forbidding them from launching armed attacks from across their borders. In 1984 both Angola and Mozambique formally signed agreements of mutual noninterference with South Africa. Within a year of these agreements, however, it was South Africa that had repeatedly and blatantly violated the accords.

During the 1980s drought, along with continued warfare, resulted in food shortages in much of Southern Africa, especially in Angola and Mozambique. The drought in Southern Africa neither lasted as long nor was as widely publicized as those of West Africa or the Horn, yet it was no less destructive. Although some countries, such as Botswana, Mozambique, and Zimbabwe, as well as areas of South Africa, suffered more from nature than others, the main features of the crisis were the same: water reserves were depleted; cattle and game died; and crop production declined, often by 50 percent or more.

Maize and cereal production suffered everywhere. South Africa and Zimbabwe, which are usually grain exporters, had to import food. The countries of Angola, Botswana, and

(United Nations photo by Jerry Frank)

South Africa's economic and military dominance overshadows the region's planning. Pictured above is the South African city of Cape Town, the chief port and legislative capital of the country.

Lesotho each had more than half a million people who were affected by the shortfalls, while some 2 million were malnourished in Mozambique. But in 1988 the rains returned to the region, raising cereal production by 40 percent. Zimbabwe was able not only to export, but also to provide food aid to other African countries. However, South African destabilization has contributed to continuing food scarcities in many parts of Angola and Mozambique, despite improved rainfall. During the late 1980s there were $4^1/_2$ million at risk for starvation in Mozambique and 3 million in Angola, while Malawi also faced food shortages, due partially to the presence of more than a half-million refugees fleeing the warfare in Mozambique. True food security will only come with peace.

HOPES FOR PEACE

Recent events have given rise to hopes for peace in Southern Africa. In 1988 Angola, Cuba, and South Africa reached an agreement, with U.S. and Soviet support, which has led to South Africa's withdrawal from Namibia and the imminent removal of Cuban troops from Angola, where they have been supporting government forces. In 1990 Namibia gained its independence under the elected leadership of the South West African People's Organization (SWAPO), the liberation movement that had fought against local South African occupation for more than a quarter of a century. After an on-again/off-again start, direct negotiations have begun between the Angolan government and Unita rebels. Direct talks are now also continuing between the government of Mozambique and the Renamo rebels, who are apparently no longer receiving official South African support (there is concern, however, that nonofficial South African interests are still helping to sustain the movement).

Perhaps the most significant opening has been in South Africa itself. The release of prominent political prisoners, like Nelson Mandela, the unbanning of the ANC and PAC, and the lifting of internal state-of-emergency restrictions have raised hopes for a negotiated end to white minority rule. Direct talks between the government and the ANC are on-going and have so far led the latter organization to suspend its armed struggle. This development has caused further hope throughout the rest of Southern Africa that the era of regional destabilization, along with white rule in South Africa itself, may be coming to a close. However, major obstacles remain to the realization of peace agreements in Angola and Mozambique as well as South Africa.

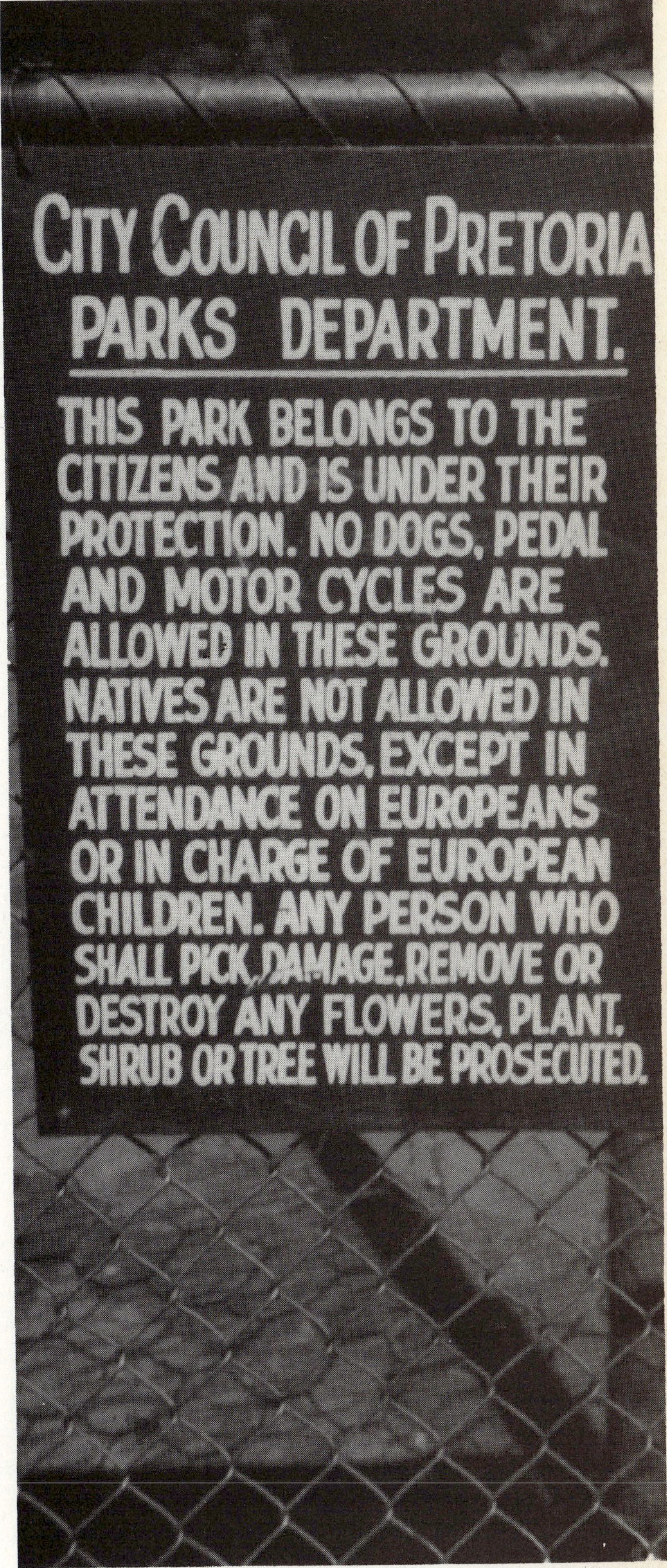

(United Nations photo)

In recent years apartheid, the South African government's policy of racial discrimination, has caused increasing unrest among blacks.

Angola (People's Republic of Angola)

GEOGRAPHY

Area in Square Kilometers (Miles): 1,246,699 (481,351) (larger than Texas and California combined)
Capital (Population): Luanda (1,100,000)
Climate: tropical and subtropical

PEOPLE

Population
Total: 8,535,000
Annual Growth Rate: 2.9%
Rural/Urban Population Ratio: 79/21
Languages: official: Portuguese; others spoken: Ovimbundu, Kimbundu, Bakongo

Health
Life Expectancy at Birth: 42 years (male); 46 years (female)
Infant Death Rate (Ratio): 200/1,000
Average Caloric Intake: 83% of FAO minimum
Physicians Available (Ratio): 1/13,029

Religion(s)
47% traditional indigenous; 38% Roman Catholic; 15% Protestant

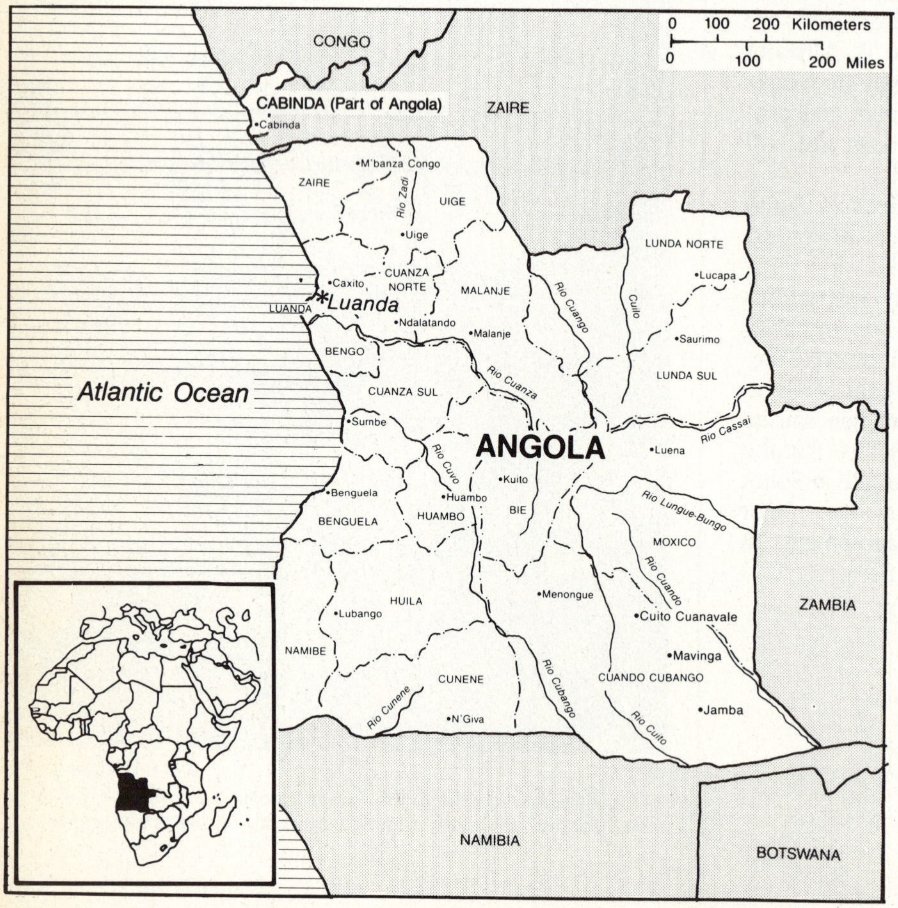

CABINDA

The tiny enclave of Cabinda, separated from the rest of Angola by a 25-mile strip of Zairian territory, is home to about 85,000 people. It is also the location of most of Angola's current petroleum output, which accounts for 86 percent of the nation's export earnings. Most of the oil is pumped from offshore fields by the Gulf Oil Corporation, whose royalty payments to the Marxist MPLA government in Luanda are the government's leading source of income. Ironically, this American company's installations have had to be guarded by Cuban troops against attacks from UNITA rebels, who are backed by the U.S. Central Intelligence Agency (CIA). There is also a small secessionist movement in the enclave, which is sponsored by the United States' regional ally, Zaire.

Education
Adult Literacy Rate: 41%

COMMUNICATION

Telephones: 40,000
Newspapers: 1

TRANSPORTATION

Highways—Kilometers (Miles): 73,828 (45,877)
Railroads—Kilometers (Miles): 3,189 (1,982)
Commercial Airports: 2 international

GOVERNMENT

Type: Marxist people's republic; one-party rule
Independence Date: November 11, 1975
Head of State: President Jose Edouardo dos Santos
Political Parties: Popular Movement for the Liberation of Angola-Labor Party
Suffrage: universal for adults

MILITARY

Number of Armed Forces: 100,000
Military Expenditures (% of Central Government Expenditures): n/a
Current Hostilities: civil war

ECONOMY

Currency ($ U.S. Equivalent): 29.62 kwanzas = $1 (fixed rate)
Per Capita Income/GNP: $600/$5 billion
Inflation Rate: n/a
Natural Resources: oil; diamonds; manganese; gold; uranium
Agriculture: coffee; sisal; corn; cotton; sugar; manioc; tobacco; bananas; plantains
Industry: oil; diamond mining; fish processing; brewing; tobacco; sugar processing; textiles; cement; food processing; construction

FOREIGN TRADE

Exports: $2.9 billion
Imports: $2.5 billion

ANGOLA

Angola is potentially one of the richest countries in Africa, but 15 years of civil war have reduced this nation of $8^{1}/_{2}$ million people to ruin. Since 1975, the year of the state's independence from Portugal, some 500,000 Angolans have perished due to the direct and indirect effects of the conflict. Up to a million others have fled the country, while another million or so are internally displaced. According to a report by the human-rights organization Africa Watch, tens of thousands of Angolans have lost their limbs "because of the indiscriminate use of landmines by both sides of the conflict." Angola's relatively small and impoverished population could not have perpetuated such carnage were it not for the long history of external interference in the nation's internal affairs. The United States, the Soviet Union, South Africa, Cuba, Zaire, and many others have helped to create, and continue to sustain, this tragedy.

THE COLONIAL LEGACY

The roots of Angola's current suffering lie in the area's colonial underdevelopment. The Portuguese first made contact with the peoples of the region in 1483. Initially they established peaceful trading contact with the powerful Kongo kingdom and other coastal peoples, some of whom were converted to Catholicism by Jesuit missionaries. But from the sixteenth to the mid-nineteenth centuries the outsiders primarily saw the area as a source of slaves. Angola has been called "the mother of Brazil" because up to 4 million were carried away from its shores to that country, chained in the holds of slave ships. With the possible exception of Nigeria, no African territory lost more of its people to the trans-Atlantic slave trade.

Following the nineteenth-century suppression of the slave trade, the Portuguese introduced internal systems of exploitation that very often amounted to slavery in all but name. Large numbers of Angolans were pressed into working on the coffee plantations owned by a growing community of white settlers, while others were forced to labor in other sectors, such as diamond mines or public-works projects.

Although the Portuguese claimed that they encouraged Angolans to learn Portuguese and practice Catholicism, thus becoming "assimilated" into the world of the colonizers, they actually made little effort to provide education. No more than 2 percent of the population ever achieved the legal status of "assimilado." The assimilados, many of whom were of mixed race, were concentrated in the coastal towns. Of the few interior Angolans who became literate, a large proportion were the products of Protestant, non-Portuguese, mission schools. Because each mission tended to operate in a particular region and to teach, usually in the local language, from its own syllabi, an unfortunate by-product of these schools was the reinforcement (the *creation,* some would argue) of ethnic rivalries among the territory's educated elite.

During the late colonial period three major liberation movements emerged to challenge Portuguese rule: the National Front for the Liberation of Angola (FNLA), the Popular Movement for the Liberation of Angola (MPLA), and the National Union for the Total Independence of Angola (UNITA). Although all three sought a national following, by 1975 each had built up an ethnoregional core of support. The FNLA grew out of a movement whose original focus had been limited to the northern Kongo-speaking population, while UNITA's principal stronghold was in the largely Ovimbundu-speaking south-central plateaux. The MPLA had its main backing among the assimilados and Kimbundu speakers, who were predominant in Luanda, the capital, and in the interior to the west of the city.

From the beginning all three movements also cultivated separate sources of external support. The MPLA, which had incorporated local members of the Portuguese Communist Party, enjoyed Soviet Bloc backing, while for a number of years UNITA received most of its arms from the Chinese (via Zambia) and thus adopted an appropriately Maoist posture. Despite its ties to Portugal through the North Atlantic Treaty Organization (NATO) alliance, the United States occasionally provided covert support to the FNLA, which also had consistent backing from Zaire. The armed struggle against the Portuguese began in 1961, with a massive FNLA-inspired uprising in the north and MPLA led unrest in Luanda. To counter the northern rebellion, the Portuguese resorted to the saturation bombing of villages, which during the first 12 months of fighting left an estimated 50,000 dead (about half of the total number killed throughout the anticolonial struggle). From the beginning, however, the liberation forces were as much hampered by their own disunity as by the brutality of Portugal's counterinsurgency tactics. Undisciplined rebels associated with the FNLA, for example, were known to massacre not only Portuguese plantation owners, but many of their southern workers as well. Such incidents contributed to UNITA's split from the FNLA in 1966. There is also evidence of UNITA forces cooperating with the Portuguese in attacks on the MPLA. Besides competition with its two rivals, the MPLA also encountered some difficulty in keeping its urban and rural factions united.

CIVIL WAR

The overthrow of Portugal's fascist government in 1974 led to Angola's rapid decolonization. Attempts to create a transitional government of national unity

(United Nations photo by J. P. Laffont)

The war for independence from Portugal led to the creation of a one-party state.

The Kongo state develops
1400

The Kongo state is contacted by the Portuguese
1483

Queen Nzinga defends the Mbundu kingdom against the Portuguese
1640

The MPLA is founded in Luanda
1956

The national war of liberation begins
1961

Angolan independence from Portugal
1975

South African-initiated air and ground incursions into Angola
1976

President Agostinho Neto dies; Jose dos Santos becomes president
1979

1980s–1990s

UNITA leader Jonas Savimbi visits the United States; U.S. "material and moral" support for UNITA resumes

Savimbi and dos Santos shake hands in Zaire, opening the door to direct peace negotiations, but the war continues

The MPLA renounces its commitment to Marxist-Leninism but affirms the need for its continued monopoly of power

between the three major nationalist movements failed. The MPLA succeeded in seizing Luanda, which led to a loose alliance between the FNLA and UNITA. As fighting between the groups escalated, so did the involvement of their outside backers. Meanwhile, most of Angola's 300,000 or more white settlers fled the country, their sudden departure triggering the collapse of much of the local economy. With the notable exception of Angola's booming offshore oil industry, most economic sectors have since failed to recover their pre-independence output, as a result of the war.

While the chronology of outside intervention in the Angolan conflict is a matter of dispute, it is nonetheless clear that by October 1975 up to 2,000 South African troops were assisting the FNLA-UNITA forces in the south. In response, Cuba dispatched a force of 18,000 to 20,000 to assist the MPLA, which had earlier gained control of Luanda. These two events proved decisive during the war's first phase. On the one hand, collaboration with South Africa led to the withdrawal of Chinese and much of the African support for the FNLA-UNITA cause. It also contributed to the U.S. Congress's passage of the so-called Clarke amendment, which abruptly terminated the United States' direct involvement. On the other hand, the arrival of the Cubans allowed the MPLA to gain the upper hand on the battlefield quickly. Not wishing to fight a conventional war against the Cubans by themselves, the South Africans withdrew in March 1976.

By 1977 the MPLA'S "People's Republic" had established itself in all of Angola's provinces and was recognized by the United Nations (UN) and most of its membership as the nation's sole legitimate government; the United States numbered among the few who continued to withhold recognition. However, the MPLA'S apparent victory did not bring an end to the hostilities. Although the remaining pockets of FNLA resistance were overcome following an Angola-Zaire rapprochement in 1978, UNITA has maintained its, largely guerrilla, struggle.

Until 1989 UNITA's major supporter was South Africa, whose destabilization of the Luanda government was motivated by its desire to keep the Benguela Railway closed (thus diverting traffic to its own system) and harass Angolan-based South West Africa People's Organization (SWAPO) forces (see the country report on Namibia). Besides supplying UNITA with logistical support, the South Africans repeatedly invaded southern Angola, and on occasion they infiltrated sabotage units into other areas of the country. South African aggression in turn justified Cuba's maintenance, by 1988, of some 50,000 troops in support of the government. In 1986 the U.S. Congress approved the resumption of covert material assistance to UNITA via Zaire.

An escalation of the fighting in 1987 and 1988 was accompanied by a revival of negotiations for a peace settlement between representatives of the Angolan government, Cuba, South Africa, and the United States. In the spring of 1988 South African forces were checked in a battle at the Angolan town of Cuito Cuanavale. Subsequently, South Africa agreed to withdraw from Namibia and to end its involvement in the Angolan conflict. It was further agreed that Cuba would complete a phased withdrawal of its forces from the region by July 1991. Hopes for further progress were raised in June 1989, when it appeared that Angolan President Jose Dos Santos and UNITA leader Jonas Savimbi had agreed to a framework for a negotiated settlement. However, by 1990 a short-lived ceasefire had given way to intensified fighting.

Despite the confident predictions of some that UNITA could not survive without South African support or, alternatively, that the MPLA government would quickly fold without its Cuban protectors, neither side in the conflict appears to be capable of a military victory in the near future. The United States has continued, and has probably escalated, its arms deliveries to UNITA, while the MPLA government has built up a sophisticated military, which it can keep supplied through its oil revenues in the unlikely event that it should lose its Soviet backing. Both factions, as well as the Soviets and Americans, have declared themselves in favor of a negotiated settlement. Such an outcome may be in the offing, but in the meantime a bit more of the Angolan nation dies with each passing day.

DEVELOPMENT

More than four-fifths of Angola's export revenues currently come from oil. There are important diamond and iron mines, but their output has suffered due to the war, which has also prevented the exploitation of the country's considerable reserves of other minerals. Angola also has enormous agricultural potential, but currently only about 2% of its arable land is under cultivation.

FREEDOM

The human-rights records of both UNITA and the MPLA are dismal. Savimbi has been known to have critics within his movement burned as witches, while many of the MPLA cadres who fought against the Portuguese were purged in 1977, in the aftermath of an alleged coup attempt.

HEALTH/WELFARE

According to a 1987 UNICEF report, the war has caused a serious deterioration of Angola's health service, resulting in lower life expectancy, 43 years overall, and an infant-mortality rate that is the highest in the world—200 per 1,000.

ACHIEVEMENTS

Between 1975 and 1980 the Angolan government claimed that it had tripled the nation's primary-school enrollment, to 76%. However, by 1984 the official figure had fallen back to 44%, as a result of the war.

Botswana

GEOGRAPHY

Area in Square Kilometers (Miles): 600,372 (231,804) (about the size of Texas)
Capital (Population): Gaborone (96,000)
Climate: arid; semiarid

PEOPLE

Population

Total: 1,225,000
Annual Growth Rate: 3.7%
Rural/Urban Population Ratio: 79/21
Languages: official: Setswana, English; others spoken: Khoisan; Kalanga; Herero

Health

Life Expectancy at Birth: 58 years (male); 64 years (female)
Infant Death Rate (Ratio): 43/1,000
Average Caloric Intake: 90% of FAO minimum
Physicians Available (Ratio): 1/7,900

Religion(s)

50% traditional indigenous; 50% Christian

Education

Adult Literacy Rate: 60%

THE KGOTLA

By tradition, all political and judicial decision-making within a Tswana community has to be aired in an open public forum known as the *kgotla*. This institution, somewhat analogous to the proverbial New England town meeting, has long served as a foundation of Tswana democratic ideals, as expressed in this common axiom: "A chief is a chief by the people." Politicians running for office in Botswana today know that they must visit and speak at kgotlas in their areas. In Botswana's cities, "freedom squares" provide an urban counterpart to the traditional kgotla. At the freedom squares, party candidates speak out on issues to crowds of onlookers. This heritage of debate and democracy may, in part, explain the strength and success of Botswana as a functioning parliamentary democracy.

COMMUNICATION

Telephones: 17,900
Newspapers: 4

TRANSPORTATION

Highways—Kilometers (Miles): 11,514 (11,098)
Railroads—Kilometers (Miles): 712 (441)
Commercial Airports: 3 international

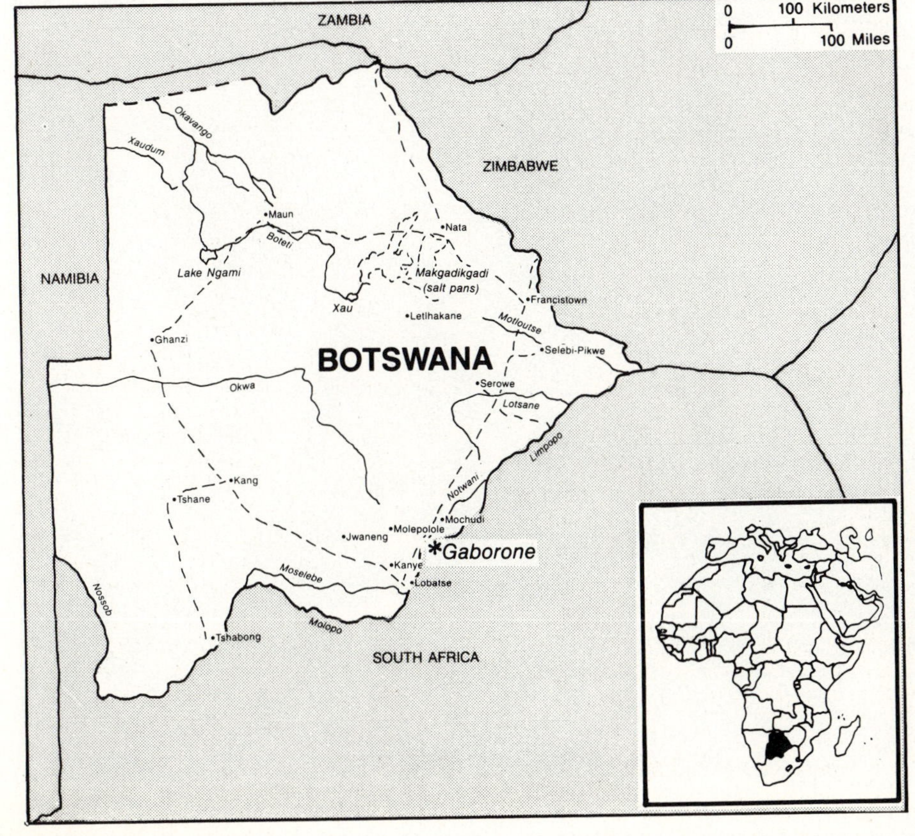

GOVERNMENT

Type: parliamentary republic
Independence Date: September 30, 1966
Head of State: President Quett K. J. Masire
Political Parties: Botswana Democratic Party; Botswana National Front; Botswana People's Party; Botswana Independence Party; Botswana Progressive Union
Suffrage: universal over 21

MILITARY

Number of Armed Forces: 4,650
Military Expenditures (% of Central Government Expenditures): 2.2%
Current Hostilities: none

ECONOMY

Currency ($ U.S. Equivalent): 1.8 pulas = $1
Per Capita Income/GNP: $1,600/$1.87 billion
Inflation Rate: 11.4%
Natural Resources: diamonds; copper; nickel; salt; soda ash; potash; coal
Agriculture: livestock; sorghum; corn; millet; cowpeas; beans
Industry: diamonds; copper; nickel; salt; soda ash; potash; frozen beef; tourism

FOREIGN TRADE

Exports: $1.3 billion
Imports: $1.1 billion

BOTSWANA

Botswana has been the Cinderella story of postcolonial Africa. In 1966 the country emerged from 80 years of British colonialism as a drought-stricken, underdeveloped backwater with an annual per capita income of $69. Over the past quarter-century the nation's economy has grown at an average annual rate of 13 percent, one of the world's highest. Infrastructure has been created and social services expanded. Whereas at independence the country had no paved roads, today major settlements are becoming increasingly interlinked by ribbons of asphalt and tarmac. A vibrant city has emerged at Gaborone, the nation's capital. New schools, hospitals, and businesses dot the landscape. Such growth has translated into improved standards of living for most Botswana citizens. However, the gap between the small, but growing, middle class (and the few truly wealthy) and the majority who remain poor is also widening, resulting in social tension.

Botswana's economic success has come in the context of its unbroken postindependence commitment to political pluralism, respect for human rights, and racial and ethnic tolerance. Freedom of speech and association have been upheld. Yet the country's internal strengths remain vulnerable to the external uncertainties of international markets, weather, and the policies of its neighbors, especially South Africa.

HISTORY

Most of Botswana's people share (Se)Tswana as their mother tongue, a language that is also commonly spoken in much of South Africa. There also exist a number of minority communities—Kalanga, Herero, Khalagadi, Khiosan groups, and others—but contemporary ethnic conflict is peaceful and relatively modest. During the nineteenth century most of Botswana was incorporated into five Tswana states, each centering around a large settlement of 10,000 or more people. These states, which incorporated non-Tswana communities, survived through agropastoralism, hunting, and their control of trade routes linking Southern and Central Africa. Lucrative dealing in ivory and ostrich feathers allowed local rulers to build up their arsenals and thus deter the aggressive designs of South African whites. However, European missionaries and traders were welcomed, leading to a growth of Christian education and the consumption of industrial goods.

A radical transformation took place after the imposition of British overrule in 1885. Colonial taxes and economic decline stimulated the growth of migrant labor to the mines and industries of South Africa. (In many regions, migrant earnings remain the major source of income today.) Although colonial rule brought much hardship and little benefit, the twentieth-century relationship between the peoples of Botswana and the British was complicated by local fears of being incorporated into South Africa. For many decades leading nationalists championed continued rule from London as a shield against their powerful, racially oppressive neighbor.

ECONOMIC DEVELOPMENT

Economic growth since independence has been largely fueled by the rapid expansion

(United Nations photo by E. Darroch)

Botswana, like many other African nations is susceptible to periodic drought. The country, however, has a good supply of underground water and the governmental competence to utilize this resource. In the picture above antelopes drink from a hole dug to allow water seepage.

Tswana establish themselves in Southern Africa
1400s

Invading groups of Nguni and Southern Sotho threaten the Tswana
1820s

Afrikaners begin to encroach on Tswana land north of the Orange River
1839

The British establish colonial rule over Botswana
1885

Botswana gains independence
1966

1980s–1990s

Seretse Khama, the nation's first president, dies in office and is succeeded by Quett Masire

Elections in 1984 and 1989 result in landslide victories for the Democratic Party; the National Front is major opposition party

South African raids kill Botswana citizens and South African exiles; new security laws are passed

of mining activity. Botswana has become one of the world's leading producers of diamonds, which typically account for 80 percent of its export earnings. Local production is managed by Debswana Corporation, an even partnership between the Botswana government and DeBeers, a South African-based global corporation; DeBeers's Central Selling Organization has a near monopoly on diamond sales worldwide. The Botswana government has a good record of maximizing the local benefits of Debswana's production. In 1987 it acquired a 5-percent share of DeBeers (global), along with 2 seats on its board.

The nickel/copper/cobalt mining complex at Selibi-Pikwe is the largest nongovernment employer in Botswana. Falling metal prices and high development costs have reduced the mine's profitability, but high operating efficiency has assured its survival. Other mining activities include coal (the largest reserves in Africa, but of low quality), gold, and asbestos. A soda-ash extraction complex is under construction, while additional mineral reserves, such as chrome, manganese, and platinum, are believed to exist.

Given that mining can only make a modest contribution to local employment, Botswana's future is very much dependent on the growth of its currently small manufacturing and service sectors. Meat processing is now the largest industrial activity besides minerals, but efforts are under way to attract overseas investment in both private and parastatal production. Botswana already has a liberal foreign-exchange policy and plans to establish an export-processing zone at Selibi-Pikwe. The nation's first auto-assembly plant was opened in Gaborone in 1990. Small-scale production is encouraged through government subsidies. Almost 90 percent of Botswana's exports go to Europe, while more than 70 percent of its imports come from South Africa.

AGRICULTURE

Agriculture is still the leading economic activity for most Botswana citizens. The standard Tswana greeting, *Pula,* ("Rain") reflects the significance attached to water in a society prone to its periodic scarcity. Botswana suffered severe drought during the 1980s, which—despite the availability of underground water supplies—had a devastating effect on both crops and livestock. Some 1 million cattle, one-third of the national herd, are believed to have perished. Small-scale agropastoralists, who make up the largest segment of the population, were particularly hard-hit. However, government relief measures were effective in preventing famine. The government also provides generous subsidies to farmers, but environmental constraints hamper efforts to achieve food self-sufficiency even in nondrought years.

Commercial agriculture is dominated by livestock. The Lobatse abbatoir, opened in 1954, stimulated the growth of the cattle industry. Despite periodic challenges from disease and drought, beef exports have become relatively stable. Much of the output of the Botswana Meat Commission has preferential access in the European Community (EC), although there is some concern regarding the potential for future reduction in the European quota. Because most of Botswana's herds are grazed in communal lands, questions about the allocation of pasture are a source of local debate. There is also growing concern about possible overgrazing.

THE SOUTH AFRICA PROBLEM

South Africa remains a lingering problem. Since the nineteenth century Botswana has sheltered refugees from racist oppression elsewhere in the region. This has led to periodic acts of aggression against the country. Attacks from South Africa greatly increased during the 1980s, when Botswana became the repeated victim of overt military raids and covert terrorist operations. Recent events within South Africa have led to a considerable easing of tensions, which hopefully will prove to be more than transitory. In the meantime, Botswana has tightened its security; a number of South African commandos and agents were captured in 1989.

Given its economic dependence on South African imports, Botswana cannot afford to impose trade sanctions against its neighbor, but it has urged the international community to do so. Gaborone is the headquarters of the Southern African Development Coordination Council (SADCC), which is working to reduce the economic dependence of its 10 member nations on the apartheid state.

DEVELOPMENT

Since independence, primary education has become nearly universal. By 1991, 70% of primary graduates are to gain access to secondary education. A university, several other tertiary institutions, and 70 vocational centers have also been established.

FREEDOM

Democratic pluralism has been stengthened by the growth of a strong civil society. Numerous new organizations representing diverse interests—labor unions, women's rights coalitions, professional associations, vocational brigades, etc.—have emerged. There is a growing independent press. Since independence, there have been no political killings or detentions.

HEALTH/WELFARE

The national health service provides medical, dental, and optical care for all Botswana residents. More than 90% of the population live within 10 miles of a health-care facility. Efforts are now being made to upgrade facilities and staff. Malnutrition remains a major concern, and automobile fatalities a growing one.

ACHIEVEMENTS

The UN's 1990 Human Development Report singles out Botswana among the nations of Africa for significantly improving the living conditions of its people. In 1989 President Masire was awarded the Hunger Project's leadership prize, based on Botswana's record of improving rural nutritional levels during the 1980s despite 7 years of severe drought.

Lesotho (Kingdom of Lesotho)

GEOGRAPHY

Area in Square Kilometers (Miles): 30,344 (11,716) (about the size of Maryland)
Capital (Population): Maseru (80,200)
Climate: temperate

PEOPLE

Population

Total: 1,755,000
Annual Growth Rate: 2.6%
Rural/Urban Population Ratio: 88/12
Languages: official: English and Sesotho; others spoken: Xhosa, Zulu

Health

Life Expectancy at Birth: 59 years (male); 62 years (female)
Infant Death Rate (Ratio): 80/1,000
Average Caloric Intake: 107% of FAO minimum
Physicians Available (Ratio): 1/12,280

Religion(s)

80% Christian; 20% traditional indigenous

THE SESOTHO LANGUAGE

Since the mid-nineteenth century Sesotho has been a leading literary language in Africa. Basotho writers have produced a wealth of prose, poetry, and nonfiction in their vernacular. The *Leselinyane La Lesotho*, first published in 1863, is sub-Saharan Africa's oldest continuous vernacular newspaper. Thomas Mofolo's play *Chaka* and Paulas Mopeli's novel *Blanket Boy* are among the many works that have been translated for international audiences. Sesotho also continues to be a major medium in music, journalism, and broadcasting. The South African government has promoted a separate Sesotho alphabet for use among Sotho peoples living in South Africa; this has created one more barrier for South Africans who have tried to encourage reconvergence among various regional dialects.

Education

Adult Literacy Rate: 59%

COMMUNICATION

Telephones: 5,400
Newspapers: 3

TRANSPORTATION

Highways—Kilometers (Miles): 5,167 (3,203)
Railroads—Kilometers (Miles): 1.6 (0.99)
Commercial Airports: 1 international

GOVERNMENT

Type: constitutional monarchy
Independence Date: October 4, 1966
Head of State: Major General Justinus Lekhanya (head of the governing Military Council)
Political Parties: banned in 1986
Suffrage: universal over 21

MILITARY

Number of Armed Forces: 2,000
Military Expenditures (% of Central Government Expenditures): 8.6%
Current Hostilities: none

ECONOMY

Currency ($ U.S. Equivalent): 2.55 malotis = $1
Per Capita Income/GNP: $245/$512 million
Inflation Rate: 15%
Natural Resources: diamonds; water; agricultural and grazing land
Agriculture: mohair; corn; wheat; sorghum; peas; beans; potatoes; asparagus; sheep; cattle
Industry: carpets; woolen apparel; candle making; pottery; jewelry; tapestries; tourism; mining

FOREIGN TRADE

Exports: $55 million
Imports: $526 million

Lesotho emerges as a leading state in Southern Africa
1820s

Afrikaners annex half of Lesotho
1866

The Sotho successfully fight to preserve local autonomy under the British
1870–1881

Independence is restored
1966

The elections and Constitution are declared void by Leabua Jonathan
1970

An uprising against the government fails
1974

The Lesotho Liberation Army begins a sabotage campaign
1979

1980s–1990s

South African destabilization leads to the overthrow of Jonathan by the military

Pope John Paul II's visit is accompanied by the hijacking of a bus carrying pilgrims; the hijackers are killed by South African commandos

King Moshoeshoe II is exiled by Major General Justinus Lekhanya, who promises elections by 1992

LESOTHO

The beauty of its snow-topped mountains has led visitors to proclaim the Kingdom of Lesotho as "the Switzerland of Africa." Unlike its European namesake, however, this small independent enclave in the heart of South Africa has enjoyed neither peace nor prosperity since the restoration of its independence in 1966. Listed by the United Nations as one of the world's Least Developed Countries, each year the lack of opportunity at home causes half of Lesotho's adult males to seek employment in South Africa. Foreign aid and a share of customs collected by South Africa are the next-largest sources of revenue. The overt and covert intervention of South African interests in local affairs has been pervasive.

POLITICAL DEVELOPMENT

Lesotho is one of the most ethnically homogeneous nations in Africa; almost all of its citizens are Sotho. The country's emergence and survival were largely the product of the diplomatic and military prowess of its nineteenth-century rulers, especially its great founder, King Moshoeshoe I. During the 1860s warfare with South African whites led to the loss of land and people and acceptance of British overrule. For nearly a century the British preserved the country, but they also taxed the inhabitants and generally neglected their interests. Consequently, Lesotho remains dependent on South Africa.

Shortly after independence, the Conservative National Party (BNP) prime minister, Leabua Jonathan, placed King Moshoeshoe II under house arrest and later temporarily exiled him. The rival Congress Party (BCP) won the 1970 elections, but Jonathan, possibly at the behest of South Africa, declared a state of emergency and nullified the results.

During the early 1980s armed resistance to Jonathan's dictatorship was carried out by the Lesotho Liberation Army (LLA), an armed faction of the BCP. The Lesotho government maintained that the LLA was aided and abetted by South Africa as part of South Africa's regional-destabilization efforts. In fact, by 1983 both the South African government and the Catholic hierarchy were becoming nervous about Jonathan's establishment of diplomatic ties with various communist-ruled countries and the growing sympathy within the BNP for the ANC. South African military raids and terrorist attacks targeting anti-apartheid refugees in Lesotho became increasingly common. Finally, a South African blockade of Lesotho in 1986 led to Jonathan's ouster by his military.

Jonathan's rule had been the source of great resentment and his overthrow was generally welcomed. But skepticism of the new regime runs deep. Most Sotho have spent time in South Africa and have thus suffered under apartheid. Both in its rise to power and subsequent policies, Lesotho's ruling Military Council, led by Major General Justinus Lekhanya, has been closely linked to South Africa. The Catholic Church has put pressure on the government to return to civilian rule, and some military leaders want to return to the barracks. There is also military and civilian support for the still-exiled Moshoeshoe II, who is believed to be sympathetic to the ANC.

Lekhanya has sought legitimacy by promising elections by 1992. However, the general's own reputation has been tarnished as a result of his being linked to the fatal shooting of a university student in 1988; many suspect him of being guilty of murder.

Lesotho is economically integrated with South Africa, which accounts for 90 percent of the nation's exports and 97 percent of its imports. Producers of wool (the largest export after labor) must rely on South African marketing boards. South African companies control Lesotho's small tourist and diamond industries. The Lesotho National Development Corporation actively seeks to attract further South African investment. The Highland Water Scheme, the biggest local development project ever launched, will provide hydroelectric power to South African industry. Besides being in a customs union with South Africa, Lesotho's currency, the maloti, is tied to the South African rand (which is also legal tender in Lesotho).

Many have long dismissed Lesotho as a South African homeland with international recognition. However, most Sotho are proud of their nation's heritage, although there is also widespread belief that it will never be truly independent until apartheid is abolished. Whether Lesotho would politically unite with a postapartheid South Africa is uncertain.

DEVELOPMENT

Despite an infusion of international aid, Lesotho's economic dependence on South Africa has not decreased since independence; indeed, it has been calculated that the majority of outside funds expended on various projects aimed at increasing local self-sufficiency have actually ended up paying for South African services.

FREEDOM

Since the suspension of the Constitution in 1970, there has been widespread abuse of human rights. Many incidents of repression have involved the nation's security forces, which have long had close ties to their South African counterparts. After the 1986 military coup, a general amnesty for political prisoners was granted. Some exiles have returned, but abuses continue.

HEALTH/WELFARE

With many young men working in the mines of South Africa, much of the resident population relies on subsistence agriculture. Despite efforts to boost production, malnutrition, aggravated by drought, is a serious problem.

ACHIEVEMENTS

Lesotho has long been known for the high quality of its schools, which for more than a century and a half have trained many of the leading citizens of Southern Africa. The national university at Roma was established in 1945 and for a while served as the main campus of the University of Botswana, Lesotho, and Swaziland, until it resumed its autonomous status in 1976.

Malawi (Republic of Malawi)

GEOGRAPHY

Area in Square Kilometers (Miles): 118,484 (45,747) (about the size of Pennsylvania)
Capital (Population): Lilongwe (220,000)
Climate: subtropical

PEOPLE

Population

Total: 9,157,000
Annual Growth Rate: 1.8%
Rural/Urban Population Ratio: 88/12
Languages: official: Chichewa, English; others spoken: Nyanja, Yao, Sena, Tumbuka, others

Health

Life Expectancy at Birth: 48 years (male); 50 years (female)
Infant Death Rate (Ratio): 130/1,000
Average Caloric Intake: 97% of FAO minimum
Physicians Available (Ratio): 1/53,000

Religion(s)

75% Christian; 20% Muslim; 5% traditional indigenous

JOHN CHILEMBWE

In 1915 John Chilembwe of Nyasaland (now Malawi) struck a blow against British colonialism and died in the attempt. Chilembwe was a Christian minister who had studied in South Africa as well as in the United States. He had returned home to establish the Providence Industrial Mission and to build a great church. His feelings against the British settlers developed from the injustices he had seen: European takeover of lands for plantations, poor working conditions for laborers, increased taxation, and, especially, the recruitment of Africans to fight and die in World War I. He rallied a few followers and planned an uprising, which led to the deaths of three settlers and the imprisonment or deaths of the Africans involved or suspected of involvement. Chilembwe appears to have planned his martyrdom. This uprising was the first effort in Southern Africa to resist colonialism and yet maintain many of the aspects of society that had developed from its influence.

Education

Adult Literacy Rate: 27%

COMMUNICATION

Telephones: 36,800
Newspapers: 4

TRANSPORTATION

Highways—Kilometers (Miles): 13,135 (8,143)
Railroads—Kilometers (Miles): 789 (489)
Commercial Airports: 2 international

GOVERNMENT

Type: republic; one-party state
Independence Date: July 6, 1964
Head of State: President-for-Life H. Kamuzu Banda
Political Parties: Malawi Congress Party
Suffrage: universal over 21

MILITARY

Number of Armed Forces: 7,250
Military Expenditures (% of Central Government Expenditures): 1.6%
Current Hostilities: none

ECONOMY

Currency ($ U.S. Equivalent): 2.67 kwachas = $1
Per Capita Income/GNP: $180/$1.4 billion
Inflation Rate: 31.5%
Natural Resources: limestone; uranium potential
Agriculture: tobacco; tea; sugar; corn; peanuts
Industry: food; beverages; tobacco; textiles; footwear

FOREIGN TRADE

Exports: $292 million
Imports: $402 million

Malawi trading kingdoms develop
1500s

Explorer David Livingstone arrives along Lake Malawi; missionaries follow
1859

The British protectorate of Nyasaland (present-day Malawi) is declared
1891

Reverend John Chilembwe and followers rise against settlers and are suppressed
1915

The Nyasaland African Congress, the first nationalist movement, is formed
1944

Independence under the leadership of Hastings Banda
1964

Diplomatic ties are established with South Africa
1967

Ngwazi Hastings Kamazu Banda becomes president-for-life
1971

1980s–1990s

Austerity measures are enacted; creditors reschedule debts

An upsurge in attacks on Malawian exiles in Zambia

An influx of Mozambican refugees is accompanied by drought and food shortages

MALAWI

Although officially a republic, Malawi has evolved into a de facto absolute monarchy under its President-for-Life Dr. Ngwazi Hastings Kamuzu Banda. Unlike a true monarchy, however, there is in Malawi no clear successor to the aging (born in 1898) Ngwazi ("Great Lion"). During the early months of independence, in 1964, Banda purged his Cabinet and ruling Malawi Congress Party of most of the leading young politicians, who earlier had promoted him to leadership in the nationalist struggle. Since then many others who once seemed close to the throne have lost their positions—or worse. A second generation of Malawians is now growing up with the knowledge that an unkind thought toward their president-for-life could prove fatal. In recent years dozens of exiles, along with their families, have been kidnapped and/or killed in neighboring states; within Malawi itself, citizens generally avoid any discussion that might be deemed sensitive.

DEVELOPMENT

Banda has not survived merely through repression. Until 1979 the country enjoyed a respectable economic growth rate, averaging 6 percent per annum. Almost all of its growth came from increased agricultural production. As was the case during the colonial period, the postindependence government favored large estates specializing in exported cash crops. Tobacco, sugar, and tea consistently have accounted for more than 80 percent of the nation's export earnings. While in the past the estates were almost exclusively the preserve of a few hundred white settlers, today many are controlled either by the state or by local individuals, with Banda himself being the largest landholder.

During the 1970s the prosperity of the estates helped fuel a boom in industries involved in agricultural processing. By 1985 some 19 percent of Malawi's gross domestic product was in manufacturing, a figure that has since declined to 12 percent. Malawi's limited economic success, prior to the 1980s, came at the expense of the vast majority of its citizens, who survive as smallholders growing food crops. By 1985, 86 percent of rural householders farmed on fewer than 5 acres. In addition to land shortage, peasant production has suffered from soil depletion, low official produce prices, and lack of other inputs. The northern half of the country, which has almost no estate production, has been neglected in terms of government expenditure on transport and other forms of infrastructure. For generations many Malawian peasants have turned to migrant labor as a means of coping with their poverty, but in recent years there have been far fewer opportunities for them in South Africa and Zimbabwe.

THE RENAMO BURDEN

Under pressure from the World Bank, the government since 1981 has modestly increased its incentives to the smallholders. Land alienation was largely halted and produce prices were increased. Although welcome steps, these reforms would have been insufficient to overcome the continuing impoverishment of rural households under even the best circumstances. In fact, Malawi's entire economy has, for the past decade, been in a state of crisis, due to the effects of warfare in neighboring Mozambique. The activities of Renamo rebels across the border have largely deprived landlocked Malawi of access to the Mozambican ports of Beira and Nacala. In addition to the loss of its transport routes, Malawi has been burdened by a massive influx of Mozambican refugees, now numbering about 1 million.

The effects of Renamo's destabilization have contributed to growing cooperation between Malawi and neighboring Frontline States. In the past the Frontline States (Angola, Botswana, Mozambique, Tanzania, Zambia, and Zimbabwe) have been suspicious of Malawi's close relations with South Africa. Malawi also had close ties with the Rhodesian and Portuguese colonial governments in the region. Prior to 1986 Malawi to a greater or lesser degree also allowed its territory to be used by Renamo. However, since then small contingents of Malawian troops have helped to reopen partially the rail line to Nacala. Malawi has also given Mozambican officials access to the refugee camps within its borders. While internal reform and an end to the civil war in Mozambique would be beneficial to Malawi, the nation's long-term prospects for development are dependent on its relations with other neighboring states.

DEVELOPMENT

After decades of relative neglect, educational opportunities have increased in recent years; today two-thirds of Malawian children receive some schooling. However, secondary education is limited to a small elite. Adult literacy is only 27%.

FREEDOM

Banda has instilled in Malawi a climate of fear, which allows for little freedom. Exiled opposition groups include the Malawi Freedom Movement (Mafremo) and the Socialist League of Malawi (Lesoma). To date these movements have been largely ineffectual, but they could become important in the post-Banda era.

HEALTH/WELFARE

Malawi's health service is considered expectionally poor even for an impoverished country. The country has the fourth-highest child death rate in the world, while more than half of its children under age 5 are stunted by malnutrition.

ACHIEVEMENTS

Although it is the poorest, most overcrowded country in the region, Malawi's response to the influx of Mozambican refugees has been described by the U.S. Committee for Refugees as "no less than heroic." Unlike some of its better-endowed neighbors who have faced far smaller influxes, the Malawi government has so far resisted pressures for the forced repatriation of the refugees.

Mozambique (People's Republic of Mozambique)

GEOGRAPHY

Area in Square Kilometers (Miles): 786,762 (303,769) (about twice the size of California)
Capital (Population): Maputo (882,000)
Climate: tropical to subtropical

PEOPLE

Population

Total: 14,566,000
Annual Growth Rate: 2.6%
Rural/Urban Population Ratio: 91/9
Languages: official: Portuguese; others spoken: Yao, Tubbuka, Batonga, Makua

Health

Life Expectancy at Birth: 45 years (male); 49 years (female)
Infant Death Rate (Ratio): 138/1,000
Average Caloric Intake: 78% of FAO minimum
Physicians Available (Ratio): 1/52,206

Religion(s)

65% traditional indigenous; 22% Christian; 11% Muslim; 2% others

WOMEN AND THE MOZAMBICAN REVOLUTION

Women played an important role as both fighters and support personnel during Frelimo's struggle against the Portuguese. Since Mozambique's independence they have become increasingly prominent in social areas that were once exclusively male domains. One-sixth of the membership of the 1983 Frelimo Congress consisted of women. In general, Frelimo (26 percent of whose members are women) and its affiliate the Organization of Mozambican Women (OMM) have actively sought to end gender discrimination. Education and job opportunities have been opened up; working women have been guaranteed 2 months of maternity leave; a Family Law has given women protection in cases of divorce, desertion, and child custody; and rules against sexual harassment have been vigorously enforced. Despite progress in these and other areas, Mozambican women, both within and outside the OMM, have become increasingly militant in demanding greater empowerment from the still nearly all-male national leadership.

Education

Adult Literacy Rate: 32%

COMMUNICATION

Telephones: 59,000
Newspapers: 2

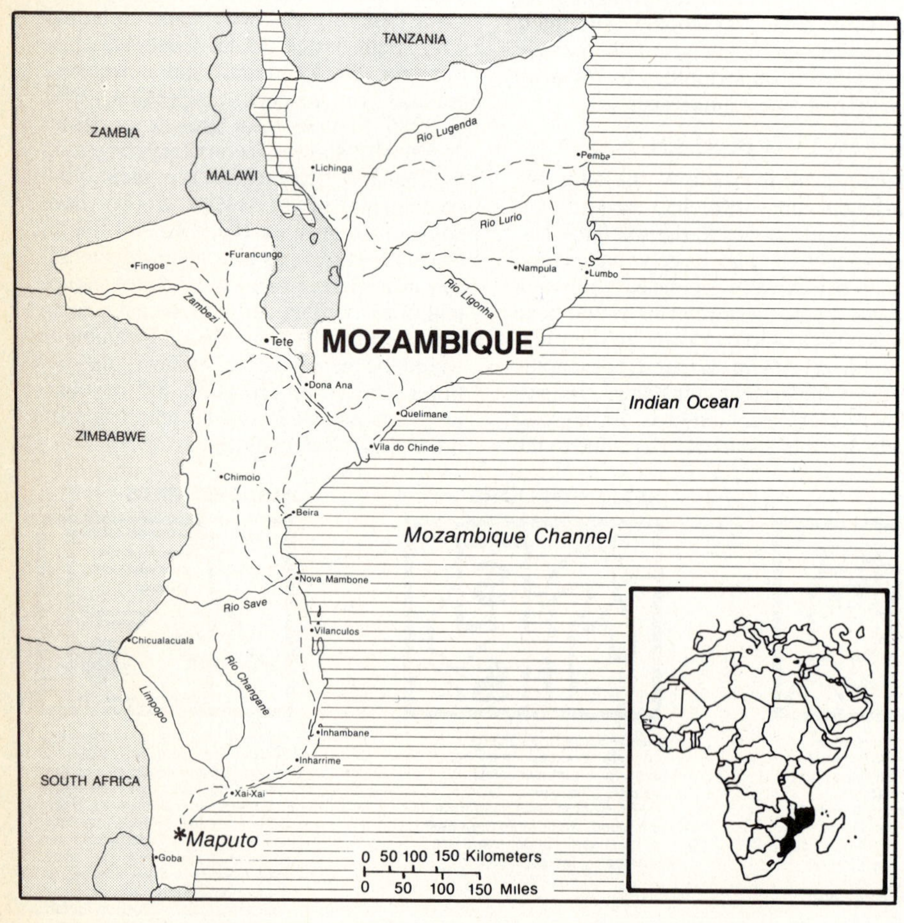

TRANSPORTATION

Highways—Kilometers (Miles): 26,498 (16,465)
Railroads—Kilometers (Miles): 3,288 (2,038)
Commercial Airports: 3 international

GOVERNMENT

Type: republic
Independence Date: June 25, 1975
Head of State: President Joaquim Chissano
Political Parties: Mozambique Liberation Front (Frelimo)
Suffrage: not yet established

MILITARY

Number of Armed Forces: 65,000
Military Expenditures (% of Central Government Expenditures): 8.4%
Current Hostilities: rebel attacks; attacks by South Africa

ECONOMY

Currency ($ U.S. Equivalent): 800 meticais = $1
Per Capita Income/GNP: $110/$1.6 billion
Inflation Rate: 81%
Natural Resources: coal; iron ore; tantalite; flourite; timber
Agriculture: cotton; tobacco; cashews; sugar; tea; copra; sisal; subsistence crops
Industry: processed foods; textiles; beverages; refined oil; chemicals; tobacco; cement; glass

FOREIGN TRADE

Exports: $100 million
Imports: $764 million

MOZAMBIQUE

For more than a quarter-century Mozambique has been bled by war. Between 1964 and 1974 Frelimo, the Mozambique Liberation Front, struggled against Portuguese colonial rule. At the cost of some 30,000 lives, Mozambique, in June 1975, gained its independence under Frelimo's leadership. Although the new nation was one of the least-developed countries in the world, many people were optimistic that the lessons learned in the struggle could be applied to the task of building a dynamic new society based on Marxist-Leninist principles.

Unfortunately, Mozambican hopes for any sort of postindependence progress were quickly sabotaged by the Mozambique National Resistance (MNR, or Renamo), which was originally established as a counterrevolutionary fifth column by the Rhodesian Central Intelligence Organization (see the country report on Zimbabwe). By 1989 up to 700,000 people had died as a result of the rebellion, including more than 100,000 purposely murdered by Renamo. It is further estimated that, out of a total population of 15 million, some 3 million people have been internally displaced, while more than 1 million others have fled to neighboring states. No African nation has paid a higher price in its resistance against white supremacy.

THE COLONIAL LEGACY

Although some parts of Mozambique were occupied by the Portuguese for more than 400 years, most of the country only came under colonial control during the early twentieth century. Thereafter the territory was developed as a dependency of neighboring colonial economies, rather than that of Portugal itself. Mozambican ports were linked by rail to South Africa and the interior colonies of British Central Africa—that is, modern Malawi, Zambia, and Zimbabwe. In the southern provinces, most men, and many women, spent time as migrant laborers in South Africa. The majority of the males worked in the gold mines. For its assistance in recruitment, the mining companies paid the Portuguese an annual sum in gold bullion.

During the early decades of this century most of northern Mozambique was granted to three predominately British concessions companies, whose abusive policies led many to flee the colony. For decades the colonial state and many local enterprises also relied on forced labor. After World War II new demands were put on Mozambicans by a growing influx of Portuguese settlers, whose numbers swelled during the 1960s, from 90,000 to more than 200,000. Meanwhile, even by the dismal standards of European colonialism in Africa, there continued to be a notable lack of concern for human development. At independence, 93 percent of the African population were illiterate. Most of those who had acquired literacy or other skills had done so despite the Portuguese presence.

Although a welcome event in itself, the sudden nature of the Portuguese empire's

(United Nations photo by Paul Heath Hoeffel)

Mozambique has been at war for 25 years. The resulting drain on natural resources, the displacement of approximately one-fifth of the population, and the persistent drought have led to the necessity of importing food to stave off famine.

Portuguese explorers land in Mozambique
1497

Mozambican laborers begin migrating to South African mines
1800–1890

The Frelimo liberation movement officially launched
1962

Frelimo's leader, Eduardo Mondlane, is killed by a parcel bomb
1969

The liberation struggle is successful when the Portuguese revolution brings independence
1975

1980s–1990s

A South African commando unit attacks Maputo; increased Renamo attacks on civilian and military targets

President Samora Machel is killed in a mysterious airplane crash; Joaquim Chissano becomes president

Mozambique increases diplomatic efforts for peace in the region

collapse contributed to the destabilization of postindependence Mozambique. Because Frelimo had succeeded in establishing itself as a unified nationalist front, Mozambique was spared an immediate descent into civil conflict, such as that which engulfed Angola, Portugal's other major African possession. However, the economy was already bankrupt due to the Portuguese policy of running Mozambique on a nonconvertible local currency. The rapid transition to independence compounded this problem by encouraging the sudden exodus of almost all of the Portuguese settlers.

Perhaps even more costly to Mozambique in the long term was the polarization between Frelimo and the former regime's African supporters, including about 100,000 who had been active in the regime's security forces. The rapid Portuguese withdrawal did not help the difficult task of reconciliation. While the "compromised ones" (former regime supporters) were not subjected by Frelimo to bloody reprisals, their rights were circumscribed and many were sent, along with prostitutes and other so-called antisocial elements, to "reeducation camps." While the historically pro-Portuguese stance of the local Roman Catholic hierarchy would have complicated its relations with the new state under any circumstances, Frelimo's Marxist rejection of religion initially alienated it to some degree from many believers.

TROUBLED INDEPENDENCE

Frelimo assumed power without the benefit or burden of a strong sense of administrative continuity. While it had begun to create alternative social structures in its "liberated zones" during the anticolonial struggle, these areas had only encompassed a small percentage of Mozambique's population and infrastructure. But Frelimo was initially able to fill the vacuum and to launch aggressive development efforts. Health care and education were expanded, workers' committees successfully ran many of the enterprises abandoned by the settlers, and communal villages coordinated rural development. However, efforts to promote agricultural collectivization as the foundation of a command economy generally led to peasant resistance and economic failure. Frelimo's continued ability to adapt and implement many of its programs under trying conditions has largely been due to its disciplined mass base; the party's membership today stands at about 200,000.

No sooner had Mozambique begun to stabilize itself from the immediate dislocations of its decolonization process than it became embroiled in the Rhodesian conflict. Mozambique was the only neighboring state to impose fully the "mandatory" United Nations economic sanctions against Rhodesia. Between 1976 and 1980 this decision led to the direct loss of half a billion dollars in rail and port revenues. Furthermore, Frelimo's decision to provide bases for the fighters of the Patriotic Front led to a state of undeclared war with Rhodesia as well as its Renamo proxies. Unfortunately, the fall of Rhodesia did not bring an end to externally sponsored destabilization.

Throughout the 1980s Renamo continued to enjoy the support of South Africa. By continuing Renamo's campaign of destabilization, the Pretoria regime gained leverage over its hostile neighbors, for the continued closure of Mozambique's ports meant that most of their traffic had to pass through South Africa. In 1984 Mozambique signed a nonagression pact with South Africa, which should have put an end to the latter party's support of Renamo. However, captured documents and other evidence indicate that direct South African support for Renamo continued, at least until 1989. In response, Zimbabwe and to a lesser extent Malawi and Tanzania contributed troops to assist in the defense of Mozambique.

In its 1989 Congress, Frelimo formally abandoned its commitment to the primacy of Marxist-Leninist ideology and opened the door to further political and economic reforms. The government, with the Catholic Church and the governments of Kenya and Zimbabwe acting as mediators, has also opened direct talks with Renamo. While recently improved relations with South Africa have given rise to guarded optimism about the eventual success of on-going Frelimo-Renamo talks, it is not at all clear whether the latter has the capacity to function as anything other than a large-scale terrorist group. Even if peace should come, the wounds of war will take decades to heal in Mozambique.

DEVELOPMENT

To maintain minimum services and to recover from wartime destruction, Mozambique relies on the commitment of its citizens and international assistance. Western churches have sent relief supplies, food aid, and vehicles; the United Kingdom is training a small number of Mozambican soldiers; and the United States has sent humanitarian aid.

FREEDOM

Mozambique established campaigns against abuses by the security forces and against corruption, as a response to popular complaints. President Joaquim Chissano offered an amnesty to Renamo rebels in 1987. On-going constitutional changes have liberalized the political climate and could lead to the establishment of a multiparty state.

HEALTH/WELFARE

An immunization campaign that vaccinated 95% of Mozambicans against measles, tuberculosis, tetanus, and small pox has begun to have positive results. But civil strife, widespread Renamo attacks on health units, and food shortages have drastically curtailed health-care goals and have led to Mozambique having the highest infant-mortality rate in the world.

ACHIEVEMENTS

Between 1975 and 1980 Mozambique's illiteracy rate declined from 93% to 72%, while classroom attendance more than doubled. However, progress slowed during the 1980s due to Renamo attacks, which by 1988 had destroyed more than 2,600 schools. In 1989 UNESCO estimated that the rate of illiteracy remained at 68%.

Namibia

GEOGRAPHY

Area in Square Kilometers (Miles): 824,292 (318,261) (twice the size of California)
Capital (Population): Windhoek (110,600)
Climate: arid; semi-arid

PEOPLE

Population
Total: 1,600,000
Annual Growth Rate: 2.7%
Rural/Urban Population Ratio: n/a
Languages: official: English; others spoken: Ouambo, Kavango, Nama/Damara, Herero, Khoisan, German, Afrikaans

Health
Life Expectancy at Birth: 57 years (male); 63 years (female)
Infant Death Rate (Ratio): 120/1,000
Average Caloric Intake: n/a
Physicians Available (Ratio): 1/4,736

Religion(s)
70% Christian; 30% traditional indigenous

POSTAPARTHEID DEVELOPMENT

Many view Namibia's independence as a test case for the end of apartheid in South Africa. For this reason, the country is being closely monitored to see what types of policies its new African leaders will adopt with regard to economic development, foreign investment, and human rights. Whites in South Africa perceive Namibia as a window to their own postapartheid future. The new government in Namibia is, however, grappling with the difficult problems of restoring an economy severely distorted by apartheid and providing jobs for thousands of demobilized freedom fighters and other soldiers who fought on the side of South Africa.

Education
Adult Literacy Rate: 99% whites; 16% nonwhites

COMMUNICATION

Telephones: 62,800
Newspapers: 11

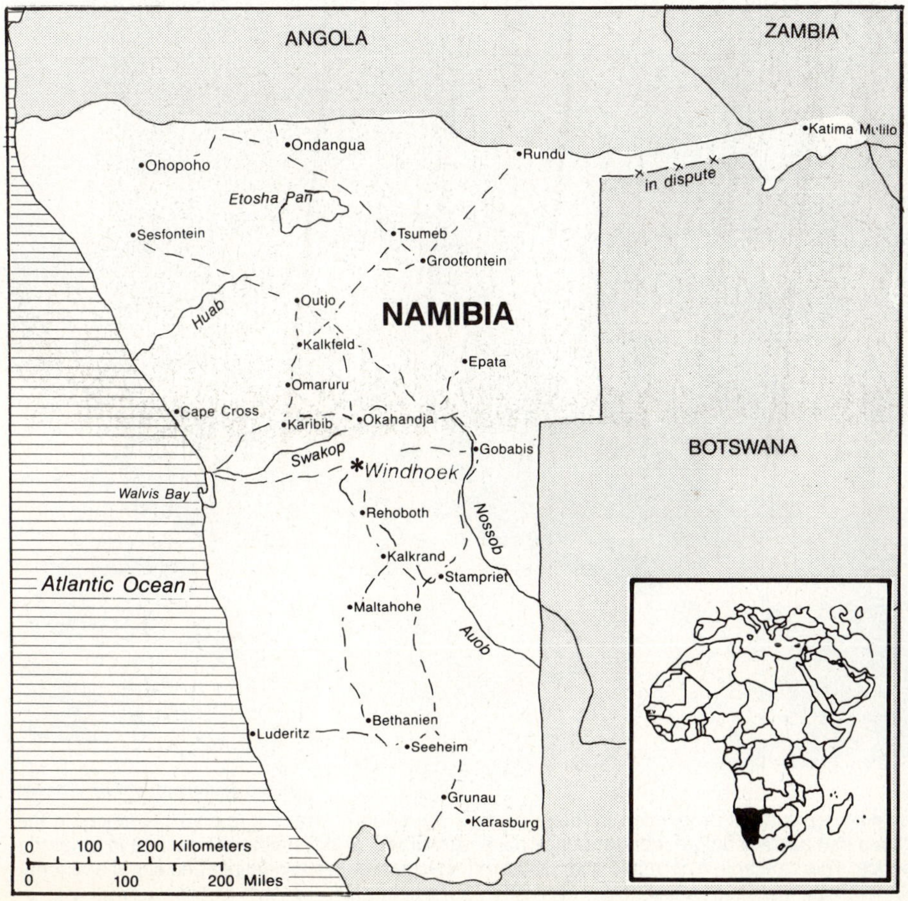

TRANSPORTATION

Highways—Kilometers (Miles): 54,500 (33,866)
Railroads—Kilometers (Miles): 2,340 (1,454)
Commercial Airports: 4 international

GOVERNMENT

Type: democratic
Independence Date: March 21, 1990
Head of State: Presigent Sam Nujoma
Political Parties: Action Front for the Preservation of the Turnhalle Principles; Federal Party; Democratic Turnhalle Alliance; South West Africa People's Organization; United Democratic Front
Suffrage: universal

MILITARY

Number of Armed Forces: n/a
Military Expenditures (% of Central Government Expenditures): n/a
Current Hostilities: none

ECONOMY

Currency ($ U.S. Equivalent): 2.55 South African rands = $1
Per Capita Income/GNP: $1,245/$1.5 billion
Inflation Rate: 15%
Natural Resources: diamonds; copper; lead; zinc; uranium; silver; cadmium; lithium; coal; possible oil reserves; fish
Agriculture: corn; millet; sorghum; livestock
Industry: meat canning; dairy products; leather tanning; textiles; clothing; mineral concentrates

FOREIGN TRADE

Exports: $935 million
Imports: $856 million

NAMIBIA

Namibia is Africa's newest country: it became independent on March 21, 1990. Its transition from Africa's last colony to independent state marked the end of a century of often brutal colonization, first by Germany and later by South Africa. The German colonial period (1884–1917) was marked by the annihilation of more than 60 percent of the African population in the southern two-thirds of the country, during the anticolonial uprising of 1904–1907. The South African period (1917–1990) witnessed the imposition of apartheid and a bitter 26-year war for independence between the South African Army (SADF) and the South West Africa People's Organization (SWAPO). During this war countless civilians in the northern areas of the country were harassed, detained, and abused by South African–created death squads known as *koevoet* (the Afrikaans word for "crowbar").

BATTLE OF CUITO CUANAVALE

Namibia's independence was the result of South African military misadventures and U.S.-Soviet cooperation in reducing tensions in the region. In 1987, as it had done many times before, South Africa invaded Angola to assist Jonas Savimbi's National Union for the Total Independence of Angola (UNITA) movement. Their objective was Cuito Cuanavale, a small town in southeastern Angola, where the Luanda government had set up an air-defense installation to keep South African aircraft from supplying UNITA troops. The SADF met with fierce resistance from the Angolan Army and eventually committed thousands of its own troops to the battle. In addition, black Namibian soldiers were recruited and given UNITA uniforms to fight on the side of the SADF. Many of these proxy UNITA troops later mutinied, because of their poor treatment at the hands of white South African soldiers.

South Africa failed to capture Cuito Cuanavale, and its forces were eventually surrounded. Faced with military disaster, the Pretoria government bowed to decades of international pressure and agreed to withdraw from its illegal occupation of Namibia. In return, Angola and its ally Cuba agreed to send home troops sent by Havana in 1974, after South Africa invaded Angola for the first time. Key brokers of the ceasefire, negotiations, and implementation of this agreement were the United States and the Soviet Union. This was the first instance of their post–Cold War cooperation.

ECONOMIC PROSPECTS

A plebiscite was held in Namibia during early November 1989. Under United Nations (UN) supervision, more than 97 percent of eligible voters cast their ballots—a remarkable achievement, given the vast distances many had to travel to reach polling stations. SWAPO emerged as the clear victor, achieving 60 percent of the votes cast, with the rest divided among a range of political parties, ranging from avowed white supremacists to ardent socialists.

(United Nations photo by J. Isaac)

Much of Namibia is arid, but the importance of developing agricultural production in those parts of the country where it is possible is key to the economic future of Africa's newest country. The sanctions that applied before independence have been lifted, and Namibia is now free to enter the potentially profitable markets in Europe and North America. This worker in a cornfield near Grootfontein is part of this essential agricultural economy.

Germany is given rights to colonize Namibia at the Conference of Berlin
1884–1885

Herero, Nama, and Damara rebellions against German rule
1904–1907

South Africa assumes League of Nations mandate
1920

The UN General Assembly revokes the South African mandate; SWAPO begins war for independence
1966

Bantustans, or "homelands," are created by South Africa
1968

A massive strike paralyzes the economy
1971

The Western Five contact group is formed to negotiate for South African withdrawal from Namibia
1977

An internal government is formed by South Africa
1978

1980s–1990s

Defeat at Cuito Cuanavale leads to a South African agreement to withdraw from Namibia

SWAPO wins UN-supervised elections; a new Constitution is approved

World leaders gather to witness Namibia's independence

Namibia is a sparsely populated land; it is twice the size of California but with a population of only 1.6 million people. More than half of its residents live in the northern region known as Ovamboland. Rich in minerals, Namibia is a major producer of diamonds, uranium, copper, silver, tin, and lithium. Recently a large gold mine began production. The end of hostilities opens up northern parts of the country to further mineral explorations where oil and coal deposits are believed to exist.

Much of Namibia is arid. Until recently pastoral farming has been the primary agricultural activity, with beef, mutton, and goat meat the primary products. Independence brings with it an end to international sanctions applied when South Africa ruled the country, thus clearing the way for Namibian agricultural goods to potentially lucrative markets in Europe and North America. Shrewd investors have already taken advantage of the potential. The day after independence, for example, a company signed an agreement with the new government to develop a sugar industry in Ovamboland where rainfall is more plentiful and wetland agriculture possible.

CHALLENGES

Despite the economic promise, the fledgling government of Namibia faces severe problems. It inherits an economy structurally perverted by apartheid to favor the tiny white minority. With a glaring division between fabulously wealthy whites and the oppressively poor black majority, the government has the daunting problem of promoting economic development while at the same time encouraging the redistribution of wealth. Apartheid ensured that managerial positions were filled by whites, leaving a dearth of qualified and experienced nonwhite executives in the country. Another structural perversion is black unemployment, conservatively estimated at more than 33 percent. Useful employment must be found for these people, lest they become a fatal burden to the state's social-service structure. The end of the war has exacerbated this problem, since the demobilization of both SWAPO freedom fighters and the soldiers recruited by South Africa introduces tens of thousands of young people into the labor pool. Indications of the potential problems this group may pose is seen in the crime gang known as the Botsotsos, made up of former members of the *koevoet* death squad. This armed and organized group is apparently responsible for much of a recent crime wave sweeping the capital, Windhoek.

Another major problem lies in Namibia's total dependence on South African infrastructure. South Africa used Namibia as a classic colony, treating it as a captive market for South African goods while extracting as much of its resources as possible. As a result, all rail and most road links between Namibia and the rest of the world run through South Africa. Pretoria also maintains its occupation of Walvis Bay, Namibia's only port. In the past the South African government has used its control of the region's transportation system to sabotage economic development in countries such as Botswana, Zambia, Zimbabwe, Mozambique, and Swaziland. The possibility of Namibia falling prey to this tactic in the future is quite real.

The government of President Sam Nujoma has taken a hard look at these and other economic problems and has embarked on a program to solve them. SWAPO surprised everyone during the election campaign by modifying its previously strident socialist rhetoric, calling for a market-oriented economy. Since taking power the government has sought membership in the International Monetary Fund (IMF) and has proposed a code for foreign investors that includes protection against undue nationalizations. A conservative white businessperson, Otto Herrigel, was named minister of finance in a move that calmed the business community.

At present the government is actively seeking both foreign investment and foreign aid from Western countries. Scandinavia and countries from the European Community (EC) have shown considerable interest. France and Germany in particular have led the way in both investment and aid to the world's newest country. SWAPO appears to be well on its way to making the transition from revolutionary organization to pragmatic leader of a democratic society. Its new attitude is best summed up in a quote by Hage Geingob, a prominent SWAPO official and now president of the National Assembly. "To distribute wealth," he said in an interview, "you must first create it."

DEVELOPMENT

The new government has instituted English as the medium of instruction in all schools. Prior to independence, English was discouraged for African school children, as a means of controlling their access to skills necessary to compete in the modern world. This effort requires new curricula and textbooks for the entire country.

FREEDOM

The Namibian Constitution is considered a model of democratic government. Universal suffrage and a strong emphasis on human rights are prominent throughout the document. Freedom of the press, freedom of speech, an independent judiciary, and provisions against discrimination in any form are constitutional guarantees.

HEALTH/WELFARE

The social-service delivery system of Namibia must be rebuilt to eliminate the structural inequities of apartheid. Health care for the black majority, especially those in remote rural areas, will require significant improvements. Public-health programs for blacks, nonexistent prior to independence, must be created.

ACHIEVEMENTS

The new government, led by President Sam Nujoma, has received high praise for its efforts at racial and political reconciliation after a bitter 26-year war for independence. Nujoma led these efforts and astonished a number of observers with his political and consensus-building skills.

South Africa (Republic of South Africa)

THE AFRICAN NATIONAL CONGRESS

The African National Congress (ANC) was founded in 1912, in response to the taking of land from Africans and the introduction of "pass laws" controlling their employment and movement. For 50 years members carried on peaceful resistance to apartheid by organizing protest marches, supporting workers' demands and strike actions, and creating independent schools and services. ANC goals are expressed in the Freedom Charter, which states that "South Africa belongs to all who live in it, black and white . . ." and calls for "one man, one vote" and the abolition of the color bar. These beliefs caused the arrest of thousands and the trial of ANC leaders for treason. When the ANC was banned and Nelson Mandela, Walter Sisulu, and others were sentenced to life imprisonment, the ANC went underground in the 1960s, planning sabotage against military and political targets and organizing resistance. The ANC and Nelson Mandela, who since his release in 1990 has acted as the movement's de facto leader, gained supporters and stature as internal resistance against the apartheid state grew during the 1980s. Since coming to office President F. W. de Klerk has implicitly recognized the fact that the ANC is now the leading voice of his country's nonwhite majority.

GEOGRAPHY

Area in Square Kilometers (Miles): 1,222,480 (437,872) (about twice the size of Texas)
Capital (Population): Pretoria (administrative) (822,000); Cape Town (legislative) (1,900,000); Bloemfontein (judicial) (231,000)
Climate: temperate; semi-arid; arid

PEOPLE

Population

Total: 39,550,000
Annual Growth Rate: 2.6%
Rural/Urban Population Ratio: 45/55
Languages: official: Afrikaans, English; others spoken: Xhosa, Zulu, Sesotho, Tswana, other Bantu languages

Health

Life Expectancy at Birth: 61 years (male); 67 years (female)*
Infant Death Rate (Ratio): 52/1,000*
Average Caloric Intake: 116% of FAO minimum*
Physicians Available (Ratio): 1/1,757*

Religion(s)

81% Christian; 19% Hindu and Muslim

Education

Adult Literacy Rate: 50% blacks; 99% whites

COMMUNICATION

Telephones: 4,500,000
Newspapers: 39

TRANSPORTATION

Highways—Kilometers (Miles): 188,309 (116,751)
Railroads—Kilometers (Miles): 35,434 (22,018)
Commercial Airports: 3 international

GOVERNMENT

Type: republic
Independence Date: May 31, 1910
Head of State: President Frederick W. de Klerk
Political Parties: National Party; Progressive Federal Party; New Republic Party; Conservative Party; Labour Party; Afrikaans Weerstand Beweging; Cape Democrats
Suffrage: universal at 18, but voting rights are racially based

MILITARY

Number of Armed Forces: 92,500 standing; 150,000 ready reserves; 130,000 paramilitary commando volunteers; 61,000 police
Military Expenditures (% of Central Government Expenditures): 5%
Current Hostilities: civil unrest

ECONOMY

Currency ($ U.S. Equivalent): 2.55 rands = $1
Per Capita Income/GNP: $2,380*/$83.5 billion
Inflation Rate: 12.3%
Natural Resources: gold; diamonds; mineral ores; uranium; fish
Agriculture: corn; wool; wheat; surgarcane; tobacco; citrus fruits; dairy products
Industry: mining; automobile assembly; metal working; machinery; textiles; iron and steel; chemicals; fertilizer; fishing

FOREIGN TRADE

Exports: $21.5 billion
Imports: $18.5 billion

*Figures for blacks and whites, when separated, vary greatly.

SOUTH AFRICA

This decade may prove to be a turning point in the long, tragic history of racism in South Africa. For nearly 3½ centuries the territory's white minority has expanded and entrenched its racial hegemony over the nonwhite majority. Since 1948 white supremacy has been consolidated into a governing system known as apartheid ("separatehood"). South Africa's rulers now claim that they are no longer committed to upholding apartheid.

In 1990 political restrictions inside the country were significantly relaxed through the unbanning of anti-apartheid resistance organizations, most notably the African National Congress (ANC), the Pan Africanist Congress (PAC), and the South African Communist Party (SACP). Today there is hope that on-going talks between the government, the ANC, and other parties will contribute to the emergence of a new, nonracial, South Africa. But there are major obstacles to such an outcome.

South Africa remains a deeply divided country. In general, the ruling whites enjoy relatively affluent, comfortable lives, while the nonwhites survive in a state of impoverished deprivation. The boundary between these two worlds is legal. Nonwhites have never been treated as full citizens, a de facto reality that under apartheid remains a de jure policy goal. Apartheid's core concept is the denial of citizenships rights to members of its three subordinate race classifications: "Bantu" (black Africans), "Coloureds" (people of mixed race), and "Asians." (Many members belonging to these groups prefer the common label "Black," which the government now commonly uses in place of Bantu as an exclusive term for black Africans, hereafter referred to as blacks.)

THE ROOTS OF APARTHEID

White supremacy in South Africa began with the Dutch settlement at Cape Town in 1652. For a century and a half the domestic economy of the Dutch Cape Colony, which gradually expanded to include the southern third of modern South Africa, rested on a foundation of slavery and servitude. Much like the American South before the U.S. Civil War, Cape colonial society was racially divided between free white settlers and nonwhite slaves and servants. Most of the slaves were Africans imported from outside the local region, though a minority were taken from Asia. The local blacks, who spoke various Khiosan languages, were not enslaved. However, they were robbed by the Europeans of their land and herds. Many were also killed, either by European bullets or diseases. As a result, most of the Cape's Khiosan were reduced to a status of servitude. Gradually, the servant and slave populations, with a considerable admixture of European blood, merged to form the core of the so-called Coloured group.

At the beginning of the nineteenth century the Cape Colony reverted to British control. During the 1830s the British abolished slavery and extended legal rights to servants. As in the American South, emancipation did not end racial barriers to the political and economic advancement of nonwhites. Nonetheless, even the limited reforms that were introduced upset many of the white Cape Dutch (or "Boers"), whose society was evolving its own "Afrikaner" identity. Today some 60 percent of the whites and 90 percent of the Coloureds in South Africa speak the Dutch-derived Afrikaans language. During the mid-nineteenth century thousands of Afrikaners, accompanied by their Coloured clients,

(United Nations photo)

The system of apartheid makes it impossible for most black South Africans to share in South Africa's economic prosperity.

escaped British rule by migrating into the interior. They established two independent republics, the Transvaal and the Orange Free State, whose Constitutions recognized only whites as having any civil rights.

The Afrikaners, and the British who followed them, did not settle an empty land. Then, as now, most of the people living in the area beyond the borders of the old Dutch Cape Colony were blacks who spoke languages linguistically classified as Bantu. While there are nine officially recognized Bantu languages in South Africa, all but two (Tsonga and Venda) belong to either the Sotho-Tswana (Pedi, Sotho, Tswana) or Nguni (Ndebele, Swati, Xhosa, and Zulu) subgroupings of closely related dialects.

Throughout the eighteenth and nineteenth centuries the indigenous populations of the interior and eastern coast offered strong resistance to the white invaders. Unlike the Khiosan of the Cape, these communities were able to preserve their ethnolinguistic identities. However, the settlers eventually robbed them of most of their land as well as their independence. Black subjugation served the economic interests of white farmers and, later, industrialists, who were able to coerce the conquered communities into providing cheap and forced labor. After 1860 many Asians, mostly from what was then British-ruled India, were also brought into South Africa to work for next to nothing on sugar plantations. As with the blacks and Coloureds, the Asians were denied civil rights.

The lines of racial stratification were already well entrenched at the turn of the twentieth century, when the British waged a war of conquest against the Afrikaner republics. During this South African, or Boer, War, tens of thousands of Afrikaners, blacks, and Coloureds died while interned in British concentration camps. The camps helped defeat the Afrikaner resistance but left bitter divisions between them and pro-British English-speaking whites. However, the nonwhites were the war's greatest losers. A compromise peace between the Afrikaners and the British Empire paved the way for the emergence, in 1910, of a self-governing Union of South Africa, made up of the former British colonies and Afrikaner republics. In this new state, political power remained in the hands of the white minority.

"GRAND APARTHEID"

In 1948 the Afrikaner-dominated Nationalist Party (NP) was voted into office by the white electorate, on a platform promising apartheid; the party has remained in power ever since. Under the apartheid system, existing patterns of segregation were reinforced by a vast array of new laws. So-called pass laws, which had long limited the movement of blacks in many areas, were extended throughout the country. Black men and women were required to carry "passbooks" at all times to prove their right to be residing in a particular area. Under the Group Areas Act, more than 80 percent of South Africa was reserved for whites, who now make up no more than 15 percent of the population. In this area, blacks remain confined to townships or white-owned farms where, until recently, they were considered to be temporary residents. If they lacked a properly registered job, they were subject to deportation to one of the ten "homelands."

Under apartheid, the homelands—poor, noncontiguous rural territories that together account for less than 13 percent of South Africa's land—are the designated "nations" of South Africa's blacks, who make up more than 70 percent of the population. Each black is assigned membership in a particular homeland, in accordance with ethnolinguistic criteria invented by the white government. Thus, in apartheid theory, there is no majority in South Africa but, rather, a single white nation, which in reality has remained divided between speakers of Afrikaans, English, and other languages, and 10 separate black nations. The Coloureds and the Asians were consigned a never clearly defined intermediate position as powerless communities associated with, but segregated from, white South Africa. The apartheid ideal was that each black homeland would eventually become independent, leaving white South Africa without the "burden" of a black majority. Of course, black "immigrants" could still work for the "white economy," which would remain reliant on black labor. To assure that racial stratification was maintained at the workplace, a system of job classification was created, which reserved the best positions for whites, certain middle-level jobs for Asians and Coloureds, and unskilled labor for blacks.

Until recently the NP ruthlessly pursued their ultimate goal of legislating away South Africa's black majority. Four homelands—Bophutatswana, Ciskie, Transkie, and Venda—were declared independent. The 9 million blacks who were assigned as citizens of these pseudo-states, which have not been recognized by any outside country, do not appear in the 1989 South African census, even though most live outside of the homelands. Indeed, despite generations of forced removals and influx control, today there is not one magistrate's district (the equivalent of a U.S. county) that has a white majority.

While for whites apartheid has been an ideology of mass delusion, for blacks it has meant continuous suffering. During the 1970s alone, some $3^1/_2$ million blacks were forcibly relocated because they were living in "black spots" within the white area. Many more have at some point in their lives fallen victim to the pass laws. Within the townships and squatter camps that ring the white cities, families have survived from day to day, not knowing if the police might burst into their homes to discover that their passbooks are not in order.

Under apartheid, blacks are as much divided by their residential status as by their assigned ethnicity. In a relative sense, the most privileged are those who have established their right to reside legally within a township like Soweto. Township dwellers have the advantage of being able to live with their families and seek work in a nearby white urban center. Many of their coworkers live much farther away, in the periurban areas of the homelands. Some in this less fortunate category spend as much as a third of their lives on Putco buses, traveling to and from their places of employment. Still, the periurban homeland workers are in many ways better off than some of their male colleagues, who are confined to crowded worker hostels for months at a time while their families remain in distant rural homelands. There are also millions of female domestics who generally earn next to nothing, living away from their children in the servant quarters of white households.

Further down the black social ladder are those living in the illegal squatter camps that exist outside the urban areas. Without secure homes or steady jobs, the squatters have been frequent victims of nighttime police raids. When caught, they are generally transported back to their homelands, from whence they will usually try once more to escape.

The relaxation, since 1986, of influx-control regulations has eased the tribulations of many squatters, but their lives still remain insecure. Yet even the violent destruction of squatter settlements by the state has not stemmed their explosive growth. For many South African blacks, living without permanent employment in a cardboard house is preferable to the hardships of the rural homelands. Nearly half of all blacks live in these areas, where unemployment is over 80 percent and agricultural production is limited by marginal and overcrowded environments.

Recent changes have tended to accentuate the importance of these residential patterns. Although their wages on average remain only a fraction of those enjoyed by whites, many township dwellers have seen their pay rise over the past decade, partially due to their own success in organizing strong labor federations. At the same time, life in the homelands has become more desperate as their populations have mushroomed.

Apartheid is a totalitarian system. An array of security legislation gives the state vast powers over individual citizens, even in the absence of a state of emergency, such as existed throughout much of the country between 1985 and 1990. Control is also more subtly exercised through the schools and other public institutions. An important element of apartheid has been Bantu Education. Beyond being segregated and unequal, black educational curriculums have been specifically designed to assure underachievement by preparing most students for only semiskilled and unskilled occupations. The schools are also divided by language and ethnicity. A student who is classified as Zulu is taught in the Zulu language to be loyal to the Zulu nation, while his or her playmates may be receiving similar instruction in Tsonga or Sotho. Ethnic divisions are also often encouraged at the workplace. At the mines, ethnicity generally determines which job and hostel one is assigned to.

LIMITED REFORMS

During 1982–1983 there was much official publicity about reforming apartheid. Yet the NP's moves to liberalize the system were limited and accompanied by increased repression. Some changes were simply semantic. In official publications, the term "apartheid" was replaced by "separate development," which was subsequently dropped in favor of "plural democracy."

A bill passed in the white Parliament in 1983 brought Asian and Coloured representatives into the South African government, but only in their own separate chambers, which remained completely subordinate to the white chamber. The bill also concentrated power in the office of the presidency, which eroded the oversight prerogatives of white parliamentarians. Significantly, the new dispensation com-

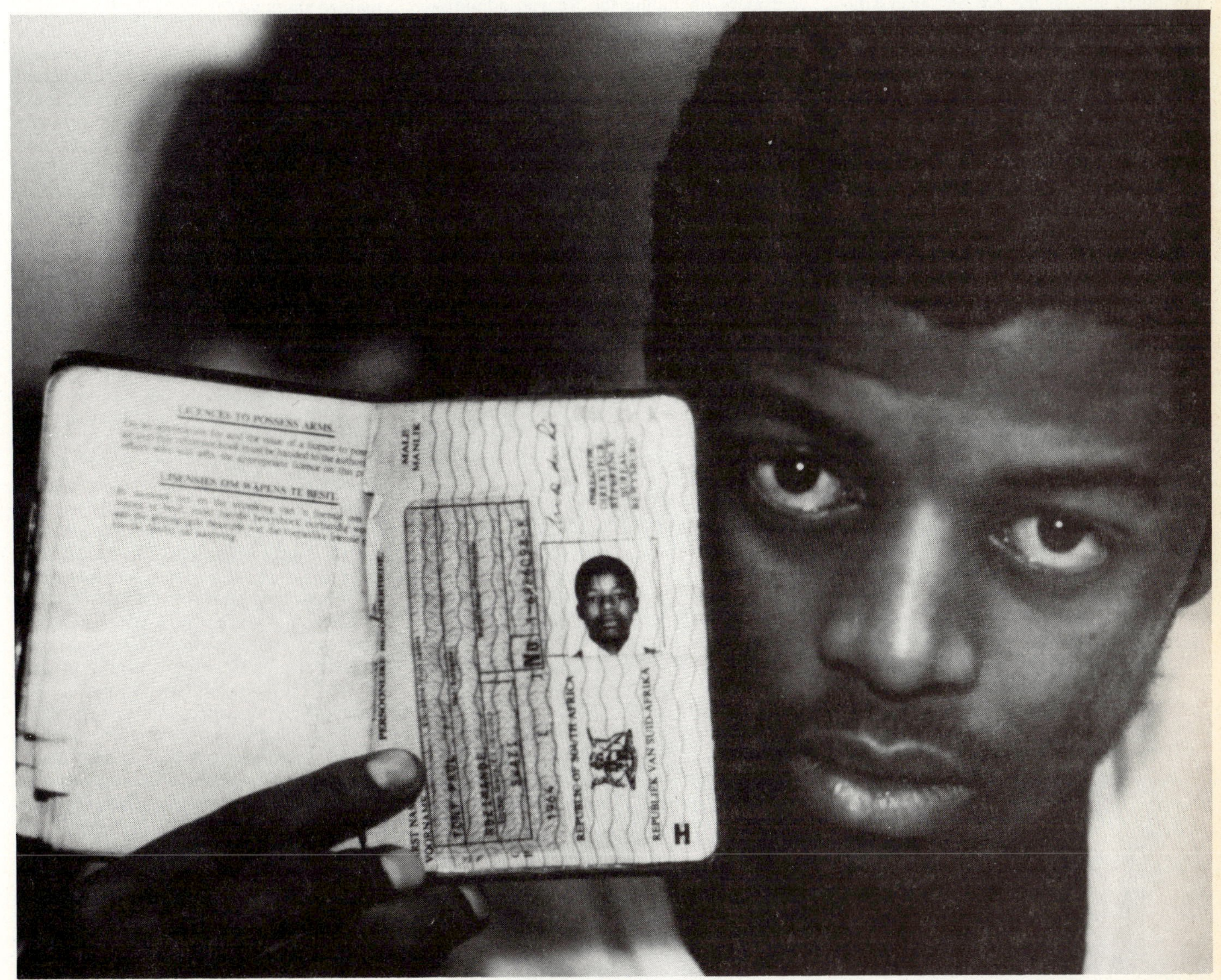

(United Nations photo)

Apartheid consists of hundreds of laws that allow the ruling white minority in South Africa to segregate, exploit, and terrorize the vast majority. Black South Africans are required to carry passes that determine where they may live.

Migration of Bantu speakers into Southern Africa
1000–1500

The first settlement of Dutch people in the Cape of Good Hope area
1652

The British gain possession of the Cape Colony
1815

Shaka develops the Zulu nation and sets in motion the wars and migrations known as the Mfecane
1820s

The Boer War: the British fight the Afrikaners (Boers)
1899–1902

pletely excluded blacks. Seeing the new Constitution as another transparent attempt to divide-and-rule, while offering them nothing in the way of genuine empowerment, most Asians and Coloureds refused to participate in the new political order. Instead, many joined with blacks and a handful of progressive whites in creating a new organization, the United Democratic Front (UDF), which opposed the Constitution.

In other moves, the NP has gradually done away with examples of "petty" apartheid. In many areas, signs announcing separate facilities have been removed from public places, although new, more subtle, signs have often been put up to assure continued segregation. Gas stations in the Transvaal, for example, now have their facilities marked with blue and white figures to assure that patrons continue to know their place. Another example of purely cosmetic reform was the legalization of interracial marriage. Although it is no longer a crime for a man and a woman belonging to different racial classifications to be wed, under the Group Areas Act it remains an offense for such a couple to live in the same house. In 1986 the hated passbooks were replaced with new identity cards. Unions were legalized, but in the Orwellian world of apartheid, their leaders were regularly arrested. The UDF was not banned but was forbidden from holding meetings. Although such "reforms" were meaningless to most nonwhites living within South Africa, some outsiders, including the Reagan administration, were impressed by the "progress."

BLACK RESISTANCE

Resistance to white domination dates back to 1657, when the Khiosan first attempted to counter Dutch encroachments on their pastures. Throughout the first half of the twentieth century the ANC, which was founded in 1912 to unify what up until then had been regionally based black associations, and other political and labor organizations attempted to wage a peaceful civil-rights struggle. An early leader within the Asian community was Mahatma Gandhi, who pioneered his strategy of passive resistance in South Africa while resisting the pass laws. During the 1950s the ANC and associated organizations adopted Gandhian tactics on a massive scale, in a vain attempt to block the enactment of apartheid legislation. Although ANC President Albert Luthuli was awarded a Nobel Peace Prize, the NP regime remained unmoved.

(United Nations photo)

Resistance groups have gained international recognition in their struggle against the South African regime.

The year 1960 was a turning point. Police massacred more than 60 persons, firing on a passbook-burning demonstration in Sharpeville. Thereafter the government assumed emergency powers and banned the ANC and the more recently formed PAC. As underground movements, both turned to armed struggle. The ANC's guerrilla organization, the Umkonto we Sizwe ("Spear of the Nation") attempted to avoid taking human lives in its attacks. Poqo ("Ourselves Alone"), the PAC's armed wing, was less constrained in its choice of targets but also proved less able to sustain its struggle. By the mid-1960s, with the capture of such figures as Umkonto leader Nelson Mandela, active resistance had been all but fully suppressed.

During the 1970s a new generation of resistance emerged. Many nonwhite youths were attracted to the teachings of the Black Consciousness Movement (BMC), led by Steve Biko. The BMC and like-minded organizations rejected the racial and ethnic classifications of apartheid by insisting on the fundamental unity of all oppressed black peoples (that is, all nonwhites) against the white power structure. Black consciousness also rejected all forms of collaboration with the apartheid state, which brought the movement into direct opposition with homeland leaders, like Gatsha Buthelezi, whom they looked upon as sellouts. In the aftermath of student demonstrations at Soweto, which sparked months of unrest across the country, the government suppressed the BMC. Biko was subsequently murdered while in detention. During this crackdown thousands of young people fled South Africa. Many joined the exiled ANC, helping to reinvigorate its ranks.

Despite heavy-handed repression, internal resistance to apartheid continued to grow. Hundreds of new and revitalized

The Union of South Africa gives rights of self-government to whites **1910**

The African National Congress is founded **1912**

The Nationalist Party comes to power on an apartheid platform **1948**

The Sharpeville Massacre: police fire on demonstration; more than 60 deaths result **1960**

Soweto riots are sparked off by student protests **1976**

1980s–1990s

Unrest in the black townships leads to the declaration of a state of emergency; thousands are detained while violence escalates

Frederick W. de Klerk replaces Pieter W. Botha as president; anti-apartheid movements are unbanned and political prisoners are released

Talks begin between the ANC and the government; the state of emergency is lifted in most areas, and the ANC suspends its armed struggle

organizations—community groups, labor unions, religious bodies—emerged to contribute to the struggle. Many became affiliated through coordinating bodies such as the UDF, the Congress of South African Trade Unions (COSATU), and the South African Council of Churches (SACC). SACC leader Archbishop Desmond Tutu became the second black South African to be awarded a Nobel Peace Prize for his nonviolent efforts to bring about change, but in the face of continued oppression, black youths, in particular, became increasingly willing to use whatever means necessary to overthrow the oppressors.

The year 1985 was another turning point. Arrests and bannings of black leaders led to calls to make the townships "ungovernable." A state of emergency was proclaimed by the government in July, which allowed for the increased use of detention without trial. By March 1990 some 53,000 people, including an estimated 10,000 children, had been arrested. Many detainees have been tortured while in custody. Stone-throwing youths have, nonetheless, continued to challenge the heavily armed security forces sent into the townships to restore order. At least 7,000 youths have died in the unrest.

PROSPECTS FOR A NONRACIAL SOUTH AFRICA

Despite the government's ability to marshal the resources of a sophisticated military-industrial complex to maintain its totalitarian control, the NP has been forced to consider giving up apartheid along with its 4-decade monopoly of power. Throughout the 1980s South Africa's advanced economy was in a state of crisis, due to the effects of unrest and, to a lesser extent, sanctions and other forms of international pressure. Under President Pieter W. Botha, the NP regime stubbornly refused to offer any openings to genuine reform.

However, Botha's replacement, in 1989, by Frederick W. de Klerk has opened up new possibilities. The unbanning of the ANC, PAC, and SACP has been accompanied by the release of many political prisoners. As many had anticipated, since gaining his freedom in March 1990, ANC deputy leader Nelson Mandela has emerged as the leading advocate of a nonracial South Africa. More surprising has been the de Klerk government's willingness to engage in serious negotiations with the ANC and other groups. By August 1990 the ANC felt that the progress being made justified the formal suspension of its armed struggle.

Many obstacles continue to block the transition to a postapartheid state. For one thing, although the government seems prepared to accept some form of power sharing, it remains opposed to the concept of one person, one vote in a unified state. Instead, de Klerk's NP appears to favor some form of dispensation that will preserve major elements of white privilege and power. The ANC, UDF, Cosatu, and SACP, which are loosely associated as the Mass Democratic Movement (MDM), are loyal to the nonracial principles of the 1955 Freedom Charter. While there exist possibilities for a future compromise between the NP and Charterists, at present they remain far apart.

Other groups are currently opposed to negotiations. Critics of the ANC fear that the apartheid regime is not yet prepared to agree to its dismantlement and that the on-going talks can only serve to weaken black resistance. On the opposite side of the spectrum are powerful elements in the white community who remain openly committed to their continued racial supremacy. In addition to the Conservative Party, the principal opposition in the white Parliament, there are a number of militant racist organizations which are prepared to resort to terrorism to block reforms. At least some within the South African security establishment are also seeking to sabotage the prospects of peace. Another wild card is Buthelezi's Inkatha Party and other smaller black groups that have aligned themselves in the past with the South African state. Thousands have been killed in on-going clashes between Inkatha and MDM supporters, which have allegedly been encouraged by the police.

Perhaps the greatest barrier to the creation of a nonracial South Africa will not be in reaching a consensus in its favor, but rather finding a means to translate the vision into reality. Even under the best of circumstances, it will not be easy for South Africans to dismantle the legacies of apartheid. Remarked one observer surveying the township he had grown up in: "They no longer need their laws."

DEVELOPMENT

In anticipation of a new, postapartheid, economy, the debate between advocates of various economic approaches has become increasingly serious. Many believe that the state must play a major role in righting the economic injustices of apartheid. Others believe that only a freer private sector can best create the necessary economic opportunities.

FREEDOM

Under apartheid, nonwhites have been systematically denied basic freedoms, and even white critics of the state have faced severe restrictions. The political opening in 1990 has created in some respects a freer atmosphere. However, police repression and death squad activities continue.

HEALTH/WELFARE

State health and educational facilities remain segregated. Those reserved for whites are far superior on average than those for nonwhites. Black schools have been periodically hit by politically motivated student boycotts, but since 1987 most students have opted to remain in the classroom.

ACHIEVEMENTS

As government-selected black leaders step down and security and services are reduced in the black townships, local "people's governments" are emerging. At risk to their lives, black representatives join in larger committees to make decisions for the townships, and communities attempt to educate the youth.

Swaziland (Kingdom of Swaziland)

GEOGRAPHY

Area in Square Kilometers (Miles): 17,366 (6,704) (slightly smaller than New Jersey
Capital (Population): Mbabane (administrative) (52,000); Lobanta (legislative)
Climate: temperate; subtropical; semiarid

PEOPLE

Population
Total: 779,000
Annual Growth Rate: 3.1%
Rural/Urban Population Ratio: 74/26
Languages: official: English, Siswati; others spoken: Zulu, Sesotho, Nguni

Health
Life Expectancy at Birth: 48 years (male); 55 years (female)
Infant Death Rate (Ratio): 126/1,000
Average Caloric Intake: 97% of FAO minimum
Physicians Available (Ratio): 1/9,731

Religion(s)
60% Christian; 40% traditional indigenous

NCWALA

Visitors to Swaziland are frequently impressed by the pageantry associated with many of its state occasions. The most important ceremonies take place during the lunar *Ncwala* month in December and January. This is a time when the nation reaffirms its bonds with the royal house. As the month begins, runners are sent to collect water from the ocean and various rivers, thus reestablishing their historic association with the Swazi. The main festival lasts for 6 days and includes the king's tasting of the first fruits, blessings to the ancestors, and prayers for rain. During the entire period there is ritual dancing—the most important of which is performed on the fourth day by the king and other members of royalty.

Education
Adult Literacy Rate: 68%

COMMUNICATION

Telephones: 15,400
Newspapers: 2

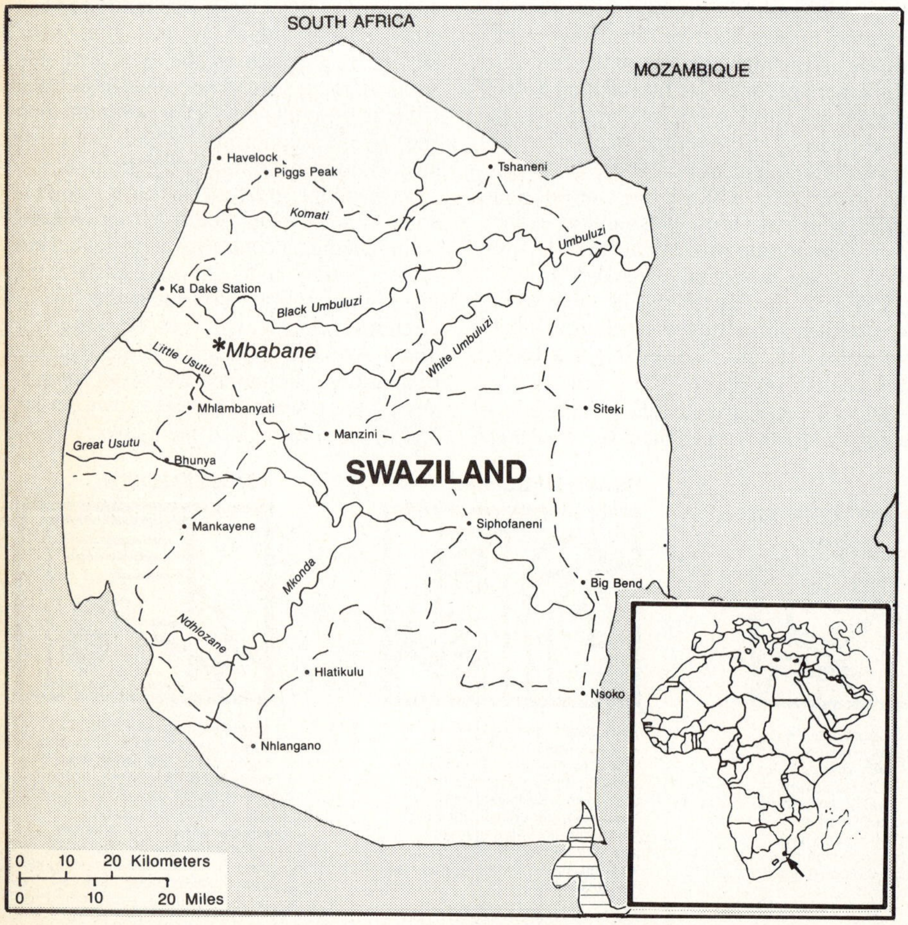

TRANSPORTATION

Highways—Kilometers (Miles): 2,853 (1,769)
Railroads—Kilometers (Miles): 292 (181)
Commercial Airports: 1 international

GOVERNMENT

Type: monarchy
Independence Date: September 6, 1968
Head of State: King Mswati III
Political Parties: banned
Suffrage: universal for adults

MILITARY

Number of Armed Forces: n/a
Military Expenditures (% of Central Government Expenditures): n/a
Current Hostilities: none

ECONOMY

Currency ($ U.S. Equivalent): 2.55 emalangenis = $1
Per Capita Income/GNP: $750/$539 million
Inflation Rate: 17%
Natural Resources: iron ore; asbestos; coal; timber
Agriculture: corn; livestock; sugarcane; citrus fruits; cotton; rice; pineapples
Industry: milled sugar; cotton; processed meat and wood; tourism; chemicals; machinery, beverages; consumer goods; paper milling; mining

FOREIGN TRADE

Exports: $394 million
Imports: $386 billion

Zulu and South African whites encroach on Swazi territory
1800s

A protectorate is established by the British
1900

Independence is restored
1968

Parliament is dissolved
1973

1980s–1990s

King Sobuza dies; efforts to annex South African homeland territories collapse

King Mswati III is crowned, ending the regency period marked by political instability

The political status quo is challenged by strikes and stepped-up agitation from the underground People's United Democratic Movement

SWAZILAND

Swaziland is a small, landlocked kingdom sandwiched between the much larger states of Mozambique and South Africa. Many casual observers have tended to look upon the country as a peaceful island of traditional Africa that has remained seemingly immune to the continent's contemporary conflicts. This image is a product of the country's status as the only precolonial monarchy in sub-Saharan Africa to have survived into the modern era.

Since the founding of the kingdom in the mid-eighteenth century, the fortunes of Swaziland have been shaped by the intervention of outside forces. From 1902 until the restoration of independence in 1968, the country was a British colonial protectorate, despite sustained pressure for its incorporation into South Africa. Local white settlers, who at the time made up only 2 percent of the population but who controlled more than two-thirds of the land, largely favored such a transfer.

Throughout the colonial period the ruling House of Dlamini, which was led after 1921 by the energetic Sobuza II, served as a rallying point for self-assertion on the key issues of regaining control of alienated land and opposing union with South Africa. Sobuza's leadership in both struggles contributed to the overwhelming popularity of his royalist Imbokodvo Party in the elections of 1964, 1967, and 1972. In 1973 Sobuza, faced with a modest but articulate opposition party—the Ngwane National Liberatory Congress—dissolved Parliament and repealed the Westminster-style Constitution, characterizing it as "un-Swazi." In 1979 a new, nonpartisan Parliament was chosen. However, authority remained with the king, assisted by his advisory council, the Liqoqo.

Sobuza's death in 1982 left many wondering if Swaziland's unique monarchist institutions would survive. A prolonged power struggle increased tensions within the ruling order. Members of the Liqoqo seized effective power and appointed a new Queen Regent, Ntombi. However, palace intrigue continued until Prince Makhosetive, Ntombi's son, was installed in 1986 as King Mswati III, at the age of 18. The new king approved the demotion of the Liqoqo back to its advisory status and has ruled through his appointed prime minister and Cabinet.

One of the major challenges facing any Swazi government is its relationship with South Africa. Under Sobuza, Swaziland managed to maintain political autonomy while accepting economic dependence on its powerful neighbor. The king also kept a delicate balance between the apartheid state and the forces opposing it. However, during the 1980s this balance tilted. A Swazi-South African nonaggression pact resulted in a greater degree of cooperation between the two countries' security forces in curbing suspected African National Congress (ANC) activists. A land deal was also made that would have transferred supposedly Swazi Homeland territories within South Africa to Swaziland, in the process giving the kingdom access to the sea. In the face of strong protests from the affected population, South Africa reneged on the agreement, following Sobuza's death. Despite this setback, the two governments continue to cooperate.

THE ECONOMY

Swaziland's economy, like its politics, is the product of both internal and external initiatives. The nation has since independence enjoyed a high rate of economic growth, led by the expansion and diversification of its agriculture. Success in agriculture has promoted the development of secondary industries, such as a sugar refinery and a paper mill. There has also been increased exploitation of coal and asbestos. Another important source of revenue is tourism, which depends on weekend traffic from South Africa.

Swazi development has relied on capital-intensive, rather than labor-intensive, projects. As a result, disparities in local wealth and dependence on South African investment have increased. Local employment as well as revenues have recently been expanded by attracting international investors looking for a politically preferable window to the South African market. A notable example of corporate relocation is Coca-Cola's decision to move its regional headquarters and concentrate plant from South Africa to Swaziland; the plant only employs some 100 workers, but it accounts for 20 percent of foreign-exchange earnings. There have also been cases of supposedly Swazi enterprises engaging in "sanctions-busting" through relabeling operations. Foreign criticism and local self-interest have motivated the Swazi government to curb such activities.

DEVELOPMENT

Much of Swaziland's economy is managed by the Tibiyo TakaNgwana, a royally controlled institution established in 1968 by Sobuza. It is responsible for the financial assets of the communal lands (upon which most Swazi farm) and mining operations.

FREEDOM

The current political order restricts many forms of opposition, although its defenders claim that local councils, *Tikhudlas*, allow for popular participation in decision-making. The leading, banned, opposition group is the People's United Democratic Movement, which calls for democratic reforms and is sympathetic to the ANC.

HEALTH/WELFARE

Swaziland's low life expectancy and high infant mortality rates have recently resulted in greater public-health allocations, which in 1989–1990 accounted for 15% of recurrent expenditures. There has also been a greater emphasis placed on preventive medicine.

ACHIEVEMENTS

Education accounts for a 28% share of government spending, the largest item in the budget. Enrollment is currently 100% for the primary-school and 43% for the secondary-school age groups. The University of Swaziland was established in the 1970s and now offers a full range of degree and diploma programs.

Zambia (Republic of Zambia)

GEOGRAPHY

Area in Square Kilometers (Miles): 752,972 (290,724) (slightly larger than Texas)
Capital (Population): Lusaka (818,000)
Climate: tropical to subtropical

PEOPLE

Population

Total: 8,113,000
Annual Growth Rate: 3.2%
Rural/Urban Population Ratio: 45/55
Languages: official: English; others spoken: Bemba, Nyanja, Tonga, Lozi, others

Health

Life Expectancy at Birth: 55 years (male); 58 years (female)
Infant Death Rate (Ratio): 80/1,000
Average Caloric Intake: 90% of FAO minimum
Physicians Available (Ratio): 1/9,881

Religion(s)

51% Christian; 48% traditional indigenous; 1% Hindu and Muslim

KAUNDA'S "HUMANISM"

Ever since his son Kambarage was arrested for the fatal shooting of a Tabeth Mwansa, a 20-year-old woman, President Kenneth David Kaunda has been faced with the difficult fact that a murder conviction in his realm carries a mandatory death sentence. However, the architect of Zambian socialism appears to have found a typically "humanitarian" solution to this unwelcome dilemma.

Africa Confidential reports that in May 1990 the Zambian penal code was quietly amended so that in cases of murder, the court "shall decide the fate of a convict by regarding his social class. The class of a convict shall determine whether he deserves a death sentence or a fine where there are extenuating circumstances." An anonymous Zambian lawyer is quoted as saying, "What this piece of legislation means is that when a man in the street, as people without money are referred to, commits murder, he or she will go straight to the gallows, while leaders and their children, including company directors, will get away with murder even when it is proved without a doubt."

Education

Adult Literacy Rate: 76%

COMMUNICATION

Telephones: 71,700
Newspapers: 2

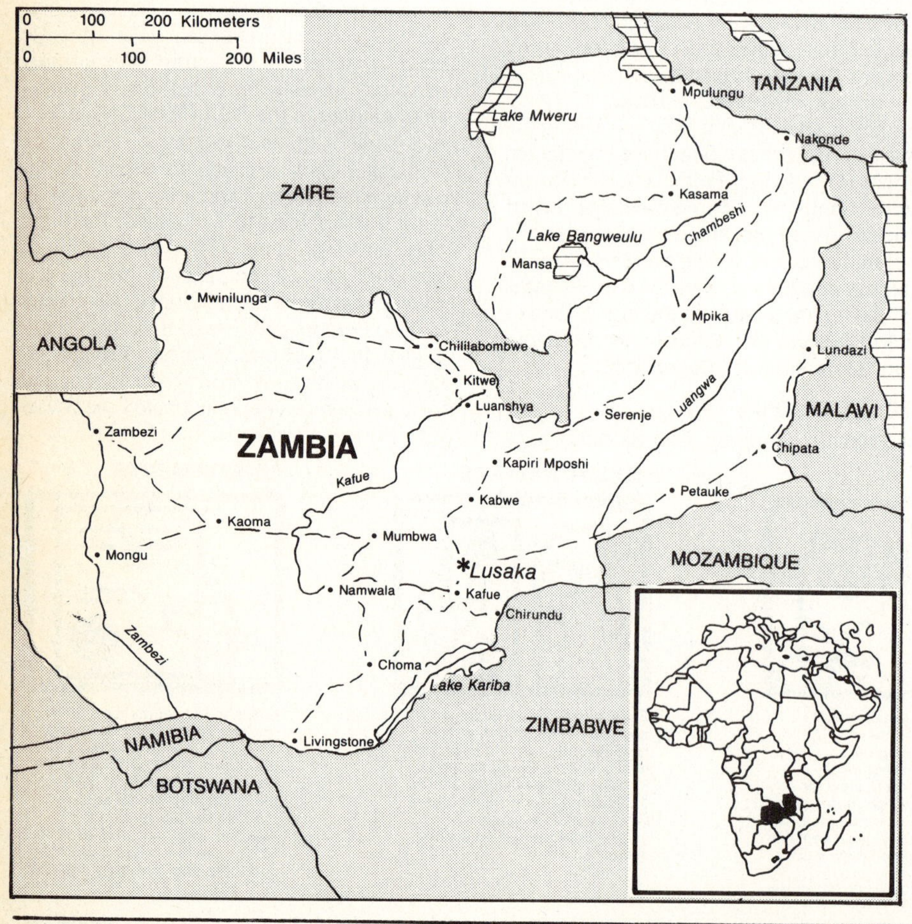

TRANSPORTATION

Highways—Kilometers (Miles): 36,370 (22,549)
Railroads—Kilometers (Miles): 1,266 (785)
Commercial Airports: 2 international

GOVERNMENT

Type: republic
Independence Date: October 24, 1964
Head of State: President Kenneth David Kaunda
Political Parties: United National Independence Party
Suffrage: universal for adults

MILITARY

Number of Armed Forces: 19,500
Military Expenditures (% of Central Government Expenditures): n/a
Current Hostilities: none

ECONOMY

Currency ($ U.S. Equivalent): 21.78 kwachas = $1
Per Capita Income/GNP: $530/$4 billion
Inflation Rate: 56%
Natural Resources: copper; zinc; lead; cobalt; coal
Agriculture: corn; tobacco; cotton; peanuts; sugarcane
Industry: foodstuffs; beverages; chemicals; textiles; fertilizer

FOREIGN TRADE

Exports: $1.1 billion
Imports: $687 million

Rhodes' South African Company is chartered by the British government **1889**

Development of the Copperbelt **1924–1934**

Federation of Northern Rhodesia, Southern Rhodesia, and Nyasaland is formed; still part of British Empire **1953–1963**

Zambia celebrates independence **1963**

Nationalization of 51% of all industries occurs **1969**

Zambia becomes a one-party state under the United National Independence Party **1972**

Kenneth Kaunda calls for a major emphasis on rural reconstruction, in his "watershed" speech **1975**

1980s–1990s

South African raids on Zambia

IMF conditions lead to riots; more than 30 are killed

As the economy deteriorates, rumors of Kaunda's retirement or overthrow prove unfounded

ZAMBIA

On June 30, 1990 Zambians poured into the streets in celebration of the reported overthrow of President Kenneth Kaunda. Their mood quickly changed as it became clear that the coup attempt had been crushed. The event, however, exposed the weakness and unpopularity of Kaunda's one-party regime, putting its long-term survival very much in doubt.

Since independence Zambia has been governed by Kaunda's United National Independence Party (UNIP). During much of this period the nation's economy, along with the well-being of its citizenry, has steadily declined. The government has consistently blamed Zambian setbacks on external forces beyond its control. There is a good deal of justification for this position. Until 1975 the high rate of return on Zambia's copper exports made the nation one of the most prosperous in Africa. Since then fluctuating, but generally depressed, prices for the metal and the disruption of landlocked Zambia's traditional sea outlets, as a result of strife in neighboring states, have had disastrous economic consequences. Nonetheless, it has long been apparent that internal factors have also contributed to Zambia's decay, while creating barriers to its recovery.

THE ONE-PARTY STATE

From the early years of independence Kaunda and UNIP showed little tolerance for the political opposition. In 1972 the country was legally transformed into a one-party state in which power was concentrated in the hands of Kaunda and his fellow members of UNIP's Central Committee. Since 1976 the government has ruled with state-of-emergency powers. Although the regime has not been as repressive as such neighboring states as Malawi and Zaire, torture and political detention without trial are common.

In its rule, UNIP is supposedly guided by the philosophy of "humanism," a term that in Zambia is equivalent to "the thoughts of Kaunda." Although it was once a mass party which had spearheaded Zambia's struggle for majority rule and independence, UNIP today stands for little other than the perpetuation of its own power.

RURAL DECLINE

An underlying economic problem has been the decline of rural production, despite Zambia's considerable agricultural potential. The underdevelopment of farming is rooted in colonial policies that favored mining to the exclusion of other sectors. Since independence the government has continued to neglect the rural areas, in terms of infrastructural investment. Until recently Zambian farmers were paid little for their produce, while the urban diet was maintained through government subsidization of imported food. The result has been a continuous influx of individuals into the towns, despite a lack of jobs, and falling food production. Today 55 percent of all Zambians are urban, one of the highest figures in Africa.

Zambia's rural decline has severely constrained the government's ability to meet the challenge imposed by the depressed international price of copper between 1975 and 1987. Copper and its by-product, cobalt, have consistently accounted for more than 90 percent of Zambia's export earnings. Falling prices have thus resulted in severe shortages of foreign exchange and in mounting indebtedness. The government, during the 1980s, began to devote greater attention to rural development. Agricultural production has risen modestly in response to increased incentives. Meanwhile, the size and desperate condition of the urban population has limited the government's ability to eliminate food subsidies and impose other harsh austerity measures advised by the International Monetary Fund; rising maize prices in 1986 set off riots which left at least 30 people dead.

By 1990 the government's continuing economic crisis had dovetailed with rising agitation for a return to multiparty democracy. Despite the president's attempts to label multiparty advocates as "misfits, malcontents, drug-peddlers and dissidents," the movement has grown, with the support of Zambia's major labor federation, its powerful Roman Catholic Church, and a number of prominent UNIP backbenchers. In May 1990 Kaunda announced that the issue would be put to a referendum. The following month, severe riots culminated in a coup attempt. Shortly thereafter Kaunda, in an about face, canceled his planned referendum and agreed to allow the legal formation of opposition parties.

DEVELOPMENT

Higher producer prices for agriculture, technical assistance, and rural-resettlement schemes are part of government efforts to raise agricultural production. The agricultural sector has shown growth. However, financial inputs are needed, and much maize is smuggled over the border to Zaire, reducing Zambia's potential for recovery.

FREEDOM

Amnesty International reports that opponents of the government are detained without trial, tortured, and the death penalty is maintained. A 1988 crackdown on the black market was perceived by many as an anti-Asian political move in an election year.

HEALTH/WELFARE

Life-expectancy rates have increased in Zambia since independence, as a result of improved health-care facilities. In 1986, 80% of primary-age children attended school; about 1 out of 4 went on to at least some secondary education. AIDS looms as an increasing health hazard.

ACHIEVEMENTS

Zambia has long played a major role in the fight against white supremacy in Southern Africa. From 1964 until 1980 it was a major base for Zimbabwe nationalists. Namibia's SWAPO and South Africa's ANC have also had headquarters in Zambia's capital of Lusaka.

Zimbabwe

GEOGRAPHY

Area in Square Kilometers (Miles): 390,759 (150,873) (slightly smaller than Montana)
Capital (Population): Harare (730,000)
Climate: subtropical

PEOPLE

Population
Total: 10,392,000
Annual Growth Rate: 3.3%
Rural/Urban Population Ratio: 75/25
Languages: official: English; others spoken: (Chi) Shona, (Si) Ndebele, others

Health
Life Expectancy at Birth: 59 years (male); 63 years (female)
Infant Death Rate (Ratio): 65/1,000
Average Caloric Intake: 86% of FAO minimum
Physicians Available (Ratio): 1/8,267

Religion(s)
75% Christian; 24% traditional indigenous; 1% Muslim

ZIMBABWE'S AGRICULTURAL SUCCESS STORY

In 1988 the New York-based Hunger Project awarded Zimbabwean President Robert Mugabe its Africa Prize for Leadership for the Sustainable End of Hunger. While recognizing the importance of leadership, though, most acknowledge that credit for the success of Zimbabwe's food production lies with the peasant, communal, and commercial farmers. Peasant farmers have boosted their maize production 1,000 percent since independence, with their share of agricultural production rising from a share of 8 percent to 64 percent. White commercial farmers also increased their output by 300 percent. Government loans, building of grain depots for storage, and improved roads, as well as resettlement for landless Zimbabweans, have encouraged thousands to increase productivity. The UN Food and Agriculture Organization (FAO) has targeted women farmers and encourages cooperative projects.

Education
Adult Literacy Rate: 74%

COMMUNICATION

Telephones: 247,000
Newspapers: 2

TRANSPORTATION

Highways—Kilometers (Miles): 85,237 (52,964)
Railroads—Kilometers (Miles): 2,743 (1,704)
Commercial Airports: 2 international

GOVERNMENT

Type: socialist state
Independence Date: April 18, 1980
Head of State: Executive President Robert Mugabe
Political Parties: Zimbabwe African National Union and Zimbabwe African People's Union (merged); Zimbabwe Unity Movement
Suffrage: universal over 18

MILITARY

Number of Armed Forces: 64,500
Military Expenditures (% of Central Government Expenditures): 6.2%
Current Hostilities: none

ECONOMY

Currency ($ U.S. Equivalent): 2.28 Zimbabwe dollars = $1
Per Capita Income/GNP: $470/$4.6 billion
Inflation Rate: 7.4%
Natural Resources: gold; chrome ore; coal; copper; nickel; iron ore; silver; asbestos
Agriculture: tobacco; corn; sugar; cotton; livestock
Industry: mining; steel; textiles

FOREIGN TRADE

Exports: $1.6 billion
Imports: $1.1 billion

ZIMBABWE

Zimbabwe achieved its formal independence in April 1980 after a 14-year-long armed struggle by its disenfranchised black African majority. Before 1980 the country was called (Southern) Rhodesia; a name that honored Cecil Rhodes, the British imperialist who masterminded the colonial occupation of the territory in the late nineteenth century. For its black African majority, Rhodesia's name was thus an expression of their subordination to a small minority of privileged white settlers whose racial hegemony was the product of Rhodes conquest. The new name, Zimbabwe, was symbolic of the greatness of their nation's precolonial roots.

THE PRECOLONIAL PAST

By the fifteenth century A.D. modern Zimbabwe had become the center of a series of states that prospered through their trade in gold and other goods with Indian Ocean merchants. These civilizations left as their architectural legacy the remains of stone settlements known as zimbabwes. The largest of these, the so-called Great Zimbabwe, lies near the modern town of Masvingo. Within its massive walls are dozens of stelae topped with distinctive carved birds, whose likeness has become a symbol of the modern state. Unfortunately, early European fortune seekers and archaeologists destroyed much of the archaeological evidence of this site, but what survives confirms that the state had trading contacts as far afield as China.

From the sixteenth century the Zimbabwean civilizations seem to have declined, possibly as a result of the disruption of the East African trading networks by the Portuguese. Nonetheless, the states themselves survived until the nineteenth century, and their cultural legacy is very much alive today, especially among the approximately 80 percent of Zimbabwe's population who speak (Chi)Shona.

Zimbabwe's other major ethnolinguistic community is the (Si)Ndebele speakers, who today account for about 15 percent of the population. This group traces its local origin to the mid-nineteenth-century conquest of much of modern Zimbabwe by invaders from the south, under the leadership of Umzilagazi, who established a militarily strong Ndebele kingdom which was subsequently ruled by his son.

WHITE RULE

Zimbabwe's colonial history is unique in that it was never under the direct rule of a European power. In 1890 the lands of the Ndebele and Shona were invaded by agents of Rhodes's British South Africa Company BSACO). During the 1890s both groups put up stiff resistance to the encroachments of the BSACO settlers but eventually they succumbed to the invaders' guns. In 1921 the BSACO administration was dissolved and Southern Rhodesia became a self-governing British Crown colony. "Self-government" was, in fact, confined to the white settler community, which grew rapidly but never numbered more than 5 percent of the population.

In 1953 Southern Rhodesia was federated with the British colonial territories of Northern Rhodesia (Zambia) and Nyasaland (Malawi). This Central African Federation was supposed to evolve into a "multiracial" dominion, but from the beginning it was perceived by the black majority in all three territories as a vehicle for continued white domination. As the Federation's first prime minister put it, the partnership of blacks and whites in building the new state would be analogous to a horse and its rider: no one had any illusions as to which racial group would continue to be the beast of burden.

In 1963 the Federation collapsed, as a result of local resistance. Black nationalists established the independent "nonracial" states of Malawi and Zambia. For a while it appeared that majority rule would also come to Southern Rhodesia. The local black community was increasingly well organized and militant in demanding full citizenship rights. However, in 1962 the white electorate responded to this challenge by voting into office the Rhodesia Front (RF), a party determined to uphold white supremacy at any cost. Using already existing emergency powers, the new government moved to suppress the two major black-nationalist movements: The Zimbabwe African People's Union (ZAPU) and the Zimbabwe African National Union (ZANU).

RHODESIA DECLARES INDEPENDENCE

In a bid to consolidate white power along the lines of the neighboring apartheid regime of South Africa, the RF, now led by Ian Smith, made its 1965 Unilateral Declaration of Independence (UDI) from any ties to the British Crown. Britain, along with the United Nations, refused to recognize this move. In 1967 the UN imposed mandatory economic sanctions against the "illegal" RF regime. But the sanctions were not fully effective, due largely to the fact that they were flouted by South Africa and the Portuguese authorities who controlled most of Mozambique until 1974. The United States for a number of years continued to purchase Rhodesian chrome openly, while many states and individuals engaged in more covert forms of sanctions-busting. Initially the Rhodesian economy actually benefited from the porous blockade, which encouraged the development of a wide range of import-substitution industries.

With the sanctions having only a limited effect, and Britain and the rest of the international community unwilling to engage in more active measures, it soon became clear that the burden of overthrowing the RF regime would be borne by the local population. Beginning in 1966 ZANU and ZAPU, as underground movements, began to engage in armed struggle. Initially the success of their attacks was limited, but from 1972 the Rhodesian Security Forces were increasingly besieged by the nationalists' guerrilla campaign. The 1974 liberation of Mozambique from the Portuguese greatly increased the effectiveness of the ZANU forces, who were allowed to infiltrate into Rhodesia from Mozambican territory. Meanwhile their ZAPU comrades launched attacks from bases in Zambia. In 1976 the two groups became loosely affiliated, as the Patriotic Front.

Unable to stop the military advance of the Patriotic Front, which was resulting in a massive white exodus, the RF attempted to forge a power-sharing arrangement, which preserved major elements of settler privilege. Although rejected by ZANU and ZAPU, this "internal settlement" was implemented in 1978–1979. A predominately black government took office, but real power remained in white hands, and the fighting only intensified. Finally, in 1979, all of the belligerent parties, meeting at Lancaster House in London, agreed to a compromise peace, which opened the door to majority rule while containing a number of constitutional provisions designed to reassure the white minority. In the subsequent elections, held in 1980, ZANU captured 57 and ZAPU 20 out of the 80 seats elected by the "common roll." Another 20 seats, which were reserved for whites for 7 years as a result of the Lancaster House agreement, were captured by the Conservative Alliance, the new name for the RF. ZANU leader Robert Mugabe became independent Zimbabwe's first prime minister.

THE RHODESIAN LEGACY

The political, economic, and social problems inherited by the Mugabe government were formidable. Rhodesia had been divided into "two nations": one black, the other white. Segregation prevailed in virtually all areas of life, with the facilities open to blacks being vastly inferior to those open to whites. The better half of the national territory had also been re-

Heyday of the gold trade and Great Zimbabwe
1400s–1500s

The Ndebele state emerges in Zimbabwe
1837

The Pioneer Column: arrival of the white settlers
1890

Chimurenga: rising against the white intruders ending in repression by whites
1895–1897

served for white ownership. In this white area, large commercial farms prospered, growing maize and tobacco for export as well as a diversified mix of crops for domestic consumption. In contrast,the black areas, formally known as Tribal Trust Lands, suffered from inferior soil and rainfall, overcrowding, and poor infrastructure. Most adults had little choice but to obtain seasonal work in the white areas. Black workers on white plantations, together with the large number of domestic servants, were particularly impoverished. But, until the 1970s, there were also few opportunities for skilled blacks as a result of a de facto color bar, which reserved the best jobs for whites.

Despite its stated commitment to revolutionary socialist objectives, since 1980 the Mugabe government has taken an evolutionary approach in dismantling the socioeconomic structures of old Rhodesia. This cautious policy is, in part, based on an appreciation that these same structures support what by regional standards is a relatively prosperous and self-sufficient economy. In addition, the government's hands have, to some extent, been tied by the Lancaster House accords, wherein private property, including the large settler estates, cannot be confiscated without compensation. In its first years in office the government, nonetheless made impressive progress in improving the livelihoods of the Zimbabwean majority by redistributing some of the surplus of the still white-dominated private sector. With the lifting of sanctions, mineral, maize, and tobacco exports expanded and import restrictions were eased. Workers' incomes rose, and a minimum wage, which notably covered farm employees, was introduced. Rising consumer purchasing power benefited local manufacturers. Health and educational facilities were rapidly expanded, while a growing number of blacks began to occupy management positions in the civil service and, to a lesser extent, in businesses.

Zimbabwe had hoped that foreign investment and aid would pay for an ambitious scheme to buy out many white farmers and to settle African peasants on their land. Funding shortfalls resulted in only modest resettlement. However, despite periodic drought, through a combination of incentives and investment the government has been able to boost peasant production significantly.

In addition to its professed concern to make its essentially market economy serve as an engine for a supposed transition to socialism, the Zimbabwean government has faced the classic dilemma of all industrializing societies: should it continue to use tight import controls to pro-

(Oxfam America photo)

In Zimbabwean organizations, as in many African institutions, decisions are often made by consensus, arrived at after long discussions.

Southern Rhodesia is proclaimed a British Crown colony
1924

Unilateral Declaration of Independence
1965

Armed struggle begins
1966

Elections following cease-fire bring victory to ZANU-PF and an end to the war

1980s–1990s

National elections give ZANU a large majority; Parliament abolishes reservation of seats by race

Robert Mugabe becomes executive president and offers a unity settlement to ZAPU

Violence mars the 1990 election; Mugabe claims a mandate for a one-party state but lifts the long-standing state of emergency

tect its existing manufacturing base, or should it open up its economy in the hopes of enjoying a take-off based on export-oriented growth? The unique diversification of local industry during the sanctions period has encouraged continued protectionism. While many Zimbabwean manufacturers would be vulnerable to greater foreign competition, the limits of the local market have undoubtedly contributed to the stagnating output and physical depreciation of local industry in recent years.

POLITICAL DEVELOPMENT

Since independence the Mugabe government has promoted reconciliation across the racial divide. Although the reserved seats for whites were abolished in 1987, the white minority, who now make up less than 1 percent of the population, are well represented within government as well as in business. Unfortunately, Mugabe's ZANU administration has shown less tolerance of its political opponents, especially ZAPU. ZANU had originally been a breakaway faction of ZAPU. At the time of this split, in 1963, the differences between the two movements had largely been over tactics. But elections in 1980 and 1985 confirmed that followings of both movements had become ethnically based, with most Shona supporting ZANU and Ndebele supporting ZAPU.

Initially ZANU agreed to share power with ZAPU. However, in 1982 the alleged discoveries of secret arms caches, which ZANU claimed ZAPU was stockpiling for a coup, led to the dismissal of the ZAPU ministers. Some leading ZAPU figures were also detained. The confrontation led to violence and very nearly degenerated into civil war. From 1982 to 1984 the Zimbabwean Army, dominated by former ZANU and Rhodesian units, carried out a counterinsurgency campaign against supposed ZAPU dissidents, in the largely Ndebele areas of western Zimbabwe. Hundreds of civilians were killed and thousands more fled to Botswana, including for a period the ZAPU leader, Joshua Nkomo.

From the beginning Mugabe has made it clear that he intends to use his party's electoral mandate to create a one-party state in Zimbabwe. With his other black and white opponents compromised by their past association with the RF and its internal settlement, this has largely meant coercing ZAPU into dissolving itself into ZANU. But the increased support for ZAPU in its core Ndebele constituencies during the 1985 election led to a renewed emphasis on the carrot over the stick in bringing about the union. In 1987 ZAPU formally merged into ZANU, but their shotgun wedding has made for an uneasy marriage.

With the demise of ZAPU, new opposition forces have emerged. Principal among these is the Zimbabwe Unity Movement (ZUM) led by former ZANU member Edger Tekere. In the 1990 elections, ZUM received 15 to 20 percent of the votes in a poll that saw a sharp drop in voter participation. The election was also marred by serious restrictions on opposition activity and blatant voter intimidation. The deaths of ZUM supporters in the run up to the election reinforced the message of the government-controlled media that a vote for the opposition was an act of suicide.

Mugabe claims that ZANU's latest victory gives it a mandate to establish a one-party state. He argues that such a step is necessary to build national unity. There is, however, opposition to such a move within his party as well as in the battered, but not broken, opposition. Many ZANU members are content with their party's de facto monopoly of political power, while others imply that a consolidation of the party's primacy will free it to pursue more revolutionary policies. To some radical critics, however, a one-party state would constitute the final step in the betrayal of the Zimbabwe revolution by an authoritarian government whose true allegiance lies with the bourgeoisie. That these and other views continue to be the subject of vigorous debate underscores the fact that there has developed within Zimbabwe a strong civil society that is at least resistant to the centralization of power.

The political controversies facing Zimbabwe should not overshadow its accomplishments. In its first decade the new nation has succeeded in providing for the expanded welfare of the majority of its citizens, especially in the areas of health and education. While preserving the vibrancy of the domestic economy, it has also, so far, been able to find peaceful nonracial solutions to the legacy of the "two nations."

DEVELOPMENT

Peasant production has increased dramatically since independence, creating grain reserves and providing exports for the region. The work of communal farmers has been recognized both within Zimbabwe and internationally.

FREEDOM

In July 1990 the government lifted the state of emergency that had been in effect since the days of the Federation. Human-rights activists in Zimbabwe hope that this step will lead to further human-rights progress. The futures of freedom of speech and association in the country are threatened by calls for a one-party state.

HEALTH/WELFARE

Since independence, expenditure on health has risen to 4% of GDP and education to 12% of GDP. As a result, most Zimbabweans now enjoy access to medical facilities, while primary-school enrollment has multiplied fourfold and literacy rates have improved. Higher education has also been greatly expanded.

ACHIEVEMENTS

Since independence, Zimbabwe's capital city of Harare has become an arts and communications center for Southern Africa. Many regional as well as local filmmakers, musicians, and writers based in the city enjoy international reputations. And the distinctive malachite carvings of Zimbabwean sculptors are highly valued in the international art market.

Articles from the World Press

Annotated Table of Contents for Articles

Topic Guide to Articles

TOPIC AREA	TREATED AS AN ISSUE IN:
Human Rights	9. Cooperation Pays Off 20. Apartheid's Other Injustice 21. Namibia's Combatants Seek New Role in Society
Independence	16. Southern Africa: Regional Bloc Seeks Boost for Weak Economies 17. Botswana: Democracy and a Buoyant Economy 18. Zimbabwe Braces for Shifts in Regional Leadership Role
Labor	9. Cooperation Pays Off
Military	2. The African Crisis: The Internal Leakages
Natural Disasters	14. The Horn of Famine
Natural Resources	4. Population Explosion Putting Africa in Peril 12. Favored Few Tap Zaire Wealth
Philosophy	8. BaKongo Cosmology
Politics	5. Africans Call for Accountable Government 10. Africa's Great Black Hope 17. Botswana: Democracy and a Buoyant Economy 18. Zimbabwe Braces for Shifts in Regional Leadership Role
Political Reform	2. The African Crisis: The Internal Leakages 5. Africans Call for Accountable Government 10. Africa's Great Black Hope 11. Mozambique: From Dogma to Doubt 17. Botswana: Democracy and a Buoyant Economy
Political Unrest	6. Poised Between Reform and Further Decline
Population	4. Population Explosion Putting Africa in Peril
Private Enterprise	15. Cattle Camp in South Sudan
Race	20. Apartheid's Other Injustice
Refugees	21. Namibia's Combatants Seek New Role in Society
Religion	8. BaKongo Cosmology
Science	8. BaKongo Cosmology
Turmoil	10. Africa's Great Black Hope 14. The Horn of Famine 21. Namibia's Combatants Seek New Role in Society
Trade	10. Africa's Great Black Hope
Violence	6. Poised Between Reform and Further Decline
Women	7. Lines of Descent 9. Cooperation Pays Off
Youth	9. Cooperation Pays Off

Article 1

THE WORLD TODAY
NOVEMBER 1990

Black Africa: from aid dependence to self-sustaining growth

Tony Hawkins

The adage that in economics only the answers change, the questions are the same, is disturbingly applicable to Africa in the 1990s. The problems of African development have been analysed ad nauseam since the World Bank's sober assessment of the sub-Saharan economy, *From Crisis to Sustainable Growth*, was released towards the end of 1989. The subsequent debate has generated little heat and even less light. Few have faulted the Bank's analysis. So widespread and deep-rooted is Afro-pessimism that it is now impossible to read anything on regional economic prospects without being subjected to a litany of dismal economic statistics. Whether the authors be from the World Bank, the United Nations, the Economic Commission for Africa (ECA) or Western politicians, academics or businessmen, the effect is the same.

There is broad agreement on the nature of the problems, though deep-seated disagreement as to its causes. Africans, on the whole, continue to blame the external environment for the region's economic failure, supported by the interventionists and apologists for socialism. Bankers, businessmen and, increasingly, the donor community, while accepting that reduced protectionism and strong growth in the industrialised countries are necessary preconditions for economic revival in Africa, argue—pragmatically—that the solution lies in policy reform in Africa itself.

The problems are obvious: the population is growing too fast; the foreign debt burden is unmanageable; exports, investment and employment have stagnated or fallen; agriculture has under-performed. For many, the most disturbing aspect of Africa's economic decline is the absence of serious new policy initiatives to deal with the crisis. The depressing news is that a decade of policy-based lending has left the continent poorer than it was before structural adjustment medicine was first administered. The ECA blames this on inappropriate adjustment strategies and the foreign debt burden. But it seems clear that without structural adjustment the situation would have been far worse. Structural change takes time—decades rather than years. It is still too early to ask for the jury's verdict.

A loss of nerve at this juncture is just what Africa does not need and cannot afford. The search for new prescriptions in a deteriorating situation is both laudable and understandable but it is also dangerous, since those African policy-makers who have embraced the Western solution with varying degrees of enthusiasm and conviction are already under pressure at home. To suggest that the policies they have fought to implement against often bitter opposition from doctrinal hardliners should now be changed would destroy their credibility altogether.

To be fair, the World Bank has not suggested that. Structural adjustment is alive, even if it is not very well. A major reason for its lacklustre performance is the lack of political commitment on the part of many—if not most—African governments forced against their better judgment to swallow Washington's medicine. A second is operational—the difficulties of sequencing and implementing structural adjustment policies.

In the search for strategies to make structural adjustment work faster and more effectively, some grasping after straws is apparent. It is difficult to read the Bank's 1989 Report without concluding that the prospects for informal sector development are being oversold; that the savings and investment targets are unrealistically high; that the resource-inflow targets are out of reach, and so on. The Report's credibility is undermined, too, by the Bank's unwillingness to acknowledge the seriousness of the Aids crisis, certainly in so far as East, Central and Southern Africa are concerned, while the exclusion of the region's most powerful economy—South Africa—is a measure of political expediency rather than logic.

It is a sign of the times that the Bank's courageous call for improved 'governance' attracted so many adherents so quickly. Scarcely was the ink dry on the Report when Western donors, who in the past had preferred discreet silence on so sensitive an issue, began to suggest that in future economic aid might be withheld from countries that failed to meet the 'good governance' test. There are few better examples of the 'thundering herd' syndrome.

But this sudden conversion to a cause, ignored for 30 years, was largely fortuitous. It arose partly from a growing sense of desperation over the African economy, but more pertinently from the demise of superpower rivalry in Africa. So long as the Russian or Cuban threat existed, the end of defeating Communism justified the means of bolstering corrupt dictatorships. Indeed, even with Moscow and Havana retreating in disarray, President Mobutu's regime in Zaire still commands aid, if not support, because of its perceived contribution to the resolution of the Angolan crisis.

The 'chattering classes' of the media and the political, diplomatic and academic communities have been quick—too quick—to conclude that political revolution in Eastern Europe will be replicated in Africa. Street protests in Francophone Africa, President de Klerk's bold initiatives in South Africa and unrest in Kenya and Zambia in the first half of 1990 certainly lend support to this assessment. But unlike Eastern Europe, no government has yet fallen. Admittedly, leaders in some one-party states—Presidents Houphouet Boigny in Ivory Coast, Mobutu Sese Seko in Zaire, Haile Mariam Mengistu in Ethiopia and Joachim Chissano in Mozambique—have been reluctantly forced to accept multi-party democracy, but the yawning gulf between words and deeds, characteristic of so many of Africa's economic reform programmes, will manifest itself in the political field during the 1990s.

Not only are there good grounds for questioning the sincerity—and capacity—of those who have promised change to achieve it, but for every leader who has embraced multi-partyism there are two who have flatly rejected it. President Robert Mugabe insists that one-party states are more democratic than pluralist ones; in Togo, President Eyedema says his people do not want it. President Mwinyi of Tanzania rejects it.

The initial reactions of Presidents Daniel Arap Moi in Kenya and Kenneth Kaunda in Zambia to street unrest in their two countries was to intensify repression. Under pressure from Western donors both have since softened their positions, but tactics should never be confused with strategy. In a continent where in the past 30 years there have been only one or two examples of ballot box-determined political change, those who believe that democracy is about to break out will be proved wrong.

In any event, the fact that political unrest in some African countries has closely followed the Eastern European revolutions is an inadequate explanation. Political ferment in Africa has a far longer pedigree. It is the result of a combination of economic failure and political paralysis.

The twin pillars of post-colonial Africa—the command economy and the one-party state—were viable only as long as economic growth kept ahead of population growth so that living standards were improving. Until the first oil price shock in 1973–74 African economies had just about managed to keep their heads above water. Immediately thereafter, economic decline was cushioned by foolish bankers and well-intentioned, though largely unsuccessful, aid agencies.

The full cost of externally-funded, largely unprofitable investment became apparent only in the 1980s, by which time it was obvious that, between them, the bankers and the donors had saddled the region with an unmanageable debt burden. Worse still, much of the foreign capital was poorly invested. Tanzania, one of the region's top aid recipients, recently embarked on a $1.2bn road rehabilitation programme designed to regain the standards existing in the mid-1970s. During the 1980s, sub-Saharan Africa received nearly $100bn in official development assistance. During that time income per head fell by more than 1 per cent a year. There can be no more stinging indictment of the aid community.

In 1990, living standards throughout the region are no higher than they were at independence 30 years ago. The seeds of political change were sown, not when protesters took to the streets in Prague, East Berlin and Budapest in the autumn of 1989 but in the preceding 10 to 15 years—a period of sustained economic decline.

African protesters are motivated more by economic deprivation than the denial of political choice. Their hope is that by changing the government—and possibly also the political system—they will improve their economic situation. In that way Africa is no different from the West, where elections are won and lost on interest and tax rates, unemployment and inflation.

It is misleading to suggest that African leaders disregard the linkage between economic progress and political systems. They understand it very well. It is not just President Kaunda who has argued that the adoption of multi-party democracy in Zambia would not increase the price of copper or cocoa. A change of government in Zambia will help the economy only if Mr Kaunda's successor is more committed to economic reform, and more competent to carry it through.

In fact, the reverse could very well turn out to be the case. In all probability a 'popular' Zambian leader who ousted President Kaunda would abandon the harsh austerity policies necessary for the revival of the Zambian economy. The partially successful structural adjustment programmes in Ghana and Nigeria have been imposed by undemocratic military regimes. The return to civilian rule in Nigeria in 1992 could well spell the end of economic reform, since the politicians will feel obliged to reflate the economy in an attempt to win voter support.

But even if it could be demonstrated that African economies would function better with multi-party democracy (as has indeed been the case in Botswana and Mauritius, though both are essentially atypical), this assumes that the requisite political infrastructure for a multi-party system is available. It is not. The political systems the colonialists left behind when they left the continent in such haste were the fruits of expediency. There were no serious attempts to design appropriate systems.

Those who drew attention to this at the time, such as Sir Roy Welensky, Prime Minister of the Federation of Rhodesia and Nyasaland, were contemptuously dismissed by the 'chattering classes' as paternalists, racists, reactionaries. 'One man, one vote, once', said Welensky. In a continent littered with one-party dictatorships, where free and fair elections occur only when supervised from outside by the UN or the Commonwealth, that prediction, so scornfully rejected at the time by the men of Whitehall, is now grudgingly acknowledged.

Worse, not only did the colonial powers leave behind an unmanageable political system and undeveloped economies, but they compounded the felony with their adoption of a double standard of political conduct, of which perhaps the most devastating example is that of Zaire. It was Belgium's panicky scuttling of its colonial responsibilities in 1960 that created the chaos from which the corrupt Mobutu dictatorship emerged. It would be comforting to believe that Belgium's recently-expressed outrage at the conduct of the Mobutu regime, nurtured for 20 years by successive Belgian and American governments, marked a sincere policy change rather than the desire to pay lip-service to the new democracy of the post-communist world.

As the Soviet threat recedes so the West has at last found the courage to speak out against African dictatorships. Even then it was left to the World Bank to set the tone. Few dispute its commonsense assertion that 'good governance' is an essential precondition for economic development. Much more difficult is how to achieve it. The World Bank provides little guidance on this score. Donors are taking up the World Bank's challenge by threatening to add political conditions to the economic conditionalities stipulated by the Bank, the IMF and a growing number of bilateral donors, before they will disburse aid.

Unhappily, demands for political conditionality are flawed on several counts. First, the concept is undefined. African leaders are right to reject the facile distinction between multi-partyism and single-party states. Recent experience in Romania is a reminder that there is far more to a free society than multi-party elections. Zimbabwe's 1990 elections, conducted on a first-past-the-post Westminster constituency model, left the minority with hardly a voice in parliament, despite the fact that only 56 per cent of the electorate voted for President Mugabe.

African leaders justify single-party rule on the ground that it prevents the emergence of tribally or ethnically driven political parties. But one-party rule has signally failed to prevent tribalism and regionalism degenerating into civil conflict. It is now time to seek alternative mechanisms — proportional representation, decentralisation, federalism, vetoes for minority groups. All of these are ideas that will have to be investigated in the 1990s. Sadly, though, only in South Africa is there any serious discussion of a constitutional dispensation designed to counter the worst excesses of African governments.

Second, there is a problem of objective measurement. The debate over easing sanctions against South Africa illustrates the point. How much reform is enough? How far does a government have to step out of line before political conditionality is cited as justification for withholding aid?

Third, for all their sermonising on governance, donors remain reluctant to apply the yardsticks of political conditionality. Whitehall's evident embarrassment over President Moi, Nordic reluctance to pull the plug on Zambia and on American equivocation over Zaire, all reflect the fact that conditionality decisions are far from unidimensional. Verbal sabre-rattling by the British and American governments over aid to Kenya has still to be translated into any sort of action, while the French have reportedly agreed to sell arms to Mr Moi.

Then there is the aid lobby's complaint that it is wrong to punish a country's poor and underprivileged for the misdeeds of its government—unless, of course, that country is South Africa. The aid lobby holds that President Moi's repressive policies do not justify withholding aid from 25m Kenyans. This argument would carry more weight had aid programmes been more successful in channeling assistance to the world's needy than they have, as shown in the World Bank's 1990 World Development Report. It is unconvincing, too, since there are many ways in which aid can be provided to a country in a manner that expressly demonstrates disapproval of the ruling regime—as in the South African case.

The self-interest of the aid lobby itself is a potent consideration, too. Exporters, consultants, academic researchers, university research foundations, research institutes and educational institutions all have a vested interest in maintaining aid flows. They, like businessmen with fat export contracts with Iraq, have no sympathy with political conditionality.

In one of the most positive and constructive contributions to the sterile debate over African economic development, Sir William Ryrie, Executive Vice-President of the International Finance Corporation, the private-sector arm of the World Bank group, suggested that 'the gigantic misuse of aid funds' might have something to do with the fact that almost all of them were transferred by methods that avoided the discipline of the market.

Unfortunately, this valuable comment begs the question: how to increase the use of market mechanisms to channel aid to Africa's indigenous private sector, as distinct from its benefits being appropriated by exporters, consultants, and 'researchers' in the donor countries? The weak link in the proposal is the assumption that viable private sectors exist in recipient countries.

This emphasis on the role of the private sector—the argument that self-sustaining growth is most likely to be achieved where governments and donors between them create an 'enabling environment'—falls short in most African countries because no private sector worthy of the name exists. There is a vibrant private sector in Nigeria, Zimbabwe, Kenya and Ivory Coast, but elsewhere non-government economic activity is largely limited to that of the informal sector.

The typical African private-sector profile is three-tiered: a handful of Western multinationals, many of whom reluctantly agreed to state participation in their African affiliates; some medium-sized 'local' firms, often owned by expatriates, especially Asians; and a huge informal sector, largely comprising peasant farmers.

Throughout the region the private sector has been a target of government policy because of its foreign links or ownership. In Kenya private-sector localisation has taken the form of increasing equity participation by local businessmen, many of whom have what are euphemistically called 'powerful political connections'. In Zimbabwe private sector 'independence' has been progressively eroded as the state or the ruling ZANU-PF party has purchased controlling equity stakes in major industrial and commercial activities. Similar patterns apply in Kenya and Malawi.

Aiding the private sector tends to take the form of bolstering the two upper tiers—multinational affiliates and the medium-sized locally-owned enterprises. Frequently, too, the IFC and similar agencies have found themselves financing joint ventures effectively controlled by African governments. There are few opportunities for financing wholly privately-owned enterprises, unless these are foreign-controlled.

This leaves the donors with the task of building not just an enabling environment but the private sector itself. The optimists believe this is less intimidating than might be thought. There is, we are told, no shortage of entrepreneurship in Africa. Unfortunately, this is another half-truth. There is no shortage of entrepreneurship in retailing, or in the import-export business—in which the export content is usually minimal—or in transport or hotels. But finding viable entrepreneurship in manufacturing, mining (other than tiny enterprises), sophisticated service industries like tourism, banking and so on is very difficult indeed.

Given the dismal performance of governments—recipients and donors—in Africa, the Ryrie argument for an enhanced private-sector role is at least worth a try, unpromising though the existing market environment might be. Like the World Bank's new-found enthusiasm for informal sector development, it may smack of grasping at straws, but the private sector can hardly do a worse job than the donors.

Official assistance should be used to relieve the debt burden, to rehabilitate the infrastructure without which there can be no sustainable growth in Africa, to train managers, technicians and—above all—trainers, not in Washington or Stockholm but on the job in their home countries or at the African training institutions. The donor community should go back to basics and undertake the functions traditionally handled by the state. This is a better way of creating an enabling environment than tying assistance to the degree of media freedom or the number of legal political parties.

The suggestion that donors with a disastrous decade of failure behind them should do more in the 1990s does not stand up. If it is right to privatise, to roll back the frontiers of the state in Europe and North America, then surely it is also right to roll back the activities of the official donors, too? Try visiting an upmarket hotel in Africa and count the number of 'official' visitors, funded by governments or donor agencies, relative to the number of businessmen there. The private sector is swamped by officialdom, not just African officialdom, but donor officialdom.

The World Bank—and others—argue that too much government smothers private initiative. So does too much aid, especially poorly targeted aid. If every dollar spent by donors on socio-economic 'research' and consultancy reports on African issues were spent on training Africans, the return on investment would be substantially higher. So high is the proportion of African imports funded by aid that export-marketing by OECD manufacturers is more about 'tapping into' aid programmes than selling Africans what they want to buy. Export salesmen do not need to know anything about market conditions in Kenya or Nigeria, as long as they know whom to contact in the relevant Ministry for Overseas Development.

Ghana, Tanzania and Mozambique are prime examples of aid dependence. Take the foreign funding away and the economic restructuring dutifully praised by IMF and World Bank teams will collapse in short order. The challenge for Africa and the aid lobby in the 1990s is to achieve what was always the intention: a self-sustaining society, rather than a poverty-stricken, aid-dependent Tanzania. Sir William Ryrie is right to champion private enterprise and investment whose neglect over the past 20 years tells us so much about the failure of African economies.

Article 2

African Letter, May 1–5, 1990

THE AFRICAN CRISIS: THE INTERNAL LEAKAGES

George Ayittey

The columnist, a native of Ghana, is a fellow at the Hoover Institution, Stanford University, U.S.

"A bucket full of holes can only hold so much water for a while. Pouring in more water makes little sense because it will all leak away. To the extent that there are internal leakages in Africa (corruption, senseless civil wars, defective leadership, government wastes, and hideous tyranny) pouring in more foreign aid won't save Africa. As a first order of priority, the leaks must be plugged."

Ever since the crisis emerged, African leaders, officials and intellectuals have drawn up various proposals or solutions for discussion.

Among them include: allocation of more foreign aid to Africa, partial cancellation of Africa's $230 billion foreign debt, a demonstration of greater political will on the part of the donors, the formation of debt cartels, formation of a new international order, and even repudiation of the debt. The astute reader will notice that most of these proposals have one thing in common: they all look to be outside (external) for Africa's salvation. These measures will help some but it would be foolish to pin all our hopes on the generosity and altruism of foreigners.

What can we do to help ourselves? Are there any internal sources of funds we can tap to ease the crisis. Certainly! What follows is one such INTERNAL SOLUTION. Remember that Africa receives about $8 billion in aid from all sources. Let's see if we can obtain more than that from within Africa itself.

First, Africa spends about $12 billion a year on the purchase of arms and the maintenance of the military. What do African leaders use the army in Africa for? To slaughter and oppress the African people! In August, 1988, the Somali Government dropped bombs on its own citizens in the northern part of the country when they demanded relief and freedom from President Barre's 20-year despotic rule. In the same month, the military government of Burundi massacred an estimated 20,000 Hutus.

Soldiers chasing fleeing Hutus machine-gunned and bayonetted many of them.

Cut the size of the army in Africa. The soldiers can't even do battle with ill-trained armed robbers in their own countries, let alone save their nations from well-equipped foreign invaders. Costa Rica has no army; yet it has not been invaded by any foreign forces. Reducing military expenditures would save close to a stupendous $12 billion for development. Foreign exchange saved is foreign exchange earned!!

Second, at least $15 billion in capital flees Africa annually. Morgan Guaranty Trust of New York estimates that, Nigeria's $32 billion foreign debt would have been only $7 billion, had there been no capital flight. Multiply that by 51 African countries and that $15 billion is even an underestimate. Part of the capital fleeing Africa present money legitimately earned by Africans but who have no faith in their countries (because of political and economic instability) to invest there. The rest is booty, money illegally transferred abroad by corrupt government officials. Most annoying, it is these same officials who draw up grandiose investment codes to attract and beseech foreigners to come and invest in Africa.

Third, at least $5 billion annually could be saved if Africa were able to feed itself. It now imports about 40 percent of its food needs. It used to be self-sufficient in food production in the 1950s and even export food. Nigeria, for example, used to export palm oil. Sierra Leone also used to export rice. Not anymore.

Tanzania used to export food in the 1960s. It is now an importer. The weather was not the culprit. The true causes of Africa's agricultural decline were the defective policies that exploited and oppressed peasant farmers, the productive class.

Fourth, another $5 billion can be saved from wastes and inefficiencies in Africa's 3,200-odd state enterprises. Add $3 billion in savings from the civil service itself through staff deployments. In 1986, some 30 percent of the Civil Service staff in Liberia were declared redundant.

Fifth, the civil wars raging on in Africa exact a heavy toll in lost output and destroyed property. The Government of Mozambique, for example, admits that the war there has cost over $4 billion, not counting output lost and the destruction of the economy. The war in Angola costs the country over $1 billion annually. Then there are the wars in Ethiopia, Sudan, Somalia, Uganda and so on. How much do you think these stupid wars cost Africa annually? Put down $10 billion.

Incidentally, the leaders of these war-torn countries refuse to sit down at the negotiating table. They would rather continue with the war. By the way, aren't we the same people who are calling upon the apartheid regime in South Africa to sit down at the negotiating table with the ANC? Do you detect any inconsistency here? Oh, but that's difference. The peasants of Angola, Ethiopia, Mozambique, Somalia, Sudan, or Uganda see no difference. They are fed up with these senseless wars. More than 200,000 Angolan peasants have died or have had their legs amputated for stepping on mines. In southern Africa, more than 400 children die each day. Nobody seems concerned. Meanwhile, useless idiots, armed with a few bazookas continue to blow up their African countries in behalf of foreign ideologies while the intellectuals perform high-octane verbal acrobatics as to which superpower is meddling in Africa affairs.

Now, if all these costs are totalled, they come up to $50 billion which may be compared with the $8 billion Africa receives in foreign aid. Which is a better alternative?

Article 3

AFRICA NEWS
October 22, 1990

Africa: A Turning Point?

As the last decade of the century gets underway, Africa's prospects for the year 2000 appear bleak. But amid the gloomy projections of increased famine, disease and conflict, new voices are pressing the continent's leaders—and their foreign funders—towards political and economic reforms.

"We want our governments to reprioritize—to spend more for the social programs that benefit children and less on wars and weapons," said Loatile Seleka, a 20-year old youth leader from Botswana, speaking at the World Summit for Children, held at the United Nations on September 29th and 30th in New York. "We intend to pressurize them in every way we can."

But African governments face international pressures that compete with the demands of their citizens for increased expenditures on schools, health care and other services to improve living standards. The demand from foreign aid donors is for budget cuts and austerity.

The 20% decline in average income during the 1980s has eroded living standards in many parts of the continent to levels that existed when most of the countries became independent in the 1960s. Part of the debate now taking place is whether the economic reforms being implemented in over 30 countries under the auspices of the International Monetary Fund and the World Bank can reverse the downward trend and nudge the continent onto the path of growth.

"The 1990s will either see Africa further marginalized from the global economy, sliding further down the development scales, or the new decade will see Africa slowly reviving, taking actions needed to bring about recovery and receiving the assistance necessary to sustain it," says Edward V. K. Jaycox, World Bank vice president for Africa.

As figures presented to the World Summit for Children indicate, Africa's problems could readily worsen, if the resources are not found to attack the causes and if the population explosion continues.

Of the 28 children who die around the world each minute, seven are in Africa. As in the rest of the world, two thirds of the 10,000 African children dying daily perish from preventable causes – diarrhea, measles, tetanus and acute respiratory infections.

The 71 leaders at the World Summit endorsed a plan of action committing their governments to a range of programs for "the survival, protection, and development of children in the 1990s." One model is a United Nations immunization campaign launched in 1985, with a goal of reaching 80% of the world's children by the end of this year. James Grant, executive director of Unicef (United Nations Children's Fund), told a summit briefing the goal is likely to be reached.

Worldwide expenditure of $2.5 billion a year throughout this decade could prevent 50 million child deaths, Unicef says. Unicef puts the amount needed in context by pointing out that $2.5 billion is what American tobacco companies spend on advertising annually and what Soviets spend on vodka each month – and what the world puts into military expenditures every *day*.

According to World Bank President Barber Conable, there are signs that "donors are willing to make special efforts to increase concessional assistance and debt relief to support Africa's economic reforms." Speaking to African finance ministers and central bank governors during last month's World Bank and International Monetary Fund (IMF) annual meeting, he said Africa's moves towards economic reforms and the response by donors is cause for "guarded optimism" about Africa's outlook.

But there continues to be widespread concern about the social impact of IMF-inspired reform policies, particularly on the most powerless sectors of the population, especially children. Structural adjustment, as these reforms are known, generally entails reduced expenditure on health, education, and water resources. Unicef has led a campaign to give structural adjustment "a human face" by incorporating protections for the poor and vulnerable into the reforms. Unicef also insists that "human indicators" be considered alongside economic performance measurements in evaluating whether structural adjustment is succeeding or failing. "Many studies have shown that investment in human resources is in fact the surest way to achieve and sustain long-term economic growth," Unicef says in a presentation prepared for the Summit.

Unicef advocates debt relief as a principal means of easing pressures on adjusting countries and of improving living standards for the poor. "It would take only a little more than $6 billion spent on health, nutrition, water, and sanitation to save the lives of 18 billion African children by the year 2000," says Stephen Lewis, a Canadian diplomat who is special advisor on Africa to United Nations Secretary General Javier Perez de Cuellar.

With Africa's finances already stretched to the limit, where can $6 billion be found? "You can't say it will come from trade or investment – they're going down," Lewis says. "You can't say it will come from foreign aid – it's stagnating. You can't say it will come from exports – commodity prices are plummeting." The only possible source, he argues, is debt relief. Sub-Saharan African countries are expected to spend an estimated $9 billion each year throughout this decade on debt payments.

But the World Bank's Jaycox says Africa's debt problem is being "overblown." Since the debt payment obligations are not now being met by many countries, he argues, debt relief will not free new funds. And he concedes that there are not any other untapped sources for Africa either. "There are no more doors to open for Africa," he says.

That makes the newest added pressure – rising oil prices – a clear danger. With most of Africa already engaged in austerity reform programs, there is not "a lot of room for further adjustment on their part," Jaycox says. However, the Bank and the international donor community have "virtually guaranteed" that countries implementing reforms "won't be underfinanced," he says. So he expects Africa's oil import countries to receive some additional assistance.

The Bank has also promised "a significant expansion" in support for improvements in education, health, nutrition and family planning, President Conable said in a letter to Canadian Prime Minister Brian Mulroney, on the eve of the Summit for Children. Mulroney, one of the initiators of the meeting, had appealed to the heads of numerous international agencies to pledge increased backing for programs to aid children.

Article 4

Guardian Weekly, June 3, 1990

Population explosion putting Africa in peril

In his long and distinguished career, 86-year-old René Dumont has acted as an adviser to the United Nations and the Food and Agriculture Organisation. Here, he suggests that unless urgent action is taken black Africa may succumb to the combined perils of a fast-deteriorating environment, outdated farming techniques and galloping population growth.

Mother Nature has given black Africa a poor deal. First there is the climate. The greater part of the continent, from the southern Sahara to eastern and southern Africa, has a semi-arid climate which in periods of drought can easily become arid.

In the equatorial zone, on the other hand, excessive rainfall washes the goodness from arable land and encourages cryptogamic diseases, while the presence of the tsetse fly rules out stock-farming and therefore animal traction.

The greenhouse effect has caused a further deterioration of the climate by intensifying droughts and tornadoes. Ethiopia is now in an even more disastrous situation as a result of the poor 1989 harvest than it was in 1984. Soil erosion, which was particularly drastic in 1978, only accentuates the damage already caused by lack of rainfall.

Whereas Asia boasts 133 million hectares of irrigated land, Africa has a mere 8 million, half of which is located between Egypt and Sudan. This makes the possibility of a green revolution remote, especially as tropical African peasants have no experience of piped irrigation, a technique that cannot be acquired overnight.

Most soil in Africa is poor. In the case of sandy soils, like the *dior* in Senegal, which have a low clay content, fertility depends on the amount of humus present. Traditional farming used to maintain humus by letting land lie fallow for long periods and then ploughing in the natural vegetation that had grown on it.

But, with the rapid population growth in Africa, this practice is now in decline and in some cases has even been abandoned. As a result, and because no manure, compost or green fertilisers are added, such sandy soils have been totally depleted.

Lack of humus encourages erosion on a vast scale. Erosion is caused not only by rainfall, which although rare, can be very violent and creates gullies on any farmland with a slope of about 1 per cent of more, but also by wind, which finishes off the job by removing the soil's finest elements. In the last 50 years, sandstorms have tended to be more intense and to last longer, with the result that they are extending farther and farther into so-called humid zones.

This is how the bankruptcy of the environment—the term is Lloyd Timberlake's—has affected arable land in Africa. An ever-greater number of people plough more and more land, because they have no means of increasing yields. So they cultivate marginal land, which is more arid and therefore more fragile. This has the effect of destroying the plant cover of areas previously reserved for stock-farming.

An increasing number of farmers try to maintain bigger and bigger herds in an attempt to survive. As there is no fodder, the animals exhaust the pasture land, then destroy edible shrubs branch by branch when no other resources are available.

The end result is what is known as desert. At the 1977 Nairobi world conference on desertification, the rich countries were called upon to finance steps that would halt the destruction of mankind's heritage in this way. They refused. Six million hectares of land are lost to the desert every year, at a cost estimated at between ten and 20 times that of prevention (about $2.5 billion a year, or 0.2 per cent of world military spending).

The estimated amount of tropical forest lost every year used to be 11 million hectares. But in 1987–1988 that figure doubled. The coastal forests of western Africa, from Casamance in Senegal to Zaire, have shrunk by more than half since 1950.

Ivory Coast's original 15 million hectares of forest have shrivelled to around 3 million. In conjunction with the greenhouse effect, this decline has resulted in lower annual rainfall in the coastal forest area and, more importantly, in the Sahel: in many cases it is now between 20 and 25 per cent lower than it was in 1968.

Yet several regions of black Africa have great agricultural potential. Around the great volcanoes of Cameroon and Nigeria and, to an even greater degree in eastern Africa, there is fertile soil and plentiful rainfall; alluvial deposits, while not as fertile as those of the Nile Valley, can be highly productive when properly irrigated.

Animal traction, which originated in Asia, arrived in Europe and was thence introduced to the Americas; but it scarcely spread at all to tropical Africa. The foreign powers that arrived on the continent, either via the Sahara or by sea on the eastern or western coasts, were interested mainly in conquest or trade.

None of them bothered to introduce the swing-plough or more importantly, the wheel (so there were no carts or wheelbarrows or indeed, later on, bicycles): farming was the job of slaves, and for that reason is still despised as an activity today.

Another reason for farming's poor "brand image" is that it is still largely carried out by women, particularly in the case of food corps. Women have to endure punishing work in the fields. Worse, they have to carry everything, either on their backs or on their heads, without the help of the wheel. Thirty years after most African countries gained independence, women are still virtual beasts of burden.

This state of affairs effectively rules out any possibility of improved agricultural techniques or more intensive farming. When the practice of laying land fallow was abandoned in Europe, farmers planted fodder crops instead, which enabled them to increase their number of livestock and therefore their energy resources—as well as producing more manure, which has such a crucial bearing on humus content.

But it is hard to see how that kind of agricultural revolution could be carried out in villages which have no means of transport. In France, I myself succeeded in spreading 30 tonnes of manure per hectare with the help of two draught horses pulling two-tonne cartloads.

In Africa, the same task carried out by women, each carrying 30 kilos on her head, would require 1,000 trips to and from the field. And if it was three kilometres away (as is often the case in Africa), the distance covered on foot would be 6,000 kilometres.

The imperial nations wanted to obtain tropical products from the countries they colonised. France encouraged and protected ground-nut growing in Senegal by providing peasants with very cheap broken rice from Indochina. As they no longer needed to rely on millet, they extended ground-nut farming. That is why the only staples eaten in Dakar are rice—and bread.

When Senegal became independent, the new regime was hungry for foreign currency, mainly so its more affluent members could enjoy the delights of the consumer society (expensive cars and other status symbols). It adopted a policy of giving priority to export crops, which so monopolised resources that development suffered as a result.

From 1958 to 1977, coffee and cocoa beans sold well or very well. But the stabilisation funds—they ought to be called "peasant exploitation funds"—diverted the extra revenue into the hands of the powerful, who were able to indulge their every whim. As a result the peasants did not have the resources to intensify their production, protect their soil or extend the growing of food crops.

When coffee and cocoa prices slumped in 1977, the so-called "Ivorian miracle", which is usually described as having taken place between 1964 and 1977, quickly evaporated. It now looks as if it may end in chaos.

Although such crops will never be capable of fuelling true growth, their price collapse has not been a "natural" development. As far back as 1980, it was widely known that traditional cocoa producers (chiefly Ivory Coast and Brazil) had already produced a world glut.

Yet the World Bank, which claims to employ 20,000 "highly qualified" experts, decided to finance large cocoa-bean plantations in Indonesia and Malaysia. In 1989 those two countries produced 200,000 tonnes of (surplus) cocoa, with higher yields and at a lower cost than in Africa.

When I put my criticism to Lindel Mills of the World Bank in October 1989, he replied: "But we want cheap cocoa, don't we?" Whom exactly does he mean by "we"? Why the rich of course.

Yet cocoa accounts for only 10 per cent of the price of chocolate. If we paid only a little more for our chocolate, producers would be able to get better prices. That would need a general agreement, of which there has been much talk in the last 25 years. Any failure to reach such an agreement must be laid at the door of the United States, Switzerland and West Germany, which have resorted to blocking tactics.

Cotton and ground-nuts do not bring in big profits. That is why their cultivation has been left to African peasants. Cotton growers, it is true, are given carefully selected seed and appropriate technical advice, and can purchase fertilisers and pesticides on credit. They know, too, that they will be able to sell whatever they produce.

It is a very different story with cereals, primarily because the much larger areas involved would make such arrangements more costly. Whereas between 1942 and 1946 France set up remarkable research institutes for cash crops (oil-seed and fibre plants, coffee, cocoa, tropical fruits and rubber), it was not until 1960 that it established a similar institute for food crops. It has not been possible to make up for that delay.

Food self-sufficiency has been the proclaimed priority of all African governments since the Lagos Plan of 1980; yet the trend has been the other way. There are, it is true, a number of obstacles in the way of development. I am a critic of the established world economic order; but as it is likely to persist for quite some time I am obliged to advise my African friends to live with it.

They have a slightly better chance of exerting leverage on a more local level, where tyrannical and profligate regimes have generated abuses which I have consistently denounced—but which the French overseas aid authorities seem only too willing to ignore or even perpetuate.

Having said that, I should stress that the real problem facing black Africa as we near the end of the 20th century is the population explosion. Many Africans refuse to face the facts, and their failure to do so could well cost them dearly.

The tropical part of Africa (excluding the Maghreb, Egypt and South Africa) had about 100 million inhabitants at the turn of the century. Its population has increased fivefold in the last 90 years, a quite unprecedented rate in the history of mankind.

Much more serious is the fact that at the present rate of increase (3.3 per cent a year) black Africa's population will double within 21 or 22 years. If that rate were to continue until beyond the year 2012, the population would double again and reach a staggering 2 billion (or the equivalent of the world population in 1930). We must not forget that it takes ten to 15 years for any concerted action to change population patterns to have any appreciable effect.

In the course of a recent lecture tour in seven black African countries, I actually met people who claimed that Africa was underpopulated. They pointed out that the Netherlands, for example, has a much higher population density.

But it all boils down to a question of development. In the 30 years or so since independence, farm output in Africa has increased in only a few cases by more than 2 per cent a year, and more often by less than that figure, whereas the Food and Agriculture Organisation advised countries to aim for 4 or even 6 percent.

The World Bank estimates that a quarter of sub-Saharan Africans live in a state of "chronic food insecurity"—in other words, they constantly go hungry. To make the present population growth rate acceptable, food production will have to be much more than doubled in the next 22 years.

We will never be able to guarantee world food security to a durable degree unless our excessive use of fossil fuels—the cause of the greenhouse effect—and galloping population growth are both drastically reduced. What is more, it will never be possible to increase health and education resources, which are already sadly lacking, at a corresponding rate.

There are, it is true, glimmers of hope. I met many agronomists, technicians and researchers who are doing sterling work in Africa. I am aware of the efforts made by many non-governmental organisations in the field, though I felt obliged once again to criticise them for not taking sufficient account of—and sometimes even denying—the population explosion.

At the present rate of increase (3.3 per cent a year) black Africa's population will double within 21 or 22 years. If that rate were to continue until beyond the year 2012, the population would double again and reach a staggering 2 billion

Recent developments have unfortunately shown that unless something is done the worthiest efforts are bound to be thwarted by the deteriorating environment, the greenhouse effect and above all uncontrolled population growth.

One can only assume that Pope John Paul has no idea of how serious the population situation is: during a visit to various African countries in February, he once again condemned birth control. I find that flabbergasting. Equally, the French overseas aid authorities have done almost nothing to warn the Africans of the population problem—and have criticised my own position, which they describe as Malthusian.

I came back from my recent tour of the continent with the feeling that the North has no right to abandon peoples who in many cases have been steered towards bankruptcy by the policies of the rich countries, including France. The only solution now is for everyone to pull together—but the Africans themselves must take the lead. Flattery is not a good way of encouraging them to do so.

Article 5

AFRICA NEWS
March 26, 1990

DEMOCRACY

Africans Call for Accountable Government

It was planned a year and a half ago. But last month's conference on Popular Participation in Development, held in Arusha, Tanzania, coincided with a worldwide wave of democratic fervor that gave the gathering an added sense of urgency.

"For us in Africa," said Adebayo Adedeji, who heads the United Nations-sponsored Economic Commission for Africa (ECA), "popular participation is not a mere slogan. It is a matter of life and death."

Convened by the ECA along with a host of non-governmental organizations, the meeting attracted 500 participants, many from grassroots groups such as trade unions, youth and women's organizations – constituencies whose views were evident in the final conference declaration.

The emphasis on people power was visible in the seating arrangements at Arusha's international conference center. After passing through an entrance hall crowded with booths displaying homemade wares and locally-based technologies, governmental and UN representatives were directed to seats in the wings, while delegates from non-governmental organizations were placed front and center under a huge banner that read: "The People."

Over the next five days, participants discussed Africa's development crisis in overtly political terms. The delegates "explicitly identified the lack of participatory processes as the primary cause of Africa's unyielding, decade-long economic catastrophe," says Salim Lone, editor of the UN publication *Africa Recovery*.

"People kept referring to events in Eastern Europe," says Carol Capps of Church World Service, an ecumenical relief and development agency. "The feeling was, if those entrenched governments can change, why can't African governments?"

The conference adopted a 13-page charter that says African governments must "yield space to the people." But recognizing the reluctance of governments everywhere to cede power voluntarily, the charter calls on African people themselves to press for democracy and "to establish independent people's organizations that are genuinely grassroots, democratically administered and self-reliant."

"I think one result of this," Capps predicts, "will be that non-governmental organizations in Africa will increase both in number and strength."

Conference participants recognized that such a course would not be easy. Mazide N'Diaye, president of an umbrella network of voluntary development organizations known as FAVDO (Forum for African Voluntary Development Organizations), said that non-governmental organizations have learned that most African countries leave little room for people's initiatives. But it is increasingly evident that African governments cannot meet the needs of their people, N'Diaye said, so people must organize themselves to fill the gap.

Reflecting the prominence of discussions about the role of women, the charter says that the attainment of equal social, economic and political rights for women must be a central feature of democratic and participatory development.

Ruth Engo-Tgeja, a conference organizer who works with Unifem, the UN agency for women's affairs, said that women's issues must be viewed in a new way. In the past, she said, such priorities as water pumps and day care centers were seen as matters of women's rights. "The more we think about these issues," she said, "the more we believe getting water for the community is not a woman's right. It is a community right . . . [Day care] should be a mainstream problem and not a women's problem."

Having women in decision-making structures, Engo-Tgeja said, insures a responsiveness to important community concerns. She pointed to the Arusha meeting as a case study of that process. Women on the conference coordinating committee, she said, "were able to bring out issues that could not be perceived by our male colleagues" – issues that were later adopted as part of the charter.

The conference theme of popular participation ensured that the question of democracy would be firmly linked to the debate on economic development issues. Hassan Sunmonu, Secretary-General of the Organization of African Trade Union Unity, said that structural adjustment programs (SAPs) have been imposed – by international institutions and by African governments – without the agreement of Africa's people. Although economic reforms are needed, Sunmonu said, the SAPs that have been mandated by the International Monetary Fund and the World Bank haven't worked, because they put the heaviest burdens on the poorest citizens.

Boaz Mpazi/Africa Recovery

Hassan Sunmonu, Secretary-General of the Organization of African Trade Union Unity.

Conference delegates generally appeared to share Sunmonu's view that the economic growth rates and increased exports advocated by SAPs have done little to achieve the goal of alleviating poverty.

Labor unions have played a brave role in exposing the myth of SAPs, Sunmonu said, but governments have responded with arrests and repression. "Our members have paid the price for telling the truth," he said.

The Arusha conference charter condemns the suppression of dissent. It defends the right to strike and calls for a halt to widespread bans on youth and student organizations and the "arbitrary" closure of educational institutions. It cited ten indicators of popular participation, including media freedom, protection of the environment and flourishing grassroots movements. The charter also carries a warning to unrepresentative governments, noting that "the forces of freedom and democracy are contagious."

More than a few delegates expressed uneasiness at the reception they might receive upon returning home. But the response of a Tanzanian government representative, who said the host country would not only endorse the charter but would seek ways to implement it, ended the meeting on a note of cheer. It was left to the ECA's Adedeji to issue a challenge to the delegates themselves. "No one else will solve our problems for us," he told the group. "Achieving a turnaround in our society is our primary responsibility. Let us show the increasingly skeptical world that we can make it and that we are determined to make it."

– John Manuel

Article 6

WORLD PRESS REVIEW ● NOVEMBER 1990

Poised Between Reform And Further Decline

Cries for democracy are also moans of economic pain

FINANCIAL TIMES

MICHAEL HOLMAN

Liberia's slide from dictatorship into anarchy is terrible, even by the standards of a continent used to upheaval. But far from being an aberration, Liberia could prove to be just the first of several states to collapse under the weight of economic mismanagement and ethnic tensions, compounded by policy failures on the part of the superpowers and aid donors. Other wars in sub-Saharan Africa highlight the continent's fragility: Angola, Mozambique, Sudan, Somalia, and Ethiopia are torn by conflict. Uganda has yet to recover from Idi Amin. Chad and Libya may again come to blows. Senegal and Mauritania keep an uneasy peace. Almost wherever one looks, from Angola to Zambia, from Mali to Mozambique, the ossified political structures of post-independence Africa are cracking.

From across the continent come calls—endorsed by Western governments, aid donors, and lending institutions—for a multi-party system. Political adjustment is catching up with the economic-adjustment programs being introduced. But the cry for democracy is as much a moan of pain caused by the economic failures over three decades of independence. Africa is delicately poised between reform and further decline.

The causes of the upheaval are complex. The most frequent explanation invariably couples the renewed search for freedom in Africa with the revolution in Eastern Europe. "The wind blowing in from Europe has begun to sweep Africa. We should not moan over it; we should even rejoice over it," as French President François Mitterrand has said. Even the Organization of African Unity, that club of autocrats so tolerant of one another's failings, conceded that it was necessary "to democratize further our societies and consolidate democratic institutions."

But there are more important influences than Eastern Europe that are driving Africans to the barricades: France is reappraising its relationship with Francophone Africa. The superpower rapprochement is causing reverberations in southern Africa and the Horn of Africa in particular, as well as leaving several African leaders anxious about dwindling patronage from foreign powers. South Africa's search for a constitution that accommodates the aspirations of the majority, while coping with the fears of minorities, is gripping the attention of the rest of Africa. Above all, a decade or more of sharp economic decline has made impoverished citizens throughout the continent angry with their rulers and impatient to find leaders who have alternatives.

Certainly, Eastern Europe's revolution encouraged opposition movements. It undermined belief in centrally controlled economic systems—although the examples of Tanzania and Zambia had already done that. And as regimes in East Germany and elsewhere collapsed, the governments in Angola, Mozambique, and Ethiopia lost reliable allies. South Africa is a unique case. Government officials there acknowledge a two-fold impact that proved decisive in persuading President F.W. de Klerk to embark on radical change: Mass demonstrations against elitist governments in Eastern Europe evoked the worst white South African nightmare. And the collapse of communism encouraged Pretoria in the belief that it was safe to unban the South African Communist Party.

There are, however, critical differences between the experience of Eastern Europe and the process under way in Africa that limit the appropriateness of any comparisons. The former has an industrial proletariat with considerably more muscle than that of the peasants in Africa's predominantly agricultural economies. Essential to the success of the East European revolution was the fact that the region's metropolitan power—the Soviet Union—was preoccupied by its own domestic crisis and had made it clear that it would not intervene.

For Africa, a similar process took place two to three decades ago, when Belgium, France, Britain, and Portugal decided that the price of the colonial relationship was too high. Post-independence Africa then enjoyed a brief peri-

From the independent "Financial Times" of London.

od of democracy, before voters discovered that the district commissioner had been replaced by the party functionary and the bureaucrat. The latter two are proving far more difficult to dislodge.

Alone among the colonizing powers, France has kept up a willingness to intervene militarily and financially if a former colonial protégé is in trouble. This willingness may now be in doubt, a factor that will prove far more significant to political change in Francophone Africa than anything that happened in Eastern Europe. Although France retains an extraordinary historical and cultural link with Africa, it is finding the financial responsibilities of underwriting the French African Community franc, used in more than a dozen former colonies, increasingly onerous. France is also giving notice that its military involvement in Africa may be more limited than in the past. The prospect of losing the military umbrella—some 9,000 French troops are based in Francophone Africa—is as disconcerting to current leaders as it is encouraging to their opponents.

The impact of the superpower rapprochement is still being felt. The obvious benefits have been the negotiations that led to Namibia's independence and the boost given to the peace process in South Africa. As Namibia begins independence with a multi-party constitution, and the world demands the same from South Africa, opposition leaders in the region are asking: Why not us? But détente has implications beyond southern Africa. Aid and security have long been linked. As Africa ceases to provide cockpits for superpower conflicts by proxy, aid to certain countries will decline. It already has in Somalia. Leaders of countries such as Zaire, who adroitly played on tensions between Washington and Moscow to build up aid levels, are now getting less support, while their opponents receive a sympathetic hearing.

The rapprochement has also left a potentially dangerous power vacuum. In the Horn of Africa, this could well be filled by Israel—which is almost certainly supplying arms to Ethiopia's President Mengistu Haile Mariam—or by one or more of the Arab states. This would exacerbate, rather than resolve, the conflicts.

Most African governments are resigned to the prospect that future aid from international donors such as the World Bank will carry political as well as economic conditions. Neither the bank nor governments such as the U.S. and Britain, which have endorsed this approach, have so far drawn up formal political criteria. But on the list would be issues ranging from the state of the local press to whether a recipient is a one-party or multi-party state. One of the first countries to face such a test has been Kenya, where opposition leaders have been detained and President Daniel arap Moi has entrenched the authoritarian ruling party. During unrest in July, Washington made it clear that aid could be reduced if reforms did not take place. Britain issued a similar message, *sotto voce*.

Whatever the roots of the African unrest, one thing is

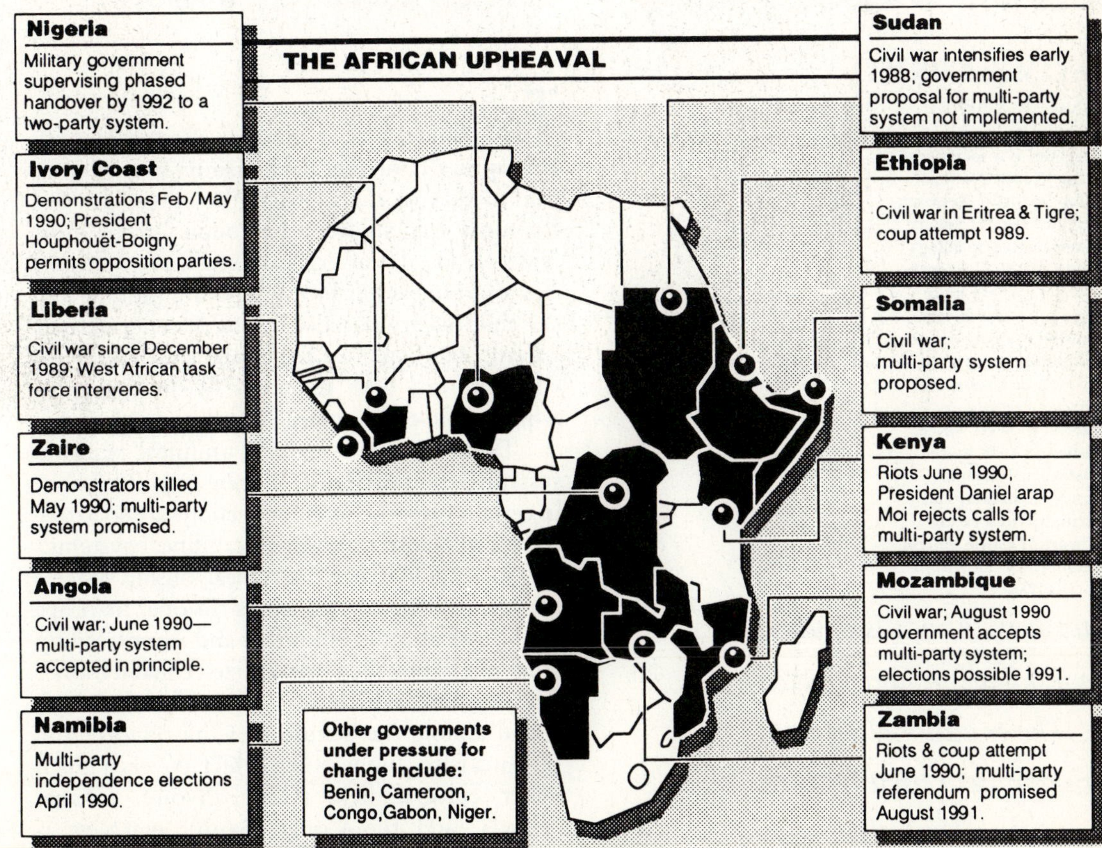

Multi-party signals should be treated with caution: The continent may be not waving, but drowning.

clear. Despite World Bank-supported economic-reform programs adopted in varying degrees by about two-thirds of sub-Saharan Africa, the continent remains in deep economic crisis. The bank's report on Africa, released one year ago, pointed out that the region's economies must grow at least 4-5 percent annually for a "modest" improvement in living standards. This target requires a 4-percent-a-year increase in real terms of official development assistance, together with further debt relief. It would represent a total bill to the Overseas Development Agency of $22 billion a year at 1990 prices by the year 2000, the bank estimates. Many economists believe that this underestimates Africa's needs, but even this comparatively cautious goal may be hard to attain.

Donor fatigue has set in since the 1980s. Nor are aid flows helped by the spectacle of the World Bank and the Economic Commission for Africa, the United Nations body that acts as the continent's think tank, quarreling over the type of medicine the patient needs. There are growing doubts that the bank's "model patients" are, in fact, going to recover. After seven years of external assistance running at an annual rate of $500 million, Ghana, for example, is a long way from passing the key test: Can growth be sustained without substantial aid?

And even if the patient pulls through, will there be sufficient external support for the 40 or more sub-Saharan countries that need varying degrees of help? It seems unlikely. Private investment is negligible, and the needs of Eastern Europe overshadow Africa's. Meanwhile, the voice of the Africa lobby carries less and less weight.

Africa's marginalization is not just its own affair. In an interdependent world, all places are vulnerable to one another's misfortunes. African deforestation may contribute to global warming; plants that could provide important genetic material for research may be lost; diseases such as AIDS know no boundaries; Moslem extremism in Africa, a potentially destabilizing issue in Nigeria, could pose a new terrorist threat. These may seem to be problems that can be addressed in time. But the "multi-party" signals from Africa should be treated with caution: The continent may be not waving, but drowning, with more than Liberia soon to go under.

Article 7

The UNESCO Courier, July 1989

Lines of descent

MANGA BEKOMBO PRISO

MANGA BEKOMBO PRISO, of Cameroon, is a sociologist with the French National Centre for Scientific Research (CNRS) and the Ethnology and Comparative Sociology Laboratory of the University of Paris X, where he is engaged on research into lineal kinship systems and the development process in Africa. He was co-editor of *Marriage, Fertility and Parenthood in West Africa,* published in 1978 by the Australian National University, Canberra, and a contributor to a recent Unesco work, *Famille, Enfant et Développement en Afrique* (1988).

Modern legislation in Africa is tending to encourage individualism and weaken social cohesion. The traditional African family is adapting to new circumstances and proving more resilient than once seemed likely.

THE children of a modern Western family belong legally neither to the family of the father nor to that of the mother; they are, first and foremost, the children of a couple. In the most widespread of the African kinship traditions, however, lineal kinship systems are the rule and the children are attached to one or other of their parents' families. The father and the mother are therefore not both members of the family to which their children are linked.

There are two main unilineal kinship systems—the matrilineal and the patrilineal—but in certain cases the interconnections are so extensive as virtually to constitute bilineal systems.

Societies in which matrilineal kinship systems are the rule are of two kinds. In one, marriage as an institution is unknown and is replaced by what might be called "recognized cohabitation". This system, which is comparatively rare, is found among the Senufo of Côte d'Ivoire and Burkina Faso. In the other, which covers a much wider cultural field (Côte d'Ivoire, Ghana, Nigeria, and the Congo Basin), marriage is recognized and the wife leaves her home to live in the home of her husband or her father-in-law.

In this case, the mother's brother rather than the natural father is considered to be the true father of the children.

Patrilineal societies are by far the most common, and it is with them that we are primarily concerned here. In contrast to modern societies which tend to stress the natural, biological link, African traditional societies lay emphasis upon a contractual social link based on the notion of the "parental role", which may be played by several people.

All the true sisters of the "genetrix" (natural mother), and women of the same age group, may be considered to be her children's "mother". Similarly, children will address all the genitor's brothers and close friends as "father". The child is, above all, the child of the lineal group to which he or she belongs. Members of the paternal or maternal clan, as well as the husband's other wives, share in rights and duties with regard to the child.

As well as the importance attached to the child/maternal uncle and brother/sister relationships, the particularly loving, "friendly" relationship between grandparents and grandchildren should also be noted. The grandson is the mirror image of the grandfather and thus becomes the "little husband" of his grandmother. Similarly, the granddaughter who bears her paternal grandmother's name becomes the "mother" of her own father. These relationships are more than just a game and people around them adopt attitudes towards the children which correspond to the status of the personages the children enact.

Marriage strategy

The organization of a marriage involves a number of phases. First of all, the head of a group of marriageable young men offers the head of the potential bride's clan a series of services or gifts of food or other objects—including a particularly valuable one, which is wrongly called the dowry— and in exchange receives the desired girl. The first group then decides which of the boys will marry the girl, while the second group decides who is to receive the dowry and thus, in his turn, be in a position to acquire a wife.

By virtue of the dowry paid, the husband's clan acquires right of paternity over children of the marriage. In return, the bride's clan obtains an extension of its territorial rights and the right of intervention in the affairs of the clan to which it has become linked through the person of the bride. Normally, the dowry goes to the bride's brother, preferably born of the same mother and her immediate senior or junior. Otherwise it goes to another brother from the maternal home or to another son of the same father, or to a cousin.

The brother who receives the dowry will have a special relationship with his sister's children. His wife, bought with this dowry, is obliged to be submissive in relation to the sister-in-law thanks to whom she was able to get married. In some societies in central Cameroon, the two sisters-in-law are regarded as husband and wife and address each other in these terms.

The new bride sets up home on the territory of her husband's clan, usually on the father-in-law's property where the son may have his own huts. She is received by her mother-in-law who completes her education, teaches her the customs

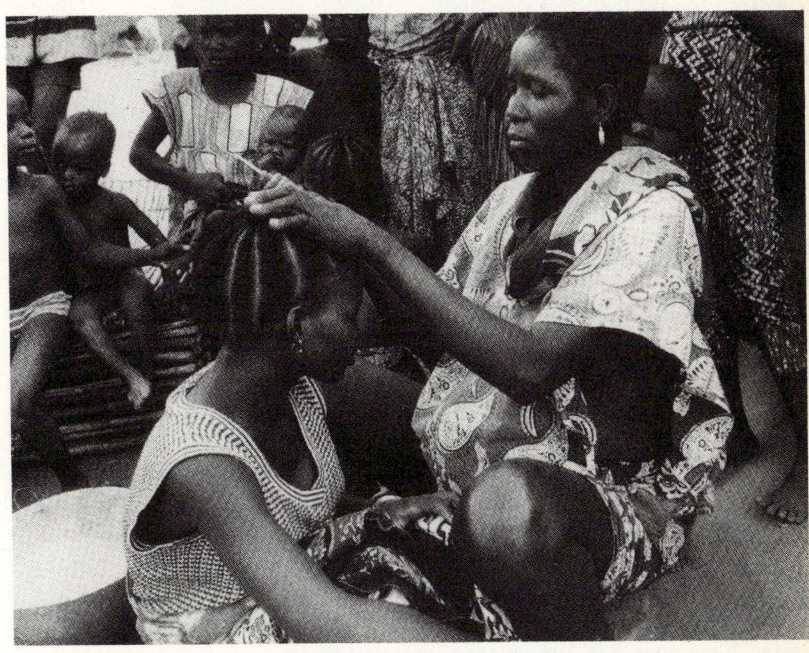

"African traditional societies lay emphasis upon a contractual social link based on the notion of the parental 'role', which may be played by several people."

of the family and, later, declares her fit to manage her own "kitchen".

The mother-in-law refers to her daughter-in-law in the same terms she uses in speaking of her husband's other wives who are junior to her. Wives of this category belong by right to the female founders of the household—usually the first two wives. The ambition of these founding wives is to produce a line, if not a lineage, with a distinct name. To do this they have to gather together as many young women as possible who will produce many children—their sons' wives and other women, generally from their own former village, whom they bring and eventually place at their husband's disposal.

The man attempts to obtain other women from households that are already established. Thus, polygamy is as much the business of the husband as of his consorts and seems to be less an expression of the man's power and wealth than a means of perpetuating a form of society.

Polygamy makes it possible to achieve two apparently opposed objectives. It signifies a man's ascent in the social hierarchy (the man most envied is the man at the head of the largest community), and it also tends to divide that community into matrifocal-based households each seeking autonomy (lineages attached to a single founder-wife).

In the traditional African setting, marriage is a matter of considerable importance. It is through marriage that the constituent elements of society reproduce themselves and that groups and individuals further a complex strategy. Women play a crucial role in this process, since they gather together and control other women as wives and companions for brothers, sons and husbands.

The community and its households

The African family to which this process gives rise is an extended family which may consist of fifty to a hundred people living in a single domestic community. The men of the community form a sub-group organized in a hierarchy based on social position and order of birth. The hierarchical aspect is, however, moderated by a collective sense of the equality of all who can claim descent from the same ancestor.

The women's group consists, on the one hand, of the unmarried girls and widows of the lineage and, on the other, of women introduced into the community by marriage. The women's sub-group is organized into a hierarchy based on age and also, for the wives, on the order of arrival and status conferred upon them by the ritual of marriage.

Thus the adults of the community consist of the male group, linked by blood, and the female group composed of women from different families who are united by a common duty of solidarity with the group that accepted them.

The children have different prospects before them. The boys will remain to ensure the continuation of the lineage. The girls will leave to found new lineages but without breaking with their parents. For although a woman remains an outsider in her husband's family, she maintains close links with her group of origin within which she retains both duties and privileges.

In practice a woman spends as much time with her parents as in her adopted group and remains very independent of her husband. Her husband may have the right to repudiate her for misconduct or sterility, but she too can decide to leave her husband on the grounds of lack of security or incompatibility with his way of life. In the latter case her brothers and fathers must assume responsibility for the consequences.

The woman who founds a household is considered to be the mother of all the children born in it, including those born to her husband's other wives. The children of the "same mother" rank in the hierarchy in accordance with the chronological order of their mother's marriage and the importance of the ritual with which the household was founded. The autonomy of the household increases with the age of the first-born son, the father's heir presumptive, and the arrival of other women and children. The eldest son will thus become the head of the household of which his "mother" is the mistress.

The household can thus be seen as a specific area in which the mother, the son and the mother's brother occupy the leading positions.

In traditional African societies, despite decades if not centuries of contact with the outside world, the totality of social relationships, including economic relationships, are governed by kinship. Social scientists who imposed blueprints for the evolution of these societies that were inspired by European history have been surprised by the durability of this phenomenon. According to these blueprints, a small degree of industrialization, accelerated urbanization, the introduction of schooling and conversion to Christianity and the insertion of African countries into the world political and economic order should have brought a complete upheaval in the family structure.

However, the old attitudes and practices have not disappeared; they have simply been adapted to suit the conditions of modern life. The authority of the leaders of the lineages remains sociologically stronger than that of the state. Polygamy persists, even if it is now practised more discreetly, with wives being dispersed in different places. The rules of the unilineal kinship system are still applied despite modern legislation which recognizes the family as consisting only of two parents and their children.

Many legal dispositions, primarily those relating to the individual ownership of property, are profoundly impregnated with modern notions of individualism which clash with the African tradition whereby the community is the main component of all identity.

The step from the right of the family community to occupy land to private, individually owned property has dealt a blow to the cohesion of the family group. Now the eldest son is no longer content to manage a shared land heritage; he is tempted to appropriate it for himself by establishing the title deeds in his own name. In so doing he runs the risk of becoming engaged in a long and tortuous legal process in which he will be in opposition to his brothers and sisters. This often leads to the breaking up of the patrimony into separate parcels of land, or its liquidation. These frequent legal procedures break the previously indestructible link that united the members of the community among themselves and with their ancestors.

Furthermore, the appearance of the modern, centralizing state has rendered superfluous many of the functions of the family head. The transmission of title deeds and responsibilities has become less important than that of goods and property left by bequest. This makes it important to distinguish between biological children who are entitled to inherit directly, from the brother's children (in patrilineal societies) and from the sister's children (in matrilineal societies).

Students walking home after school near Addis Abeba, Ethiopia

The new African family

All this is leading to a strengthening of the process of individualization and to the break-up of traditional family unity. This does not mean, however, that the traditional African family is being transformed into the small, Western-style, nuclear family. Rather it is giving rise to single-parent families built around either the father or the mother. The movement towards individualization clashes with the need to be a part of a network of solidarity which, for the most part, remains the lineage. Some individuals join associations based on age or social position which offer their members social assistance and psychological support.

These few examples demonstrate the limits of change in the social and family fabric. This resistance to change may be explained in terms of an underlying rejection of individualistic ideology or of the limitations of state power. It seems likely, however, that the encounter between Western ideology and traditional social values will give rise to new family structures fashioned by a society undergoing a rapid transformation.

Article 8

The World & I
SEPTEMBER 1988

BAKONGO COSMOLOGY

Complex ideas of the universe from the heart of Africa were little recognized until recent decades

Wyatt MacGaffey

European visitors to Africa have often been reluctant to credit the people they meet with the capacity for abstract or systematic thought. In the 1880s, travelers and missionaries with experience of the Lower Congo believed "the ideas of the natives" amounted to no more than "a ruinous heap." Said one, "There is no coherence in their beliefs, and their ideas about cosmogony are very nebulous." Anthropologists have concurred: "One would seek in vain in [Kongo] culture for large and coherent conceptions and structures such as would give the human reality they incarnate the prestige accorded in Africa and elsewhere to other civilizations."

Yet, some African civilizations have indeed earned prestige for the complexity of their cosmologies and the refinement of their moral and symbolic systems. The ideas of the Dogon of Mali and the related Bamana (Bambara), noted also for their sculptures, have been studied for decades by a school of anthropology founded by Marcel Griaule. The Dogon had a graded series of initiation lodges in which wisdom was progressively revealed to a religious elite. In the best-known of his publications, *Conversations with Ogotemmeli*, Griaule describes how the Dogon assigned a learned elder to explain the origin and mysteries of the universe to him.

But where no hierarchy of religious elite existed —such as in the Lower Congo—there was no social basis for the development and authentication of cosmological knowledge. We also expect to learn about a cosmology from myths and to recognize myths by the miraculous events that occur in them, in which sacred beings and divine heroes shape the world. But in Lower Congo we find no narratives of this kind.

Instead of asking whether the BaKongo or any other people have a cosmology, we could assume that they must have one, because all social interaction necessarily presupposes some ordering of the world in space and time, specifying the place of human actors within it. If two Americans meet, for example, they are usually unaware that they think anything about "cosmology" or that, if they did, it would have any relevance to their interaction. Nevertheless, to interact at all, they must know or assume certain fundamental things about each other. It is necessary to know, for example, whether the person one is addressing is alive or dead. Usually that is no problem, though it is possible to be mistaken; comedies and thrillers both exploit the shock value of such mistakes. The difference between life and death also has serious public consequences, since a live person has civil rights and legal responsibilities that a dead person does not.

The difference between life and death is not a given in nature, however; that is, it is not in all cases a simple matter of observation. In the last two decades, Americans have repeatedly asked their courts and legislatures to decide just what the difference is. The beginning of life is as difficult to identify as the end and has given rise to as many controversies. The language used by parties to these disputes is often overtly religious, in a denominational sense, but even if it is not, their emotional tone and their feeling that these issues are fundamental tell us that we are in the domain of religion.

Cosmological distinctions about the order of the universe, the place of humankind within it, and the nature and varieties of human beings vary from one society to another. They may or may not be true in some scientific sense. Since they are fundamental to social life and experience, it is difficult if not impossible for the members of the society to step outside their assumptions, which they take to be given

ELISOFON ARCHIVES: NATIONAL MUSEUM OF AFRICAN ART

Traditional BaKongo wood carvings.
A crouching figure on a round bell.

realities, or to imagine what life would be like in a different universe.

Kongo cosmology

The BaKongo, who live in the western Zaire province of Lower Zaire (called in colonial times Lower Congo) and in adjacent parts of both northwestern Angola and the People's Republic of Congo, may number some three million people. Their territory, on the Atlantic threshold of the Zaire basin—the heart of Africa—has been deeply influenced by relations with Europe going back more than five hundred years to the first arrival of Portuguese ships on the coast in 1483. After the creation of the colony of the Belgian Congo in 1908, most Kongo men, and many women, went to school, became Catholics or Protestants, and entered wage labor. Their political party, Abako, led by Joseph Kasa-Vubu, was one of the most effective forces in the fight for national

ELISOFON ARCHIVES: NATIONAL MUSEUM OF AFRICAN ART

Carved head for an ivory staff.

independence, obtained in 1960. In Zaire today they are among the best educated and most influential groups.

In 1970, most BaKongo believed that the universe is divided into the two worlds of the living and the dead, separated by water and related to each other in such a way that when the sun sets among the living it rises among the dead. The movement of human life resembles that of the sun, in that after being born into this world and spending a lifetime in it, the soul passes into another existence in the alternate world. The other world is very much like this one. In fact, it is in a sense identical to it, since after dark, when the living go to sleep, the dead wake up and go about their daily occupations in what they think of as day, in the same houses that the living use, cultivating the same fields and cooking at the same hearth. There are also differences, however; in some ways the dead contrast with the living. Since they are older and can see in our world as well as their own, they are more powerful, They do not suffer from disease as we do, and they have become white rather than black.

Kongo cosmology is in fact more complex than

this, but the sketch suffices to suggest that the fundamental concepts of time, life, death, and race are entirely different from those taken for granted by Americans or Europeans. In this cosmology, since the land of the dead is like another village, and not really very far away, it is remarkable rather than epoch-making that individuals may be able to go there and return to this world, to die and rise again from the dead.

The land of the dead is the village cemetery in the adjacent forest, but it can also be entered through certain caves and deep pools. The water that divides the worlds may be any pool or stream—the Zaire River or the Atlantic Ocean. In one of the most powerful applications of this cosmology, America, the land on the other side of the ocean, is the land of the dead to which Africans go when they die, changing their skins and becoming white.

The cosmology of divided worlds is an abstract model that enables the BaKongo to comprehend and interpret the facts of history and geography, human social experience, and relations of power. As we shall see, they use it to understand international relations, a dispute between two villages, or their own dreams. As the grammar of their thinking, it has not itself, until recently, been the object of their intellectual scrutiny. As an interpretive schema, it is mobilized when the urgencies of events demand it, and it may be applied differently by different individuals, drawing different conclusions.

The Kongo cosmology was first set out in print by Fu-kiau kia Bunseki in 1969, in a short work entitled *The MuKongo and the World in Which He Circulates*, written in KiKongo and published with a French translation. Fu-kiau, a young man with a good secondary education, was prompted to write by his conversations with the anthropologist J.M. Janzen. Fu-kiau was not a hoary Ogotemmeli steeped in tradition, but a man whose contact with outsiders was such that he could appreciate their problem in understanding the Kongo perspective. A diagram of the universe, similar to Fu-kiau's and labeled in KiKongo, has been found in use among Afro-Cubans in Cuba.

Fragmentary elements of Kongo cosmology have long been discussed, only to be relegated to footnotes as oddities instead of being taken seriously as parts of the missing system of Kongo religion. Europeans, representing a civilization that sees itself as obviously superior to all others in its moral, scientific, and political achievements, have naturally been reluctant to admit that they were seen by Congolese as spirits of the dead, their morality as witchcraft, their science as magic, and their politics as cannibalism. It is still more difficult to admit that there may be some truth to this perspective.

EMIKO OZAKI/THE WORLD & I

The BaKongo are found in the region between Pointe Noire in the north, Stanley Pool and the Kwango River in the east, and Luanda in the south.

Personal experiences

Kongo cosmological thinking was brought home to me personally when my wife and I lived in Matadi, the main port of Zaire, situated at the head of navigation on the Zaire estuary. It had about 180,000 inhabitants in 1970, many of them sailors who regularly traveled to Antwerp, New York, Houston, and even Japan on Belgian and Zairean merchant ships. Many more worked in the docks, and most of them had opportunities for contacts of various sorts with the crews of foreign ships. The town was also the seat of Protestant and Catholic missions established there since its founding in the 1880s. My host was a relatively prosperous man, an electrician, who could afford to keep a substantial household, including two wives and twelve children.

As I walked across the marketplaces of the town, I would be followed by a murmur of explanation from one marketwoman to another. "*Ndombe kena!* He's black!" People would tell the story: My host, the electrician had formerly owned a bar. To raise money for it, he had sold me his nephew, by witchcraft, to persons unspecified (missionaries, perhaps), who had transported me to America. I had become white in the land of the dead, had made good to the point of being able to marry a white lady, and had now come back to demand a reckoning; that explained why I was living in my "uncle's" house without paying any rent, why I was willing to eat local food, spoke authentic KiKongo and asked all those questions about local tradition—I was trying to recover my roots.

Sometimes people would put the question to me directly, in French or KiKongo: "Monsieur, is it true that you are black?" Others brought me photographs of recently deceased relatives to ask how they were getting on in the States. I had to reply that unfortunately we had so many immigrants arriving in America every day that it was hard to keep track of them all. Not everybody thought the same way. My host and his wives insisted to their friends that I was a *real* white man, and students from the secondary school, upwardly mobile all, noting my nondescript clothes and the fact that I went about on foot, would sometimes sneer at me as a bankrupt, poor white.

Even these skeptics had not really abandoned the traditional cosmology; the land of the dead has its native population, people whose ancestors were always white, in addition to those who have been imported as slaves by witchcraft. "Monsieur, were your ancestors black or white?" A matter of common puzzlement is the skin-change: Does it happen immediately or gradually? A black American evangelist visiting Kinshasa was asked about his light-brown color; how did he get that way? Embarrassed to recall a presumptive history of plantation miscegenation, he said that it came gradually, and his questioner went away satisfied.

The view of myself that I encountered in Matadi was not new to me. Five years before, I had lived in the village of Mbanza Manteke which, though rural, is no more remote from contact with Europe than is Matadi. A famous Protestant mission was established there in 1879, and since the turn of the century its male inhabitants have worked in cities like Kinshasa or Matadi. It gradually became clear that people expected me to take a siesta at noon, not just because that had been the habit of the missionaries when they lived there, but because for white people, as the BaKongo saw it, noon was really midnight, so of course they needed to sleep. Likewise, the European custom of sea-bathing was understood as a means of restoring one's health by contact with home base, as it were, the land beyond the water. My neighbors would call me "dead man" and laugh, somewhat uneasily.

At that time—1964—the U.S. government saw itself as engaged in a struggle with the Russians for the hearts and minds of the Congolese. The United States Information Agency took care to provide local newspapers with accounts, in French, of the presidential elections, in order to demonstrate the virtues of democracy. Some of the villagers read these accounts with great interest and asked me questions to further their understanding. It turned out that they interpreted what they read in terms of their cosmology, in which not only the universe but any part of it may be thought of as divided into two opposed worlds. They gathered that Mr. Johnson, representing North America and therefore a white man, was contending with Mr. Goldwater, a black man, the leader of South America.

At the same time, they knew all about Sputnik, alerted by radio, and they would draw my attention to satellites passing overhead. They greatly admired both the Russians and the Americans, who could produce such marvels. But they had no use for communists, such as the Belgians, who were nothing but witches and incapable, they were sure, of building so much as a railroad locomotive. Later, the Americans were to be congratulated on flying to the moon, something Kongo magicians could also do, but the trouble with magicians was that one was never sure they were not up to mischief with their remarkable feats. Just what were the Americans doing on the moon, anyway? I was never able to answer this question satisfactorily.

Rituals and dreams

Cosmology is revealed not only in such personal experiences but also through the analysis of rituals. Kongo rituals proceed in a space that has first been laid out as a microcosm, sometimes by drawing a diagram on the ground. The simplest and most common diagram is a cross, not to be confused with the Christian cross. A person taking an oath, for example, may mark a cross in the dirt with his finger, then stand on it to swear. The transverse line corresponds to the bound-

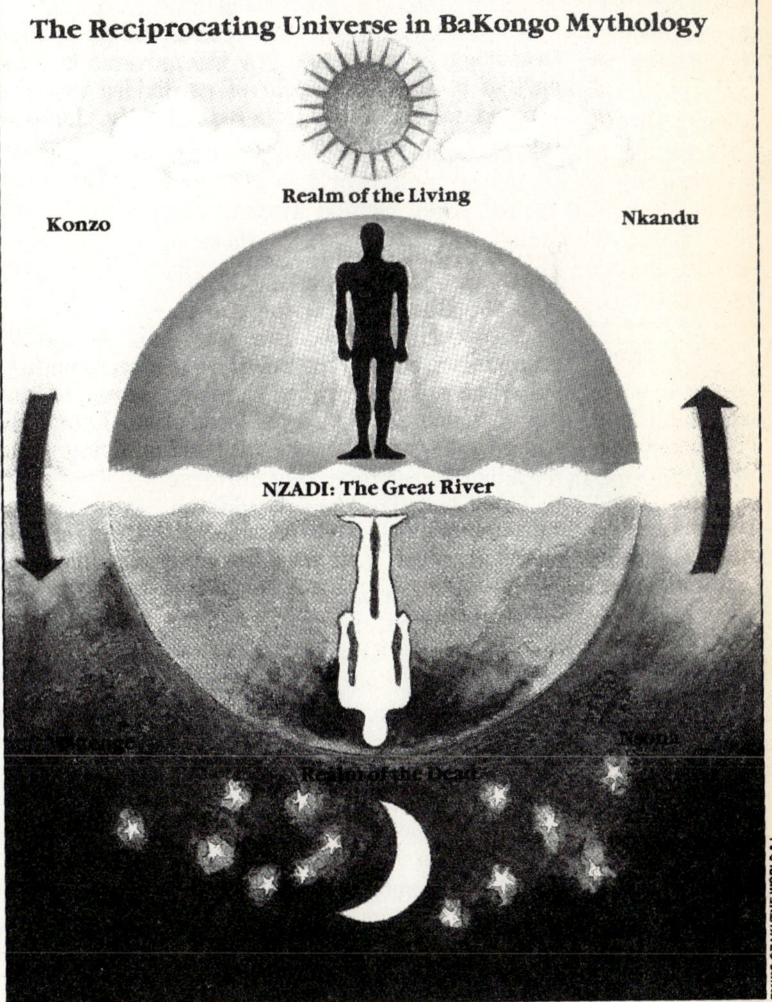

ary between the worlds; the intersecting one, to the path of forces moving between them. In some of the complex rituals performed in precolonial times, initiates were described as spending several days, weeks, or even months in the land of the dead under the water. What in fact they did was to spend the time in a specially built enclosure or distant camp. When they emerged from seclusion, they were considered to have been reborn, able to speak the secret languages of the dead and endowed with miraculous powers.

Their cosmology is so necessary to the organization of their culture and so taken for granted by them that the BaKongo do not recognize it as a topic or "problem." Conversely, once we have been alerted to it, the evidences of it are everywhere. The cosmology that the foreigner finds surprising is treated merely as the setting for transitory ingenuities, as in the riddle, "What black man went to Europe and became white?" Answer: a manioc root left soaking in the water for three days (to remove the acid) and then peeled.

In dreams, the soul may see something of the other world, so dreams are taken seriously as glimpses and warnings of the occult forces at work in our lives. To dream of trucks, trains, or ships is a sinister warning that someone will be "traveling." In the 1930s, when trains were new to the country, people would go down to the station to watch for recently deceased relatives passing through on their way to Matadi and beyond. Only people with special sinister powers, however, are actually active in the night world, while their bodies lie asleep in bed. They include witches, and also chiefs, who must have powers like those of witches in order to be able to defend the community against them.

ELISOFON ARCHIVES: NATIONAL MUSEUM OF AFRICAN ART

A typical inland BaKongo village.

Kongo history through Kongo eyes

The BaKongo tell no stories of the kind that the Western ear recognizes immediately as myths. In a cyclical or reciprocating universe such as Fu-kiau describes, one would not expect to find an account of its origin. What one does hear, in many hotly contested versions, are the stories of the origins of the clans in Mbanza Kongo. Mbanza Kongo, located in what is now northern Angola, was the capital of the Kingdom of Kongo when the Portuguese visited it at the end of the fifteenth century. The kingdom disintegrated after the battle of Mbwila in 1665, the capital itself being reduced to no more than an important village to which the legendary majesty of the past still faintly clung.

In modern Kongo, everyone derives his or her social position from membership in his or her mother's descent group or clan. Clan membership specifies the range of partners it is possible to marry and indicates where one has rights to land and residence. In asserting a claim to land or to political office, the head of a clan recites its tradition of origin, in which it usually appears that the founding chief left Mbanza Kongo, crossed the great river (*nzadi*), and arrived at the clan's present territory where, there being no other inhabitants, he "swept up the droppings of the elephant" and founded his own *mbanza*, or central place. The story tells his magical deeds, such as crossing the river on a raffia mat. It reports what clans he met along the way, whose sister he married, and so on. The representatives of other clans are supposed to be able to confirm the truth of these events and thus the property rights that the story legitimates.

Since, in a general sense, such stories might well be true, historians have generally treated them as accounts of actual migrations in which the BaKongo dispersed over their present territory from their original home. Scholars assumed that the river was the Zaire (Nzadi) and dismissed the magical events as accretions on a historical core. In fact, the supernatural references are among a number of clues showing that the stories are the missing myths, that they are narrative versions of the model of the divided worlds of the Kongo universe. In both the stories and the model, the essential movement in time is a crossing from one world to the other across the water that divides them.

The slave trade and the Christian missions

From the mid-seventeenth century to about 1890, the history of Kongo is bound up with the slave trade. Trials for ritual offenses, often violations of cult rules specially designed to trap the unwary, fed a thriving internal trade in slaves. Political losers and troublemakers could be sold to another village nearer the coast, with replacements acquired from further inland. At the coast, European slave traders established depots by treaty with chiefs who could guarantee orderly conditions of business and a steady supply of slaves in exchange for guns, cloth, liquor, and other goods.

This trade is understood by modern BaKongo as witchcraft; or rather, "witchcraft" is, among other things, what the BaKongo call slave trading. Witches, who are one's evilly intentioned neighbors, acquire sinister powers from the other world that enable them to operate "at night," that is, in unseen, occult ways. They steal the souls of victims, often relatives, who in the daylight world will be seen to die shortly afterwards. These souls may be eaten by members of the witch's coven, each of whom is obliged to provide a meal for the others in turn. This belief is the basis for stories interpreted by foreigners as cannibalism; there was never any actual cannibalism among the BaKongo.

Instead of being "eaten," stolen souls may be sold for an unholy profit, which explains, in Kongo eyes, why some people get rich. Victims should be sold, like slaves, at some distance, so that they cannot make their way home. Most victims of witchcraft end up in America, where they are supposedly put to work in factories making textiles and automobiles. Their souls would go to America anyway, after a normal death, but witchcraft sends them there prematurely.

Described and understood as witchcraft, the slave trade is believed to have persisted into the twentieth century. All relations with Europe and America, collectively referred to as *Mputu,* are understood in the same way. When Protestant missionaries arrived in the 1880s, they were seen as practicing a new form of the same trade. To be converted meant to be initiated into a magical conspiracy, similar to the traditional cults, in which the initiates learned how to become powerful and wealthy. In exchange, as in other cults offering sinister competitive advantage over one's neighbors, the converts had to hand over the souls of one or more relatives. These victims the missionaries kept stored, it was believed, in attics, trunks, or boxes, until the time came to ship them to America. In 1912, when a certain Swedish missionary began to build a brick house, the local people said, "It's all over, he's building a warehouse for souls." And when schoolchildren began to learn the French terms for parts of the body, many people fled as far away as Brazzaville.

Despite this dubious reputation, the Protestants did win many converts. So did the Catholics, who came later, so that since the 1930s virtually all BaKongo have been Christians. Nevertheless the reputation exists. In 1980, in Kisangani, about one thousand miles northeast of Kongo territory, rumor explained the recent arrival of Baha'i missionaries in that area by saying that the government had incurred an enormous foreign debt in building the new international airport there and had had to allow a new group to harvest souls in order to pay it off.

The economics of imperialism

The production of export goods by local labor, organized by the Belgians in the earliest stages of colonial rule, continued the same extortion of souls by other means. I was told in 1970 that ivory and rubber, the principal exports at the turn of the century, were merely the containers for souls being shipped overseas. Later on, when the cultivation of urena was introduced (and required), the fact that some people's bundles of fiber weighed surprisingly heavy when sold to Belgian traders proved that the victims of witchcraft had been stowed in them. Amid the nationalist fervor of 1960, a Kongo newspaper published an article, in French, demanding the immediate return of all Kongo people who had been transformed into a chemical product as merchandise.

It was believed in 1970, in Matadi and elsewhere in Lower Congo, that some individuals, willing to do anything to get to America and become rich, would volunteer for this traffic. They would enter into an agreement with a foreign technician about to go home on leave and eager to do a little business on the side, such that he would take them with him to sell in Mputu. Industrial accidents in the port of Matadi were popularly explained in this way. Elsewhere I was told of certain deep pools into which ambitious persons anxious to reach the land of the dead would throw themselves, to return later as newly arrived but "locally made" white technicians or managers.

In the office of a certain magical healer, I was told a whole colonial history. The office was a murky little shed in Matadi; around the walls hung various obscure bundles, a small stuffed crocodile, a turtle shell, and a calendar from the Dime Savings Bank of Brookline. On the healer's desk stood a glass full of ballpoint pens awaiting medication so that their schoolboy owners would be able to pass their examinations. The story:

> This trade was not created by black people but by the Catholic missionary. From the time of our ancestors it was our custom to sell people, but they did not die entirely. They were sold to the Portuguese, who stuffed them into ships for transportation to Belgium. When they arrived there, the Belgians sent out a notice to all the nations, saying, "What shall we do with these people? for they are worthless." Then the Protestant missionary said, "It is not proper to kill them; they should be sent to an island with water on every side, where they will die of hunger, and that will be the end of them." So they signed an agreement and put the people on ships and cast them away on an island where there was a forest

with no food in it, and the sea on every side.

But truly God does not sleep. He gave them civilization, and skyscrapers sprang up, and food appeared, and every needful thing. When the Belgians came to see what had happened, they found nothing but skyscrapers, with no room anymore to plant food. And so it is to this day.

So the Catholic priest considered that something else should be done, saying, "This time, when we buy someone, we had better finish him off for good." When a man dies he has no means of knowing he is going to Belgium. Lots of people when they have been traded have the idea that now they are going to be rich, they will have their own magic. But when one has gone to Europe, that's where his name is; as for a return here, there is none—he wants the white man's ways.

Later the priest, seeing how things were, sent a message to the colonial government, saying, "The medicines the people use, which give them power, should be taken away." So now in Belgium they have a whole house full of our things, though they have no idea how to use them.

It would be a mistake to treat this story as fantastic or even simply wrong. Despite the unfamiliar idiom, we can recognize in it references to both Manhattan and the Royal Museum of Central Africa at Tervuren in Belgium. More importantly, the story conveys a far more accurate picture of the extraction of labor from Africa for the benefit of the developed world than does the usual self-serving account of Europe's "civilizing mission" and the white man's burden.

The sources of cosmology

A system of belief does not descend ready-made from the sky, nor can we explain either its origin or its present strength by saying that it is a relic of the traditional past. Their cosmology seems real to the BaKongo because they live it; their daily experience confirms it. If we examine that same life sociologically, we find that the sociological models of political organization and marital alliance exhibit the same structure as the cosmology.

Every free man or woman belongs to a matrilineal clan, a group whose members trace their descent from an original female ancestor. The group is exogamous, meaning that everyone must look to some other group for a spouse. In practice, the members of any one clan marry into many other clans, but if we were to construct a model of the marriage system, it would be necessary to show only one other clan in order to demonstrate the principle. The marital alliance extends into other matters as well. For example, every group needs at least one other to testify to the truth of its traditions and its property claims. Though every individual belongs with his mother in one group, his father necessarily belongs to the other, where he has certain religious and political functions to fulfill, and so on.

This simple, egalitarian model is well established in Kongo thought and expressed in a variety of proverbs, such as "Where the needle goes, the thread follows," and "Whence the pig escaped, they return the piglet." It is also embodied in a number of figures of speech, found among many Central African peoples, that describe the relationship between two clans as being like the two banks of a river. The role of a married woman in linking them is compared to that of a canoe going to and fro. The similarity to the model of the reciprocating universe is clinched by the term *nzadi*, which means not only "large river" but "in-law." Hence the riddle, "What large river is full to overflowing, but we don't fall in?"

The reciprocating universe is thus real to BaKongo because they literally live it.

In 1921, Simon Kimbangu arose as a prophet in Lower Congo, preaching the Gospel, healing the sick and casting out witchcraft. So began one of the best-known African religious movements of modern times, surviving Belgian repression through several decades and giving rise to many variants. One of the

ELISOFON ARCHIVES: NATIONAL MUSEUM OF AFRICAN ART

A symbolic power-figure made of wood and iron nails.

strongest Kimbanguist themes concerns the expected return of the "King of the Americans." A hymn says, "When the King of the Americans comes, to announce the King of Kongo, our sufferings will have been noticed."

Not understanding Kongo cosmology, the Belgians took this millenarian expectation literally, attributing it to the nefarious influence of Marcus Garvey or of the American government, eager to take over the Belgian colony. In fact it meant that BaKongo expected the hand of God, working through his prophet Kimbangu, to turn the world upside down, so that the ancestors from across the water (the Americans) would return, and disease and oppression would end. Similar ideas guided popular understanding as national independence approached in 1960. Many people thought they would become white, and some of them knocked politely on the doors of European residences asking to see the kind of accommodations they would be moving into. The Europeans thought them naive, as no doubt in a sense they were, though not in the sense that was attributed to them.

A longer discussion would show that the whole cosmology is intriguingly more complex than I have shown here. Like other cosmologies, Kongo ideas of the universe are not in a simple sense either true or false. Component propositions may be refutable, but the system, as part of the fabric of a way of life, is self-confirming. As that way of life changes, so will it become implicit in the cosmology. Such a process happens not because of any universal tendency but because of particular local events. More and more BaKongo individually live urban, bureaucratic lives to which the clan system is becoming irrelevant. More radically, the government of Zaire has taken legal, economic, and political steps to destroy local social structures such as the one described here.

Additional Reading

Wyatt MacGaffey, *Religion and Society in Central Africa*, Chicago, 1986.

Robert Farris Thompson and Joseph Cornet, *The Four Moments of the Sun: Kongo Art in Two Worlds*, Washington, 1981.

Wyatt MacGaffey is John R. Coleman Professor of Social Sciences at Haverford College.

Article 9

AFRICA NEWS
November 28, 1988

Cooperation Pays Off

Six days a week, Selina Adjebeng-Asem rises at 5 a.m., and she rarely goes to bed before 1 a.m. In the 20 hours that constitute her work day, the Ghanaian sociologist and mother of three teaches classes to 350 undergraduates at Nigeria's Ife University, makes four round-trips to her children's schools to deliver them to morning and afternoon classes – feeding them lunch in between – does the family shopping, cooks an evening meal, checks her children's homework before putting them to bed, and, finally, burns the midnight oil with academic chores like writing and reading. On Saturdays, Asem rests. "That is my day," she says, smiling. "Nobody better talk to me."

As daunting as Asem's schedule may seem, her position as one of Africa's highly educated professional women relieves her of the arduous physical labor that is a constant feature of most African women's lives. And Asem is the first to insist that she is not unique, even among the women in her socio-economic class. "All average working women [in west Africa] are doing what I'm doing," she says. "They wake at about 5 and are asleep, at the earliest, by 11. We cope somehow, and we hope that nature will continue to be good to us so that we can survive."

At the annual African Studies Association conference in Chicago last month, Asem joined other scholars in examining some of the problems faced by African women, along with the strategies some are using to better their lot.

Across the board, according to the participants at the Chicago meeting, African women tend to be better off when they cooperate with each other, formally or informally. In Ghana, for instance, University of Michigan anthropologist Gracia Clark founded a women's agricultural cooperative whose members have combined government encouragement, sage financial advice and traditional social structures to run a successful business.

The Hadasko ("hard working") Women Farmers' Association was born in 1981, when an official from Ghana's National Council for Women and Development visited Damongo, in the northwestern district of Gonja. The official recommended that the women of Damongo form a cooperative in order to take advantage of government funds that were available to collective farms. Under Flt. Lt. Jerry Rawlings, Ghana's government has favored the agricultural sector of the economy, and there has been a strong push toward getting more women involved in farming.

The Hadasko association, which grows cassava and processes it into gari, a staple food in many parts of Ghana, has quadrupled its membership to 200 women in seven years. It operates without men and without outside assistance because the women – who, traditionally, have been ineligible for bank loans because they don't own property – have found strength in their reputation. Although the cooperative will guarantee to repay a bank loan taken out by a member, it automatically ousts any member who defaults on a loan without good cause. Thus, the project has earned a reputation among local bankers as an excellent risk. And that trend, according to Gracia Clark, applies to women's cooperatives in other parts of Ghana. "Banks lend to women and like lending to women," Clark says, "because women pay the money back."

Hadasko is also successful, Clark says, because it draws upon Damongo's existing power structure. First, the group poses no threat to local men because farming was never a "male domain." And second, the association institutionalizes a preexisting relationship between the community's women. The cooperative is split into work groups of five to ten members each, and within each group, women help each other, not only with work-related tasks, but with childbirth, domestic problems and other personal matters. Each group is led by a respected, generally older, member of the community – a woman who would traditionally be looked to as an advisor.

Finally, of course, Hadasko has succeeded because the Ghanaian government encourages such initiatives. But even in Kenya, where

Almasy-Vauthey/Unesco

Primary schoolchildren in Lagos, Nigeria. At many African secondary schools, boys outnumber girls by almost two to one.

authorities have been less willing to support women's groups, Hilarie Kelly of UCLA founded a nomadic group whose women come together under the aegis of a sacred ritual to cooperate on economic projects and to work out problems.

The Orma, Muslim cattle-herders who live near Kenya's border with Somalia, are gradually settling into a more sedentary life style that, Kelly says, affords women "more occasion for cooperative labor and leisure." But settling into villages has also meant an increase in interpersonal tensions, and since Islam, as the Orma practice it, does not encourage women to gather to discuss problems, Orma women have turned to an institution that pre-dates their community's conversion to Islam.

The *gaas eba* (meaning "blessed shade," and so named because meetings are held under trees) is led by women elders, and it has so much power as a ritual expression of the woman's "role in regulating the sacred forces behind fertility, rain, milk production, peace and tranquility," Kelly says, that "men cannot prevent their wives from attending." But, even though Orma women also acknowledge the ritual importance of *gaas eba*, the institution is evolving, in some neighborhoods, into a series of regularly held meetings where women can address various secular concerns. The *gaas eba* serves as a conduit for complaints from women to male village elders; and sometimes, Kelly says, a women's *gaas eba* receives permission to punish an "especially offensive or abusive husband whose behavior is taken as an insult against all women, as thus against domestic peace."

The *gaas eba* has also, in some cases, spawned women's cooperatives for the sale of milk. Some of these are now competing successfully with other cattle-herding groups, and even with the government's Kenya Cooperative Creameries.

While the Ghanaian and Kenya collectives highlight the power women can seize when they work together, there are few national women's initiatives active in Africa. Many African governments have established organs for the consideration of women's issues, but so far, little impact has been made on the daily lives of women on the continent.

One Kenyan academic at the Chicago conference blamed women themselves for not pushing their own concerns at the national level.

"Where were the women's organizations?" the academic asked, after explaining that a law that would have made wife-beating illegal in Kenya was thrown out of court because it was "traditional" for men to "discipline" their wives. Citing the recent decision by Kenya's ruling Kenya African National Union to take the once-powerful women's organization called *Maendeleo Ya Wanawake* under its mantle, the academic complained that other such groups "have not taken the lead in helping women either to seize the rights they do have or to fight for others."

Selina Adjebeng-Asem, who spoke at a recent gathering Duke University in North Carolina, agrees that women must take the lead and help themselves. But she insists that attempts to "liberate" African women are doomed to failure unless men are also liberated.

"I belong to a number of organizations that are women-based," Asem says, "but I don't think that is where the problem lies. The problem lies in the society. We would be defeating our purpose by making it just a feminine issue. The only reason we ask women to get involved is because it concerns us, and men are not going to go out of their way to look at our problem. But when it becomes a mainstream problem, then men are going to look at it."

Asem's particular interest is in gender inequalities in the Nigerian work force, and she believes that more women must get more education in order to break into technical fields in significant numbers.

"People will tell you that we don't have a women's problem in Nigeria," Asem says. "I mean, nobody is discriminating against any woman. If you can get education, you can get a job. And if I have a faculty position and have the same qualifications as [a man], I get the same salary. There's no discrimination."

But the problem for many Nigerian girls, Asem says, is getting the education in the first place. Many families place great emphasis on educating sons, but keep their daughters at home "cleaning and doing dishes and helping Mommy take care of the babies." Other girls, especially the daughters of Nigeria's Yoruba trading women, often leave school young in order to join their mothers in the street markets.

When educating children represents a financial sacrifice – as it does for more and more African parents as the continent's debt crisis deepens – school fees are allocated to sons. "There is something in our community," Asem says, referring to west Africa, "that believes that male stands for power, stands for continuity. So even women want to educate their male children more than their female children – because they will carry the family line. They are the symbols of the family."

According to Asem, not only does the drop-out rate for Nigerian girls increase as they go further in school, but those women who do complete degrees are "sexually segregated" into "female ghettoes" like nursing, teaching and clerical work. She and the other members of a professional women's group make regular visits to secondary schools, where they talk to first-year female students about the opportunities that are available in technical fields.

Asem admits that the task of sensitizing the next generation of west Africans—male and female—to women's issues won't be easy. The pressure on women to conform to existing norms is "incredible," Asem says. Most of her women students are afraid that if they get all the education they want and need to compete with men for high-level jobs, they will be unable to find husbands when they are ready to marry. And in Africa, Asem says, "a woman must marry. A woman must have children."

But Asem thinks Africa's current economic woes may actually help women decide to go on in school. "I hope and believe that all these inflationary trends are going to make men accept more qualified women as wives. I think that the woman who has more education and a fatter pay packet will stand a better chance of getting a husband than the one that stops by the way." Asem also counsels women to get more education as a hedge against failed marriages, since women often bear primary responsibility for providing for their children.

While Asem doesn't think Nigeria needs a "women's movement" on the Western model, she does believe that individual women can affect a lasting change in the way society views women's roles.

"Who makes society but us?" Asem asks. "And who can change society but us? You just stick your neck out and say, 'I'm not doing this,' 'I'm going to go ahead and do that.' Believe me, by the time two or three people have become deviates, society is bound to accept us for what we are."

"Just go ahead and do exactly what you want to do," Asem advises her students, male and female. "Just do it."

Yosef Hadar/World Bank

Women planting groundnuts at a seed multiplication farm in Nigeria.

Article 10

World Monitor, August 1990

AFRICA'S GREAT BLACK HOPE

In a continent struggling for survival, Nigeria strives to learn from disaster and show the way out.

Blaine Harden

Blaine Harden, the Washington Post's bureau chief in Eastern Europe, wrote from sub-Saharan Africa for four years. He distilled this article from his forthcoming book, "Africa: Dispatches from a Fragile Continent," © Blaine Harden, to be published in October by W. W. Norton & Co.

AFRICA'S MOST POPULOUS country is its brightest hope. Nigeria is an odd place to find a silver lining. It is infamous, even among Nigerians, for being loud, dirty, violent, and corrupt. Its reputation is not unlike that of the United States at the end of the last century—and that is my point. In spite of its all-too-visible failings, I believe that Nigeria's mix of talent, resources, and gall will one day pull the country up out of Africa's own bleak social and economic category: the Nth World.

After coming to know Nigeria, I found myself more and more intolerant of a soft-focus stereotype of Africa that continues to captivate the West. The Oscar-winning movie "Out of Africa" was a paean to love lost among white colonialists. Time magazine devoted its most extensive African coverage of the 1980s—twenty pages of purple prose and color pictures—to an essay that rhapsodized about lions in the tall grass, sagacious pastoral warriors, and "miles and miles of bloody Africa."

This is anachronistic claptrap. Many Westerners have fixated on a self-glorifying illusion, a tranquilizing chimera that justifies ignorance of modern Africa while sanctifying the purchase of khaki pants at Banana Republic stores.

ELEPHANTS AND EXPORTS IN DECLINE

There are countless reasons to despair for Africa, by which I mean black Africa. In the 45 countries south of the Sahara and north of South Africa, at the end of the 1980s per capita income was lower than it was 30 years earlier. Seventy percent of the world's poorest nations are in black Africa.

Africa is the most successful producer of babies in recorded history and the world's least successful producer of food. Gains made in health and education in the 1960s have been lost in many parts of the continent to economic anemia and a population growth rate that is still accelerating. Central and Eastern Africa have emerged as the world epicenter of AIDS. The Sahara Desert creeps south and the Kalahari north, moving 100 miles closer each year as desertification and erosion spread. West African rain forests are rapidly being chopped down for hard currency. About half the 1.4 million elephants that roamed Africa in 1980 were killed by the end of the decade, shot and carved up by ivory poachers with automatic assault rifles and chain saws.

Africa's export earnings declined massively in the past decade. The foreign debt burden, relative to Africa's income, was the highest in the world. Interest payments bled away one of every three dollars Africans earned. The region became more dependent on foreign assistance than any other part of the developing world. Outside investment dried up.

Yet there is more to modern Africa than a vast, flat plain of failure. A learning curve can be discerned. Governments have finally started to sift sense out of nonsense. They have, in the words of former Nigerian President Olusegun Obasanjo, begun "to accept that an unjust international order will not change simply because of the euphony of their own rhetoric..."

Many African leaders have stopped blaming their problems on the legacy of colonialism. They have openly admitted that their countries are bleeding from self-inflicted wounds. As in the Soviet Union and Eastern Europe, smothering state control is being lifted from the marketplace. Farmers in many reforming countries are being paid a decent price to grow food, and they responded in the later half of the 1980s with record crops. These tentative efforts have won the attention of rich countries, and Africa's share of world development aid has nearly doubled in recent years.

THE RUSSIANS ARE NOT COMING

For the first time in the post-independence era, the continent is no longer a chessboard in a global cold war. The Russians are no longer coming. Africa is not a region that the United States can win or lose to communism. It seems to have been tacitly agreed, by the Soviets and the Africans themselves, that communism is irrelevant and unworkable. In the last year of the 1980s, American-Soviet diplomatic cooperation laid the groundwork for South African withdrawal from Namibia. Soviet refusal to back endless civil war in Ethiopia has pressured the government there to make peace overtures to rebels (although the fighting continues).

More fundamentally, Africa's learning curve is etched into the everyday lives of human beings caught up in the fitful process of shifting from one set of rules to another. Hundreds of millions of Africans are lurching between an unworkable Western present and a collapsing African past. Their loyalties are stretched between predatory governments and disintegrating tribes, between arbitrary demands of dictators and incessant pleadings of relatives, between commandments of the Bible and obligations to the ancestors. At its heart, the great experiment in modernity that continues to rattle Africa goes on inside individuals, as they sort out new connections with their families, their tribes, and their countries.

Though continuously battered, African values endure. They are the primary reason why, beyond the sum of Africa's dismal statistics and behind two-dimensional images of famine victims on TV screens, the continent is not a hopeless or even sad place. It is a land where the bonds of family keep old people from feeling useless and guarantee that no child is an orphan, where religion is more about joy than guilt, where when you ask a man for directions he will get in your car and ride with you to your destination—and insist on walking home.

The short, squalid history of independent black Africa is that of traditional cultures being forced and forcing themselves to accommodate Western ideas and technology. It has been a halting, confusing, demeaning process.

Nigeria—with its wealth, its huge pool of educated people, its aggressiveness—has invented itself at a higher velocity than the rest of black Africa. It certainly has not been any smoother, just faster.

Last year, three decades down the freedom road, Nigeria, as usual, was frantically falling apart. Africa's most populous nation was flailing about in exuberant desperation, struggling not to drown in its daily bath of chaos and self-flagellation, avarice and wild-eyed pride. The president, Ibrahim Babangida, a gap-toothed general with an

President Babangida has a more sophisticated economic mind than any other leader on the continent.

endearing smile, was telling the assembled fat cats and stuffed shirts at the Oxford and Cambridge Club Annual Spring Lecture in Lagos that they—the privileged elite—were a major reason for the country's plight:

"You will, perhaps, agree that the worst features in the attitude of the Nigerian elite over the last three decades or more have included: factionalism, disruptive competition, extreme greed and selfishness, indolence and abandonment of the pursuit of excellence. Indeed, a companion cult of mediocrity—deep and pervasive—has developed and, with it, a continuous and, so to speak, universal search for excuses to avoid taking difficult decisions and confronting hard work, and a penchant for passing the buck."

Meantime, that is to say, in the last year of the 1980s, rioters exploded into the sewer-lined streets of Lagos, burning cars, looting supermarkets, trashing government offices. They were protesting something they called SAP, a four-year-old structural adjustment program which, by order of the unelected general with the endearing smile, was removing make-believe government subsidies and making every Nigerian (except a growing number of generals and selected members of the Oxford and Cambridge Club) miserable.

NO STOMACH FOR DOWNWARD MOBILITY

The young rioters, many of them college students, halted tens of thousands of cars and trucks at morning rush hour on Lagos freeways to hand out green leaves ripped from city shrubbery. The leaves betokened solidarity among the panicky middle class. They were symbols of an angry people with no stomach for the kind of downward mobility that the rest of black Africa passively accepts.

Hundreds of demonstrators seized the moment and gave the economic riots a peculiarly Nigerian twist. While denouncing SAP in the name of the downtrodden common man, they extorted cash from fellow sufferers stuck in traffic. Police shot about a hundred rioters and arrested 1,500 others before the trouble ebbed, and Lagos traffic accelerated to its normal maddening crawl.

Other pots boiled over. Nigeria was making a third run at democracy. The first try had foundered in 1966 because of incompetence, the second in 1983 because of greed.

President Babangida, having vowed to give power back to civilians, decided to ban all former politicians from taking part in the proposed "Third Republic" on the grounds that they were likely to be fools or thieves. If the "old breed" even joined a political party, the general decreed, they would spend five years in prison.

Even as things fall apart, pots boil over, signals cross, Nigerians somehow are managing to meld themselves into that most unusual of black African entities—a real nation. Against all odds, things come together.

Out of the Biafran war of the late 1960s, which was Africa's bloodiest tribal conflict, has come a lasting tribal peace—a feast of forgiveness remarkable in world history. Out of the berserk corruption of Nigeria's oil boom has come a gutty, sober-minded program of economic reform. Out of the two-time failure of democracy has emerged a moderate military regime that is orchestrating its own dissolution in favor of elective government. Out of six military coups, and after the assassination of three heads of state, Nigeria has wound up with an extraordinarily beneficent Big Man—President Ibrahim Babangida.

President Babangida has a more sophisticated economic mind than any other leader on the continent. He is a former tank commander and happens to be a nimble politician. While imposing a hated economic adjustment program on Africa's most disputatious people, he managed to remain personally popular. Most remarkable for an African Big Man, the general promised to step down in 1992 and the promise was believed.

REASONS FOR CONCERN

As the '90s began, there were no guarantees that any of Nigeria's gains would endure. There were sound reasons to fear catastrophe.

Like Sudan, Nigeria is rent by religion. It is divided north and south between Muslims and Christians, and economic hard times have ratcheted up religious tension.

Coups always threaten. Babangida sanctioned the execution of 10 military officers who conspired in 1986 to overthrow him. (He personally has been on the winning side in three coups, including the one that brought him to power in 1985.)

Nigerians deeply resent poverty. They have watched in disbelief and anger as their average annual income was sliced in half, from $670 to $300, in the past decade. The country slipped from low middle-income status to what it really is: a least developed country. The kind of strikes and economic riots that erupted in late 1980s will probably recur.

And yet Nigeria—horrible, ugly, boastful, coup-crazed, self-destructive, too hot Nigeria—is black Africa's principal prospect for a future that is something other than despotic, desperate, and dependent. If the world's poorest continent is going anywhere, Nigeria is likely to get there first. Two reasons are size and wealth.

The place is not a banana republic. One of every four Africans is a Nigerian. An estimated 114 million people lived in the country in 1989. The population is growing at a rate that is among the highest in the world. In less than 50 years, Nigeria will have at least 618 million people—close to the present population of all of Africa, more than double the population of the United States.

Besides sheer numbers, Nigeria has world-class wealth. The country's gross national product is bigger (in years when the world oil price is strong) than that of white-ruled South Africa and more than half that of all black Africa combined. It is the world's ninth largest oil producer and ranks fifth in natural gas reserves.

Below ground there are about 40 years worth of oil and a century worth of natural gas.

A UNIVERSITY-TRAINED ELITE

Above ground there is a wealth of well-trained and frighteningly ambitious humanity. There are an estimated 2 million university-trained professionals. They constitute the largest, best-trained, most acquisitive black elite on the continent.

Finally, many Nigerians have a penchant, indeed a mania, for self-criticism. They obsessively pick apart the failures of their leaders and of themselves. Titles of popular books by Nigerians include "Another Hope Betrayed," "The Trouble With Nigeria," and "Always a Loser—A Novel About Nigeria."

"It Wouldn't Be Nigerian If It Worked," howled a headline that typifies the Nigeria press, which is at once the best and most irresponsible, most boorish and brilliant in Africa. A letter to the New Nigerian newspaper by O. Gbola Ajao, a teacher at the College of Medicine in the city of Ibadan, said:

"Some years ago we were asking about developing a tourist industry in Nigeria. What a laugh! How will any foreigner in his right mind want to come for vacation in a place like Nigeria? Even those of us born there are always looking for one excuse or another to get out of the place."

The government in 1984 invented WAI—the War Against Indiscipline—which amounted to an official declaration that Nigerians are intolerably rude, messy, and violent. WAI posters were distributed throughout the country, urging people to queue in line, pick up their garbage, stop sleeping on duty, stop armed robbery, stop drug pushing, stop fighting, be nicer. Novelist Chinua Achebe upped the ante on national self-flagellation by writing:

"Nigeria is not a great country. It is one of the most disorderly nations in the world. It is one of the most corrupt, insensitive, inefficient places under the sun. It is one of the most expensive countries and one of those that give the least value for money. It is dirty, callous, noisy, ostentatious, dishonest and vulgar. In short, it is among the most unpleasant places on earth!"

DICTATORS ARE LAMPOONED

All true, and yet dictators—Big Men in the African mold—are not acceptable in Nigeria. They are lampooned in newspaper cartoons. They are overthrown. Babangida could not survive if he were to back away from his promise of a return to democracy.

Although they have badly botched it up when they achieve democratic rule, Nigerians refuse to settle for anything less. After 30 years of independence, civilians have been in power for 9 years, generals for 21, and the national consensus is that only democracy works.

Nigerians refuse to commit a corrosive crime common to most of black Africa—passive acceptance of tyranny. It is no accident that half the continent's newspapers, half its journalists, one-quarter of its published books, a Nobel laureate in literature, and a growing number of world-class novelists and poets are Nigerian.

"The worst sin on earth is the failure to think," writes Nigerian novelist and television producer Ken Saro-Wiwa. "It is thoughtlessness that has reduced Africa to beggardom, to famine, poverty and disease. The failure to use the creative imagination has reduced Africans to the status of mimic men and consumers of the products of others' imagination."

Nigerians foul up, but on their own initiative, not on other people's orders.

"Nigerians are not rational," Prince Tony Momoh, a wealthy businessman, influential traditional leader, and minister of information in Babangida's government, told me. "We would prefer to go hungry to being told what to do. I can't think of any other African country doing such an irrational thing. But there is more to a Nigerian than reasoning."

Nigerian pride careens off in self-deluding directions. There was talk, in the oil-boom years, of Nigeria's becoming a superpower. Until poverty nixed it, the country longed for a "black bomb." A former foreign minister, Bolaji Akenjemi, said in 1987 that "Nigeria has a sacred responsibility to challenge the racial monopoly of nuclear weapons."

Akenjemi, in another prideful vein, instructed Nigerian ambassadors around the world to open the doors of their embassies to all people of African origin. Expatriate Africans should come to view Nigeria in the same way that Jews view Jerusalem—as a shelter "for blacks in the diaspora," the foreign minister said.

He ordered his diplomatic corps never to hold an official dinner without reserving one-third of the guest list for Africans. Akenjemi either did not know or, more likely, did not care that most Africans view Nigerians as the loudest, most obnoxious people on earth. Akenjemi was sacked by Babangida for talking too much.

Like most other outsiders on their first trip to Lagos, when I got off the plane in 1985, I was scared. The city was hideous. It was like the post-nuclear-war backdrop for the movie "Road Warrior," only hotter, uglier, smellier.

I went to a Chinese restaurant where it proved impossible to order a meal for less than $100. Lagos was then the most expensive city in the world.

(The Union Bank of Switzerland surveyed 49 cities in 1985 and found that goods and services in Lagos cost more than anywhere else. The survey found that, exclusive of rent, it cost $2,010 a month to survive. That was $410 more than in New York City. Rent for a two-bedroom Lagos apartment was then $85,000 a year, three years payable in advance. All this changed dramatically with Babangida's economic reform. In 1988 Lagos ranked 71 on a list of the world's most expensive cities.)

WORLD'S MOST TWISTED ECONOMIC ORDER

Lagos was also part of the world's most twisted economic order. I sat one afternoon in a steamy back-alley saloon with a jet-lagged baby-clothes smuggler who was sipping iced palm wine.

"What I feel is better to fly with than anything else is baby wear," he told me, explaining his six trips a year to Taiwan. He explained the advantages of baby wear for a Nigerian trader: a profitable haul could be stuffed in a couple of suitcases. Customs inspectors at Lagos airport usually did not demand duty or bribes to clear booties and bibs. Nigerians would line up to pay 500% markups for baby clothes.

The key to the smuggler's existence was government price controls on air tickets and the grossly overvalued Nigerian currency, the naira. The smuggler bought naira on the black market with dollars, paying one-quarter price. He then bought air tickets with naira, paying about one-eighth the world real price. He flew first class, if he could get a ticket. Airlines reported "saturation bookings." One-tenth of the nation's discretionary income, $350 million a year, went for air tickets. The warped monetary system was driving economists around the bend.

"The government's overregulation of the economy is creating these opportunities for private gain at the expense of the society in general," complained Ishrat Hussein, a World Bank representative who had been sent to Lagos to do what then seemed impossible—persuade Nigerians to live within their means. "The traders are paying no taxes. There is no way local industry can compete with these imported goods. Consumers must pay outrageous prices. I call it private affluence, public squalor."

I went back to Nigeria four more times over the following four years. On each trip I escaped Lagos to travel to the north, east, and west of a country that is the size of California, Nevada, and Arizona combined.

Each time I returned to Nigeria, I confirmed that the impossible had occurred.

Nigerians stopped lying to themselves.

They struggled to retool the economy so it would run on what they actually earned, rather than on what they wished they earned.

The naira, for decades a symbol of Nigerian manhood, was devalued again and again.

A corrupt import licensing regime, which had spawned a parasitic elite of millionaires who did nothing but bribe bureaucrats, was scrapped.

Farm prices were increased, and agricultural production, after a 20-year nose dive, jumped sharply.

Africa's most ambitious program to sell off government-owned business was launched.

The baby-clothes smuggler was forced out of business.

Nigeria—a country that has been synonymous with all that was pompous, self-deceiving, and mindlessly extravagant in post-independence Africa—became in the later half of the 1980s an African model for free-market reform.

It was an impressive but agonizing adjustment.

Almost everyone was getting poorer. The price of the cassava-based staple food, which many Nigerians had long shunned as a poor man's food, jumped fourfold in two years. The middle class could not afford spare parts to fix cars. So it walked. Onetime high rollers who owned Mercedeses and BMWs swallowed their pride and entered the *kabukabu* trade, turning their onetime symbols of success into overcrowded taxis. Nigerians who used to shake their heads in disgust about reports of famine in Ethiopia were forced to live with hunger. College graduates were eating one meal a day. Hospitals around the country reported increasing malnutrition among children.

I talked to scores of Nigerians, middle class and poor, who found no point to their misery. "I do not understand what this is all about," the Rev. Ebenezer Okwuosa, pastor of a poor parish in the town of Uli in overcrowded eastern Nigeria, told me in 1988. Food and transport costs in Uli had doubled in just eight weeks. The minister asked me, "How can my government say there is no money?"

After the civil war of the 1960s, the second cleansing cataclysm that helped forge Nigeria into a nation had been an avalanche of money. Sudden hikes in the world price of oil in the 1970s and early '80s opened the floodgates, and $100 billion poured into the coffers of the Nigerian government in a decade. It was more money in less time than any black African nation had ever seen or was likely ever to see again. The cost of all that wealth (a typically Nigerian oxymoron) proved greater than the Biafran war. When the boom finally fizzled in the mid-1980s, the country had an $18 billion foreign debt. A generation was weaned on avarice. Corruption hypnotized the national psyche.

A LESSON LEARNED

Yet even money-mad Nigerians could not dispose of $100 billion without making a few socially useful purchases. In contracts laced with kickbacks, a vast highway system was built, along with more than 20 new universities. Primary school enrollment tripled. As recently as 1985, more than 100,000 Nigerian families were sending one or more children abroad to university. As greed lured Nigerians into cities, it broke down tribal and sectional differences. Ambitious men could not afford traditional hatreds. US economist Sayre P. Schatz, who analyzed Nigeria's situation, speculated that "pirate capitalism" in Nigeria helped speed "formation of a bourgeoisie that is truly national rather than regionally or tribally based."

The most important legacy of the oil boom was not what it bought, but what it taught. The squandering of Africa's greatest fortune sobered Nigerian leaders to the folly of too much government. It was a primer in the social cost of unbounded private greed when married to uncontrolled bureaucratic power. A new national Constitution, completed in 1989 as part of the preparations for the planned return to democratic rule, pointedly scaled back the role of the government. It deleted language describing Nigeria as a "welfare state" and excised clauses saying that Nigerians have a right to free primary, secondary, and adult education, and to free medical care.

The oil bust forced the country to cut its imports by two-thirds. Overstaffed government marketing agencies for cocoa and other cash crops were eliminated. Farmers began getting more money for their labor. All this, of course, is standard World Bank advice for sick African countries. But Nigeria turned to it not because it was ordered to do so, as have so many other African nations that go through the motions of reform in order to secure more loans. Humiliating experience—wasting a unique windfall that might have catapulted the country out of the third world—forced Nigeria to learn the hard way. The lesson seems to have stuck. In 1985, when I first went there, the country was a joke among economists who specialized in Africa. At the end of the decade, Tariq Husain, the World Bank representative in Lagos, told me that Nigeria was taking reform more seriously than any other country on the continent.

THIRD TRY AT CIVILIAN SELF-RULE

After Babangida seized power in a bloodless coup, as foreign debts mounted and oil revenues continued to shrink, it became clear that prideful opposition to reform would bankrupt and isolate the country. Unable to overcome nationalistic opposition to an International Monetary Fund loan, Babangida outwitted it. In one of the neatest economic maneuvers in African history, the general told the IMF that Nigeria did not want the loan. Then, as the country rejoiced in having told the IMF where to go, the military government implemented what Babangida described as "our structural adjustment program produced by Nigerians for Nigerians." It was far stricter than what officials from the IMF or World Bank had dared demand, and it earned the country relatively generous rescheduling agreements with Western creditors.

An indomitable national spirit and a natural distaste for dictatorship, however, have not been enough—thus far—for Nigeria to lay the groundwork for a working democratic government. For the third run at civilian self-rule, in the hope that it might give democracy a better chance, Babangida's military regime had tried to phase in elected government, starting with local, then regional, then national elections.

At the same time, the general has attempted to treat his nation's social distemper with a government agency called the Directorate for Social Mobilization, or Mamser. It was supposed to do for politics what the defunct War Against Indiscipline was supposed to have done for garbage—clean it up. Babangida ordered Mamser to "eradicate all those features of our behavior in the past which have made our society a byword for disharmony, dishonesty, distrust, and disservice, and a haven for those who prefer to embrace and to promote in their conduct the least attractive traits in human nature."

To lure cynical, apathetic, and newly impoverished voters to attend a nationwide series of Mamser "political awareness" rallies, the military jazzed them up with performances from well-known Nigerian pop musicians. The military also

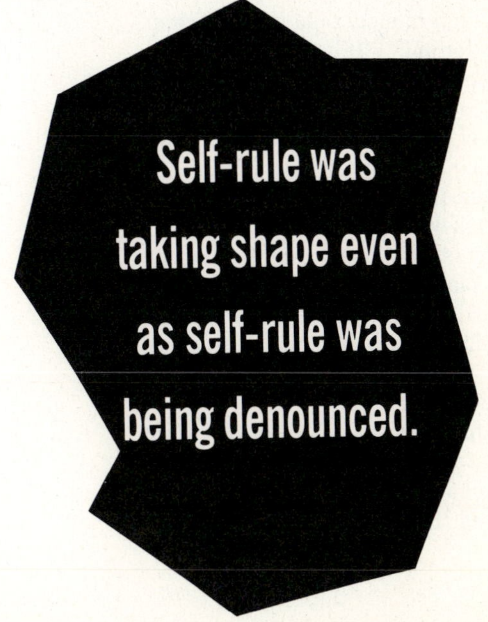

invited local obas, chiefs, and emirs to come and speak their mind. The result was a political consciousness-raising exercise marked by unruly crowds, wildly contradictory speeches, and bare-chested musicians with dreadlocks, who made fun of pudgy generals and sang about how living in Nigeria was like "living in prison." The rallies proved less cures for social distemper than testimonials to it. Unimaginable or impermissible virtually everywhere else in black Africa, the rallies could have come off only in Nigeria.

I attended one such rally along with a gaggle of generals in combat fatigues; a handful of emirs in flowing white robes, turbans, and dark sunglasses; several hundred civil servants who had been let out of government offices to learn about honesty; and 15,000 or so pushy adolescents who were desperate to dance.

The generals, the traditional leaders, and the government workers sat in shaded bleachers. Everyone else stood (and sometimes fainted) in noontime heat.

A SINGER DENOUNCES WASTEFUL WAYS

Squads of "Mamser Youth," teen-agers employed and outfitted by the government to give an image of responsible political awareness, were deployed to help police with crowd control. They wore bright blue slacks, white sneakers, and T-shirts urging "Be orderly," along with caps exhorting "Shun Waste and Vanity."

The chaos began when an insouciant reggae singer named Christy Essien jumped onto a stage erected in the middle of a vast asphalt military parade ground. In floppy camouflage fatigues, high-top Army boots, and a grass skirt, she gave the generals a mock salute. Then she rapped in pidgin about how voters should cheat the politicians who try to cheat them.

"If him bring you money, take am and chop. Make you no vote for am." ("If he tries to buy your vote, take the money and buy food. Then vote for someone else!")

This rally, one of scores held across the country in 1989, took place in Abuja, a new capital city planned in the mid-1970s when the country was stumble-down drunk with oil money.

As much as any other venue in Nigeria, the city was an apposite place to denounce the wasteful ways of the bad old politicians. Abuja has a 1,000-room, five-star Hilton Hotel with marble in every room, satellite-fed television, and imported gourmet chefs in the kitchen.

Several months after that rally in Abuja, in apparent disgust at the 30 political associations that his countrymen had come up with, General Babangida ordered the politicians to funnel their ambition into two political parties created by the military government: the National Republican Convention and the Social Democratic Party. "One a little to the right of center and one a little to the left." At the time I wrote these words, it seemed doubtful, to say the least, that soldiers could forge the structures of an elected government by imposing them from above.

A CHIEF SPEAKS OUT

In any case, the only effective speaker at the pro-democracy rally in Abuja was a Nigerian who could not be bothered with democracy. His Royal Highness, Chief of Karibi, Alhaji Abubakar Mamman, waddled slowly to the speaker's platform, sheathed in layer upon layer of white muslin, turbaned, wearing gilded sandals, and carrying an ornately carved walking stick. The chief spoke slowly and with considerable precision. He addressed his remarks to the military government, as represented by the rotund senior military officer seated in front of him, Maj. Gen. Gado Nasko. Chief Mamman proceeded to tell General Nasko that the rally was a waste of time.

"Can we really embrace political awareness in this country at this time when hunger, illiteracy, and unemployment threaten us?" the chief asked, as the querulous crowd, for the first time, actually listened to a speaker. "What about the problems of armed robbery, train robbers, cocaine dealers, and others who have robbed us? After 29 years of independence, we have not gone far."

"Your assignment," the chief said, referring to the military government's crusade to instill disciplined democratic values in Nigerians, "is too much for you."

His Royal Highness returned to his seat amid deafening applause. At a rally intended to inculcate democratic awareness, an unelected hereditary ruler thrilled voters by arguing that such awareness was impossible. Self-rule was taking shape even as self-rule was being denounced. Nigeria, once again, was falling apart while coming together. Its future was confused and terrifying and limitless.

Whether in Nigeria or elsewhere, the Africans themselves are the only way to make sense of the news out of Africa. More than any other people on earth, their future is in jeopardy and they deserve the attention of the rest of us. It is premature, I think, to pass final judgment on their experiment. Scrawled on the tailgates of exhaust-belching trucks that rumble through the back roads of West Africa is a grass-roots admonition to those inclined to write the continent off. It says: "No condition is permanent."

Article 11

Guardian Weekly, December 16, 1990

Mozambique: from dogma to doubt

Frédéric Fritscher

While peace negotiations are continuing in Rome between his government and the rebels of the Mozambican National Resistance (Renamo), President Joaquim Chissano of Mozambique has begun to abandon old Marxist dogmas and steer his country, ruined by years of civil war, along the road to political pluralism. It was on December 1 that the country's new constitution based on multi-party rule took effect.

MAPUTO—With the exception of Mozambique Avenue, which winds between the estuary and the airport on the outskirts of the capital, Vladimir Lenin Avenue is the longest road in town. It runs parallel to Karl Marx Avenue, which is just as wide, but shorter, and does not cross Mao Zedong Avenue where the American Cultural Centre and the USSR's Novosti Press Agency are housed in the same block. Naturally, Friedrich Engels also has his avenue—the United States ambassador lives there. Mozambique has sacrificed much to socialist theoreticians.

"Let us study and become acquainted with an instrument for liberating the people." "Fight for victory and the triumph of the Revolution." The black letters of the slogans painted on the walls on July 24th Avenue are beginning to flake away. Sometimes you come across great militant frescoes which also testify to the socialist fervour of the early years of independence.

Revolutionary paintings have however failed to protect Maputo from the slings and arrows of time. The city is falling apart. The roads are pitted with potholes. Buildings are in a state of advanced disrepair. Worksites abandoned by the Portuguese colonial rulers when the country gained independence in 1975 have been left in the same state. On the road to the beach, between Maputo's disused motor-racing track and the concentration camp architecture of the new residence housing South Africa's trade mission employees, the concrete skeleton of an unfinished 24-storey-high luxury hotel reaches into the sky waiting for walls that will never come.

Yet the charms of Lourenço Marques, formerly a holiday resort so appreciated by South Africa's middle class, are once more beginning to show from beneath Maputo's leprous scab. People seeking a certain type of leisure flock to what is left of the Navy Club, the Maritime Club and the Costa do Sol complexes. The cafe terraces are inviting. The markets and shops are well-stocked. Which was not the case just a few years ago.

The first effects of the economic rehabilitation programme launched in January 1987 with the International Monetary Fund's and the World Bank's backing are beginning to be felt. Unfortunately, not everybody is benefiting from them. In the shadow of Frelimo (Mozambican Liberation Front), the country's single ruling party, a privileged class has prospered, while the rest of the population has become poorer. The establishment has benefited indirectly from massive worldwide financial support. Corruption, formerly the exception, is now rapidly becoming the rule.

"Previously there was nothing, but we had money," said Eusebio, a cab driver who owned a shiny new Peugeot 405. "Today the shops are full, but we can't buy a thing."

At the Mercado do Povo, the people's market, a live chicken costs 6,000 meticals (£3.60). A doctor earns 100,000 meticals (£60) a month and a company driver barely 30,000 meticals (£18).

The strikes that broke out in December 1989 in protest against a dramatic reduction of the purchasing power flared again in February with the announcement of a new round of price increases. The cost of basic foodstuffs shot up steeply: 64 per cent for rice, 25 per cent for maize and so on. The government attempted to get on top of the situation by legalising the right to strike while at the same time taking the strikers in hand with the help of the single official union. But it was mid-March before conditions returned to normal.

In such circumstances, it is difficult to get the public to appreciate the reforms currently being introduced. And yet, Mozambique is in the course of resolutely turning its back on its erstwhile ideals. Frelimo's sixth congress in July 1989 sounded the death knell of "Marxism-Leninism." The National Assembly has just adopted a new constitution founded on multi-party rule. The Republic of Mozambique, which is no longer a "people's republic", has a new national anthem. The liberalisation of the economy has begun with the privatisation of 31 state-owned enterprises. And most important of all, the government is starting to talk to those who had always been branded in the local press as "armed bandits"—supporters of Renamo. Mozambique's late president, Samora Machel, must be turning in his grave.

President Chissano, who has been in office since 1986, firmly grasped the nettle when in January 1990 he proposed debates on a new constitution. The discussions lasted three months. Big public rallies did not produce the expected results, unlike meetings at places of work where union mobilisation was completely effective. Public radio covered the debates with great frankness and the official daily, Noticias, happily published the discussions. The party college even came out in favour of multi-party rule.

It was not yet in the bag, however. While the politburo, which was theoretically close to the President, went along with the transition to multi-party rule, the central committee members on the other hand dragged their feet and resigned themselves to taking the step only in mid-August after a stormy session, because they were convinced they would come out on top at the next elections thanks to Chissano's good public image and the strong position of the state apparatus in the country.

The long parliamentary debate in early October revealed new splits in Frelimo. Chissano himself had to step in to oppose some politburo members who supported "black power" and were looking for a subterfuge to keep whites and Indians out of responsible posts. Such a policy would have led to a xenophobic campaign likely to jeopardise liberal reforms, and the reconciliation with the dissidents and Portuguese businessmen who were being asked to return to Mozambique and invest there.

In the end, on November 2 the deputies adopted a new constitution largely inspired by Algeria's February 1989 constitution. This is not surprising. The two countries have very close ties, and most Mozambican leaders have been through Frelimo's office in Algiers between 1962 and 1975, or have spent some time in training camps that Algeria had long made available to liberation movements.

The deputies now have to examine laws governing the establishment and the functioning of political parties as well as a new election code. Legislative and presidential elections, based on universal suffrage have as of now been announced for 1991. This testifies to a fine optimism, to put it no higher, on the part of the authorities.

The country has in fact been devastated for years by a cruel civil war which has affected a third of Mozambique's 13 million population. True, Frelimo forces, backed by the Zimbabwean army, have been inflicting severe setbacks on Renamo in recent months, gradually regaining control of rural areas held until now by Afonso Dhlakama's rebels, mostly in Zambezi province. But as things stand, with communications still to be restored and millions of Mozambicans displaced from their homes and villages, organising elections seems quite unreal.

For the first time in 15 years there is a ray of hope on the horizon. After months of unsuccessful attempts the government and Renamo are talking directly. In August 1989, President Chissano asked the Christian churches to establish contacts with Renamo and at the same time named as his mediators the presidents of Kenya and Zimbabwe who in June arranged to hold a Frelimo-Renamo meeting in Blantyre, Malawi.

But the meeting did not take place. Noting the failure of a purely African initiative, Chissano went through the Santo Egidio Catholic community, which is well established in the country, to resume talks with Renamo. The first contacts took place in Rome in July. Present at the talks were Italy's former secretary of state for cooperation Mario Raffaelli (Italy is Mozambique's leading financial backer) and Jaime Gonçalves, archbishop of Beira, who belongs to the same Ndau tribe as Afonso Dhlakama, the rebel leader.

The first conversations did not result in a ceasefire, but they were "frank and open". A further meeting was set for mid-August. As on the previous occasion, the two delegations were led by Mozambique's Transport Minister Armando Guebuza and Renamo's Raul Domingos, who is in charge of foreign affairs. They agreed to meet again soon, but still there was no ceasefire.

Renamo dragged its feet about coming to a third meeting which finally began on November 9 in Rome under Italian auspices. The rebel movement's hesitations reflected the disarray in which Chissano's initiative had plunged it. The Mozambican President had in fact cut the ground from under Dhlakama's feet, for a new constitution had been the latter's constant demand. What else was there basically left to negotiate apart from the withdrawal of Zimbabwean troops, except—perhaps—a transitional stage that would stave off elections for a few years to give Renamo time to find and train the managers it so badly needs?

During the transition period, Chissano could appoint a government of national unity consisting of men acceptable to Renamo. This solution is not as far-fetched as it may seem. Mozambique is one of the world's poorest countries and can no longer afford to abide by a "logic of war".

(December 1)

Article 12

AFRICA NEWS
January 29, 1990

Favored Few Tap Zaire Wealth

At a time when Africa is actively courting American business, U.S. firms have found their path to one of Africa's largest mining companies blocked by an unorthodox arrangement with a New Jersey food broker.

President Mobutu Sese Seko of Zaire has granted a lucrative contract to a company controlled by one of his long-time American supporters, Grover Connell. Under the agreement, Connell Rice and Sugar Company holds exclusive rights to procure most of the equipment, spare parts and other items obtained in the U.S. by Gecamines, the government-owned mineral giant in Zaire.

To the handful of diplomats, bankers and corporate officials who have known about it, the Connell contract illustrates the extent to which U.S. relations with Zaire revolve around a group of prominent Americans, whose ability to do business there is based on personal ties to Mobutu, and whose financial interests are closely intertwined with efforts to win friends and influence for Zaire and its leader.

Although not a public figure, Grover Connell is a wealthy businessman with good political connections. On Capitol Hill, he is well-known for an unusual $84,000-a-year seminar program, under which members of Congress have been receiving honoraria for visiting Connell headquarters in Westfield, New Jersey. According to data compiled by Common Cause, Connell Rice disbursed $2,000 each, the legal limit, to 39 House members and three Senators in 1988 and paid out the same amount in 1987.

Zaireans have the fifth lowest incomes in the world.

The program makes Connell the largest corporate donor of Congressional honoraria, a controversial channel for political contributions. (Under the pay-raise legislation adopted by the House of Representatives in December, members are now barred from accepting honoraria, but the Senate still permits the practice.) Only four large trade associations, led by the Tobacco Institute, gave more to members of Congress than Connell did in 1988, the last year for which figures are available.

Earlier this month, four House members who have received Connell honoraria travelled with Grover Connell to Zaire, where his company handles the largest share of U.S. government food aid contracts under the Food for Peace program.

Zaire, a strategically-located central African nation bordering nine other countries, has one of the world's most impoverished populations and one of its most flamboyantly wealthy leaders. Since seizing control of the former Belgian Congo in a 1965 CIA-backed coup, Mobutu has held virtually absolute sovereignty. He also relies heavily on support from Western governments, particularly France and the U.S. – and sometimes from Belgium, Zaire's former colonial ruler with whom relations have been stormy.

Successive American administrations have backed Mobutu on the premise that he is the only leader capable of holding together the vast nation – about the size of the U. S. east of the Mississippi River – and a treasure house of minerals.

But Mobutu's reputation for human rights abuses, lavish spending and corruption has tarnished his public image. "Congress has restricted aid to Zaire partly because it is a plutocracy where resources are diverted from their assigned destinations and have historically been so," Rep. Howard Wolpe, chairman of the House Africa subcommittee said last year. "We have seen, in this subcommittee, evidence that literally hundreds and hundreds of millions of dollars have vanished into the hands or the bank accounts of the president and his collaborators."

According to diplomatic sources, Connell Rice and Sugar has been collecting a 30% commission on Gecamines purchases in the U.S. since the contract was signed in early 1988. The purchases normally average about $5 million a month, providing annual earnings for the Connell company of more than $15 million. These fees are

Rebecca Kohler/Africa News

"far out of line with anything anyone else is charging," says one knowledgeable official. Although he expressed his willingness to talk with Africa News, Connell repeatedly failed to be available for an interview.

There was heavy resistance to the Connell contract at Gecamines, says the official. "They had no desire to have this rice dealer charge them for something they had been doing for themselves," the official says. But Mobutu – whose photograph appears on the frontispiece of the annual report – effectively controls the company by appointing its top officials. And he apparently wanted the contract signed.

At the World Bank and International Monetary Fund, where Zaire is seeking assistance to meet payments on its crippling $8 billion foreign debt, Connell's lock on procurement and his price tag have caused dismay. Gecamines is by far the country's largest business, producing copper and cobalt worth about $800 million to $1.3 billion a year (depending on market conditions) and providing up to three-quarters of Zaire's export earnings.

Because of its vital role in contributing foreign exchange to Zaire's ailing economy, Gecamines is kept under close scrutiny by the international lending institutions, and irregularities have been uncovered throughout the mining company's history.

Although the contract with Connell is seen as "perfectly legal," according to one knowledgeable official, there is concern that the high commissions are reducing revenues that are badly needed for Zaire's overdue loan payments and for budgetary outlays under an IMF economic stabilization program.

Following protests by Zaire's lenders and donors, Gecamines payments to Connell have been reduced, the official says. A number of Gecamines suppliers are now refusing to work through Connell and are making sales directly to the mining company, as they did before the contract was signed, industry sources report.

Still, the contract is regarded as part of a continuing pattern under which Zaire's budget and its mining revenues serve as a "private pool of funds for Mobutu and his friends," in the words of one senior international economist.

"Frankly, I'm not sure what the hell is happening to that money," says a lending institution officer. But many officials are convinced the funds are somehow being rerouted to seek greater support for Zaire in Washington and around the country.

For more than a quarter of a century, Mobutu has assiduously wooed America's leaders. He has been a frequent visitor to the White House since 1963, when, as head of the army but not yet head of state, he was received by John F. Kennedy. He has already managed three separate encounters with President George Bush – more than any other African head of state – twice at the White House last year and once at Emperor Hirohito's funeral in Tokyo.

Bush is probably the closest friend Mobutu has had in the Oval Office. By Mobutu's count, the two men have met 15 times since Bush first visited Kinshasa in 1972 while serving as U.S. ambassador to the United Nations. Bush has sailed on Mobutu's luxurious Zaire River yacht, and the Zaire president has been included in a congenial family dinner at the Bush retreat in Kennebunkport, Maine.

Mobutu told interviewers last year that Bush came to "know Zaire's problems by heart" during his year as head of the CIA.

On the Democratic side, Mobutu's most important and longest-standing relationship has been with New York diamond magnate Maurice Tempelsman, a leading political fundraiser who is also current chair of the African-American Institute. His business involvement in the country is as old as the Mobutu government.

Over the years, Tempelsman has served as an important intermediary with both Democratic and Republican administrations and has negotiated business deals in Zaire worth hundreds of millions of dollars for American, South African and Japanese firms.

More recently, the Zaire leader has developed ties with several members of the Congressional Black Caucus, particularly the immediate past chair, Mervyn Dymally of California. In 1988, at Dymally's request, Mobutu contributed $250,000 to a California charity, Coalition for a Free Africa (CFA), founded by Dick Griffey, a friend and campaign contributor to both Dymally and former presidential candidate Jesse Jackson.

Mobutu has also made extensive use of paid lobbyists to plead his case in Washington. Currently, Zaire employs two firms. One of them, van Kloberg and Associates, headed by Edward J. van Kloberg, III, has a history of representing controversial governments, among them Zaire's closest East European ally, Romania. Zaire's other contract is with Black, Manafort, Stone, and Kelly, a public relations company with high-level Republican ties which also represents the Unita rebel movement of Angola, headed by Jonas Savimbi.

Some of Zaire's earlier Washington representatives were drawn from the world of the fabulously wealthy. In the mid-1980s, they included Nael el-Assad, a relative of Saudi Arabian arms merchant Adnan Khashoggi, once one of the richest non-head-of-states in the world; and Robert Maheu, the ex-FBI man who helped the CIA recruit a Mafia hitman to try to kill Fidel Castro and in the 1970s served as chief assistant to that decade's richest American, the late Howard Hughes.

Altogether, Zaire has spent over $3 million in the past five years seeking to influence American policy. But the debate in Washington has shifted very little. Each administration has continued supporting Mobutu, seeing him as the only viable option for protecting the interests of Zaire, while his critics in Congress have fought to restrict and reduce foreign aid.

The latest and most serious challenge to the Zaire leader on Capitol Hill is the near-total aid cutoff – on grounds of "uncontrollable corruption" – proposed by Rep. Ronald Dellums (D-CA), who chairs the Congressional Black Caucus. When he first introduced the legislation in 1988, Dellums received the backing of most of his Caucus colleagues and many other members as well. But Mobutu has made inroads into that support by aggressively reaching out to the Caucus membership.

At the center of the effort has been Mamadi Diane, a Guinean-born businessman who heads a shipping brokerage firm, Amex International, which is the agent for U.S. government food aid shipments to Zaire.

Diane and Connell have business connections dating back to the mid-1970s, when Diane worked for the St. John International Company. Connell was part owner of an affiliate company, St. John Maritime, which was implicated in the Tongsun Park Koreagate rice-buying scandal.

Park, a U.S.-educated Korean businessman, gave hundreds of thousands of dollars to members of Congress, both to boost support for South Korea's military dictatorship and to win Food for Peace contracts for his business associates. He was convicted of making bribes, but charges against Connell were dismissed in 1979, after Park withdrew his allegations that Connell knew about the scheme.

Today, all three men have close ties to Mobutu, as well as overlapping African involvements. Diane serves as shipping agent for Food for Peace consignments to Zaire, while Connell Rice supplies much of the food.

Park's precise relationship with Mobutu remains a mystery, but he appears to be playing both a political and a business role. When Rep. Dan Burton of Indiana, the ranking Republican on the House Africa subcommittee, stopped off in Zaire after visiting Savimbi in Angola last year, he says he was surprised to encounter Park at Gbadolite, Mobutu's presidential palace. Last June, according to columnist Jack Anderson, Park was present when Paul Manafort met with Mobutu to secure the lobbying contract.

Both Connell and Diane have been active in promoting Congressional visits to Zaire. The four members of the House who accompanied Connell there this month include two liberal Democrats from his state, Robert Torricelli and Robert Mrazek, as well as Mike Espy, a black Democrat from Mississippi, and Bill Lowery, a Republican from California. Torricelli has received $6,000 in honoraria from Connell over three years, Lowery $4,000 and Mrazek and Espy $2,000 each.

Two years ago, Mrazek authored a letter to Mobutu, co-signed by 47 other House members, which expressed disquiet about "persistent reports of widespread government corruption and human rights abuses." Torricelli and Espy were among the co-signers. Mrazek says he is still concerned about political freedoms in Zaire, but he is hopeful of a "more forthcoming attitude on the part of the Zairean government with respect to human rights." Mrazek says his airfare was paid out of Congressional travel funds; while in Zaire the four Congressmen were guests of the Zaire government.

Diane has organized trips to Zaire for Dymally and other black members of Congress, and he has actively lobbied Zaire's cause on Capitol Hill. In 1988, he established the Zaire American Research Institute (ZARI) in Washington, D.C. to "promote friendship, cooperation, and improved relations" and to engage in research and disseminate information, according to incorporation papers filed with the District of Columbia government. The organization's 1988 tax records indicate that initial funding of $100,000 was used to open an office on K Street and hire an executive director, Marva Jo Camp, who had been an aide to Dymally. Last year, Camp was replaced by Glenwood Roane, an attorney who has been director in three African countries for the U.S. Agency for International Development, AID.

Funding for the institute has come from Zaire businessmen, Roane said in an interview. The largest contributor has been Bemba Saolona, chairman of Zaire's principal business organization. Bemba is widely regarded as one of Mobutu's closest advisors and business associates. He owns a string of manufacturing, agricultural and distribution companies, as well as SCIBE, the country's second largest airline.

Roane says Bemba contributed about $90,000 to ZARI in 1989 – out of a total budget of some $220,000. Another $12,000 was given by the General Motors subsidiary in Zaire, GMAZ. In addition, Bemba provided air transport for a group of black mayors who were taken to Zaire by ZARI in June. In May, ZARI received an $80,000 transfer from the Swiss Bank account of Idrissa Toure, a Guinean believed to be associated with Diane in several business ventures.

In the coming year, Roane says, ZARI will concentrate on helping Zaire formulate a "responsible policy" for handling its immense rain forest. "President Mobutu is fully aware of the importance of that resource," Roane says, "and we want to move quickly to assist efforts to preserve it." Whether Zaire can obtain a reduction of its debt by promising to preserve its forests, in the sort of "debt-for-nature" exchange that international lending agencies have been discussing with Brazil, is undetermined. But ZARI hopes to coordinate an international conference to examine all aspects of the rain forest question to be held in Zaire late this year.

While ZARI and Diane have concentrated on the Black Caucus, van Kloberg has focussed on improving Zaire's image among other members of Congress and in the news media. Working under a two-year, $300,000 agreement, the firm made most of the arrangements for Mobutu's official trip to Washington last July, which included not only an Oval Office visit but also meetings on Capitol Hill and a session with reporters at Blair House. Van Kloberg also handled a follow-up trip by the vice prime minister, Nimy Mayidika Ngimbi, whom Mobutu has put in charge of "citizen's rights and liberties."

More recently, the firm has put together two issues of a newsletter, *Zaire News* and plans to establish a Zaire-American friendship committee, composed of prominent figures from both countries.

After his June visit, Mobutu beefed up the PR effort. He signed a one year, $1 million contract with Black, Manafort, Stone and Kelly immediately following his departure from the U.S., where he reportedly was angered by criticisms of his government in news reports and from members of Congress. The Black Manafort firm has managed three successful visits for Jonas Savimbi, whose warm welcome here is something that has eluded Mobutu. Charles Black and Paul Manafort, the firms' principals, played leading roles in the Bush presidential campaign of 1988, alongside their former partner, Lee Atwater, the Bush campaign manager and current chair of the Republican National Committee.

In the forefront of the campaign against Mobutu over the past two years has been the Rainbow Lobby, a Washington, D.C.-based group affiliated with the New Alliance Party but unconnected to Jesse Jackson's Rainbow Coalition. The Rainbow Lobby has actively promoted the Dellums Bill and has forged links with leading Zaire opposition figures. The group has attacked Dymally for his Zaire-related activities, and Dymally has responded in kind.

Last year, Glenwood Roane of ZARI sued the Lobby for defamation in connection with remarks made by Howard University professor Nzongola Ntalaja at a Rainbow Lobby-sponsored seminar. But Roane has recently dropped the suit. In another counter-attack, a forthcoming article in the magazine *American Spectator* by David Brock, who is highly critical of Mobutu's Congressional adversaries, alleges that the Lobby "set up" Rep. Gus Savage (D-IL) to keep him from joining the Black Caucus defections from the Dellums bill. Savage has been accused by a Peace Corps volunteer of sexually molesting her during a visit Savage made to Zaire with Diane last year.

Van Kloberg has led the campaign against the Rainbow Lobby and is credited with achieving results on Capitol Hill for his controversial

Steve Askin/Africa News

President Mobutu's Fond de Roi *"Palace of the Kings" in Brussels, Belguim – is one of his many mansions.*

client. Black Manafort's role, on the other hand, remains fuzzy. "We never see them at all," says one administration aide. As with the Connell contract with Gecamines, insiders are asking what the firm is doing to earn its high fee. Black Manafort officials won't comment on their activities.

Dymally's role in obtaining gifts and contracts in Africa for political associates has provoked questions about possible conflicts of interest, including a complaint to the House Ethics Committee from the U.S.-Congo Friendship Committee, a Rainbow Lobby ally.

In June, the *Journal of Commerce* reported that Dymally had written to Ugandan President Yoweri Museveni, protesting his government's decision to hire as its agents for food aid shipments "a firm other than Amex International," Diane's company.

Dymally has also intervened with the Angolan government to obtain oil shipping contracts for Dick Griffey, who owns Solar Records and the African Development Public Interest Corporation (ADPIC), a Hollywood trading company. Griffey says during one trip to Luanda, Dymally introduced him to Angolan officials and said "the best way" for the government to resolve its problems with the United States is "to make contact with the African-American community" and "to find a black American and do business with him." Angola has been seeking to convince Washington to end its support for the Unita insurgency and normalize diplomatic relations.

On another occasion, the *Washington Post* has reported, Dymally used a meeting in Washington with Angolan oil minister Pedro de Castro Van-Dunem Loy to ask that Luanda expedite processing of a $12 million shipment already agreed to for Griffey's ADPIC.

In 1988, Griffey's Coalition for a Free Africa paid part of the expenses for part of an African tour which took him to seven nations, and later to Brazil. During his travels, Dymally says he sought to raise additional funding for CFA. So far, the only sizeable donation the coalition has received beyond Mobutu's $250,000 is some $300,000 contributed by Griffey, according to Virgil Roberts, Griffey's general counsel and president of ADPIC.

Dymally also sought an oil contract in Angola for Camp, the former ZARI executive director and part-time Dymally aide. He made the request in a letter to Angola's ambassador in New York Manuel Pacavira.

Both Griffey and Dymally adamently dispute charges that they are involved in conflicts of interest or profiteering at Africa's expense. Dymally insists that his efforts are a legitimate and important part of his role as a black political leader. "I see nothing wrong with helping black businessmen get contracts in Zaire or anywhere else," Dymally said in an interview. Criticism of him for these actions "is all racism," he says. White Americans and Europeans have a corner on most business opportunities in Africa," he charges, "and they don't want to share them."

Griffey says he is not getting involved in Africa to make money. The $250,000 Mobutu contribution to CFA had "nothing to do," Griffey says, with his business activities.

"I'm going to do something that helps the people," he says. "I see Africa as the new frontier, the world's richest continent, the world's poorest people."

Article 13

WORLD HEALTH, March 1990

EQUATORIAL GUINEA
Hope for the future

Patricio Rojas

Dr Patricio Rojas is the WHO Representative in Malabo, Equatorial Guinea.

An emergency situation – this is how the national authorities have described the present state of health and health services in Equatorial Guinea, a small country with a population of 340,000 situated on the Gulf of Guinea, in Central Africa.

A decade under a repressive regime (1969-1979) left the public services virtually derelict and brought about the collapse of internal and external communications, a drastic drop in agricultural production (cocoa, wood, coffee), the drying up of foreign investment and a steady exodus of the few nationals who had been trained for the

(WHO/P. Rojas)

Street scene in the capital, Malabo.

production, service and administration sectors. Violations of human rights forced nearly one-third of the country's population into exile. The end of the dictatorial regime in 1979 afforded a chance to draw up plans for democratic rule and national recovery aimed essentially at ending the social and economic chaos, revitalising national development and improving the living standard.

But in spite of tremendous efforts and the sustained support of friendly countries and international agencies, the country's situation remains critical. Thus for instance there has been no significant improvement in indicators of health and the quality of life in recent years. Indeed, some of these indicators remain alarmingly low: infant mortality is estimated at 145 per 1,000 and no more than four per cent of the population has access to drinking water.

Equatorial Guinea is confronted by a whole range of health problems, from the virtual ruin of most of the physical infrastructure in the health sector to acute shortage of all types of resources. The absence of any integrated health development strategy has also prevented more rational use of technical and financial assistance from bilateral and international agencies. So the real challenge is to define objectives, establish priorities and draw up realistic action plans at a point where the country's needs are pressingly urgent.

Drastic problems call for bold measures. In Equatorial Guinea, general mobilisation is under way to promote health development from the highest political level down to the People's Councils throughout the country, of which there are more than 1,500. The overall objective is to establish a health infrastructure based on primary health care in the next four years; the government and health workers have joined forces with ordinary people of the country to try to make Health for all a reality by the year 2000.

WHO has actively helped the health authorities based in the capital, Malabo, to identify priority problems and channel human, material and financial resources to tackle them. Efforts are afoot too to draw up strategies for the health sector, to coordinate the best possible use of resources from bilateral cooperation and international agencies, to involve other agencies of the UN system in health programmes, and to concentrate WHO resources in priority areas and encourage inter-agency projects to deal with urgent problems.

Three-phase scenario

WHO's technical cooperation programme for Equatorial Guinea has steadily been intensified. A three-phase scenario for health development promulgated by the Regional Office for Africa gives due attention to the needs of the local, intermediate and central levels of the health sector. Four projects funded by UNDP, UNICEF and the World Bank are now under way, with WHO as the executing agency. In a country where diarrhoea, malaria and measles have a high epidemiological profile, the need to strengthen basic programmes to control these diseases is urgent. Meanwhile, the infrastructure for primary health care must be developed, as the only means of extending the activities of these programmes and achieving adequate coverage of vulnerable groups. WHO's technical assistance concentrates precisely on these programmes, both in their technical aspects and in the more general areas of management and administration.

WHO is now putting into effect six projects funded from the regular budget and four with extra-budgetary funding which address the country's most urgent health needs. In addition, a special fund has been approved by the Regional Committee for those countries which qualify as the least developed in Africa. In the case of Equatorial Guinea, this fund has been used to build or rehabilitate health centres for urban fringe areas, to equip emergency units in the national referral hospitals, to provide supplies of essential drugs and to strengthen the Ministry of Health as an institution.

Since coordination is vital to ensure that all resources available for health are properly used, WHO has forged close contacts with the bilateral cooperation agencies at work in the country, particularly with the Spanish Cooperation Agency, which maintains 70 per cent of the primary health infrastructure in all parts of the country.

EQUATORIAL GUINEA adjoins Cameroon and Gabon on the Western coast of Africa. Covering 10,800 square miles, including the island of Bioko (formerly Fernando Po), it has a population of 340,000 and its capital is Malabo. ■

These efforts and resources alone will not suffice to guarantee the success of health development activities. Indeed, without the organized involvement of the community in these tasks it would be difficult, if not impossible, to lay the foundations for any improvement in health anywhere. Fortunately, Equatorial Guinea has a strong and extensive network which is well-fitted to mobilise communities in health activities. With the agreement of the People's Councils, the projects of WHO and other agencies are bringing about a community-based infrastructure for health, which is the key to attaining Health for all. And so, although the health situation is still far from being under control, it is nevertheless possible to look to the future with a considerable degree of optimism.

Article 14 *Guardian Weekly,* December 16, 1990

The Horn of Famine

Julian Summers

Famine is again threatening a huge area of Africa, from Ethiopia through Sudan and Chad to Niger in the west, with hundreds of thousands of deaths possible in a repeat of the 1984–5 disaster in which a million people died in northern Ethiopia alone.

From the hot desert floor outside the Red Sea port of Assab our Hercules climbs into the sky and heads inland. For an hour, the plane flies north-east across the Danakil desert. Then, out of the arid, featureless plain below rises the massive eastern escarpment of the Ethiopian highlands, like an island rising from a sea. Our plane does not so much land at Asmara as the earth comes up to meet it.

Touching down is a dangerous exercise. Since February last year the Eritrean People's Liberation Front (EPLF) has shelled Asmara's airport from the hills and valleys beyond on an almost daily basis. But the aircraft is on the ground for just 12 minutes: in that time, 20 tons of flour are off-loaded by a team of 30 porters, straight on to a truck backed into the rear of the aircraft. As the relief food heads for the distribution centres in the city, the Hercules is already on its way back to Assab to reload.

Two planes repeat the hazardous journey from Ethiopia's only operable port to the Eritrean capital four times each day, seven days a week. Since rebel forces occupied Eritrea's own port of Massawa earlier this year, the United Nations' airlift has represented the only life-line for the people of Asmara and surrounding countryside. For these million and a half people, home is a besieged enclave afloat on its high plateau above EPLF-controlled territory, another island rising from the arid lowlands. It is an island supplied from the air.

But the 160 tonnes of food the planes bring in daily is not nearly enough to feed a population which has seen the harvest fail four times in the years since the famine of 1984–85. To reach the one million people currently affected by food shortages in the government-held enclave, at least twice that quantity of food would be needed.

The ring round the highlands is squeezing the life from Eritrea's capital. It is perhaps the most beautiful city in Africa: set at 8,000 feet on the lip of the great escarpment, it is an Italian-designed art deco masterpiece of jacaranda and palm lined avenues and villas wreathed in bougainvillaeas, a planned city populated by a gracious African people. The highland air is clear and in the perfectly preserved avenues of the city people used to stroll each evening to its cafes and squares to enjoy the temperate climate.

But now when dusk falls the city simply goes to sleep. There is no electricity, no diesel fuel for generators or vehicles, and no water in the mains. In the darkness, looking out on the once prosperous city, you might well be deep in the countryside. And what to European eyes looks at first like Asmara's quaint 1930s calm—its simple, stylish shop fronts and car-free avenues frozen in time, like an illustration from the French primer we used to have at school—is revealed not as peace but as the quiet of the grave, brought on by 30 years of war.

Eritrea has always had a structural food deficit. Settled agriculture has been practised for at least three thousand years on these lands, the seat of Ethiopia's ancient Axumite civilisation.

But so intense has been the tilling of the soil over the years that it is now exhausted. While Eritrea's strong, industrial base and good roads meant that in earlier times it could afford to buy in grain from the more fertile central and south of Ethiopia, the war of secession—which effectively began when Emperor Haile Selassie annexed the territory in 1961—has all but destroyed the economy.

Eritrea now depends on international food aid, but as the EPLF's military campaign grinds on the problem of delivering that food grows ever more acute.

At Geshnashum, a small village 20 miles to the north of Asmara just off the main road to Keren, the effects of the 10-month siege and disruption to the food supply from Massawa are beginning to bite. In the three weeks before our visit, 30 people had died, and in the ad hoc clinic set up in the schoolroom, eight more patients suffer in silence on intravenous drips.

The killer is not famine alone: this rural area, like the one to the west of Asmara, is in the grip of a malaria epidemic which is extremely unusual for these highlands. In a good time the young and fit would be expected to resist the incursions of this lowland disease. Six years of recurrent famine, and the recent deprivations of the siege, mean the malaria epidemic has claimed even the strongest, now weakened by persistent malnourishment.

Walking around the village among the young crowd animated by our visit are four small children, each carrying an even smaller child on their back. These four are infants suffering severe malnutrition: three have swollen legs and belly, the tell-tale signs of kwashiakor, the other the sunken eyes and skeletal frame of marasmus. It would nearly always be possible to seek out a malnourished child in the poorer rural villages of Ethiopia and Eritrea. But four, without looking, is an indication of how advanced is the famine now stalking these beautiful, blighted lands.

On each succeeding visit to Asmara and the highlands of Eritrea you find yourself thinking: people cannot go on this way, something has to give. But on each return conditions have grown a little worse, and people have continued along the knife's edge with astounding resilience. This time though the signs of impending disaster are overwhelming.

For the second year running, the rains have failed disastrously in the highlands. Only about one-tenth of the normal rain fell, and its erratic pattern has sabotaged any hope of a harvest. On the road south of Asmara to Adi Quala and Tigray, the crops in the field stand thin and uneven, balding in patches as if grown old. Farmer Tewolde Seyoum is harvesting as we pass, sooner than normal because he can expect no further growth from his still immature crops. He shows us a head of t'eff, the staple cereal for all of highland Ethiopia, and rubbing it between his palms separates the grain. There is a meagre yield of tiny, reddish seed, less than half of what he would usually expect. Indicating a donkey laden with his freshly cut crops, he says he expected just five kilos of t'eff from that bundled load. From his entire landholding, he anticipated just 50 kilos of cereal.

"It is enough to feed my family for only a couple of months," he said. "After that we'll have nothing."

The story is the same throughout Eritrea, much of Tigray and Wello to the south, and the province of Haraghe in the east. As many as two million people in Eritrea and at least as many again in Tigray and Wello face famine.

The only part of the north country which expects a good harvest in 1990 is the traditionally fertile western region of Tigray, Shire.

For the second year running the rains have failed from the Horn of Africa through the Sahel. In addition, wars in Eritrea and Ethiopia, southern Sudan and eastern Chad have displaced millions of people, disrupted food production and absorbed the major part of government budgets.

On the road which runs through Tewolde's land from Shire, Tigrayan merchants with droves of donkeys laden with t'eff are making their way north from their more fertile fields to take advantage of prices driven sky high by the siege in Eritrea.

Merchants tell us that a 100-kilo sack of t'eff bought in Shire for 230 Ethiopian Birr, or around £60, fetches 570 Birr from merchants in the town of Adi Quala, just inside Eritrea. Once transported to Asmara itself, these entrepreneurial merchants can expect to sell again at 700 Birr, or £185.

It is good business for the merchants but, ironically, eastern Tigray will probably be in need of this food later in the year to meet shortages brought on by its own drought and a possible 50 per cent crop failure.

In Asmara, the pragmatic and undramatic head of the Catholic Secretariat, which administers the only relief programme in the government enclave by means of the Hercules airlift, shows not a moment's doubt when asked to describe the seriousness of the people's plight. Franciscan priest Abba Paulos Fessehaye says, "This famine will be the worst in 10 years. People are dying already."

Once again then, Abba Paulos and supporting relief agencies like Cafod are soliciting food and funds from western donors to sustain food deliveries into next year. But while all the agencies are much better prepared now than five years ago to face the crisis, the logistics grow ever more complex.

The EPLF's own relief wing, the Eritrean Relief Association (ERA), and its equivalent in rebel-held Tigray, Rest, will be bringing food across the border from Sudan. But the actions of the Islamic military government there, with its support for Iraq, have antagonised Western donor governments and may interfere with ERA and Rest's operations. Sudan's own food shortages may also place pressure on stocks being transported through its territory to other destinations.

The remarkable "Southern Line" operation, in which a consortium of the Ethiopian churches co-ordinates the trucking of food from Assab through the front line into rebel-held northern Wello and Tigray, will also be sustained as long as military positions hold.

Together with internal purchases of surplus grain in places like Shire, and the cross-border operation, these proven methods—given donor support—should not head off the worst that the drought can bring.

It is in the besieged highlands around Asmara that disaster lies in wait. With the airlift bringing in only half of the food needed, most beneficiaries in the city are surviving on half rations every two months. Added to their gnawing hunger are the shortages of water and fuel, the rocketing prices, the limited freedom, the aerial bombardment of artillery and mortar.

But these are city people, and their capacity for survival, either through the help of relatives outside or the work of merchants and contrabandists, means they have coped this far, 10 months into the siege. The farmers of the outlying villages have far fewer of these advantages, and it is they who are suffering first.

For one Hercules to fly in its 80 tons each day for a month from the coast at Assab into the enclave costs donors around $1 million. At that price, the argument in favour of funding the other two aircraft needed to sustain the people is undermined by the difficulty of raising the money from governments when there is a much more sensible solution to the logistics equation.

That is the mounting of an across-the-lines relief operation from Massawa into Asmara and the highlands, a journey of less than a day. It would be infinitely more efficient than either the airlift or the option of extending the trucks on the Southern Line into Eritrea from Assab, a six-day journey.

But the political and military stalemate has stalled hopes of re-opening Massawa since the EPLF turned away a United Nations' survey team which had come to inspect the damage inflicted on the port by heavy fighting and subsequent air-raids by the Ethiopian Air Force. After years of criticism for preventing food from reaching the starving, the Ethiopian government's apparent new flexibility, and the high degree of accountability achieved for food aid distributed within government areas, has put the Eritrean nationalists on the defensive.

Negotiations to re-open Massawa continue, and in the meantime the people of besieged Asmara wait for some conclusion, any conclusion, to the war. In its 30-year course, the war has been characterised by long periods of stalemate punctuated by spells of frenetic military activity. The EPLF claims they could take Asmara whenever they wish. Fighting is now centred around Decemehare, on the road to Tigray, and at Ghinda.

Twelve years ago, the Eritrean nationalists held the whole of the territory except Asmara itself. With a massive input of weapons from the Soviet Union, the Ethiopian army rolled them back to the lowlands by stages over the next years. There is no guarantee that the war is nearing its end; even now.

While the two intransigent regimes battle with each other, and with their internal divisions, their territories are bled to death. On the day we left Asmara, the shells were coming down again near the airport. Thirty had landed the evening before, all in the field adjoining the airport road, and as we waited on the apron for the Hercules to appear in the sky overhead, another three shells came down behind the sandbagged containers which act as offices for the relief operation.

When the shelling ended, energetic porters came running over to show the shrapnel they have collected, brutal lumps of sharp metal still too hot to hold, tossed from palm to palm in display. The EPLF are too media astute to shoot down a UN relief aircraft, and they shell the area around the airport this morning probably just to ginger up the authorities.

But it is a dangerous game to play. Two weeks ago a bus waiting at the security checkpoint on the road to the airport was hit, and 18 civilians are reported to have been killed. Earlier this year, many more civilians were killed by the bombing of Massawa.

Now, in Asmara and the high plateau which surrounds it, Abba Paulos says people welcome the sound of exploding shells and gunfire because at least it means something is happening which might bring the war to an end.

For these besieged people who have known only fighting, their worst enemy now is time.

Article 15

The Christian Science Monitor, February 23, 1990

Cattle Camp in South Sudan

Despite six years of civil war, the Dinka people live with dignity and purpose

By Robert M. Press

Staff writer of The Christian Science Monitor

BOR, SUDAN

SUDDENLY there it is: a Dinka cattle camp.

From behind curtains of white smoke from dozens of small fires, cattle emerge, ambling in from the bush, heading unescorted toward their tethering pegs, where they wait patiently for women to slip a rope over their long, curved horns, and tie them down for the night.

It is an ancient scene, among the survivors of an ancient, seminomadic people. After all the devastation of six years of civil war in southern Sudan – the deaths, the fleeing, the unchecked cattle diseases that in some areas have nearly wiped out entire herds – the Dinka way of life persists: a life of dignity, purpose, and, before the war, a life of peace.

Dinka who still have cattle are doing what they've always done: caring for their beloved animals,

SHIRLEY HORN – STAFF

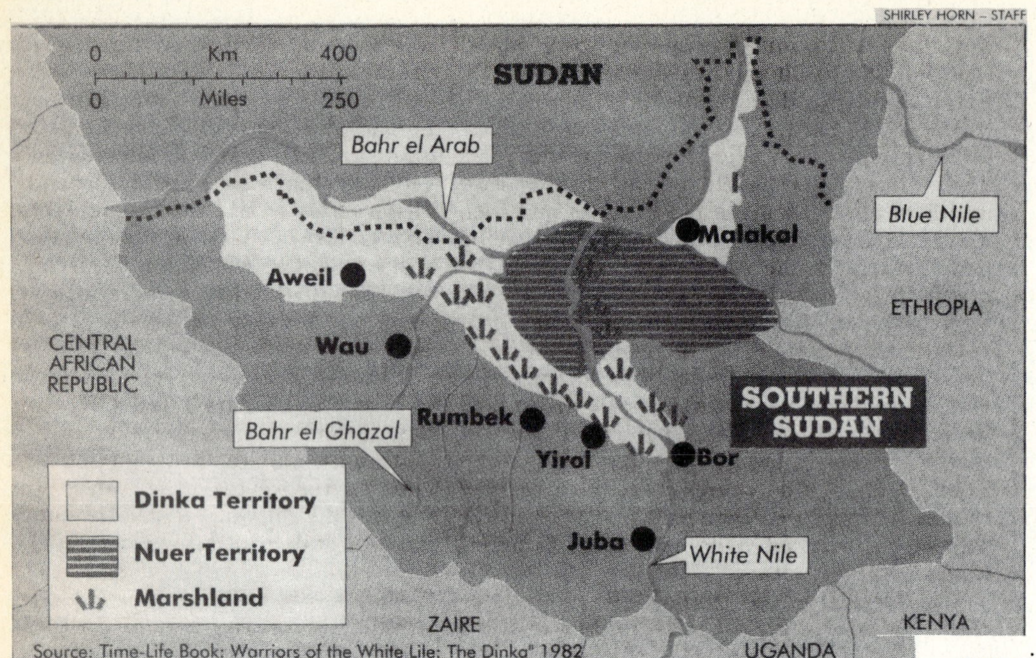

Source: Time-Life Book: Warriors of the White Lile: The Dinka" 1982

sleeping next to them at night, grazing them by day.

Cattle shape the daily routine of the Dinka, their culture, and even their language. Many Dinka names are words of different colors of cattle. Their animals provide milk, wealth, payment for brides, and a sense of pride to the owners, who decorate the horns of favorite oxen with tassels.

One of the largest and most isolated ethnic groups in Africa, the Dinka comprise some 20 tribes, sharing a common language, and living in 150,000 square miles of flat savannah in southern Sudan along the White Nile and some of its tributaries.

Here in one of their camps, alongside the road north to Bor – a road lined with occasional twisted, burned ruins of trucks and even a tank that once belonged to the Arab-controlled central government – there is still a sense of calm.

Dinka and visitors warmly greet each other. I reach out, questioningly, and touch a face covered with white ash, a ghostly cosmetic on the man's black skin. A teenage boy leads me to one of the dozens of small campfires, and shows me how to pick up the cooled ash and rub it on my face. Dinka apply the ash as a protection against the flies that swarm around the cows. Smoke from the fires keeps mosquitoes at bay.

Women in the camp are clad in one-piece, loose-fitting cloths that usually tie over one shoulder. Most of the men and boys are naked. Before the war, they started wearing shorts. But now, with the economy destroyed, few Dinka have money for clothes.

The people still wear their brass anklets, ivory necklaces, bracelets, and earrings (both men and women). One Dinka stands proudly adorned in a handsome, beaded, corset-like waistband of red, white, and blues.

Dinka men are the main source of recruits for the Dinka-led rebel Sudan People's Liberation Army (SPLA), which is fighting for a greater political voice for southerners in a united Sudan. But, as in most wars today, civilians, not fighters, are by far the main victims.

In 1988, more than 250,000 people died in southern Sudan, primarily because of starvation resulting from the war's disruption of farming, according to the United Nations. Many were Dinka. More than a million southerners have fled to other parts of Sudan or Ethiopia, seeking safety and food.

Majok Gani, a Dinka herdsman, is sitting on the ground, carving a wooden cattle prod. At first he is suspicious of the visitors, then he decides to make a plea for help. "Because of this war, our boys are not studying. There is a school here [in a nearby village], but no teacher, no chalk, no exercise books."

Wani Lado, another Dinka, says: "We have no clothes, no shoes, no salt, no sugar. You can help. Collect these talkings [words] to inform your people."

But, slowly, life is improving a little for the Dinka and others in rebel-secured areas of the south.

Cattle and child vaccination teams are reaching some areas. Schools, though with few supplies, are opening in many villages, often under trees or in grass huts. And because of UN and other relief food, and improved local crops, malnutrition in rebel areas is now minimal, according to UN officials, though government-held towns in the south, including Juba, remain critically dependent on deliveries of food aid.

Even as the two Dinka herdsmen make their appeals for additional help, children in the camp laugh excitedly at visitors. Several boys strike dance poses, curving their arms to portray the horns of the cattle that continue to be the center of Dinka life in Sudan.

Article 16

The Christian Science Monitor, July 12, 1990

SOUTHERN AFRICA

Regional Bloc Seeks Boost for Weak Economies

By John Battersby

Staff writer of The Christian Science Monitor

MAPUTO, MOZAMBIQUE

MEMBERS of a 10-nation southern African economic bloc – formed 10 years ago to reduce economic dependence on South Africa – are considering involving Pretoria in the effort to revive their regional economy and build a viable market.

"A democratic South Africa is naturally welcome to regional institutions like SADCC," said Pascoal Mocumbi, the Mozambican foreign minister, in a recent Monitor interview. "South Africa is the most developed country in the region and as such should be part of such a grouping."

This new attitude of Mozambique, a key member of the bloc, reflects both the ongoing political reforms in South Africa and a growing realization among African leaders that international trends – like the economic unification of Europe and the democratization of the Eastern bloc – will reduce prospects for foreign aid and investment in Africa.

But officials of the Southern African Development Coordination Conference (SADCC) insist that South Africa will not be admitted to its ranks until a nonracial and democratic government has been established.

"It has always been the position of SADCC that a post-apartheid, democratic South Africa will be an automatic member," spokesman Kgosinkwe Moesi told the Monitor from the SADCC secretariat in Gaborone, Botswana.

"South Africa is an integral part of the region and has a very important role to play because of its infrastructure and natural resources," said Mr. Moesi. "These can be useful in achieving the very goals that SADCC is striving toward."

SADCC will conclude its 10th anniversary celebrations with a summit in Gaborone Aug. 24. SADCC chairman Quett Masire, the President of Botswana, said at the start of celebrations last April, "We have confounded the cynics and maligners, who argued that SADCC was not viable without South Africa."

SADCC was formed as a loose alliance of independent states in response to what members saw as a South African policy of destabilization aimed at economic domination of the region.

SADCC's executive secretary, Simbarashe Makoni, says members – once heavily dependent on South African ports and rail routes – had succeeded in diverting 50 percent of their trade through SADCC countries. The group has also made headway in establishing interstate airlinks, telecommunications, and power connections.

For the first half of SADCC's existence, South African sabotage of existing rail links to various southern African ports forced a reorientation of trade through South Africa.

A United Nations report published last November calculated that South Africa's destablization policy had cost its SADCC neighbors over $60 billion between 1980 and 1988.

Angola, at war with the Pretoria- and US-backed UNITA rebels, topped the list of victims with $30 billion in losses. Mozambique, fighting a 15-year war with South African-backed Renamo guerrillas, followed with $15 billion. During the same period, some 1.5 million lives were estimated to have been lost through war and famine – 900,000 in Mozambique alone.

SADCC Snapshots

SHIRLEY HORN – STAFF

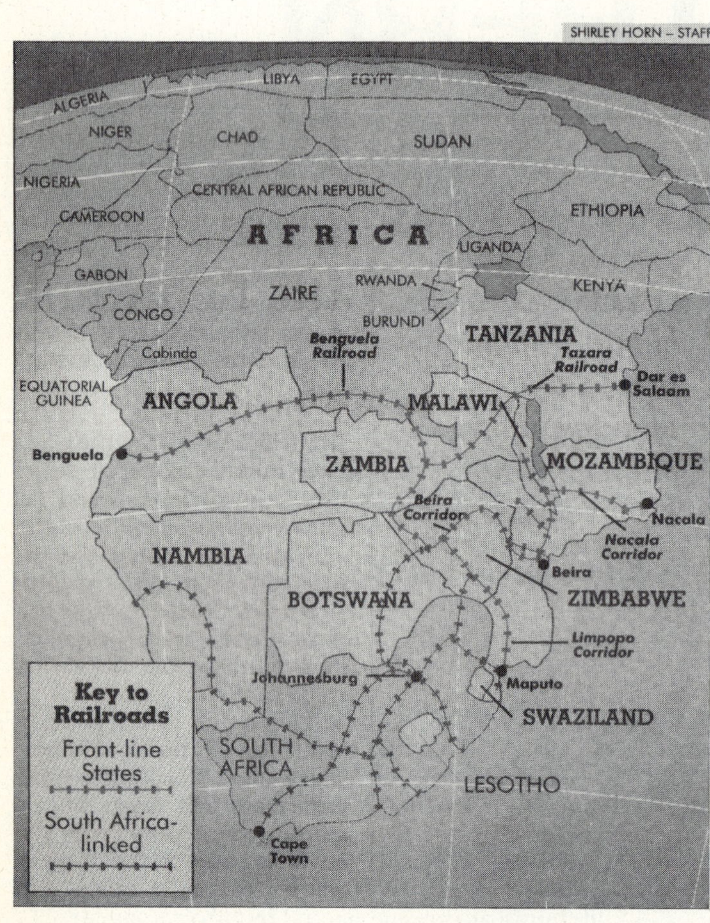

ANGOLA
Nominally Marxist-Leninist state has begun talks with US-backed UNITA rebels. Largest and most efficient Army in sub-Saharan Africa. Major export: oil. Pop.: 9 million.

BOTSWANA
Economic policies have resulted in one of the most buoyant economies in region. Resisted South African pressure to sign nonaggression pact. Mainly desert. Exports diamonds. Pop.: 1.3 million.

LESOTHO
Kingdom ruled by military junta. Migrant workers employed in South African gold mines account for 40 percent of GNP. Pop.: 1.8 million.

MALAWI
Under autocratic rule of leader Hastings Banda since 1964. Hosts 1 million refugees from Mozambique. Pop.: 8.4 million.

MOZAMBIQUE
Former Marxist state with devastated economy embracing reforms. Rich agricultural potential. Exports: cashews, prawns. Pop.: 15.7 million.

NAMIBIA
SADCC's newest member. Dependent on South African transport links. Africa's most democratic constitution. Exports: diamonds, uranium. Pop.: 1.5 million.

SWAZILAND
Landlocked kingdom bordering South Africa. Signed nonaggression pact with Pretoria. Pop.: 0.7 million.

TANZANIA
Only SADCC state beyond South Africa's sphere of influence. Provided alternative transport route via Tazara railway. Pop.: 24 million.

ZAMBIA
Close to economic collapse after drop in copper prices. Ruled by Kenneth Kaunda, popular as African statesman, but not in Zambia. Export: copper. Pop.: 7.8 million.

ZIMBABWE
Strongest SADCC economy. Nominally socialist, but pragmatic policies have retained confidence of whites. Against the trend, President Mugabe seeks creation of one-party state. Exports: coal, nickel and tobacco. Pop.: 9.8 million.

SOUTH AFRICA has aspired in recent years to become the engine of regional economic growth. In pursuit of that goal, Pretoria has had to respond to SADCC's success in winning Western diplomatic support. Giving aid to SADCC enabled Pretoria's Western trading partners to find a satisfactory compromise between full-scale sanctions and an internationally unpopular failure to act in the face of apartheid.

Mozambique and Angola have been major recipients of $3.2 billion in aid already given to SADCC countries. A priority project has been the rehabilitation of Beira port in Mozambique.

JOHN VAN PELT – STAFF

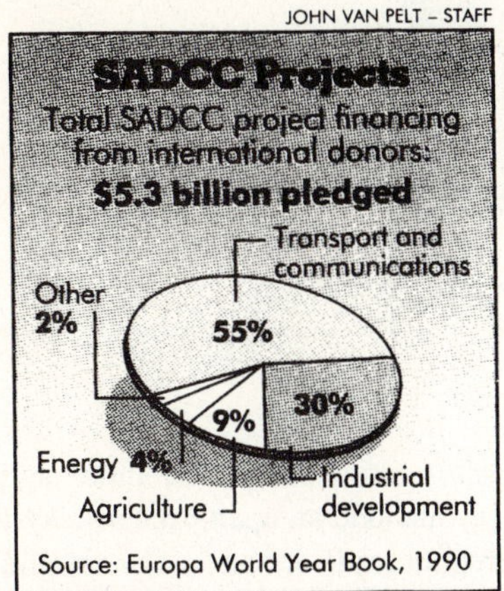

Funds have been used to restore sabotaged rail routes like the Benguela line in Angola, Mozambique's Beira corridor to Zimbabwe and Nacala line to Malawi, and the Limpopo corridor between Maputo and Zimbabwe. Besides transport, SADCC has projects in energy and manpower development, agriculture, and industry.

Yet South African trade with the member nations—Namibia became the 10th member in March this year—has grown steadily. In 1986, trade with South Africa amounted to 30 percent of total SADCC imports and 7 percent of exports. In contrast, trade between SADCC members amounted to only 4 percent of the group's total foreign trade.

SADCC officials insist that there can be no direct cooperation with South Africa until apartheid has been scrapped. SADCC has helped persuade South Africa to make political changes through its success in mobilizing economic aid to the region and focusing Western diplomatic pressure against Pretoria's destabilization policy.

At its April meeting, SADCC leaders began making long-term preparations for the eventual integration of a post-apartheid South Africa.

The leaders warned, however, that it would be naive to expect that the mere abolition of apartheid would lead to economic growth in the region. Some experts say the type of political settlement in South Africa will determine the quality of the regional relationship in the post-apartheid era.

"If a power-sharing arrangement stops short of genuine majority rule, the SADCC countries would be wise to stand back," says Rob Davies, economist at the Center for African Studies at Eduardo Mondlane University in Maputo.

"Then they will have to continue their economic struggle in an adversarial relationship with South Africa.

"But if a post-apartheid South Africa follows enlightened policies, it may create the conditions for SADCC states to work together with South Africa to transform regional economic relations," he said.

Article 17

The Christian Science Monitor, July 12, 1990

Botswana: Democracy And a Buoyant Economy

Ross Dunn

Special to The Christian Science Monitor

GABORONE, BOTSWANA

Botswana, a rare example of capitalism and democracy in Africa, has played a leading role in the Southern African Development Coordination Conference (SADCC). Quett Masire, President of Botswana, is the current chairman of the group. His predecessor, Sir Seretse Khama, was the first chairman of the conference, which established its headquarters in 1980 in Gaborone, Botswana's capital.

Botswana was one of the continent's poorest nations at independence in 1966. It now has Africa's fastest growing economy, and stands out on a continent suffering from scarcity, mismanagement, and debt. As one of Africa's few multiparty democracies, its politics are characterized by open debate, efficient government, and a free-market philosophy.

Economic success followed the discovery of diamond deposits in 1967, one year after independence. And in 1989, for the fourth successive year, Botswana was the world's leading diamond producer by value.

Prudent management and use of the diamond wealth has been important to the country's stability. While wealth is still unequally distributed, international observers have recognized effective government efforts to care for all citizens during the 1981–87 drought.

Botswana faces little of the intertribal conflict that has divided many other African nations. Officially, the country has eight tribes. But the strength of allegiances between them has made the nation virtually one tribe. Richard Mannathoko, chief executive of British Petroleum-Botswana, says that Botswana's tribes developed a system for resolving intertribal conflict that was tailor-made for the transition to Western-style parliamentary democracy.

After a record output last year, it is believed that revenue from the diamond mines has begun to plateau. But unemployment has not been reduced, and new labor-intensive industries are needed.

Finance Minister Fergus Mogae says that investments by Heinz and Colgate are examples of US interest. Botswana wants investment to create broad economic growth, and reduce dependence on diamonds, which in 1988, accounted for 73 percent of Botswana's exports. The country's foreign exchange reserves stand at a remarkable $2.4 billion.

But President Masire says, "I am little disappointed that they [US investors] didn't move in a little more aggressively." Botswana's assets include an open exchange system, cheap labor, and preferential trade access to Europe and the US through the Lomé Convention and the Generalized System of Preferences.

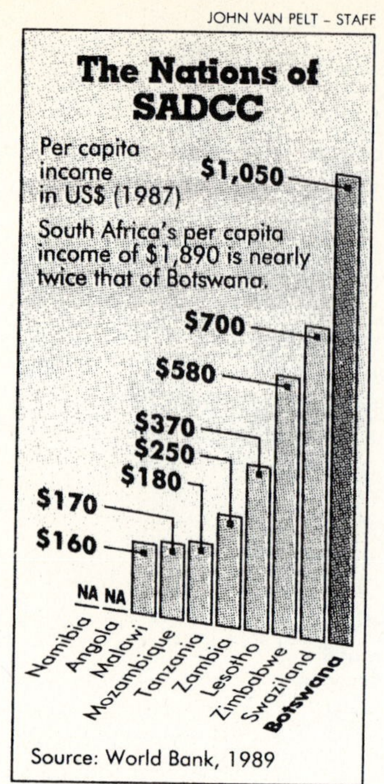

Article 18

The Christian Science Monitor, July 12, 1990

Zimbabwe Braces for Shifts In Regional Leadership Role

By Colleen Lowe Morna

Special to The Christian Science Monitor

HARARE, ZIMBABWE

ZIMBABWE, a leading member of SADCC, is looking forward to the emergence of a majority-ruled South Africa with both anticipation and fear.

Once white-ruled itself, Zimbabwe has campaigned vigorously for an end to apartheid in South Africa. But as that day draws closer, Zimbabweans are increasingly aware that a new South Africa will dwarf this country's star role in regional affairs, as well as threaten its fledgling industries.

Zimbabwe's strong economy and central location have given the country an unofficial leadership role in SADCC, the 10-member South African development Coordination Conference. It has the largest industrial sector and boasts the most-educated leadership in the SADCC grouping. Gaining full independence from Britain in 1980, Zimbabwe emerged just as SADCC was formed. Zimbabwean President Robert Mugabe has been a high-profile figure in African affairs, and as head of the "Nonaligned Movement."

Because of SADCC's emphasis on shared responsibility, Zimbabwe, which coordinates the portfolio responsible for food security in the region, is not officially more prominent than the group's other nine members.

But "right now Zimbabwe is the biggest fish in a small pond," says an economist at the University of Zimbabwe. "When South Africa comes in [joins SADCC as a black-ruled state], not only will the size of the pond increase dramatically, but it will be as though a whale – maybe even a shark – has been put into it."

"Although this is not a popular thing to say right now," he says, "it is not clear that the economic impact of a free South Africa will be less harmful than the economic impact of overt destabilization."

Zimbabwean business leaders fear that better political relations would lead to cheap South African goods flooding its markets and pushing them out of business. Many of Zimbabwe's industries, which grew up under the artificial protection of pre-independence (1980) sanctions, are inefficient and badly in need of new equipment.

These industries would also find it difficult to compete with South Africa in regional markets. Although South Africa has continued to trade with its neighbors, it has been shut off from countries further afield, like Tanzania, and those which have barred South African products, like Angola. Some South African goods still reach these countries through indirect and black market routes.

Zimbabwe's industry and commerce minister, Kumbirai Kangai, told a recent business meeting here that the country's industries would soon be competing with South Africa in regional markets and would have to "arm themselves with aggressive marketing and professional practices or risk folding." A similar theme has been echoed by other government officials. A businessman in Harare says that "developments in South Africa will only be positive if we are innovative enough."

Before Zimbabwe (then Rhodesia) became independent, the country coexisted with its prosperous neighbor by finding niches – like manufacturing special types of furniture or electronic goods – where it had competitive advantages, a Zimbabwean banker says.

The likelihood of a free South Africa emerging, according to the banker, has simply highlighted the need for Zimbabwe to push ahead with a much-talked-about trade liberalization plan. Zimbabwe's finance minister, Bernard Chidzero, announced at a Confederation of Zimbabwe Industries meeting this week that the Cabinet has approved a policy framework including trade liberalization, but will not release the details until later this month.

Article 19

INSIGHT / OCTOBER 1, 1990

South Africa Steps Along a Minefield of Alliances

SUMMARY: Since the South African government lifted the ban on the African National Congress in February, alliances have been in a state of flux. The ANC's old ally and bankroller, the Soviet Union, has been sidling up to Pretoria. The ruling National Party has been trying to broaden its base. Militants on both sides are feeling left out. And Zulus are fighting the backers of the ANC in the townships.

The office looks like any other in Johannesburg's bustling financial district. People mill around the lobby and engage in conversations that occasionally burst into laughter.

Then a deliveryman arrives with a bundle of freshly printed handbills emblazoned with the hammer and sickle. A burly white man embraces a younger black man and fires questions: "How was jail?" and "Have you got a job yet?" A scholarly looking Indian teases a group of blacks by recalling how he smuggled food to them on "the Island."

As any South African could tell you, he is referring to Robben Island, where the government once imprisoned its most feared dissidents. And the participants in this banter are not just any white-collar working stiffs; they are the career revolutionaries of the African National Congress, just back from prison or exile.

Joe Slovo, head of the South African Communist Party and reputedly white South Africa's most hated man, bounces around in search of a fax machine. Walter Sisulu, prison comrade of Nelson Mandela and elder statesman of the liberation movement, ducks through a door under a sign warning that the rest rooms are not for public use. Once the scourge of the diamond-studded burghers of Johannesburg, these men now ride the same elevators, simmer in the same traffic jams and rush about trailing identical briefcases — except that theirs are stuffed not with gold-share prospectuses but with plans for turning South Africa's economy upside down.

In unbanning the ANC and its allies in February, Pretoria made a happy meal of 30 years of demonizing rhetoric. The ruling National Party has traditionally portrayed the black liberationists as stooges of Moscow in a scheme to grab South Africa's minerals and control Western shipping around the Cape of Good Hope. Now the Nats are trying to sell white voters on a whole new idea, that the ANC is a worthy partner in building the "new" South Africa.

"The communist bogey was set up for electioneering purposes. We didn't think deeply about it," says Gen. H. de V. Du Toit, a former chief of military intelligence. He adds with a shrug: "We got most of this from the States."

If the old way of seeing things has outlived its usefulness, there is a history that lingers on. Though a Munich insurance company is paying for the ANC's new Johannesburg headquarters, the Kremlin remains the group's biggest bankroller. As recently as July, Slovo assured the faithful that money was still flowing from Moscow. And within days of Mandela's release from jail, the congress issued a circular claiming that a delegation had just returned from the Soviet Union and "all their military requirements were met in full."

The white government is trying to overlook such indiscretions. Says Foreign Ministry Deputy Director-General Rusty Evans: "One can sympathize with an organization's need for funding, especially when there's only a limited amount available domestically."

If anything, the African National Congress seems mildly bewildered by its sudden emergence into the sunlight. After a generation of clandestine carryings-on in foreign capitals, conspiratorial habits die hard. Since Mandela's release, a lively debate has developed over how to provide jobs and upward mobility for blacks. But the ANC's contribution, drafted by a British Marxist and leaked to the press, ignores economics and instead rants about foiling the capitalist plot to keep South Africa as part of the "imperialist system."

Then there is the "armed struggle." The government's overwhelming military superiority has always meant that it was a dead letter. But some militants have a hard time letting go anyway. No sooner had the Pretoria Minute been signed, formally ending the armed struggle, than Chris Hani, leader of the ANC's military wing, threatened to "seize power by force." During her recent travels abroad, Winnie Mandela repeatedly brandished a rhetorical AK-47. Back home, armed infiltrators are still being intercepted at the borders.

Wielding the "Spear of the Nation" conferred a status that some surely miss. The leaders of the ANC's armed wing were heroes to young blacks and got to dispose of an estimated $80 million a year in Soviet aid. "The military types were the Soviet Union's closest allies in the past. Now they are in danger of being left by the roadside," says Northern Illinois University's Daniel Kempton, author of a recent book on Soviet-backed liberation movements in Southern Africa.

Understandably, the idea of negotiation offends the amour propre of some lifetime revolutionaries. The ANC was a member of the Khartoum Class of 1969, a Soviet-sponsored gabfest in which a single liberation group from each African colony was dubbed "authentic." Other attendees included guerrilla leaders from what was then Rhodesia, Mozambique and Angola. Except for the South Africans, all engaged in combat in overthrowing white rule.

While visiting abroad, a young Johannesburg political scientist was recently mistaken for an ANC activist by a senior official of the Zimbabwean ruling party. The Zimbabwean, after recounting his own experience in the 30,000-man guerrilla force that drove the Rhodesian government from power, offered an unflattering appraisal of the ANC's martial virtues. "They have a very low opinion of their South African counterparts," says the political scientist.

Besides being reluctant to give up the chance for glory, the military wing houses some of the ANC's most radical viewpoints. Hani and his predecessor as the armed wing's commander, Slovo, are leaders of the South African Communist Party, which has been allied with the ANC since 1960. Many Communists are white or Indian, and their educational credentials and organizational skills give them influence beyond their numbers. According to London's Africa Confidential newsletter, 28 out of 35 members of the ANC's National Executive Committee are Communists.

Since it was legalized in July, the SACP has turned itself into a regular political party. Though its vote-getting pull has yet to be tested, it could prove robust. The red flag is waved with enthusiasm at township rallies, and many of the so-called Young Comrades take an openly pro-Soviet line. An analyst at the South African Institute of Race Relations figures the Communists could draw 1 million votes at election time.

At the same time, the party may be losing its clout in the ANC, which for years has been urged by Western well-wishers to drop the Communist tie. Over the years Slovo earned a reputation as a hardened Stalinist and knee-jerk defender of Soviet foreign policy. Then the Berlin Wall tumbled, and suddenly he began singing the virtues of multiparty democracy and private enterprise (while still insisting on the "moral superiority" of communism over capitalism).

This was too much for Pallo Jordan, the ANC's formidable information minister. He publicly rebuked the Communists for their past defense of tyranny and questioned the sincerity of their conversion. "There are a lot of Stalinists [within the congress] running around doing penance right now," says an analyst with a liberal Johannesburg think tank.

On the other hand, South Africa's most trenchant newspaper, Business Day, has frequently called attention to what it considers the ANC's totalitarian baggage, picked up in years of wandering through the netherworld of African revolutionary politics. For whites, one of the most sensitive issues is cultural freedom and diversity. But in a harangue to the Grahamstown Arts Festival, ANC Culture Minister Barbara Masekela warned the white sponsors that in the future they would be expected to pay obeisance to "majority culture."

More ominously, the ANC continues to cling to the notion that South Africa's 27 million blacks must speak with one voice, that of the African National Congress. Sisulu insists black differences must remain buried at least until a new constitution is ratified. "Perhaps differences will grow once we are in government. But even after negotiations, unity will be needed to put right the [economic] situation."

That will be too late to air crucial issues that divide the black majority. Not all blacks agree with the ANC's vision of a unitary South Africa governed by a strong central bureaucracy, its antipathy for capitalism or its ideology of nonracialism. The Pan-Africanist Congress, a radical black faction whose motto is "one settler, one bullet," claims a rapidly growing membership and has had several bloody skirmishes with Mandela supporters in recent weeks.

More horrific still is the burgeoning violence between followers of Zulu Chief Mangosuthu Buthelezi and allies of the African National Congress. More than 3,000 have died since 1985 in Natal province, a largely Zulu-populated area. Now the battle has spread to the crowded townships of the Transvaal and taken a more openly tribal cast. In less than a week in late August, 500 people were killed in battles fought between Zulus and Xhosa with spears, axes and automatic weapons. (The ANC's leadership is disproportionately drawn from members of the Xhosa tribe.)

Buthelezi has never been forgiven for forswearing exile and armed struggle and trying to win a Zulu place in the sun through negotiation. Now that the ANC itself has decided on the wisdom of talk, it would deny Buthelezi's Inkatha Freedom Party (which has 1.7 million members) a separate seat at the table. If the ANC gets its way, Buthelezi's group will have to push its views — in favor of federalism and free markets — from under the ANC umbrella.

Still, there is a good reason why the ANC's antidemocratic tendencies are less troubling to the white regime than in times past: They are no longer backed by the military resources of the Soviet Union and its regional allies.

Says the Foreign Ministry's Evans: "The steps taken by this government are quite dramatic. These things would have been impossible if the Soviet Union had an overt policy of undermining South African sovereignty, as in the past it did have."

In South Africa, the traditional Soviet approach was a spoiling operation. As elsewhere, the Kremlin's foreign policy consisted almost entirely of arms shipments and agitprop aimed at empowering extremists and thwarting compromise. In Ethiopia, Mozambique and Angola, the Soviets reaped a richly deserved whirlwind: incompetent and unpopular regimes that imposed a terminal drain on Soviet resources.

At least when it comes to South Africa, the Soviet Union is singing a new tune, and it is not hard to guess why. The two countries account for most of the world's gold production and much of its platinum and diamonds as well. For decades, Pretoria and Moscow have cooperated surreptitiously in marketing gold and diamonds; now they see much broader scope for market-rigging and developing the technology to rejuvenate tired mines.

Mark Swilling, an analyst at the Center for Policy Studies at Johannesburg's Witwatersrand University, recently visited Moscow. "There are significant forces in the Soviet Union that want trade links now," he says. "They see the possibility of putting together a cartel with South Africa on the world stage, and they don't care who the government is."

In cozying up to Pretoria, Moscow has auctioned off much of the ANC's bargaining strength. In 1986, Soviet academics conspicuously began pooh-poohing the armed struggle and talking about "group rights," a constitutional scheme to entrench white power that even Pretoria now rejects as retrograde. Two years ago, the Kremlin badgered Angola into signing a U.S.-brokered deal that kicked the ANC guerrillas out of their last military bases in the area. Since then, they have cooled their heels in Tanzania and Uganda, 1,000 miles from the nearest target. The same deal is sending the Cubans packing from Angola, thus removing the only conventional force in the region capable of challenging the South African Defense Forces.

"South Africa is in the strongest position since the instability started in the 1960s," says Chester Crocker, the State Department official who negotiated the Angola-Namibia accords. "The Cubans are going home, the armed struggle has been discredited and Pretoria can bring its boys home from the border."

President Frederik W. de Klerk has seized the opportunity offered by Moscow's imperial retreat to defang and domesticate his black opposition. But can he also democratize it, thereby avoiding the African pattern of corrupt and arbitrary rule?

Besides all the usual tribal divisions, South Africa must cope with a huge and palpable economic gap between blacks and whites. "It's very difficult to have a functioning democracy when the largest part of the population feels done in economically," says Erich Leistner, director of the Africa Institute of Pretoria University and a longtime student of regional affairs.

He outlines the problem facing the white establishment: "In the near future there will be a black president and black ministers in government with real clout, not just Uncle Toms, so the black population can see they have a real say in government. We must hope that business and cultural leaders can convince blacks with these responsibilities that it's not in their interest to go for a socialist system."

The real danger, he adds, will come after the postapartheid honeymoon. Most blacks will wake up and discover they are still poor, and radical politicians will accuse moderate black leaders of selling out. "It's difficult now to sketch a path to deal with that complex political problem," Leistner says.

Yet there are reasons for hoping that South Africa can succeed where others have failed. For one thing, it has a large black middle class whose members are fully aware of the disasters elsewhere on the continent. Many have jobs, homes, families and even businesses they consider worth protecting, and they have already had their fill of chaos in the 1980s.

Witness the popularity of Nomavenda Mathiane, a Soweto journalist who writes about the suffering of ordinary people in the township's political turmoil. Under the arbitrary rule of the Young Comrades, schools have been turned into centers of agitation, breeding a generation of militant illiterates. Parents are forced to join rent strikes, work stoppages and boycotts that endanger their homes and jobs, and gangs of activists go door-to-door demanding children for use as fodder in violent demonstrations. The price of dissent from this comradely order is the "necklace" (a gasoline-soaked tire placed around the victim's neck and ignited) and the firebomb.

Having spent a generation stoking the terrors of white South Africans, the National Party is a past master at making electoral hay from the dread of social disorder. That could stand them in good stead in the first postapartheid election, slated for 1994. "Blacks will see that de Klerk is still the fount of power. The vast majority of people would welcome a return to stability," predicts Gen. Du Toit.

And unlike Zimbabwe, where the white community has largely retreated from politics, South Africa's rulers have made it clear they do not intend to give up the ghost or settle for tokenism. "Last year it was the skin game: group rights and a white veto," says Swilling. "This year the Nats are talking about majority rule. They are looking to represent a coalition of minorities at the bargaining table."

In late August, the Natal branch of the National Party became the first to open its rolls to blacks. If de Klerk has his way, others will soon follow. By some estimates, the party can hope to pull in the 20 percent of black voters who are middle-class and conservative as well as a large share of Indian and mixed-race voters. In any likely constitutional arrangement, that would give the Nationalist coalition enough parliamentary clout at least to veto the wilder impulses of an ANC majority government.

That is, assuming de Klerk can bring enough white votes to the table with him.

In a recent by-election, the Conservative Party, which rejects the idea of talking with blacks, scored impressive gains, and new supporters are flowing into the ranks of paramilitary organizations sworn to uphold

> "In the near future there will be a black president. We must hope business leaders can convince blacks it's not in their interest to go for a socialist system."

white rule by violence. These groups take aim at de Klerk's core constituency, the majority of whites who are descended from the earliest Dutch settlers. "The Afrikaner *Volk* is divided like never before," says John Barratt, director of the South African Institute of International Affairs.

Boosting fears of white terrorism are rumors that behind the latest wave of township killings lies a "third force": Neither Inkatha nor ANC, the mysterious vigilantes have been likened to Renamo, the Mozambican rebel group that has received support from white extremists in South Africa. Unsigned letters have started to appear in South African newspapers muttering about "secret armies" and invoking the spirit of the Boer resistance to British rule at the start of the century.

The apartheid-loving right is said to have strong support in South Africa's heavily armed and ill-disciplined police force (although de Klerk recently sweetened their pay envelopes with a 70 percent raise) and in the rural areas. Moreover, most white men have had military training, and many are involved in mining, which gives them access to explosives and the expertise to use them.

"Sociologically, the conditions are absolutely right" for terrorism, says Swilling. "You've got a highly motivated group with a total worldview that includes God, the Land and the *Volk*. They have a passive base, which leads them to resort to armed force to extort concessions." As a result, Swilling's liberal think tank is pushing the idea of a *Boerstaat*, or white homeland.

But others believe the paranoia will quickly evaporate as it becomes clear that South Africa is not another Angola or Mozambique. Five million strong and economically indispensable, South Africa's whites are a golden goose that Mandela and company cannot afford to kill.

At defense headquarters in Pretoria, a naval intelligence officer is wrapping up a briefing on the tumultuous state of his country's neighbors. He is optimistic that South Africa's fate will be different: "We may have to accept a change in our privileges and national identity, but that's more than outweighed by the possibilities opening up. Nothing really important is going to change."

— Holman Jenkins Jr. in Johannesburg

Article 20

WORLD • WATCH
MAY • JUNE 1990

APARTHEID'S OTHER INJUSTICE

Crowded, arid, and poor, South Africa's racially contrived homelands are among the world's most degraded lands.

ALAN B. DURNING

Alan B. Durning, senior researcher at Worldwatch Institute, studies the relationships between poverty and environmental decline and tracks environmental movements worldwide.

In 1652, Dutch settlers put ashore at the Cape of Good Hope and built a small town, a way station on the trade route to the Orient. Foreshadowing all that was to follow, they soon planted a hedge around their encampment and forbade the region's aboriginal people, the Khoisan, from remaining inside. Ever since, the colonists and their descendants have been pushing that hedge out in larger circles.

With the Land Act of 1913, the Dutch, by then known as Afrikaners, completed their appropriation of the 438,000-square-mile region today called the Republic of South Africa. The act gave the newcomers 87 percent of the national territory, relegating blacks to the so-called Native Reserves it established on the remaining 13 percent (see map). In 1948, the white voters of South Africa elected the white supremacist National Party, which, capping a long history of racist legislation, transformed the policy of racial separatism into the institutionalized oppression of apartheid.

Pretoria soon systematically began crowding blacks not wanted in the white economy into the bits and pieces of South Africa reserved by government fiat for the region's original inhabitants. By design, these reserves, now euphemistically called "homelands," were the least fertile in the country. Today, they rank among the world's most degraded lands.

Homelands or Wastelands?

Few observers north of the Limpopo River realize that apartheid has been as devastating for South Africa's environment as for its people. In much of the country, in the words of novelist Alan Paton, "the earth has torn away like flesh."

The ecological results of apartheid's policy of "separate development" are written all over the tortured topography of the homelands. As one U.S. Agency for International Development official in neighboring Swaziland puts it, "Many of the homelands bear more resemblance to the face of the moon than to the commercial farms and game preserves that cover the rest of the country."

With 6 percent of its territory under protection as parks or game reserves and a professional conservation corps unequaled in Africa, the republic has long cultivated its image as the continent's conservation leader. But the facts bear a different witness: South African farmers lose 20 tons of topsoil for each ton of crops they produce. The nation's southwestern deserts are marching to Pretoria, expanding across one and a half miles of exhausted pastures a year. And its overuse of pesticides, including Agent Orange components 2,4-D and 2,4,5-T, endangers farm workers and the food chain alike.

In these regards, South Africa is not alone. Modern history is all too full of societies that have squandered their patrimonies. South Africa's assault on the environment *is* exceptional, however, in its motivations and its rapaciousness. Racist policies, and the extraordinary means to which the state has resorted in maintaining them, have doomed the nation's ecology to suffer as have few regions of the world.

"The Land Is Breaking"

Today, with apartheid apparently closer to its demise than ever before, a reckoning of its ecological toll can help reveal the path toward a new South Africa where black and white live together in a greener land.

As historian Francis Wilson and health specialist Mamphela Ramphele of the University of Cape Town write in *Uprooting Poverty,* their comprehensive review of the plight of South Africa's poor, "Almost everywhere the land is breaking under the burden that has been laid upon it."

Because few comprehensive surveys of land degradation within the reserves have been conducted, it is hard to get an accurate fix on the extent of the devastation. What data do exist, however, show a frightening picture.

When the government's Ciskei Commission gave its report a decade ago, 46 percent of the land in that reserve was classified as moderately or severely eroded and 39 percent of its pastures overgrazed. In Lesotho, an impoverished country surrounded by South Africa and similar to the homelands in history, ecology, demography, and economic dependence, 10 percent of the original farm land is now barren waste and almost 90 percent of grazing and croplands suffer unsustainable rates of soil loss.

Indeed, the destruction of Lesotho's vegetation is so severe it can be seen from orbit. American geographers L.A. Lewis and L. Berry write: "A Landsat image of the boundary area between Lesotho and the Republic of South Africa shows the boundary as though it were a natural geologic feature."

Similar land degradation is apparent in most homelands, as anecdotal evidence amply confirms. In the Msinga district of the kwaZulu homeland, erosion gullies called *dongas* have grown into small valleys and topsoil is scarce. KwaZulu farmer Creina Bond Alcock reports, "Old fields have vanished completely in some parts of Msinga, opening up extraordinary expanses of stone." Sunduza village in the Transkei homeland is scarred with *dongas* 65 feet deep, and in the once-fertile Lebowa homeland boulders occasion-

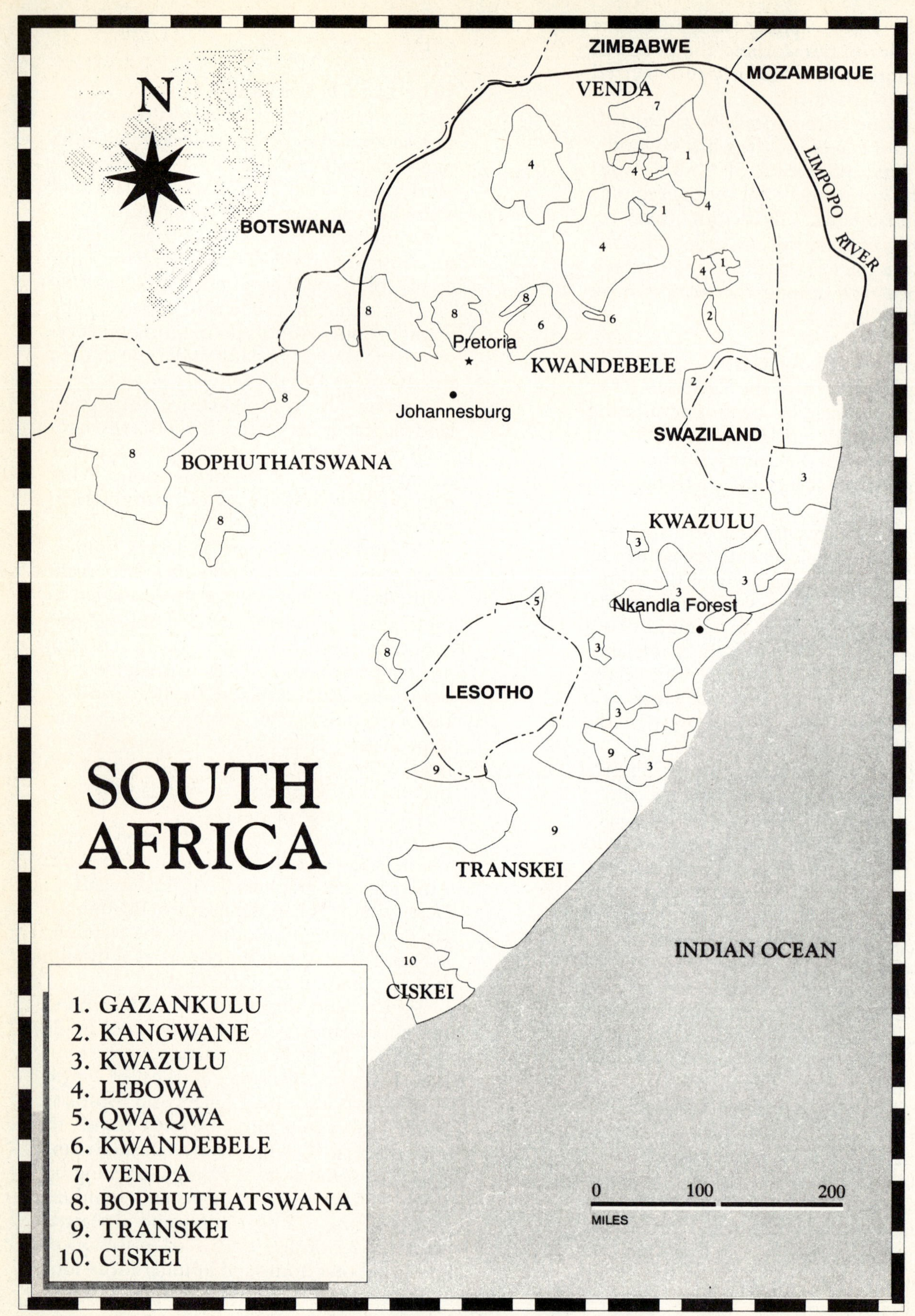

N
ZIMBABWE
MOZAMBIQUE
VENDA
LIMPOPO RIVER
BOTSWANA
Pretoria
KWANDEBELE
Johannesburg
SWAZILAND
BOPHUTHATSWANA
KWAZULU
Nkandla Forest
LESOTHO
SOUTH AFRICA
TRANSKEI
INDIAN OCEAN
CISKEI
1. GAZANKULU
2. KANGWANE
3. KWAZULU
4. LEBOWA
5. QWA QWA
6. KWANDEBELE
7. VENDA
8. BOPHUTHATSWANA
9. TRANSKEI
10. CISKEI
0 100 200
MILES

ally roll down denuded mountain slopes and crush the huts below.

The forests, too, are overburdened. Two-thirds of South Africans use wood for fuel, but because of the extreme population pressures in the homelands, wood is increasingly difficult to come by. Researcher Anton Eberhard of the University of Cape Town surveyed fuelwood gathering in four reserves and found that women typically make a trek of three to six miles every other day, collecting loads that weigh about 65 pounds. In the homelands, writes energy researcher Mark Gandar, "If wood gathering is counted as part of food preparation, more effort is put into the preparation of food than the growing of it."

With per-capita consumption of fuelwood at 1,100 to 1,800 pounds annually, forests in the homelands don't stand a chance. Twenty years was all it took for fuelwood gathering to strip the forests from the remote slopes of Lebowa's Leolo Mountain. In Qwa Qwa, forests exist only as a part of history.

KwaZulu boasted 250 distinct woodlands a half-century ago; today it has scarcely 50. A century ago, Cetshwayo—the great Zulu warrior who led his tribe against white troops set on subjugating them—was buried deep in the Nkandla forest. The forest's receding edge is now scarcely visible from his grave.

The Racial Roots of Decline

Environmental decline in the homelands has four interlocking causes, and all of them trace their roots to apartheid. First, the 10 homelands are situated in fragile environments—regions best suited as rangeland. From the very beginning, blacks were given land where topsoil is thin, rainfall scarce and unpredictable, and the ground sloping and rocky. Borders were carefully drawn, and sometimes redrawn, to exclude anything of value: industrial sites, transport lines, mineral resources—and fertile land.

The result is that the reserves, now theoretically independent from Pretoria to one degree or another, have become landlocked archipelagos scattered across the map of South Africa. A geographic survey of kwa-Zulu reveals 48 large and 157 small tracts, and one of Bophuthatswana's six segments is 200 miles from the others.

Second, apartheid forces the land to support an astronomical number of people. Of South Africa's nearly 40 million people, 29 million are black, 5 million are white, and the remainder are classified as either "colored" or "Indian." Perhaps slightly more than half of the black population lives crowded into the reserves, held there by apartheid.

Overpopulation in South Africa's reserves is a political phenomenon, enforced by the white minority government. Not only are blacks forbidden from moving out of the homelands, South African scholars believe that nearly 3.5 million additional blacks were pushed in between 1950 and 1983 to bring about the state's goal of territorial separation of the races.

Meanwhile, birthrates in the homelands are higher than elsewhere in the country, because the extreme poverty to which apartheid consigns blacks leads couples to have larger families in an attempt to gain economic security. The African population of the nation has quadrupled during this century, rising even more steeply within the homelands.

All told, forced relocations and natural increase combine to give the homelands an average population density higher than all but three African countries. White rural areas are at most one-tenth as heavily populated.

Perhaps the most telling demonstration that the homelands are overburdened arises by comparing their agricultural potential with their population. During World War I, a government commission surveyed the agricultural carrying capacity of the small reserve of Qwa Qwa and estimated that the area was already overcrowded at 5,000 inhabitants. Today, Qwa Qwa is home to more than 500,000 people. Likewise, the Ciskei has about nine times as many inhabitants as it can support in subsistence agriculture.

With population growth and land degradation in the reserves, per-capita food production has fallen dramatically, so much that the homelands are now net importers of food. In the late 1940s, Bophuthatswana's farmers were harvesting around 250 pounds of maize and sorghum for each resident of the reserve. In the late 1950s, they were taking in 180 pounds per person; in the early 1970s only 110 pounds. Today, the harvest is undoubtedly spread even thinner.

Third, the homelands suffer a labor shortage. Seemingly paradoxical, this problem is a result of the fact that few of those present are in their peak working years. In South Africa's bizarre migrant labor system, the destitute lands provide the white economy with reservoirs of cheap black labor. Some 70 percent of homeland income is earned in the white economy by unskilled workers who cram buses for hundred-mile daily or weekly commutes, or who spend most of their lives working hundreds of miles from home.

The homelands, then, are home mostly to the young, the old, and the infirm. In the 1960s, when "removals" were near their peak, many elderly blacks were consigned to these areas because the government considered them, in the words of one cabinet minister, "surplus appendages." A detailed survey in one region of kwaZulu found that most inhabitants were children or elderly and that 81 percent of working-age inhabitants were women, mostly mothers who could not leave their children to work far away. These women, struggling to provide for so many, are too hard-pressed to undertake land-conserving projects.

As the poor get poorer, the land is worn down to bare rock. In South Africa, blacks are disenfranchised not only politically but ecologically

Finally, poverty itself makes land conservation difficult. A decade ago, two researchers at the University of Stellenbosch ranked the 57 nations for which income distribution data were available. South Africa came in dead last—it is probably the most inequitable nation on earth. In a nation where whites enjoy the same affluence as Americans, half of the population—80 percent in the homelands—lives beneath the poverty line.

Cut out of the prosperous South African economy by apartheid, and living hand to mouth, farmers in the homelands lack the cash to make long-term investments in protecting their land. With average disposable income of around $150 a year—1/16th the white average—they simply cannot afford to buy fencing to control grazing, hire laborers to help terrace sloping fields, or invest in tree planting to conserve soil and water.

These four elements—bad land, overpopulation, labor scarcity, and poverty—combine to form a vicious circle of environmental and economic impoverishment. As the poor get poorer, the land is worn down to the bare rock. In South Africa, blacks are disenfranchised not only politically but ecologically.

A Glimmer of Change

Today, the apartheid system is crumbling at the edges. Since the election of President Frederick W. de Klerk in 1989, racial separatism has been on the retreat. History reminds us, of course, that apartheid is like a chameleon: The nomenclature of South African racism has evolved endlessly to blend with international opinion. In official parlance, "apartheid," for instance, was replaced early on by "separate development," then "separate freedoms," "plural democracy," and "vertical differentiation."

"50,000 white farmers have 12 times as much land for cultivation and grazing as 14 million rural blacks."

This year's changes are real, though. The security apparatus has been weakened, most public places desegregated, political prisoners freed, political organizations unbanned, and promises of further reforms made. A peaceful transformation now seems possible where a year ago only bloodshed could be foreseen. The path ahead is tortuous, but South African society, divided as it is, has begun the journey.

On the negotiating table are the very pillars of apartheid: the Land Act of 1913 and the mock-independence of the homelands; the Population Registration Act, which requires every citizen to be racially classified at birth; the Group Areas Act, which keeps blacks segregated in cities; and the denial of black suffrage.

Abolishing each of these will have important environmental benefits. The rural segregation of the homeland system leaves South Africa with a pattern of land ownership more concentrated than any on the seven continents. As former *New York Times* correspondent James Lelyveld puts it, "50,000 white farmers have 12 times as much land for cultivation and grazing as 14 million rural blacks."

The homelands structure is already beginning to tremble. A coup d'etat in Ciskei in March pushed out a black leader loyal to Pretoria and replaced him with a group of officers who call for the dissolution of the homeland's titular independence. The news of their power grab brought throngs of celebrators into the open in the towns and villages of the reserve.

Days later in Bophuthatswana, tens of thousands marched through the dusty streets demanding an end to the sham of independence that has made them foreigners in their country of birth. In Transkei, a referendum is to be held later this year on whether to renounce the independence enforced by Pretoria and apply for reunification with the republic.

When democracy comes to the nation, the fiction of homeland self-rule will no doubt go by the wayside—the question will be how best to reverse the 300-year trend toward concentration of land ownership in white hands. A swift and just redistribution of the nation's land would attack the central problem that drives rural decline.

Reason to Hope

Thoughts of a greener future are certainly optimistic, but they are not idle speculation. There are reasons for hope, including the dramatic growth in environmental awareness in the nation. The white population experienced an environmental awakening in 1989 similar to that in Western democracies in 1988. It culminated in the formation of Earthlife Africa, the first nationwide environmental group working on a broad range of ecological issues.

Significantly, whites as well as blacks are beginning to blame apartheid for the nation's environmental problems. Earthlife, a nonracial organization with a growing black membership, sees the creation of a post-apartheid democratic society as, in the words of member Henk Coetzee, "a precondition for clean and healthy living conditions for all South Africans."

Concern for an environmentally sound economy is now voiced often in the black liberation movement as well, though more quietly. Max Sisulu, head of the African National Congress's (ANC) Department of Economics and Planning and son of ANC leader Walter Sisulu, issued a statement last November on the black political body's environmental priorities. Sisulu showed how apartheid has exhausted the land in the reserves and emphasized the ANC's commitment to sustaining the environment that supports humankind: "The present generation has a responsibility to future generations to preserve the environment. . . . The ANC believes environmental reconstruction constitutes a major task of a free and democratic post-apartheid South Africa."

Bold words are easy for those out of power: there is no guarantee that a majority-ruled government will implement the reforms of the land distribution system needed to protect the earth and provide for the people. Nonetheless, a solution of the race issue will be the single most important step toward a solution of the land issue.

The emancipation of South Africa's people and land may have begun on February 11th, when Nelson Mandela was released from prison in Cape Town. That day he lamented, "Apartheid's destruction on our subcontinent is incalculable." He was referring, presumably, to the devastation of black lives and families, but his words could apply just as easily to the once-beautiful countryside of the reserves, lands that can be healed only by a flowering of equality.

Article 21

The Christian Science Monitor, September 17, 1990

Namibia's Combatants Seek New Role in Society

But unemployment is already 35 percent, making jobs scarce

By John Battersby

Staff writer of The Christian Science Monitor

ONGULUMBASHE, NAMIBIA

NAMIBIA'S 23-year-old bush war is over, but the new government is facing a dilemma over how to incorporate the 30,000 or so combatants who fought on both sides back into national life.

"With the removal of the South African Army, a huge vacuum was left in the north of the country," said Information Minister Hidipo Hamutenya.

Thousands of former fighters have joined the estimated 35 percent of unemployed Namibians. "The people want to see a quick solution to the problem of unemployment and they are looking to the government," he said. "But the process is not as quick as we would like it to be."

Since Namibia gained independence six months ago, the British Army has begun training a 10,000-strong Namibian armed force made up of former South West African People's Organization (SWAPO) guerrillas and ex-soldiers of the South African-led South West African Territorial Force. SWAPO never disclosed the number of guerrillas in its military wing, the People's Liberation Army of Namibia (PLAN), but it is estimated at more than 10,000 fighters.

At an emotion-charged ceremony in this remote Ovambo village on Aug. 26, about 20,000 SWAPO supporters commemorated the 24th anniversary of Namibia Day, which marked the beginning of SWAPO's military struggle.

Veterans of the "battle of Ongulumbashe" – the first encounter with South African security forces – were decorated and senior SWAPO officials lauded the role played by the armed struggle. "The aim of the armed struggle was independence," said Namibian President Sam Nujoma. "We have accomplished that mission ... and it now remains our task to transform and develop our country for the benefit of all its people."

Former PLAN guerrillas are reluctant to speak out publicly about their plight. But one articulated the feeling of many former fighters in a candid interview with the pro-SWAPO daily, The Namibian. "We sacrificed our lives to serve in PLAN," said Maria Emmanuel of Karasburg who served in the frontline of battle for five years. "We gave up the chance of going to school, and now we can't get jobs because we don't have an education. We have military training but now they tell us we can't join the Army."

Mr. Nujoma said in a Monitor interview that it will not be possible to absorb all former guerrillas in the new Namibian Army. "The government will have to introduce its own projects in the next few months. Otherwise, the situation will become intolerable," he said.

Information Minister Hamutenya said international aid donors were taking a long time to release funds pledged at a New York conference in June, and that projects would take a while to establish.

He said the government hoped that about 15,000 former fighters from both sides could be employed in a construction training program and an agricultural scheme. Both ventures would fall under the Defense Ministry.

The end of the fighting has restored a semblance of normality to the lives of the dominant Ovambo tribe in the arid north, which is home to one third of the country's 1.3-million people.

But many Ovambo families – most of whom live in tribal villages made of grass huts – have been divided by the war. Returning PLAN fighters often find they have brothers or sisters who served in the Pretoria-led administration. Others had been maltreated or tortured in SWAPO detention camps or in South African-run jails.

"National reconciliation must also take place within the shattered families of the north," says a Lutheran missionary near the former South African military base at Oshakati.

The Ovambos, who bore the brunt of the war, lived under a dawn-to-dusk curfew in constant fear of reprisals by the dreaded South African counter-insurgency unit Koevoet or "Crowbar."

Thousands of civilians were caught in the conflicts that claimed the lives of some 20,000 people, more than half of them PLAN guerrillas.

Despite the new-found peace, the deep scars of war are creating new tensions in the overcrowded and underdeveloped north. The crime rate has soared on the back of rising unemployment. Skirmishes between former political adversaries are frequent.

This is particularly the case in the northeastern Kavango and Caprivi provinces where special police who are former PLAN guerrillas clash frequently with local sympathizers of the opposition Democratic Turnhalle Alliance, which won 21 of the 72 elected seats in the Constituent Assembly.

The special police were formally disbanded by Prime Minister Hage Geingob on Sept. 3 following mounting complaints from travelers in the north who were stopped at makeshift roadblocks, searched, and harassed. The special force is to be replaced with newly-trained members of the Namibian Army, but the controversy has highlighted the government's dilemma over what to do with former PLAN fighters.

Hamutenya estimates that between 50,000 and 60,000 Namibians were directly dependent on the war effort for their livelihood including some 25,000 combatants who were demobilized. Forty-three thousand Namibian exiles were repatriated in June last year.

In addition, thousands of civilians in the north made a living from selling goods and services to the soldiers. Many of the "cuca shops" which sold drinks to the soldiers are battling to survive today. The once thriving taxi industry in the north is also depressed.

But for the time being, residents of the war-ravaged north are content to be rid of the South African security forces and are still savoring their new-found freedom. "Business is not what it used to be," conceded Aupopa Ashipali who owns a small discotheque in Oshakati. "But we've got our freedom."

Article 22

The UNESCO Courier, September 1989

Shaka Zulu, a living legend

KALAME IYAMUSE BOSCO

Kalame Iyamuse Bosco is a Ugandan writer based in Paris. His doctoral thesis, on order and chaos in the African novel, will be published shortly.

SHAKA Zulu is an outstanding example of a historical figure who became an epic hero. In the epic of which he plays the central role, his birth, rise and fall are closely associated with those of the Zulu empire.

History relates how the Zulu were a small clan of the Ngunis, a Bantu people which migrated to southern Africa from the north around 1300 AD and settled in the Vaal regions east of the Drakensberg mountains. The migration trek of the Ngunis was led by Malendela, who had two sons, Quabe and Zulu. Little is known of Zulu except that he became the progenitor of the nation which bears his name. Chroniclers sum up his heritage in these terms: "He left the world cumbered with a grave and richer by a nation. And therein lie his monument and his fame. No feats, no follies, not one word of praise of him is recorded."

A great nation deserves to be born in more splendid circumstances, however, and this is why the epic of Shaka is so important. In it Shaka is attributed with achievements so towering that they qualify him to usurp from Malendela's son the role of father of the Zulu people.

Birth of a hero

Shaka was conceived during a pre-marital relationship, and his mother Nandi, a member of the Lengani royal family, only later became the third wife of his father Senzangakhona, king of the Zulu. Before his birth, the elders had declared that his mother was not pregnant but merely harboured *ishaka,* an intestinal beetle. This "beetle" later became an emperor.

This beginning of the legend, locating moral fault in the conception of Shaka as the root cause of his problems, is important for the structure of the epic in that it prepares for Shaka's odyssey of initiation. In fact, Shaka was not really an illegitimate son, since among the Zulu people premarital conception was only considered a crime among the lower strata of society. It was tolerated among the aristocracy and both Shaka's parents were aristocrats.

Shaka's early childhood was unhappy. His mother's name, Nandi, meant "the Sweet One", but she hardly lived up to it. Wilful, sharp-tongued and authoritarian, she was despised by many, including her husband. Her beauty and her inferior position in the Zulu royal house provoked a mixture of jealousy, hatred and scorn, and Shaka too was treated with derision. This hostility brought together mother and son. Shaka adored his mother and this bond was further strengthened when the two went into exile.

Banished by Senzangakhona, mother and child were badly received in Nandi's family. Their sufferings actually became much worse since a discarded wife had no place in the social hierarchy. In addition, a child, and especially a boy, belonged by priority to his father's clan. Shaka was made to feel the full force of his mother's humiliation. He was often scolded and beaten for no valid reason. Defended by nobody but his mother, he developed into a tough, self-reliant personality. He was said to have killed a hyena and saved the girl it was carrying off, and to have performed other youthful feats of bravery. Shaka was condemned to enter adulthood prematurely. From this point, the various oral and written renderings of the epic diverge.

There are two major written versions. According to one, written by Thomas Mofolo in 1908, Shaka falls into the hands of Issanoussi, an all-powerful medicine man who helps him complete his initiation.

The second written version of the Shaka epic is a poetic rendering by Mazisi Kunene, who is himself a Zulu. This version is closer to the historical facts and to the Zulu literary tradition.* Unlike Mofolo, whose version of Shaka's exploits emphasizes the role of magic, fantasy and suprahuman forces, Kunene dwells more on Shaka's political, military and visionary qualities. He takes us directly from Shaka's childhood to his military apprenticeship under his protector and mentor, Dingiswayo, the enlightened king of the Bathethwa, in whose army Shaka becomes a recruit.

The rise of Shaka

Shaka's intelligence soon brought him to the attention of Dingiswayo. Above all he distinguished himself as a skilled military leader with ideas which would revolutionize the art of war. He advocated the use of the short, wide-bladed stabbing spear instead of the long throwing spear, claiming that a soldier who threw his spear not only disarmed himself, but also armed his enemy. The long spear was also cumbersome and ineffective in close combat. According to Shaka, a good soldier should be a well-trained professional, hardened and experienced in the techniques of combat. Dingiswayo listened to his proposals and gave him the command of a group of young volunteers who soon proved far superior to all the other troops. Shaka also did away with the leather sandals that not only reduced the soldier's speed but also made his feet soft and vulnerable. His soldiers toughened their unshod feet by dancing on hard ground littered with thorns.

Shaka then tried to impress on the soft-hearted Dingiswayo the idea that an enemy should either be completely destroyed or forced to declare allegiance to him, and that the art of war should be geared to this goal. To this end Shaka proposed the use of a "cow-horn" formation in battle. Three divisions should be engaged in battle. The bulk of the army should make a frontal attack with fresh reserve forces at the rear. The other two divisions should lie in wait, one on the left and the other on the right. Once the enemy was engaged in the frontal attack, the other two divisions should close in, encircle him and cut off his retreat. Dingiswayo was reluctant to put these revolutionary ideas into practice, and Shaka had to be patient.

* Originally written in the Zulu language, Mazisi Kunene's *Emperor Shaka the Great* has been published in English as part of the Unesco Collection of Representative Works by Heinemann Educational Books Ltd. (1979). Its publication has not yet been authorized in South Africa in its original form.

The return to Zululand

Shaka's glory could not be complete until he returned to Zululand as legitimate heir to his father's throne. Before his death, Senzangakhona had named the cowardly leader Sigujana as his heir. With the blessing of Dingiswayo, Shaka marched to claim control over Zululand. His venture was successful. At the head of his invincible regiment and flanked by his two trusty lieutenants Mgobhozi and Mqoboka, Shaka entered his father's royal palace and ushered in a new era.

He was now in a position to put his revolutionary military and political ideas into practice. Bound by respect and loyalty towards Dingiswayo, he waited for the latter's death before pursuing expansionist policies. When Dingiswayo was slain by Zwide, the dreaded king of the Ndwandes, Shaka waged war against Zwide.

He lured Zwide's army into a trap by making a tactical retreat which enabled him to gain better fighting ground and to wear out his enemy through fatigue and famine. Zwide's army depended on provisions collected or looted in the battle areas, whereas Shaka had formed a brigade of young men to look after the provisioning of his forces during mobile warfare. Since Shaka had previously devastated the zones along which he lured the enemy, Zwide's army inevitably succumbed to starvation. His army destroyed, Zwide is said to have disappeared in the open mouth of a mountain and to have been carried along an underground stream to the land of the evil dead.

Having conquered the strongest of his adversaries, Shaka now began to strengthen and expand his empire. He had already formed regiments on the basis of age: the *uFasimba,* a brigade of sixteen- to twenty-year-olds, the *isimPholo* (the "bachelors' brigade" of twenty- to thirty-year-olds) and the *amaWombe* (the "battlers", comprising married men up to forty years old).

In Shaka's empire, hierarchy was based on merit. More than ever before he made heroism a central part of the Zulu ethos. A recognized hero exercised greater political authority than a born prince. Later this caused conflicts between him and his brothers, but it was a guarantee of equal opportunities for all who served under him. Anyone who defended the interests of the Zulu nation became Zulu, and it is often said that most of his generals and close comrades were not of Zulu descent.

Shaka's death was the result of heinous intrigues by his envious brothers, Dingane and Mhalangana, with the complicity of Mbopha, his army commander. His death is seen by many African authors as the ultimate betrayal and the murder of a Christ-like figure. The two brothers leapt from their hiding place and stabbed him from behind. Mbopha struck at the astonished Shaka from the front as he fell. Afraid that he would rise again, the three assailants continued stabbing at him furiously even after he was dead. They then placed guards around his corpse in case he should rise from the dead.

Just before his death the visionary Shaka is said to have pronounced the words: "So, my brothers, you are killing me? And you, Mbopha, son of Sithayi! You think you shall rule Zululand after my death. No, you shall never rule over it."

Shaka is a figure of the pre-colonial era, which colonial historians have often endeavoured to reduce to a subsistence level of village exploits. His image is a challenge to this prejudice. African poets such as Léopold Sédar Senghor of Senegal and playwrights such as Zambia's Twanyanga Mulikita have composed works inspired by the Shaka epic. In all these plays and poems, Shaka is depicted as the hero of an Africa seeking to overcome tribal divisions before the onset of colonial domination. There is often an underlying theme that the hero will rise again.

Credits

GENERAL AFRICA

Page 170 Article 1. From *The World Today,* published by the Royal Institute of International Affairs in London.

Page 173 Article 2. Reprinted from *African Letter,* May 1-5, 1990, p. 3.

Page 174 Article 3. Reprinted from *Africa News,* Volume 34, Number 2. © 1990 Africa News Service.

Page 176 Article 4. From *Guardian Weekly,* June 3, 1990, p. 16.

Page 178 Article 5. Reprinted from *Africa News,* Volume 33, Number 4-5. © 1990 Africa News Service.

Page 180 Article 6. Reprinted from *World Press Review,* November 1990, pp. 30, 32, 34.

Page 182 Article 7. Courtesy of *The Unesco Courier,* July 1989, pp. 22-27.

Page 186 Article 8. From *The World & I,* September 1988, pp. 512-521. Reprinted with permission from *The World & I,* a publication of The Washington Times Corporation, copyright © 1988.

Page 193 Article 9. Reprinted from *Africa News,* Volume 30, Number 11. © 1988 Africa News Service.

WEST AFRICA

Page 196 Article 10. From *World Monitor,* August 1990, pp. 31-36, 39-41. From *Africa: Dispatches from a Fragile Continent,* by Blaine Harden. Copyright © 1990 by Blaine Harden. Reprinted by permission of W. W. Norton & Co.

Page 203 Article 11. From *Guardian Weekly,* December 16, 1990, p. 14.

CENTRAL AFRICA

Page 204 Article 12. Reprinted from *Africa News,* Volume 33, Number 1. © 1990 Africa News Service.

Page 209 Article 13. Reprinted from *World Health,* March 1990.

EAST AFRICA

Page 211 Article 14. From *Guardian Weekly,* December 16, 1990.

Page 213 Article 15. Reprinted by permission from *The Christian Science Monitor.* © 1990 The Christian Science Publishing Society. All rights reserved.

SOUTHERN AFRICA

Page 215 Article 16. Reprinted by permission from *The Christian Science Monitor.* © 1990 The Christian Science Publishing Society. All rights reserved.

Page 217 Article 17. From *The Christian Science Monitor,* July 12, 1990, p. 10. Copyright © 1990 by Ross Dunn.

Page 218 Article 18. From *The Christian Science Monitor,* July 12, 1990, p. 10. Copyright © 1990 by Colleen Lowe Morna.

Page 219 Article 19. By Holman Jenkins, Jr. From *Insight,* October 1, 1990, pp. 8-11. Copyright © 1990 by Holman Jenkins, Jr./Insight.

Page 222 Article 20. Reprinted by permission of *World •Watch,* May/June 1990, pp. 11-17. Copyright © 1990 Worldwatch Institute.

Page 227 Article 21. Reprinted by permission from *The Christian Science Monitor.* © 1990 The Christian Science Publishing Society. All rights reserved.

Page 229 Article 22. Courtesy of *The Unesco Courier,* September 1989, pp. 44-47.

Glossary of Terms and Abbreviations

Acquired Immune Deficiency Syndrome (AIDS) A disease of immune-system dysfunction assumed to be caused by the human immunodeficiency virus (HIV), which allows opportunistic infections to take over the body.

African Development Bank Founded in 1963 under the auspices of the United Nations Economic Commission on Africa, the bank, located in Côte d'Ivoire, makes loans to African countries, although other nations can apply.

African National Congress (ANC) Founded in 1912, the group's goal is to achieve equal rights for blacks in South Africa through nonviolent action. "Spear of the Nation," the ANC wing dedicated to armed struggle, was organized after the Sharpeville massacre in 1960.

African Party for the Independence of Guinea-Bissau and Cape Verde (PAICG) An independence movement that fought during the 1960s and 1970s for the liberation of present-day Guinea-Bissau and Cape Verde from Portuguese rule. The two territories were ruled separately by a united PAIGC until a 1981 coup in Guinea-Bissau caused the party to split along national lines. In 1981 the Cape Verdean PAIGC formally renounced its Guinea links and became the PAICV.

African Socialism A term applied to a variety of ideas (including those of Nkrumah and Senghor) about communal and shared production in Africa's past and present. The concept of African socialism was especially popular in the early 1960s. Adherence to it has not meant governments' exclusion of private-capitalist ventures.

Afrikaners South Africans of Dutch descent who speak Afrikaans and are often referred to as Boers (Afrikaans for "farmers").

Amnesty International A London-based human-rights organization whose members "adopt" political prisoners or prisoners of conscience in many nations of the world. The organization generates political pressure and puts out a well-publicized annual report of human-rights conditions in each country of the world.

Aouzou Strip A barren strip of land between Libya and Chad contested by both countries.

Apartheid Literally, "separateness," the South African policy of segregating the races socially, legally, and politically.

Arusha Declaration A document issued in 1967 by Tanzanian President Julius Nyerere, committing the country to socialism based on peasant farming, democracy under one party, and self-reliance.

Assimilado The Portuguese term for Africans who became "assimilated" to Western ways. Assimilados enjoyed equal rights under Portuguese law.

Azanian People's Organization (AZAPO) Founded in 1978 at the time of the Black Consciousness Movement and revitalized in the 1980s, the movement works to develop chapters and bring together black organizations in a national forum.

Bantu A major linguistic classification for many Central, Southern, and East African languages. Also, a derogatory term for Africans, used by the South African government.

Bantustans Areas, or "homelands," to which black South Africans are assigned "citizenship" as part of the policy of apartheid.

Basarawa Peoples of Botswana who have historically been hunters and gatherers.

Berber The collective term for the indigenous languages and peoples of North Africa.

Bicameral A government made up of two legislative branches.

Black Consciousness Movement A South African student movement founded by Steve Biko and others in the 1970s to promote pride and empowerment of blacks.

Boers The Dutch word for farmers of Dutch-German-French descent who settled in South Africa after 1652. See also *Afrikaner*.

Brotherhoods Islamic organizations based on specific religious beliefs and practices. In many areas, brotherhood leaders and their spiritual followers gain political influence.

Cabinda A small, oil-rich portion of Angola separated from the main body of that country by the coastal strip of Zaire.

Caisse de Stabilization A marketing board that stabilizes the uncertain returns to producers of cash crops by offering them less than market prices in good harvest years while assuring them of a steady income in bad years. Funds from these boards are used to develop infrastructure, to promote social welfare, or to maintain a particular regime in power.

Caliphate The office or dominion of a caliph, the spiritual head of Islam.

Cassava A tropical plant with a fleshy, edible rootstock; one of the staples of the African diet. Also known as manioc.

Chimurenga A Shona term meaning "fighting in which everyone joins," used to refer to Zimbabwe's fight for independence.

Coloured The South African classification for a person of mixed racial descent.

Committee for the Struggle Against Drought in the Sahel (CILSS) A grouping of eight West African countries, formed to fight the effects of drought in the region.

Commonwealth of Nations An association of nations and dependencies loosely joined by the common tie of having been part of the British Empire.

Congress of South African Trade Unions (COSATU) Established in 1985 to form a coalition of trade unions to press for workers' rights and an end to apartheid.

Copperbelt A section of Zambia with a high concentration of copper-mining concessions.

Creole A person or language of mixed African and European descent.

Dergue From the Amheric word for "committee," the ruling body of Ethiopia after the revolution in 1974.

East African Community (EAC) Established in 1967,

this organization grew out of the East African Common Services Organization begun under British rule. The EAC included Kenya, Tanzania, and Uganda in a customs union and involved common currency and development of infrastructure. It was disbanded in 1977, and the final division of assets was completed in 1983.

Economic Commission for Africa (ECA) Founded in 1958 by the Economic and Social Committee of the United Nations to aid African development through regional centers, field agents, and the encouragement of regional efforts, food self-sufficiency, transport, and communications development.

Economic Community of Central African States (CEEAC, also known as ECCA) An organization of all of the Central African states, as well as Rwanda and Burundi, whose goal is to promote economic and social cooperation among its members.

Economic Community of West Africa (CEAO) An organization of French-speaking countries formed to promote trade and regional economic cooperation.

Economic Community of West African States (ECOWAS) Established in 1975 by the Treaty of Lagos, the organization includes all of the West African states except Western Sahara. The organization's goals are to promote trade, cooperation, and self-reliance among its members.

Enclave Industry An industry run by a foreign company that uses imported technology and machinery and exports the product to industrialized countries; often described as a "state within a state."

Eritrean Peoples' Liberation Front (EPLF) The major group fighting the Ethiopian government for independence of Eritrea.

European Community (EC, or Common Market) Established in 1958, the EC seeks to establish a common agricultural policy between its members as well as uniform trade and travel restrictions among members. A common currency is planned for 1992.

Evolués A term used in colonial Zaire (Congo) to refer to Western-educated Congolese.

Food and Agricultural Organization of the United Nations (FAO) Established in 1945 to oversee good nutrition and agricultural development.

Franc Zone This organization includes members of the West African Monetary Union and the monetary organizations of Central Africa that have currencies linked to the French franc. Reserves are managed by the French treasury and guaranteed by the French franc.

Freedom Charter Established in 1955, this charter proclaimed equal rights for all South Africans and has been a foundation for almost all groups in the resistance against apartheid.

Free French Conference A 1944 conference of French-speaking territories, which proposed a union of all the territories in which Africans would be represented and their development furthered.

French Equatorial Africa (FEA) The French colonial federation that included present-day Congo, Central African Republic, Chad, and Gabon.

French West Africa The administrative division of the former French colonial empire that included the current independent countries of Senegal, Côte d'Ivoire, Guinea, Mali, Niger, Burkina Faso, Benin, and Mauritania.

Front for the Liberation of Mozambique (Frelimo) Liberation forces established in 1963 to free Mozambique from Portuguese rule; after 1975 the dominant party in independent Mozambique.

Frontline States A caucus supported by the Organization of African Unity (consisting of Tanzania, Zambia, Mozambique, Botswana, and Angola) whose goal is to achieve black majority rule in all of Southern Africa.

Green Revolution Use of Western technology and agricultural practices to increase food production and agricultural yields.

Griots Professional bards of West Africa, some of whom tell history and are accompanied by the playing of the kora or harp-lute.

Gross Domestic Product (GDP) The value of production attributable to the factors of production in a given country regardless of their ownership. GDP equals GNP minus the product of a country's residents originating in the rest of the world.

Gross National Product (GNP) The sum of the values of all goods and services produced by a country's residents at home and abroad in any given year, less income earned by foreign residents and remitted abroad.

Guerrilla A member of a small force of irregular soldiers. Generally, guerrilla forces are made up of volunteers who make surprise raids against the incumbent military or political force.

Harmattan In West Africa, the dry wind that blows from the Sahara Desert in January and February.

Homelands See *Bantustans*.

Horn of Africa A section of northeastern Africa including the countries of Djibouti, Ethiopia, Somalia,and Sudan.

Hut Tax Instituted by the colonial governments in Africa, this measure required families to pay taxes on each building in the village.

International Monetary Fund (IMF) Established in 1945 to promote international monetary cooperation.

Irredentism An effort to unite certain people and territory in one state with another, on the grounds that they belong together.

Islam A religious faith started in Arabia during the seventh century A.D. by the Prophet Muhammad and spread in Africa through African Muslim leaders, migrations, and holy wars.

Jihad "Holy war" waged as a religious duty on behalf of Islam to rid the world of disbelief and error.

Koran Writings accepted by Muslims as the word of God, as revealed to the Prophet Mohammed.

Lagos Plan of Action Adopted by the Organization of African Unity in 1980, this agreement calls for self-reliance, regional economic cooperation, and the creation of a pan-African economic community and common market by the year 2000.

League of Nations Established at the Paris Peace Conference in 1919, this forerunner of the modern-day United Nations had 52 member nations at its peak (the United States never joined the organization) and mediated in international affairs. The league was dissolved in 1945 after the creation of the United Nations.

Least Developed Countries (LDCs) A term used to refer to the poorest countries of the world, including many African countries.

Maghrib An Arabic term, meaning "land of the setting sun," that is often used to refer to the former French colonies of Morocco, Algeria, and Tunisia.

Mahdi The expected messiah of Islamic tradition; or a Muslim leader who plays a messianic role.

Malinke (Mandinka, or Mandinga) One of the major groups of people speaking Mande languages. The original homeland of the Malinke was Mali, but the people are now found in Mali, Guinea-Bissau, The Gambia, and other areas where they are sometimes called Mandingoes. Some trading groups are called Dyoula.

Marabout A Muslim saint or holy man, often the leader of a religious brotherhood.

Marxist-Leninism Sometimes called "scientific socialism," this doctrine derived from the ideas of Karl Marx as modified by Vladimir Lenin; it is the ideology of the Communist Party of the Soviet Union and has been modified in many ways by other persons and groups who still use the term. In Africa, some political parties or movements have claimed to be Marxist-Leninist but have often followed policies that conflict in practice with the ideology; these governments have usually not stressed Marx's philosophy of class struggle.

Mfecane The movement of people in the nineteenth century in the eastern areas of present-day South Africa to the west and north as the result of wars led by the Zulus.

Mozambique National Resistance (MNR, also known as Renamo) A South African-backed rebel movement that attacks civilians in attempting to overthrow the government of Mozambique.

Muslim A follower of the Islamic faith.

Naam A traditional work cooperative in Burkina Faso.

National Youth Service Service to the state required of youth after completing education, a common practice in many African countries.

National Union for the Total Independence of Angola (UNITA) One of three groups that fought the Portuguese during the colonial period in Angola, now backed by South Africa and the United States and fighting the independent government of Angola.

Nkomati Accords An agreement signed in 1984 between South Africa and Mozambique, pledging that both sides would no longer support opponents of the other.

Non-Aligned Movement (NAM) A group of nations that have chosen not to be politically or militarily associated with either the West or the communist bloc.

Non-Governmental Organization (NGO) A private voluntary organization or agency working in relief and development programs.

Organization for the Development of the Senegal River (OMVS) A regional grouping of countries bordering the Senegal River that sponsors joint research and projects.

Organization of African Unity (OAU) An association of all of the independent states of Africa (except South Africa) whose goal is to promote unity and solidarity among African nations.

Organization of Petroleum Exporting Countries (OPEC) Established in 1960, this association of some of the world's major oil-producing countries seeks to coordinate the petroleum policies of its members.

Pan Africanist Congress (PAC) A liberation organization of black South Africans that broke away from the ANC in the 1950s.

Parastatals Agencies for production or public service that are established by law and that are, in some measure, government organized and controlled. Private enterprise may be involved, and the management of the parastatal may be in private hands.

Pastoralist A person, usually a nomad, who raises livestock for a living.

Polisario Front Originally a liberation group in Western Sahara seeking independence from Spanish rule. Today, it is battling Morocco, which claims control over the Western Sahara (see *SADR*).

Popular Movement for the Liberation of Angola (MPLA) A Marxist liberation movement in Angola during the resistance to Portuguese rule; now the governing party in Angola.

Rinderpest A cattle disease that periodically decimates herds in savanna regions.

Saharawi Arab Democratic Republic (SADR) The Polisario Front name for Western Sahara, declared in 1976 in the struggle for independence from Morocco.

Sahel In West Africa, the borderlands between savanna and desert.

Sanctions Coercive measures, usually economic, adopted by nations acting together against a nation violating international law.

Savanna Tropical or subtropical grassland with scattered trees and undergrowth.

Senegambia A confederation of Senegal and The Gambia signed into agreement in December 1981 and inaugurated on February 1, 1982, to be ruled by a Cabinet of five Senegalese and four Gambians.

Sharia The Islamic code of law.

Sharpeville Massacre The 1960 pass demonstration in South Africa in which 60 people were killed when police fired into the crowd; it became a rallying point for many anti-apartheid forces.

Shengo The Ethiopian Parliament.

Sorghum A tropical grain that is a traditional staple in the savanna regions.

Southern African Development Coordination Conference (SADCC) An organization of nine African states (Angola, Zambia, Malawi, Mozambique, Zimbabwe, Lesotho, Botswana, Swaziland, and Tanzania) whose goal is to free themselves from dependence on South Africa and to cooperate on projects of economic development.

South West Africa People's Organization (SWAPO) Angola-based freedom fighters who have been waging guerrilla warfare against the presence of South Africa in Namibia since the 1960s. The United Nations and the Organization of African Unity have recognized SWAPO as the only authentic representative of the Namibian people.

Structural Adjustment Program (SAP) Economic reforms encouraged by the International Monetary Fund which include devaluation of currency, cutting government subsidies on commodities, and reducing government expenditures.

Swahili A widespread *lingua franca* in East Africa; an African-based Afro-Arab language and culture.

Tsetse Fly An insect that transmits sleeping sickness to cattle and humans. It is usually found in the scrub-tree and forest regions of Central Africa.

Ujamaa In Swahili, "familyhood." Government-sponsored cooperative villages in Tanzania.

Unicameral A political structure with a single legislative branch.

Unilateral Declaration of Independence (UDI) A declaration of white minority settlers in Rhodesia, claiming independence from the United Kingdom in 1965.

United Democratic Front (UDF) A multiracial, black-led group in South Africa that gained prominence during the 1983 campaign to defeat the government's Constitution, which has given only limited political rights to Asians and Coloureds.

United Nations (UN) An international organization established on June 26, 1945, through official approval of the charter by delegates of 50 nations at a conference in San Francisco, California. The charter went into effect on October 24, 1945.

United Nations Development Program (UNDP) Established to create local organizations for increasing wealth through better use of human and natural resources.

United Nations Educational, Scientific, and Cultural Organization (UNESCO) Established on November 4, 1946 to promote international collaboration in education, science, and culture.

United Nations High Commission for Refugees (UNHCR) Established in 1951 to provide international protection for people with refugee status.

United Nations Resolution 435 Voted in 1978, this resolution calls for internationally supervised elections and independence for South African-ruled Namibia.

Villagization A policy whereby a government relocates rural dwellers to create newer, more concentrated communities.

World Bank A closely integrated group of international institutions providing financial and technical assistance to developing countries.

World Health Organization (WHO) Established by the United Nations in 1948, this organization promotes the highest possible state of health in countries throughout the world.

Bibliography

RESOURCE CENTERS

African Studies Centers provide special services for schools, libraries, and community groups. Contact the center nearest you for further information about resources available:

African Studies Center
Boston University
270 Bay State Road
Boston, MA 02215

African Studies Program
Indiana University
Woodburn Hall 221
Bloomington, IN 47405

African Studies Educational Resource Center
100 International Center
Michigan State University
East Lansing, MI 49923

African Studies Program
630 Dartmouth
Northwestern University
Evanston, IL 60201

Africa Project
Lou Henry Hoover Room 223
Stanford University
Stanford, CA 94305

African Studies Center
University of California
Los Angeles, CA 90024

Center for African Studies
470 Grinter Hall
University of Florida
Gainesville, FL 32611

African Studies Program
University of Illinois
1208 W. California, Room 101
Urbana, IL 61801

African Studies Program
1450 Van Hise Hall
University of Wisconsin
Madison, WI 53706

Council on African Studies
Yale University
New Haven, CT 06520

Foreign Area Studies
The American University
5010 Wisconsin Avenue, N.W.
Washington, DC 20016

African Studies Program
Center for Strategic and International Studies
Georgetown University
1800 K Street, N.W.
Washington, DC 20006

REFERENCE WORKS, BIBLIOGRAPHIES, AND OTHER SOURCES

Africa South of the Sahara 1990 (updated yearly) (London: Europa Publications, Ltd.).

Africa on Film and Videotape 1960–1961, A Compendium of Reviews (East Lansing: Michigan State University, 1982).

Africa Today, An Atlas of Reproductible Pages, rev. ed. (Wellesley: World Eagle, 1987).

Scarecrow Press, Metuchen, NJ, publishes *The African Historical Dictionaries*, a series edited by Jon Woronoff. There are more than 40 dictionaries, each under a specialist editor. They are short works with introductory essays and are useful guides for the beginner, especially for countries on which little has been published in English.

Colin Legum, ed., *Africa Contemporary Record* (New York: Africana) (annual). Contains information on each country for the reporting year.

Africa Research Bulletin (Political Series), Africa Research Ltd., Exeter, Devon, England (monthly). Political updates on current issues and events in Africa.

Chris Cook and David Killingray, *African Political Facts Since 1945* (New York: Facts on File, 1983). Chronology of events; chapters on heads of state, ministers, parliaments, parties, armies, trade unions, population, biographies.

MAGAZINES AND PERIODICALS

African Arts
University of California
Los Angeles, CA
Beautifully illustrated articles review Africa's artistic heritage and current creative efforts.

African Concord
5–15 Cromer Street
London, WCIH 8LS, England

Africa News
P.O. Box 3851
Durham, NC 27702
A weekly with short articles that are impartially written and full of information.

Africa Now
212 Fifth Avenue, Suite 1409
New York, NY 10010
A monthly publication that gives current coverage and includes sections on art, culture, and business, as well as a special series of interviews.

Africa Recovery
DPI, Room S-1061
United Nations
New York, NY 10017

Africa Report
African American Institute
833 UN Plaza
New York, NY 10017
This bimonthly periodical has an update section, but most of each issue is devoted to broad-based articles by authorities giving background on key issues, developments in particular countries, and United States policy.

Africa Today
Graduate School of International Studies
Denver, CO 80208

The Economist
P.O. Box 2700
Woburn, MA
A weekly that gives attention to African issues.

Newswatch
62 Oregun Rd.
P. M. B. 21499
Ikeja, Nigeria

UNESCO Courier
UNESCO, Place de Fontenox
75700 Paris, France
This periodical includes short and clear articles on Africa, often by African authors, within the framework of the topic to which the monthly issues are devoted.

The Weekly Review
Agip House
P.O. Box 42271
Nairobi, Kenya

West Africa
Holborn Viaduct
London, EC1A Z FD, England
This weekly is the best source for West Africa including countries as far south as Angola and Namibia. Continent-wide issues are also discussed.

NOVELS AND AUTOBIOGRAPHICAL WRITINGS

Chinua Achebe, *Things Fall Apart* (Portsmouth: Heinemann, 1965).
This is the story of the life and values of residents of a traditional Igbo village in the nineteenth century and of its first contacts with the West.

———, *No Longer at Ease* (Portsmouth: Heinemann, 1963).
The grandson of the major character of *Things Fall Apart* lives an entirely different life in the modern city of Lagos and faces new problems, while remaining committed to some of the traditional ways.

Okot p'Bitek, *Song of Lawino* (Portsmouth: Heinemann, 1983).
A traditional Ugandan wife comments on the practices of her Western-educated husband and reveals her own lifestyle and values.

Buchi Emecheta, *The Joys of Motherhood* (New York: G. Braziller, 1979).
The story of a Nigerian woman who overcomes great obstacles to raise a large family and then finds that the meaning of motherhood has changed.

Nadine Gordimer, *July's People* (New York: Viking, 1981).
This is a troubling and believable scenario of future revolutionary times in South Africa.

———, *A Soldier's Embrace* (New York: Viking, 1982).
These short stories cover a range of situations where apartheid affects peoples' relations with each other. Films made from some of these stories are available at the University of Illinois Film Library, Urbana-Champaign, IL and Boston University Film Library, Boston, MA.

Cheik Amadou Kane, *Ambiguous Adventure* (Portsmouth: Heinemann, 1972).
This autobiographical novel of a young man coming of age in Senegal, in a Muslim society, and, later, in a French school, illuminates changes that have taken place in Africa and raises many questions.

Alex LaGuma, *Time of the Butcherbird* (Portsmouth: Heinemann, 1979).
The people of a long-standing black community in South Africa's countryside are to be removed to a Bantustan.

Camara Laye, *The Dark Child* (Farrar Straus and Giroux, 1954).
This autobiographical novel gives a loving and nostalgic picture of a Malinke family of Guinea.

Winnie Mandela, *Part of My Soul Went With Him* (New York: W. W. Norton, 1985).
Details the personal and political saga of the wife of jailed ANC leader Nelson Mandela, an activist in her own right.

Ousmane Sembene, *God's Bits of Wood* (Portsmouth: Heinemann, 1970).
The railroad workers' strike of 1947 provides the setting for a novel about the changing consciousness and life of African men and women in Senegal.

Joyce Sikakane, *A Window on Soweto* (London: International Defense and Aid Fund, 1977).

Wole Soyinka, *Ake: The Years of Childhood* (New York: Random House, 1983).
Soyinka's account of his first 11 years is full of the sights, tastes, smells, sounds, and personal encounters of a headmaster's home and a busy Yoruba town.

Ngugi wa Thiong'o, *A Grain of Wheat* (Portsmouth: Heinemann, 1968).
A story of how the Mau-Mau Movement and the coming of independence affected several individuals after independence as well as during the struggle that preceded it.

INTRODUCTORY BOOKS

A. E. Afigbo, E. A. Ayandele, R. J. Gavin, J. D. Omer-Cooper, and R. Palmer, *The Making of Modern Africa,*

vol. II, *The Twentieth Century,* 2nd ed. (London: Longman, 1986).
An introductory political history of Africa in the twentieth century.

Gwendolen Carter and Patrick O'Meara, eds., *African Independence: The First Twenty-Five Years* (Bloomington: Indiana University Press, 1985).
Collected essays surrounding issues such as political structures, military rule, and economics.

Basil Davidson, *The African Genius* (Boston: Little, Brown, 1979). Also published as *The Africans.*
Davidson discusses the complex political, social, and economic systems of traditional African societies, translating scholarly works into a popular mode without distorting complex material.

______, *Let Freedom Come* (Boston: Little, Brown, 1978).
A lively and interesting history of Africa in the twentieth century.

John Fage and Roland Oliver, *Cambridge History of Africa,* 6 vols. (New York: Cambridge University Press, 1975).
Comprehensive descriptions of regional histories.

Bill Freund, *The Making of Contemporary Africa: The Development of African Society Since 1800* (Bloomington: Indiana University Press, 1983).
Recent African history from an economic-history point of view, with emphasis on forces of production.

Adrian Hastings, *A History of African Christianity, 1950–1975* (Cambridge: Cambridge University Press, 1979).
A good introduction to the impact of Christianity on Africa in recent years.

Goren Hyden, *No Shortcut to Progress: African Development Management in Perspective* (Berkeley: University of California, 1983).
An assessment of development in relation to obstacles, prospects, and progress.

John Mbiti, *African Religions and Philosophy* (Portsmouth: Heinemann, 1982).
This work by a Ugandan scholar is the standard introduction to the rich variety of religious beliefs and rituals of African peoples.

Phyllis Martin and Patrick O'Meara, eds., *Africa,* 2nd ed. (Boomington: Indiana University Press, 1986).
This collection of essays covers history, culture, politics, and the economy.

J. H. Kwabena Nketia, *The Music of Africa* (New York: Norton, 1974).
The author, a Ghanaian by birth, is Africa's best-known ethnomusicologist.

Chris Searle, *We're Building the New School: Diary of a Teacher in Mozambique* (London: Zed Press, 1981; distributed in the United States by Laurence Hill & Co., Westport).
A lively book that shows that the lives of students and teachers in the nation of Mozambique are both exciting and difficult.

Timothy Shaw and Adebayo Adedeji, *Economic Crisis in Africa: African Perspectives on Development Problems and Potentials* (Boulder: L. Rienner, 1985).

J. B. Webster, A. A. Boahen, and M. Tidy, *The Revolutionary Years: West Africa Since 1800* (London: Longman, 1980).
An interesting, enjoyable, and competent introductory history to the West African region.

Frank Willett, *African Art* (New York: Oxford University Press, 1971).
A work to read for both reference and pleasure, by one of the authorities on Nigeria's early art.

COUNTRY AND REGIONAL STUDIES

Tony Avirgan and Martha Honey, *War in Uganda: The Legacy of Idi Amin* (Westport: Laurence Hill & Co., 1982).

John E. Bardill and James H. Cobbe, *Lesotho: Dilemmas of Dependence in Southern Africa* (Boulder: Westview Press, 1985).

Gerald Bender, *Angola Under the Portuguese: The Myth and the Reality* (Berkeley, University of California Press, 1978).

William Bigelow, *Strangers in Their Own Country* (a curriculum on South Africa), 2nd ed. (Trenton: Africa World Press, 1989).

Allan R. Booth, *Swaziland: Tradition and Change in a Southern African Kingdom* (Boulder: Westview Press, 1984).

Marcia M. Burdette, *Zambia: Between Two Worlds* (Boulder: Westview Press, 1988).

Gwendolen Carter, *Continuity and Change in South Africa* (Gainesville: African Studies Association and Center for African Studies, University of Florida, 1985).

Christopher Clapham, *Transformation and Continuity in Revolutionary Ethiopia* (Cambridge: Cambridge University Press, 1988).

Maureen Covell, *Madagascar: Politics, Economy, and Society* (London and New York: F. Pinter, 1987).

Toyin Falola and Julius Ihonvbere, *The Rise and Fall of Nigeria's Second Republic, 1979–1984* (London: Zed Press, 1985).

Robert Fatton, *The Making of a Liberal Democracy: Senegal's Passive Revolution, 1975–85* (Boulder: L. Rienner, 1987).

Foreign Area Studies (Washington, DC: Government Printing Office). Includes country study handbooks with chapters on history, politics, culture, and economics, with maps, charts, and bibliographies. There are more than 20 in the series, with new ones added and revised periodically.

Marcus Franda, *The Seychelles: Unquiet Islands* (Boulder: Westview Press, 1982).

Sheldon Gellar, *Senegal: An African Nation Between Islam and the West* (Boulder: Westview Press, 1982).

Joseph Hanlon, *Mozambique: The Revolution Under Fire* (London: Zed Press, 1984).

Tony Hodges, *Western Sahara: The Roots of a Desert War* (Westport: Laurence Hill & Co., 1983).

P. M. Holt and M. W. Daly, *A History of Sudan: From the Coming of Islam to the Present Day* (Boulder: Westview Press, 1979).

Allan and Barbara Isaacman, *Mozambique from Colonialism to Revolution, 1900–1982* (Boulder: Westview Press, 1983).

Richard Joseph, *Democracy and Prebendel Politics in Nigeria: The Rise and Fall of the Second Republic* (Cambridge: Cambridge University Press, 1987).

Michael P. Kelley, *A State in Disarray: Conditions of Chad's Survival* (Boulder: Westview Press, 1986).

David D. Laitin and Said S. Samatar, *Somalia: Nation in Search of a State* (Boulder: Westview Press, 1987).

J. Gus Liebenow, *Liberia: Quest for Democracy* (Bloomington: Indiana University Press, 1987).

Tom Lodge, *Black Politics in South Africa Since 1945* (New York: Longman, 1983).

David Martin and Phyllis Johnson, *The Struggle for Zimbabwe: The Chimurenga War* (Boston: Faber & Faber, 1981).

Norman N. Miller, *Kenya: The Quest for Prosperity* (Boulder: Westview Press, 1984).

Malyn Newitt, *The Comoro Islands: Sturggle Against Depencency in the Indian Ocean* (Boulder: Westview Press, 1984).

Julius Nyerere, *Ujamaa: Essays on Socialism* (Dar es Salaam: Oxford University Press, 1968).

Thomas O'Toole, *The Central African Republic: The Continent's Hidden Heart* (Boulder: Westview Press, 1986).

Jack Parson, *Botswana: Liberal Democracy and the Labor Resource in Southern Africa* (Boulder: Westview Press, 1984).

Deborah Pellow and Naomi Chazan, *Ghana: Coping with Uncertainty* (Boulder: Westview Press, 1986).

Bereket Habte Selassie, *Conflict and Intervention in the Horn of Africa* (New York: Monthly Review Press, 1980).

Study Commission on U.S. Policy Toward Southern Africa, *South Africa: Time Running Out* (Berkeley and Los Angeles: University of California Press, 1981).

Rachid Tlemcani, *State and Revolution in Algeria* (Boulder: Westview Press, 1987).

Michael Wolfers and Jane Bergerol, *Angola in the Frontline* (London: Zed Press, 1983).

Rodger Yeager, *Tanzania: An African Experiment* (Boulder: Westview Press, 1983).

Westview Press specializes in country studies and has many additional ones forthcoming.

Sources for Statistical Reports

U.S. State Department, *Background Notes* (1990).

C.I.A. *World Factbook* (1990).

World Bank, *World Development Report* (1990).

UN *Population and Vital Statistics Report* (January 1989).

World Statistics in Brief (1990).

Statistical Yearbook (1990).

The Statesman's Yearbook (1990).

Population Reference Bureau, *World Population Data Sheet* (1989).

World Almanac (1990).

Demographic Yearbook (1989).

Index